FALL & ASCENT

FALL & ASCENT

INDIVIDUATION IN THE
MALAZAN BOOK OF THE FALLEN

MICHAEL WOODS

Fall and Ascent: Individuation in The Malazan Book of the Fallen

© Copyright 2025 Michael Woods

All Rights Reserved.

No part of this book may be reproduced in any form without written permission from the author, except in the case of brief quotations embodied in critical articles and reviews.

The material in this book is provided for educational and informational purposes. Nothing within the text is meant as a substitute for direct expert assistance. If such level of assistance is required, the services of a competent professional should be sought.

Fair Use. Copyright Disclaimer under section 107 of the Copyright Act of 1976, allowance is made for "fair use" for purposes such as criticism, comment, news reporting, teaching, scholarship, education and research. Fair use is a use permitted by copyright statute that might otherwise be infringing.

ISBN: 978-1-7635938-0-0

Cover art by David Toros

Section divider image by Freepik.com

When a summit of life is reached, when the bud unfolds and from the lesser the greater emerges, then, as Nietzsche says, "One becomes Two," and the greater figure, which one always was but which remained invisible, appears to the lesser personality with the force of a revelation.

C.G. Jung, *The Archetypes and the Collective Unconscious*

Contents

FOREWORD XV

INTRODUCTION 1

HEROES AND ARCHETYPES: INDIVIDUATION AS A PROCESS OF
    TRANSFORMATION 9

THE BOOK OF THE FALLEN AS TRANSFORMATION 27

PROD AND PULL: BIRTH IN CHAOS, GOOD AND EVIL IN *GARDENS
    OF THE MOON*...43

WINDBLOWN SANDS: THE ANIMUS AND THE COLLECTIVE IN
    DEADHOUSE GATES..69

FORCES OF NATURE: THE ANIMA AND THE MOTHER IN *MEMORIES
    OF ICE*..105

STIR THE ASHES: SHADOW WORK AND THE FATHER IN *HOUSE OF
    CHAINS*..157

CIVILISATION IN TRANSITION: SYMBOLS, INNOCENCE, AND THE
    LIGHT IN THE DARK IN *MIDNIGHT TIDES* 219

WE ARE THE FALLEN: BIRTH AND RENEWAL IN *THE BONEHUNTERS* 265

CLIMBING INTO THE LIGHT: INITIATION AND THE DEATH OF THE
    CHILD IN *REAPER'S GALE* 307

SEEDS IN THE ASHES: WITHDRAWAL, RECONCILIATION, AND THE
    MIDDLE PASSAGE IN *TOLL THE HOUNDS* 343

WHAT IS, WAS: ALCHEMY, FIRE, AND RENEWAL IN *DUST OF DREAMS* 381

UNCHAINED HEARTS: REDEMPTION, CONJUNCTION, AND RETURN
    TO CHILDHOOD IN *THE CRIPPLED GOD* 421

CONCLUSION 455

PRIMARY REFERENCES 465

BIBLIOGRAPHY..466

ABOUT THE AUTHOR 469

Expanded Contents

FOREWORD XV

INTRODUCTION 1
    INDIVIDUATION 2
    MALAZAN: COMPASSION IN THE INDIVIDUATED SOUL 4
    THE WRITER AND READER AS HERO 5
    SOURCES AND MAP 6

HEROES AND ARCHETYPES: INDIVIDUATION AS A PROCESS OF
    TRANSFORMATION 9
    STORY AND RITE 9
    ARCHETYPES 10
    INSTINCTS AND COMPLEXES 13
    EGO AND SELF 19
    DEATH AND REBIRTH: THE HERO AND INDIVIDUATION 22

THE BOOK OF THE FALLEN AS TRANSFORMATION 27
    THE CYCLE OF INDIVIDUATION AND THE CYCLE OF THE BOOK OF THE FALLEN 31
    BALANCE 35
    THE CRIPPLED GOD: STRIVING FOR COMPASSION 38

PROD AND PULL: BIRTH IN CHAOS, GOOD AND EVIL IN *GARDENS OF THE
    MOON* 43
    GANOES PARAN 46
    CROKUS 51
    SORRY 55

Rallick Nom	56
Lorn	59
Whiskeyjack	63
Conclusion	65

WINDBLOWN SANDS: THE ANIMUS AND THE COLLECTIVE IN *DEADHOUSE GATES* 69

The Whirlwind	71
The Chain of Dogs	73
Felisin	78
Mappo and Icarium	92
Crokus	98
Fiddler	98
Lostara Yil	100
Cotillion	100
Stormy	101
Conclusion	102

FORCES OF NATURE: THE ANIMA AND THE MOTHER IN *MEMORIES OF ICE* 105

Ganoes Paran	111
Mhybe	120
Children of the Dead Seed	126
Silverfox	128
Toc and Envy	130
Burn as Terrible Mother	137
Gruntle and the Cat	139
Bridgeburners and Grey Swords	143
Whiskeyjack	144
Korlat	147
Moon's Spawn	149
The Crippled God	150
Conclusion	153

STIR THE ASHES: SHADOW WORK AND THE FATHER IN *HOUSE OF CHAINS* 157

Ganoes Paran	163
Karsa Orlong	166
Felisin / Sha'ik	186

HEBORIC	191
BIDITHAL	193
THE BONEHUNTERS	194
TAVORE	196
FIDDLER / STRINGS	199
COTILLION	200
CROKUS / CUTTER	203
LOSTARA YIL	206
ONRACK	209
SCILLARA	214
CONCLUSION	216

CIVILISATION IN TRANSITION: SYMBOLS, INNOCENCE, AND THE LIGHT IN THE DARK IN *MIDNIGHT TIDES* 219

UDINAAS	220
FEATHER WITCH, ENTROPY, AND CONSCIOUSNESS	221
UDINAAS (CONTINUED)	223
SEREN PEDAC	230
BRYS BEDDICT	237
RHULAD SENGAR	241
AWE AND THE COIN	251
TRULL SENGAR	253
DIFFERENTIATION AND INTEGRATION: BALANCE, OPPOSITION, AND CONSCIOUSNESS	258
THE CRIPPLED GOD AND FORGING	260
CONCLUSION	262

WE ARE THE FALLEN: BIRTH AND RENEWAL IN *THE BONEHUNTERS* 265

SCILLARA	267
APSALAR	271
COTILLION	274
CUTTER	275
KARSA ORLONG	276
MAPPO RUNT	278
LOSTARA YIL	282
FIDDLER AND THE FOURTEENTH	283
BOTTLE	285
CORABB BHILAN THENU'ALAS	288
TAVORE	290
GANOES PARAN	294
HEBORIC	299

- The Moon 301
- Goddesses 303
- Trull Sengar 304
- Conclusion 304

CLIMBING INTO THE LIGHT: INITIATION AND THE DEATH OF THE CHILD IN *REAPER'S GALE* 307

- Rhulad 309
- Redmask 312
- Seren Pedac 315
- Chaos and Transcendence 319
- Kettle 321
- Magic as Metaphor for Metaphor 324
- The Hunted 326
- Yan Tovis / Twilight 329
- Janath 330
- The Bonehunters 333
- Beak 335
- Nimander 337
- The Crippled God 338
- Conclusion 339

SEEDS IN THE ASHES: WITHDRAWAL, RECONCILIATION, AND THE MIDDLE PASSAGE IN *TOLL THE HOUNDS* 343

- Anomander Rake and Mother Dark 346
- The Eye 350
- Crokus Younghand 351
- Nimander 356
- Endest Silann 360
- Dying is Archetypal 362
- Spinnock, Seerdomin, and the Redeemer 365
- Kallor 368
- Traveller: Grief 371
- Stonny and Murillio 374
- Barathol and Scillara 376
- Gruntle 377
- The Bridgeburners 378
- Conclusion 379

WHAT IS, WAS: ALCHEMY, FIRE, AND RENEWAL IN *DUST OF DREAMS* 381

- Kalyth 384
- Fire and Dragons 389
- Setoc 390
- Badalle and The Snake 392
- Blood and Wounding 398
- Tavore 399
- The Bonehunters 402
- Fiddler 406
- Ash and Coagulation 408
- Icarium 409
- Tanakalian 411
- Yedan Derryg and Yan Tovis 413
- The Maternal and Conjunction 416
- Lostara Yil 417
- Conclusion 418

UNCHAINED HEARTS: REDEMPTION, CONJUNCTION, AND RETURN TO CHILDHOOD IN *THE CRIPPLED GOD* 421

- Tavore 423
- Badalle 429
- Ganoes Paran 431
- The Crippled God 432
- Forkrul Assail 436
- Fiddler and the Bonehunters 440
- Cotillion and Lostara Yil 443
- Twilight – The Watch 445
- Tanakalian 447
- Brys and Aranict 450
- Setoc and Humanity 451
- Ending 453

CONCLUSION 455

PRIMARY REFERENCES 465

BIBLIOGRAPHY 466

ABOUT THE AUTHOR 469

Foreword

I was around twelve when my father, who was a chef, decided to go back to school, finishing high school, then getting a B.A., then an M.A. and finally, after eighteen years (while working as a waiter to keep his family afloat), his PhD in psychology. Through my teen years, the house was full of university text books related to his studies. I read many of them. That would, of course, have included Jung. My ancillary interests in mythology had awakened by then, and I am sure I can track a path to my eventual studies in anthropology, although all of that was formative in only the vaguest sense. In any case, that was a long time ago; nor can I say, definitively, that Jung was a conscious intention behind the creation of The Malazan Book of the Fallen, or the stories within it.

That said, story is a complicated thing, one that has narrative continuities that cross many if not all cultures. Not just narrative continuities, but psychological ones as well. If I were to think about the elements of The Malazan Book of the Fallen and perhaps my fiction writing in general, that I am most proud of, they lie with the psychological verisimilitude of the characters. I often get notes from readers highlighting certain character storylines (Felisin, Ganoes Paran, Seren Pedac, etc), and these readers are often clinicians, therapists, and psychologists, or are experiencers of comparable trauma. They see some truth in those fictional characters and their ordeals.

The magic of Jung, of course, is found in that very universality he explored, the subtextual language of our lives which seems to characterise consciousness, and its passage through time. We seem to function via more than one heart-beat. In our lives we rise and fall many times, with pauses between each movement; we move to unseen currents, and the internal landscape of our lives deceive us with notions of sameness, all the while changing without surcease.

Not counting the eight years I needed to find a publisher for *Gardens of the Moon*, the essential writing of the ten-book series took about eleven years. I was freed to do this at age 41 – a bit late for the start of my writing career. But it may be that I needed to wait that long in order to bring to the effort a certain maturity. In any case, this was very much a mid-life endeavour, though it took me past that by the end. My sense upon completion was of a vast weight lifting from my shoulders. I felt I had done all I could, to the best of my ability, with the genre. All that followed was but reiteration. Or, in the case of the Kharkanas Trilogy, a focused descent into language itself.

Anyway, that's all background. This book in your hands, dear reader, is extraordinary, and it seems The Malazan Book of the Fallen was well-suited to a Jungian analysis.

To the extent that I was being deliberate in my formulation of archetypes, well, I do know that I wanted to dismantle the hero's journey as promulgated by Campbell; or, rather, to truncate it for my characters, so that no single character could serve to carry the reader through the entire journey. I preferred to think that the hero's journey, if such a thing was necessary, would belong to the reader, and only 'completed' if that reader did not bail part-way through the series. That to complete the reading was itself the journey, heroic or otherwise. And, knowing that, I fully expected to lose readers along the way.

My most pressing internal requirement was to deliver something worthwhile to the reader who did stay with me until the very end. That was probably the primary pressure I was feeling as I neared completion.

I'd like to convey my appreciation for highlighting the function of The Snake and its conjoining with the Bonehunters, to entwine the two serpents into the symbol of healing. Pretty much no-one else has caught any of that. As for Tavore, the avoidance of her point-of-view was essential, for reasons of literary effect as much as anything else, though her reluctant role as Mother was certainly in my mind (and Fiddler as the father), so I suppose I was channelling some Jung after all. The metatextual elements of Badalle and the power of language was of course not accidental. To write is to doubt. And faith will ebb more readily than rise, especially with a long, long project.

It may be that any lengthy work, substantive of text in other words, can sustain Jungian analysis, at least in respect to fiction. That said, I am relieved that The Malazan Book of the Fallen proved such fertile soil for the endeavour.

As one last note to readers of this work: perusing this analysis prior to reading the source material in its entirety, is not advised. If you are familiar with Jungian analysis, that's wonderful, but not necessary. Michael Woods sets each stage with a comprehensive grounding in Jungian theory, and it's more than enough to carry you through.

It is my hope that this book signifies the beginning of a conversation rather than its conclusion. There's plenty more to delve into or expand upon in a Jungian context. That, of course, is not due to some special quality of The Malazan Book of the Fallen, but to Jung's extraordinary insight into the human condition.

Now, enough of me. Inevitably, the author must step to one side, and let the work speak for itself.

Be well, and be forgiving of others and of yourself.

Steven Erikson

Victoria, British Columbia,

December, 2024

Introduction

This text came about because it was a set of ideas that gnawed at me over many years. I couldn't let it go. Or rather, I was drawn to return. The unerring pull of a primordial force at the other end of a chain. The call to adventure, perhaps.

Reading the *Malazan Book of the Fallen* by Steven Erikson was a formative experience for me, and that has only been confirmed with each reading, as life has wrought its changes. But there was always a sense that the fullest interpretation was just beyond reach of my understanding or experience. I felt that there was an elusive underlying structure, or arc, in the novels that I needed to pin down, or at least name. I've been circling around this understanding for some time, and this text is the closest I can come to adequately understanding the books, and the feeling that I have undergone in reading and studying them.

Individuation is necessarily an idiosyncratic process, much of the change occurring internally, and yet such growth can be understood as being itself archetypal in its movement. So interpreting the Book of the Fallen as this one thing is quite easy, because all life is the process of individuation, and literature at its heart is simply an account of life; it is also hard to refute because it is my own experience and interpretation.

However, I will contend that Erikson is very intentional in his writing, and while he may not have specifically set out to write ten volumes about individuation from the Jungian perspective, the overall arc of the process and the spirit of the endeavour is very much part of his intention.

Individuation

Individuation as a concept is a little slippery. Jung's terminology has been built on by a couple of generations of "Jungian" analysis and thinkers, the terms defined and worked through post fact by people trying to make their own sense of Jung's thoughts and journey, often seeking to package them for easy consumption. That was in part Jung's intention; it was never his place to formalise structures and definitions, and reading his work and seeing his understandings develop throughout his practice and across his lifespan is both enlightening and daunting. Having read Jung's work both as an undergraduate student of psychology and later as an adult thrashing about for sense and healing, I can attest that diving headfirst into the Collected Works of C.G. Jung can be tricky. Writings about Jung's concepts are often more lucid and enlightening, (i.e., easier), at least for my modern mind to consume, than the originals, even if they sometimes lack the nuance.

Individuation is, in short, psychological growth, a movement from ego-centredness to ego-transcendence, a fulfilling of potential. In his own words,

> In general, it is the process of forming and specializing the individual nature; in particular, it is the development of the psychological individual as a differentiated being from the general, collective psychology. Individuation, therefore, is a process of differentiation, having for its goal the development of the individual personality.[1]

Individuation is characterised by conscious movement, an aware integration of the unconscious processes and forces in life. It has as its goal psychological wholeness. Marie Louise von Franz distinguishes it from the general nature of growth:

> One aspect of [individuation] is an unconscious process, a growing up, a maturation, and a movement toward death. At first sight, this says nothing more than that from an acorn an oak develops, from a calf a cow, from a child an old person; but there is another aspect—and only this is individuation in the strict sense of the word—a process of developing consciousness, which, continually broadening its frame of reference, works toward the conscious realization and active fulfillment of an original fundamental wholeness.[2]

---

[1] Jung, C. G., CW6 [757]
[2] Von Franz, 1997, p. 133

We can see in von Franz's passage above a couple of challenges that run through Jungian texts. First, the concept is both so universal as to be almost self-explanatory, while at the same time it is only strictly this other thing which almost eludes definition. Certainty pervades the writings of Jungian analysts, and yet the contradictions are hard to ignore. Jung's own writings were not without contradiction—they are a record of his thoughts throughout his career, his own changes and turmoil. My challenge here is to maintain a consistent approach to the concepts and terms, while not losing the richness of their meaning; at the same time to reflect through this text how my own understanding is being reshaped as this very journey is undertaken.

We will take as a starting point the notion that individuation is the fulfilment of self. This is in our psychological character and our soul. It is a goal that is strictly unattainable, yet worthy of our striving, for the very process of a conscious journey imbues a life with meaning, gives us a target in the dark. This conception takes into account the notion of the fundamental growth of a being (as of seed to tree) as being part of individuation, for the biological and psychological milestones we pass through life, seemingly patterned by genetic unfolding, are the foundation from which the conscious mind can flourish and seek wholeness. One who remains a child is unlikely to be searching for spiritual awakening at midlife, for example. All, of course, depends on the outer conditions, too, the safety and security of the social context, the basic needs fulfilled.

As definitions go, it's not neat. But it's a process, and we'll orbit and refine our understanding as we go. Better broad than formal, so it rings true for most.

But one central point we will keep dancing around is that of meaning, our search for it, its value for our life. The process of individuation is guided by our own individual values, interests, and the resonance of truth in our search—maybe we can call it conscience. It seems as though we have built in guide rails at the unconscious level that keep us moving in the right direction. Meaning might not keylight the end goal, but is a feeling we can attune to.

Individuation then is both the journey and the destination of life's movements. Each stage of life might be compared with the hero's journey—the coming to consciousness of a child, growth to adulthood, the pivot of midlife, death—and individuation is the archetypal, guiding process that, when consciously approached, can provide and deepen life's meaning through its movements and challenges. Like life, it is never-ending, drawn by time's arrow. But being patterned, the journey recurs with variation at each of life's stages and through life's challenges. Each time around, we deepen our consciousness, and therefore deepen life's meaning. It is a reread on this unavoidable ride, and the conscious hero straps on sword and shield to respond to the call to adventure.

Malazan: Compassion in the Individuated Soul

Fantasy literature allows for deep study of life through metaphor for society, and for the individual. Invoking gods, magic, and imagined cultures and technologies provides the author a canvas upon which to symbolise the aspects of our own civilisation, indeed aspects of our own souls, in the same way myths and stories, folk tales and legends have always functioned as lessons, inviting the listener (or, lately, the reader) to step into the mind of a protagonist and learn by living out acts of heroism, misfortunes, and misdeeds.

Steven Erikson's *Malazan Book of the Fallen* (hereafter Malazan, or the Book of the Fallen, or just the Book) is a ten-volume work of fantasy literature replete with heroic journeys and narratives of growth. Its cast of characters is as wide as its breadth of setting, and this variety allows the author to play with notions of the hero and variations on the theme of individuation. These narratives play out thematically across the arc of the Book as well as in the minutiae of the characters' stories.

That notion of growth is one of the very themes of the Book of the Fallen, and the elliptical movement through life of separation and return, from child to adult and back again. Additionally, the coming to compassion of the individual, which requires the experience of empathy is a theme that rings through the series. These themes are part and parcel of finding meaning in a Jungian sense—for individual growth as well as value for the collective. Conscious growth of an individual, through confrontation and integration of the unconscious and its archetypes necessarily results in a more compassionate being, and perhaps a more compassionate society.

The Writer and Reader as Hero

Malazan has been part of my own individuation. As mentioned, I couldn't let the ideas go, but it has also changed as I entered new phases of life. First read as a young adult and receiver of culture, I am now at the midway point of life, a father, and creator and bearer of culture. There is a pressing need to understand the journey I took, and why it has stayed with me. The understandings I came to, that are still in some sense elusive, needed to be brought to conscious understanding so I can begin to remove its enchantment. That's another way of saying I haven't quite figured out yet what it is I want to say. And I think that's okay. To strive to question reveals.

Reading ten books takes time, and time brings change. My first reading of Malazan occurred when it was first published, across the course of a decade and more. We readers grew with the characters, our changes occurred alongside the heroes, and it couldn't be otherwise.

If reading the books is something, writing them is its own epic. Erikson's own individuation is on full display in the evolution of the narrative as the books unfold. Even a journey undertaken with definite intention is going to reveal hidden things as it progresses, the unconscious peering through the cracks. While we can't pretend to know how the writer changed through the process, some of that growth is reflected in the characters and the story itself. Malazan is a reflexive work, and Erikson's awareness of his audience and his intentional drawing of them along with him on the journey signifies his elderhood.

The criticism could nevertheless be levelled that my interpretation is somewhat forced; the series of books is big enough, and the concept of human growth universal enough that such an interpretation can easily be found by digging deep enough and bending enough quotes to fit my purpose. Indeed, I am leery of literary criticism—if you squint hard enough you can read anything through your blurred vision of a passing mention into a particular narrative, no matter how unconsciously the original text is written. But I contend that there is intention on Erikson's part, to a greater or lesser degree, to undertake and explore the journey of individuation, and that that intention unfolds in the narrative. Even if everything beyond the merest intention is unconsciously done by the author, the success of it as an individuation arc for himself underlies the success of it for the reader, and within the story itself. In other words, that intention and conscious writing is sufficient to demonstrate that this interpretation is true and meaningful.

And, too, the degree and depth, the elliptical nature of the story is itself the work, and it reveals itself. That working through is both proof of, and the very work of, an individuation process.

At the very least, understanding the books through this interpretation empowers a reader to apply a different lens to character, to understanding the other. And the greater the methods of interpretation and understanding at our disposal, the more likely we are to pause, to imagine, moreover to listen, and see how we and all others around us are part of the same striving, a journey of heroic proportions towards greater consciousness. Jung believed that this process was an innate purpose of the soul. Erikson's work plays it out for us, inviting empathy for even the smallest character and the simplest creature in his world, empowering us on that process by never letting us forget that part of our nature, even when it hurts.

Sources and Map

This book will explore the concept of individuation and Jungian concepts as they seem relevant for understanding the interpretation herein. I don't pretend to carry out a comprehensive survey of these ideas, only what is necessary to make the connections. Jung flew by feeling and meaningfulness more than by strict definition and compartmentalisation.

It is also tricky in part because Jung wrote of such universals. While this analysis is firmly grounded in Jungian concepts, and of matters of humanity elucidated by Jung, I refer more often to later sources building on and exploring the concept of individuation, his understudies, those that hew close to the spirit of the original writings and deepen our understanding.

Much of the work in recent decades on Jungian concepts, particularly the notion of archetypes, strays too far from Jung's own exploratory process, formalising and presenting with certainty the ideas that Jung expressed more often from his gut feeling than a formal thesis. As well, we must remember that Jung's collected writings and lectures span his entire adult life and career, through which changes and growth occurred, throughout a tumultuous period of history. Some of the contradictions in Jungians' work come about from cherry-picking quotes from the collected works, much of it is the all-too-human need to proscribe formal definitions and categorisations on concepts that Jung himself acknowledged elude neat definition. Indeed, I have no doubt I will be just as guilty of that in the coming pages. But there is truth that precedes our ability to express it, and I will aim to stay true to the feeling of Jung's work, because that is what will resonate with me and my fellow readers.

So while the collected works of Jung is the primary bibliographic material, the texts referred will be predominantly later Jungian analysts, leaning towards works which have solidified my own understanding of the individuation process, and are interesting and accessible reads in their own right. I particularly commend Marie von Franz's work on interpreting fairy tales, for anyone interested in fairy tales or fantasy literature, for its incredible interrogation of symbolically dense folk tales. Other sources which were important in my reading and appear frequently in reference are Jolande Jacobi's *The Way of individuation*, Edward F. Edinger's *Symbol and Archetypes* (particularly the first part), and Emma Jung's *Animus and Anima*. Robert Johnson's short but incredibly rich writings are modern and elucidating for understanding Jungian concepts, standing out for their depth and concision, and frequently based around interpretations of mythology.

Plenty of online resources will provide a broad understanding of the concepts sufficient to consume (or challenge) this work. Avail yourself of the *Jung Lexicon* by Daryl Sharp, available online.[3] Rather than further muddy any terminology with wordy definitions, I prefer to rely on the feeling. The gist will do.

Furthermore, I will attempt not to be swamped by details of plot, relationship, or timeline in Erikson's novels, again only describing what is necessary to enable the interpretation I invite. My presumption is that the audience for this work is predominantly readers of those books, who already know such minutiae, probably better than me. In the rare case that a reader is here for the Jung and cares little for Erikson, then the concision of detail will prove a strength.

We will begin with a brief look at the hero and individuation, touching on the concept of archetypes and the unconscious, and showing how the journey of stages is typical of individuation. This should fulfill any background required.

Then we will dive a little deeper into Malazan, expanding on the idea of the Book of the Fallen as its own journey of individuation, and how the hero's journey is central to that. Some of the Book's deeper themes will be elucidated: the striving for balance, and the approach to compassion. The underlying arc of the Crippled God as an invitation to compassion will here be explained.

---

[3] https://www.psychceu.com/jung/sharplexicon.html

Thereafter, we will work through Erikson's novels in order, showing how each work provides a unique insight into the individuation process. We will explore through the characters in each of the novels, and we will return to them at different stages of their (and our) journey. The novels have thematic relevance to the journey, and this provides the perfect canvas upon which to explore the process. Quotes from within the novel being discussed in a chapter will be referenced by page number, while the odd reference of another novel from the book cycle will be abbreviated clearly (e.g., *GotM* for *Gardens of the Moon.*)

In approaching the books this way, we will learn as we go, much like naïve heroes. Each book is teachable in what it adds to an understanding of the individuation process, even as it represents a further step in the reader's and writer's own journeys.

There will be character arcs that weave throughout the ten books and show the various stages of growth in deeper detail and variation. Some characters move out of our focus, inviting us to fill the gaps. Other stories highlight aspects of the journey, and some focus the overall themes of the individual books. The themes of the books themselves is its own cyclical journey.

Heroes and Archetypes: Individuation as a Process of Transformation

Story and Rite

One of the deep powers of story is how it models and guides. Empathy, that peculiar consequence of consciousness that lets us cast our mind beyond its own shell, draws us through time and worlds into tales of others' imagining. Information activates within us through story, and that prepares us for knowing what to do when the time comes, when the call to adventure rings out. It is through listening and contemplation—a luxury our fast modern society doesn't prioritise—that we learn the story's lessons.

Hero stories are embodied by listening, reflecting, journeying time and again as a tale is relived or retold. And the stories remain relevant because life proceeds, and repeats. "Indeed, it is most important that children and adults should be exposed to myth and ritual, because helpful archetypal images are in this way activated in the unconscious."[4] A reread is valuable.

The higher purpose in us, our greater consciousness and meaning in life, is shown to us by the hero or protagonist; that very consciousness imparts the nature and ability to use the knowledge that we gain by hearing those stories.

What makes a story mythical is its resonance, the depth of its draw on the culture that belongs to it. Martin Shaw tells us how the power of story and myth is cultivated over time and through repeated telling:

> Though on one level myth is not really about "a long time ago" (but a kind of numinous present), we know that the opening

---

[4] Harding, 1965, p. 36

up to its images through many communities and over long stretches of time deepens the power and intricacy of its disclosures. Repetition has enormous weight. So although the myths usually refer to eternal concerns, the repeated practice of invoking that very "timelessness" is one of the elements that gathers psychic vigor to the telling, like moss around a stone. It's very mysterious.[5]

Esther Harding describes in her exploration of the Babylonian creation myth how the recounting of tales and myths is at once performative and immersive. The teller and the listeners participate in a very real sense by the deep impressions created by archetypes resonating. "If the narrator is touched by the archetypal images in the story, the audience will also be seized by them."[6] The same role is fulfilled by religious ceremony, and in fact literalised in some ways, as in the baptism or the taking of communion, the participant experiences and embodies redemption of the Christian myth.

Because the Book of the Fallen is written consciously and humanely, it activates archetypes and resonates with the reader's instincts. It is an effective conveyor of its message, and provides an impactful experience through taking the journey.

In the Malazan world, Erikson tells his stories across time and place. There are many heroes for us to witness, and experience the story of individuation from a variety of perspectives, through different lenses, and with tweaks and twists on the themes. Also, the very fact of the greater story cycle itself being a grand story of chaos to wholeness—growth, death, and rebirth—is itself a kind of repetition. Erikson chimes the symbolic bells time after time, using that repetition and relatedness to not so much drive the point home as invite the reader in, opening himself and the reader up to receptivity. It is not a matter of forcefulness, it is preparing the ground to accept the life-giving rain of psychic attention.

Archetypes

Archetypes are the contents of the unconscious, that being the spiritual background upon which our conscious lives exist. They are symbolic

---

[5] Shaw, 2014, p. xviii
[6] Harding, 1965, p. 36

expressions of the unconscious: dynamic, alive, charged symbols. We observe them indirectly through patterned behaviour in the collective and in individuals.

Fundamental to the thinking of Jung was the directive purpose of life, the search for meaning. Part of this was the notion that consciousness is always expanding as we develop, both as individuals, and as a culture or civilisation more broadly. The grander movement is played out in miniature within each of us—theme and variation. Jung believed the collective unconscious was part of the instinctive heredity of humanity, which bestowed on us the capacity to tap into deeper shared unconscious life and fulfill that potential.

Through investigation of dreams and imagination, of himself and patients, as well as study of the social and cultural conditions of his time, Jung discovered that the manifestation of unconscious forces, in the form of symbols and characters, drew close parallels to the images and motifs pervading mythology, folktales, and religious stories as far back as we can ascertain. Being so deeply ingrained in our collective psyche, Jung proposed that this shared ocean of imagery was part of our psychological heredity. Where instinct instantiates a physical drive, archetypes do so for the spirit.

Though in the background of our psychic lives, these unconscious forces can act upon our conscious self, the ego. Jung posited that archetypes represent an antinomy between spirit and matter, or the psychic and physical worlds. This suggests they are not separate, but complementary, in tension and always seeking balance and cross talk.

Indeed, one cannot be conscious of something without its apparent opposite – light and dark, death and life, good and evil.

> Nearer to consciousness and more easily grasped by it is the phenomenon of a pair of opposites in which two distinct figures belong together as complementary aspects of a single whole. In myths and fairytales such pairs appear as heaven and earth, sun and moon, hostile brothers, twins, angel and devil, tree of knowledge and tree of life, etc. In creation myths as well, the constituents and creatures of the world are brought into being as pairs of opposites: light and darkness, land and water, life and death, male and female.[7]

Archetype refers to the deep unconscious contents, instinctual patternings, but we more commonly understand it to mean the archetypal images that are manifested by the unconscious, and can take the form of

---

[7] Jaffé, 1970, p. 25

symbols or characters: the wise old man, the witch, the anima and animus. However, I will aim to cleave close to Jung's own notion of archetype as the precursor of such images, rather than the consciously experienced or culturally constructed representation of them. The hero archetype is not the central figure that our deeper self latches on to, but the journey it takes and the instinct that makes us relate to it.

The archetypes are important because Jung's analytical process was based on working through them to approach individuation, both in analysis and of its own course in a life well-lived. Individuation is a kind of spiritual dialogue—a bringing to consciousness, owning (or rather accepting) those aspects of the unconscious—both personal and collective.

Integrating the archetypes is a process of bringing up, but not fully identifying with, an unconscious force, then creating distance, a kind of elliptical orbiting. This circularity or spiralling is a theme that frequently appears in Jungian psychology. We aim for a sense of balance and, being a dynamic process, it is thus never ending. Integration and differentiation are in a constant dance or dialogue.

> The aim of the individuation process is a synthesis of all partial aspects of the conscious and unconscious psyche. It seems to point to an ultimately unknowable, transcendent "centre" of the personality, which—paradoxically—is at the same time its periphery—and is of the "highest intensity", possessing an extraordinary power of irradiation. This centre and periphery Jung calls the Self, and he terms it the origin and fulfilment of the ego.[8]

Central to the individuation process is the development and rounding out of aspects of the self. I won't go into Jungian typology here (popularised along with psychological testing in the second half of last century), but the concept is instructive. We bring to consciousness the under-utilised aspects, balancing the poles of our personality—for example, the intellectual incorporates the sensational, the introvert opens to extraversion. These aren't necessarily dichotomous, but on a spectrum, so the aim is balance. A healthy ego finds balance by communing with the under-utilised aspects. That communication with the unconscious parts is a vital aspect of the individuation process, as one needs to understand their self and be able to flex and balance the aspects where necessary.

> "out of the unconscious rise contents and images, and they

---

[8] Jacobi, 1967, p. 49

> show themselves to the conscious mind as though secretly asking to be grasped and understood, so that 'birth' may be accomplished and 'being' created" says Aniela Jaffe. "If consciousness fails, the images sink back again into the dark, into nothingness, and everything remains as if unhappened. But if it succeeds in grasping the meaning of the images, a transformation takes place"[9]

Bringing the unconscious symbols to consciousness doesn't necessarily mean they are assimilated by the ego. Indeed, a story can be written and be 'just a story'. But if the image is noticed, then a change takes place in understanding. Approaching story with consciousness, and growing consciousness through the living of story, creates the potential for an individuating ego.

Instincts and Complexes

Jung continually tried to articulate the nature of archetype, and there is certainly a recognition that archetypes are known through their action, rather than in and of themselves. Late in his career, Jung wrote:

> They are immemorially strange and unknown, and yet we seem to have known them from everlasting; they are also the source of a remarkable fascination that dazzles and illuminates at once. They draw us like a magnet and at the same time frighten us; they manifest themselves in fantasies, dreams, hallucinations, and in certain kinds of religious ecstasy.[10]

The very notion of archetypes is abstract, and while we can use metaphors and anthropomorphisation to represent them in a story, or as a story, in the real world their validity is shown in their effects, mainly through symbols and complexes. Story makes them relatable, and personal. You express the archetype—the hero, for example—within your own life. Experience manifests as meaning.

We might question how archetypes differ from any other instinctive drive. Indeed, Jung wrote of archetypes in relation to instinct, whose drives

---

[9] Ibid. p.44
[10] Jung, C.G., CW16 [501]

and narratives underpin many of our actions, development, and maturation: "The primordial image might suitably be described as the *instinct's perception of itself*, or as the self-portrait of the instinct."[11] And elsewhere: "Archetypes are systems of readiness for action, and at the same time images and emotions."[12] In other words, they function much as biological instincts. Jung simply chose to focus on the symbolic, emotional form at which they collide with consciousness – the form in which a conscious, planning mind can reckon, realise, and communicate such unfoldings.

> Myth is the primordial language natural to these psychic processes, and no intellectual formation comes anywhere near the richness and expressiveness of mythical imagery. Such processes deal with the primordial images, and these are best and most succinctly reproduced by figurative speech.[13]

We already have the primordial images—prey, predation, parenting—so the instinct to play hunt or build a nest is enacted in narrative form. Children at play act out things that have meaning – nursing, cooking, whatever has meaning in the world around them. It is the interaction of what we invest with meaning and what lights up instinctive faculties that creates personality. And a complex develops around these things as experience is shaped.

As consciousness develops, such expectations take the form of a narrative, or range of possibilities of such. Imagery crystallises in response to experience and learning, as the psyche corresponds the inner expectations to the outer world. Indeed, "there is good reason for supposing that the archetypes are the unconscious images of the instincts themselves, in other words, that they are *patterns of instinctual behaviour*."[14]

Perhaps, then, we can think of archetypes as the interface between the instincts and cultural or social representations. The outer world and life experience activates instinct, but it does so through the action of archetypes, which instantiate complexes using the language of symbols. While complexes, those interactions between outer and inner world, are the manifestations of archetypes in the individual, the language they speak is symbol.

Esther Harding, in exploring the birth of consciousness in the Babylonian creation myth, describes how such mythologies are mirrored in

---

[11] Jung, C.G., CW8 [277]
[12] Jung, C.G., CW10 [53]
[13] Jung, C.G., CW12 [28]
[14] Jung, C.G., CW9i [91]

the mind, and that their interaction throughout history shapes the vessel of consciousness:

> The mythologems represent the archetypal patterns that underlie the development of history, but they also underlie the development of human consciousness in its particular form in each individual. Our chief interest in the ancient stories and cosmogonic myths stems from the fact that while they give legendary accounts of the beginnings of the world, they are also records of the gradual evolution of consciousness in man. They contain, as it were, the history of man's experience vis-à-vis life with all its problems as well as its fulfillments, whether these be inner or outer. The age-old experiences of the human race have left imprints in the capacities of individuals—inborn patterns of behavior that we call instincts. In addition, there are patterns of functioning in the psyche that express themselves in images and are recorded in many forms of story.
>
> These inborn patterns, or archetypes, are of course inaccessible to consciousness, but their images are readily observed and, indeed, they underlie our dreams, our fantasies, and our understanding of other people, as well as of life itself.[15]

We can see, then, the overlap of instinct and archetype, and how the overall patterns might be inherited.

Complexes give form to the archetypes, almost like the medium through which the archetype expresses itself in our psyche. Typically, a complex is defined as a group of related images, bound together by a particular emotional valence—a positive or negative mother complex, for example. We could understand them as functional units within the psyche, almost as proto-personalities themselves, formed by interactions between unconscious contents and life experiences.

As we grow, our associations form and constellate together. Memory and experience, positive and negative, collate around a set of image associations. Social and cultural associations are incorporated into the complex, and indeed our own peculiar biological inheritance. This complex, as a set of impressions, expectations, emotions, and memories associated with the archetypal images, then modulates our behaviour and our interaction with the outer world—and the responses from the world in turn reinforce and shape the complex. This is the inner and outer worlds in constant dialogue.

---

[15] Harding, 1965, p. 46

All this interaction is happening simultaneously on all these different levels, in the psyche, within your biological genome, and culturally/collectively. This is why it can be hard to pin down the archetype, or what its place or role really is, and it seems to be abstracted out from the various factors. Perhaps it is a translating function, or a system activating function when experience triggers instinct or vice versa. But suffice to say, the archetype itself is usually not the active factor, though it is a convenient shorthand. Most often we are talking about a complex or a symbol. Where necessary I will dissociate the ideas, though I will often use terminology loosely in aid of understanding. In a sense, we have to generalise and ambiguate to some degree, because without generalisation we'd get lost in infinite nuance.

Symbols, too, are both dynamic and material. They arrive from the world about us, attracting consciousness which strives to interpret them. They set consciousness in motion, and contribute to the formation of a complex. We assimilate the unconscious contents contained in the symbol, culminating in views, orientations, and concepts. In the unconscious are instincts that have indefinite forms until life experience and the back and forth within the world and unconscious construct a complex that gives shape to a notion of what it is to be, say, a person, what a mother is, a father, a face.

So you can project a pole of the complex. For example, we might say Felisin projects her negative animus complex onto Beneth. I will use somewhat interchangeable language, because we aren't really interested in the functional healing of these characters, more understanding the broad dynamics so we can discuss individuation at a higher level of abstraction. So for simplicity we might say, for instance, that Crokus projects his anima onto Challice D'arle. But were we to get down and dirty we could say that his ego is under the possession of his anima complex, which (the complex) is projected onto her. Or, more abstractly, that he has a neurosis that is rooted in the anima complex. While the latter interpretations might interest me or a staunch Jungian analyst, I'll lean to the simpler forms at the risk of losing a little nuance for the gain in readability. When I do dive into the nuance, it is likely because I have decided the further distinction is useful for interpretation, or I've just got carried away.

The images you use to colour a dynamic will affect how you interpret it, so I am creating as well as interpreting. I'm not going full postmodern in saying every interpretation is equally valid. But there is a possibility that an interpretation can overlap with author's intention such that it both enlightens and expands—that's achieved here. And I think Erikson, or at least Kruppe, would approve of my own embellishments.

Returning to individuation, we can say that it is the instinct to grow towards optimal functioning and an effective state of adaptation to the world. This can partly be fulfilled by dealing with the complexes, conscious appreciation of their role in our psyche, and so removing roadblocks to totality.

Complexes are said to have an archetypal core. Archetypes, as anticipations and expectations (psychic instincts, to make an unnecessary distinction) interact with experiences, repeated behaviour patterns, memories, and so on, and the individual's particular genetic predispositions and responses, and so the complex forms. This in turn mediates the person's response pathways, updating their anticipations, therefore playing a role in behaviour and relation to the world. While this explanation seems a little like a black box description, it has been found useful clinically, and it grounds the (perhaps unnecessary) abstraction of archetypes.

As splinter personalities, or energy diversions, the complexes can respond without our conscious intention. To some degree this is useful, for we don't want to expend conscious energy unnecessarily (thus the value of pain reflexes and so forth). But if a complex is negative (i.e., if adaptation has been harmed in response to neglect or trauma) negative reactions may occur prior to conscious awareness. Think of someone who is quick to anger, or how your emotions flare in response to a phrase a parent had favoured.

Scrabbling to tie it all together: archetypes drive unconscious expectations, are expressed in culture through symbols, and act through an individual as a complex.

Part of the therapeutic process is integrating the complexes. Something repressed, or grown out of trauma, or other negative childhood experience, can be avoided or projected out to others. Symptoms of such are anything that encounters fear, shame, or resistance. Such negative complexes lie in the shadow, and work is needed to acknowledge and express such negative feelings, before healing can begin. Unattended, deep structures, systems of belief, rationalisations, and a whole host of defence mechanisms can be built up in response to, and as a way of working around confronting those aspects.

But why, you might be wondering, is any of this relevant, or necessarily bad, outside of the therapeutic context (and arguably in that context itself)? How does it highlight something about a person or a character?

We might be aware that the collective unconscious can sweep people into mass movements, drawing a culture's or a social unit's energies away from progress. Similarly, at the individual level, say a projection of a complex draws energies away from the underlying purpose of growth. It takes away from the unfulfilled potential in a person. We might fail to adapt to the outer world, or fail to adapt to the inner world. The depths of the unconscious, collective or personal, can cause a mental illness, or temporary destabilising effect on the conscious ego, such as in a midlife crisis, or a tumble into addiction or other neurosis.

All of this theory was developed at the coalface of psychotherapy, so is often more concerned with the potential neuroses and psychoses that might develop through adaptive failure. Your reactions might be unconscious, you might have hangups with your family, history, memories and so forth, living in delusion, be captured by obsessions that draw you away from reality. But on the other side of the equation, conscious appreciation and synthesis of aspects of the individual can enable them to understand and thus escape such negatives and, further, direct their psychic energies towards growth and fulfilment.

So this is more than a mere intellectual exercise, a mapping of a theoretical formation onto a body of literature. When we understand or contextualise human psychodynamics, we give a language and a framework for the infinite variation we see: the patterns, the likenesses and contrasts—to account for some of the variation, and to understand why we relate.

Archetypes reveal how our psychic nature is determined by underlying patterns, which influence experience. In truth, this definition of archetypes is little different to instinct, as we currently understand it. Jung, his followers, and contemporaries, perhaps working from different notions of what constitutes instinct, or trying to distinguish the realms of physiology and psychic nature, held this notion of archetype up against instinct where perhaps no distinction is truly necessary.

Our current psychological paradigm recognises better the interactions between the biological, psychological, and sociocultural realms. Perhaps it could even be said we overemphasise the psychological and in fact devalue the biological, associating it with baseness and preconscious nature, something to be overcome. But the biological nature does not like to be denied, the hound within us will howl for release. Instinct and archetype then, are both explanations for the predetermined responses, expectations and anticipations, and narratives.

If anything, we might think of archetypes as the layer of translation between instinct and the symbolic images and representations that manifest in the conscious mind. If we consider instinct to be fundamentally biological, the very notion of archetype is only necessary once consciousness evolves, the psyche differentiating itself from pure physiological instinct. But of course, they are never truly separate, and all of our understandings and the effects of the unconscious are always working and interacting at all levels – biological, psychological, and sociocultural.

The representations found in myth and folktales, as well as those at the individual level in dreams and fantasies, are no less well understood if rendered as instinct than by archetypes. I will use both terms somewhat interchangeably, again with clarity the focus. But this digression is necessary to (hopefully) avoid clouding the notion of archetypes, to remove some of the mystique.

Jung pointed out a distinguishing feature of an archetype is its feeling value, which sets it apart from other images, and perhaps from other forms of instinct. This hints at the presumed numinosity of the images once they enter consciousness. But whether this feeling value arises after the symbol achieves consciousness, and the very nature of it stimulates the feeling, we can't say. The feeling may be merely a conscious rationalising what is an otherwise subconscious impulse.

It is safe at this stage to acknowledge Jung's bringing of the term archetype to common usage, and to use it as part of a broader definition of instinct.

Ego and Self

Just as matter seeks balance and equilibrium, so does the psyche. This balance in an individual can be represented at the level of conscious and unconscious as the dance between ego and Self.

Ego is the conscious manifestation of the individual, how we experience our ongoing narrative in the world. Self, a somewhat problematic term, even when capitalised, can be viewed as the unconscious ideal of the individual, and corresponds to an internal image of a deity.

Von Franz here summarises the Self as a directional expectation of the psyche, and thus makes clear that it is an important guide to the individuation process: "it is the 'divine spark' residing in the depths of the psyche of every human being. From this center also emanate the ultimate resolves of conscience, when a person seeks to be guided not by conventional morality but really by his 'inner conscience.'"[16] From the Self arises the impulse to individuation, giving the ego at once an ideal and an actuating energy. It represents the wholeness towards which we strive, and the font of energy upon which we draw.

In a lecture, Von Franz used the metaphor of a pine tree, whose seed represents the Self, with all its potential for perfect upright growth of the archetypal pine. But depending on when and where the seed falls, how far it is blown, the nature of the soil, the wind that bends the sapling, the bump of an animal, and how it faces the sun, the growth of the tree is unique and individual, varying from the Self potentiality.

I'll take the metaphor a step further. The roots of a tree, too, grow in their individual way, depending on the nature of the soil, the climate and the rain, growing around obstacles like submerged rocks and the like. The mycorrhizal web in the soil is the unconscious, winding and writhing great distances through field and forest, the greatest store of the soil's carbon, it interacts with the roots of the trees, feeding them and feeding from them, improving the health of the tree and thus helping it fulfil its potentiality by improving the roots' ability to take up nutrients and expand further. We don't even know it is there, but sometimes when we dig in the soil, we see its networks in white starburst. Now, the mycorrhizal network also passes messages along its immense length, helping the trees 'speak' to one another. Furthermore, sometimes, almost without warning, the network will break the surface, a mushroom bursting up through the soil, just as the unconscious is wont to do.

We also know that the higher a tree wishes to grow, the deeper its roots must go to anchor it. And what is its purpose, after all? To be fruitful.

Edinger discusses the ego-Self axis in depth. The take away is really that during the individuation process the ego seeks both to differentiate itself from the Self (just as the conscious individual does from its primordial wholeness) but also to maintain connection through conscious attention to the symbols and processes of the unconscious. By doing so, we are in charged tension at all times, a reciprocal relation between conscious and unconscious.

Differentiation is not total separation. In early life (the first half) the

---

[16] von Franz, 1997. *The Self-Affirmation of Man and Woman*, para 23.

progressive differentiation can be felt as an alternation between inflation and alienation. The latent, young ego is completely identifying with the self. I am the world, its centre and its entirety. The perfection and wholeness of the original state, dwelling in Eden. The glossy spine uncracked. It is the selfishness of the child in its innocence. This is inflation because it presumes itself to be all.

Then, alienation. Exiled from paradise, permanent wounding and separation occur. Herein is the idea that individuation, or the growth of consciousness more generally, entails a wounding. The spur to a self-reflecting ego in later life is often an injury or a failing, parental death, a marriage breakup. Growth occurs at the stages of life that are riven by doubt and uncertainty, and often it is trauma or loss that elevate us to a new level. The wounding is often an incitement, but also there is the fact that an increase in consciousness is a two-sided coin. With consciousness comes responsibility, doubt, the knowledge of death.

Individuation is therefore an ongoing series of separations and returns, in effect maintaining the link of the ego and Self. Too much separation can lead to psychic illness; too little, the same. Again, we are looking at notions of balance and chains. Difficulty arises because we swing too far in one direction or the other, and we tend to overcompensate. "Inflation or alienation become dangerous conditions only if they are separated from the life cycle of which they are parts. If either becomes a static, chronic state of being, rather than a part of the comprehensive dynamism, the personality is threatened."[17] Edinger is showing that while alienation and inflation are necessary dynamics, it is the constant balance and dynamism itself that are important and healthy in a growing consciousness.

The Self can be reckoned as an image of wholeness. Discovery and experience of the Self is the goal of individuation (of course, without inflation of the ego by identification with that godlike Self).

> The Self can be defined as an inner guiding center, which does not coincide with our consciousness and which can only be further explored through dreams, which show that it works toward a lasting expansion and maturation of the personality. To begin with, however, this great center in us is no more than an inborn potentiality. In the course of a lifetime it can be realized to a greater or lesser degree, depending on whether the ego is willing to pay attention to its messages.[18]

---

[17] Edinger, 1972, p. 62
[18] von Franz, 1997. *The Individuation Process*, para 9.

Myths and rituals are replete with archetypal images, and relate to transpersonal categories. The story of Christ reads like the ultimate individuation arc, a hero story. In studying a religion, the practitioner takes part in ceremony and thereby acts out the process, the role, much as a reader subconsciously acts out the stories he or she reads. We all play heroes when we hear a tale spun, and thereby learn the attributes of heroic endeavour, of growth, and of the bounds and mores of society, as well as strengthening our self-image when conflict occurs.

This could indeed be the very purpose and importance of story in human history, its shaping role, and in some way explain why archetypes are so, well, archetypal. So infused with power and so widespread. In coming out of chaos, we are searching for solidity—we are building identity.

Death and Rebirth: The Hero and Individuation

Work on individuation in Jungian analysis focuses often on dreams and fantasy, though expression of the archetypes is also found in myth and folk tales. Fantasy literature therefore functions as a nice platform to stir up some of the important symbols.

"Psychological development in all its phases is a redemptive process. The goal is to redeem by conscious realization, the hidden Self, hidden in unconscious identification with the ego."[19] Growth is the hero story. Or rather, the hero's journey is a stand-in for the individuation process, a personification. I would go as far as to say the hero's journey is merely an example of an individuation arc, which is why it resonates deeply and across time and place, but not universally.

Jacobi notes that the "first requisite for maturation is the stability of the ego and the strengthening of consciousness."[20] These are the preconditions for undertaking the second half of the individuation process, the movement from the first half of life to the descent towards death. She speaks here of the overall life as one of growth towards wholeness in preparation for death.

However, we can consider stages within the life itself as their own journeys following the same archetypal pattern. The journey is ever repeating,

---

[19] Edinger, 1972, p. 103
[20] Jacobi, 1967, p. 27

fractal, or at least staged in some conception. Jacobi discusses it as being conceived in 2, 3, 4 and so on, even up to 10 distinct stages. This is mirrored by the Book of the Fallen being cyclical, the deaths and rebirths of characters, their heroic journeys always ending and beginning. Fantasy makes such metaphors literal: rebirth, a lens which Erikson uses to approach the problem of the rebirth of psyche through the humanising lens.

The simplest story is in two stages: there and back. Fraction it as you will, but the gist is it's not linear. Change is the thing—change and return. What good is growing without a community to bring that knowledge back to?

> Often the transition from the first to the second half of life is accompanied by other kinds of disturbances and serious upheavals. Divorce, change of profession, change of residence, financial losses, physical or psychic illnesses of all kinds characterize the readjustment or forcibly bring it about…difficulties in life, sudden entanglements, dangers and tests of courage, all of which have to be faced and conquered, form as it were an organic part of the analytical work.[21]

It sounds a lot like the hero's journey. The journey out in the first half of life, the return in the second, after the trials and the descent into shadow, whereupon one returns changed, focused more on the spiritual realm than the physical.

But it is not just the descent towards death. Indeed, if life's transitions, or any change and upheaval, can be seen as a death and rebirth, then the preparation of the psyche for the greater sense of meaning is itself a preparation that recurs. "This [the fundamental wholeness which is the goal of individuation] appears already as potential wholeness in early childhood in the form of symbols in dreams and fantasies which manifest again and again in periods of transformation such as puberty, the midlife period, and in times of crisis."[22]

We can define life in terms of distinct phases, but it is also dependent on situations. Trauma, tragedy, the death of a loved one do not politely wait for our readiness. Sometimes we are pulled like reluctant heroes upon the course of psychic growth. At other times, our readiness is inherent, and circumstances simply allow us to fulfill that potential.

The hero is symbolic of the aspects of individual growth that are the stepping out from the old life, and the bringing home of the new. Its broad applicability to aspects and stages of life is therefore obvious, though the hero

---

[21] Jacobi, 1967, p. 23
[22] von Franz, 1997. *The Cosmic Man*, para 1.

archetype itself is not enough to contain all the possibility of individuation. We can't just keep slaying dragons, cleaving away all that is part of us, of culture. There would be no foundation, no stability, just energies focused on seeking, ever seeking, for the new without the time to appreciate what we have and what we had.

Individuation is a striving for differentiation, a fulfilment as of a seed to a tree, of growth potential. We have already discussed the metaphor of a tree's growth as distinguishing the ideal concept of Self. That growth is also itself a journey, here discussed by Jacobi, with emphasis on the challenges, and the right way of approaching those challenges, as the courageous uptake of the adventure:

> Like a seed growing into a tree, life unfolds stage by stage. Triumphant ascent, collapse, crises, failures, and new beginnings strew the way. It is the path trodden by the great majority of mankind, as a rule unreflectingly, unconsciously, unsuspectingly, following its labyrinthine windings from birth to death in hope and longing. It is hedged about with struggle and suffering, joy and sorrow, guilt and error, and nowhere is there security from catastrophe. For as soon as a man tries to escape every risk and prefers to experience life only in his head, in the form of ideas and fantasies, as soon as he surrenders to opinions of "how it ought to be" and, in order not to make a false step, imitates others whenever possible, he forfeits the chance of his own independent development. Only if he treads the path bravely and flings himself into life, fearing no struggle and no exertion and fighting shy of no experience, will he mature his personality more fully than the man who is ever trying to keep to the safe side of the road.[23]

Much focus on individuation is therefore on the transition of mid-life, the inflection point between life and death. The two halves of life, like the movement of the sun across the sky, like phases of the moon. There is growth, zenith and descent.

> In the secret hour of life's midday the parabola is reversed, death is born. The second half of life does not signify ascent, unfolding, increase, exuberance, but death, since the end is its goal. The negation of life's fulfilment is synonymous with the refusal to accept its ending. Both mean not wanting to live, and not wanting to live is identical with not wanting to die.

---

[23] Jacobi, 1967, p. 16

Waxing and waning make one curve.[24]

A reckoning occurs at midlife, where the growth of the first half encumbers the person with so much psychic baggage that the weight becomes undeniable, but also at that stage the ego has presumably developed enough that the confrontation with these facts is possible. Physically, mentally, culturally, much change occurs at this point. The descent of the second half becomes undeniable, almost as though we feel the gravitational pull returning us to the earth.

However, the fractal journey occurs right from birth, of becoming conscious as a child, the separation from the mother, the growth to adolescence which entails another psychological separation, the second half of life, then presumably at death. Indeed, Jung states that "individuation is practically the same as the development of consciousness out of the original state of identity."[25]

Failure to take an accounting leads to neurosis. Mid-life is often associated with a change from physical to spiritual development. If we are stuck in one or the other, with too much emphasis on one or the other, there are problems. "Generally speaking one can say that whereas the first half of life is, in the nature of things, governed and determined by expansion and adaptation to outer reality, the second is governed by restriction or reduction to the essential, by adaptation to the inner reality."[26] Perhaps Jung's focus on individuation being part of the second half of life was due to the first half being such an expansive instinctual expression of growth, while we must apply conscious action and attention to overcome inertia in the second half. All cries out for balance. Likewise, stasis at any point of the hero's journey is problematic.

Any staging of course is artificial, as blurred as any definition of shadow and light. It is a continuum rather than a clear distinction. As such, it may be thought that one is in all stages of individuation at the same time, for different parts of their self. Similarly, the process within the characters, each of their heroic quests as we might think of it, play out across the Book, microcosms of the grander narrative, each representative of the author's own quest and workings.

---

[24] Jung, C.G., CW8 [800]
[25] Jung, C.G., CW6 [762]
[26] Jacobi, 1967, p. 25

The Book of the Fallen as Transformation

Fantasy speaks to a reader directly through symbols, metaphor, imagery, the very stuff of Jung's psychology. It speaks by creating a space in the reader that the real, mimetic world and its rules might otherwise occupy. Into that space the heart and soul can rush. It creates a more direct connection to the unconscious. Marie von Franz's studies of folk and fairy tales revealed that they work in a similar way upon the listener to fantasy, but perhaps even denser, at the pure image level. Fantasy is beyond conscious reality which, we could argue, does not make it unreal, or less real, but more so.

And so, like the dreams and artwork through which Jung's analysis took place, the fantastic is a canvas upon which to entertain the soul's journey. Erikson has spoken about his goal in writing the Book of the Fallen as an exercise not in answers, but in asking the right questions – this is a soul in discovery. Finding the right questions requires an unlearning of what you thought you knew, a rebirth of sorts. That process of discovery is shared with us as readers.

"The psyche is the theatre of all our struggles for development. It is the organ of experience pure and simple. The affirmation of these struggles is "life"; negation of them means isolation, resignation, desiccation."[27] The Book of the Fallen is the theatre of Erikson's struggle for development, and as readers it becomes our own. In that sense, the details matter less than the experience itself (it's not the destination, but the journey). Just as in any form of therapy—dream or art therapy for example are lenses through which to honestly explore the self—we can use the Book (and indeed any great literature, though here it is executed with deep intention) as the theatre of our individuation process.

The naive ego state can be in identification with the world, as though it

---

[27] Jacobi, 1967, p. 14

is all a projection of your own mind. Writing can be individuation because by letting the world of your own creation loose, you no longer identify with it as an inflation of the ego. It is being released, after coming to fullness and fruition. Erikson essentially needed to write the Book of the Fallen to both incorporate it and free himself from it. All these elements of the unconscious, this enormous story riddled with archetypes, is brought to his consciousness and worked through, the page a dream state. To write, then, is both catharsis and assimilation. He has developed a healthy link with that unconscious world. Had he not written it (to completion) the unconscious drives would have remained and reared up, begging to be written. Indeed, we can witness characters' doubts, regressions, despite their early intention, even to the end of the tale when characters ponder the futility of the journey.

The plethora of stories within the Book allows Erikson to deconstruct the hero myth, and to explode it into a universal rendering of the growth process by focusing on parts, breaking it, reshaping its various constructs. These magnifications function to provide intensive experiential study of various parts of the individuation process.

In any work of literature, perspective is an important tool in allowing the reader to identify with characters. Fantasy provides an interesting study, because we are no longer bound by the constraints of real-world sociocultural and historical contexts. Fantasy is ruled by metaphor and myth. Multiple points of view gives us many perspectives but also the responsibility of finding some coherence, an overarching narrative, a truth: we put ourselves into it as much as it infuses us.

The hero corresponds to the ego: "the hero or heroine, that is, in general the main figure in a myth or fairy tale, with whom the hearer or reader of the tale usually tends to identify emotionally."[28] However, von Franz further describes how the hero in fairytales is also somehow undifferentiated, thus giving him or her a universality. In other words, the hero is archetypal, part of the collective unconscious. Further still, their often magical nature, their divinity, also makes them symbolic of the Self—the ideal nature of man, that which we identify with the god-image. In this way, the hero or heroine is a lesson in the evolution of the ego, a guide for how to attain that Self.

Erikson, rather than seeking a universal, impersonal hero image, gets down and mucky with many characters. The individuality expressed through each hero and heroine gives us instead variations of the story, many lessons.

That is what we do intuitively, we seek a coherent narrative, order from chaos, we neaten and enumerate. That search is how we make sense of the

---

[28] von Franz, 1997. *In The Black Woman's Castle*, para 2.

world around us, it is our coming to consciousness, the very basis of an empathic being. We seek virtue in hope that it reflects on us. Isn't the very notion of an anti-hero loaded by such assumptions? Why do we need to distinguish those less desirable traits, if not to relegate them to the shadow?

We empathise with the hero, because that is how we interact with narratives. We identify, even when these undesirable traits make us squirm. And by upsetting norms, by challenging our worldview, an author has the power to reshape the landscapes of moral possibility—a very individual form of worldbuilding, if you will.

Von Franz quotes Max Lüthi discussing fairy tales as pure forms of opposition. Good triumphs over evil because of its purity of character. These narratives lack "concrete detail and reality; they reflect little depth of experience, little of the complexity of human relations, little shading, but in compensation for this poverty of content, they are clear and incisive in form."[29] Erikson's world and characters, in contrast, are replete with shading. All grey; no black and white. In fact, when one character or culture is in imbalance, its flaws are highlighted, such as the Forkrul Assail, who represent justice and order but taken to an extreme. Where fairy tales are direct communications at the level of symbol, from the unconscious, closer to dream, Erikson's journey is a circumnavigation of the shadowy borderlands between conscious and unconscious, the place where we are challenged from both sides, in which we learn and grow.

That said, von Franz tells how, while good and evil are implicit in both the self and nature, it is often at the whimsy of chance or fate whether good triumphs and the devil is downed. This can come in the form of the help of animals, pure luck, or a force of nature.

> Sometimes we have the impression that fairy tales merely reflect a conflict between opposing images of God or opposing dominants of the unconscious mind. But usually we can discern ... that the essential for man is to grasp the principle of individuation in the center of his own psyche; that is, the inner creative germinal point where the progressive tendency toward humanity and wholeness, inherent in both the bright and the dark power of God, strives for fulfillment.[30]

In other words, the narratives provide outer bounds, and the listener's instincts home in on the right path for him or her.

Fairy tales are archetypal, and as Marion Woodman says, the characters

---

[29] von Franz, 1997. *The Problem of Evil in Fairy Tales*, para 2.
[30] Ibid. para 52.

and creatures within them are personifications of psychic energy. Fantasy literature can be both sprinkled with metaphorical aspects, or represent personifications entire. That opens up a breadth of interpretive possibility—there is universality, but it is also personal. Both Erikson's intention and our readings as receivers of this myth and its tales are personal in the interpretations. My reading may not resonate with you, or the deep resonance may ring a bell but the final interpretation not sit right. You may see other stories that resonate more strongly with you. Therein lies the beauty, the depth, the rereadability of the Book.

> In this way, every individual tale illuminates a quite definite aspect of the collective unconscious, and this is where the meaning and living function of that particular tale lies. This also explains why there are so many relatively similar fairy tales, that is, why from a relatively constant set of building blocks—like the image of the witch, the hero, the helpful animal, etc.—peoples build ever new fairy-tale structures; in the integral just-so-ness of every individual tale there is a special meaning, which is sought out by the collectivity at a particular time and which can be delineated by following the "thread" of that tale in the process of interpretation. The curious thing that emerges in doing this is not only the fact that all the archetypal images in a tale are contaminated—and thus with enough amplification interconnections can be shown to exist between all of them—but also that the "thread," the "how" of the story's movement, itself seems to circumambulate a single meaning or content.[31]

Von Franz talks about how a fairy tale is never fully understood. In part, that is because variations imposed by an individual's telling can shift meanings, or take them out of context. But there is also a value in it because the tales are circling around a universal meaning. Likewise in dream interpretation, fully intellectualising a dream's meaning would deaden the symbols. Room must be left for feeling, for mystery.

But along with this, cultures of story that are felt more than known become a canon of tales, and the sheer volume of story itself highlights the archetypal patterns. One story is not enough to understand a hero's journey, and simply studying one tale to death would remove some of the divinity. Putting many stories together, "you get a kind of intuitive mapping of the structure of the collective unconscious and the possible structures and

---

[31] von Franz, 1997. *In The Black Woman's Castle*, para 11.

processes in it."[32] Erikson's cast of characters gives us this volume of stories. It is the Book of the Fallen, a history of those who have taken the fall, so to speak. By enveloping ourselves in this world and all of the characters' journeys, we are most effectively able to glean the deeper underlying pattern.

The obvious metaphor is how the facts of the story are gleaned through the perspectives of the characters. No one character has all the information, though each approaches it with a different perspective. We circle around a truth by taking on all those perspectives, and indeed we can determine how much weight we ascribe to each viewpoint. That is how a personal touch is appointed to a reading, and it doesn't make any one reading lesser or more valuable.

The oral tradition is redolent of the power of story. Sitting around a fire, listening to your tribe members tell such stories of the sun stealers and the underworld, yes, you would learn the messages, the fables, but I suggest you would learn as much from the experience itself—that contact with the storyteller—observing the unspoken such as the connections amongst your tribe, the very reverence held by the stories. You would relate just as strongly to the teller themselves: witnessing their emotions, their frailties and fortitude, take comfort from the obvious fact that they are undergoing the journey themselves with each rendering. And the storyteller could not help but be aware of this heroic power.

The Cycle of Individuation and the Cycle of the Book of the Fallen

Jung's individuation is a western conceptualisation of the journey, the growth process, or at least we could say that he presents a western lens through which to view that universal process. Erikson, in exploring his multitude of heroes and cultures is allowing himself play space to explore different manifestations. Of course, postmodernism would insist that his own lens is necessarily enforcing an interpretation, but one of the strengths and freedoms of fantasy is that its very nature can render it objective in that sense. Tweak one variable and see what difference it makes. In this way, fantasy can explore

---

[32] Von Franz M.-L. , 1997a, p. 21

those universalities without professing to understand all the varieties of experience in our world.

Jacobi described the individuation process as simply as the difference between 'I do' and 'I am conscious of what I do', and thus as a bringing of oneself to awareness: recognition and development of the ego. By holding a mirror up to the reader, and by extension documenting his own journey, Erikson demonstrates that process, undertakes it, and guides it, all at the same time. Reading it and rereading it is akin to the rigour of learning and reciting a long oral story.

> Jung lays great stress on the decisive role played by consciousness and its capacity for insight, though he rigorously rejects its dictatorship and constantly demands that attention be paid to the "messages" sent up from the unconscious depths. Work on the psyche in his view aims at giving these messages their due and, over and above that, at strengthening consciousness so that it shall be equal to the demands made upon it on the great journey of life, the "quest of the hero", through encounters with the contents of the unconscious.[33]

We could say these messages, the contents of the unconscious, are the symbols in literature working upon us, just as dream images work upon us. It is by engagement with the symbolism, the deep process of reading and understanding each hero's journey and the imagery in the books, by engaging our empathy, that the distinction can be made between simple self-awareness (i.e., that one is reading a book) and conscious self-awareness (that one is undergoing that very journey described). Such consciousness is what Erikson promotes as a writer. One must write consciously: imagery is intentional, style and word choice are conscious decisions and therefore moral decisions.

> Edinger: "Stated in the broadest possible terms, individuation seems to be the innate urge of life to realize itself consciously. The transpersonal life energy, in the process of self-unfolding, uses human consciousness, a product of itself, as an instrument for its own self-realization."

The meaning of the text will become clear as we dive into the books themselves. The overall thematic cycle from chaos to wholeness, through death and rebirth, and the touch with the collective and building the family, all playing out on many levels.

---

[33] Jacobi, 1967, p. 19

Consciousness, its very nature, and the shifts we undergo as we grow, could be seen as a growth of self-perception. This occurs as much on the societal, collective level as the individual. When something perceives itself as separate from the unity, it achieves consciousness (or at least, it can). The child realises it is separate from the mother, thus self-awareness, consciousness. The adolescent is not the centre of the world, thus removing the inflation of the ego to god. And so on. Metafiction is thus self-awareness of the reader and author. Not only do we take this journey together, but we nurture awareness of it, a conscious dialogue between fiction and life, symbols and reader. It makes the process and the experience purposeful and meaningful in the growing of our consciousness.

> The individuation process, as a universal law of life, exhibits an archetypal pattern which remains more or less constant and regular. The signposts and milestones on the way are specific archetypal contents and motifs whose sequence cannot, however, be determined in advance and whose manifestations vary from individual to individual....The symbolism of birth, life, death, and rebirth is part of the pattern of the individuation process. From the remotest times man has tried to express it in the imagery of myths and fairytales, in rituals and works of art, to capture the archetypal events in forms that are valid for all men.[34]

We could see individuation as metaphor for life, life's stages, and all growth and transformation. A fulfilling of potential in growing to a new stage, phase, or reality. Change occurs even without conscious awareness, but with intentional attention to the integration of the unconscious the person can realise great psychic potential, and therefore deepen meaning. Grandiose as it sounds, this connection with the divine, the unconscious, should be a humbling experience, approached with honesty and empathy.

Fantasy literature speaks to us in archetypal ways, and its resonance is in part due to that representation of growth and transformation. Ursula LeGuin, in *The Child and the Shadow*, spoke about fantasy as being:

> The guide of the journey of self-knowledge, to adulthood, to the light...It also seems to me that most of the great works of fantasy are about that journey; and that fantasy is the medium best suited to a description of that journey, its perils, and rewards. The events of a voyage into the unconscious are not describable in the language of rational daily life: only the

---

[34] Ibid. p. 60

symbolic language of the deeper psyche will fit them without trivializing them.[35]

The Book of the Fallen is itself a grand cycle from chaos to wholeness, death and rebirth. Erikson invites us to pick up what pieces we might, what resonate with us, absorbing as well what discomfits us. The images and journeys chosen by the writer, spoken in that symbolic language, leave space for individual interpretation. And that space is the imaginative possibility. As growing and learning humans (still, as an adult) we explore those consequences – we grow compassion.

But this cycle is one that is worked through over and again. Growth does not halt with the finding of the treasure. It is incumbent upon the conscious being to seek deeper meaning and wholeness, and Jung spoke of this as an almost necessary drive. "The goal of individuation, the realisation of the self, is never fully attained…'Successful individuation' is never total, it is only an optimal achievement of wholeness."[36]

Rebirth is, of course, a theme of the Book of the Fallen. It is inherent in the hero story, individuation, and growth. It occurs at each stage—constantly, we might say. Death and rebirth is always occurring. So rebirth appears in each volume of the Book in some way. Beginning with the startling death of Ganoes Paran, which is a signpost that this sort of thing will be occurring.

Erich Neumann described how the world's myths mirrored the growth and the very existence of human consciousness, beginning with wholeness. As a snake biting its own tail, we eventually return to that wholeness. The process of individuation, of a life lived consciously, allows for the journey that began in unconsciousness to end in conscious wholeness.

Erikson is fully aware of this fractal, cyclical nature in the Book, and indeed the vast tapestry of stories alone allows room for rereading and new interpretations. There is always a deeper connection, more of the deep collective that can be apprehended by a person, and it can always be maintained that a richer life can be achieved, that more meaning can be extracted from it. This doesn't make the journey of individual growth a fool's errand, rather it maintains consciousness and encourages deeper journeying. Much like the counsel to be like Christ is never in itself achievable, but the striving arguably leads to a constant bettering of the devotee.

While that very openness is a get out of jail card, as you can basically impute these meanings onto any story with the semblance of an arc of

---

[35] Le Guin, 1979, p. 61
[36] Jaffé, 1970, p. 83

character, my purpose here is to show intentionality on Erikson's part, at least an intentional working through of the issues and archetypes. That openness is also a strength here, as Erikson can tell the story from many viewpoints, playing with the variables as he goes.

It is easy to see how, if you view the tale differently, you can attribute any number of stages to it. In a sense, we have to accept that there is not a specific breakdown, though I will refer to stages at various points. As it is all a continuum, we may linger at one stage of the journey longer than others. This metaphor itself can be played with quite readily when one is particularly long-lived, or undead.

> The individuation process, as the way of development and maturation of the psyche, does not follow a straight line, nor does it always lead onwards and upwards. The course it follows is rather "stadial", consisting of progress and regress, flux and stagnation in alternating sequence. Only when we glance back over a long stretch of the way can we notice the development. If we wish to mark out the way somehow or other, it can equally well be considered a "spiral", the same problems and motifs occurring again and again on different levels.[37]

Erikson speaks of elliptical writing, wherein a problem is approached and returned to, with change. This is on a small scale the hero's journey of departure, change, and return. On a wider scale, the Book follows that same pattern, as we take the journey and return changed. Many stories, and rereads allow for multiple passages at a problem, seeing an argument from different perspectives. This itself is necessary for honest self-analysis, and growth.

Balance

A theme in both Jung's psychology and the Book of the Fallen is that of balance. There being no straight lines and neat separations, life and the archetypes being dynamic, the journey recurring, the seeking of balance is always necessary. In a way, that dance itself is the work of achieving psychic wholeness, as we strive to balance the integration of unconscious forces with

---

[37] Jacobi, 1967, p. 34

the autonomy of the ego.

Jacobi writes of Jung's understanding of the individuation process being concerned with both conscious and unconscious aspects of the psyche "in their delicately balanced and creative interaction with the conscious mind." This is made metaphorical in Malazan. The dynamic mobility suggested, the tension and stagnation, could be seen as order and chaos, fundamental to magic, and the final order out of which compassionate humanity emerges.

Jacobi continues:

> The beginning and end of psychic life are in his view inseparable, bound together at every moment in the thousand-branched stream of psychic energy which pours without cessation through all the reaches of the psyche.
>
> In this psyche the energy is kept in a state of constant dynamic mobility by a subtle mechanism of self-regulation and compensation, balanced between tension and stagnation.[38]

The lifelong individuation process is one of balancing the biological life with the psychic life. Of coming to a greater depth of meaning in the soul, so that death can be approached with humility, having lived a life in its fullest capacity of humanity. Jacobi again:

> The more biological a life is, particularly in its second half, the more it can be said to "come to an end", and the more powerfully those late years are shaped by the spirit, the more it can be said to "come to completion". Generally speaking, there is a polar relationship between the two forms of life, since the one often develops at the expense of the other.[39]

Again here, we could draw a metaphor of spirit/psyche as the magical balance to the physical world. Indeed, in Erikson's world magic itself is a literal balancer. He uses it to level the playing field, so to speak.

And indeed, magic itself has a balancing force, otataral. The chaotic forces of magic, itself both order and disorder, needs a counterbalance, "Negation to creation, absence to presence" (*DoD* p.250). Though even otataral has within it a life, an element of blood and chaos, so we can see that there are layers to the dance of balance and counterbalance. This play of balance in the metaphor of magic is just one way Erikson realises the theme. Chaos and order are the overarching forces in tension, just as in the human

---

[38] Ibid. p. 13-14
[39] Ibid. p. 16

psyche. "There are many words for this struggle. Order against chaos, structure against dissolution, light against dark, life against death. But they all mean the same thing." (*HoC* p.681)

Jung spoke of insoluble problems, and that seemingly intractable situations could leave us stuck because we are focused on outer solutions to those problems, and remain so even when it is obvious that no such solution exists. The true solution in such situations is an inner solution: the acceptance of the very fact of no outer solution to a problem, that the way forward is the very psychic growth that this paradox has engendered. This realisation can be hard, can leave us embittered, and can stay with us for years. We can bear psychic and physical scars because of it.

Jungian psychology sees the challenges of the life, conflict, not as failures or misfortunes but as necessities to growth, challenges to a dynamic system that has fallen into stagnation. "The self is made manifest in the opposites and in the conflict between them; it is a *coincidentia oppositorum* [coincidence of opposites]. Hence the way to the self begins with conflict."[40] The response of that system and its ability to adapt are the markers of its strength, its heroic aspects. A stable, perfect, unchallenged world is staid and decrepit. A soul without loss is a soul that hasn't grown. Conflict is the spur to attention and intention, and therefore to growth.

The fundamental growth with which we all begin, of course, is the separation from the mother, both physically at birth, then psychologically as the child grows. In later life, such separations recur at different stages: the physical release of growing into adulthood, the second half of life from the first, and so on. Recall the dynamics of ego and Self, where integration and separation are carried out consciously, to avoid the inflation or alienation of the ego. Von Franz spoke of these dynamics: "If you take the human personality as a sphere, with the Self embracing the whole sphere and also being the self-regulating factor in the centre, any deviation will have compensations."[41] She points out that these compensations are often expressed psychically in dreams or fantasies.

Chaos is not simply the antithesis of balance, but it creates a mobility in the world. The striving for balance is at heart the state of nature, the very dynamic through which psychic growth occurs, whereas order in and of itself is unnatural, a form of stasis. Chaos and order pull against one another, and the tension between the two is the inner conflict through which the ego asserts itself.

---

[40] Jung, C.G., CW 12 [259]
[41] Von Franz, 1980, p. 16

Tension between opposites is often resolved through the spontaneous creation of a new symbol reconciling them. Think shadow as reconciling dark and light. It is as though the mind is forced into an untenable situation so that something new and creative can come into existence. Similarly, a culture may be in stasis when a hero rises to raise the mass consciousness or brings culture to the collective. In the Book of the Fallen, magic is a potent metaphor, and this idea of a creative force arising in response to a need is flirted with in the series. The warren of Shadow, for example, "only appeared following the Emperor's assassination at Laseen's hand." (*GotM*, p.123) It is as though warrens, houses, holds and so on are the archetypal manifestations of a collective psyche, symbols arising in response to the chaos of the unconscious. "…the power of Chaos, the paths that lie *between* warrens" (*GotM* p.119). Indeed, it seems magic is an ordering force as well as a pathway, and a symbol upon which to project the underlying archetypal force and thus restrain it—use it consciously.

And so in the Book of the Fallen, Erikson uses various images and even entire cultures as metaphors for this dynamic psychic system's striving for balance. A character may hold too much suffering on themselves, and it has to break. Another may be too strong in his convictions and see comeuppance from fate or the gods. These are the normal dynamics of character, of humanity, but Erikson uses his grand tapestry to explore these ideas in depth, to stretch the tension, to see how much a person can bear until they break. He is exploring his own degree of psychic strength and challenging the reader to speculate upon their own.

The Crippled God: Striving for Compassion

The underlying story for the Book is one of redemption for Kaminsod, the Crippled God. The arc of this God is a background process in the novels which we are led to, and either during or by the end of the process we see that the focus of this storyline is compassion. Although the final novel is titled *The Crippled God*, that storyline is somewhat underneath the main action. Here we will put it at the fore, because it is a crucial demonstration, and underpins the drive in the novels towards compassion.

What he represents is not a great villain, but an invitation to compassion. It is the culmination of the themes that are worked through: redemption, growth, and picking up pieces of a story to achieve individuation, the death and rebirth of the hero, the notion of balance. The Crippled God's redemption is not explicitly addressed, and indeed Tavore, who we do not get much insight into, is the hero who is most responsible for seeking to redeem the god's heart. As readers we are wracked with doubts and misinformation, challenged to witness, and by staying with that pain we are able to accept the redemption when it arrives. We have changed.

> As this process goes on, it gradually becomes clear that a hidden goal-orientation is at work in it, which is bringing about a slow psychic growth. This is a process of self-realization, of becoming oneself. A more comprehensive, more mature personality becomes visible and also tangible to others.[42]

The Book of the Fallen is working at both a conscious level of the hero stories, and at the unconscious level, with the stories guiding us through the process beneath consciousness, and the underlying goal of redeeming the Crippled God itself creates a journey towards compassion. Could one function without the other? It is a demonstration of the effect of the individuation process, while at the same time a guide for those who approach it with an open heart.

If we consider the greater tension between chaos and order, then the existence of the Crippled God in the Book is the external force that pushes the system out of its equilibrium. It is the psychic wound that triggers growth. "A third force, to change forever the eternal war between order and dissolution...A master demanding the worship of imperfection." (*HoC* p.682) The Crippled God's nature is a recognition of the necessity of suffering to growth. Perfection is a futile goal, so is sleepwalking through ignorance. In similar fashion, the individuation process is also a recognition of the necessity, or at least the growth potential of struggle and suffering. We must fall before we ascend.

> Because man fears the mighty and continuous effort bound up with this task and if possible shuns every sacrifice, there are even in the "natural" individuation process all kinds of degeneracies and deformations. Precisely because it is nature-bound, its manifestations may be "sick" and defective. It may for instance be blocked (by psychosis), inhibited (by alcoholism or other cravings), it may be bogus, superficial, infantile, or prematurely interrupted (by death, accident, war),

---

[42] von Franz, 1997. *The Individuation Process*, para. 4.

it may be hindered by degeneration, perversion, etc.[43]

In myth and folklore, gods often show up as uninvited guests, travellers, or as beggars and so forth. This invites the realisation of the divine within the earthly, compassion for the distasteful and mundane. This is what Erikson draws on with the Crippled God, and is characteristic of the portrayals throughout the series of those entities residing within our collective shadow. We are invited to have compassion for all sorts of undesirable characters and entities. We are shown that they, too, are taking a journey. On the face of it, the Crippled God was seeking a place in the Malazan world. The divine often appears requesting lodging, and it is those who offer the visitor hospitality that receive a blessing. Showing compassion, being in touch with the unconscious, is the sign of strength. Ganoes Paran, as Master of the Deck, fulfills this role when he accommodates the Crippled God's new House of Chains in the Deck, sanctifying the Crippled God and assimilating his shadow.

Edinger discusses the attitude to weakness and suffering in the Christian myth, showing that this is essential to individuation:

> A real transvaluation of ordinary values is brought about. Strength, power, fullness, and success, the usual conscious values, are denied. Instead, weakness, suffering, poverty, and failure are given special dignity. ...Psychologically understood, we have here, I think, a clash between the goals and values of two different phases of ego development. Preoccupation with personal honor and strength and the despising of weakness is inevitable and necessary in the early stages of ego development. ...It is in the later phases of psychic development, when a fairly stable and mature ego has already been achieved, that the psychological implications of the Christian myth are especially applicable.[44]

In a similar way at the beginning of our reading, just as we are having our expectations of genre tropes overturned, born in naivete into a chaotic world, we are not ready to understand and embody the compassion required to redeem the Crippled God in our own hearts. At this earlier stage we need to distance ourselves from that which is distasteful, from the suffering. We must initially separate ourselves, seeing it as the 'other', so that a reunification may occur. By taking this extensive journey, Erikson guides us so that it might be achieved for the reader as well. But just as the perfection of Christ cannot be

---

[43] Jacobi, 1967, p. 17
[44] Edinger, 1972, p. 153

attained in reality, it is not a failing of us if we don't achieve compassion the first time around, or if we lack compassion for someone or something. We can always take the journey again. There is always more growth that can occur.

There are many creation myths that depict the beginning of things with the scattered parts of a giant or a cosmic being. This represents the preconscious wholeness that exists before ego develops, before differentiation occurred. The primordial or cosmic man being dismembered and then returned to wholeness is a return to light – often resembling the bringing of culture, or a new phase of psychological development. The reunification of the cosmic one is a work of redemption. Here Von Franz discusses the concept:

> the idea prominently emerges of an evolution that corresponds to the development into consciousness of all humanity. This, however, can also be understood only as an inner psychic process in the individual, for each individual always encounters himself initially as a chaotic miscellany of hereditary components, a particle of a mass and the mass itself, which can reach unity only through becoming conscious.[45]

The work of wholeness for the Crippled God is therefore a redemption motif that carries through the Book of the Fallen. It also represents an individuation for the heroes who partake, and in our and the writer's work it proposes that the collective understanding of compassion for this being we were led to believe was the 'other' may indeed develop consciousness for all of us, the collective. The arc brings to consciousness what was chained in the unconscious. A shared attention to the shadow and the god's reunification can change the world.

But first, let us return to the beginning, take the journey again.

---

[45] von Franz, 1997. *The Cosmic Man.* 'The Quaternary Structure…' para 8.

Prod and Pull: Birth in Chaos, Good and Evil in *Gardens of the Moon*

The overwhelming experience in beginning this series is of being thrust into chaos. We are trying to find our feet both in this place, this world, and with the many characters we are presented, their histories and relationships.

We open at Mock's Hold, the centre of the empire's birth. Though we don't know much of its origin, it certainly appears that chaos reigns now in the empire – a pogrom, soldiers appearing to be bemoaning the lack of control in the situation. "Chaos itself. If one force is ascendant in this time it is surely that…" (*TBH*, p.678) The wild swing of Mock's Vane hints at its influence from unpredictable sources beyond what is seen.

Chaos is necessary as a starting point. From chaos, all is created. It is the impetus for the balance to be found in order.

The defamiliarization of the structure of this opening novel is itself a representation of the chaos of being born into this world. We are rudderless in a storm, characters and motivations are unclear, magic battles raging. We intuitively seek order in narrative, seek a perspective upon which to anchor ourselves, but Erikson demands that we ride the chaos—he stretches the reader to a limit, showing us that this is not going to be comfortable. "Through the gamut of life we struggled for control, for a means to fashion the world around us, an eternal, hopeless hunt for the privilege of being able to predict the shape of our lives." (457) But this privilege is denied us. What bare mastery we have is slippery and unpredictable, riven by chaos. "A young person has not yet acquired a past, therefore he has no present either. He does not create culture, he merely exists. It is the privilege and task of maturer people, who have passed the meridian of life, to create culture."[46] We begin

---

[46] Jung, C.G., CW10 [272]

with chaos and seek balance, thus growing in the process.

"I want to be a soldier. A hero." (5) Ganoes Paran's youthful announcement conditions the reader to expect the hero narrative, that sympathetic anchor point. But we also know a soldier and hero are not the same thing, and that is something he will quickly learn. There is in this the arrogance of the inflated ego. What he wants is the state of completed heroism, the lure of the whole self. To take the role of a hero, however, is to undertake the journey and to grow in the process.

In early life (we could casually denote the first half) the progressive differentiation of an individual can be felt as a series of alternations between inflation and alienation, as described by Edward Edinger[47]. Just like the child from the mother, we are exiled from paradise—permanent wounding and separation occur. In myth this is represented both through the individual and at the broader scale by creation stories. Life, then, is an ongoing series of separations and returns. The goal of the conscious, maturing mind is to maintain the link between ego and Self, as too much alienation leads to psychic illness, and not enough separation the same. We are looking at notions of balance and chains.

The latent, young ego completely identifies with the Self. I am the world, its centre, and its entirety. The perfection and wholeness of the original state, dwelling in Eden. The glossy spine uncracked. It is the selfishness of the child in its innocence, the adolescent in his egocentricity. It is inflation, because it presumes itself to be all, it projects the archetype of the hero, the end of the journey, onto the Self. Erich Neumann likens this virgin state to a cosmic wholeness, where the creation myths take place. Separation of the ego has not yet occurred, not yet differentiated itself from the unconsciousness of pure image. Light emerges from the darkness of the unconscious.

So we are thrust into chaos at the beginning of the story with no frame of reference. In a sense all stories begin that way, but arguably when we know the patterns, we use the same old archetypes, we are just travelling down a well-worn rut of stuff we have already assimilated. Erikson challenges us here by pulling away that foundation, or at least causing some discomfort. And that discomfort is necessary in the individuation process. We have an inherent aversion to it, just like we are searching for the pattern, seeking the obvious hero and the bad guy.

Sorcery that "fray[ed] the fabric between the worlds. Whatever dwelt beyond, in the Warrens of Chaos, felt close enough to reach out and touch." (49) Again, we are just starting to get a foothold here, we can still sense that

---

[47] Edinger, 1972

chaotic birth. This is not just about the scattering of the narrative, the shaken sense of time at the siege of Pale, but a recognition that chaos is a beginning.

Jolande Jacobi writes of the transition to life's second half, the work of individuation in a spiritual sense, and why this venture is often troubling:

> "In most of the cases the lack of a tenable philosophy of life or of a religious foundation is also apparent — which, in this critical phase, when everything gets unsettled and needs to be built up again, would provide a secure foothold. As a rule there is no proper relationship to the suprapersonal as a support, so that the crises are due to actual conflicts in the present and not to those rooted in the past."[48]

For us as readers, with this rebirth into a novel world, it is a similar lack of foundation.

In a way it turns out Paran is right, despite the seeming arrogance, because he does do the hard work eventually, and that marks him as a hero. It is more that we have to go down with him in his descent, but even this is sudden and unfamiliar as a reader. So first he must separate from the identification with self, before he can integrate, and in undertaking that part of the journey a separation is made between this hero and the reader, and despite his recurring character in the series that close identification is never truly regained. We intuitively understand the fragility of such identification.

> "Life may be compared to a piece of embroidery, of which, during the first half of his time, a man gets a sight of the right side, and during the second half, of the wrong. The wrong side is not so pretty as the right, but it is more instructive; it shows the way in which the threads have been worked together."[49]

In rereading, we take the journey again, see the back side of the embroidery. We are no longer expanding and exploring, but synthesising our understanding. The end point of the second half of life is, of course, a known destination.

> "At this point the second phase of the individuation process begins, when the ego, having become consolidated during the first phase, turns back in order to gather new vitality from contact with its origin, the creative background of the psyche, and to cast anchor in it this time for sure. After having broken away from the domain of the Self, the ego must re-establish a

---

[48] Jacobi, 1967, p. 43
[49] Schopenhauer, as quoted in Jacobi, Ibid. p. 25.

connection with it so as not to remain rootless and lifeless."[50]

So I begin to question, perhaps Paran's character is not simply representative of the upset expectations, he just takes us the hard way. He does end up being the hero, it's just that we are shown that that hero might not look like we think when we are young and naïve.

Gardens of the Moon is fundamentally about good and evil, though is conspicuous in its absence of an obvious hero and an obvious villain. It is all grey, just shades. That puts us in a naïve state, a childlike ego where our projections are freely given. It is interesting in and of itself to whom we apply our hero projection – the boy soldier, the orphan, the Eel, the Bridgeburners. There is no full identification of good and evil possible, but that also means there is no right and wrong answer.

That forced identification with a naïve ego state does two things. It readies us for the journey ahead, taking us out of our preconceived ego, and it also upends the expectations of the genre and to some extent story more generally.

Ganoes Paran

Gardens of the Moon opens with the wide-eyed innocence of young Ganoes Paran atop Mock's Hold, surrounded by empire stalwarts. Naïve and expectant, he is a stand-in for our own pure state. On first reading I didn't get that, I just wanted to identify with someone, something. Next we see him, his innocence is gone, all swept away by the aftermath of an encounter with the shadow (in this case the Hounds of Shadow), the representatives of dark, unknown forces at work to unsettle the Empire. He has seen death and depravity, and it has taken away the child in him.

In the aftermath of the massacre, he thinks about his sudden ascent to the role of aide to Adjunct Lorn, and speculates "his father and sisters were bound to be impressed." (33) It is immediately interesting that although he has attempted to separate himself from the family's social structure, he still seeks approval there, marking for us the fact that he is still a child.

But more, Marie Louise von Franz, Jungian scholar of folklore and

---

[50] Jacobi, 1967, p. 42

myths, says in a fairy tale we must count the main figures, the princes and princesses, brothers and sisters, and note who is missing. Here we have four – Ganoes, his father, and his two sisters. The mother is missing from his speculation. That, according to von Franz, is symbolic of a psychic gap, and signifies that compensations will be taking place. It also indicates where wholeness might be found – in a fairy tale it might be a king seeking a wife or somesuch.

In the Malazan Empire, the feminine principle has been lost to unconsciousness. The story that unfolds across the series speaks in many ways to a redemption of the feminine aspects, as the collective has pushed out the feminine life-giving principle. We will see how this plays out with the Paran sisters in later books. Suffice to say that the siblings Paran are often stand-ins for the Empire, and even for its enemies. The mother is alive, we learn later, but strangely absent here.

In youth, nominally in childhood, some people are carried along by unconscious processes, the instinctive patterns of life. Not yet ready to develop their own individuality. "The true process of individuation—the *conscious* relationship with the great inner man or one's own psychic center— usually begins with an injury or some state of suffering…"[51] One gets the sense that Paran is striving to forge an identity here, with his choice to join the military an attempt at separation from the expected path his nobility affords. Yet the military comes with its own structure and predetermination. In fact, the comfort of the military and its structure could be likened to a maternal embrace. He hasn't yet suffered the wound or shock that forces him upon the individual life path.

"He'd been someone else so many times…a thousand faces…" (110) Sounds heroic enough. But really what we're seeing here is the adolescence, a period of transition, where the old is left behind but the new isn't yet fully formed. Many paths to choose from. Who to become?

As he is sent to join the Bridgeburners, we know Paran's life is in danger as the knowledge of previous dead captains of the squad comes to light. Indeed, he even confronts the squad with the matter when he meets them, trying to get ahead of the problem. So it is not a surprise when an attempt is made on his life. It is a surprise, however (especially to a naïve reader such as myself on first reading) when the attempt succeeds.

When this wounding does occur, it is an attack by shadow—Sorry possessed by a shadow god—and this is symbolic of the archetypal shadow rising up to precipitate the individuation journey. As he lies unconscious,

---

[51] von Franz, 1997. *The Individuation Process.* 'The First Encounter…' para. 5.

important members of the Bridgeburners discuss his situation. His wounding is a trauma, both body and mind, while the healing that has brought him back to the world has only healed his physical body. So here is the necessary wounding that occurs to spur his individuation. He is brought back to life, through the meddling of Oponn, the gods of chance or fate. His sword is named Chance. So from relative stasis to the clash with shadow and chance, Paran's life quickly moves from a solid path to chaos.

This move from fixed to chaotic, and the distinction of mind and body shows in Paran a state of alienation. The separation is forced, his mind and body split too far, and the break too sudden. This alienation results in him feeling alone in the world, and while there is a sense that his individuality and firm decision to set off on his own path comes with a necessary loneliness, his current standing marks him as apart in ways he is never really able to mend.

As such, he is surprised to find humanity reflected first in Toc, then Tattersail, then later in Coll. These discoveries are like an adolescent venturing out of the protective circle of the family, forming bonds in the social environment. But he loses Tattersail, almost immediately, and this loss he takes upon himself. He feels again a sense of abandonment. She is reborn in a child's body. This theme, beyond mere rebirth, but variations of shifting bodies and the continuum of child-adult is one that will recur, and bear watching through the series. Erikson is striking chords around the notion of transformation. The return to childhood for his lover also mirrors Paran's own immaturity, perhaps bringing them more on a level. He becomes vengeful, his red knight on the charge. But his confidence leaks from him, both the weakness of his condition and the realisation that he is not yet ready to fulfill what is required of a matured hero.

Paran finds himself acting unconsciously, unaware that repetition isn't healing. He thought he had found certainty in his pursuit of vengeance against Hairlock and Lorn, but only succeeds in blaming himself again when Toc is killed: "my every move seems a desperate search for someone to blame, always someone else. I've made being a tool of a god an excuse, a justification for not thinking, for simply reacting. And others have died for it." (446) What we see with these realisations is that he is confronting his own egocentrism. His conviction in his goal is gone, and he has to live through the pain and the loss now, but the acceptance lays the groundwork for his freedom.

For with alienation comes the flipside of the coin: Paran realises he is unchained and is free to make decisions, especially as he sees the chained all around him within Dragnipur, the warren within Rake's sword. He pulls the god Oponn in, a metaphor for actively drawing upon the unconscious, making it conscious and working with it. This is really a realisation of his autonomy, where before he felt at the whims of other people, a tool, and his goals were almost developed by default, his desire for vengeance barely even his own. He realises his own strength when he enacts the beastly aspect of himself – his shadow aspect. This is a first encounter with the shadow within himself. While he has seen the shadow revealed in the world, particularly in the massacre at Itko Kan, and it has acted upon him in his assassination attempt, this represents his first encounter with it internally, consciously. Though the work of integrating the shadow is long, this initial glimpse is often necessary to shake the youth out of their state of arrogance or stasis. When he finds himself back on the plain, in mundane life, that empowerment has surely changed him, as he senses the presence of the beast within him.

As he accepts his journey to be that of saving the squad, he thinks of his regrets, and equates them to the masks he's worn. He recognises that in the Adjunct, too. He knows they are both lacking humanity because they've played roles that weren't their real self. They haven't really lived.

At this time they are both realising their compassion—or rather, they are seeing its potential within them, for neither have truly journeyed to its full realisation. Both of them are still just potential at this point. But they are still continuing on with their prior goals. There is inertia when we've been unconscious for so long. Helplessness can be mistaken for futility.

He meets Coll in the Gadrobi Hills, and says, "It was never a life before, only the palest shadow of what I've now found." (477) This is the result of separation—his empowerment is still very new—but already he recognises the immense potential of humanity. With freedom comes responsibility for oneself, and Paran knows that when he was enacting a life path laid neatly for him he was no agent in his existence. Note both he and Coll are mourning an old life. This tale is full of mirrors.

Free, he approaches situations with honesty and openness, and, though separate and by all accounts alone, he finds in Coll a friend. It tells us something about the courage in taking that first step of separation from the old life, and gives comfort, because in approaching with true compassion one will find support, friendship.

When he is called upon to defend the Azath at the fete, he questions again whether he is only a tool. The T'lan Imass, Tool, tells him the Azath is "Too young, not yet of strength to imprison that which called it into being," (613) There are brilliantly subtle dynamics here, where the ancient one is guiding Paran to aid the forces of balance, which are not yet ready to contain the chaos approaching. For Paran himself, the very act has the same consequence at a personal level—balance and stability do not just occur now that he has attained some maturity, but it must be actively sought, which strengthens him against the chaos of his new life stage. "*Defend?* Against that? The choice was taken from him." (613) Initially it is out of his control, but the demands of this mythical battle elicit awareness of his agency, from a submission to helplessness, a regression to his old thinking perhaps: "A tool, nothing more. All I have done, all I have survived, to reach this." (613) Then the hound rises up within him, his beastly shadow aspect, though notably he almost loses control of his nature and must be reined in by Tool. He has not yet integrated his shadow aspect, as that is a longer process, but his awareness and acceptance of it allows him to draw strength from it and defeat the Finnest.

Paran undergoes this battle while he is unconscious at the fete—a conflict in his unconscious. We are seeing anthropomorphised forces of power, archetypal symbols, showing us that fantasy is metaphor. Characters and symbols as stand-ins for archetypes do literal conflict, serving as analogy for the transformation of the ego.

Paran has essentially come of age after his battles within the unconscious, even though he has not yet attained the full psychological status of adulthood. From having no control over his life to releasing his bonds—he has embraced independence. He has undergone a death and rebirth, akin to separation at adolescence, and now he is able to exert his influence upon the world—twice, within Dragnipur and with the Finnest. He is in touch with the unconscious, in dialogue with it. He can call upon the gods.

He finally has a literal dialogue with the shadow, in the form of Cotillion. "He ducked beneath a tree into shadow…" (620) Just as this occurs, he is briefly attacked by another hound, who then backs off. He has passed a first test, if you will, of the confrontation with his shadow, and he is seen not as a helpless creature but as a threat, if not yet an equal. He finds that Cotillion is not remorseful, but hardened, cold. Cotillion, too, will recover his humanity in time, though we literally don't know who he is at the beginning of the story. Paran gives Cotillion his sword, Chance, symbolic of his no longer willing to be moved by fate and whimsy. He is taking conscious control of his journey.

He bears the body of the Adjunct in his arms, a fitting end to his state of being used. At the end he muses, "Agent for the Adjunct once, now a soldier. Finally, a soldier." (655) What he thought was the end goal is merely the beginning of his agency over his life.

Crokus

The story of Crokus Younghand initially sets us up to expect the fairy tale motif that an ordinary 'hero' becomes king, often by redeeming a princess. Our expectations are again playing a part here, as we expect him to come to his place in the world, or at the very least to win the rich daughter of the noble.

Crokus's parents died when he was a child, and is raised by his uncle Mammot. Excited by the edge of danger, he has latched on to the group of the Phoenix Inn, even Kruppe as a mentor. By the time we meet him, we see his frustration that nothing is changing, and he feels outed by Rallick and Murillio's secret plotting. Lacking feminine influence, he casts around for danger, and lands on Challice D'arle – the lofty maiden, the white virgin in the high tower, the grail. He gazes upon her sleeping form when he robs her, and is ensnared in a mythical trance. Mammot lights up at his passing interest in education—a year, though, seems a long time for a pining youth. He has decided to go through with it, it seems, but makes the fatal mistake of trying to undo the past.

When Crokus steals back into Challice's room to return her jewels, he is shown both as the caricature of the intrepid hero, and as briefly aware of the numinosity and duality of the anima projection: "He listened to her soft, regular breathing behind him—*like the breath of a dragon...*" (393) He blurts out the claim that he will line up as a suitor, and when she laughs it shatters what's left of the fantasy he's created.

In addition to playing with the notion stealing the dragon's treasure, this seems like an inversion of fairy tales, such as the Swan Maiden, where a hunter returns to the site of bathing sisters and possesses one, hiding her swan mantle so that she'd stay human and not return to swan form. Crokus doesn't get to possess Challice, and in aiming to return her trinkets appears to be denying his nature and anima possession. However, one crucial notion in such stories is that the feminine is there to be redeemed, the swan suit itself is an enchantment, so in a subtle way Crokus undermines her chance at redemption and sets a pattern in himself. Either way, he is off-kilter since the moment he first left Challice's window, and his physical and mental faculties are not at their sharpest. Crokus doesn't get time to fully withdraw his projection of the anima upon Challice, and seems on the verge of becoming aware of his projection, of raising his consciousness.

And then he meets Sorry. Here is the earthy side of his projections. He recognises her as a killer who is unfazed by the death she deals, sees the blood on her knife. Is she the opposite of Challice D'arle? Certainly they counterbalance one another—flipsides of a two-headed coin. The fantasy and the reality, or even poles of an archetype.

This fateful meeting comes about when he sets off outside the city with Kruppe, Coll, and Murillio (his own heroes), in a mocking call to adventure: "No reason to be so glum, lad. Consider this a mighty adventure." (421). But like so much since his possession of Oponn's coin, Crokus's notions are overturned. His heroes are defeated, they all ride mules but for Coll who, acting out former glory charges like a red knight. And it is Adjunct Lorn, in the midst of uncovering her own humanity, who defeats them, with Crokus the last standing and needing to take responsibility. In the aftermath, they find Sorry dazed and no longer possessed—Crokus reacts initially to her as a threat, but then riding with her back to the city finds some comfort in her presence.

Crokus displays the moodiness that might be attributed to adolescence, but here is typical of being anima possessed: he gets angry at Sorry asking questions, he's irritable, snappy. She needs a name, and he offers the name Challice at first, then that of his matron goddess, Apsalar – he realises it is a mistake, and wants to withdraw his projection, but she takes it and doesn't give it back. He is conflating his anima projection with the veneration of a goddess. This unconscious projecting of goddess-like power on her is instinctive, unconscious, and Sorry, being an empty vessel, and probably the influence of having already had godlike power from her own literal possession by Cotillion, takes it. This projection entrenches their power differential, and he finds it hard to claw it back.

He goes with Apsalar to K'rul's belfry. She is stuck to him now. He's still irritable, and there is conflict within him because she doesn't fit the anima projection he has created based on Challice. His image of the girl in the tower didn't need to be integrated with reality. Now he is bringing the new girl to a different tower, this one with shadows, stories, a past. His resistance is clear as he argues with her going up the stairs, doesn't want her experience to contradict his. She looks at the moon and tells him the fantasy about gardens in the moon's oceans, the full and peaceful life promised. In that moment, all his projections are transferred to her. "Why not?" (532) These tales reflect escapist fairy tales, a naivete that she proceeds to lose, or never had because it got taken away from her. Again, notions of innocence and pure birth, even though this opening salvo is anything but.

Then at the Fete, he is falling apart. His plan to confront Challice ends comically, as his nature as a thief demands he literally steal the girl because he is unable to meet her at her level. Apsalar is gone. Mammot, too, isn't what he thought. The rug has been pulled from under our young hero. Even loyal Kruppe foresaw his death – though it turns out this was likely the symbolic death begetting rebirth in his change of life. He is traumatised by the sudden revolt of his world, and the death of Mammot. Easy then to escape into another life.

Crokus has his unseen protectors, many of them, but as he is being trailed by Lorn, the Crimson Guard—literally invisible protectors—become clear to him. His fate was not in his hands, not in control. The unseen forces are an analogy for his unconscious.

He saves Baruk by attacking Vorcan, and this is achieved by throwing bricks. This is an apt symbol. Bricks are of the earth, so we could say that Crokus is coming back down to earth, his feet back on the ground as Challice suggested at the Fete. He is aware now of the unconscious forces, has taken back his projection from Challice, and it has been moved to Apsalar, who is more of an earthy figure than the airy Challice, maiden of the tower.

We follow Crokus's development (or lack) in later books. His relationship with Apsalar changes. He doesn't want her to become someone, i.e., he can't take back his projection. He has invested in her the power of his anima, raised her up as a goddess, and the removal of that stability if she grows pulls him from a place he hasn't allowed himself to grow out of.

Edinger discussed how challenges to the ego-Self axis can result in lack of self-acceptance. This is the Cutter-Crokus character, not wanting to exist or be himself. No parents, with his world balanced around uncle Mammot, and all his identification with the people and the city results in his alienation when he finds the world bigger than him. That loss of Self, a lack of central identity, results in his projections coming easily, falling hard for the women in his life and the strong identification with the Phoenix Inn crew. Later, he becomes someone else, or at least rejects himself and his identity and, adrift, needs to find himself, gain a solid foundation for his ego to latch on to.

He feels the call to action in the chance to leave the city, perhaps, or maybe it is just his obsession/projection drawing him along. Either way, the effect is a parting, a casting out from the paradise his inflated ego had previously created. "Darujhistan seems smaller. Almost insignificant." (551) That is the fall for Crokus. And while sometimes it can be taken voluntarily, sometimes it must be forced (this can be through injury, loss of someone, a job, house, so on).

Of course, there is shadow at work too. The darkness of the unconscious. This manifests itself in his violent lashings out – the verbal ones and the knifework. We see later, when he returns to Darujhistan, that he has grown, but his shadow hasn't been fully integrated – it is still out of his control and he attacks his old friend, Rallick. Indeed, he says he hurts people around him. He also falls back to Challice, in an attempt to take back the residual projection of his anima. It is hard work for him, and that can probably be read as a result of his alienation/abandonment as a child. Not to say it is hopeless, just that the work is harder.

In time, Cutter will confront the fact that none of us is equal even to our own expectations. He will never achieve the idealised divine Self, none of us will. Though we will orbit around it, and keeping it as a potential, a guide, is itself valuable. This is the Jungian idea that we aim for divinity, and we will achieve greater wholeness if only by maintaining that impossible to reach target. Similarly, cultures have ideals which they strive for, and that is how Jung considered religious mythology: it gives both a collective myth, the values of the collective, as well as the central hero myth in many cases. Christ as the divine Self in the Christian mythology, for example.

Despair precedes redemption. Crokus, and later Cutter, views himself as beyond help, and of course we see him wallow in it for a while. He is following the traditional pattern, but perhaps his own abandonment makes the rise from that underworld more difficult. Edinger described how when a child is rejected, the damage to the ego-Self axis predisposes them to later alienation. It becomes more all-encompassing. In Cutter's case, the world and family he had built for himself was fragile, and its shattering and the following alienation was akin to his entire world falling apart. See his sense of betrayal when Meese warns him the D'Arles blame him for killing a guard, and his surprise that Challice is waiting for another at the Fete—these are taken as personal slights.

For a time he then rejects opportunities to build connection, because he is not ready, or not accepting of his ability to repair. But that foundation was there in Darujhistan all along, but when he returns it is he who has changed. Perhaps the nature of growth is to see that value where we previously hadn't. Things change, of course, and are tainted with a new set of eyes, but perceiving the imperfections and accepting it regardless, whether in the self or others, is a sure sign of a maturing character.

Development of consciousness takes the form of a series of

inflated/heroic acts, provoking rejection, followed by alienation, repentance, and renewed inflation. It is a cycle resulting in incremental growth in consciousness in the early years. Later, the same pattern typifies psychic growth (and perhaps material growth in the first half of life). In that sense, alienation is a necessary prelude to awareness of the self. There must be despair before growth can occur—a separation, a descent into the underworld, a death preceding a rebirth. Without separation of ego and Self, one cannot perceive the numinous self. We need separation to see it. Repair then takes place through a reconnection of the ego-Self axis.

There is a tension between wanting a story to be a certain way, and allowing it to change with individual tellings. It is the universal patterns that make a story memorable and relatable, yet with variation it reflects the teller and the society. That tension is often what is playing out when a story doesn't resonate with us, or when we get mad that our hero has died. 'It is not supposed to be that way!' we cry. We want to preserve. And yet the nature of change, of our growth as readers is much like individuation itself—we need to be wounded, to be challenged for any change in understanding to occur.

Sorry

Sorry is worth discussing, though much of her tale is other people's perceptions and projections of her. Perhaps this is inevitable as she is not herself any more, rather a possessed aspect of Cotillion, with a little of herself and Rigga in the background, though dormant. At times an individual can also be the lodestone of an entire culture's projections, with figures such as Marilyn Monroe or Princess Diana the oft-cited examples, and arguably monarchs play such a role. This is like an eruption of the archetype into the collective psyche. But here we are only discussing the individual level.

Sorry has Rigga the Seer within her, warring for her with Cotillion. Sorry notices this when she feels something for Crokus – the knowledge that she won't kill him. Rigga, though we mightn't have liked her, was still more human than Cotillion, at least at this time. That little burst of the unconscious when Whiskeyjack utters the word *'seer'* was enough to arouse that aspect of herself. And though Cotillion's possession wants to quash that remaining glimmer of humanity, it can't. I think there is a lesson here for Cotillion.

So the girl is an extension of Cotillion at first, and we see her as the projection of Whiskeyjack's harsher side. And of course we have discussed how she is Crokus's projection of the feminine elevated to goddess status. And now her tale begins, as she must find herself, assimilating all those aspects that have been unwittingly projected on to her. Her quest is to gain some semblance of self that is not merely defined by other people.

Rallick Nom

Rallick Nom is in despair. As Crokus is trying to backpedal his past by returning Challice's trinkets, Rallick is pondering how his life is essentially ending when he inevitably will descend into the catacombs to meet the guild leader, Vorcan, accepting his job—his fate?—as a clan leader.

His job will be secured, but his humanity gone. He sees no growth or potential for himself, no way to arise from the depths. No hope, no life possible for himself, he is carrying out his task and job as mere duty. He is lacking the feeling function that will allow him the potential of rebirth, to see the gift of hope in those catacombs so he may rise up changed.

He considers that his helping Coll would be an act of humanity, but I feel he doesn't believe that deep down. It is just another sense of duty, fulfilling his role because it is what he's good at. "Could that right the wrong, could it even the scales of retribution? No, but it might return to a man his life and his hope." (399)

This is midlife crisis, or its anticipation, which leaves him in a strange purgatory zone. "For himself, Rallick, such gifts had long since been lost, and he was not the kind of man to stir the ashes…Nor would he recognize hope if it came to him. Too much a stranger, too long a ghost." (399) Interesting to note, after his reflections, the next person he sees is Crokus. Crokus, for whom the righting of wrongs is also in question. Crokus, who will later return to Darujhistan a new person, a flame born anew, but feeling a stranger.

He confronts Crokus here, warning him away from the thief's life, telling him it's no heroic way. Who knows what effect this had the impressionable Crokus, who indeed worships Rallick in a way? Perhaps here is Rallick's power to take a life, his words a wounding that will enable Crokus to let go of his old life and spur his decision to leave the city.

Later he is out to kill Ocelot, to spare Coll. "Coll's death…would strip from Rallick his last claim … to what? To humanity. The price of failure had become very high." (497) Why has he changed at this point? Before it was only duty, but it has become personal for him. He is a double here for Paran's shift in saving someone else in the name of maintaining humanity. It could be that Rallick never truly considered the possibility of failure, of the consequence of loss, and having that realisation has shaken him from his lethargy. Or simply he needs the success, Coll's survival, to maintain his aloofness. It is interesting that in this moment he covers himself with otataral dust, a kind of masking.

"He began his ascent." (497) Out of the depths of his hopeless despair, and also a sly hint perhaps that he is rising to the level of ascendant within the story. In his scrap for survival with Ocelot, he must cut his own braid, and is stabbed in the chest – wounded and transformed.

Rallick and Murillio both feel a weariness after their actions at the Fete. Coll has been avenged. Murillio feels lost. His physical life is complete, now he has to confront the midlife malaise, where the expansion and accumulation in the physical realm loses its power and the growth of the psychic life in the second half takes precedence. Rallick is the same, but as already intimated, he has achieved some sort of transformation, and has within himself the power to act.

Both Rallick and Murillio are immediately searching for meaning in the wake of their successful plan. They have been living their life for someone else's benefit. To scale the heights and find it empty, this is the midlife hump.

As he rests at the Azath house, Rallick has a feeling that "what grew here was right, and just" (649). He can rest easy knowing he has affected justice. But there is still growth to occur, he is simply not ready to take the next steps on his journey, or doesn't know where to go. This is shown symbolically when he is seen to stop the growth of the Azath by his presence, and Vorcan tasks him to stay put there. "You will remain here, thus holding it in stasis." (606) It is also an acknowledgment of Rallick's influence, particularly on Crokus, who must escape the influence of those like Rallick around him, holding his growth back.

Sometimes when we arrive at midlife, or when we have achieved a milestone we set out to achieve, we can be riven with ennui and depression. The achievement itself is not as satisfying as we thought, because it was the process in arriving at the goal that was transformative. Furthermore, people can be stuck having laid out their journey and when they arrive they do not know what to do next—this is more typical of the midlife crisis, as we can be so focused on the outward goals, the cultural process, that with the turning toward spiritual side, there is a great emptiness—the process didn't achieve wholeness, and now we must pivot to a new process entirely, that of psychic growth.

Rallick's state of mind is not really indicative of these crises, rather he is taking a moment to reflect. "He knew that the door would open for him, and it did." (650) Where does his certainty come from at this stage, that the Azath house would open for him? We could speculate that during his process he has consciously attended to the nature of his journey, his plans for going into the catacombs and such, and this has strengthened and prepared him. He has already begun his ascent.

In a way, his end mirror's Paran's, lifting the unconscious woman, Vorcan, and carrying her. Only, Paran was on the wrong path, and his woman is dead. He is filled with uncertainty. Rallick feels just, a sense of certainty in his path, even if the destination is unclear, and Vorcan is merely unconscious. Then he ends up in the Finnest house. Frozen, another state of stasis.

Korlat appears here for the first time, and she says of the Azath house: "The Azath will not be touched, for it is new, a child." (651) Balance is being sought by this new entity, born of chaos.

Jung's contention was that duality is necessarily human, and that part of the work of individuation was to perceive both what is good and evil in the self. "To confront a person with his shadow is to show him his own light."[52] Good and evil are both contained in the self, are both part of the wholeness of being, of our character, and to deny the evil, the shadow side, is to repress it, which merely allows it to come out in other manifest forms. Perhaps it could be argued that the collective shadows manifest as the nation's shadow. And therefore that the shadow of those of the empire manifest as the empire's motives of domination and control. That the helplessness of the individuals is compensated by the domineering control of the 'nation-state'.

Gardens of the Moon is chaos, but it is also original wholeness, so we can see that it is at once both ends of the spectrum. There is still some comforting initial wholeness in, say, the inn at Darujhistan where Crokus is about to be pulled from his bubble. Erikson is riffing on themes. Of course, this theme develops further throughout the series, as we see childhood, separation, and so on in different ways at different times in the series. It's fractal, or at least a spiral orbit. But this is the very important point that must be noted. These

---

[52] Jung, C.G., CW10 [872]

ideas of departure and return, the elliptical approach, separation and unification – are all hallmarks of the individuation process. Themes, just as psychoses, will reemerge at different points, take on a different meaning depending where one is at in their life, just as the reading of these books has different meaning for me at the midpoint of my life than it did as an adolescent. Changed, we approach them differently, view them through a different lens.

In much the same way, childhood psychoses might reemerge for parents. My own inflations, identifications with unconscious elements recur as my children develop. Similarly, the same sort of echoes typify the hero, who returns changed. A true hero wouldn't retire, were there more dragons to be slain—and there are always more dragons.

So we are left in a state of alienation at the close of *Gardens of the Moon*. We have witnessed and experienced both the initial wholeness and its shattering, with a journey in the offing. We have experienced chaos and being cast adrift that toyed with our expectations. But alienation is not an end in itself. This is not a world of meaninglessness—but that meaning must be sought. Without the separation, without the fall that alienation prompts, there can be no attaining of higher consciousness, no growth.

And so where to from here? We must find our grounding, we must build some sort of identity. To do that we need a foundation, a family.

Lorn

There is a curious section in the middle of the book, when Adjunct Lorn arrives at Pale, where a core of characters are all undergoing a transition. Toc and Tattersail both release an old part of themselves as they identify more with the 2nd army, foreshadowing both their impending rebirths. Paran has had his literal death and rebirth. Even Tool, the Imass, accepts a new name as a shedding of his old self. Lorn's last shreds of humanity are crushed beneath the role and title of Adjunct: "The woman named Lorn…ceased to exist the day she became the Adjunct." (285)

Lorn is the predecessor for Tavore, but also her foreshadowing in every way. Lorn is hard, but we see her humanity in the end, when she breaks down for Ganoes. Exactly what happens to Tavore.

Initially she is hard and opaque, but we see a little cracking in her surface.

First, Toc sees a brief glimpse of her humanity when he senses her heartfelt loss at her horse's death. We then watch briefly as her shadow becomes conscious when she recalls Tattersail's role in her family's death. We see its rage boil up when they meet, then it is crushed again. As Toc observes at the dinner scene: "The woman named Lorn had risen…to find justice and in that last act reclaim its life—and it had been denied…by the thing known as the Adjunct." (285) If anything, this death of Lorn is the inhumanity of empire. She is incorporated into the collective psyche, the rational, rule-based empire, and it deadens the humanity in her.

Interestingly, "the woman named Lorn" (418) appears one more time in the book, as Lorn and Tool approach the Gadrobi Hills. Lorn is riven with doubts about freeing the tyrant, and she is trying to quell her sense of guilt with the affirmation that she is not personally at fault, and only an extension of the empire's will. For all the quashing of her humanity achieved at the dinner, it rises up again, but she has been reminded how to push it away.

This foreshadows what happens to Sorry, whose human side is also trying to rise up at the same time in the book. We thought Lorn, the human identity, had died again. But humanity is more powerful – Tool has drawn the humanity from her, perhaps, made her confront herself once more, but it is close to the surface. Or can we say that the drive for humanity is unkillable?

"Success…demands discipline, Adjunct," (324) Tool tells her when she is lax in her response to him. This rang to me like a foreshadowing. She is the prototype for Tavore, who does have the discipline for her long journey. The shadow creates danger when it overpowers the ego, so it must be projected or internalised. Tavore is strong, and holds the shadow for her people, the army, but here Lorn has identified her ego with a persona (the Adjunct), and when the shadow of her past was raised she could only reaffirm the persona.

Both her arms are wounded, one in the attack of the Barghast when Tool rescues her, and then Murillio's rapier when she attacks Crokus's crew. She is disarmed. She is the weapon hand of the empress, but without the means to fight, what is left? If anything, the rising to the surface of that humanity shows how hard it is to maintain that coldness all the way to the end, which sets us up to be even more impressed by Tavore. It raises our expectations.

As she walks through the crowds of Darujhistan's fete, she ponders her insignificance. She recognises the faces about her, realising she is part of a collective consciousness. Unconscious becomes conscious, and she sees herself as part of that mass, and that is when humanity breaks through again. Her tale has been one of fighting the façade of her persona: she is unable, in the end, to suppress the life in her, Lorn shedding the mask of the Adjunct.

When we try to suppress our humanity, the defences will break. We can't suppress what must come up in us. Psychic illness arises not from the suppressed contents, but from their denial in consciousness. For Lorn, it is a neurosis of questioning her legacy and her self-worth. Too young, perhaps, for a midlife crisis, but that is the nature of her questioning. Her tale is not that much different from Rallick Nom's. Her end is similar to Rallick's except he killed the assassin and his life became his own. The assassin gets her, here in the form of the Crimson Guard and Meese and Irilta, and she has only regrets as she bleeds out. Living someone else's life, the unlived life.

At the end she is lifted into Paran's arms, an echo that will recur at the series end. Without her armour, he realises, she is light. There is not much of her humanity, it was all in the outer shell, the persona.

At the beginning of the fourth book of *Gardens of the Moon*, Kruppe wanders a landscape in his dream. He ponders the tundra, the colours, the contrast of the barren ground and the brightly starred sky overhead. He wonders if it is a creation of his mind. "Are these visions of instinct, then, unfurled in this dream for a purpose?" (330) He sees the stars, witnesses a herd of beasts. "Has he travelled back, then, to the very beginning of things?" (330)

There is an oft-quoted passage of Jung's from *Psychological Aspects of the Mother Archetype* which demands to be quoted in full:

> " 'But why on earth,' you may ask, 'should it be necessary for man to achieve, by hook or by crook, a higher level of consciousness?' This is truly the crucial question, and I do not find the answer easy. Instead of a real answer I can only make a confession of faith: I believe that, after thousands and millions of years, someone had to realize that this wonderful world of mountains and oceans, suns and moons, galaxies and nebulae, plants and animals, exists. From a low hill in the Athi plains of East Africa I once watched the vast herds of wild animals grazing in soundless stillness, as they had done from time immemorial, touched only by the breath of a primeval world. I felt then as if I were the first man, the first creature, to know that all this is. The entire world round me was still in its primeval state; it did not know that it was. And then, in that one moment in which I came to know, the world sprang into being; without that moment it would never have been. All Nature seeks this goal and finds it fulfilled in man, but only in

the most highly developed and most fully conscious man."[53]

The similarity of these passages is striking, as they serve the same purpose—to recall the awe of the birth of consciousness from ancient memory. Jung's of course gives context, he is asking the question why consciousness should exist, and in the expression of the world about him finds the answer. Kruppe wonders whether his world is a creation of him or whether it exists independent of him. He then oversees the birth of the divine child, Silverfox, and the scene is therefore another expression of the theme of birth. If this was not intentional homage by Erikson, then we can confidently say that it is a case of what Jung termed synchronicity.

It is also a further extension of the idea raised by the elder god K'rul's earlier appearance in Kruppe's dream. The notion that K'rul has been gone a long time because nobody worshiped any more, and that the god was only awakened by a drop of blood in his temple, bears strong similarities to many of our own beliefs. Marie-Louise von Franz makes note of this:

> A god nobody believes in, or prays to or thinks about is nothing, nonexistent. For instance, the Egyptians always took their god statues to the Nile and washed them, put cream over them and then carried them back into the temple. That was their way of saying, "If we don't do something, if the gods are not renewed by our activity, then they would just rot away in a corner of the temple. They would be nothing." It's our consciousness that is necessary. That's why it is so important to be conscious of the life of the archetypes, because if we are not conscious of the autonomous life of the archetypes in the psyche, then they are seemingly nonexistent and, in fact, even destructive.[54]

This demonstrates the difference between awareness of the archetypes and actually making room for them. We may even ritualise them so that they exist in reality, and can be assimilated into the ego. Not only is it the role of religion in society and for the individual, but any form of ritual may provide stability in life. Making time and space for those otherwise unconscious aspects brings them to awareness and out of the nowhere zone where they might fester and burst forth unprepared, resulting in personal illnesses and psychoses, as well as ill-fated cultural movements, extremism, and the like.

Kruppe's dream acts as an altar, his point-of-view a space where we can reflect, and more specifically the author can reflect in a self-conscious way.

---

[53] Jung, C.G., CW9i [177]
[54] Von Franz, 1999, pp. 99-100

Whiskeyjack

Whiskeyjack stands in many ways for the Bridgeburners, and in some ways for the empire itself. Following the prologue with Ganoes Paran, where Whiskeyjack himself makes a brief appearance, the story begins in earnest at the aftermath of a battle, and the Bridgeburners are destroyed, dying. There is the literal smell of chaos in the air, and the reader is thrust relentlessly into the messiness of the world, reinforcing the aspect of initial chaos.

For Whiskeyjack it is the chaos of middle life, which is brought thematically into focus later in the series, but suffice to mention that the questions and motives differ from the naïve hero attaining adulthood, but it is still the expression of the same inbuilt human drive. In some ways this passage of life as part of individuation is additionally discomforting because the past is so deeply worn, expectations are set, just as a reader might be motivated to search for the familiar bones of story structure. But here it is not to be found, and thus Whiskeyjack's story has the ring of tragedy about it from the outset. He has seen too much, but that doesn't leave him better prepared to find his way, to find patterns of sense in the chaos.

Adjunct Lorn, wounded in her shoulder, ponders the notion of control. "Through the gamut of life we struggled for control, for a means to fashion the world around us, an eternal, hopeless hunt for the privilege of being able to predict the shape of our lives." (457) Whiskeyjack, as another martial figure, reflects this same tension between the order of the empire and its armies (his persona as soldier), and the inexorable nature of the world eating away at that sense of control. But where Lorn is lacking humanity and it comes upon her, Whiskeyjack already has that core of compassion and is trying hard to hold onto it in the face of his circumstances, and trying to hold it for the Bridgeburners too.

Whiskeyjack projects his shadow on Sorry:

> "When he had looked upon Sorry at Graydog, the source of his horror lay in the unveiling of what he was becoming: a killer stripped of remorse, armored in the cold iron of inhumanity…in the empty eyes of this child, he'd seen the withering of his own soul." (341)

He confronts the dark aspects of his own life, and then confronts or admits the friendship he feels – he's letting his feeling side in – personalising the death that is about to happen as a result of his command. This is a working through. He is identifying with that projection.

But he doesn't trust himself. He urges himself to "Step back from that chasm." (342) He bites his cheek hard enough to bleed – he needs a wound, but he is too literal, and thinks he needs to feel it physically. He hasn't confronted the deeper wounding which is his losses already, of other friends, his old life.

Then he reveals his headaches. The worry and the ruminating has physical effects, of course, and it would be interpreted as a manifestation of those feelings. But there is more, he gets Mallet to magically heal his headache and his bitten cheek. He is in a state of avoidance, again stepping back from the chasm. He and his body are trying to reify a wound for him to work through, something with a mundane solution, but he is not ready to journey through it.

In the mythological sense, we sometimes take a dive but come up too soon. James Hillman described it as a kind of drowning. Let the flood take you and drown, for if you are not down there long enough you won't return with the treasure—you won't retain the power that transforms. We are just paying lip service to the journey into the darkness. Whiskeyjack needs to push through his pain, for though he is aware of it he is not assimilating it. And as a result, all the losses, all the pain of his friends is weighing on his soul. This comes from a place of compassion, but the service of others at the expense of one's own growth is all too common. We can stay and look after the parents, or we can leave and grow. The hero can defend the village, or he can leave to slay the dragon.

The squad offer Whiskeyjack friendship in turn, to take their own suffering back from him, their own share of the pain of loss. He agrees that he was wrong about Sorry, but he still can't let go of his conviction of the possibility of evil in humanity. There needs to be more to restore his own humanity. He has seen the depths of the shadow, and you can't put a lid on that, the notion that it also exists at some level in oneself.

First, he needs a wound, one that will mark him. One that can't or won't be healed away. He gets that when he is wounded at the fete, a broken leg.

Note, it is Fiddler's speech that is the fulcrum point for Whiskeyjack. Fiddler here rises up, when until now he has been fairly low-key. "…when you take away everybody else's humanity, you take away your own." (500) This is Fiddler's rallying cry, and it is a statement he lives by throughout the series. It is also explored to varying degrees in other characters. How much can we hold for other people? Fiddler will be the standard bearer for this as the series progresses. He will be the counterbalance for Tavore as the Bonehunters seek to redeem the Crippled God. "It's that hurt we feel that makes us keep going…" (500) His humanity lives on the ground level. He is down in the dirt with the soldiers.

Conclusion

> " 'I am lost. In this world. In this time.'
>
> Rake grunted. 'You are not alone in those sentiments, Eldering one.'" (629)

K'rul's rebirth, of blood, triggers old deep forces that will add chaos to this world. One further image of birth to contend with here is the Gedderone Fete, a spring celebration, the time of renewal and birth out of darkness. No wonder in the chaos of this rite the forces converge to begin anew. And Empire itself can be considered a form of rebirth, the scouring away of the old, killing the king to renew culturally.

A rebirth is a birth from chaos, not in the sense of creation out of the formless chaotic pre-existence, but in that the old life has descended into chaos because it doesn't match the instinctive maturational state the body expects, or is mismatched with the social context, or indeed if the unconscious is urging new expression of the self. In the breath of seeming pause and the clear light following a transformation, the time before may be recalled as chaos.

Why is the hero important in all this, why is the hero narrative important? Because Erikson is not only taking us on multiple hero journeys, and ours and his in the form of an individuation process, but because he is directly portraying the notion that heroism is not as the fantasy genre has typically made it to be—the soldier, the boy king, the risen orphan etc., but rather that heroism is often unseen, unwitnessed, be that quiet notions of a hand on a shoulder, or a total sacrifice of humanity that nobody would ever see or understand. Heroism doesn't need a witness, and that is why the Book of the Fallen is the witness for us, or Kruppe is, or Circle Breaker. Not just as the process, the journey, the archetype, but as the valency of heroism.

All change is a death and rebirth, all change is transformation, and all transformation requires a sacrifice—of the old, in death, or of some image, something of value. Erikson is not only exploring these aspects of the hero, but in true hero-story fashion, doing so while showing us what it is to live a heroic life, to make a heroic change. Showing us how to sacrifice for change and transformation, as well as the consequences when you don't.

The drive to seek a hero, one to identify with, is a primal urge driven by the collective unconscious. The divine figure or hero is present in so many cultures and communities, that its necessity cannot be denied. So what Erikson is pushing against here is not just expectations but a real underlying psychic urge. Interestingly, it is that very antagonism within the self that is necessary for growth. So where a mere upsetting of expectations would be an intellectual curiosity, the withdrawing of a central hero figure instigates a psychic drive to seek wholeness again. This tension created forces us to take back our hero projection—in effect, it could lead us to question all our projections of the hero archetype, whether in our lives or in cultural representations. This arouses insight into ourselves, and our judgments of others, which is exactly the mindset that Erikson wants us to adopt before we set off on this journey. This conscious, open state is replete with love, compassion.

By identifying with a hero, the world and its events are drawn by that perspective into a more simplified one, of good and evil, dark and light. By withdrawing that identification, Erikson early on makes it clear that we shouldn't, or makes us unable to identify and thus get firm perspective on good and evil. That is the very point. Destabilising our perspective and thus drawing attention to the interplay of identification, chaos, good and evil.

In my first reading, as an adolescent, this destabilisation was too much, and I didn't make it through the novel. I wasn't ready for the instability, I needed the perspective, or the identification with a hero. Mostly, I hadn't been trained to trust, or to read in such a way. So this is the birth of a reader. And it is the birth of the writer, in a sense, as Circle Breaker launches himself upon the world, Erikson salutes us at the water's edge.

> "You see therefore that the conscious and the unconscious, the opposites of the psyche, are torn apart through consciousness. Thus an original unconscious totality or harmony is disturbed, and that is how these people believe it happened,

this tragedy of mankind in discovering consciousness."[55]

In containing all possibility of good and evil, the tension of the opposites, the characters in this book are true symbols in the Jungian sense. Meaning for a reader depends on the state of consciousness in that reader, their stage of life or the journey of individuation, the way a character is assimilated. We conjoin the opposites, then allow them to part again. This is the flux of symbol and archetype in the psyche.

Gardens of the Moon gives us questions. Even when as a reader we accept we aren't getting spoonfed answers in these books, we still have to sit with the discomfort of not knowing, and in fact never get all the information. It will never come together in a neat form, the sweeping reveal. On reading again, I realise that much of my discomfort was in the different facts from different perspectives, and it took some time to realise it is not a puzzle, but that conflict is as essential in perspective as in anything else. That discomfort is the tension of growth. It is responsibility, a burden.

Jung's rallying cry was that we must live with the opposites within us. We must bear the fact that each hero, each soul, has within it both the potential for great good and great evil. And that fundamentally we are all connected by the heredity of humanity, through the unconscious. Erikson has showed this in *Gardens of the Moon*, and my own early readings can attest that the ambiguity may make you turn away. The challenge now stands before the reader whether to accept and empathise, no matter what will be seen, or will we be swallowed by the mass unconscious?

Now we leave the garden, the fall has begun.

---

[55] Von Franz, 1997a

Windblown Sands: The Animus and the Collective in *Deadhouse Gates*

Deadhouse Gates is a book about the collective, how we are bound, and it gives us a shared experience, a common myth, from which we as the readers can journey forth. In it we will also explore the Jungian notion of the animus.

It is about chains and blank slates, notions of history, and, as in all stages, rebirth. We are at once the accumulation of our history, paths set that may be seen as fate, but also a blank book. We are our genetic, collective heredity, influenced by the culture around us, and also individuals, carving out some sense of self.

These are the questions that plague a newly awakened soul. Am I at the whims of fate, or do I write my own history? Am I chained? Can I give that chain a yank and take charge of my own story?

Does the individual even exist without the collective? Are we fundamentally individuals that form a collective, or do we grow out from our collective nature? Jung suggested the latter:

> Man as an individual is a very suspicious phenomenon whose right to exist could be questioned by the biologist, since from that point of view he is significant only as a collective creature or as a particle in the mass. The cultural point of view gives man a meaning apart from the mass, and this, in the course of centuries, led to the development of personality and the cult of the hero.[56]

This mirrors the growth of the individual's consciousness from the state of initial, paradisal unconsciousness. But just the same way the process of indiv-

---

[56] Jung, C.G., CW5 [259]

iduation is an ongoing push and pull of separation and return, there is a give and take between the individual and the collective.

The startling image that opens the book foreshadows the exploration of the seemingly mindless collective: a swarm of flies collected as one, heralding death. There is going to be death in this tale…and we are chained together in all sorts of unseen ways. What is the power that organises us so? What is any power that moves us? Chains are an important image, but are chains just a way of binding? They are an important symbol throughout the series. Are we all bobbing on the waves of collective unconscious heredity, or are we merely a collection of individuals, separate and unbound? How much say have we over our own fates?

The acolyte of Hood approaches the chained prisoners. The flies that swarm over him herald death, but it turns out there is nobody beneath. At the book's conclusion, crows swarm Coltaine, and when they disperse, there is no Coltaine left. Is the individual then a creation of the collective?

We also see D'ivers for the first time in *Deadhouse Gates*, many that become one. Rats and desert wolves are our first exposure. This is the counterbalance to the Soletaken, the one-to-one animal shapeshifting in Malazan. The D'ivers also invite the question of what the individual is within the group. Are they all of one mind, or only aspects of it? Do the individuals have their own ego self?

The collective relates to psychic factors in a society, or humanity more broadly. In a sense, the conscious personality is built up out of factors in the collective unconscious but that are felt to be personal. As we are a set of nation states, fractured societies, it mostly refers to our identified society or culture. However, the collective unconscious is shared by humanity at large.

The collective unconscious "contains the whole spiritual heritage of mankind's evolution, born anew in the brain structure of every individual."[57] It is where the archetypes reside, and from whence charged symbols and mythological motifs arise in the personal conscious. This is distinct from the collective consciousness which relates to the norms of a society, the spirit of the age, its religions and philosophy. As the prevailing mode of society, it is often the case that individuals within it are somewhat unconscious. It is safe to operate within society's strictures, more so the smaller and more insular society is, or the less flexible its norms and rules. As such, within the bounds of collective consciousness, transformation of the individual is less likely.

It is in the interest of individuals to act and live unconsciously to some extent. Instinct preserves energy by reducing deliberation and decision

---

[57] Jung, C.G., CW8 [342]

making, the very energy intensive process of conscious thought. So being part of a collective means there is a drive to yield to the collective thought, but this ever wars with the instinct for individuation, for separation and differentiation.

Archetypes have been assimilated into societal consciousness within the collective consciousness. Sometimes, though, something from the unconscious can erupt through, instinctive forces entrancing the masses. The rise of Nazism is an oft-cited example, which occurred while Jung was working.

So how does one go about maintaining individuality and selfhood against these competing forces? How do we individuate, and prevent ourselves identifying with others' perceptions, and modes of being?

In *Deadhouse Gates*, Erikson offers us two instructive forms of collective. First, the Whirlwind uprising, which represents the collective consciousness.

The Whirlwind

Symbols rise up into the collective consciousness – they can take possession of a culture if not brought to consciousness and integrated. Jung was working from the beginning of the 20th century right through the two world wars, and the rise of Nazism is explored often in his writings. It is an example of a cultural archetype bursting into the collective consciousness to ill effects.

Undercurrents of the Whirlwind appear early in *Deadhouse Gates* can be likened to glimpses of the unconscious. The pictographic symbols used by those fomenting the uprising can be seen as the upwelling of the symbolic language of the psyche. They fade quickly, reminiscent of dreams. And they are ignored at one's peril. Duiker sees signs of the Whirlwind uprising on the walls, but with inertia the Empire carries on, unknowing, and is met with violence.

As well as being a metaphor for this working of the collective consciousness, the Whirlwind is itself an example of a collective being developed, for the Seven Cities peoples. A shared purpose, the overthrow of their occupiers, and a mother symbol to rally around.

Religion is the most immediate example of the collective experience. It serves many purposes: a shared story, and shared experience in the rituals and celebrations themselves, social life. The rituals often enact an important counterpoint to the regular life, e.g., mass ritualises the journey of Christ, and provides balance to people by enacting that dark side. Religion is also a safe space in which to worship, a vessel for all the projections.

How, then, is the collective important for individuation? It is a counterbalance to the individual pursuit of growth. The community is both a foundation, and that to which the hero returns with the treasure. A conscious person steps beyond the mass psychology of the collective consciousness—separating from the collective—but on returning in a state of higher consciousness hopefully lifts the consciousness of the community in turn.

Jung hints at the value of religious or collective ceremony for the individual in *Man and His Symbols*, on the universal hero myth:

> "The narration or ritual repetition of sacred texts and ceremonies, and the worship of such a figure with dances, music, hymns, prayers, and sacrifices, grip the audience with numinous emotions (as if with magic spells) and exalt the individual to an identification with the hero."[58]

In this way, the ritual and the collective give the shared experience of numinosity, but also shine light on the individual as a hero, giving guidance, and balancing the notions of the group and differentiation.

Duiker reflects on how a city might be conquered, but there is an inability to overcome the deep history, which is ineluctable as the present falls into the past. "Perhaps victory is not achieved by overcoming that enemy, but by joining with it, becoming one with it." (46) There are layers of history, our shared heritage. We can't rise beyond our cultural and psychic history, but may be conscious of it, so integrating it and perhaps that would make us feel less overwhelmed, but able to contextualise ourselves better.

The Whirlwind represents the growth of collective out of disparate alienation. We are presented with its symbols, a mundane representative, and the god itself. "The Book of Dryjhna holds the heart of the Whirlwind Goddess…" (106). So, another heart to be redeemed, along with the Crippled God's. This theme recurs in the series. And it is interesting to note that it is Kalam, a Bridgeburner, along with Fiddler, who are instrumental in bringing about the return of this god's heart.

Sha'ik, the earthly representative of the Whirlwind goddess is herself a symbol of rebirth. Were the Seven Cities peoples able to renew their culture through assimilating this symbol, they would be able to throw off their oppressors, rise anew and as one, in unity. Whether through their lack of consciousness, a focus on the vengeance and petty back and forth, the

---

[58] Jung C. , 1964, p. 68

pillaging and outbursts we see, or through the deflecting power of first Coltaine and, later, Tavore, or whether the Sha'ik reborn they get in Felisin is just not strong enough, we can't be sure, but it seems the people finally fail. The image of Sha'ik is also twisted by cynical powers who want to use it for personal gain.

Being part of the empire is being part of a collective, but it's not just the soldiers, as the Whirlwind shows us. It's all the refugees, the residents that get caught up in it. The coastal guards and outposts. All the plans like rescuing Heboric that go awry in the midst of mass movements. "For all their self-importance, they were but grains of sand in a storm vaster than anything they could comprehend." (232) These are all forgotten tales, far from the hero narratives we witness. People on both sides are dying in service to an idea, part of the collective consciousness.

The Chain of Dogs

The second instructive form of the collective in *Deadhouse Gates*, the Chain of Dogs, builds the suprapersonal both within the book and for the readers. It is the creation of collective identity in the face of disparate chaos. In so doing, it shows the value of the collective as a bolster against both inflation and alienation, and is representative of our beginning journey as readers – we are identifying with a collective. We have a story on which to hang our hats, a memory hook, an echo. It is something we experience together, its growth as well as its tragic end, and that unites us and protects us as readers, and joins us with the writer, who indeed shares in the growth and fall with us.

This story is a collective experience that we witness, but doesn't become the story itself. That is why it must end. It must fall back into story (myth) because were we to stay in the Chain of Dogs, no growth would occur. We need the betrayal, the fall (note that it is literally the Fall of Coltaine, bringing home the biblical allusion). The Chain of Dogs is in some way a building of collective identity in which ego can form. We need to experience a collective that we can then differentiate from. The choice of Duiker for the point-of-view for this part of the story also reinforces that sense of being both part of, and separate from, the Chain of Dogs, maintaining just enough distance.

Deadhouse Gates is also about history, and shows how history itself is a collective. Duiker is required as witness and narrator, otherwise we wouldn't see all the peripheral lives that contributed to the Whirlwind, to the epic moments that follow. It is an alert that the great moments of history, including in Malazan, won't necessarily be attributed to a POV hero, even though there are many on display. And therefore Coltaine, unwitnessed, is the precursor to Tavore's quest across the desert. Indeed, the Bonehunters are born when she literally reverses the Chain of Dogs.

Duiker's soldiering days are behind him, and so witnessing the horror of the uprising tests his faith in humanity. "In self-defense, his soul withdrew, deeper, ever deeper." (207) The collective consciousness is capable of such horror, and the individual must create the boundary for the self or else become swallowed by it. Coltaine provides another answer: in the face of his own charges trying to pull him down, in spite of ingratitude, he continues.

It is noteworthy, too, that Duiker's journey in following the initial stages of the Chain of Dogs, striving to join with it (those stages which remain unseen) is like his return to the village. He has separated from the collective, and thus stands outside of it, can understand it and view with objectivity. That is his gift in this stage of the journey.

Duiker witnesses swarms of capemoths, a singleminded mass drawn by death, as heralded by the flies in the prologue. He reflects that their nature is just like the numb killer's mindset. The attitude the soldier needs to see the other as enemy is a return to the collective consciousness, projecting its shadow onto the others. At one point he imagines a face in the cloud of capemoths. We see what we expect to see, and that is especially so when we are part of the collective. The many D'ivers also have a singularity of purpose, a mindless migration, unquestioning it seems, drawn as by instinct.

So the collective is at the same time a literal coming together and integration of the many, and symbolic of the synthesis of the parts of the individual. Although the unity and integration of the unconscious is a goal for the individual, the collective remains of great import.

> "As the individual is not just a single, separate being, but by his very existence presupposes a collective relationship, it follows that the process of individuation must lead to more intense and broader collective relationships and not to isolation."[59]

Jung understood the tension that is created between the individual and collective as individuation occurs, that these were not in opposition but rather were differently focused. Each has the power to move the other.

---

[59] Jung, C.G., CW6 [758]

Jung believed there was psychic value in religion. Religious practice, and collective processes more generally, protect the individual from alienation. They provide solidity and a representation of the Self/deity on which the ego can relate and draw. It allows a return to, and reconnection with, the Self, a safe space through which to allow the individual to grow. "When the collective psyche is in a stable state, the vast majority of individuals share a common living myth or deity… Each individual projects his inner God-image (the Self) to the religion of the community."[60] Without the collective to form a vessel for the archetypes, they would be projected elsewhere.

Like the other uprisings in the novel, Coltaine came to power by unifying the Wickan clans against the empire. He is already a lodestone for the collective. The Seventh army has a rivalry with the Wickans in training. Coltaine is able to use his experience uniting people to strengthen them through wearing them down. He finds their inner gold by breaking down the layers.

We then see the contrast of collectives at the battle of Sekala Crossing, when the Wickan warlocks raise the spirits of an ancient battle. Those spirits, cursed to repeat their final moments, chained to the repetition of their history, and the mothers killing their own children, we are told are kin slaying kin. There is a need to create other, a differentiation instinct, both from the collective and from that which we don't like. The mental contortions required to carry out such battles must be severe. "They would have done to their victims what was done to their own families," (358).

The Wickans are the counterpoint, their history being the same pointless fighting, but "the Emperor, as our enemy, united us" (357). The collective is raised, and such differences can be transcended. By setting aside their cycles of war and vengeance, developing a new identity, they lift one another up— the beauty of a greater collective. We, too, are being shown the way to accept all the aspects of this collective, and in doing so sharing its purpose. To its logical end, we could presume that a great enough consciousness could unite all humanity.

The journey of the Chain of Dogs is itself like a repetition of history. There is the illusion of progress, each day the same, no end to the quest. This is mirrored in the novel by Kalam's thoughts as the Imperial Warren seems to go on and on: "when gnawing hunger and thirst grew constant and unappeased, when exhaustion pulled at every step, the notion of time sank into meaningless; indeed, it revealed itself as something born of faith, not fact." (458) And Felisin: "We shamble like animated corpses, cursed in a

---

[60] Edinger, 1972, p. 65

journey without end." (455) Contrast this with Icarium, though, who despite an inability to achieve progress believes there is an end, and whose faith still lies in the purpose, the goal.

At its darkest points, Duiker doesn't believe the Chain will make it, or at least can't see the end beyond their own dust. "Coltaine trains them as he would beasts, and they don't even realize it." (425) We, too, are being trained, our belief being built by the objective witnessing of Duiker. At this point, he is convinced they will fail. And yet, we are defiant. We want him to be wrong. By not showing us inside Coltaine, Erikson allows us to retain our faith, it is something we construct and share as readers. Were we to see inside his point of view, there would likely be some doubts, and that would be enough to put cracks in our faith.

Suffering joins us, forges a collective. Duiker takes Corporal List through the wagons of the sick and wounded. "The endless struggle laid bare. Gone is the idyllic, the deceit of self-import as well as the false humility of insignificance. Even as we battle wholly personal battles, we are unified." (477) Now Duiker has reawakened his faith, and is trying to convince Corporal List. He was enlivened by his crawl in an underground, given some life by the water he found there.

This notion of being a seemingly undifferentiated part of a mass is reflected in the swarm of butterflies the Chain goes through to reach Vathar crossing. "They migrate. Creatures of instinct. A mindless plunge into fatal currents. A beautiful, horrifying dance to Hood. Every step mapped out." (597). This image mirrors not only the capemoths Duiker saw at the Whirlwind's beginning, and the flies in the prologue, but the Path of Hands, the instinctive journey of the shapeshifters, following a path prepared. On Coltaine's death, we are again witness to an echo of that initial image. The crows descend on Coltaine "like flies swarming a piece of flesh… And when they rose, exploding skyward, the warleader of the Crow Clan was gone." (768)

Coltaine becomes a living symbol. He is both demon and saviour, or maybe both. We see in him something beyond human. He is a living function of a symbol, as Jung would say, the integration of the collective consciousness and collective unconscious. His character has potency because both the Chain and the Whirlwind soldiers view him as something other than human. Their projections come from the unconscious—a belief in saviours and a belief in demons respectively. His ascendancy, as such, is the recognition of him as a living symbol, redolent with archetypal meaning, and that meaning may be different for different individuals because a true symbol contains that manifold potential. As an energised symbol, Coltaine is raised from representation to something religious. Later in the series we hear about the birth of cults revolving around the Crow Clan, the feathers, etc. He is not a sign for a hero figure or demon any more, but a symbol that stands for the heroic archetype, a fine but important distinction.

By witnessing, we and the other characters have raised him with the energy of the unconscious. This also is how the experience binds us, coming from the same unconscious place, even though we may recall (or picture) it differently, though our remembrance may be represented by the cross, or the feathers, or so on. The energy is transferred, in what Jung described as a magical way.[61] We may transfer some energy from a river, but we won't capture its flow. The redirection of energy into ritual is a culture maker: through ritual and religion—energy invested in a symbol—meaning is created out of psychic forces that would otherwise be fear, superstition, base instinct.

The inaction of High Fist Pormqual, the betrayal at the Chain's end, fails to answer for all that we have seen and felt. We as readers feel that there must be some victory, though not only does the army fail to save Coltaine and the chain, it is also then sacrificed itself. The depth of this betrayal, witnessed, strikes us deeply.

Coltaine becomes an even more powerful symbol because he is punished for doing the right thing. He has not transgressed in our eyes—though the locals may see him as representative of a transgressing force, the Empire. He has acted virtuously, selflessly, and defeated the odds. ("I would make no wager." (713)) And so we feel better and better about him as time goes on, seeing him as an ascending spirit not just because the point of view characters do but because the evidence is presenting itself to us. So the floor falls away from us when the unjust end arrives. That betrayal is intensely felt for us. We may reflect as he is raised upon a crucifix that Christ, too, was punished most decisively despite his virtue.

As long as Coltaine lived, he was the projection of self for all—Chain and readers alike. He was our god, upon whom we projected that archetype. He needed to fall so that separation could occur, and we could retrieve our projection, begin to find that inner god, to grow.

Of course, another side to the collective and the raising of an archetypal symbol is the curious memory of the masses. Heroes become myth after the fact. Mythological motifs are often applied post hoc to a lived life, infusing it with great power. How has Coltaine's memory changed by the time we read it? Charged symbols are alive, and story has value in itself as a living thing. It

---

[61] *On Psychic Energy*, CW8

can have value greater than the event itself, or the life. Arguably, the Christ story has a mythical value regardless of interpretation or factual reality. Duiker needs to tell the story, because in that way not only does it live on, but it births itself as myth.

Coltaine, in giving Duiker the vial that ensures his rebirth, recognises that the myth is greater than its players. This is heroic self-sacrifice for the betterment of the collective. "All that we have done avails the world naught, unless the tale is told." (712) It is an acknowledgment that the telling of an archetypal tale defies the physical history of the hero themselves. "It is not the Empire's soldiers the Empress cannot afford to lose, it is its memory." (735)

We as readers now have a shared awakening of unconscious symbols, a shared experience which has chained us together, forged us. We watched and felt, we took the journey together. This binds us as a collective as part of a shared mythology. It gives us something to anchor us as the Book of the Fallen progresses, and also resonates with meaning at references to the Chain of Dogs or Coltaine throughout. It also prepares us for the symbol that is Tavore.

At its heart, the Chain of Dogs also foreshadows our very journey, shared, that we as readers will be taking in reading Malazan. Daunting, though not impossible, without question those who survive it will be changed by the experience. Erikson uses sleight of hand to answer the falls that we see—by offering moments of compassion. They are the answer to the pain of the fallen. And in so doing, with the experience inviting individuation, he raises us all up.

Felisin

The animus is the complex in women that is counterpart to the anima in men, which is explored more fully in *Memories of Ice*. The anima is covered in greater detail in Jung's collected writings, in large part because that is what he was most familiar with. This bias and lack of clarity, perhaps reflective of Jung's times, hasn't been completely redressed since. Where the anima is the animating spirit, the animus was sometimes referred to as the soul, which seems like an ambiguous distinction. However, it is the notion of it being masculine in energy which is latched on to. The prime imprinter of the archetype in women is typically the father.

For functional purposes, we can better understand it as the relating function in women, rather than the oversimplified notion of it being an inner man. It is archetypal, in the sense of it being an ancestral experience of men. More specifically, the archetype translates to consciousness through the symbol of a man or men.

Von Franz, comparing it to men's anima, notes its range of characteristics:

> Her [anima's] counterpart in the woman is the animus, a derivative of the father image. It manifests negatively as prejudices, rigid opinions, traditional spiritual patterns, brutality, and other forms of masculine inferiority. It manifests positively as buoyancy, creativity, and steadfastness of character.[62]

And Jung himself describes the nature of its manifestation:

> "it expresses itself in the form of opinionated views, interpretations, insinuations, and misconstructions…the animus too has a positive aspect. Through the figure of the father he expresses not only conventional opinion but equally what we call "spirit," philosophical or religious ideas in particular, or rather the attitude resulting from them. Thus the animus is a psychopomp, a mediator between the conscious and the unconscious and a personification of the latter."[63]

This notion of mediation between the conscious and unconscious, as that relating function between the ego and the archetypes, is of most relevance and interest. The same holds true for the anima in men, which also should be understood primarily as a relating function.

In Felisin, we have an example of the dynamics of the animus, its projections onto others, and its wounding, such that her ability to relate is adversely affected. Felisin is already numb when we meet her. She has a lot she needs to suppress, and the life she soon finds seems an easy fit. Our immediate impressions of her are of abandonment and the horror of, first, the Cull, and then abuse by the masses, and of Baudin's beheading of the lady. She is left naked and numb, and the sense of abandonment is compounded by the fact that her sister, Tavore, was instrumental in bringing her down.

---

[62] von Franz, 1997. *The Discovery of Meaning in the Individuation Process*. Para 21
[63] Jung, C.G., CW9ii [32-33]

We had already suspected the mother is missing in the Paran family, and we further learn early on here that the father has died. The sense of abandonment will be strong in this situation, particularly in a child (Felisin is only 15 or thereabouts). The loss of a father might lead to an animus complex constellating, as there is no figure to receive her projections—the father being generally the first carrier of the projection of the animus. So its growth becomes held, and the gaps are filled with a kind of desperate clutching at whatever replacement figures are available.

While trying to avoid putting too much weight into an over-analysis, we can say that Ganoes has disappeared on Genabackis, and the father has soon after died. Tavore has allegedly compensated for the shame by disavowing family and becoming adjunct (though from Lorn's story we can hope that this is just a persona, the human beneath is not truly dead.) This leaves Felisin and mother, who was strangely not spoken of in *Gardens of the Moon*. Lacking masculine influence, exacerbated by the early trauma of losing her father, there is a vacuum in Felisin, and a compensation is created where the animus is amplified in negative ways. Immediately, she will cast about for fathers, and she has both the spiritual side in Heboric, and the apparent warrior, or masculine strength, in Baudin. Though note they are both negatively aspected, Heboric being a fallen priest, and Baudin a monster, a murderer.

The negative animus complex can lead to a spiral of self-hate, and desire for revenge, as well as idealisation of others. There being a mismatch of thought and actions, inertia results, and contact with the world—the real world—can be avoided in an attempt to block traumatic memories, or simply to prevent a confrontation that will expose the worldview to scrutiny. This can in turn lead to passivity and self-obsession. Perfect for Felisin, then, that she lands upon Beneth, an animus projection of a king figure, to facilitate and reinforce that sense of disconnection and self-hate.

The Cull, as described by Heboric, is a welling up of unconscious forces, the collective rebelling against the nobility. The people lining the walk to the ship are enveloped in mass consciousness, their rage one of 'us against them', with no personal feeling for the individuals they hurt. The mockery of justice is a reversal to appease the collective shadow. "Stripped away civilization itself, leaving nothing but the chaos of savagery." (11) Riots and looting occurred, but organised, a pressure valve being released. Alas, the true feelings, discovery of their underlying source, remains unconscious when it is manufactured in this way. Compare with the conscious uprising in Seven Cities, which this is clearly meant to mirror.

Felisin makes herself a vessel for men. Her passivity is obvious in the very first line we see of her at Skullcup: "Felisin lay unmoving..." (86) She is intellectualising all of it. She has learned fast on the slave ship, and we are apprised of the workings of the prison camp and her arrangements with Beneth in almost lifeless matter of fact. "What we women have to overcome in our relation to the animus is not pride but lack of self-confidence and the resistance of inertia. For us, it is not as though we had to demean ourselves, but as if we had to lift ourselves."[64]

Because of her trauma, she is at once withdrawn and lashing out. This is her animus at work, as it both rationalises the trauma and acts as a protector psychologically, externalising the cause of her pain. Both animus and anima (the equivalent feminine unconscious aspect of men) even in their negative manifestations can provide a protective power over a consciousness that is too weak from what might otherwise overwhelm it. Here Felisin's animus encircles her to provide some protection from the trauma she has already undergone. It is important that we question how we feel about her acts hereafter, but were it not for that strong protective force, I suspect the girl wouldn't have made it.

The ego can be thought of as balancing the roles of the psychic functions, both with the outer and inner worlds. If we don't relate to the inner (i.e., through animus and anima), neurosis occurs, we begin to lose self-regulation. As a result, ego builds up and contracts from both the outer and inner worlds. The skin of the ego thickens. Sometimes this can take the form of a persona, (a mask or armour) with which the ego identifies. It becomes a compensatory mechanism for inability or refusal to relate to the inner world, thus focusing the energy on the relation to the outer.

Felisin acts out a rebellion against the father figures of Heboric and Baudin. She is resentful, and wants to be independent, but is fearful of Beneth, and so she verbally darts Heboric and Baudin, a safer outlet. "Don't father me, old man." (93) She does have insight, in dialogue with herself after hurting Heboric: "I've no wish to be so cruel." (95) But she can't help it, can't stop. She is in the possession of the animus complex.

Her sense of abandonment is exacerbated when she feels excluded by Heboric and Baudin's plotting, but she also knows intuitively that they are a lifeline for her. While they and their connection to her are not going anywhere, the abandonment she feels, combined with the attempt at psychic separation, leads to a complete sense of alienation, that she is truly on her own. This is the result of too much withdrawal and over-differentiation. She thinks that to harden herself is to survive, but they represent her humanity in

---

[64] Jung E., 1955, p. 23

some way. We see the reciprocity in her actions keeping them alive: she gets Heboric to work the tiller instead of pulling carts. This role, directly connected to the earth, is a grounding. Perhaps we can read this as drawing her projection from Heboric back down to earth.

Of course, predominantly Felisin projects her ill-formed animus image upon Beneth. Their arrangement appears like a comforted state for her, yet it is in reality a blissful lack of awareness. "I am the king of Skullcup, you'll be my queen." (88) Emma Jung describes how the projection can be, in a sense, functional, in that it results in a relationship based on dependence and lack of conflict. But the downside is the woman remains in a state of unconsciousness.

> "Such a total transference of the animus image as that described above creates, together with an apparent satisfaction and completeness, a kind of compulsive tie to the man in question and a dependence on him that often increases to the point of becoming unbearable. ...a man to whom the animus image has been transferred is expected to take over all the functions that have remained undeveloped in the woman in question, whether the thinking function, or the power to act, or responsibility toward the outside world."[65]

Indeed, Felisin relies on Beneth to do things for her, to be her action in the outer world, looking after Heboric, and such. She mentally justifies it as making a trade, but I feel a case can be made that that is a rationalisation upon which she justifies her continued lack of desire to increase her self-consciousness, to make conscious her animus side. Von Franz describes this as a "strange passivity and paralysis of all feeling, or a deep insecurity that can lead almost to a sense of nullity."[66] In this state of possession, we can convince ourselves the thoughts and feelings belong to the ego, rather than to an unconscious force. Beneth beats her, and the wounds of her body match the wounds to her soul. As such, she takes it passively, accepts it, and is immediately forgiving of Beneth.

The animus can give both an insistent conviction spoken aloud, or she might be outwardly very feminine but "obstinate, cold, and completely inaccessible."[67] We can see aspects of both ends of this continuum in Felisin, depending upon who she speaks to. Perhaps as her confidence falters she retreats one way or the other. To assimilate the animus, she must eventually

---

[65] Jung E., 1955, p. 10
[66] Jung C.G., 1964, p. 191
[67] Jung C.G., 1964, p. 189

question her own convictions.

> "When this discrimination between the image and the person sets in we become aware, to our great confusion and disappointment, that the man who seemed to embody our image does not correspond to it in the least, but continually behaves quite differently from the way we think he should. At first we perhaps try to deceive ourselves about this and often succeed relatively easily, thanks to an aptitude for effacing differences, which we owe to blurred powers of discrimination. Oftentimes we try with real cunning to make the man be what we think he ought to represent. Not only do we consciously exert force or pressure; far more frequently we quite unconsciously force our partner, by our behavior, into archetypal or animus reactions."[68]

Reality creeps in, and Felisin begins to prod at Beneth, seeking reactions, trying to draw out the image of the strong, controlling hero. There is a clash between the archetypal image and the reality, because in reality no individual can match up to the pure archetype. Similarly men dominated by their anima side never manage to find a woman that lives up to the idealised anima image.

Felisin needs to integrate this aspect of herself, to fully grow past that stage of projection. It is perhaps a blessing that when the Whirlwind comes to Skullcup, Beneth is taken from her, allowing escape, but this has the negative side effect of disallowing a conscious distinction from him (along with that integration of the archetypal image). And so, while we are rid of Beneth, so to speak, his impact stays with her. (To say nothing of the basic emotional trauma of seeing a loved one, conflicted though the relationship was, taken.)

I quote here Emma Jung at length again, for she describes well the process and dynamics of withdrawing a projection, which is as applicable here as for men's equivalent the anima, as well as other archetypal projections that will be referred to throughout.

> "The first stage on the right road is, therefore, the withdrawal of the projection by recognizing it as such, and thus freeing it from the object. This first act of discrimination, simple as it may seem, nonetheless means a difficult achievement and often a painful renunciation. Through this withdrawal of the projection we recognize that we are not dealing with an entity outside ourselves but a quality within; and we see before us the task of learning to know the nature and effect of this

---

[68] Jung E., 1955, p. 11

> factor, this "man in us," in order to distinguish him from ourselves. If this is not done, we are identical with the animus or possessed by it, a state that creates the most unwholesome effects. For when the feminine side is so overwhelmed and pushed into the background by the animus, there easily arise depressions, general dissatisfaction, and loss of interest in life. These are all intelligible symptoms pointing to the fact that one half of the personality is partly robbed of life by the encroachment of the animus."[69]

With such an identification, we can live within fantasy or dream, finding it hard to tell the difference between it and reality. Felisin's unconsciousness, her incapacity, is here represented by the drug addiction, but in her soul it is a dependence upon the unconscious animus. Her image of herself is at odds with reality—she imagines herself the queen of Skullcup, but in truth is a fading child-image. No doubt the feelings of abandonment, and her noble birth, help build walls about this self-image, the expectation that she was more, her noble birth glossing her own mirror despite her insistence on separation.

We are reminded that separation must also remain conscious in some way. Because the past cannot truly be separated, to presume it has been excised only invites it to worm its way back in less healthy ways. A woman must integrate the animus, by making conscious that part of herself, allowing it to function in a healthy way, neither repressing it nor allowing it to devour her.

Were he an ongoing point of view character, there would likely be much to write about Beneth in reflection, his own infatuations and anima possession. It is commonly described that when one partner is possessed by the animus or anima, it can draw out the opposing force in the other. I strongly suspect there is a lot of unconscious possession in Beneth, too. It could also be noted that the men about Felisin aside from Beneth—Heboric and Baudin especially, but also Pella the young guard—represent phenomenological aspects of her animus image, presenting together a council of wisdom, passing judgment upon her.

On making their escape, a swarm of bloodflies descends on Felisin and Heboric, a callback to the book's opening image of the fly-priest in the round. Flies swarm down and Felisin covers herself in mud (another earthing image) but too late, they cover her, and there is blackness, silence, nothingness. This is the first step of her scouring and rebirth.

---

[69] Jung E., 1955, p. 13

Of Sinker Lake, "It was said that the water was cursed and to dive into it was to disappear. Some believed a demon lived in its depths." (91) There is something foreboding and mythical in the lake, and therefore no surprise that a rebirth occurs when she swims through it, a mythological drowning. The idea of a bath or a dipping as cleansing of bewitchment is frequent in fairytales. In general, going under water is an analogy for going into the unconscious, a return to the womb. For Felisin, it is the cleansing of the dust and grime of Skullcup, and a preparation for raising the soul up, baptism. "It was not nearly enough." (189)

As she watches another collective massing, the beetles in the desert basin, Felisin reflects on her disfiguration and her dreams of rivers of blood. There is something oddly passive about her in the desert, still, though flashes of a queenly humanity are bursting through. She is reflective, analytical, though there is still a childish inaction. "Tension between what was real and imagined" (236). The river of blood seems a comforting embrace, it gives a purpose that she otherwise lacks. The river as an image or symbol is also the unconscious, the collective. It flows of its own accord like the masses. What is real is her lack of purpose, a strong ego consciousness with which to fend off the collective psyche.

She begins to lash out, but now with a cutting insight she previously lacked. Something has been born within her, or accepted, perhaps even something severed, and with it has arrived a certain wisdom. She professes to know about the faults of both Heboric and Baudin, reading them like books. She has certainty that Baudin is hiding food, but she is wrong. Her certainty begins to get a shaking when the foundational concept she'd had—that her actions had kept them all alive at Skullcup—is challenged. At that point she doesn't have much left upon which to form rationalisations. And she believes herself beyond saving. "Salvation was for others." (264)

It is notable at this point she is beginning to speak in poetic turns, simultaneously blunt and sharp. Her language is redolent with metaphor—the edge that binds psyche and matter. Poetry is a ritual act of feeling, important for the feminine side, so something has worked in her rebirth.

She takes Baudin to her bed which, while an act of cunning, may also be a reaching out of her feminine instinct which has been rejected. She rationalises it as manipulation but self-punishment is part of it. Either way, her plot to kill Baudin in that scenario fails, yet another nail for the delusions she has been cloaked in about her own power and agency. Her helplessness is mirrored to her by Baudin's anticipation of her post-coital attack, and then by Gesler's blank rejection of her when their rescue arrives. She had wrapped herself in notions of her power within a small world at Skullcup, but it was all fake, all rationalisation. She is as helpless now as she was chained in the round—and, like the herald of death, she is finding nothing beneath her façade.

Here she is searching for meaning: "There has to be a way to reflect something other than hate and contempt./No, not a way./A reason." (287) She has scoured away the old, all illusions dispelled. She understands that how we act in the world is so often driven by the life inside. The reason often arises in the very search for meaning itself. Poetry is her way, I think. Her driving forces of vengeance and spite, but lacking power and direction, makes her an empty vessel. "We command nothing, not even our next step in this mad, fraught journey." (387)

Fire sears them as they leap from the Silanda, another rebirth image. Baudin protects her from the flames, but she is in a state of surrender. Is it conscious surrender? "Felisin did not struggle. Seeing that no escape was possible, she almost welcomed the bites of fire…" (389) The pockmarks fade, those from the bloodfly bites.

"I haven't changed," (390) she says when they discover Baudin's transformation. This is psychically true. Her rationalisation when Baudin's role as a bodyguard is revealed is a defence mechanism aimed to deny change. She wants to hold on to her vengeance because that is all she has left giving her momentum. Baudin walks off, and Felisin's negative animus is welcoming her retreat, rather than surrender or admit reliance. It tells her she never needed anyone, that she was always alone. It is just another abandonment that reinforces her psychic chains.

"I feel…emptied, with nothing left in me to rebuild." (450). Had Felisin known she was protected, she would have remained a child. There would have been only dependence, if indeed she survived at all. Her trauma was pivotal in her growth. The unconscious found aspects upon which to assert itself, to protect her, and while it was all undesirable, she survived. She is hardened, changed, but part of growth is the very acceptance that the purity of before-times is not attainable again. It is how we live with those newly assimilated parts of ourselves that determines who we are going forward.

"Yet the cast of her mind remained fraught. She had run out of hope." (514) Of all the darkness she has encountered, she seems to be at her lowest point in the caves—escape from Skullcup, rescue from the island, all of it hasn't helped. She had to feel the futility, the abandonment, the powerlessness over again to reach that low. This is a call to individuation. But she hasn't integrated the animus effectively, she is moving on without all the pieces in place, and in that sense she will remain broken. "You cannot be remade unless you are first broken," she tells Heboric (567).

"She wondered if the gift of revelation—of discovering the meaning underlying humanity—offered nothing more than a devastating sense of futility." (515) Felisin is so convinced that she needs to be independent that she equates surrender at the psychic level with death and meaninglessness. She identifies with the persona she has constructed, she thinks she is the armour. But she is forced to have faith in Heboric's ghost hands as they descend the cliff face together, risking the fall. Something that can't be seen or felt, or rationalised away. She must surrender to his magic, and let Heboric bear her down.

She then cradles Baudin's head on her thighs as he dies—obviously a mothering gesture, and a cracking of the lack of feeling that she had felt up to then. "Armor can hide anything until the moment it falls away. Even a child. Especially a child." (529) In this moment the admission of Baudin's care for her breaks her open, she surrenders finally to feeling. It also foreshadows the armour that hides her from her sister at the end of *House of Chains*. We can read Baudin as being focused and singleminded, or we can also assume that, like us, he can see the humanity in her, see that she is not all gone, indeed that their final moment together is reflection of their recognition in one another, brief though it is, of their respective humanity. Baudin is genuine in believing that she is worth saving, despite everything.

Beneth's death had resulted in her shifting the warrior/protector projection to Baudin. This only served to increase the resentment she felt towards him, as she tried to draw out of him the same respective projection that Beneth gave her. Holding him in death is also the regret for not being there for Beneth. Heboric should probably be let go too as a projection, but he sticks around. She fathers him, with his disability and lack of faith, a reversal. The absence of the mother that we speculated about may be a hole that she is trying to fill, but she does so clumsily.

The psyche drives towards individuation, change, and when repressed or stymied, it will enact change of its own accord. This will often arise in unpredictable or unhealthy ways, compensating for the lack of consciousness of the individual. In Felisin's case, her feeling attributes are so stymied that her urge to care (seen in glimpses) pours through like a river of blood as the lust for power.

She is stuck in her body, held down, in the sense of its mundane form. She is unable to make the psychic separation because her sense of abandonment has removed her agency, not to mention her actual experiences. Lacking a ritual of initiation, she sees the death of the old as a death in truth, rather than a relationship between herself, her body, the world. Because she is so young her adolescence is interrupted by this trauma and upheaval, so she hasn't been able to make a psychic transformation typical of that period. That weakness allowed identification with the animus. But she needs that growth to become more conscious of her values and feeling side, strengthen her ego.

The animus has tyranny over her, control of her body. Surrender of control results in possession. Absence of the mother and mothering in recent times leaves room for the possession of the archetypal mother. Indeed, accepting the goddess, surrendering to her, is a kind of return to the womb, a paradisal state of unconsciousness. It is also of interest to note the notion of the breath of the Whirlwind, as animus, spirit, is an animating or inspiring force.

With Baudin's death, she has also lost her psychic protection, of the warrior aspect of her animus. Lacking protection, the great mother rushes in. Seeking feeling and power, the archetype tries to fill the void. Her desire for vengeance, to show the world, is ready to rise up, being the counter to her erstwhile passivity, and the unconscious symbolised by her drugged state.

The animus can impart a feeling of always being right. Barbara Hannah described how overcoming the animus is in part acceptance of the suffering of releasing certainty. "But at the same time, in place of the certainty the animus lent us before, we have a dim feeling that in all this doubt, suffering and uncertainty, there is somewhere a purpose, perhaps even a divine purpose, that it is not all in vain."[70] We feel that with the insertion of Sha'ik reborn, the animus in her is doubling down, her certainty and attained wisdom strengthening itself even as the Seer's influence widens her horizons. Heboric suggests: "You're still in that rush of power, Felisin, and it's deluded you into thinking it's delivered wisdom as well." (650) She is not strong enough to integrate the powers of the seer with the opinions she holds, and she is trying to ride the power instead of surrendering to it.

Young women often project their animus on to a movement as an expression of their own ideas. That cause or movement allows her to generate, or animate, energies that aren't finding expression in her inner world. Felisin is perhaps engaging in this sort of outsourcing of her libido (life energy) in attaching to the Apocalypse. Of course, she rationalises this as the means to take vengeance on her sister. It allows her to have a voice, an effect on the world.

---

[70] Hannah, 2000, p. 102

I think in Felisin we see that she has developed her ego, even though it may seem that she is treading old ground, or trying to. Her path is in a sense set by her negative animus complex, and her rationalisations remain, but her feeling, mothering instinct and the quality of her armour serve, at least temporarily, to strengthen her and give her some control over her life. I see this as a positive stage of individuation. Indeed, she is reborn, and though the trappings of power she is offered eventually prove to be tragic—she regresses to childhood—she has ascended from powerlessness and futility to something more, and been gifted insight from that connection to her unconscious.

Furthermore, it seems as the goddess begins to accept her there is tentativeness, a dance. Felisin's strength of character, the armour or persona she has constructed, enables her to maintain some of herself, to fend off what would otherwise be a consuming rush of power. "A deal has been struck. Power granted—so many visions—yet Felisin remains, her rock hard, scarred soul floats free in the vast Abyss." (669) I suspect that in Baudin's death, the exposure of the child within, and the mothering nature she is showing, she has transformed enough to not be a mere vessel. On arrival at the camp she says she will speak for the orphans, give them a name. Again, a maternal instinct. This nature puts her to some extent on a level with the Whirlwind goddess.

It is also notable that the only animus figure left is Heboric, the wise man archetype, the spirit father. Her council of animus projections has died about her. She has begun to assimilate it, but it all seems too late, though we see its potential in her capacity for reflection, creativity and so on. Though we can already sense the replacement of her council of animus men in Leoman, Toblakai, and the high mages in the rebellion. Heboric has also been reborn, and his connection to the ghost world of the past is a kind of spirit connection for Felisin, too, though more earthly and grounded (in history) she presumes, than the Whirlwind goddess. She may even be relying on him, as animus, as the go-between for her and the goddess—the connection to the unconscious and that is another reason she remains herself in the face of the goddess's numinosity.

In Felisin Younger, the orphan she has named, she is recognising her feeling aspect, and projecting her unlived life onto another. "A poet's eye. In some ways, as I might have become, given the freedom..." (820) It would be important for her individuation, her wholeness, to try and integrate that child aspect of herself. Heboric weeps for the child Felisin never was.

Sha'ik immediately retreats to Raraku, a childlike withdrawal. We can see here that though she has been reborn, is powerful, and has attempted to cast off and project away the child within her, the child that she was, it will not be escaped. She first needs to overcome her fear, needs the maternal embrace of Raraku and the goddess's power to overcome the fear of her sister, enable her to act.

Felisin's story continues in *House of Chains*, where more is to be said, but for now, suffice it to mention that she adopts Felisin Younger, another attempt at human form of motherhood, though there too she falls short of expectations. And again she is surrounded by a council of wisdom, though in a different form, again with Heboric, a connection to her previous manifestation, as well as Leoman, Toblakai, and Bidithal, as the various aspects of her animus council. Her task there is partly to exert and maintain control.

> "To discriminate between oneself and the animus, and sharply to limit its sphere of power, is extraordinarily important; only by doing so is it possible to free oneself from the fateful consequences of identifying with the animus and being possessed by it. Hand in hand with this discrimination goes the growth of consciousness and the realization of the true Self, which now becomes the decisive factor."[71]

Where the book of the Whirlwind was empty for Leoman, Felisin feels she doesn't need to open it. The presumption is that all she had to do was escape the old story, but escape is not enough, we must write our own future, and it is necessarily going to be shaped and influenced by what has come before. Sometimes we merely act out the old story ad infinitum, and this identification with the earlier stage of development disallows full transformation. Of course, as Sha'ik she is simply a vessel again, now a godlike projection for the collective, the dark aspect of the Great Mother. Failing to integrate our own complexes, we become more available for the projections of others. "…as if she was nothing more than a vessel filled with water." (561) And, "A crucible fired clean, empty." (602)

Perhaps this is Felisin's fate, her early abandonment drawing her ever back to a childish state, that which she understood at some level cannot be hidden by armour, and she remained a child unto her death at the hand of Tavore. Tavore's actions killed the child in her, foreshadowing her ending.

To look at it another way, in the Whirlwind Felisin feels the genuine love of a mother figure, that she had not received. Finally (even though it is in the

---

[71] Jung E., 1955, pp. 38-39

form of a river of blood) there is the offer of a comforting embrace, without dire purpose, offering itself as much to her, not to use her like tyrants and abusers.

> "Detached from the dead gods of the past, we lose all and find all, for in the moment of surrender the living god and goddess enter. We move from a place of total abandonment to a place where we can never be abandoned. In that moment of knowing, soul and Self are one. No longer dependent, no longer afraid or needy, we are given the gift of love.
>
> Jung calls this the path to individuation."[72]

Felisin has shed the old life and surrenders to the embrace of the new. Regardless that we experience the Whirlwind goddess as a witch figure, a dark mother, it is a synthesis for Felisin, a new stage on her path. "Felisin surrendering herself yet again. Remade. Reborn." (604)

Of course, we could say the empty book is a metaphor for her new life being an open book, the idea fulfilling her plans for revenge. But such basic motivations don't tell us why she is able to be Sha'ik, why the psychodynamics work. The character dynamics at a deeper level give her narrative an authenticity, and help us to understand how the patterns repeat in her life, how she fails as mother and, ultimately, in her quest for revenge.

To summarise then, the animus in Felisin used, we suspect, her lack of maternal love, as well as her expectation to be pampered as a noble, and her feeling that she is better and smarter than others, to possess her, leading her to enjoy her seeming queenhood in Skullcup. Her egotistical superiority over the failed priest in Heboric, and the lowborn criminal thug in Baudin, as well as the duality of her fear and the one-dimensionality of Beneth, allowed her barbed superiority to thrive. Her rationalisations weakened as they proceeded across the desert, where she continued to lash out and use her old tricks, and latched on to vengeance as a purpose—though her unconscious feeling instinct broke through in her care for Baudin and the orphans. This maternal nature, as well as the hardness of her ego's defences, allow her to fend off full possession of the goddess, maintaining, and even individuating her own self as she comes to power.

It is a fabulous character arc. We can see, at least, that Erikson's work is an astounding summation of psychodynamics. At most, it shows the conjunction of Jung's psychology and the growth of personality, the tendency towards individuation, and the complications therein. There is nothing linear

---

[72] Woodman, 1990, p. 138

here. Furthermore, we can see that individuation is as natural and applicable a concept as the hero archetype.

Mappo and Icarium

Icarium has no memories, his unconscious all buried. Mappo tries to keep it for him, holding his unconscious. When we recall Fiddler's words to Whiskeyjack in *Gardens of the Moon*, about bearing the weight of others' humanity, it is no surprise that Fiddler and his crew run into Mappo and Icarium.

Who is chained to whom? Icarium's legacy is a type of chaining. Just as we are part of a collective, we are part of the collective of history. We are necessarily a result of all our ancestors (our ascendants). Again, whether we see those chains as heavy bindings, or merely a string of links connecting us to a rich history, depends. Icarium's heritage and history bind him, even though he is not conscious of the memories.

Similarly, we are not always aware of the unconscious forces that act upon us. Icarium seeks symbols…he is following a path. He is trying to raise consciousness even as Mappo diverts him. Is Mappo's course of action the right decision? Is it moral? It benefits the collective, sure, but at the expense of the individual, it seems. But it also protects Icarium the individual. It is Mappo's journey to answer these questions in turn.

There are no good answers, and as we have discussed, this tension is often where consciousness grows. It is a trigger for the individuation process. As von Franz says, the initial crisis of the individual is in seeking something that is "impossible to find or about which nothing is known."[73]

Iskaral Pust tells the travellers that time is "Irrelevant. Importance lies solely in the deeds done, the goals achieved." (115) The weight of history is a relevant theme in this novel. Seven Cities, the histories of the characters, Heboric and Duiker as historians, and Icarium's puzzling of his own history, trying to piece together symbols.

The labyrinthine underworld of Iskaral's caves represents very well a shadow world. The directions to the library, for example, make no sense, nor does Mappo's solution. The works they find in Iskaral's library are from a

---

[73] Jung C, 1964, p. 167

civilisation "mired in minutiae." (118) Often what remains of our history is not its minutiae, but its symbols. Mappo tells how this search for answers was on the contrary a mask for their meaninglessness. Perhaps this is us – overeducated, indebted, sifting through signs (not symbols) hoping to find them charged with meaning, so that there may be some underlying purpose. The cultural and civilisational amnesia we live under is our refusal to acknowledge the unconscious.

Memory is itself a story that prepares for the future. So is growth possible with no memory, no reflection? We can't change our perception without the foundation from which to launch change. Fiddler's conch shell exploding reveals a rush of civilisational memories. The weight, which has been building in the background, has become immense, the strain of Icarium's forgotten memories, alongside those of Apsalar, and in a sense the feelings of our culture's forgotten history. The song of the shell is a release valve, a breath of peace in the chaos.

Cultures may see gods as time itself, or vice versa. The rhythm of the seasons, the sun's passage, and so on, were markers of memory. It also represents the heroic journey, the rise and fall, the rebirth. These rhythms are themselves mythical symbols of the journey, and Icarium's notion that writing replaces memory tells us that in breaking down, in specialising and dissecting, we are concretising something that is otherwise numinous. "The power that resided in the telling of tales, the ritual unscrolling of memory." (575) Indeed, it is perhaps of some relevance here that at least in our world the earliest form of timekeeping would likely be a sundial or gnomon, which use the cyclical movement of shadow to depict the rhythm of time.

Time is also necessary for causality. Icarium's obsession with time is in that sense a search for meaning. There is a logic and a flow. Without it, perhaps we are not able to perceive our world. "All that we were has led us to where we are…but tells us little of where we're going." (611) Without history, perhaps the future is only futility. It is time's past, present, and future that create a life, a self, a culture.

This story thread is also about literacy and memory. There is a sense that what we have lost with literacy is the depth of meaning. Words are cheap when ink is free. We lose the overarching meaning without the culture to bind us.

Culture—those signs we mistake for symbols of archetypes – can replace real discourse with the unconscious. Deeper study dilutes meaning, and as a result we don't leave room for the numinous.

Mappo is really trying to stop Icarium learning everything, because it is the search itself that gives meaning, it is not just that the things he will find will destroy him. He knows that Icarium has purpose, and that purpose will disappear if he finds answers. The answers can never live up to the search. This is played out in metaphor as Icarium takes on Pust's charge to find the broom. There is an innocence in his willingness—a hero leaps to take quests. "It was not the goal of the search we were to value, but the journey." (210) Then Pust does a reading, showing "renewal, a resurrection…You must begin a journey. Soon." (213). The Rope card at the beginning of the reading seems to suggest Apsalar as Sha'ik, but this is just the first misdirection.

Icarium wants to witness the rebirth. Just like the quest, he is undertaking these hollow goals. Looking for signs, when what he needs are charged symbols with real meaning. They lack meaning if they are not conscious. It is the difference between narrative and symbolic story. The more an image is concretised, or used cynically, the more the power drains from that symbol.

We must be willing to sacrifice, to pay the price. But Icarium has no identity with which to pay. Again, this is metaphor for our society—we lack cultural memory. The gestures we undertake are hollow. Mappo balks at the point of entering Tremorlor, when he has revealed his mission to Icarium, but Icarium stays firm. Again, sacrifice of the self is heroic, and must be undertaken for growth to occur, advancement of the collective culture. It often means ending a comfortable balance of life. That is the charge of the hero, not content to rest forever in the glow of his treasure, lest all stagnates. Icarium's willingness to accept that burden, just as he took on Pust's frivolous quests, is more heroic, even though he is arguably less burdened by the anxiety attached to a history. Mappo's reluctance is understandable.

Mappo reflects on his choosing by the Nameless Ones and his village's destruction—by Icarium, we understand. He has taken an individuation journey already, unwilling to be stymied by the village life of traders he left, separating from the collective. Then he joined another tribe, and was similarly caught in a cycle of warring and vengeance. He was bored of that life, too, felt himself pegged to a tree. Life can reach plateaux, and we pine for new growth, quickly tiring of the new life we've made.

So Mappo returns to find his village has been destroyed, his kin murdered. The task before him was not to be of vengeance, he is being offered the chance to prevent future occurrences. Mappo, being conscious of the static cycle of war and vengeance, fits this role. But he suspects he would not have taken the calling had not his village been destroyed – a dreadful wounding.

"You will be an unpainted hide, Mappo. The future will offer its own script, writing and shaping your history anew." (251). We have here questions of our individual power and responsibility in defining the collective, the role of a hero, and of what influence we have in turn as part of a collective. Do we have to be outside of it to shape its story? Is forgetfulness, that hide scraped clean, the best reaction to past trauma? Can we learn if we do not confront our past? The historian would argue not. Icarium's quest suggests the drive for that knowledge and growth is innate and irrepressible. Again, if we reflect on our own culture, we are in the habit of silencing that which discomfits us. Repress that thirst for knowledge, deny one side of our opposites, and the culture will tear itself apart looking for answers.

Icarium recounts a dream of the Nameless Ones when they encounter a body at Tremorlor. No Jungian analysis would be complete without at least mentioning dreams, though here we won't analyse the contents, suffice to say the dream reveals a truth that was not known to the conscious world. "And as I feel my memories drift apart…away…I sense I have but dreamed. And so awaken." (658) The curiosity in Icarium's state of waking life is dreamlike. Memory fades quickly, though the source is beneath consciousness. There is a truth concealed in the unconscious mind that works away, even beneath the amnesia. Does it change our body, our spirit, even if forgotten? There is a profound truth in the continuation of unconscious life, its suppression or expression, despite our ignorance. The ability of unconscious memory to hold pain is analogised in Corporal List's visions, his own dreams revealing the history of a Jaghut family, and the emotion infects both him and the place they travel. Icarium's story is cultural amnesia, but loss of history and meaning won't hold the unconscious energy down forever.

Mappo believes Icarium was responsible for the destruction of his village, yet wars within himself to keep from Icarium that understanding, the power within him. He is Icarium's shadow, gatekeeping the unconscious, repressing his rage. He is the carrier of the burden of things forgotten; indeed, his bag can hold a lot of hidden content. Both characters are frozen, not able to raise things to consciousness. "They studied each other, their eyes searching the altered reflection before them, one set plagued with innocent questing, the other disguising devastating knowledge." (409)

A counterpoint to the doubt is the notion that Icarium's life now has meaning because he has a quest, a goal that he progresses towards each day. Our question, and Mappo's, is whether that is true to Icarium's humanity. Is it still life, if out of time? His search for self is, in fact, the archetypal quest of the individual. Are we to presume it is bereft of meaning because we know the answers are not to be found?

Is life the illusion of progress, or does the passing of time trick us into the illusion of futility? Duiker, with an impending battle, reflects: "We go to partake of death. And it is in these moments, before the blades are unsheathed, before blood wets the ground and screams fill the air, that the futility descends upon us all." (490) It is only in a life lived that meaning is made. A life avoided, or ended without stepping forth on the journey, well, there we might question futility. Stuck in old patterns, like war and vengeance, a way out can seem impossible.

A similar cast of mind infects Felisin, when she is at her nadir:

> "We do naught but scratch the world, frail and fraught. Every vast drama of civilizations, of peoples with their certainties and gestures, means nothing, affects nothing. Life crawls on, ever on…It's the ignorant who find a cause and cling to it, for within that is the illusion of significance. Faith, a king, queen or Emperor, or vengeance…all the bastion of fools." (515)

We don't all have to be ascendants or famed wanderers to change and shape the world. In a sense, you have to be able to surrender to the greater forces of the world, let them sweep you along before being able to shape them in turn. But her sense of futility may actually be a sign that Felisin is experiencing surrender, or that what she assumes she is doing when she allows herself to be used is being conflated with the sacred surrender required to be at one with herself. So there is a fatalism in her. She doesn't yet know that surrender should not result in futility, but growth.

There is also something curious in Icarium as the builder of timekeeping mechanisms being himself out of time, by virtue of lack of memory. The repetition and cycles of the years represent rebirth, the mythical renewal and regeneration of the world. The old is purged and purified, "a combustion, an annulling of the sins and faults of the individual and those of the community as a whole."[74] Is Icarium thus unable to be reborn, reliving his sins and guilt unconsciously, through the eyes of those around him?

Against the theme of time's repeating, historical cycles, the reliving of them, this being outside of time seems to me a hopeful one. If it is not relived, one cannot exist within his suffering, or that which he has caused others. But does that keep him below a threshold of humanity, thus driving in turn his search? Fiddler suggests: "Without history there's no growth…" (403) But would that very knowledge at once fulfil Icarium and drive him mad? Making him whole and tearing him apart.

---

[74] Eliade, 1949, p. 54

Conversely, he is and remains a myth, archetype. There is no fall, no evolution of his history, though he is still alive, and very much associated with the passage of time.

History is a burden. Cultures that view time as cyclical replay the birth of the cosmos with the passing of a year, thus purging and regenerating the year past. Christ's redemption cleaned the slate of man's sin. Icarium's history still weighs upon him, his construction of time's intricacy not allowing a release, and so his past reveals itself like ancient cities from under windblown sands. Through full regeneration each year, we would start anew in a nascent state, absent all notions of history and responsibility. Icarium, unable to go into his darkness, unable to take the fall, never has the opportunity to rise above his current state of individuation.

Layers of history, lives built upon lives. The death of the imperial warren, the old city in the caves, those ruins beneath the deserts. This weight affects us. As we grow through our stages, as individuals or as a culture, we do not ascend free of burden, return to a virgin state. The baggage builds—without history there is only ignorance. Each transition must perforce be harder, a greater battle. The chains heavier and the strength (of character) required to carry them up to another level of consciousness.

Finally, Mappo thinks, "I cannot escape my cowardice." (779) Yet we understand it is not cowardice, but friendship. Bravery, in fact. But he is stuck either way. In typical fashion precipitating individuation, there is no good answer for Mappo, still. But we can say that he remained true to what his heart told him. Was his unwillingness to sacrifice his own comfortable life his failure to grow, or taking the way that is morally true to himself the beginning of growth? "My selfish desires made a mockery of my integrity, my vows." (779) Others' value systems have driven him thus far. We want him to be right in his decision, but we also want the protection of the collective, preventing the dangers Icarium represents. Finally, his ability to take the fall, make his own sacrifice, prevents his transformation. We may return to peace for a time, but what is unconscious has had a taste of freedom, and will continue to simmer. He has now set for himself a pattern, and is vulnerable to inaction.

Crokus

In *Deadhouse Gates*, we are only just checking in with Crokus, mostly seeing him from the outside as he matures. "Like it or not, lad, you've got some growing up to do." (107)

He can't speak for Apsalar, though he thinks he knows her mind, insists she's just a fisher girl, even though his projection of goddess nature suggested there was so much more. Fiddler finally understands that Apsalar's life is her choice. He holds Crokus back from pursuing her, and guarding her against Iskaral Pust.

Later, as they prepare to track her through the desert, Fiddler reflects on Crokus's knife technique, sees a new maturity in it. That realisation of letting her be, allowing her to follow her father, changes him. He has to let go of his notion of her as an empty vessel for his projection. But he deals with it in part by withdrawing and in part with externalised violence. We need to give that rage and violence a container, or an outlet, but cannot let it define us.

Mappo later comments: "I may well be underestimating the young man. He's grown within himself." (579) It remains to be seen the nature of this growth, whether that is a growth that has turned inwards, not able to accept and thus shutting himself from the external world.

Crokus admires Icarium's forwardness, his loss of the past. Perhaps he sees in it, and in the potential of Icarium's rage, something he might adopt. He thinks he can excise his own past and thus be heroic. But again he is stuck in a projection – one cannot cast off one's past, any more than can be someone we admire.

Sorry: "As if I have no self unstained…I am no mere girl any more…I choose my own causes, Father." (659) She is asserting her selfhood, which inevitably will find her at odds with the static idealisation Crokus has constructed.

Fiddler

Fiddler has parted company with the Bridgeburners, a necessary separation on his own journey of individuation. "One must be dumped out of the psychic containers that keep one unconsciously identified with family, tribe, party, church and country."[75]

Fiddler muses on their still being soldiers of the empire. "Malaz isn't the Empress, and the Empress isn't Malaz." (106) We know that service to the empire is something of meaning for those that are part of it, even if the deeds are not objectively honourable. We learned in *Gardens of the Moon* that the tools of the empire are part of the machine (an organic body), and that they can lose their humanity, as seen in the Adjunct, and Paran to an extent. But we also know that Fiddler is very conscious of maintaining humanity.

He thinks in parting with Kalam about their shared goals, that it was friendship that bound them. Now, alone, or at least parted from his squadmates, he is lacking the collective. He later builds that up again as part of the Bonehunters. It is no surprise that he is in disguise as a Gral tribesman, someone out of place. He is a mirror of Crokus here. The lad needs to grow, and Fiddler needs to accepts his elderhood. They both miss their crew.

Fiddler is protecting children, first in Ehrlitan when he received Kimloc's blessing, and then in G'danisban. In a literal way he is also protecting Crokus and Apsalar who are little more than children. He knows, he is conscious of that role, and he had spoken to Whiskeyjack of compassion, of holding others' pain for them. It's not mere duty for Fiddler; he's doing it because it's right.

He has the gruff exterior of a certain reluctance, but we get a chance to learn who he really is, what he represents. He changes little in *Deadhouse Gates*, but finds situations that allow him to express his fathering role. "*Children are dying*" is the phrase that echoes through this novel, and Fiddler is one of our bulwarks against it.

When they enter Raraku, it is a mothering embrace, a wing wrapped about them. "She's found her father." (531) He also steps into Mappo's way to offer succour for Icarium, who, finding his mechanism in a dead city, regresses to childlike nature. "Voice of a lost child…child's worst fears." (575) This role is one that Fiddler is outwardly uncomfortable about at first, but he acts with instinct and certainty.

---

[75] Edinger, 1986, p. 25

Lostara Yil

We meet Lostara Yil as she is tracking Kalam, her role one of deception. "Bluster could be its own disguise, arrogance a mask hiding an altogether deadlier assurance." (136) But, too, masks can hide more masks.

Lostara's story begins with certainty, she is cold, brutal. She opens up to her feeling side, here in the form of a dance. She has to let herself go to be fully in the shadow dance. Certainty becomes doubt, becomes despair, and must be rebuilt consciously.

We know less about her history. The Red Blades are turncoats in a sense, natives of Seven Cities fighting for the empire, another layer of masking. Lostara kills Sha'ik, which we could see as her symbolically repressing the consciousness of the mother figure, and doing so on behalf of her people. In that fight she takes a head wound from Karsa Orlong, symbolising an attack of the animus, the head being the centre of the intellect, the logos.

She then meets Pearl, a grey dusty figure appearing as if by magic, a trickster, and together they follow Kalam into the Imperial warren, a kind of descent into the underworld. She is hardened, merciless, dutiful, and it appears that she needs to integrate masculine and feminine, find life in her body, creativity. The relationship with Pearl is an outward expression of her internal antagonism. Her journey across the Book of the Fallen will be to shift her abandonment in the negative sense to a positive abandon—freedom, spirit.

Cotillion

With his possession of Sorry, we know that Cotillion already has some experience with children being used for his (House's) purposes. Then he meets Panek.

For the first time we get a more internal look at Cotillion, taking him down to a level we can understand. We could consider him in the second half of life. Ascendancy, and even life after death can be seen as metaphors within this fantasy world as the latter half, or the descent if you will, towards the end. His life's achievements and constructive accumulation have been completed.

He now has to learn to reintegrate the child in himself. His humanity.

He says of Kalam (revealing for both) "Like me, he is haunted by helplessness." (749-50) We do not immediately think of Cotillion as helpless, rather as prudent and instrumental. But we can see now that he is reaching out through his flailing attempts at humanity for some firm hold on the world. He has become evanescent like the shadow realm he inhabits.

"When I Ascended, Lady, it was to escape the nightmares of feeling… Imagine my surprise that I now thank you for such chains." (750) He has focused on the rational, practical aspects of life. Cotillion's journey of individuation is therefore perhaps the most explicit in the series. He must reintegrate his feeling aspects. First, through his anima (perhaps a failed attempt with Sorry, or he has imprinted upon her) and his shadow—then find a container for it. He becomes Lostara's shadow.

Panek asks him if he has his own children. "A daughter. Of sorts…We had a falling-out, I'm afraid." Panek suggests forgiveness is necessary, and we learn that it is she who must forgive Cotillion.

Stormy

"Nobody. Nobody at all." (197)

While our time with Stormy is relatively brief, and we don't get similar depth of study later in the series, in *Deadhouse Gates* the old marine's story is a nice thematic rounding out of the book's ideas. He must come to believe in himself, or accept himself as something. Anything.

He is reborn by burning away his self. He is touched by Heboric's godly ghost hand, healing a possibly deadly wound. "Heboric plunged a ghostly, loam-smeared hand directly into the wound." (282) There is suspicion that power, even the god Fener himself is passed into Stormy's keeping with that touch. "Something passing through…Was it Fener himself?" (293)

He wanted to hide away as part of the collective, just a soldier, part of the unconscious mass.

Legana Breed gifts him his sword, a legacy. Though he also says of Stormy that his soul is insufficient to breach the wound in the warren. He is aware of Breed's sacrifice—the Imass had volunteered endless pain. "Existence without meaning…" (331) Heboric says. Stormy is to be filled with purpose; he has to live up to the legacy he has had thrust upon him, live with meaning in Legana's stead.

Conclusion

Picture a chain whose ends are conjoined, thus forming a loop like a snake devouring its own tail. Each link in the chain is formed in the same shape, thus creating a self-similarity we associate with fractal images. We could imagine that each link is like a life in the grander link of the collective. Each circles round from birth to life to death to rebirth, like each season exists within a solar year. That is how the rebirth of the individual occurs, too, in its passages of life—childhood, adolescence, adulthood, senescence. One could even say each day that we awake is a rebirth of the conscious mind, and within the day...so you see. A chain not only binds, it connects us, revealing how alike we are, part of something greater, even as we are singular.

Deadhouse Gates offers us the notion that redemption, rebirth, is possible, even in the most hopeless situation. Felisin is reborn. Apt saves the children. The dogs are healed by Mappo. Duiker is saved by the magical vial. Coltaine and the warlocks have their souls collected by crows. All the help that the Chain of Dogs receives – the Trygalle Trade Guild, the Khundryl and Kherahn tribes who escort and help the refugees – these are all instances of compassion. Here is an enemy, a poison in foreign lands, but compassion can still be shown, and it can live on even if only in symbol and story. This is crucial preparation for our understanding the Crippled God.

In the process of individuation, it is important that we not get beyond ourselves. Only by reminding ourselves and remaining human, in spite of the numinosity of the unconscious, in spite of awareness of my fallibility and incompleteness as a human, can we open ourselves to the unconscious. In this process we balance the mundane humanity with the godliness of the Self. That very consciousness and balance is the goal of the individuation process.

We think of the collective, of our tribe, not just because it is historically important, but because we cannot be separated from that context. No matter how much individual will we preserve and exert, we do not exist in isolation. "[T]he totality—the fullness of man—is not in the separate member, but in the body of the society as a whole; the individual can be only an organ."[76] Also, the hero has to bring the treasure back somewhere, or what is the point?

---

[76] Campbell, 1949, p. 354

A culture hero changes the culture; he doesn't win the treasure for self-exaltation.

Individual and culture is a bidirectional balance, they affect each other, bound by chains. Strong heroes can shift the culture, the collective. They have a stronger gravitational pull. If they align with archetypes, or are able to represent them symbolically for the culture, they act as symbols and exert more pressure. Coltaine effectively achieves that in this story.

With the increase in population, over-density in many of our living spaces, etc., it is easy to lose the comprehension of meaning for the individual. How hard it is to separate from the mass when the mass is so all-encompassing. Asserting selfhood and maintaining consciousness in the face of the collective is also a protective mechanism against that mass consciousness and cynical manipulations of its weaknesses. "The world lives on, beyond us, countless unravelling tales." (782)

Awareness of the Self, such as in the individuated person, can create feelings of connection between people, because knowing the self enhances empathy. That is what we are doing here in these books. In individuating, you work between and within the collective and individual levels. It expresses the balance between inner and outer self, or the conscious and unconscious. Further, projections that might otherwise fracture the social unit can be apprehended consciously. von Franz suggests individuation has a positive contagious effect, "as if a spark leaps from one to another."[77]

> "Only this wholeness [consciousness creatively allied with the contents of the unconscious] of the individual can make possible a fertile and living community. Just as in a certain sense a sound body is the foundation for a sound spirit and psyche, so a sound individual is the basis for a sound community."[78]

The tension between individual and collective can manifest in another way, through the draw of the collective on the individual as a protective mechanism for the collective. In Jung's Visions Seminars, he discusses how when a woman begins controlling her animus, or a man his anima – we could say when any individual begins to ascend beyond the mass mind of the collective – she or he is like a sheep who strays ahead of the flock. The other sheep see it as a wolf, and thus it becomes open to attack. The individuating soul is an attack on the herd instinct of us as social creatures. We could

---

[77] Jung C., 1964, p. 224
[78] Neumann, 1955, p. xlii

understand the openness to attack as coming both from beyond the flock, as in a real wolf – the devils of the unconscious – but also from the projections and accusations of the flock itself.

With the existence of community there is a tension between the individual and the life of the collective, the responsibility we bear towards it. This creates anxiety, and can be destructive, but that tension is necessary. In an extreme, polarised world, it is easy to have the balance too far in either direction, too egocentric or too unconscious. Imbalance can be destructive to community, as well as self-destructive, and yet these poles are self-reinforcing and we can swing between them rather than find balance. The seeking of that balance is the work of balancing and living in the tension that is part of the process of individuation.

Forces of Nature: The Anima and the Mother in *Memories of Ice*

Water is life; the ocean is mother.

Memories of Ice begins with the receding of the ocean, that mother disappearing from the T'lan Imass, yet her waters nourish the land while at the same time revealing what is buried beneath.

When life is frozen, it is in stasis. Again, there is a duality, for it is both preserved but also prevented from growing.

The ranag and ay, ancient beasts fossilized beneath the ocean's silts: "The surface is shaped by what lies beneath" (25) says Bonecaster Pran Chole. This is the unconscious. "We are the clay…" The Imass, warring against the Jaghut, are driven by instinct, their original purpose maybe forgotten, much as animals are instinctive, not driven by conscious motive.

Archetypes rise out of the depths of the collective unconscious. The mother complex and the mother archetype are powerful and important because the mother is typically the primary caregiver – and/or by her absence it is formed – so there is a lot of psychic baggage attached, before anything else happens.

Jung himself did not lay out his theories in systematic ways; most of that work has been done by others that have built on his ideas. In his writings, and logically, there is substantial overlap between the Mother and Anima archetypes. The mother is an imprinter of attachment and identity. As development proceeds, the anima grows away from the mother out into the world. For the anima, the mother is the most prominent image. She is the first carrier of the anima projection.

> "The mother-child relationship is certainly the deepest and most poignant one we know. . . . It is the absolute experience

of our species, an organic truth as unequivocal as the relation of the sexes to one another. Thus there is inherent in the archetype, in the collectively inherited mother-image, the same extraordinary intensity of relationship which instinctively impels the child to cling to its mother."[79]

Readers may be struck by a certain quaintness, even primordiality in the terminology and gendering of the terms used. Of course, language has difficulty representing such abstractions as archetypes without resorting to metaphors and images. But there is a deep biological and cultural truth to the distinction of masculine and feminine, and our understanding of such instincts is rooted deeply in our genetic and cultural heritage. That truth transcends the socio-political zeitgeist, and if one is willing to accept the language and run with the feeling, call on those instincts, that truth can be accessed with a minimum of discomfort.

Neumann argues the value of exploring the notion of the feminine archetypes for both the individual and culture, in his preface to *The Great Mother*:

> "The investigation of the special character of the feminine psyche is one of the most necessary and important tasks of depth psychology in its preoccupation with the creative health and development of the individual.
>
> But this problem of the Feminine has equal importance for the psychologist of culture, who recognizes that the peril of present-day mankind springs in large part from the one-sidedly patriarchal development of the male intellectual consciousness, which is no longer kept in balance by the matriarchal world of the psyche."[80]

He continues:

> "Not only does our concern with the archaic world of the archetypes—though they are seemingly anachronistic and far removed from the everyday reality of modern man—provide the foundation for all psychotherapy; it opens up to man a

---

[79] Jung, C.G., CW8 [723]
[80] Neumann, 1955, p. xlii

view of the world that not only enriches his own personality but also gives him a new perspective on life and on mankind as a whole."[81]

Jung, writing about the Mother archetype, shows us the very extent of its associations lends credence to the numinous nature of the mother throughout humanity.

> "The qualities associated with it are maternal solicitude and sympathy; the magic authority of the female; the wisdom and spiritual exaltation that transcend reason; any helpful instinct or impulse; all that is benign, all that cherishes and sustains, that fosters growth and fertility. The place of magic transformation and rebirth, together with the underworld and its inhabitants are presided over by the Mother. On the negative side the mother archetype may connote anything secret, hidden, dark; the abyss, the world of the dead, anything that devours, seduces, and poisons, that is terrifying and inescapable like fate."[82]

Kilava takes the children from the hunted Jaghut to send them away. She has just lost a child, and is lactating, which reminds us that instinct plays out unbidden. There is counterdependency in motherhood, and fundamentally there is an instinct to nourish. But these children end up being an offering to seal a wound.

There is an inherent duality in parenthood; we think we set free, but we entrap (sometimes unconsciously), and we are often unwilling to sacrifice ourselves in turn (our notions of the world) to free the children again. We are ever in a dance, unable to extricate ourselves from our heritage and history, unwilling to give ourselves up to it.

This is the other end of the chain to *Deadhouse Gates*, a deepening of its themes of history and burdens and heritage. The Imass and their eternal war with the Jaghut reflects this. They chose immortality to fight a war. In this way they aim to achieve preservation of memory and purpose. Mhybe wonders, "shall we ever see an end to war?" (106)

Kilava slaughtered her clan "To break the link and thus achieve

---

[81] Neumann, 1955, pp. xlii-xliii
[82] Jung, C.G., CW9i [158]

freedom..." (33) This is the extreme metaphor for pulling away, severing connections. There is a clear duality expressed in Tool's curse of that very freedom that she celebrates, and that pains her. The Matron's soul is freed as a result of Kilava's actions: children are imprisoned and the mother is freed. Mother and child are chained, in mutual sacrifice, differentiation and return.

"All is struggle, all is war for dominance." (64) The eternal war is also just life, it is destruction and rebirth, fire and fertility, fall and ascent. Tool takes umbrage with the notion of oneness with nature, which we certainly bestow upon our primordial forebears, and romanticise. There was never a blissful before-time, when life was harmony. Again, it is balance, the seeking of, the taming and shaping of chaos to fashion order; the sundering of order's chains to initiate new growth.

But nor is nature our enemy. Such an oversimplification leads to an earth rent by poison.

Choice, foresight sets us apart. Consciousness is the ability to communicate with the world not in awe, fear, or violence, but to shape it in turn.

> The projection-making factor is the anima, or rather the unconscious as represented by the anima. Whenever she appears, in dreams, visions and fantasies, she takes on personified form, thus demonstrating that the factor she embodies possesses all the outstanding characteristics of a feminine being. She is not an invention of the conscious, but a spontaneous product of the unconscious. Nor is she a substitute figure for the mother. On the contrary, there is every likelihood that the numinous qualities which make the mother-imago so dangerously powerful derive from the collective archetype of the anima, which is incarnated anew in every male child.[83]

The mother is the first carrier of the projection of the anima, and so the archetypes and complexes of mother and anima have significant overlap. In men, because the primary caregiver, the mother, is female, it is a return in a sense, finding that relationship through the feminine. It is also all around us, the world as mother. The mother archetype is generally projected inwards,

---

[83] Jung, C.G., CW9ii [26]

where the anima is projected onto others. Although with the overlap, perhaps the distinction becomes moot.

Von Franz discusses the central import of the anima being the mediator between the conscious and unconscious:

> "The anima is a personification of all feminine psychological tendencies in a man's psyche, such as vague feelings and moods, prophetic hunches, receptiveness to the irrational, capacity for personal love, feeling for nature, and—last but not least—his relation to the unconscious. It is no mere chance that in olden times priestesses (like the Greek Sibyl) were used to fathom the divine will and to make connection with the gods."[84]

As our complexes, or our translations of the archetypes into personally meaningful images and dynamisms crystallise, they become more distinct from one another and more concrete. Of course, there will still be crossover between mama and anima, for example, and too much overlap will certainly create functional difficulties in developing individuals.

The symbols we associate with archetypes also differentiate accordingly, so the anima will become less and less associated with the image of our actual mother over time. Similarly, the ego/self is initially hermaphroditic, then differentiates into male and female.

The goal of treating with the anima in man is to separate and analyse it, to integrate it as Jungians would say, otherwise it is continually projected onto others. This integration is akin to finding the magic within the self. Opening to the anima allows communication with the inner self, the unconscious, from which further integration of the archetypes can occur.

In youth, the child must first separate from the mother in a healthy manner. Failure in this stage results in infantile dependence on the projected anima, often the mother herself or a projection of the motherly aspects onto other women. The further confrontation with the archetypal projection of ancestral experiences of women that a man encounters in his young adult phase, often towards a first love, then become crucial. It is expected that much of this projection is wrapped up with the experience of the mother, both at a personal and archetypal level.

> "In the case of the son, the projection-making factor is identical with the mother-imago, and this is consequently taken to be the real mother. The projection can only be

---

[84] Jung C., 1964, p. 177

> dissolved when the son sees that in the realm of his psyche there is an image not only of the mother but of the daughter, the sister, the beloved, the heavenly goddess, and the chthonic Baubo. Every mother and every beloved is forced to become the carrier and embodiment of this omnipresent and ageless image, which corresponds to the deepest reality in a man... And, at the same time, she is the great illusionist, the seductress, who draws him into life with her Maya--and not only into life's reasonable and useful aspects, but into its frightful paradoxes and ambivalences where good and evil, success and ruin, hope and despair, counterbalance one another."[85]

As the anima image that a man carries within himself is typically drawn from the image of the mother, the mother archetype has particularly deep charge. Effective integration of the anima archetype then allows a man to relate to women as themselves, not translated through expectations and archetypal complexes. It allows for communication with the unconscious, and thus opens up the realisation that within the self is the divine aspect.

The anima can be considered to manifest a creative capacity, a positive feeling aspect associated with the feminine:

> "Now, in a man, the positive anima is the magic of life. That's why a man who is not in contact with his anima is dry, dull, intellectual and rather lifeless. I have sometimes even defined the anima as the stimulus to life. Everything that stimulates a man or fascinates him comes from the positive anima. That's why if a man has a negative relationship to his anima he becomes depressed, finds no pleasure in anything and criticizes everything."[86]

Anima as soul is the call to adventure. She is the communication between conscious and unconscious, and can be what elicits growth. "It is the mover, the instigator of change, whose fascination drives, lures, and encourages the male to all the adventures of the soul and spirit, of action and creation in the inner and the outward world."[87]

Thankfully, our intrepid hero is here to help us explore these two fused feminine archetypes.

---

[85] Jung, C.G., CW9ii [24]
[86] Von Franz, 1999, p. 116
[87] Neumann, 1955, p. 33

Ganoes Paran

Ganoes's negative mother complex affects his anima. His reintroduction in *Memories of Ice*:

> "Ganoes Paran was plagued by images of drowning, but not in water. Drowning in darkness. Disorientated, thrashing in panic in an unknown and unknowable place. Whenever he closed his eyes, vertigo seized him, knots tightening in his gut, and it was as if he'd been stripped down to a child once again. Terrified, uncomprehending, his soul twisting with pain." (92)

He is in the womb. The pain in his gut that recurs through the novel is an attachment to the wounded mother complex—an umbilical cord.

He is preoccupied by his connection to the hound of shadow, yet within the sea of chaos, there is something equally primal and instinctual: "The emotions frothing this crest … more like a child's. A child's…" (93)

He is up against problems of materiel, administration and so forth, and he is uncomfortable with the official role that has been thrust on him. It is made plainest here with the administration at the beginning of the novel, but it is the authority in the army more broadly that makes him uncomfortable. He has already discovered he is not living his own life in *Gardens of the Moon*, and now here he is saddled with more responsibility, yet he is ostensibly free.

This is the process of maturation at work, so to speak. We grow and get more responsibility in a seeming endless addition of burdens. And many of us have has the experience – maybe it's archetypal – of a job that isn't fulfilling, that doesn't do our own soul's work—the accountant who just wants to paint, for example. It can be wretched, physically debilitating. Part of us thinks we need to regain the lack of responsibility that marked earlier stages of development, and so we end up avoiding responsibility. We may flit from job to job. We may find creative ways of rationalising and undermining our growth. We may eat our own gut worrying and become resentful. It is a prison. For some, individuation means stepping outside of the system, playing by a new set of rules.

Paran is trying to convince himself it is the Hound's blood in him causing his dreams of flight and drowning, which is a pretty sure sign in a story that's not the case. "Without the ability to trust—anyone. Naught but solitude." (100) Anima is the relating function in men and Paran, being adrift from mothering forces, is in need of connection and acceptance. This is an interesting example of the dynamic of the anima developing out of the mother archetype, or being affected by it.

The various stories in *Memories of Ice* are basically summarised in his dream images: "A child screaming in darkness, a Hound howling lost in sorrow. A soul nailed to the heart of a wound…" (100-1). In fact, they are more or less variations on the same idea.

That trapped feeling can be indicative of the mother complex. "But always escape. Flight…even as the burdens settle." (94) He has lost the embrace of the empire, as have all the ostensibly renegade soldiers. He has lost Lorn, who had taken the role of maternal embrace, and then he failed to transfer his anima because Tattersail died.

The anima image is heavily influenced at first by the mother, but as the child differentiates, moves out into the world, the anima is projected onto other women, and influenced in turn by the world (this is the dynamic of the complex developing). First, or early loves, have an outsized impact on the image, and take a heavy load of projection. Tattersail is a strong influence on Paran's anima image for this reason. Conscious awareness of the image is shaped by experience and memory. Thus, Silverfox, with Tattersail's characteristics, not to mention her pre-conscious memory echoes, will interact with Paran to fire up that anima complex.

Perhaps this smacks of overanalysis of what is merely magical rebirth, but as a metaphor it sits nicely. Erikson might be imagining what a character might do in this unreal situation, but he's calling on fundamental psycho-dynamic truths—how the memory and the psychophysiology are influenced and recalled by emotional experiences. His conclusion appears to be that we might not react much differently to how we'd feel if we met someone who was a dead ringer for a high school flame.

"Self-pity could easily become a well-worn path in his thoughts, unless he remained mindful of its insipid allure." (156) Pain, paralysis, the loss of agency one feels, whether with the burdens of maturation or through illness or trauma, can infect the ego, draw self-pity. He finds out he has lost his parents, his mother (little to his surprise) took her own life, no doubt adding to his sense of abandonment. This little tidbit makes us reflect on his character all of a sudden. He says that he and his sisters are without conscience, capable of anything; he is wrong, and perhaps attributing to them some perception of his mother. Though it does set us up to view Tavore as harsh and capable, just as Felisin's perceptions did. His cold response is a conscious attempt to retreat to the coldness he claims is typical of his family, but it can itself be seen as a rut of self-pity. We must wonder again at the upbringing of the Paran siblings, what cold abandonment they felt.

> "Death and dying makes us into children once again, in truth,

> one last time, there in our final wailing cries. More than one philosopher has claimed that we ever remain children, far beneath the indurated layers that make up the armour of adulthood.
>
> Armour encumbers, restricts the body and soul within it. But it also protects. Blows are blunted. Feelings lose their edge, leaving us to suffer naught but a plague of bruises, and, after a time, bruises fade.
>
> …
>
> Memories and revelations settle in like poisons, never to be expunged." (160)

Here we have again the notion that what protects also imprisons. Memories remain beneath, calcified in our bodies, even if not conscious. That is how we remain as children. Armour is our persona, at once what we present to the world, but also what we hide behind. Fragility remains. The raw state of childhood is protected by an outer layer of civilising, but beneath that we are still, to an extent, the warring instincts of biology. Still children of mother earth, dependent, frail.

Paran's constructed armour is the attempt to bat away those final cries, to deny the child within him. The wording of his thoughts is a callback to Felisin's moments with the dying Baudin. Her attempts at armouring herself were likewise a denial, and they were shed. This is a denial of the self, a refusal to feel. The anima, as the relating function, invites a man to feel, so enter Silverfox.

He is uncertain, meeting Silverfox, this not yet fully developed anima figure. His need is essentially to regain some relation to his inner world. Whiskeyjack suggests he should try and draw out the Tattersail aspect, which of course is symbolic of his positive anima complex. Could we then suggest that Nightchill, the other soul in Silverfox, is the negative aspect of his anima complex? "Remote. Cold." (193) While he didn't know Nightchill, perhaps his anima complex has been affected by Tavore to some degree?

Silverfox, in turn, has a very explicit task for Paran: "You must find the answer for your own creation, you must find the purpose behind what you have become." (175) This is the process of individuation, in a nutshell; the quest for understanding—consciousness. The anima here, as is its wont, elicits action. He has made contact with the unconscious, and she has responded.

"Aimless, purposeless men do not undertake quests." (175)

But who better?

"I don't believe in goals – not any more. They're naught but self-delusions." (175)

That's alright, it's about the journey. Rather, it's about the peeling away of those delusions, to get at a deeper truth.

He has a sense of flight, and this is a denial of the unconscious. How affected he is by grief, by pain, we can only speculate. After Lorn's death and all he had suffered, he realised he had got his own life back. He had agency. The reticence he shows here towards Silverfox and the idea of himself as a player in the world does not jive with that sense of newfound freedom.

Silverfox tells him he is to represent the new card, he is the wanderer within the sword. In essence he must accept the ascendant nature, that all the sensations and feelings within him are part of him. His colleagues, and Silverfox, show faith in him. They sense or see that he is more than he admits. He spurns their faith, insists to himself that he will fail, in whatever it is they want. Is this merely refusal of the call to adventure? Growth is hard; with responsibility comes burden, pain, sacrifice—that is the armour he had pondered. It is about letting go of the child within.

He dreams of the child within the wound, flight, and Silverfox tells him he must run towards the child. We should always turn to that pain, face the fear, the dark, the unknown, to leave the known world and self behind. Yes, that refusal is one way of saying we fear leaving the comfort of the mother's embrace. Each separation can feel like abandonment, especially for Paran who has felt out of control and alienated already. Mhybe reflects, "Detachment is a flaw, not a virtue." (214)

As Master of the Deck, Paran can communicate with the unconscious. Essentially, within Dragnipur he has had a numinous experience. He has also had a death and rebirth, but he needs to learn how to relate, not just in the outer world, but with the unconscious. This is the role of the anima, as a mediator with the unconscious. He has to let her in, has to accept her, so that he can confront his shadow. His firm grip on consciousness has slipped. Having had the experience of slipping into unconsciousness, it becomes easier for it to happen again—a door has been opened, much like hypnotism. It happened at the Fete, when he spoke to Cotillion, and here it happens again when he is spirited away to the Azath house. Part of the initial task for him will be to hone this ability to communicate with the unconscious, to control it. That is an opening of dialogue with the anima, and allows greater access to unconscious contents.

Within the Azath house, Paran repeats his reluctance, "The House is mistaken in its faith, Raest." (228) Raest, in turn, gives him the same task as Silverfox. "Walk into the darkness…You will make the journey eventually…" (229)

He continues to withhold his feelings from the Bridgeburners under his command, his arms wrapping around his pained gut like he is literally trying to hold it all in. "He's a hard bastard…Captain might make it after all." (478) The soldiers recognise his struggle, the burden. He thinks that he should stow his feelings, to show strength, but there is something unhealthy about keeping that humanity bottled. There is resistance in him, the pain in his gut telling him to hide who he is, though we know that both Anomander Rake and Whiskeyjack, reasonable judges of character both, liked the young man.

We could again speculate that a lack of maternal influence plays a role—the expectation that the world would care for him. As a noble, that was probably a reasonable expectation, and the family passed on its responsibility. When leaving to be a soldier, he escaped that cosseting, but wasn't able to be himself. A positive maternal relation would allow him to express his instincts, neither locking them away nor getting all he wants. His grief at Tattersail, Lorn, his family, all adds further layers to his self-deception. And yet, instinct still stirs beneath.

Alongside the hiding of his pain, Paran also defends himself from the outside. "She's haunting me. Seeking my thoughts. But I'm not ready for her." (664) This dual sheltering from the outside and keeping the self within is a hardening, a calcification of the persona. Such can obviously prevent true relation to the outer world, and when it is the anima or relating function against which one defends, then an inability to relate to the unconscious also results. "Given all that he held within himself, Paran was beginning to instinctively recoil from her contact." (666) Only, the deeper instinct is to relate, and no doubt it is tugging on Paran, given his recent states of loss and loneliness. Defying the instinct is what is causing him pain. Quick Ben tells him, "You got sick, Captain, not from resisting the power forced upon you, but from resisting yourself." (786)

Sometimes, it can be the case that our ego isn't strong enough to hold what is expected of us. We may not be ready to grow into what our biology expects, or the unconscious drives may be overwhelming. In such events, we need another to help carry that weight. Trotts takes the role of leader of the Bridgeburners, and this gives Paran relief from the burden of command, the expectations, the outer connection while he deals with inner connection. Paran even finds himself critical of Trotts's decisions and leadership—this shows the value of another perspective, and thus the carrying of that burden can open up insight or reflection into oneself.

He continues to suffer under Silverfox's psychic assault as his soldiers confront him in Capustan about his knowledge, "assailed…a dark desire to be crushed lifeless beneath it – if such a thing was possible - rather than yield…No, not her. Her power that was so much more than just Tattersail." (684) The anima is not merely the image we project onto, or personify (same goes for the animus), it is a whole suite of relating functions—to ideas, people, inwards and outwards. By denying it, the buildup becomes undeniable from the unconscious. If we hide ourselves, if we don't relate.

Paran faces here his responsibility as Master of the Deck, sees powers wanting to use him again. This could also be read as a factor of being unable to relate to his own unconscious. He feels overwhelmed by the archetypal energies cracking through his defences like the blood oozing through the stones of the tenement on which he stands. We must deal with the anima (or animus) before contacting the shadow. We need to open up the channels of communication with the unconscious before we can begin to integrate those repressed or forgotten parts of the self.

He doesn't want to make a decision at the behest of these powers. "He felt himself mentally wheel round, to face that incessant, alien presence that had so bounded him. Felt himself open like an explosion." (685) This is his assuming of ego strength, it is a turning point, if you will. His turning is also a turning inward, an opening of dialogue. Because he has been used, and because he has denied communication so long, there is strength there in the force getting through to him, and he has to respond in kind. It is notable that he 'felt himself' turning, rather than actively taking the action. Indeed, "the bestial blood" (686) suggests that maybe the response is his unconscious instinct pulling him in, taking him over and flowing freely.

Maybe being open to the outside, with his grief, to his soldiers, would have allowed a more respectable dialogue to develop, but that's not how it went down. And we see how his inner strength, perhaps borne out of that earlier connection with instinct, the brush with the shadow, has allowed him to build this capable vessel on his own. While it's possible to grow and work through our complexes, even to undergo individuation by ourselves, there is value in relating, and the social aspect of our lives is crucial.

Paran is assertive in this confrontation with the unconscious, with the shadow (as we might refer to the elder gods, as he's now communicating with the Nightchill aspect of Silverfox, those gods being deep-seated, influential.) He asserts for the life of mortals, insists they will not be used. It shouldn't be manipulation, rather we must come consciously to change, that is meaningful growth, so Paran is displaying his understanding and maturity at that level. And "something other than pain and grief – I'll fight you." (686) He is taking a heroic stance here, placing himself between humanity and the collective shadow. He has integrated his bestial, instinctive aspect, each time he contacts it, it seems stronger, and now he has opened up relation to the unconscious.

He asks about Tattersail, and is informed her attentions are not focused on him. "So I was flattering myself, thinking otherwise. Dammit, Paran, you're still a fool." (689) Here we see Paran's anticipations and therefore his projections being pierced. This understanding is the beginning of him withdrawing his projections, should he make that conscious decision. He had already cut his strings from Oponn, and perhaps this withdrawal from the unconscious has given him strength.

In the square with Itkovian and Gruntle, Paran tries for levity. He is making decisions, seeming to take command. A change has come on him, just as with Gruntle, like they are both waking to their integrated selves. For Paran, this comes with recognition from his soldiers, namely Blend and Picker who agree that he knows how to command. It is notable it is these two women, along with Detoran, who set out to "straighten 'em up" (714), given that these two women of the squad were the ones who were willing to take Paran out. This is another acknowledgment that Paran has now found good communication with the feminine aspect.

His role as Master of the Deck is explicated:

> "Power...Sensitivity to unseen currents, knowledge of the interconnectedness that bound all things and everyone to everyone else. Ganoes Paran, who despised authority, had been chosen as an adjudicator, a mitigator of power whose task was to assert a structure – the rules of a game..." (759-60)

This is redolent again of the ability to traverse the unconscious, to understand there is more to life than the superficial levels of ego and persona. But really what we are seeing is discomfort with the notion of ordering chaos—living, through relating. "No wonder my body recoils, seeks to reject what has been forced upon me." (760) Power, by which he means to bemoan responsibility, adulthood.

"A position demanding a sudden burgeoning of his ego, the unassailable belief in his own efficacy. *That's the last thing I'm capable of, alas. Plagued by uncertainty, scepticism, by all the flaws inherent in someone who's chronically without purpose.*" (762) But isn't that how we all approach the task of growing up?

Denying ourselves humility, we can go through life playing adults, just children dressed up as grownups, talking in cliches, living a patterned life unthinking. Accepting burdens and meeting life level-eyed takes the shine off the giants we looked up at when we were young, but it's the only way to grow. Maybe we slow with age, as the burdens pile up, but it is strength of soul that rallies to meet that weight.

> "I can feel the pressure – the voice of countless gods, all demanding that I deny my sanction, since it seems that I am the one cursed with that responsibility…There's a lone voice crying out, deep within me, so buried as to be almost inaudible. A lone voice…I think it's mine." (782)

The ego or the conscience is asserting itself against the unconscious of the masses, of popular opinion, of easy outs. It can be hard to think through problems when we follow that lone voice of conscience, but easier in the long run on our souls. Anyway, he is able to communicate within now—hear the voice, now that he's opened up to it. He is no longer a tool, a sounding board.

When Paran sees Silverfox approaching the parley, he realises that she has stopped reaching out to him psychically. This is symbolic of the power of the projection being withdrawn. "If anything truly existed between us, it is now over." (840) His withdrawal of projection from Silverfox, and by extension from Tattersail is realised when he understands that what he gives to her isn't how his memory sits. The anima complex is shaped by experience, indeed interacts with it, and memory can amplify a fiction. But by withdrawing the projection from an external figure, he is more able to use it to communicate with the unconscious.

Paran speaks to Silverfox about the unconscious processes of emotion, how they do not deserve attachment because they are not what defines him. "I can examine myself, my every feeling, until the Abyss swallows the world, yet come no closer to mastery of those emotions within me. For they are not static things; nor are they immune to the outside world – to what others say, or don't say. And so they are in constant flux." (884) Emotions, complexes, are subject to influence from our history, memories, projections, as well as our conscious nature. By differentiating himself from being defined by those transient states, Paran is asserting again his strength of ego. He probes Silverfox here, his memory of his time with Tattersail, to test his emotional attachment, and he realises those feelings in full and can remember objectively—but in his state of projection, he idealised the time he spent with Tattersail. He is saying here that he can be dispassionate from the flux of moods and feelings, yet not deny them.

What he leaves unspoken is that if we are not to let emotions rule, then we must act. Take steps. "I've done my climb down, Silverfox, and am now climbing up the other side." (883) That conscious engagement with the depths is not achieved in one flash of insight, but must be continually worked on. There is danger in over-psychologisation of feelings and emotions, for we risk identification with fleeting states and expectation. If we identify with the emotions, they end up living us. The climb down can at times be a fall, but climbing up the other side is conscious action, it is a journey that must be undertaken in action.

> "'I admire him, Dujek. For his resilience, for his ability to examine himself with a courage that is ruthless, and, most of all, for his inherent humanity.'
>
> 'Sufficient to warrant faith, I'd say.'" (914)

He appears now able to command with ease, commutes with Quick Ben and gains his respect. He promotes Picker, and hands over Anaster to the Grey swords, along with his blessing, of course. "I can speak on behalf of the Malazans." (920) He is also in control of the unconscious, his roamings within the Deck. "Barely conscious of his own intent." (969) Mastery is in part the shift of conscious effort to unconscious.

His wounded face marks him as battle-hardened, his perfection gone, or rather his paradisal state prior to separation from the mother. He is now one of the Bridgeburners in truth, but more, he is now relatable to them. They look on his face and see not an outsider but one of their own, a shattered visage through which he can relate. "I'll carry my scars." (1035) He takes command of the Bridgeburners in Coral, and competently leads them, finding balance in his character, knowing when to command, when to speak. Crucially, too, his imperfection probably has some relevance to his understanding of the Crippled God's designs—his wound a relating factor to the wounded. This then becomes invaluable in his sanctioning of the House of Chains.

With Quick Ben, they return to the Rent at Morn, sacrifice the mother who has had her time, to redeem the child, the Jaghut sister, the feminine. To give answer to the Crippled God's poison. Pannion and Kilava both, in this scene, realise they have a way to go to forgiveness and redemption, and we see a brother and sister, kin, joined in an embrace.

And so we see in Paran in *Memories of Ice* the role of the anima. At an intrapsychic level, Silverfox as anima mediates between the Paran's consciousness and his unconscious. Opening communication with the unconscious allows the free flow of information, and a level of mastery of understanding his emotions and seeing the world through relating. Further, she is typical of a man's projections and idealisation of a woman based on the man's complex. Withdrawing those projections disentangles the outer world from the impulses and fixations of the projected complex, allowing one to relate objectively to the outer world. Paran frees himself from those infatuations, and his ability to communicate with the unconscious, his insight, stand him in good stead for approaching his shadow.

Mhybe

The feminine is at once the giver, the transformer, and the nurturer of life. So the archetypal images and symbols associated with these functions are predominantly feminine in nature, and dominated by mother images. Neumann, in *The Great Mother*, specifies that the archetypal image of the *vessel* encapsulates both the elemental and transformative nature of the vessel. In the Rhivi tongue, *mhybe* means vessel. The definition of vessel should not be equated with something inert and empty, rather that it is something whose inner workings are unknown. The elementary nature of the body, not just the feminine, as something transformative and mysterious, is a common understanding.

"The inside of the body is archetypally identical with the unconscious, the "seat" of the psychic processes that for man take place "in" him and "in the darkness"—which last, like the night, is a typical symbol of the unconscious."[88] The understanding of the body as vessel in turn results in a projection at three levels: the world as vessel, the heavens as vessel, and the underworld. The projections cause us to view the workings of the cosmos as analogous to the body and organs. Virtually a universal projection, this creates a perception of the earth mother (e.g., Burn) as well as the heavenly vault being the playground of the gods.

Indeed, it is in the function of mother that the numinosity of the Feminine as vessel becomes apparent. It is the transformer in the conception of the child, its carrier, its nurturer when it is born, and protector in the early years. Erikson's association of the Mhybe with a vessel is therefore not to denigrate her as a *mere* vessel, but to behold her as a powerful symbol. It is

---

[88] Neumann, 1955, p. 40

mentioned that she is adorned with trinkets to ease the ache in her bones, and in many cultures a distinction is made of sacral vessels by their ornamentation. Kruppe's gift of copper adornments worked by the Rhivi spirits further emphasises this, and he calls her, "Holy Vessel." (368) Copper is also a feminine symbol, being associated with Venus, healing, and youth.

Vessel is the womb in mythical symbolism. Vessel is also a means of becoming conscious, by holding feelings, ideas, and beliefs. It is less that Mhybe is being emptied than that she is holding all that unconscious for Silverfox. We ask our mother to hold too much.

Mhybe is a vessel for the mother archetype for the army. They draw from her by projecting on to her, not just the metaphor for a child feeding on a parent, which alone always struck me as too cynical. Rather, it is what we put in the vessel, what we ask it to hold, that tests its energy.

Motherhood is transformative. Neumann writes of how that transformative character is related to blood—first menstruation is an acute sign of transformation, then its cessation during pregnancy, and after, its seeming transformation to milk. Birth is the end of one transformation and the beginning of another. The human child's dependency is key to the transformation and the connection between mother and child; the relationship builds over the first year or more, and a woman becomes a mother during that time, not instantly. The physical separation of child from the womb is merely a preparation for the psychic separation that will occur over the lifespan: conscious and unconscious growth towards fullness in the woman.

Depression can come about because of the loss of the old. It may take time to become a parent, but the severing of the old life is instant. Mhybe doesn't get the full dependence of the precocious Silverfox. This is signifying the difficulty of the transition. She wasn't prepared. The differentiation of the child, on the other hand, the end of dependence, can probably be eased by conscious attention to the self as a parent, preparation for that separation. There is counter dependency in the relationship between mother and child. The mother is often not taken care of because she is expected to do the caring. As that nurturing role is not required for Silverfox, Mhybe is simply uncared for. There can be guilt about anger and resentment, and if she keeps it in, it can eat at her.

In Korlat, Mhybe, and Silverfox we have three mothers. And yet, we are all children. Nothing makes this clearer than parenthood. Daughters can end up mothering the mother. This is shown here in the relationship between Mhybe and Silverfox, but it is because of the magically accelerated development of Silverfox, rather than a psychological failure to grow in Mhybe herself.

"It is the nature of everyone here to treat every situation tactically, to push away personal feelings, to gauge, to weigh and balance." (133) Mhybe has here misread (at the least) Whiskeyjack and Korlat, who have genuine compassion for both her and Silverfox. Mhybe's sense of betrayal by her child has affected her perception of others, perhaps she is even projecting that calculating sense onto others. It affects her ability to relate, to trust. In some ways, this is the defensive instinct of the mother, but twisted into illness.

Mhybe is thrown because the power dynamic typical of mother and child has been shifted. The mother's role is to determine control over the child's body, its inputs, restriction of its movements, alongside the nurturing and comforting role. This has been taken away from her, even reversed in a sense with Silverfox's growth demanding sustenance beyond her mother's means. Mhybe therefore has lost her sense of agency, or regresses to a child herself.

"The old woman told herself she felt no resentment…" (104) Further, in response to Brood's questioning of the dynamic: "I choose to accept it." (198). There is instinct at play here. She insists she wouldn't hate, but all around her people are telling her how cruel her fate is. It is an interesting reflection of how expectations can define your experience. As a parent, there is severe cognitive dissonance in the feeling of wanting to be away from your child, because you are supposed to love and nurture it. We wonder if it makes us bad parents, bad people. No doubt this is more extreme for a mother.

"I am my daughter's web, and I am alone in that." (199) Again, I think of the unready mother. Her instinct is telling her that as a single mother, she is all Silverfox has. This mentality can destroy the self, keep her a child. "The time for me is surely past, yet those around me continue making demands of me." (202) The social world is expecting her to be responsible for the direction of the child's growth. Yet, while there is dependency, there is also the need for distancing, for release, allowing the child to grow and become its own expression of the self.

Crone tells her, "She is you more than the others." (236). We want to take responsibility for the best in our children. They reflect us, socially. The separation that occurs as children grow takes a toll on the parent as much as the child, with the realisation that this force of nature is beyond our control. We need to relinquish that control to an extent, yet still provide the strength of a framework.

Mhybe's situation mirrors Burn's, where the Crippled God is chained to Burn, a parasite, a poison, affecting the life of the Goddess. The understanding of the destructive nature of humanity on the earth can give rise to an instinct to tear it all down, to erase humanity. As Caladan Brood's burden shows us, this is not a decision to take lightly, and that attitude is symptomatic of disconnection. The compassion shown by the Andii in caring for Mhybe, protecting her, is a sense of hope in her humanity.

Mhybe is pursued in her dreams, or so she assumes. Though Kruppe urged faith in the gift of her dreamworld, she sees only threat. In the depths of depression we are unable to evaluate what's good and bad, a veil of self-abasement clouds our vision. We assume all is pain and, more, that it is deserved. "Silverfox feels abandoned by her mother. This leads to bitterness." (510) Their alienation from one another is bounced back and forth, although even in the midst of this, Silverfox we are told engages the undead dragon in Mhybe's dreamworld to rescue her from the abyss. Though alienated, there is still a protective, maternal instinct in Silverfox.

Mhybe seems to be running at the head of the pack of undead wolves. This is the gift in her dreamworld, a freedom. Like Silverfox, she is the living leading the undead. Of course, Mhybe sees in Silverfox the very thing that haunts her dreamworld, the T'lan Ay that take form about her daughter, the pack that she leads. "She may look frail and seem powerless, but there is that within her which is capable of driving the T'lan Ay away." (590) Silverfox in turn sees the helpless mother, unable to provide succour to her child. No doubt this is the very fear she faces in the impending confrontation with her own spiritual children, the T'lan Imass. They cast their reflections, then, upon one another, seeing themselves, yet fearing what the other might see.

Kruppe may dissemble, but he lands on a truth when speaking to Coll and Murillio about Mhybe's condition, and that there is mercy in his gifts: "she is not yet ready to receive such truths, alas. This is a journey of the spirit. She must begin it within herself." (622) This is as true of individuation as it is any personal growth. The conditions of the mind and its context must be ready to birth the new. Mhybe doesn't yet have the full awareness to take in the information at hand, namely that of her dreams, and no doubt her depressive state affects the interpretation of all that she receives. Rereading demonstrates this understanding of our experiences, as our interpretations and values change with time, with age. Growth follows a general trajectory, and sometimes we want to grow too fast, but the context isn't right, and sometimes we resist and the world thrusts change upon us. Mhybe's social context is supporting her in her journey—Korlat, Kruppe, all her watchers—but there is only so much that can be done in guiding her to the way out of her depths. In the end, all valuable growth must be instigated internally.

Mhybe's dreamworld itself, as an unconscious, is part of the mother figure. Where dissociation and isolation can be negative, they can also have positive valence, as in this case: protective sleep which allows for the incubation of internal growth. It is the prison as a protective circle. Mhybe is offered the opportunity of spiritual growth where she has lost out in the physical world.

She is trying to hold on to the child in herself, that which has been taken from her, and so she can't accept her own child. This disrupted transformation from youth to motherhood can appear as selfishness or rejection from the outside, but it is more a failure of adaptation.

As the dark aspects of the mother are inherent in the archetype, a failure to consciously adapt to motherhood risks those instinctive, destructive tendencies coming to the fore. I am talking here about acceptance of the feminine, its full nature and potential. This shouldn't be read as accepting traditionally defined, restrictive roles, but rather consciously integrating the full potential of the feminine nature, good and bad, transformative and destructive.

In her dream, she comes across the spirit of Toc in a cave, a wolf figure. She stands on the threshold here, not yet willing to step into the deeper layer of unconscious, the dark of the cave. They are sceptical of one another, but Mhybe sees another soul imprisoned. He is the mirror of her, a vessel that cannot take the love the mother offers. Toc tells her, presuming she is the Seer, that the Matron's child made for her a prison. Mhybe's own situation is reflected before her, inviting her to understand. She wonders if the prison she has found is the curse of all mothers, and Toc says "It is the curse of love." (823) These are the chains born of connection. The counterpoint to the fact of the mother not being able to let go is that all love demands something of the parties, that chain pulls hard, our instinctive gift and burden.

The story of Little Red Riding Hood draws interesting echoes here. The grandmother in that story, the kindly maternal figure, is devoured by a wolf, and in turn therefore expresses the devouring nature of the maternal. Mhybe flees from the wolves in her dreams, denying the dark side of maternal nature expressing itself in her unconscious. The fullness of her nature and indeed her own growth are stymied by that denial. While she is devoured in the outer world by the child, Mhybe rightly fears being devoured in her inner self. Again, there is a reversal here, where the devouring by the wolf is seen as possession by a dark spirit, Mhybe's darkness is manifest in the outer world by her bitterness and resentment, and the wolves in her dreams offer redemption.

Having had the natural withdrawal of her child fast-tracked, she has not been able to assimilate the dual nature of motherhood. For her, then, the gifts of maternal embrace in turn, the dreamworld, the womb-like tomb prepared for her in Hood's temple, are acknowledgment that she is but a child herself. "I wasn't ready. I was unprepared to give so much of myself." (1069) Her dreamworld is her embracing nature. "She sleeps, to dream." (1133) It is the revelation that she has within her that potential, that she is not merely a vessel, but a numinous container for the sacred, a nurturer of that world for the ancient gods. Observing the gathering about Mhybe, Rath'Shadowthrone observes "What bubbles in this cauldron?" (1019), and it is again worth noting that a cauldron is another womb-like symbol of conjoining, of mystery, and birth.

She reconciles nature with spirit in her absorption into the dreamworld, and this is a fulfillment of the mother nature in her. She faced her dark side, turned it on herself and out to others, but in the end saw the gift of her nature. Kruppe's gift in showing her the dreamworld was an invitation to embrace the spiritual nature in her, to experience it as a relief, a temporary freedom.

Much of this is too abstract and would ring hollow if forced onto character and progressions of growth. You can't make a character an archetype, or at least can't do it over and over in a conscious manner without abstracting away all truth, or making the character so unreal as to defeat the purpose. The characters written by Erikson are enriched from an unconscious place. They come, then, from a place of truth, a deep place. Using Jungian concepts to analyse and understand the characters and stories is done usefully after the fact, as an interpretive lens post-fact. The same could be said of trying to understand yourself, or practically applying the knowledge in a therapeutic setting. Jungian thinking is a language we can use to abstract and translate experience and problems and growth and healing, but if you say I'm going to tackle my mother complex, you're just bypassing the depth of the issue, the internal depths.

For example, a child isn't aware of the mother archetype, or the development of a complex. Silverfox might be, but she's an exception. The child does know instinct, feels it. The instinct for succour, for nourishment, warmth and attachment. Individuation, the drive to grow, to seeking meaning, is itself instinctive.

Archetypes themselves, then, are a vessel, a cultural narrative within which we can study and understand the underlying instincts and drives.

Children of the Dead Seed

"What hides at the core of that empire of fanatics?" (132)

The Pannion Empire is birthed because of a mother/matron freed by the soul of children/child. This is a mirror of Silverfox and Mhybe, to show us the counter dependency of mother and child.

Unity is not possible, the mother is devouring because the father is, well, unconscious. Absent, when it counts. The feminine here does not need to submit, surrender itself, and so remains as a devouring mother figure.

With death, "an involuntary spilling of life seed." (408) This makes a mockery of fertility cults, where both the mother as life giver and the earth as devourer and renewer in creating life are worshipped. Erikson is again highlighting the connection between death and birth.

The Pannion Seer is fixated on mother, and thus he reproduces in his society the absence of father, and the dependence on mother. But in turn he doesn't want them to connect with their masculine side. Dependence is not only carried down generations, but transferred, as the dependent child fears the mother's liberation.

Toc senses within the Pannion domin "a child betrayed…terror and pain." (493) and later in Pannion's tower sees the power behind the seer, sees its true face: "a child standing before him." (504). It is the broken relationship between mother and child, played out on both sides. The Matron who's lost her children, and the Jaghut child taken from its own mother, and to its mind, betrayed and abandoned over again. Both had been subject to pain from that abandonment, and both seek to repair it. "The sparks of need reside within her." (504) This is instinct. It will burst forth even when denied for so long.

Indeed, the Tenescowri also represent the devouring mother, or rather the Pannion Domin itself does. It is not creative or restorative, but rather destructive, leaving behind only empty cities, literally devouring what is not incorporated. The Tenescowri then are both the devouring mouth and genitals of the Domin.

The notion of feeding on the dead and conquered also suggests the power of mass movements, or the collective consciousness, to swallow up the individual. Indeed, it can devour entire societies and cultures.

Itkovian reflects on the nature of that empire, bringing up again the image of a flower:

> "Cities and governments are but the flowering head of a plant whose stalk is the commonalty, and it is the commonalty whose roots are within the earth, drawing the necessary sustenance that maintains the flower…The countryside before us…has been a wasteland for some time, sir. Thus, while the flower still blazes its colour, it is in fact already dead." (903)

We can see in this passage how the nurturing effect of the mother can be drawn on too hard, lifeforce sapped so that only the appearance of living is maintained.

The warren within the sword Dragnipur offers a counterpoint. Draconus beseeches Paran to tell Rake to take more souls, kill more with the sword, so that the wagon can continue to be pulled away from pursuing Chaos. There must come a point where so many souls are taken that there is no world left to save. This conclusion of extremes is no different to the Domin.

Compare the Malazan Empire as we saw it in *Gardens of the Moon*. While empire typically has both positive and negative outcomes, the embracing aspect of the Malazan Empire is at least acknowledged. It has the effect of rebirth, and while it is destructive of certain aspects of the colonised cultures, it is not all-devouring like the Domin here. It can be as much marriage, and while a marriage itself can be seen as conquering and devouring, in its best aspects it creates a new fullness. Pannion's need is also reflected in the hunger of the Tenescowri. Withheld nurture and nourishment, to mirror his own deprivation of motherly love.

Anaster could be seen as the eternal child, puer aeternus. A sickly, wild haired youth, who only lets his mother come close. His red lips call to mind an almost cherubic innocence. He becomes a vessel for Toc, because he is in an infantilised state of incest, unable to escape from the mother. Toc, being stronger, and having more effective communication with his anima, does escape.

Itkovian tells Anaster, "There is despair within you. I will take it from you, sir, and with it your burdens." (654) Anaster is jolted as if struck, and indeed, Itkovian has struck a nerve of truth. Anaster's development is delayed. We see his mother clawing up him, touching, holding. There is only despair, it is what is holding him together. "I am not your father," Itkovian goes on, "but I will be *as* him." (654)

But Korlat's assessment is that there is a spark of conscience in his madness. He can't bear the thought of leading the Tenescowri, and thus wants to lead it to its annihilation. In turn, he demands damnation for himself. This awareness suggests that even in the most seemingly hopeless case, there is humanity, and thus the possibility of redemption.

Silverfox

Silverfox's arc can be read as the maturation of a daughter to the fullness of feminine potential. It is an abbreviated journey from childhood to adulthood and ostensible motherhood. She represents the emergence of feminine values in culture. She is a variation of the miraculous birth, or "unholy conjoining" as Kallor terms it (128). Erikson is very deliberate in representing Silverfox as an older child, twelve summers, when Paran arrives, so there is resistance, along with Mhybe's initial insistence that she wouldn't reject her. When the army begins its march, she has "aged five years", so that she is at the end of her adolescence and on the cusp of adulthood. This is typically the transformation that is most deeply associated with separation from the mother.

The ubiquity of stepmothers in fairy tales is notable, and they usually signal that a woman is destined for individuation, must come to terms with the dark mother figure, first seen in the personal shadow and later as part of the Self.[89] The stepmother could easily be replaced with a reluctant or distant mother. In rejecting the mother, a woman rejects the source of life, her deepest nature, and because of this split, she cannot avoid the suffering which is a precondition for her individuation.

Fairy tale stepmothers represent vanity, jealousy, and bitterness as the hallmarks of her evil. From Silverfox's point of view, she could suspect that Mhybe is jealous of her youth, indeed her bitterness arising from the loss of her youthful beauty, taken so harshly by her child. In this respect, the very fact of us getting Mhybe's point of view but not Silverfox's is a curious reversal of expectations. Further, we could see her whole tale as a reversal of the fairy tale stepmother or witch (often concurrent) who devours children, a negative pole of the mother archetype. In such a fairy tale, the woman can be represented with a dark and light side, just like the polarities of the mother archetype. Silverfox has these aspects in the souls within her, Tattersail and Nightchill. There is even an aspect of the masculine within her. Her growth journey is to consolidate and synthesise these natures, to give new life to culture, particularly the Imass.

---

[89] Birkhäuser-Oeri, 1988

Renewal, or growth, comes about in the conjunction of different sides. Jungians might emphasise the opposites, but polar opposition is oversimplified; we exist on spectra which reflects the infinite possible variation in the human experience. Silverfox, in reconciling those parts of herself, in absorbing Nightchill despite others' attempts to force a one-sided nature on to her, even if that means displaying a coldness to her own mother, finds space to grow as an individual.

Her growth in a sense happens too fast. She takes the responsibility of protecting her mother. Who knows what sense of rejection she gets because Paran is denying her attempts at communication? Probably a father complex, borne out of his own mother complex. But all this responsibility and sense of abandonment is likely having effects on her own sense of security, and her ability to adopt the mother's role. The flow on effects in her own psyche might soon become apparent. We could also be seeing her attempt to integrate the masculine aspect of herself, that of Bellurdan, with her reaching out to Paran.

At the gathering, her sense of abandonment and loneliness floods out in her castigation of Pran Chole, who she feels is her father. "I will not abandon her!" (885) she says of her mother. Pain and the perceived abandonment caused her to withdraw. The instinct in her is to reconnect, but she perhaps lacks the knowledge of how. The aspect of her that is cursed with betrayal, Nightchill, makes her overly sensitive to abandonment, suspicious and mistrustful.

Kruppe speaks of the spirits within her:

> "A spirit of hard edges…Another spirit, to clasp hard the hurt of abandonment until it can find proper answer! And yet a third spirit, filled with love and compassion…And a fourth, possessing the power to achieve the necessary reparation of old wounds-" (861)

Quick Ben is surprised at the fourth, because those around her have been concerned about the souls within her. Jungian psychology considers the four as representative of a balancing function, bringing the triad into balance. Three represents a dynamic principle which is potentially brought into wholeness by the fourth. While it might be considered the reparation mentioned is of the T'lan Imass, it is also reparation of the split within her, a mending of souls towards totality. Three becoming four then marks the unity and integration of aspects of the unconscious to form an ego that is capable of greater fulfilment.

Silverfox knows the power and feeling of release when she frees the T'lan

Ay, "An effort demanding so little of herself, she was left feeling appalled." (1131-2) Fear of letting go, of dissociation, can lead us to hold too long. It is the nature of all mothers that they must in time release what they have nurtured, lest burdens accumulate. "Such gifts were hers to give. No, they are not gifts." (1132)

Toc and Envy

The anima is certainly an envious force. "…as Jung once said, envy or jealousy is the primary flaw of feminine nature. It is not only a flaw of feminine nature in women, it is also the shadow of the anima in men. As soon as a man is anima possessed, then he too is touched by jealousy and envy."[90]

The witch, representing the repressed anima, often enslaves heroes (e.g., brothers) or turns them into animals in fairy tales. This is the fate of the Seguleh. The Rent (with its maternal associations) and Toc's eye scar are mirrored. His wound, his humility and honesty, the shedding of his personae as Claw and spy, make him good at relating, thus able to avoid anima possession to a large degree. He wants to rejoin the host: "A long journey." (63) He has accepted the quest. He has a magical helper in Tool, and is confronted by a tempting woman. He escapes her influence, enters the belly of the beast, returns, is reborn.

Of course, Lady Envy is the anima. Flighty, easily offended. Toc resists the lure of the unconscious anima, and consciously separates from her. But then he gets drawn in by the mother. We could argue that he is so steadfast in denying the feminine that the more powerful force of the mother archetype rushes into that space. Lady Envy has that attribute of enchantress, holding Toc, and even the Seguleh it appears, against their will. She emasculates and even enchants the Seguleh to sleep. They are infantilised, treated as children. For them it is obviously a regression, and we can speculate that the nature of their society makes them more prone to the anima capture. There is within her the elemental feminine, like swan maidens and nixies of folk tales, drawing from the primal femininity that defines the great mother and anima archetypes.

Envy furnishes Toc with two smiles at their initial meeting, including a

---

[90] Von Franz, 1997a, p. 141

heart-stuttering smile (65). But Toc is all business. Smiles don't come easy in this world, so both our instinctive expectations and the mismatch lead us to expect that there is attraction there. But Toc isn't reeling from her playful nature, not yet. Only when she brushes against him, and he senses with his scar the subtle magic she employs with both the chiding of the Seguleh, and at his "sudden impulse to fling himself down to her feet, begging forgiveness." (71) He senses there is magic at work, manipulation of emotion. By the end of their meeting Envy has him off balance with irrational desires, right where she wants him. She also warns him against offering his indebtedness. This is curious, and hard to interpret. It could just be that she refers to her status in the world, but I also think we do not want to be in service to our unconscious archetypal figures. The transactions should be fair and balanced. If we do not pay in full, the unconscious energy can turn on us. This could be likened to Envy's quickness to anger: "Any more of this nonsense and I shall lose my temper." (67) Thus, like Toc's desire to beg forgiveness, we feel we must balance the scales, but we can't weaken and throw ourselves at the anima's feet. We need to maintain a strong ego consciousness.

The Seguleh are certainly possessed by her. They're given to random attacks, eruptions of unconscious energy. A martial race, they need to know how to feel relationships, not simply dominance behaviours. That's why they are easily ensnared: they are one-sided in their functioning. One feels they repress biological instincts in favour of cultural constructs.

"Please don't be angry with me," (179) Envy beseeches. She is certainly given to swings of emotion, or rather she is constantly pulling against Toc's emotions, keeping him off balance. Envy's draconic nature isn't yet revealed to us, though Emma Jung notes the association of serpent with anima: "Moreover, the serpent is also dangerous. Its bite is poisonous and its embrace suffocating, yet everyone knows that despite this dangerousness the effect that it exerts is fascinating."[91]

Toc, then, is right to be wary, though he suggests it is her sorcerous nature that causes it. He has, after all, a sensitivity to it through his wound.

> "She is a psychic factor that insists on being considered, not neglected as is the general tendency, since a man naturally likes to identify himself with his masculinity.
>
> However, it is not a question of either surrendering his masculinity completely to the service of the Lady Anima or

---

[91] Jung E., 1955, p. 76

losing her entirely, but only of granting a certain space to the feminine, which is also a part of his being. This he does by recognizing and realizing the eros, the principle of relationship, which means that he not only becomes aware of his feeling, but also makes use of it, because to create, and especially to preserve, a relationship, a value judgment (which is what feeling is) cannot be dispensed with."[92]

Their exchange, when he fends off her advances, and snaps at her about mocking his scars, shows his oversensitivity. She is unfazed, and accepts what she perceives to be a challenge in winning him over. We see then the dynamic of resisting too hard the entry of the unconscious. He has projected upon her a negative, witchlike power, and immediately feels he has messed up. Again, it is about relating. He is juggling that feeling aspect, not knowing how much to open up. Note the dynamic where if the anima is rejected, it will push back harder, it will fight you.

Even if not consciously formed, his sensitivities are accurate. She is full of charms and misdirection. Should she gain too much power, he will fall asleep like the Seguleh. But he shouldn't cut her off.

> "The anima as a rule is projected first upon a real woman; this may lead the man to enter upon a relation with her that he might otherwise find impossible; on the other hand, it may also result in his becoming much too dependent upon her…"[93]

Toc thinks about his loneliness having been separated from Onearm's host. It was his family, "at least what passed for family for a child born to an army" (307). Baaljagg, the ancient wolf-like ay, shares her memories of being orphaned and saved by an elder god. This is a tale of lost children as much as mothers.

Other than being a neat summation of the role of animus and anima as elemental archetypal forces within us and how initial projections play out, it leads us to question Toc's success. He separates from her, holds her at bay. He fends off her advances. But does he deny her outright? Is he repressing his anima here? He later becomes ensnared by the Matron, a symbol of the Great Mother archetype. So is this because he has not made enough allowance for his anima, or could we say that he survived that encounter and emerged into a new body (Toc Anaster) because of that encounter and

---

[92] Ibid, 81.
[93] Ibid, 81-82.

successful integration of the anima? In attaining a new body, his personality is intact, so we could assume he maintains his clearly defined ego.

Compare this with Crokus's initial projection of the anima on Challice D'arle, then failing to differentiate from it. He carries that baggage to his obsession with Sorry. He names her Apsalar, itself an attempt to control the elemental figure, but as they travel together he never really allows her in. He gets entangled with a mother figure, too, in Scillara, and later returns to home and replays many of the same dynamics over again. That story appears to be a failure to integrate the anima, which results in a stagnation of his developmental stage.

In Crokus, then, it is a failure to discriminate between the personal aspect of the anima and the archetypal concept of the feminine which the anima represents, the suprapersonal feminine. Crokus, in naming Apsalar after a goddess is conflating his personal projections with the suprapersonal goddess. Toc, conversely, holds the goddess Envy at bay, perhaps recognising the distinction between his mortal projections and the deep unconscious power of the feminine goddess. He treats her with respect, but does not allow her to overtake his ego.

Toc is then tasked with a heroic return to the mother. The Elder God, K'rul, speaks to him. "The children of the Pannion Seer are suffering. You must find a way to release them…I speak of compassion." (321) Toc going into the Matron's embrace mirrors the notion of a soul in the Rent. Toc willingly returning to the Mother (a heroic incest) frees the souls of the Pannion Seer's followers.

There is a recognition, then, that Toc is capable of compassion. This may be the reason that Baaljagg sees a companion in him. And he mentions that Tool is a friend. This openness, the willingness to relate to his outer world shows us his ego strength, the ability to integrate his anima.

Envy asks Toc if he thinks she is cruel, and he replies honestly in the affirmative. She agrees. In communicating with the anima, the unconscious in general, in a spirit of open honest communication, we avoid its capture of our soul. Toc here is not showing resistance, again affirming his ego strength.

She gets angry when he calls her a witch, that being an aspect of the negative anima. Her response itself is probably to be read as his remark having hit home. Her anger, though, quickly dissipates and she pulls him in for a kiss. She could ensorcel him for compliance but chooses not to, and he remains conscious. Again, he recognises her power but neither capitulates nor fights. "The choice must be yours, else you shall indeed be enslaved." (405)

While the anima as a function within is not strictly a woman in the man, there is a virtual image constructed with all his influences that we perceive as the archetypal image. That idealised image, heavily influenced by cultural representations, can be bewitching. Toc has the choice here to take the fantastical mythological image, though that will result in his falling into unconsciousness, missing the opportunity for growth. Sometimes in a fairy tale this may occur through outside interference, a sleeping magic or similar bewitchment, a poison or a pin in the collar.

Toc then decides to separate from Envy and the gang. His ego strength allows him to have fended off possession by the anima. He is now to make a heroic reuniting with the mother, but his further goal is returning to his village, the army. In doing so, he is swept along by the mass unconscious of the Tenescowri under Anaster. Primal, driven by instinct, hunger.

He insists as he travels with the Tenescowri that he will not eat human flesh. This is him holding to his ego strength, his identity being maintained in the rush of the mass consciousness about him. "Better to devour myself from within, to take my own muscles away, layer by layer, and digest all that I was." (492). There is a rebuilding in rebirth—to be broken down and rebuilt again. Of course, this is only an entrée to what he will undergo in the embrace of the Matron and his eventual rebirth as Toc Anaster.

His ascent to Pannion's tower is like a reverse of the descent through the layers of hell. This self-revelation layer by layer is a "mortal's solitary task." (499). In rising from the mass as individual, Toc has accepted the wolf nature within him. He doesn't fight that instinct, indeed he accepts it, and it allows him to sense the meat he has been given as well as the vision of the Jaghut behind the Pannion Seer. His ability to trust those instincts signifies his good relationship to the unconscious.

In myths, the hero often has two mothers: the mundane earthly mother, and one representing the Great Mother, who must be overcome as part of the heroic journey motif. At times, this might be represented as a battle or entering into the lair of a giant lizard-type creature, or dragon. This is seen as heroic incest—symbolic, not literal incest with the mother, and is regenerative.

> "Victory over the mother, frequently taking the form of actual entry into her, i.e., incest, brings about a rebirth. The incest produces a transformation of personality which alone makes the hero a hero, that is, a higher and ideal representative of mankind…
>
> This struggle is variously represented as the entry into the

cave, the descent to the underworld, or as being swallowed—i.e., incest with the mother."[94]

Toc's decision to leave Envy and crew, and to consciously enter the embrace of the mother (first as part of the collective of the Children, then literalised by the embrace of the Matron) is a heroic act. His ego strength in assimilating his anima allows him to take this burden heroically, rather than falling prey to it unconsciously, like Oedipus did. This allows Toc to emerge from her embrace and be reborn, and though he does not do so in a mythological heroic way of hacking his way out by strength, it could be seen that Tool's rescue, as kin, is representative of an aspect of Toc himself.

When he is taken into the Matron's embrace, Toc is held as an infant, his life reduced to sleep, feeding, toileting, though it is notable that his ego consciousness does not allow itself to regress to match the expectations of the Matron. "The cycles of his life…delusions of being a babe" (658) The Matron holds him tight and breaks him, reshaping him, or rather denying him his potential human form, keeping him malformed. His pain, his wakefulness, only encourages her to hold him tighter, and so he learns not to speak up or cry out.

"If the personal mother and father are guided solely by maternal and paternal instinct, they themselves set no bounds to their own power in relation to the child-they simply act as instinct dictates."[95] This relationship (for it is surely that despite its negative implications) between Toc and the Matron is an exploration of the deleterious effects of a mother who, being affected by her own trauma, cannot let go of the child. Submersion into unconscious instinct results in identification with the parental archetype. Harding continues: "if there is an excess of parental care—the emerging consciousness of the child may be swamped or even drowned, just as surely as it can be crushed when the parental instinct functions negatively and the parents are cruel or neglectful."[96] At its worst, the result is that the child will stay unconscious, in other words, not separate from the mother psychologically.

The journey of individuation becomes crucially important when one becomes a parent. Conscious approach to one's own growth and appreciation of the nature of relationship with the child can mitigate the potential growth of negative parental complexes, or the passing on of generational trauma. While the relationships of parent and child are founded

---

[94] Neumann, 1949, p. 154
[95] Harding, 1965, p. 38
[96] Ibid.

on what are among the most fundamental instincts, there is also an instinct in the child to separate and, no doubt, in the parent to let go at the right time—which we can see enacted by social groups in the form of ritual initiation—so there is constant tension between instinct within and between people. Perhaps the very instinct to individuate is itself the growth of consciousness through which one can nudge and moderate those instinctive pressures to better adapt to the world.

But Toc is alive within, and can watch through his soulbound kin's (Baaljagg's) eyes as his companions attempt to rescue him. His soulmate and the one he called friend seek to repatriate him from the mother's grasp. He has allies in those he related to.

The image of the wolf looking for its mate at the start of the book is about seeking a reunion with the feminine. The two beast thrones symbolise the fundamental instinctive need to integrate masculine and feminine. We now see in Mhybe's dream that Toc has escaped into a dark cave, a corner of the unconscious, where the wolf within him awaits his mate. This is the approach of wholeness resulting from his confrontation with the mother—the feminine will be integrated. This is a result of the heroic return to the mother.

His understanding is shown as he now reflects on his time with Lady Envy, and his anima projections. "He missed her. Not as a woman – not precisely, in any case. *No, the immortal face she presents, I think. Unburdened, a trickster's glint to her millennial regard.*" (827) Here is recognition that what he had projected onto the woman was something more deep-seated, something unconscious. He thinks it was bravery, taken now, humbled, but now he has a well-earned respect for the numinous nature of the feminine.

Toc is redeemed by both Mhybe (the mother) and by Tool. Even as his mind feels the gift of wounding from the released memories of the T'lan Imass, he recovers his own friendship, kinship, as Tool rescues his body. Bound by memories, Tool comes to his aid, and he is able to release the wolf within him. The wolf god in turn carries his soul to be reborn as Toc Anaster, in the body of Anaster who could never pull away from the mindless mother, who was left with so little of himself.

Burn as Terrible Mother

There are two aspects of the mother archetype: on one hand its nurturing, abundance, protection, and fertility, on the other its swallowing, devouring, dark aspect. The terrible mother is the dragon, the whale that swallows Jonah and so forth. Rapunzel, confined in the tower of witch-mother, is under its power.

The Matron, when she holds Toc, is an extreme example of the unconscious, devouring mother. In many ways, the Matron is like a child with her grasping and mewling—not too different from Anaster's mother. She also shows how pain can be passed on through generations. The parents are such powerful, numinous figures in our life—at all levels we accept their history and memories. The matron has had the pain of the rent, and unknowingly passes that pain on to Toc, in an attempt to mother him.

Neumann describes the emergence of ego and individual as a kind of birth: "the subjective experience of distress, suffering, and helplessness in every critical transition to a new sphere of existence."[97] All situations of containment ending are experienced as rejection by the mother. Birth itself is at once release and a rejection from the paradise of the womb. In discussing Mhybe, we understood the vessel symbolism; there is a duality in the vessel as being both a protective symbol, and that which contains, including the taking back of the dead. One aspect of earth as mother having a similar duality is the cave, which is a dwelling, but can be seen, too, as a tomb.

Burn's warren as seen by Quick Ben is an immense cave, a place of warmth and protection, and he sees rib-like ridges at the ceiling, suggesting he is indeed within the body of the Goddess. But Burn is also dying, and her helpers are dying as they try to hold her together, making that place a tomb.

As earth mother, Burn is fundamentally ambiguous, at the same time the source of everything and containing everything, she is self-contained. The witch of Burn's warren tells Quick Ben that Burn is sick, her dreams are fevered. People upon her work and fight in endless rhythm, but she is indifferent. The nature of mass consciousness is affected by those dreams. Should we ignore the deep abiding mythology of the earth as mother and caregiver, should we draw down the power of something not naturally of this world, the damage done sets us into endless war with our own selves, our world.

A refrain we hear about the condition of our own world is that nature is

---

[97] Neumann, 1955, p. 67

all powerful, and even were a changing climate to destroy us, the earth would continue. "She would simply begin again." (232) Perhaps it would even be a good thing. But within Caladan Brood's grip is a hammer, the power of judgment, with which he could release Burn, thus destroying life on the planet. He resists this, seeking a balance, hoping for sense. The burden of such judgment is clear, it is not a decision to take lightly, nor should we dismiss our own meaning by externalising such decisions.

Mankind, in his dependency, is as awed by the size and potential of the earth as giver and protector of life, as well as her violence, as the infant is to its mother. When that awe is lost, or ignored, alienation results.

Mhybe's rejection of Silverfox tells us something about generational dynamics. The relationship prepares her for aloofness from her own children. Holding fast to the child is the negative aspect of the mother's embrace. The Matron and Silverfox both display this. Both ensnare: the Matron crushing Toc and Silverfox not releasing the Imass, the former devouring, the latter still feeding off her own mother, literally and psychologically. These two straddle the same point: the Matron ensnares because she lost her children, and Silverfox, her mother rejecting her, also won't let her children go.

So the aspects of the Mother are along a continuum from birth, transformation, and expansion of conscious, down to stagnation, decay, and dissolution of the individual consciousness. Crone calls herself Great Mother in *Gardens of the Moon*, and here: "I am Crone, unchallenged matriarch of Moon's Spawn's cacophonous, vast murder of kin!" (116) Korlat tells Whiskeyjack of the ravens' shame of their origins. Death to birth, rot to fertility, the two poles of the mother archetype.

The crone is often the representation in folk tales and mythology of the dark side of the mother archetype. She is the one who devours life energy, as opposed to the life-giving nature of the positive side of the mother. This is why we see the great ravens as devourers of magic—they feed on the energies of others, and arose from death and chaos.

The Rent at Morn is also an aspect of the Terrible Mother. Its description is patently vulvic. It consumes souls, holds but doesn't release, all the hallmarks (clawmarks) of the negative aspect of the mother.

Gruntle and the Cat

Gruntle at first shows us a pragmatic, martial nature. When he watches Buke take commission with the necromancers, he reflects on the man's suicidal nature. He fails to bring feeling out in the man. He feels helpless, caged by his inability.

Suicide can be read as a projection onto death the realisation of the self. It is a desire for unconsciousness because there is a misguided recognition that in unconsciousness there is wholeness, the desire for a return to paradise. One will get closer to the self, because it has been disconnected, alienated. Buke looks for danger to force himself to action, as compensation for inability to feel, to confront life. He has created an endless war within himself. "Haven't you been in suffering's embrace long enough?" (143)

Gruntle, it turns out, is spurned by a woman who's gone off with another. He spars with Stonny, who in turn is likely animus possessed: "No such thing as iron petals." (147) Stonny likely holds an anima projection for Gruntle. It is notable that she is often apart from him, and he has to collect her from a drinking session or she ranges too far ahead of the caravan. So there is distance between him and his relating function, and he is unable to rein it in. This notion of releasing and holding ties in to the duality of the mother.

He can understand Buke's despair, and sees the potential failure within himself, mirroring that of Buke. He wants to draw Buke's feelings out because he wants to feel redemption is possible. He doesn't feel empowered to change the course of his own story, namely he drinks to unconsciousness, which is what caused Buke's feelings of guilt. "Took the deaths of everyone you loved to do that, and I'm terrified it might take the same for me." (272)

When Gruntle is dying from the K'Chain Che'Malle attack, he watches it, helpless. He questions why his consciousness lingers. In a sense, he welcomes unconsciousness, which is why he is critical of Buke, and why he drinks. In a state of unconsciousness he no longer feels the dissonance of not relating, of failing to act. It is an abdication.

At this point Trake has already claimed Gruntle. He is a caged animal, instinct left unexpressed for a long time. The opportunity for rebirth has arisen. The counterpoint to Gruntle's acceptance of unconsciousness is shown in Treach's death struggle, "his will to live reduced to something bestial, something that refused to recognize an end to its life." (316) This is a representation of an everlasting war as well, nature, the life and death of existence and the fight for survival.

Von Franz has written that tigers and wolves in fairy tales are often representative of repressed instinct. Psychological content has been wrongfully pushed into the body and perverted, and when an impulse comes up and is not lived out, it goes back down and tends to develop anti-human qualities. Just like is seen in animals, instincts when frustrated tend to express themselves somehow. We can learn to repress our instincts, but they cannot be escaped.

Gruntle's anger builds, his violent impulses blocked, until he goes over the edge, and becomes a tiger. Warlike impulses have been repressed, his inability to defend and control Stonny. His compensation to Treach's instinct has created a vessel for the ascendant tiger, perhaps with the aid of the Elder God K'rul, who knows Gruntle needs to activate his bestial instinct. Their conjunction is propitious. His awakening in the courtyard is a rebirth, from darkness to light—the morning, the burgeoning of consciousness. Harllo's death seems to be validation of his fears, and he doubles down into unconsciousness and unwillingness to act, refusing to take part in the fighting. He takes on Buke's self-blame. "I saw you, Harllo." (346). He blames himself because he thinks it should have been him, and he was welcoming the promise of that oblivion, which makes us wonder whether his desire to trade his soul for Harllo's is more selfish? Lacking the bestial fight for life, Treach comes in.

But he still has to be able to relate to his unconscious. He still has to open up to those instincts, to accept the part of himself that chooses not to act, or to act appropriately, at the right time. It takes a wounding of his anima, as projected on Stonny, to trigger that within him.

Again, his instincts are storming within him, struggling to find the appropriate outlet for action and healthy release of control. Overcompensation for a perceived inadequacy. Sorting out the relational problems may have woken Gruntle to the dangers, spurred him to act, but he preferred to sit back and do nothing.

Birkhäuser-Oeri conceives of the maternal as analogous to the unconscious, thus the source of consciousness:

> "There are in fact two essential sides of the maternal: one which is trying to create consciousness and existence and uses all available means to achieve that goal, and another which seeks unconsciousness and nonexistence, in other words destruction and disintegration."[98]

Gruntle's efforts to squash down his consciousness, and thus responsibility,

---

[98] Birkhäuser-Oeri, 1988, p. 22

could be seen as a desire of return to infantile paradise, where the negative side of the maternal seeks to disintegrate the individual, or prevent its growth and inevitable separation.

When Stonny is raped, Gruntle feels responsibility, but he let Stonny go. His inability to be open with her, to her—to relate, in other words: the function of the anima—results in a failure of his protection (as a captain, not as a man). Inability to act can come from a lack of internal connection with the anima. Anger at himself boils up and aids the transformation. He had bemoaned her "frustrating knack for ignoring his orders." (263)

We have all had the experience of not acting when we should have, of not saying something we felt, and then watching the consequences unravel. In extreme cases, this can lead to self-blame. Gruntle is experiencing a common duality—the inability to act, along with the acting out as compensation which can happen inappropriately, often as anger or rage. Our sense of a lack of agency results in a need to affect the world, yet we can be oppressed by the conditioned lack of agency, and inappropriate relation to the world, others, and the self, and so don't know how to act out.

Gruntle's instincts lead him to Stonny's location once the siege in Capustan breaks out. He has relegated to the unconscious the actions which he feels he should have taken—the steps of approaching and rescuing her. "It's only coincidence that Stonny's ahead," he thinks. "I'll just find the gate and pull the lass out. Won't take long." (546-7) Even when their eyes finally meet, Gruntle is frozen, perhaps in shock this time, and it is on Stonny to call him over. She tells how she carved her rapist inside out, something hanging from her weapon, in the other hand a broken rapier. These symbols are the carving out of Gruntle, his inner self breaking. "'Did you save any of him for me, lass?' She shook her head." (551)

A cat is at once a positive symbol of instinct and spirit, and can have negative associations with darkness and magic. That dual nature is itself interesting. While we are not looking here at a domesticated cat, the symbology should be similar. Maybe more primordial, violent. It is definitely a feminine symbol, and thus connected to the anima in men, as well as a move towards totality in women. This will become important when we explore Tavore Paran.

Gruntle wants to sacrifice himself, seeking wholeness. It is a search for rebirth but not wanting to pull the feeling side up, not able to relate to it. Searching for freedom and responding to life's inequity, Gruntle seeks a way out. The cat rushes in. Freedom isn't gained, but rebirth is, just not on his own terms. He still has to learn to live with it, but it has been forced upon him, rather than approaching it consciously. Sometimes our development comes unbidden, through trauma.

When Gruntle, in the midst of the siege and his own acts of revenge, sees Stonny, the jolt from his unconscious is palpable. "it was as if he had been shocked awake – as if all this time his soul had been hunkered down within him, hidden, silent…She was broken still…painfully vulnerable, profoundly wounded…" (635) Noting again that anima is equated with soul, this reflects Gruntle's own broken anima, broken because he failed to communicate with it, and the consequences ride him. In the face of resistance to change, it often does take a shock, the unconscious dragging the ego to a new stage of growth. In the face of self-destruction and retreat, this can be seen as a gift.

"Flight! Away from what I was! From all that I had been!" (579) Both Gruntle and Buke flee from themselves, and their almost opposing instinctive animal forms are different ways of resolving. Buke is allowed to fly free, spirit, while Gruntle, earthbound, is the expression of instinctive action.

It is interesting that we mostly see the aftermath of Gruntle's acts. What we understand of his fighting and transformation is seen through others' eyes, or reports. Compare to Itkovian, whose role we might remember as being the redeemer, the compassionate one, but we witness him slaughtering many Tenescowri. In a way, this adds to the mythic resonance of Gruntle and his change. "…the militia now existed more within the mind of Gruntle than they did in the real world." (635) It is perhaps worth considering whether the acts of Gruntle and his followers are indeed exaggerated retellings of the witnesses to give answer to Gruntle's shift, or rationalisations within Gruntle's own mind to account for the outflow of rage. In the square when Itkovian has acted, Gruntle seems to come to awareness. "I feel like I've just woken up." (709) He was in the thrall of the unconscious, of instinct.

Paran acknowledges that Gruntle should keep playing by his own rules, when Gruntle's irreverence for his patron god becomes apparent. Having accepted himself, his instincts, it is accepted in turn of him, if not by his god. He is more comfortable in his skin, having integrated his nature. He tells Paran, "I don't even like fighting." (778) He is reluctant to embrace power, just like Paran, but now that power has been placed upon him, accepted within, it is moderated by a reluctance to use that power.

Bridgeburners and Grey Swords

The creativity of religion and ritual are powerful holders of projection. The military and its associated activities is a big one, especially for the mother archetype, because it is containing, and nurturing, provides comfort for disparate people. It provides relation, place, and order.

Picker, accosting the merchant at the book's start, is amused by his notion of the city of Pale succumbing to the Malazan Empire's embrace. "Hear that? An *embrace*. That's a good one, old man. A motherly hug, right?" (74) We also see the maternal warmth of a nest in Spindle's hair shirt.

The whole army, having ostensibly been cut loose from the empire, is missing that motherly attachment: "The Malazans' anchor had been cut away…Almost ten thousand soldiers had suddenly acquired an almost childlike need for reassurance." (92) Paran keenly feels the disconnection. The balance has been pulled too far towards alienation.

We have from Whiskeyjack a description of the birth of the Bridgeburners in Raraku, that womb we discovered in *Deadhouse Gates*. They, too, were lost children: "A company culled from the army's cast-offs." (362). And in their final interment in Moon's Spawn, they return to a womb, that maternal sarcophagus settling in the Coral Sea. "some time soon – perhaps a month from now – it would touch the waves, somewhere in the ocean, and then, as water rushed once more into the fissures, filling the chambers within, Moon's Spawn would sink. Down, beneath the insensate seas…" (1162) This is a return to unconsciousness but across a lunar month, with its redolence of feminine mystique, the cycle of fullness, descent, and rebirth.

The Bridgeburners' undergo a ritual of passage, a funeral, "the binding that was shared grief." (1162) Their captain, Paran, steals his way into their tomb to pay homage, to offer his blessing. He is bound to them, one of them after all, joining them briefly in this maternal dark.

The Grey Swords arrive at the conjoining of the beast gods, Togg and Fanderay. They are welcomed in. Their recruiting of the women of Capustan is an act of conjunction with the feminine, a willingness to approach that totality. "Itkovian was not surprised to see a half-dozen old women gathering to meet them" (789) These are playful witches, though they also refer to the dark side of the feminine, the fear they instil. "You, a young man, are among old women, and there is nothing in the world more perilous!" (790)

The Grey Swords, after the siege of Capustan, consist of more women than men. They are to be part of the conjoining of Togg and Fanderay, an internal marriage—though marriage is not quite right, even though it is often used to symbolise this relating. It is more about complementarity, that a man would find in his inner feminine nature a sort of companionship. The martial nature of the Grey Swords, then, corresponds to a man who hasn't integrated his anima. Now it is undeniable.

When we are looking at the anima, and the same applies with the animus, we can take away some of the abstraction of the archetype, and generalise it to say that there is a problem with the relating function of the individual. So, for example, how is Gruntle relating to the people around him, i.e. hiding his care. This helps us understand Whiskeyjack, too. We are looking at how he relates to Korlat in this novel, and, more broadly, his relation to all those around him is also important. But the archetype is what imprints upon Korlat, because she is his feminine figure, a love interest, and so is inevitably compared in the psyche with the projected archetype—the complex that has been constructed in him over time and through his historical relations. It is also a practical generalisation because what we are witnessing in Whiskeyjack (or any exemplar) is not just them relating to others, but relating to himself by way of his unconscious.

The idea of a relating function in men being an inner woman is to some extent developed over a long time in culture and the individual. It is not necessary that the anima be personified as a woman, though we have the challenge of these abstract concepts being impossible to grasp, let alone speak or write about, without falling back on metaphor and symbol as a means to translate the ideas. To understand it, the anima, we turn it into an image, a personality, which is usually a woman. Because that is how our limited consciousness is able to communicate with it.

Whiskeyjack

Whiskeyjack's compassion has been challenged by Sorry, her very existence shaking his hopefulness, his faith in life. She caused him to withdraw his relating, feeling functions, to build a wall like a good mason can, and retreat to a place of safety in himself. His relating sense is challenged in *Memories of Ice* by Rake wanting to kill the mothers, the Tenescowri. He is striving to maintain some humanity. In being able to relate to Korlat, he is rescuing his inner feminine.

Jung distinguishes mother identification in the early life and the counter equivalent in women as a regression, while that of later life is a process of integration of conscious and unconscious, and necessary for individuation. Here the mother symbol doesn't refer back to life's beginnings but is more related to the creative faculties of the unconscious.[99]

Whiskeyjack's wounded thigh echoes the unhealing wound of the Fisher King. His wound is riven with meaning, it is an entry to the soul. The king wounded is a grounding. It puts him down amongst the dirt and water instead of astride a golden throne. "In stepping down among women/ and men, he found what/he'd surrendered and damned/its reawakening…" (*GotM*, 39) In *Gardens of the Moon*, Tattersail recognised the humanity in Whiskeyjack, how it was seemingly out of place given his history and the hunted nature of his squad. He wanted to see the humanity in the possessed Sorry, and it was upsetting his worldview, "leaving as his last claim to humanity his squad, a shrinking handful of the only people that mattered anymore." (*GotM*, 279)

There is a kingly virtue in the keeping of the wound, in living through it. The opportunity for quick healing is as hollow as all the veils we have in modern life to quick-fix our ills and distract from our emptiness. We are being shown that sometimes we have to journey through the pain, in fact it is almost essential for individuation that we step into that wounding. It is not a flaw in his character that makes him reject healing, it is a vital, heroic strength. We sense that, and it makes its role in his downfall all the more bitter.

Whiskeyjack feels sorrow for Mhybe. A brutal sacrifice, he reckons. It is a very mechanistic assessment. Note how this changes with his experience, with feelings drawn out by Korlat. "I'm not one to stand to one side in the butchering of a child." (198)

He has kept those markers of the Andii, and so redeems them in revealing the pieces to Korlat. "a lone, dark smooth pebble." (525) The pebbles also become symbolic of the heart, particularly for the Andii and Korlat, but for Whiskeyjack too. Though for him the symbol is awkward and foreign, and represents the hardened nature of his feeling side. Whiskeyjack is under the impression that there is strength in repressing emotions, in remaining dispassionate, much like Paran—who may have learned or introjected some of that from Whiskeyjack himself. Reflecting on his time with Korlat, he exhorts himself, "Do not embrace this wonder so tightly you crush the life

---

[99] CW5, *Symbols of Transformation*

from it." (587)

The next scene with the two of them shows a more consolidated aspect of his relating, though he is still affected by fear of losing her. Korlat confronts Whiskeyjack, assuming he knows more about Silverfox and Mhybe's suffering than he does. He responds as himself, pragmatic, not being drawn into responding through his anima, and it defuses her anger. She, too, becomes aware of her own instinctive reaction, and they communicate openly.

There's a dance—both have things hidden, yet both approach their relationship with gratitude. That is ego strength, retaining themselves yet navigating together in a shared space. The whole can be greater than the sum of the parts, and the shared can, in turn, grow the parts, too.

Freeing the feminine, feeling instinct, is often represented by freeing a maiden from a dragon. We are seeing echoes everywhere here, in Korlat's dragon nature, her realising her 'humanity' in her love for Whiskeyjack. Neumann wrote that the symbolic slaying of the mother overcomes the fear of her power. The thigh wound represents a castration, and to take on the dragon, redeeming the feminine, overcoming his own stuck feeling, is an attempt to redeem himself from that castration and the hold of the negative mother aspect.

After Capustan, Korlat takes Whiskeyjack through her warren of darkness to meet Quick Ben's image. This draws him away from his responsibility of command, and during their walk in dark, they speak loosely of their relationship. The scene is brief, but symbolic of Whiskeyjack's willingness to go down into darkness with Korlat, to let go of his martial focus for a time.

It is worth noting both that Korlat tests his faith immediately after this, and a rift forms, and that Rake brings up his wounded leg very soon after. Again, where there is a wounding in his relations, the physical wound, or it as a symbol, comes to the fore.

He doesn't let Rake kill the Women of the Dead Seed. He has to then take that burden himself. Doubt begins to assail him, and he sees himself as the monster he feared when looking upon Sorry in *Gardens of the Moon*. "The monster that stalks me is none other than myself." (811) Anaster suggests to him that this curse of self-hatred is contagious, to which Whiskeyjack agrees. Then he shuts out Dujek's approach of comfort. Whiskeyjack's doubts about himself are again beginning to harm his ability to relate, to understand others. He presumes that the soldiers only saw and didn't understand his actions. It isn't mere humility that draws this feeling, it is that he lives forthrightly and has gained respect and trust—their feelings would surprise him because he hasn't thought about his actions, he lives them in a heroic manner. And therefore he has no choice but to attract that respect. It takes Korlat's insistence that he not underestimate his soldiers' regard to make him see.

When Itkovian is riding out to the parley after the siege, he reflects on the soldiers lost: "these had been his friends. *A truth I dared not approach. Not as Shield Anvil, not as a commander. But that has changed. They are my own grief, as difficult to bear as those tens of thousands of others."* (831). This precisely mirrors Whiskeyjack's realisation in *Gardens of the Moon* of his friendship with his squad, and his ongoing attempts to reconcile those feelings as his burdens have grown.

By learning to relate, Whiskeyjack is able to comprehend the weight of what he has seen and lost, able to accept the friendship offered him by his squad, and of course then able to work the stone of Korlat's heart.

Whiskeyjack, in the final analysis, simply falls a little short of true openness. He lies by omission with Korlat before they part: "Later, Whiskeyjack would think back on his words, and wish that they had been cleaner – devoid of hidden intent." (917) He is not alerted by Korlat's intuition about Kallor's arrival. She senses a betrayal, but Whiskeyjack is too tired or dismissive. He is not open to that feminine instinct at the last, perhaps due to the distance between them as she focuses on her kin in the final march. "He noted but chose to ignore Korlat's wry disbelief" (1038).

Again, we are reminded of the Fisher King, the question not asked at the Grail Castle, failing to redeem the wounded feminine in the King. And it is Whiskeyjack's wounded leg that undoes him, allowing Kallor to best him.

But even in his death, he redeems the woman in Korlat. "What you would guard, staying with me, is the heart within you," Orfantal tells her. "Descend, Korlat, to the mortal realm." (1117) For his failings, those he fixated on in himself, he achieves after death what was growing in life. There is a lesson there, for a life well-lived.

"He had done that, for he remained the man he had always been." (1076)

Korlat

Korlat observes the Azath house at the end of *Gardens of the Moon*, and speaks the words of Mother Dark: "It is new, and what is new is innocent, and what is innocent is precious. Observe this child of wonder, and know respect."

(651) Like Mother Dark, Korlat's flaw, she says, is hope.

Korlat sees the innocence in the child. She resonates with Whiskeyjack when he defends Silverfox. She has a negative mother complex, it is true, probably like all the Andii due to their abandonment by Mother Dark we can presume, though Korlat appears to be working through it and finding her own compassion for the innocent. Because she is compassionate. She understandingly fears abandonment in herself, but it doesn't seem to affect her negatively in how she treats others.

Korlat befriends Mhybe, and she wants to reassure her (and herself) that there is a greater good. That life itself is precious, even in the midst of grief and despair. But she will go through her own doubts and return to this understanding. In this way, she is the explicit aspect of Whiskeyjack that has been repressed. Whiskeyjack wants to defend Silverfox the way he felt he should have been able to for Sorry. He is reassured that there is humanity in the child, and he acts upon it for Silverfox.

"Seek my heart and you may not like what you find" (524) Whiskeyjack gives her stones, as mentioned a metaphor for the heart. He is a mason after all, a worker of stone.

Korlat's position is consistently sympathy for the mothers. She forgives her own abandonment, sympathises for children and the weak. She walks the walk. There is life within her. Motherhood, metaphorically, even archetypally.

Her own faith has been restored with Whiskeyjack. She escorts him from the battlefield into her warren, showing her trust in him, her willingness. Soon after, she tests his faith, drawing a lie out of him. Does she test because she has her own issues of trust to deal with? We don't know much of her yet, lacking her point of view, but what we have gleaned suggests her mothering nature. Initially we might expect this testing is cold pragmatism, but her reaction to Whiskeyjack protecting the Tenescowri suggests her regret at having pressed him. She could as well have just asked rather than test, presuming as she does there is a reason for the false narrative of Dujek and Whiskeyjack as outlaws. "My vision was clouded…born of need and of love" (740)

Rake, speaking to Whiskeyjack notes "I had not expected to find in her such…renewal…To see it flowering so…" (745) The flowering brings to mind the image of the rotted flower from the prologue, its contrasting nature of fertility and decay, cycles and the maternal. Part of the power of the feminine aspect is to achieve and to serve renewal, rebirth. In a different way, perhaps, to the archetypal culture hero who might slay a dragon and bring fire. But first, a woman must redeem her own heart.

When we finally get Korlat's point of view, she is distracted, thinking about Whiskeyjack. We see her fragility, uncertainty, and get a sense of her fear of abandonment for the first time: "will you ever release me? Please. Do not. Ever." (935) She wonders why Rake and Whiskeyjack had struck such a sudden friendship, what Rake saw in the mortal. Surely it is the ability of Whiskeyjack to draw the very life from Korlat, her feminine instinct long dormant, which is just what Rake plans to do with Mother Dark.

Mother Dark had abandoned the Andii, left them in silence following a betrayal. This hardened Korlat to her relating. Despite her attempts at maternal care, there is still a coldness within her. "Women with a negative relationship to their personal mothers are often completely split off from their emotions; they cannot give warmth because they have never received any."[100] After the battle at Coral, she feels Mother Dark close in the manifestation of darkness over the city, and she realises Mother Dark's grief, only amplified by their cursing of her. The hurt and betrayal invite ever more. Finally, she does open to her humanity, released by Whiskeyjack, the mason. "A heart, once of stone, made mortal once more." (1117)

The notions brought up in Korlat's story will continue to have resonance. Her argument for the innocence of the child, the seeking and freeing of the heart, these are the ways we will need to think about the Crippled God, even if we may respond darkly to it. This is signposted throughout.

Moon's Spawn

> "...the favored spiritual symbol of the matriarchal sphere is the moon in its relation to the night and the Great Mother of the night sky. The moon, as the luminous aspect of the night, belongs to her; it is her fruit, her sublimation as light, as expression of her essential spirit."[101]

Moon's Spawn is notable for the fact that it hovers unseen above the narrative of this book, much as it literally hovers unseen over Coral until its final revelation. Moon's Spawn is the matriarchal womb of darkness for the Tiste Andii. It is perhaps their replacement for the mother they have lost,

---

[100] Birkhäuser-Oeri, 1988, p. 141
[101] Neumann, 1955, pp. 55-56

Mother Dark, who has abandoned them.

The apathy of the Tiste Andii is a counterpoint to the postnatal depression of Mhybe. Theirs is the alienation of losing the mother. As a result, Korlat refers to how children come sometimes, but it is not a creation born of intention and love, necessarily.

Both the moon and water are mythical and archetypal symbols for the maternal. Water, as maternal depths and place of rebirth, baptism. The symbolism of baptism echoes a few times throughout the series. The moon is more recognisably a feminine symbol, as counterpoint to the sun, and with its connection to the menstrual cycle. Its light is softer, and it illuminates the dark.

Moon's Spawn coming to join with the water of Coral Bay then becomes a symbol of wholeness, or at least its attempt. It is further a foreshadowing of the Andii's reconnection with their Mother Dark. Large bodies of water might also signify the unconscious, and baptism is a rebirth, a return to the womb of creation.

The Crippled God

The Crippled God is torn away from his world like a lost child, abandoned. He is called down to this one in fiery balls of destruction, broken into pieces like Osiris or Saturn. At the same time, his fall is a rebirth, of an era perhaps, comets whose image reminds us of sperm, and the continent scoured clean by fire.

The Crippled God is now isolated, alone in his tent. He has no one to relate to, and we must remember that the anima is the relating function. Of course, he's the villain here, because he wants others to suffer. "If I must suffer, so too must the gods and their world." (88) If we approached him with compassion even at this stage, he wouldn't be seen as the villain at all. This is not just about withholding our judgment because we expect there is more to the story, but we would see his suffering and understand that there is something that must be healed. The possibility is written into him even from the beginning. The notion that nobody is beyond redemption.

We implicitly assume that suffering is deserved—that is a story we tell ourselves. It is a natural consequence of individualism. For most of us, it takes the journey of the story cycle to relieve us of that notion for the

Crippled God. Ending suffering is the most important thing. The Crippled God is suffering—he turns that out onto others. It is contagious—it poisons Burn, as a metaphor.

The mission of analytical psychology is to go as deep as possible to the root psychological cause to end suffering. To heal that part that is spreading suffering. Not just cut it out—that wounds again and makes scars. While suffering might be inevitable, it is not necessary, it is not a fixed state of being. But we have said a wounding is necessary for individuation—to clarify, a wound is not necessary in the suffering that it implies, it can be a shock, a disruption of the known, a chaos to the balance, a disorder. Usually there is suffering—for it is unavoidable—but it is not the suffering that strengthens you. That is wrong. The suffering awakens you and signals, and prompts healing.

Healing heals. Suffering doesn't. The very notion that suffering strengthens you is driven by a lack of compassion. It mistakes the hardening of a scar for the growth of healing. So the Crippled God is wrong in his approach, but he needs to be healed to realise he is wrong. Part of that healing is having compassion given to him. Compassion combats unconsciousness, so that suffering may end, healing occur, and growth be achieved.

It is a form of narcissism, that notion of letting the individual further suffer because it is good for them, or work it out for themselves. Munug speaks of happiness to him, and the god replies with spite: "Assuming you have suffered enough to have earned it." (81) This is a cruel notion, and comes across that way, but it is remarkably prevalent in our society, both subtle and explicit. Generations expect the same suffering that they lived through, individuals expect that others will suffer a similar fall to justify their position, and so we unconsciously perpetuate the conditions of suffering.

There is no virtue inherent in suffering. Nor should we accept it and pretend that we can reframe our way out of it—that's a pat 'mindfulness' notion of living within suffering. Go into your suffering, accept it, we are told. Fuck that. We should all strive to end suffering, our own and others'. Suffering is good for ideologues and salespeople, because weak and hurting people are dependent and so lift others up as saviours. If someone's advice or practice is predicated on continuing, or at least not moving beyond suffering, they are unconscious or they are profiting at your expense, be it through weekly sessions, monthly subscriptions, or generational wealth transfer.

"Bear in mind, child, that the value lies in the journey, not in the goal achieved." (81) This refrain echoes through the Book of the Fallen, but here the Crippled God is twisting the notion. All the best lies have an element of truth, as they say. He is mocking Munug here, but, again, that bent interpretation is often taken in our world as a misguided truth. Munug prays: "I deserve this world's pain in unending bounty" (82). It takes such an insane villain and his unconscious adherent for us to see the irrationality of that notion. Paran tells himself, "There are no gifts in suffering." (160) and we know he is oriented towards the success not just of himself but the collective.

The Crippled God speaks to Quick Ben about Burn, that she cannot awaken while he is chained to her. This seems to imply that a goal of the story is to awaken, or bring to consciousness the nurturing of mother earth. Healing and compassion. The Crippled God says it matter-of-factly, not getting any of his pleasure at others' suffering. Yes, he wants to lash out at others to make them suffer, but there appears to be a recognition here that this is not an end in itself—that the world must still turn.

It is worth noting, too, that we are speaking here about wounding of characters in a metaphorical way, because it is a story. A wounded face is a humbling. Nor should we cut out an eye to get second sight. Perhaps in losing myth in our culture we have learned not only to inflate our egos to outer images, but also to take things too literally. We are dancing between treating the characters as if they were real, and treating them as archetypal symbols. Story allows us that playful expression, to embrace the contradiction.

Just as Tavore is foreshadowed and mirrored throughout the Book, for example by Lorn and Coltaine, so is the Crippled God. Itkovian is a specific example. He accepts people regardless, just as the Crippled God does. His acceptance is itself a form of compassion, as it is given freely. "Black-mannered Itkovian, will you ever unsheathe your true self?" (285) Itkovian, witnessing the Tenescowri, and delivering his own slaughter, is riven with horror at the nature of the Pannion Seer: "it sickened him. Filled his heart with an overwhelming hatred" (629) Compassion becomes his answer to that.

The Shield Anvil is "human heart", chosen to withstand grief, to "assume the sorrow of the world." (654) And so we might reflect on the Crippled God's ending, of the redemption of his heart. This is a metaphorical heart, a signal. Itkovian is the vision of compassion that must resonate as we come to understand that God. Itkovian later becomes Redeemer, signalling that the final redemption will be achieved by unflinching compassion.

Compassion is the recognition of pain as part of the human experience, and the willingness to meet that pain openly, with empathy and kindness. It is a response to suffering and adversity. "Within limitless reality resided the promise of redemption." (697) Itkovian takes the pain of Rath'Fener, for example, knowing there is nobody to take it from him. "Who shall embrace me?" (697)

The Crippled God wants us to live in that pain. He is in a sense the counterpoint – that pain should not be escaped, it should be suffered. In that respect, Itkovian is living as The Crippled God thinks he should. But the suffering is not an answer in itself. Itkovian thinks suffering fashions compassion: "From horror, grief must be fashioned, and from grief, compassion." (695). Perhaps the Crippled God has not yet understood that transformation, and Itkovian is a demonstration of it.

He sees the priest's life unfold before him, a narrative, when he assumes the priest's pain: "comprehension is not synonymous with absolution." (705) Itkovian encounters an alien presence, a god who would have taken the broken priest's soul, and offers to take the god's pain, too, learning something of the nature of god and mortal:

> "Immense power. Not malign, yet profoundly…different. From that presence: storm-tossed confusion, anguish. Seeking to make of the unexpected gift of a mortal's two hands…something of beauty. Yet that man's flesh could not contain that gift.
>
> Horror within the storm. Horror…and grief." (706)

If not the Crippled God himself, then this alien presence is a study in the nature of foreign gods, a demonstration of how to read the Crippled God. He is confused, not intentionally malign, and seeks to fashion a gift of the broken mortal he finds. From horror to grief. And then perhaps what the Crippled God needs to learn is the transition to compassion, or to regain it. It is the three step shift from instinct, to empathy, to humanity.

"Not one life's history unworthy of notice, of acknowledgment." (706) This seems to me the echo of the Crippled God's realisations. Itkovian, by accepting the memories of the Imass, for example, offers them hope of something greater, beyond the pain and grief of existence with only the promise of oblivion. That is also what the Crippled God offers – some sense of hope, of worthiness. Itkovian is like the archetype to which the Crippled God holds, striving for his humanity. "You are the bringer of peace, the redeemer of the fallen." (707)

Conclusion

Ice is water, fertility. As the ice melts and the flowers grow, the land heals, reawakening the feminine. The feminine principle, the descent into the collective unconscious—the instinctual world of the mother—is necessary for the healing within a person or the collective. A new spirit can emerge, reconciling the two sides of humanity: nature and spirit.

We could say overall in Malazan that the Great Mother is sweeping across the land because of the martial, rational nature. Getting consciously integrated with the feminine allows defeat or at least the balancing of the one-sided nature of warfare. Whiskeyjack and Toc do so. Togg and Fanderay do so. Gruntle accepts it. And so on. So we return to a state of balance.

We might also return to the notion of release versus ensnaring nature of the mother archetype. While we have seen it from the point of view of the children, in Toc or the Imass, the need for release comes in this novel in the many souls crying out for it. Pannion, and indeed the Matron needed release, from the Rent. The Crippled God is also needing release, being chained to the great mother earth, Burn.

Kruppe:

> "There is, all about us, ancient knowledge – that cannot be denied. Yet Kruppe wonders, are there memories? True memories? Of enlivened flesh and the wind's caress, of the laughter of children? Memories of love?
>
> When frozen between life and death, in the glacial in-between, what can exist of mortal feeling? Not even an echo. Only memories of ice, of ice and no more than that." (795)

Life, memory, is embodied. Rationality, logos, is only worth so much. Growth can't be isolated from biology any more than the individual can be isolated from the collective. Memory, then, like instinct, is truly alive and drives us.

You need to know from whence you came, otherwise you're just living in the momentary state of consciousness you find yourself in at any given time. Toc considers the finality of the T'lan Imass ending, with no spirit to embrace them, and he is distraught. That is why Itkovian's embrace is a gift. Living without the promise of something beyond themselves, without meaning beyond the stagnant mundane, what does this mean for a myth? This is mirrored by the Barghast's recovery of their spirits. In memory and myth there is meaning. History and culture intertwine to create us. Forgetting means stagnation—metaphorical when looking at the Imass, and culturally in the Barghast. The Barghast dead wander, too. "Their [young spirits] gift is comfort…the vast schism between us is time—and the loss of memory. We are as strangers…" (473)

"The Barghast must accept that growth is necessary, even if painful." (954) This is as opposed to clinging to the old life. Twist, the Moranth with the poisoned arm, chooses to live with the suffering of that limb even if it will kill him, as opposed to cutting it off to live. Sometimes there is value in dissociation, as a child from the mother, and at times we must accept some degree of suffering if it is the spur to growth. Of course, there is balance to be sought here. While the Crippled God might welcome the suffering and worship it, that is not an end in itself.

Itkovian needs to get through the memories to access and embrace the pain of the Imass. "Voices, a flood, memories…They had known them as living things." (1072) Again, embodying memory, the role of narrative. Those memories in turn give life to the land of Mhybe's dreams. The land interacts with memory, the story is in the land as much as the people. Taking away or denying history and memories deadens the land.

Our memory of childhood is scattered, isolated images and resonances. Of early infancy, there is nothing at all, yet the connections we form with the mother, indeed many instinctive patters are formulated and reinforced during this preconscious state. We had the collective and questions of chains and the blank slate in *Deadhouse Gates*, but here we have been looking at separation. Motherhood and childhood are at once and intertwining and an inevitable separation.

When there are two sides in conflict, we are moving away from static notions. Our known world, the old order, must be challenged. The next instalment will dive into this notion. In *Memories of Ice*, we are at the other end of the chain from *Deadhouse Gates*. They curl about one another, an uroborus devouring itself. Memories are burdensome, but are they defining? The child grows, but can't outrun history, which is passed on to its own children. The counterbalance of Imass memories, to the lost history of Icarium.

> "Kinship is more important than you might think. Blood-bound lives are the web that carries each of us; they make up that which a life climbs, from newborn to child, then child to adulthood. Without such life-forces, one withers and dies. To be alone is to be ill, Warlord, not just spiritually, but physically as well." (199)

Draconus reflects on the war of Chaos and order in Dragnipur, his notion that only in darkness could order be manifested. He had forged Dragnipur so that flight from Chaos sought to protect the gate, but he has realised that before Houses and Holds was not exactly wandering, "but migration. A seasonal round – predictable, cyclical. What seemed aimless, random, was in truth fixed, bound to its own laws." (972) Here we see the denial of instinct. We cannot flee from our genomic inheritance. Instinct seeks to manifest itself, in behaviours, anticipations, and patterns. Denial of those instincts, or flight from them, only serves to create neurosis. This doesn't mean we are completely at the whim of pre-patterned forces, but that denial of our unconscious expectations is dangerous, just as much as falling victim to pure unconsciousness. Chaos, then, can be seen as the removal of selfhood.

The conscious approach to individuation fulfils its potential and allows us to apperceive the instincts, their influence, not deny them or flee. If you doubt this interpretation, consider how often the word instinct appears in *Memories of Ice*. It is the deepest force of nature. It is what archetypal images represent.

In *Memories of Ice*, we become aware that mortals are stepping out from the shadow of the gods and ascendants, just as the child must go beyond the embrace of the mother. It is a generational shift, if you will. The old must make way for the new, to refresh society. "You and your fellow gods have been calling out the rules uncontested for far too long. Step back, now, and see how us mortals fare … I think you're in for a surprise or two." (786)

Standing up to face the gods, even the very notion of the Crippled God and his new House challenging the established powers, what we are seeing is the dual notion both of humanity stepping up, and of the waning of the old and the waxing of the new, the very foundation of growth and rebirth.

Beyond just stepping beyond the mother's embrace, we must also venture forth into the world. That means challenging the rules, the father. *House of Chains* is then a matter of finding that balance again. Karsa plays that out – separation, alienation, the weight of his past, and rejoining society in the Whirlwind. Of course, he has other plans for civilisation.

Stir the Ashes: Shadow work and the Father in *House of Chains*

House of Chains opens with a scene cast in greyscale. Silt and clouds, pewter sky, grey bodies and black crabs, it is drab and desolate. It is a scene of shadows.

Trull Sengar is the container for the Edur's shadow projections. The Edur are, themselves, aligned with the Shadow realm of magic. Here we see brothers, though they could as well be aspects of the same person. The repression is clear: they will not speak of him again. But there is discomfort, their instinct or perhaps their conscience tugs at them.

The shadow in the unconscious will not be ignored or repressed. It is like the roofs of the submerged city poking above the waterline, that which is unseen rising from the unconscious. Though there is a wall, it will be breached.

Jungians like to embrace the man's appreciation for the concept of circumambulation: that one might perceive something from all possible angles, thus forming a complete understanding of it. The shadow, being itself both disembodied and the embodiment of antithesis, invites such an approach. Its definition is elusive, its contents poorly understood. In trying to get at the shape of this concept, we will shine a light from all corners, from low and high, in an attempt to illuminate what structures and effects lurk back there.

Shadow is the hidden, repressed, dark side of the self, but Jung also said it was the whole unconscious in a sense. It is everything we cannot see, cannot directly know. In part this reflects his resistance to formally defining his concepts.

Robert Bly called shadow the long bag we drag behind us, which should ring bells for Karsa's long chain of souls he drags behind. Bly contends we start with a whole, round self, and everything for which we meet disapproval, we put in a bag – our anger, selfishness, sexuality, and so on. Our bag gets big, it weighs on us. And later in life when we open it, or it is opened for us by someone, say a spouse, those repressed things come out. And they've been waiting a long time.

Shadow is therefore everything that moves against custom and social mores, all the things we put in our bag. The things we repress and don't allow expression. All that we are told is bad, sinful, dirty, untrue. In this way it is a mirror of society and culture, as well as of the individual.

Leguin neatly summarised the shadow as "all that gets suppressed in the process of becoming a decent, civilized adult."[102] And it should be no surprise that aggression and sexuality constitute a large and weighty part of our shadow in civilised society. This helps to understand why Freud concentrated on these aspects of our personality and development, given their primacy as instincts and preponderance as repressed aspects.

There is a tendency of unconscious aspects of the individual shadow to be contaminated by the collective shadow. We assume that our dark characteristics are devilry. Further, and commonly, we project the shadow onto the environment, onto a group or an individual.

What we dislike in other people often shows what is in our shadow side. When a characteristic in another makes you particularly angry, that is a hint of where to look for your own shadow. Likewise, if a criticism is levelled at you that raises volatile emotions (anger, or denial), the criticism has cut close to the shadow.

I find Bly's notion (that the shadow is what we put in it) more useful, less daunting. That is our personal shadow. There is no point trying to integrate the collective shadow, that would be like trying to swallow a black hole.

> "Recapitulating, I should like to emphasize that the integration of the shadow, or the realization of the personal unconscious, marks the first stage in the analytic process, and that without it a recognition of anima and animus is impossible."[103]

So the shadow is not just the dark side of the self, the deeper potential for rage and evil—although that exists, it doesn't encapsulate the shadow. The thing with shadows is they aren't darkness itself—you can bring what is within them to focus by shining a light. That light is awareness—consciousness. The process of individuation, or the analytical process, allows

---

[102] Le Guin, 1979, p.59
[103] Jung, C.G, *The Syzygy*, CW 9ii [42]

us to make room for the shadow. We become aware of the repressed, unknown parts of the self—not just the anger and the rage and so on, but all of that which we don't know or weren't allowed to know, by society or by our own repression. Realising our dual nature, namely that both good and evil exist within us, we either constellate that duality, or repress it.

> "Whatever ground we can reclaim from the shadow is firm and fertile ground that enables us to commence building the house founded on the rock. In contrast, everything built only on the light side of the ego complex or on the persona, invariably turns out to have been built on sand."[104]

Building a house, we must extend the foundations deeply below the surface, into those unseen spaces, like the roots of a tree. If they are unstable, working against us, or not acknowledged at all, the structure is unstable.

The House of Shadow developing and growing in the Malazan world is a metaphor for the cultural shadow of that world. It comes despite the attempts at repression. Understanding the House can be seen as the individual growing, recognising their own shadow. Erikson is then using the writing of this to integrate his own shadow.

A house is a psychic space, our bounds against the world, and our reflection. Our houses are built in straight lines. Shadows are cast as stark divides, and there are many corners where they might gather, and usually a handful of crannies the light will never reach. Once, perhaps, it was carved out of rock—life itself a rich vein within the earth. Now above it, we aim to brightly illuminate that inner space, such that beyond its walls the darkness is more profound than ever.

The shadow is our unlived life, our potential, if you will. While we might recognise that there is potential for darkness within us, that is not inherent to, or defining of the shadow. Birkhäuser-Oeri noted that the shadow refers to "dark, morally inferior or primitive aspects of the psyche but also the positive aspects we are unaware of."[105] The positive aspects of the shadow have been referred by Robert Johnson as the 'inner gold.' So the shadow is all the instincts that we betray or quash. There can be evil there, you can repress an instinct to harm others. You can just as likely repress a creative talent, or education or society can train you out of instinctive desires to create or follow some passion.

We may need to open dialogue with the animus or anima, or work

---

[104] Hannah, 2000, p. 77
[105] Birkhäuser-Oeri, 1988, p. 23

through a mother complex to unleash these instincts, but here in the shadow is where they meanwhile reside.

Culture has an enormous impact on the personal shadow. What do we most likely repress but those things that would affect our outward relating to the world, thus harming our instinct to socialise? Cultures and societies have rules and norms, patriarchal notions that can be introjected as right and wrong—to keep and to bag. All the way down to etiquette, dress, and so on.

The father, as the mediator to the world outside the family, thus has a role to show and guide how to relate, and of course how not to. It is apparent therefore that the father archetype can in many ways be a conduit to the shadow.

Jacobi described the Father archetype as "an all embracing god-*image* the epitome of everything fatherly, a dynamic principle which lives as a powerful archetype in the soul of the child."[106] The Father represents authority, power, control, the collective. The animus is thus very different from the anima in a sense, though their first carriers are the contrasexual parents or carers. Anima is more likely a singular image, versus the collective image of the animus. A girl's primary caregiver is still (usually) a woman, her mother, so men are somewhat foreign to her. The patriarchy is external.

While the animus is spirit, the anima is soul. This distinction may seem ethereal but is useful. The main function is likewise relation to the unconscious but, in contrast, for the animus it is about a connection to spirit or mind as opposed to one of relationship. Balance is necessary, else all are wounded. In relationship, a weakness in one aspect or another draws out or amplifies similar or complementary psychic energies in the other. Our society, then, has historically held the feminine in its collective shadow.

While the father is representative of this repression, in the form of patriarchy, we can generalise further to say that the father as archetype is that which mediates relationship between the individual and the sociocultural world. Where the mother is a mediator of individual relationships, the father then acts as the membrane between the individual and family unit with the broader social context. He can repress with overly restrictive chains, and he can be too permissive or even absent, leaving the individual exposed to society's predation—neither extreme is helpful for healthy development.

Robert Bly and Marion Woodman in *The Maiden King*[107] speculate on the loss or absence of the positive father archetype. In men there is a loss of the ordering principle in their lives. They may fear older men, their authority, or

---

[106] Jacobi, 1925, p. 107
[107] Bly & Woodman, 1998

rebel against the principles for which they stand. Despite that, he will judge himself through their eyes, not having integrated balanced judgment. He might idealise masculinity, and his projections often fall on a perfect, unattainable woman. A woman whose masculinity is damaged may be fearful of being forthright, especially with men who represent paternal and patriarchal values. She might act like daddy's little girl, or mother to her boy-husband. She displays a childish idolisation of men, which her partner will never live up to.

Father is a more dynamic archetype, strongly determined by culture and cultural values. Where mother is stable across time and culture, remaining the world of origin, the deeply seated instinctual side of life, father doesn't have that inherent stability. This is why the animus is often a multiple, or experienced as a council or set of men in dreams. It can also be understood in fertility cults, where the symbolic king, the father archetype is sacrificed or renewed seasonally, in order to feed the earth—the mother. That short annual or seasonal lifespan of the king is equated with the need for renewal in the father archetype.

The hero, in slaying the father, overturns cultural values, ushers in the new, refreshing or rebirthing culture. Karsa Orlong's journey is one of slaying the father. He becomes the bringer of culture—though he explains it as destroying civilisation. Indeed, he goes on to kill the god of war, the old values because Fener has been replaced, so that rebirth can occur. The archetypal father wants the world to change, but the normal patriarchal stability of the objective father wants it to stay the same. Karsa wants to lead the Teblor to war, and yet he knows he must prove himself and return first.

Karsa descends to the world he didn't know, that is a perfect metaphor for the descent into the underworld, the unconscious. This part of the hero's journey is the confrontation with the shadow. And yet Karsa's character is in some ways and inversion of the hero figure is a culture bringer. He proposes upon his return to bring war, destruction of civilisation. But most importantly his quest is the overturning of the prevailing structures and norms.

"Nature has but one enemy. And that is imbalance." (28) Shadow is a homeostatic function, whose need is mitigated by proper relating through anima or animus. Confronting one's shadow is about raising consciousness, both within and in the world without. It is not simply the case that consciousness is raised by these processes of individuation, certainly not that the shadow is 'integrated', but rather what are we conscious of? Our understanding of the world relies on what we attend to, where we shine the light determines what shadows are cast.

When we raise consciousness of ourselves, we also change the way we view the world about us, become conscious of different things. Orienting our consciousness in a certain direction amplifies meaning around us, heightens our awareness and sensitivity to certain things, draws people to us. This touches on Jung's notion of synchronicity, where the 'meaning value' of things happen together, but does not rely on any extrasensory or paraconscious phenomena.

Seeing the unseen has limitations, particularly in ourselves. It is through relation that we learn, for we are social by nature. Thus the urge to connect with relating functions and understand parental archetypes prior to communing with the shadow.

Something unintegrated doesn't necessarily arise as negative emotions, or a life crisis. We can be in paralysis because of inner conflict. This is a symptom, the unconscious encouragement to give attention to something. But as always, it is an effort, to be in a place of unknowing, on the verge, to step into the dark.

Trull Sengar takes the burden of the shadow for his people. In the prologue we witness his Shorning. He is the container for his society's shadow, his brother's alter-ego, but he is cast out irrevocably. Only, the shadow cannot be denied, any more than society's structures can be burned away without resultant chaos. "His brother had shattered the balance." That energy, the instincts underpinning it, will find an outlet elsewhere. "This was a flood that would not be denied." (28)

The wall of the Nascent, where Trull is chained is a potent metaphor. On one side, the ocean, the unconscious. A flood being held back by thick battlements, bodies rotting and bloated, piling up. Attempts to separate, to cast out the unconscious or its contents, are doomed to fail. The shadow will prevail if it is repressed.

His people "knew almost nothing of our past. Our long, tortured history. And what we knew was in fact false. If only…we had remained ignorant." (329) Like Karsa Orlong, Trull has confronted the shadowed history of his people, and his chaining is one result of that. It is a haunting premonition for the Teblor.

Ganoes Paran

The Crippled God, and the people he represents—the lost, the crippled, the sick and weak—is representative of the suppressed shadow. This then is the House of Chains. It is gaining power, i.e., overwhelming the ego, and it is rising up in unpredictable, destructive ways.

Paran chooses to make the shadow conscious. As he was a kind of stand in for the reader in *Gardens of the Moon*, here as Master of the Deck, he is a kind of stand in for the world itself. Though in this book he is not present, his decision, and the building of our understanding of it, is very much working in the back of our minds. He is a presence hovering over the events. It is only as events in the book are coming to a head, shadows swirling over Raraku, that L'oric reveals Paran's decision: "A Master has come to the Deck, and that Master has just sanctioned the House of Chains." (965)

The House of Chains personifies the archetype of shadow, because it is the people we don't see. It's not just making room for the parts of the self that are negative, it's shining a light on all of which we weren't aware.

Just as the Crippled God is now bound by the rules of the great game, so working with the personal shadow brings its contents within our conscious perception. It becomes less able to exert an outsized influence on the ego. We are less exposed to the upwelling of the collective shadow. Paran allowing the House is acknowledging the repressed parts of the unconscious. No longer the 'other', outside the self, it is maintaining conscious awareness.

Paran as Master of the Deck represents a sense of control over the unconscious, those symbols (archetypes) of deep forces. His conscious standpoint is a signal that he is coming from a position of ego strength, and therefore able to safely communicate with those unconscious processes without being overwhelmed.

The idea of integrating the shadow, as it is frequently referred, is not so much about embodying or becoming one with the darker side of the unconscious, but carving out a place, shaping a vessel in which we can hold the unconscious, in which we can house the shadow. We give it space, but temper its autonomy. Civilisation and culture forces a decision between what is ego and what is shadow, and Karsa is railing against that forced decision.

Ganoes Paran, and therefore the reader, for whom his sanctioning is a symbolic integration of the shadow, has therefore taken the crucial step of recognising the shadow.

Broadly, we can define the shadow as anything in you that is not part of your conscious ego-complex. That can be either forgotten or repressed, retrievable or lost. It is also abilities and qualities that may be productive and positive, but unrealised, and this may be how Paran's discovering his ability to become Master is showing.

To shine a light on those parts of yourself, to make them conscious, or integrate them if you will, it is not enough to simply raise that awareness and then forget. You have to make it part of you, consciously or at an instinctive, automatic, operating level. It must be part of the game, so it might have a real effect on you and the world and not just work its ill-effects from…well, from the shadows. In the background of the psyche.

Note that these aspects and archetypes are not necessarily tackled in distinct stages or compartmentalised in real life. To attempt to isolate such things in a therapeutic setting, even to name them as such, would invite chaos. It would be to over-psychologise the process. We can, however, tackle them separately in service to the themes of these books.

Further, it should be pointed out that the prevailing Jungian wisdom would suggest that the shadow is the first thing to tackle in the name of therapeutic or self-improvement. I suspect because it is the most intuitive, and indeed probably the most romanticised archetype (which should itself reveal something of the nature of our culture). We have already explored Paran's anima complex, and indeed this is the more functional order of things, for the anima or animus, those relating functions of the psyche, are the mediators of the conscious self to the unconscious. If we aren't able to communicate openly and honestly with the unconscious, then what value in trying to get in touch with the shadow or alter-ego? Indeed, such an attempt may leave a naïve ego consciousness at the mercy of the shadow's depths. A light is useful when stepping out into the dark.

Jung's own words have perhaps led us astray:

> …it is a therapeutic necessity, indeed, the first requisite of any thorough psychological method, for consciousness to confront its shadow. In the end this must lead to some kind of union, even though the union consists at first in an open conflict, and often remains so for a long time. It is a struggle that cannot be abolished by rational means. When it is wilfully repressed it continues in the unconscious and merely expresses itself indirectly and all the more dangerously, so no

advantage is gained.[108]

Perhaps what is necessary is the very awareness of an unconscious, not an attempt at its integration. If our social life is grounded and relating functions are active, then we have allies, and perhaps that open conflict is avoidable. A confrontation with the shadow is certainly possible, in dream or in life, but to attempt to dive in and integrate that without developing ego strength is more likely to precipitate psychological illness.

We could further read the Edur as shadow, not just in their aspect but as metaphor. They are that which is looked upon as inferior, with the other Tiste wishing to repress knowledge of them. Their birth to Mother Dark was from the "unwelcome union of light…The Tiste Andii considered it a degradation of pure Dark, and the source of all their subsequent ills." (*DG* 290) Here we can see that Trull Sengar is portrayed in the prologue as a microcosm of the Edur. They are symbolic of the archetypal dimension of the shadow, rather than the personal aspects.

And so it is clear why the Crippled God has decided to make use of them. Their elder warren of shadow is also shattered, which again plays into that god's notion of brokenness. "There was shadow upon their souls." (*MoI* 411)

But how does a difficulty with the shadow work in life? It could be that something in the shadow is causing problems, but just as likely whatever is being acted out in the world is causing problems that might be remedied by integrating something from the shadow. Think of the poison in K'rul, in the warrens, it could be attacked by integrating the Crippled God, his House, from the shadow into the game, the ego consciousness.

Projection is a symptom—it is a signal that there is something amiss. What is the instinct being repressed in the Malazan world? Humanity, compassion, its free abundant expression to all. That's it at a broader level. Imbalance manifesting as chaos. You could trace the themes of each novel and make an argument for there being repressed instincts concordant to those. And so Erikson is exploring how each way of breaking down the

---

[108] Jung, C.G, CW14 [514]

factors and instincts responsible for manifesting the human condition can lead to complexes and imbalance, exploring them from different angles, while at the same time guiding us through a mythology that teaches us the dangers and the right approach to integrating those aspects of ourselves.

For example, a mother complex might affect our ability to relate as individuals. At a broader social level, it might lead to us neglecting the earth and allowing it to be poisoned. A father complex might lead us to adhere to rules that exclude important aspects of ourself that could address such poisons. And so on.

Karsa Orlong

Karsa could be seen as a heroic adventurer, or just as one child trying to attain adulthood, undertaking the ritual of initiation. He thinks it is the former, but really he is so dominated by his father – patriarchal baggage – that it is the latter. He is attempting to kill the child within, and to slay the father. "For the mythological hero is the champion not of things become but of things becoming; the dragon to be slain by him is precisely the monster of the status quo…"[109]

The Uryd clans, in a sense, represent a state of collective unconscious. Their introduction, in what amounts to a second prologue, is the clan's men banding together to slay a dog that went unpredictably savage: "there was nothing, nothing at all, to give cause to the sudden turn." (31) More than a metaphor for the Crippled God's poison and influence in this world, the passage reveals the dynamics of the shadow archetype. "Madness, they knew, could remain hidden, buried far beneath the surface, a subtle flavour turning blood into something bitter." (31) The clan appears to us as being unaware of the influences of the shadow. Something is poison beneath the surface of the clan, and it has found expression in one savage dog.

"Karsa Orlong lived and breathed his grandfather's tales." (32) Erikson's phrasing here instantly keys us in to the dynamics at play. Karsa wants to escape from his father and his father's story, to live his grandfather's. Synyg, Karsa's father, has already escaped his own father (Karsa's grandfather, Pahlk), choosing a humble life, not one of pillage and conquest.

---

[109] Campbell, 1949, p. 311

So it quickly becomes apparent that Karsa's heroic journey is not to overturn the prevailing archetypal father, those societal norms, but to reinforce them in defiance of his actual father. It might be assumed then that Synyg himself has already undertaken his hero's journey, already individuated to a greater degree. "Synyg, who had done nothing in his life, who tended his horses in his valley and had not once ventured into hostile lands." (32)

But it is still the father's role to confirm the child—to enact the rite of passage to the world beyond the family. Is Synyg weak, or neglectful in his role? The society works against Synyg, reinforcing the norms he appears to have shed. There is tragedy in this, because he is out on his own, a pariah, living his individuated life, yet society resists his knowledge, the treasure of fuller understanding he has brought. And his persistence in the face of that, of being the vessel for the shame of his own father and son, is truly heroic.

Synyg has successfully defended his herd from raiders, has trained his son in martial forms, but Karsa disdains him: "Karsa could find no reason for pride in such things." (33) These are merely what is expected of a man of the Uryd clan, he thinks. Karsa is stubborn, and identifies himself with the form of heroism embodied by his grandfather and the stories of that man's historic deeds. That identification is in Jungian terms inflation of the ego, a conflation of Self with a projection, so that the ego fixates and strives towards an image that is fundamentally unreal, that is not authentic to Karsa.

"Karsa would not do as his father had done. He would not do… *nothing*…Too much of the clan's reputation lived only in the past." (33) We can see the instinct at play here, of slaying the father archetype, and of renewing the culture's values. But Karsa's desires are a regression, "A return to the old ways." (33) His inflation of his grandfather's values leads him to inflate in turn his own position, his dominance, and his state of growth: "We shall weave our way to Silver Lake. To slay the children who dwell there." (33) The inflation has led to his presumption of a father role, or a mockery of it. Partly, too, he is reinforcing his own sense of fatherlessness, by assuming that role, acting out in a way that sublimates his shames as a son.

It is also interesting to note the inherent contradiction in Karsa's use of weaving, turning what should be a humble domestic act, one typically undertaken by women historically in our world, with mythical connotations of fate and the maternal, and twisting it to presage violence.

Synyg gifts Karsa the destrier, Havok, to Karsa's surprise—a kind of blessing, though he doesn't bless the journey itself.

> "What would you have me bless, son? The Seven Gods who are a lie? The glory that is empty? Will I be pleased in your

slaying of children? In the trophies you will tie to your belt? My father, Pahlk, would polish bright his own youth, for he is of that age." (41)

The warhorse ends up being a connection to home, a gift he holds on to when he later names his Jhag horse Havok, thus maintaining his father's blessing in what he carries.

The request for blessing marks an initiation, the father's responsibility to confirm the transition from the family to the outside world. "Mother would have blessed me," (41) thus we learn that Karsa's mother is dead. The girl he had hoped would bless him, too, has blessed instead his companion Bairoth, so there is certainly a feminine influence lacking in the youth's life. He is setting out on this journey with two mates, Bairoth and Delum, adrift, with no parental blessing and the sudden withdrawal of his anima projection.

Further, Synyg warns Karsa that his grandfather's blessing is self-serving: "Pahlk, Finder of the Path that you shall follow, blesses your journey." (41) Unspoken in Pahlk's words is the assurance that Karsa is staying within previously laid foundations. This is the equivalent of the mother clinging too tightly. This reinforces the notion that while Karsa assumes he is battling against his father's mentality, he is in fact ensnared by the archetypal father, in the form of his grandfather's fantasies.

Ego strength is armour against unconscious forces. The Uryd Elders' notions of madness is a good example of this:

> "At times, the elders had explained, the burdens laid upon a man by the Seven proved too powerful. A mind must be strong, and strength was found in faith. For the weak man, the man who knew doubt, rules and rites could become a cage, and imprisonment led to madness." (49)

There is much to read into this passage. First, a presaging of the Crippled God's madness arising from his chaining. We can also see in it an explication of the negative effects of the father archetype, those rules and rites, that can only be flexed by a strong ego. The notion that the gods, the Seven, are responsible for burdens plays into the presumption of power by the patriarchal figures of a society. Karsa, then, while he appears to enact faith to his god, is in truth imprisoned by his grandfather's notions of former glory, and mistakes certainty for faith.

Karsa tells Bairoth at their outset, "Your faltering courage threatens to poison us all." (51) This poison of disbelief threatens to sully the treasure of their return should they hoard the glory of their quest. Society must be changed by the hero's return, or the burden will weigh upon the hero. The

Uryd youths speak of it as the elders wanting their own piece of the glory—but this is the patriarchal bounds of culture, transforming to match. That they see it as power, a theft of glory, is their own projection, their own desire to step out beyond the grasp of the father archetype.

> "They will believe us, but only if we in turn believe them – their reshaping of the past, the blessing that was not given, now given, all the villagers lining our ride out. They were all there, or so they will tell you, and, eventually, they will themselves come to believe it, and will have the scenes carved into their minds." (51-52)

Myth retells events, reshapes history to fit a neat narrative. Thus, a successful hero quest is shaped in a similar way. It is a balance between society's strictures, how far they can be bent, how they remould in turn the hero's journey, and how the journeys prod and pull culture along its path of progress.

Karsa scorns the words of Bairoth on their journey, and the caution of Delum. He begins with no intention but the destruction and glory at the quest's end, but as they ride he learns quickly from his companions' assessments, is moderated by them, and assimilates their understanding of their enemies, thus gaining their wisdom and moderation. Upon their deaths, as they stay with him in spirit form, it is a metaphor for his adoption of their aspects making him more complete.

The brighter the light, the deeper its shadow; greater the hero, the longer. Upon their first encounter with a rival clan, Karsa, having slain seven, vows to gentle the clan. His companions then realise the audacity of his quest, the breadth of his vows. "Remind me to tell you one day, Karsa Orlong…What life is like, for those of us in your shadow." (58)

More than what is repressed and ignored, one's path through life trammels the ground, each footfall affecting the natural progression of the world in your wake. Being aware of the shadow raises an awareness not just of those actively shadowed aspects, but also makes one aware of how your actions affect others, how you construct history within and without simply by living. Conscious attention and appreciation of this makes it more apparent while it is happening, rather than letting it become a heavy psychic weight only accessible when problems arise in the long term.

When time's arrow flies, all is cause. Karsa Orlong's wake is bathed in blood – the history he makes resounds with warcries and dying screams. One cannot apprehend his whole history without knowing its effects. Thus, along with the shadow made in the course of a life, the weight of the bag one drags, there is the path its bearing gouges through the land. In the course of individuation, awareness of one's nature brings about a greater appreciation of cause and effect.

Karsa is disabused of his certainty, the fires of his grandfather's tales quenched by contact with the world. The words of the Rathyd women cut him. His world is small because he lived within an introjected image created by his grandfather's tales. Karsa is living in fantasy. His father, then, perhaps had done the job of communicating the world for him, but Karsa Orlong, stubborn, refuses to accept that his fantasy is just that. His certainty, we learn, is firm enough to deflect the outer world's blows.

Each step, Karsa's known world is peeled away. If the child's initiation, the separation from the parents, doesn't occur, the world will eventually force a split. Karsa Orlong, physically able to deal with the consequences, further rationalises his certainty.

The youths come across a cave which appears to speak to their tribes' origins. The writer of the words on the wall says they must dismantle their cities and burn their books, forget like Icarium, who is also referenced. They must return to a simpler time. This message is not just a tempering of wild progress, it is a regression. The soul strives ever forward. Karsa, in this sense, is a force of nature. "The fallen know but one challenge…and that is to rise once more." (85)

Stories can keep a tight rein on behaviour, on progress. This can be the role, or the effect, of cultural narratives, and can be the negative effect of the father archetype, the strictures of social order. There is tension between progress and erasure of the past in the Teblor. Their descent of Bone Pass, seemingly outside of time, is a metaphor for the Teblor history. Our history is part of our shadow, the descent of our genes.

After the attack at Silver Lake, when he is impaled, Karsa (though he disregards it) learns that Pahlk's story was not only a lie, he was dishonourable. It was his mischief and murder that has brought bounty hunters down on the Teblor. Rather than restoring their glory, Pahlk's ways have spelled their eventual end.

Bairoth, readying Delum for war with facepaint, appears to understand that the myth of the Uryd, the Teblor all told, is hollow. Of the elders who ready themselves for a final battle, he says:

> "The paint hides nothing – the desperation remains undisguised in their eyes. They come to the ends of their lives, and have found that those lives were without meaning. It is that knowledge that drives them from the village, drives them out

to seek a quick death." (115)

Keeping people from progress, from individual growth, there is an absence of meaning. A cultural narrative can defy instinct, powerfully so if that narrative itself seems on the surface to rely on base instinct, in this case violence and conquest.

As he is chained in a basement, the underworld, Karsa reflects on the Teblor distaste for torture and imprisonment, something that we saw in Karsa's desire to free the Forkrul Assail, Calm. Banishment is the greatest punishment, and led "usually, to death, but that came of starvation of the spirit within the one punished." (135) This again speaks to the control of narrative, where stepping outside the norm, challenging the patriarchal father archetype, is as death.

As they journey, Karsa frequently surprises the others with his insightful assessments of people, and of tactics, as well as his empathy, even though in other ways he is naïve and stubborn. His very ability to read the cave walls is startling, and his ability to read between the lines, so to speak, to draw away from the message, speaks to a mature intelligence, though rough-cut. It is leadership his mates sense, even at this early stage.

And yet, when Bairoth mourns Delum's brain damage from a head wound, Karsa is hardened against his emotions. He sees only weakness. This is redolent of a clash with fatherly values, or perhaps even the lack of maternal nurturing. Karsa has suffered both.

Synyg, unable to convey the fatherly strength required, or perhaps due to the loss of the mother, resulted in Karsa's stubbornness (raising walls to the world, hardened against sympathy and love). He failed to hold Karsa to a frame. Karsa's father imago was therefore transferred to Pahlk, whose ways represent the cynical application of a narrative that is regressive and manipulates base instinct.

As with the shadow work, the question arises, how do these psychic factors of the father archetype play out in the real world? What lessons can be applied, how do complexes develop at the interface between the outer and psychic worlds? In the process of separation from the mother, for example, we also need to separate from the archetype of the mother. This can mean understanding and integrating the symbols, perceiving the entanglements of the complex, withdrawing projections, in a way that maps the outer world experience. This can only be effectively done with conscious awareness.

None of that is to say there isn't a huge swath, perhaps even a majority of the population whose relations and attachments are so healthy and, well, archetypal, that they can skate through. Is there greater, untapped potential there? Harding describes one angle, that maybe we can be so unconscious of it that we don't realise our sights are set too low:

> That the work is just not boring instead of being stimulating, fulfilling, calling forth all his creative capacities; that the marriage is "all right" instead of being a deeply satisfying and growing relationship; that the leisure is filled with activities to pass the time instead of being joyful or interesting or wonder-provoking experiences this speaks of the penury of the times, due to the loss of a relation to the deeper values, so characteristic of Western culture today.[110]

A good portion of us, at least, do have a mismatch there, or are even aware of the unhealthy nature of our parental relations. We know this because we resonate with a story or a myth. In those cases we are dragging psychological baggage with us. Not that a wounded relationship is necessarily a bad thing, it is sometimes the very spur and necessity for growth and change, a transgression or wounding causing a separation. It is the irredeemable wounds, those that can't heal, that cause the imbalance of psychic ill-health.

> But unless one discovers how to separate from the parent archetype, as well as from the actual human parents, one will not really be free. In conscious orientation he will be his own master, able to make an external adaptation that seems to be quite adult, but in the unconscious he will still be tied to the archetype of parent; that is, he will be childish and at the mercy of impulses arising from the unconscious.
>
> This situation will obviously produce a conflict between consciousness and the unconscious impulses. If one persists in a willed attitude and disregards the inner demands of the archetype, the breach between conscious and unconscious will increase. Eventually the unconscious, which is of course far more powerful than consciousness, will begin to manifest in symptoms-symptoms of neurosis in some cases, or, in others, the individual will become increasingly self-willed and rigid, in

---

[110] Harding, 1965, p. 17

compensation for the neglected warnings from within.[111]

The conflict between conscious and unconscious lives can create problems. We intuitively know that allowing the unconscious to rule is problematic—we stay, we obey, we give up our selfhood for the paradisal state of protection by the father or the mother's nurturing embrace. Likewise, if we shun the unconscious and overvalue the wilful ego, a split—neurosis—can occur.

This, it seems, is the more common problem of our age. Our rational culture, with its relative absence of community, initiation, religious and ritual containers for the unconscious, assumes the predominance of the conscious psyche, and doesn't perceive the chains of the unconscious. They're not trying to drag us back—well, some parents might—but they certainly weigh us down.

Adolescence as a phenomenon could be seen as an extended parental hold: the instinct to separate is stymied by cultural forces, economic demands. There is the notion that the adolescent period is itself expanding, to encompass both earlier maturation and experience, and the later education. There is much to process culturally and socially, and perhaps with the speed of advancement previous generations are less and less able to facilitate separation. Whatever positives come from our complex culture and technologies, the instinctive drive to separate remains a hallmark of the adolescent period, and extending it can only increase the tension.

No wonder the desire to differentiate is so strong. But in the meantime we are bereft of the rituals and celebrations that would initiate us into the adult world. We can only build psychic walls to mimic a separation—but the voices of the parents, the father's arch tone, still can be heard over those walls.

So what are we to do? Tear it all down and start again? Doesn't that end in us just building new walls?

Sitting in his captivity, Karsa Orlong ponders the nature of slavery, and in dialogue with his captor Damisk and his fellow captives. He is working through the notions of freedom and civility. "You think I am a slave because I am in chains?" (136) His disdain for the Sunyd, a rival clan, who he thinks

---

[111] Ibid. 16

have accepted the life of slavery, is palpable. It is clear, then, that he puts choice and will above all else. His determination to free himself, and the fact that he maintains his sense of self despite the outward manifestation of chains is indicative of his ego strength, even as it also hints at the stubborn wilfulness we have already witnessed. It is also the beginning of his crusade against civilisation, which to him appears as the removal of freedom, the force of binding people in chains. This extreme view that all social order is necessarily oppressive and patriarchal certainly finds a mirror in our world.

His quest hereon becomes a kind of intellectualisation of the nature of civilisation because he refuses to recognise the enslaving narratives and mentality of the Teblor. The way for the individual, the archetypal hero, to achieve independence and individual purpose, is to differentiate from the parents. This happens first in physical separation from the mother, and later in separating from the father, or stepping beyond the father's mediating role between family and outer world. In other words, Karsa's instinctive need to slay the father, to distinguish himself from the patriarchal rule of his clan, is redirected towards slaying civilisation (an even greater father or patriarchy). This is a defence mechanism that comes about from his refusal to accept that people would choose slavery out of anything other than weakness, and more importantly, that Pahlk's narrative was wrong.

Slaying the father, as it is expressed by Neumann for example, or personified in myths and tales, is metaphorical. This may seem obvious when stated so, but if the insinuation of such tales is its finality, that the father no longer has any rule—that all custom and history is to be cast out for reasons of, say, patriarchy or historical inequity—then we are not left with much in the way of cogent reality or societal foundation at all. No more than we should destroy the earth to escape from the embrace of the mother. Much more clarity is achieved by saying we should slay the negative effects of the father complex. There is need to bring those things to consciousness and so act against the negative impacts.

Perhaps a society in which myths are deeply embedded, embodied, would not suffer from such over-literal interpretations. These archetypes are the manifestation of deep instincts, stories that guide the anticipated psychic journey of the individual as well as the collective.

Further, it is not the archetype itself that is destroyed, it is its symbolic manifestation. Just as we don't actually slay our father, nor do we dismiss the archetype, remove all notions of patriarchal structure or mother earth. The hero-struggle is the removal of dependence on the parents at this stage of life, wresting back power from the archetypes by overturning their symbolic manifestation. "He would, one day, return to his people, and he would shatter their rules." (170) This conclusion to Karsa's heroic individuation is still in the future.

Just as a rift can form with the actual parents, a wound can occur in society or culture by disregarding or damaging the relation to an archetype at the collective level. And so a further struggle ensues where that relation must be returned to balance. This is, in a sense, the narrative of life playing out at multiple levels. We separate and return, ever seeking balance within the conditions that society and culture allow, and within our individual myth and potential.

If we disregard an archetype, it will emerge from the unconscious in a new manifestation. The mother may manifest as the state or an embracing ideology. The father may take the form of a charismatic leader, as history has demonstrated. The disempowerment of individuals, denial of instinct, may cause people to be drawn to external hero figures, like comic book heroes or their large screen adaptations.

Karsa's journey after the attack at Silver Lake is various manifestations of chains being broken, and even greater ones being placed upon him. His new pal Torvald Nom likens him to a bear that broke loose of its captivity, in his eyes, "A look that says: *Chains will not hold me.*" (167) This part of the journey is as much inner as outer, and seems to signify the growth from unconfirmed adolescent to adult, or at least the attempt. He is moving through a series of obligations and strictures—impalements, nets, and other bindings. We replace one burden with another, in seeking freedom.

Finally, he is chained and bound by the Malazans. It is in his psychic bind, ensnared by chains, with no foreseeable strategy for escape, that he comes to his realisation about the nature of the Teblor and the lowlanders. So it often happens that an insoluble problem begets insight. As if the unconscious is shining a light on the self. His decision to appear broken, rather than accept passivity, forces his unconscious mind to explore inner problems.

"Borders, once defended with vicious determination, had for some reason been left abandoned." (168-169). While he is considering the Teblor physical borders, we can see that he is also touching on the nature of the father archetype, the lack of father influence allowing outside influence and vulnerability. But he could just as well be pondering his own ego walls, left exposed to truths he was not previously willing to see, and so there is a duality in the experience of growth and vulnerability.

He realises and accepts Pahlk's failings, which he had been heretofore unwilling, it seemed, to even hear. Thus he is acknowledging and preparing for a differentiation from that mentality. The separation from the father is the beginning of a new independence, marked by a sense of alienation from the actual father-figure.

> "It was not his lies that were the greatest crime, it was his lack of courage, for he had shown himself unable to wrest free of the strictures binding the Teblor. His people's rules of conduct, the narrowly crafted confines of expectations – its innate conservatism that crushed dissent with the threat of deadly isolation – these were what had defeated his grandfather's courage.
>
> Yet not, perhaps, my father's." (169)

Karsa sees in this the overbearing nature of the father archetype, the patriarchy that constricts, and which therefore results in Pahlk's and the Teblor's reliance on that father image. Without the courage to step into the world, beyond the father's care and structure, the rules and expectations, progress and growth is hobbled. And then, vulnerable to the world's predation, one is ill-prepared to face the social world.

Synyg's aloofness has prepared him for this moment of realisation, though it is a harsh love that manifests so. It might be argued that Synyg lived his purpose, his values. Perhaps with a mother to mediate the relation between the men it might have played out more forthrightly. But as it is, there is a wound between Karsa and his father. The work of mending that injury is ongoing.

His realisation here is a kind of rebirth. He understands that he will return, heroic, and would raise up the Teblor, bringing enlightenment, and balancing the conservatism he perceives in his people.

The all-powerful and terrible nature assigned to the god-father in mythology was passed down into society, its functions carried by kings and priests and mortal fathers and senior males (father-figures). "They range from physical dominance to abstract ideas. This was the origin of patriarchal rule: codes of law, rituals of religion, the rights of property and so forth."[112] It is important to note that physical dominance would have taken evolutionary precedence, by virtue of consciousness and the application of social structure appearing later in our history. The latter would have co-evolved to some extent, or been developed as rationalisations for, the psychical attributes and hierarchies. That very physical dominance conveys the power to enforce such codes. This has a protective evolutionary role, because defectors from the tribe are kept in line so as not to endanger the collective. Rules are meaningless with no power to enforce them. In other words, the conflation of physical power and patriarchal dominance should not be seen as purely cynical attempts to withhold power from women, or justifications for the same—though that is not to discount that such occurrences have of course existed. We must assume that these patterns exist and persisted to some degree because of their adaptive value.

But while that understanding may grate on our modern sensibilities, it should also be understood that therein lies the importance and power of the myths. A negative, devouring, and overbearing father archetype, and the hero who slays that power, is a warning and a roadmap. A collective embodying such myths is less likely to fall into unconsciousness and suffer such imbalance.

In turn, such power should serve as a warning to a self-aware society: heed your myths, but do not let the myths themselves become one-sided.

Humbled, chained to the wagon bed, Karsa Orlong is made a child once again. Immobile, accepting the feedings, the soothing words of Torvald Nom as he learns anew of the world around him. It is a mirror of the Mhybe in *Memories of Ice*.

This movement of his story is about his stripping away of himself, his certainty, his physical and psychological selves. Chained and gagged at the ship's mast, he dreams, and he is told by his god that his surrender is failure. His chained souls come for him. Awakening, weeks have passed, and the storm of chains comes for him, lashing at the ship and transporting them to the flooded warren, the nascent where we saw Trull Sengar, a shadow world.

He is chained to his wagon bed, floating on a still dark sea with Torvald

---

[112] Harding, 1965, p. 27

Nom at his side. Accepting his impending drowning, Karsa surrenders again, accepts his fate. Almost instantly, Torvald finds the water is not so deep.

With these manifestations of surrender and acceptance, and his honest appraisal of his father, Karsa is able to appreciate his gods in a new light. Appearing to him in a dream, his god challenges his strength once more. His certainty of the reality of the Seven as gods, likely from Synyg's words, is shaken: "But now, Urugal, I am no longer so sure—" (194)

When Torvald finally frees him from his chains, he must learn to move his body once again. This is a rebirth, unburdened. To emphasise this image, Erikson throws Karsa half way down the throat of a giant black fish—the leviathan's belly, though this one is a dark mirror of Moby Dick. And shortly after, he cuts the dead Borrug out of a shark's belly, another twist on the archetypal image.

"A year ago, words had been blunt, awkward things…but that flaw had been Karsa's alone." (209) This self-insight is symbolic of his growth. His separation is under way. The ego is separate from the wholeness of the family or tribe. "All that Karsa had experienced since leaving his village – had served as instruction on the complexity of the world." (210) His realisation is that his development has occurred as the awakening of a child. And he had to surrender to a childlike state to arrive at that. This was not, however, a regression, adoption of childish naivete, but a conscious approach to the experience and vulnerability of a child. He is still, in many ways, adolescent, and encumbered by the father, but he has come a long way. "The only answer he gave – when he gave one at all – was of violence, misdirected, a lashing out on all sides." (210) The ability to control and direct one's instincts and impulses is a hallmark of maturity.

It is interesting to reflect at this point of Karsa's story, his breaking of his chains and relinquishing of past certainty, his unwillingness to be a tool of the gods, that he has undergone a similar arc to Ganoes Paran in *Gardens of the Moon*. Where Paran achieved his growth and understanding by a mixture of luck, charisma, and friendship, Karsa has arrived by sheer strength of will. Karsa's chains are also symbolic of the negative father complex, that he is attempting to break free from. We also know of Karsa's later link with the Crippled God, himself chained, as we saw in *Memories of Ice*.

Having supped at Keeper's tower, Karsa and Torvald drink at a spring. On their walk back, Karsa is open to his feelings of friendship, his gratitude to Torvald, and his regrets for deeds and words spoken to his mates Bairoth and Delum as well as his rival tribes. It is also clear that this openness is a struggle for him, but he moves into that discomfort.

Alas, the pair are chained again, by Silgar again, and are once more on their way to Otataral island. Karsa's face is tattooed as shattered glass, and he meets Leoman, also imprisoned. Torvald once again rescues Karsa, and they escape. We see Karsa stumbling out of a long dark passage beneath Ehrlitan, one of the seven holy cities. Karsa reborn.

In the petrified grove in Raraku, Karsa carves likenesses of his Teblor gods alongside the likenesses of Bairoth and Delum. "Karsa slowly turned from the faces of the gods, and looked upon those for whom this place had been in truth sanctified. By Karsa's own hands. In the name of those chains a mortal could wear with pride." (473) The power in Karsa's hands suggests the control he has over his world and his fate. The chains, of course, are friendship, kinship. He is still closed to the outer world, for Leoman tells him that little is known of him or his people, but within, Karsa is open to relation.

He keeps his friends close, and few, but his very recognition of them, as well as his dislike of Bidithal and chains in general, shows emotional maturity. "Grief, finally unleashed. At an end, his time of solitude." (475) This openness to his repressed emotions is a breaking of his psychic chains, and allows him to progress to the next stage of his journey.

"He set out, westward, as the day was born." (484) The sun hero's journey begins anew here. Where previously Karsa set out unwitnessed, in the dark, symbolising his naivete and birth from ignorance, this time he is affirmed by his community, even if they are spirits. These journeys recur, life being likened to a series of elliptical orbits, much as each passing day.

We spoke about the night, but of course, day itself is a powerful metaphor for the journey of growth. The expression of such movements are internalisations of outer experience, and their mythologisation is not mere allegory, "they are symbolic expressions of the inner, unconscious drama of the psyche which becomes accessible to man's consciousness by way of projection—that is, mirrored in the events of nature."[113]

Jung wrote about the night sea journey as a heroic journey, indicating the

---

[113] Jung, C.G., CW9i, [7]

numinosity of the sun, which "sails over the sea like an immortal god who every evening is immersed in the maternal waters and is born anew in the morning."[114] This journey, with its associated symbols, the mystery of descent into dark, plays out in many myths and tales.

With the coming of light, consciousness is born, then the sun describes its rise, the peak of its powers at the midpoint, and then wanes in its second half in the descent towards death:

> "the daily course of the sun and the regular alternation of day and night must have imprinted themselves on the psyche in the form of an image from primordial times. We cannot demonstrate the existence of this image, but we find instead more or less fantastic analogies of the physical process. Every morning a divine hero is born from the sea and mounts the chariot of the sun. In the West a Great Mother awaits him, and he is devoured by her in the evening. In the belly of a dragon he traverses the depths of the midnight sea. After a frightful combat with the serpent of night he is born again in the morning."[115]

But then each day is not merely a replaying of the metaphoric journey—each day provides the opportunity for individuation. It is not just a metaphor for the heroic journey of enlightened consciousness and rebirth, but is in actuality an invitation to live it. Each day can no doubt be heroic if you only need to survive, but what about adults now? What treasures do we bring back to the tribe?

Progress, the chance to do it better, to redeem ourselves and others – no wonder the sun's rebirth is numinous. Of course it is worthy of worship if, once again, we are offered this gift – the world's compassion, freely given.

We shun our instincts, and the meaning that evolved in answer to those instincts and needs of survival. What are we doing to our soul when we imprison it in the confines of a meaningless pattern, deny the full expression of our instinct for meaning, for growth. The need to break free of those patriarchal bounds expresses itself elsewhere.

What happens when we deny a whole social group? A nation? A faith? A sex?

---

[114] Jung, C.G., CW5, [306]
[115] Jung, C.G., CW8, [326]

Karsa's journey beyond the rebirthing womb of Raraku is attended by Leoman with a warning, "If you must kneel before a power, first look upon it with clear eyes." (484)

"The journey had been long, but he knew his path ahead was still longer." (602) This realisation is the goal of initiation. He is stepping forth into a new state, crossing a threshold. Part of this notion of reversing or reflecting his initial journey, he crosses blades with Icarium. This is a conscious approach to the myth he only became aware of on his downward journey from home.

As he crosses the land, he ponders the systems of power, the burden of civilisation. "The notion of a life spent tilling fields was repellent to the Teblor warrior." (611) Here is a nod from Erikson to the accepted notion that the pre-agricultural life had a clear distinction, that they were barbaric times. "Wealth was measured in control over other people…Better to struggle against helplessness" (611) Karsa's conclusion is that people must be empowered, their chains removed. Those who would use power were to be defied. But there is a duality in the notion of chains and burdens—the tension between order and chaos—some structure is necessary to provide balance.

On this initiation journey, he is accompanied in his mind by Bairoth and Delum, where the first time around he was one-sided in his mentality, and had to learn to embrace the aspects that defined them. "Perhaps, in truth, no more than my mind's own conjuring." (602) From inner certainty and conflict with the outer world, he has grown to where his conflicts are internal. "You hide your thoughts now, Karsa Orlong. This new talent does not please us." (614)

Further reflections of his initial journey come. First, in the form of the wolf D'ivers, mirroring the pack of dogs he tamed—this time there is no clash, their wildness remains. He then takes a journey through a Tellann dreamworld, mirroring the descent of the Bone Pass. Across dying ice, and he walks over a field of Imass bones. Within a tower he finds Aramala, a Jaghut mother. He frees the maiden, and learns about his gods, among other things. She disabuses him of his naivete.

Karsa creates his flint sword, and confronts the Seven, his putative gods. "To live is to suffer. To exist – even as we do – is to resist." (681) Their notion echoes the assertion of Tool in *Memories of Ice*, that nature is always at war. The state of imbalance that characterises life, resistance against entropy, is here taken to an extreme, that life necessitates suffering.

> "Stone, sea, forest, city – and every creature that ever lived –
> all share the same struggle. Being resists unbeing. Order wars

> against the chaos of dissolution, of disorder. Karsa Orlong, this is the only worthy truth, the greatest of all truths. What do the gods themselves worship, but perfection? The unattainable victory over nature, over nature's uncertainty. There are many words for this struggle. Order against chaos, structure against dissolution, light against dark, life against death. But they all mean the same thing." (681)

In part what we are seeing is the T'lan Imass rationalisation for their state of war. Because they see all through the lens of war, they see this life as a battle, an unwinnable contest. No hope. One step further renders this darkly: if all is war, and suffering is inherent, then suffering is inevitable. Thus the Crippled God's assertion that suffering is itself the worthy truth.

Jung's notion is rather that such tension, the balance and imbalance in constant flux, is the action of growth—it is the energic basis of life. Life is not just witness to the unravelling of the tale, but it has its own instinctive desire to continue. Conscious awareness has furnished us with the ability to alter the balance, sometimes in unseen ways, and perhaps with enough collective power to change the world for the better. Meaning alleviates suffering, or at least makes it worthwhile. Suffering and sacrifice might be necessary, but it is answered by compassion, by love. There is meaning in spite of our smallness in the face of universal forces and the weight of history.

These Imass contend that gods seek perfection, victory over nature, and that the Crippled God would change that paradigm because all is imperfect. But perfection and control are not necessarily the same, though either could conceivably lead to the other. Growth and individuation do not cast aside imperfection, but allow for the striving towards a higher goal and state as something that is in itself meaningful even if unattainable. Accepting imperfection, then, is not surrender—it can be liberating. It can be redemptive. "No matter how brief a child's life, the love of the parents is a power that should not be denied…it is immune to imperfection." (682-3)

Of their failures, the Seven say: "Such things cannot be undone. Thus, you may surrender to it, and so suffer beneath its eternal torment. Or you can choose to free yourself of the burden." (683) Again, they are concerned that any imperfection, any flaw, is a weight carried in the shadow. Burden is to be relieved by its celebration—this is the Crippled God's way.

But we can carry our history without its burden. We can relieve suffering without making of it a virtue. This is polarised thinking, taking two extremes and setting them at odds. Such polarity creates a vacuum along the spectrum of life's nuance, and can be seen vividly in our political spheres. Jungians tend to embrace polarity and opposition, as it appeared frequently in Jung's writing. It is no less dangerous there.

This mindset is attractive because it has its own rationalisations built in. It beguiles one not to waste their energy in either direction. The lure of sublimating one's emotional response to a flaw or a wounding, rather than facing those very feelings. But sometimes the work is worthy – the burden is what gives life shape.

Furthermore, feelings of guilt, sadness, regret, like physical pain, are conscious guides. They indicate where you might be living at cross-purpose to your instincts and moral values. They are the conscience, the internal sensor that works in concert with the social world to adjust the self and life towards balance. Without reflexive awareness of those feelings, without the willingness see it and undertake change in response to it, we are simply accepting dissolution—of life, and of the self and society. To revel in the pain and suffering is to war against the instincts of life. Suffering, though inevitable, is not defining of life.

Dichotomous thinking arises because two poles are clearly seen, and it leads us to magnify small things – one small regret, celebrated, would lead not to change, but to narcissism. On the larger scale, such collective thinking would swallow the individual, because there would be no need for self-reflection. Such extremity leads the Crippled God's followers to step over from a grain of truth to a field of fanaticism. Indeed, such outward certainty often hides the threat of apostasy: "It would appear that there are acceptable levels of imperfection – and unacceptable levels of imperfection." (685)

Karsa Orlong's reversal, his own myth making, is very well symbolised by his enlivening and destruction of one of his gods. He is thus claiming sovereignty back from his people, and from the archetypal father—the notion of culture in the form of gods determining his behaviour and belief systems.

Investing Bairoth and Delum in his sword finally quietens them in his mind. It is a ritual parting with an aspect of himself, his past life. Even were this not literal for Karsa, ritual has a purpose in this way. It can externalise a psychic process, anchoring it in the real world. Here Karsa also finally internalises the nature of those two men, accepting their natures as part of his own. This is the positive side of the shadow, that within one is the potential that is unlived—Karsa always had the potential for thoughtfulness and wisdom, but he needed to journey to accept that part of himself, to integrate it after projecting it out onto his mates and their spirits.

In naming his horse Havok, he is claiming for himself the gift of his father's blessing, taking it now on his own. Confirmation can now come from his own inner self.

Riding back with the promise of delivering death, he realises "He had been indifferent for long enough, indifferent to so many things. He had reined in his spirit's greatest strengths, among them his need to make judgments, and act decisively upon them in true Teblor fashion." (842) Though the nature of his answers may appal us, it is true that repression of one's nature is a shadow function, and should be dealt with. Indifference can arise from a perceived inability to act, a feeling of helplessness, which is often a misattribution. Reawakening assertiveness can result in a realisation of one's power, no longer quashed by the chains of one's own doubts. As Heboric notes to Scillara, "Indifference destroys the soul." (835)

Karsa had a period of solitude before this journey, and now feels his power awakened once more. "A House is just another prison. And I have had enough of prisons. Raise walls around me, and I will knock them down." (844) He is now full of certainty, but there is no notion of balance there, no partial surrender or acceptance of civility. His experience has shown him that freedom must be total.

However, even this must be kept in balance. Karsa returns to the camp and begins killing because he promised to. He begins with Silgar, ending what he should have ended long ago, a sundering of his chains. After killing Febryl, he feels the ghost chains attached to him pulling him back, discouraging him. This is perhaps the control of the Crippled God, the shadow. Finally, Karsa's strength of will (or stubbornness) ends the resistance, but the chains remain instead of breaking. This is reminiscent of the struggle for independence at the cusp of adulthood—the draw of the old, the hero striking out—there is a play for control, and while independence is here achieved, full separation is avoided.

Karsa's return to the camp is itself the assertion of balance. He is a force of nature and is therefore the answer to the nest of vipers, the web of deceit that has tangled Raraku. His is the sword that cuts the Gordian Knot of intrigue and deadly intention. His growing audacity must shake even the gods. He kills the Deragoth, and it should be remembered that he announced he still wants to kill the Crippled God, but he will break his chains first. He acts on his principle, not necessarily applying a compassion to the individual beneath. It is the structure he defies.

His final scenes suggest the possibility of change. He renounces his vow to make Malazans his enemy, which suggests at least the ability of self-reflection. His tossing out 'Siballe's corpse into the newly born sea, to oblivion, strides somewhere between mercy and pragmatism. Once more, he rides west, like the archetypal sun-hero. "West, into the wastes." (1012) Like the sun, but the wastes suggest there is a slog through darkness ahead.

In conclusion, we have seen that Karsa is under the power of the archetypal father, still trying to deny the influence of the actual father. His development is therefore stymied. He has introjected the influence of his peer group, which is indicative of an inability to relate to the outside world—social/psychosocial mediation hasn't occurred in a constructive way, thus he is clinging unconsciously to that peer group where he is looking for confirmation in absence of his father's. "Lead me, warleader."

Breaking the chains can be read as an obvious metaphor for escaping the father complex. Breaking away from the capturing patriarchy. Karsa's uncanny ability to escape or be rescued means he had less need for self-reflection. It also means he is always breaking free, thus stuck in a repetition of that adolescent moment.

If a dive into the psychodynamics can be forgiven, the father affects the boy's ability to relate to the outside world through his anima—that is, through his relating function. Communicating the world in the right way is important because it prepares the child for the world's dangers and opportunities. Karsa Orlong is wounded because Synyg was weak, or simply rejected by society, and the surrogate father, Pahlk, lied and manipulated.

Adapting to the threats and opportunities inherent in the social world and natural world can be problematic without the father's confirmation. Mother can provide a bulwark against some of the negative effects, though that can often result in an overreliance on the mother's protective nurturing. We don't know when Karsa's mother died, but clearly he didn't get that protection.

Without a way to confirm himself, to individuate and thus confront his father complex and learn to relate, at least until he submits and integrates his temporary captivity, his vows are merely adolescent lashings out. He is fixed in a psychosocial phase of an angry pre-adult too bitter at the world and unable to let go of his peer group, that keeps him in an immature state.

Rather than destroy culture, the hero's job is to transform it, to bring something new to culture—building on the old, not just killing it, because that is merely chaos. Karsa's mission to destroy civilisation must be tempered, or else he is stuck in the adolescent impulse to break things. Culture, the father archetype, having buy-in from the society, thus resists change, to the extent that it will not accept being swept aside completely. Of course, that resistance, and the self-reinforcing nature of such structures, creates the possibility of tyranny, and wariness of this manifestation of tyranny justifies criticism of patriarchy.

This is almost analogous to the move to life's second half, wherein the state of external growth turns inward. Old values of ego expansion are integrated with new values – we find fullness in exploring those previously neglected aspects of ourselves. There can be immense resistance, like in adolescence, as we try to hold on to youthful ideals or live through our children—the midlife crises, neuroses.

Of course, these are all at a larger scale across the lifespan. The same metaphors can play out at a smaller scale, as any new skill or information is learned and incorporated. Our goals, broken into sub-goals, are overcome, and change and growth ensue.

Felisin / Sha'ik

> "There are folds in this shadow…
>
> hiding entire worlds.
>
> Call to Shadow
>
> Felisin" (266)

Heboric's presence allows Sha'ik to undertake negotiations with her personal animus. They have been replaced by a new set, in Leoman, Toblakai, and Bidithal and the others. The old guard, here only Heboric, is a retaining of her humanity, her old self.

Neumann talks about the spiritual aspect as a fundamental part of the feminine archetypes. "In a woman, every psychic situation that leads to an animation of the unconscious…sets in motion the unconscious patriarchal structures of the animus."[116] So we can see here the crossover between animus as the communicator of the unconscious in women, and the father or patriarchal aspects of the unconscious. In a similar way, we saw in the previous chapter how mother and anima overlap.

The contrasexual archetype in women presents differently, because there is inherently a different relationship to father, the presentation of animus as

---

[116] Neumann, 1955, p. 294

a council of figures and so on. The relating function in women is mediated by the bounds between the family unit and the social world. This is phenomenologically different to a man's relating function, which is mediated through the mother—the primary caregiver—and thus the projected image is closer. For women, whose primary caregiver is also the mother, the father, and thus the relation to the social world, is necessarily different. Much of the development in this sphere occurs before the consciousness develops in the child.

Felisin has replaced her animus council with one that is more aloof, and unprotective. They don't care about her as a person, even Karsa considered her a hapless victim (355) of the Goddess. But as cruel at times and dutiful as Beneth, Baudin, even Heboric seemed, they thought she, Felisin, the human beneath, was worth saving.

Her holding on to Heboric is not a regression, as it may seem, but a way of remaining conscious. She is giving time and attention to that part of herself she had previously neglected. When she discovers Ganoes is still alive, she sends out all but Heboric, and weeps upon him: "The child in his arms – for child she was, once more – cried in nothing other than the throes of salvation." (371) Of course, this all appears to be at a detriment to Heboric himself, and that is a truth too. It is more often that we read of women embodying the anima projections of men, as mother, nymph, lover, and so on, and this is, if cultivated, at a loss to her own development.

Like her animus, she stands aloof as a mother. We can only speculate what Felisin's real mother was like, though we have noted her relative absence. But perhaps Felisin's unconscious motive is to visit upon her adopted child, Felisin Younger, the experience of self-toughening she endured. Recall that Felisin was only a child in Skullcup, and had to make her own way, fight her own battles. Perhaps she forgets that she had protectors, or has learned to trust too much in them.

She has swapped Skullcup for Raraku. A comforting maternal embrace. She assumed futility in life, and is now in the comfort of being a mere symbol. She doesn't have to live—though there is the instinct to adopt. But she is too alienated to make it work in a healthy, functional way.

In a way, by acting as symbol she is the shadow of the Whirlwind Goddess, the collective shadow of those people. A mere symbol, and the vessel for all the failures and shortcomings. She is metamorphosed by possession by the goddess, and for her internal journey she needed to consciously assimilate the power and live on, but she didn't get the chance.

What we have seen in Felisin's adoption of the children, and her return to poetry, is the instinct of creation, of creativity. Wondering at the book of Dryjhna, she remarks to Karsa, "There is no rebirth among the ashes of his vision, and that saddens me." (358) This tells us that Felisin is still functioning at her instinctive level—that she has, in her rebirth, or despite her traumas, maintained her inner self. Instinct can be seen as a wisdom of the body. She herself has already been reborn, but she is aware that the answer is not in destruction, but in continued rebirth.

When Karsa shows her his grove of carved figures, snakes arrive. The serpent has mythological connotations, the masculine aspect of the numinous feminine we often see draped over goddesses. But here we are reminded of wisdom, of self-knowledge. The grove of stone is a petrified Eden. "Creation, Chosen One." (359) This is offered in response to her desire for rebirth.

Like Tavore, Sha'ik/Felisin remains remote to us through the first movements of *House of Chains*. In Book Four, we open with her recollections of spying and fascination with sister Tavore, and her notion of Tavore standing in Ganoes's shadow, then becoming it. So we are returning to her childhood again, a weak, frightened state, insecure, where she has already been when in Heboric's arms. Knowing of Ganoes's survival and knowing Tavore is coming render her childlike. She had hardened herself to her situation, to the world—her very identification with the goddess made her remote and ephemeral, allowed her to leave her life behind—but there is a drive towards this childhood return. Again, it is not mere regression, perhaps more a desire to repeat, to fulfill the living out of the youth she was denied. An inability to grow beyond the child she was when trauma was inflicted upon her life.

Felisin Younger reflects that the goddess sees them all as tools, that she had thought Felisin/Sha'ik reborn was different. She had seen her, the other orphans as people, and was human. But she sees now that "the Whirlwind Goddess has stolen the love from her soul." (715) And so Felisin is no longer human. But what they fail to see is that her humanity is expressed finally in her obsessive fear of Tavore.

When Sha'ik enters Heboric's tent—his newly sanctioned temple to Treach—the Goddess is driven from her. We see that the Goddess is a reification of her personal shadow. "A sudden…*absence*. Terrifying, bursting like the clearest light where all had been, but a moment earlier, impenetrable gloom. Bereft…*yet free. Gods, free – the light –*" (718) Repressed memories flood in, her guilt and regret for how she's passed on her hurt to others.

After Heboric refers to her as Sha'ik, she corrects him: "Don't call me that. I am Felisin Paran of House Paran." (719) The goddess was only ever a persona, something her inflated self-image aspired to, its power and maturity. This persona of Sha'ik has served to aid in the repression of Felisin's shadow because the integration or realisation of the shadow aspect of the self can be stifled by the shadow. Sha'ik's seeming inaction and neurotic responses to Tavore's approach are indicative of a depression arising out of a conflict between persona and shadow. Felisin has undergone trauma, and spent considerable energy trying to find defence mechanisms to harden herself and prevent collapse of herself. With Baudin's death, she had exposure to being a child again. This is central to the conflict that is holding her back, especially when we see her returns to childhood when her family is mentioned.

Persona often compensates for the nature of the shadow. When presented with the opportunity to don the mask of the Whirlwind Goddess, Felisin unconsciously grasped it. The power, where she had been rendered powerless by her situation and continued traumas, and maturity (or rather its pantomime in acting as mother to the adopted children, even perhaps as matron to the entire camp) offered by the role of Sha'ik was an ideal outlet.

Felisin is being kept from herself, her intuition and her vulnerability, her humanity. "The Goddess doesn't want me to think" (824) There is dread ceremony as she armours herself in Sha'ik's battle gear—finishing with the hands and head, all that is left of her ability to act and think. "Have I any choice in this?" (913)

She has come from a life where she had armoured herself, and it was to survive, but we have seen that a human child lived beneath. The Goddess was an escape, a further layer of armour to the world. Now, in donning Sha'ik's armour the capture will be complete, and Felisin will step out to face the world with nothing of herself remaining.

Raraku's awakening is the souls of the past making their return. The Goddess is preventing Felisin from reconciling her past, from perceiving her history as anything but pain and wounding. Preventing redemption. The Whirlwind, after all, wants only destruction.

As the final showdown with Tavore looms, Felisin's childhood is again recurring in her mind, as memories find their way to the surface. "And now the Whirlwind Wall had closed, retracted, had drawn in from the outside world," (972) so do Felisin's mental defenses withdraw. We recall Heboric in *Deadhouse Gates*, when Felisin is considering taking up the mantle of the goddess: "Sha'ik would face the Empress…History recounts similar rebellions, lass, and the tale is an endless echo." (DG 563) And so her story falls into a predictable ending. This is also similar to the endlessly repeating story of a child's rebellion from the parents.

She reflects on the madness of the Goddess, of walking a ledge atop an abyss, and she feels that in herself and attributes it to a kind of madness. That seed of madness is the betrayal in her that never healed. We have already considered how dark powers might keep one in their weakness and suffering, notably with the Crippled God. Felisin has been kept on the ledge by the Whirlwind Goddess, not allowing her to think, not allowing her to heal. The ledge she clings to is "the place…of childhood." (973) She is prevented from redemption of the child within, an opportunity to grow and express her own humanity.

Of the Goddess, too, she reflects on "Her ego armoured in hatred. She cannot look in, she can barely see out." (973) We saw in *Deadhouse Gates* how the traumas undergone wounded Felisin's ability to communicate both with the inner and outer worlds. The ego, as the control centre of the body, was no longer able to communicate with the unconscious (*The Goddess doesn't want me to think*) and has taken on a persona so buried beneath the sand, so firmly armoured, that nothing of what is within is visible. Thus, nobody was left who could see her as worthy of redemption, for she didn't let them in—save for Heboric. Now, finally, "Sha'ik reached for the helm." (973)

But as the Whirlwind goddess is killed, Felisin's armour lifting from her, she feels abandoned again, just another betrayal. "I am Felisin once more." (984) She tries to speak, to hold out her arms, but her ability to relate is gone, her body weak beneath armour too heavy, and all that was set in motion comes to its inevitable fulfillment.

In her final moments she regresses to childhood again, and draws the action out of Tavore, unwittingly forcing her into her instinctive behaviour. They are submitting to their roles. Tavore, having been doubted, must demonstrate herself to be a powerful mother.

How could we see Felisin as an aspect of Tavore's journey? We can really only speculate. She kills the caring mother within, before it can truly express itself, but also kills the child. She is cutting herself adrift as she slays Felisin, though unknowing. She is striking out alone.

People can make the mistake of thinking they can integrate the shadow by living it out. In this case, Jekyll becomes Hyde. This leads to identification with the shadow. But we need to allow it to coexist consciously, give space for it, through ritual or dialogue. Identification with it leads to destruction, and this is Felisin's downfall.

Armour is a kind of persona, or perhaps the other way around. We think of persona as that which we project to the outside world, but it is often not so conscious. It is formed when there is a clash between the expectations of the world and that which is inside, like a crust about the psyche. But it also has a dual role: not only projecting something of within, but protecting the psyche from that which it does not want to get in. Armour that works both ways.

Felisin's is a wonderful journey to read. From alienation (abandonment) she identifies with the deity. In this case literally becoming the goddess of the whirlwind. From her despair, she opens up to the transpersonal power of godhood, but it is inflated, and becomes a complex. We note how the role is ill-fitting, till her ill-fated end.

She wants to show Tavore—her need to prove is all outward, she hasn't taken back her projection and consciously turned it to growth. "But she'd never had the chance for that." (984)

If there was still any question whether Felisin was capable of compassion, worthy of redemption, it is answered in her final thoughts. Answered by her raised arms, answered by the voiceless words to her sister, answered with a final question: "I just wanted to know, Tavore, why you did it. And why you did not love me, when I loved you." (986)

She wasn't ready to accept the deity, too empty a vessel. The people that use and abuse us want us to be empty—because they can fill us with their projections. Perhaps she became emptied out by her experiences, or was it simply that she wasn't allowed to grow and become mature enough to take on the power that came to her?

The tragedy of Felisin is that she had the chance to regain her humanity – to assimilate her animus, her shadow, to relate to her own feeling side, her internal mother by redeeming the child (Felisin Younger). But she fails, instead being led by others' projections upon her, and the fate which her unconscious aspects decide for her. She could take her armour off and forgive—and perhaps in her final moments she was ready to open her arms and do just that—but by staying hidden, unconscious, she failed to grow, and thus died.

Heboric

Heboric is the shadow of Sha'ik's army: "he was their very opposite, a sordid reflection in a mangled mirror." (336) He possesses no delusions, he thinks.

In *Deadhouse Gates*, his gift of blind-sight allowed him to encounter the shadow, the forgotten and the unseen. He touched the jade statue, and gains narratorial insight into history. He became jaded, as it were, about history and humanity.

With his ghost hands he is not able to embrace, and thus feels powerless. It is akin to his faithlessness, and that makes it easy for him to lack faith in Felisin, for example. When his hands are gifted him, they are strangely ghostly, still not quite able to embrace, and his faith still needs to return to him internally.

Heboric had his fall, then pulled down his god, was gifted with new hands and descended with Felisin, became attached to her. He has had many falls, then, and probably wonders how much further he has to descend. But he has watched Felisin, and no doubt thought the same thing about her, and perhaps that gives him some confidence. "You must undertake the journey...But I know, it cannot be done alone." (468) Felisin Younger calls Heboric to adventure, to the retreading of his journey thus far, back to the source of his power, and to answers.

He seems to be welcoming the indifference promised in death when he sits at his pyre. L'oric visits and they discuss their respective secrets and knowledge of the Jade Giants, whereupon whatever L'oric tells him spins him out of his death desire. His hands, "Together, there at the ends of his wrists, they became the weight of the world." (482) From indifference, to purpose.

Heboric might be seen as the Shield Anvil for the Crippled God. (At least that the Crippled God is trying to claim him, but he won't be...) There is the connection with the Jade statue, and there is the hint in Silgar's drawing: "an elaborate pattern in the dust around Heboric's moccasins. Chains, surrounding a figure with stumps instead of hands...yet footed. The ex-priest scowled, kicking through the image as he set forth." (353) This is also indicative of his flight from the influence of the god. He fears sleep and the images brought forth in silence. He pushes away the image as he holds Felisin: "And each time the vision of his fallen god rose before his mind's eye, he ruthlessly drove it back down...his own grief would wait." (371)

He wakes from his dream of the Jade Giants, and he is marked, he assumes, by Treach. Having been a destriant, he wants to take that role: "In need of a Destriant, Treach?" (592). L'oric's discussion resulted in his feeling the weight of the world, so we should assume he is Shield Anvil. His acceptance of Treach is immediately different to his resistance to the other god.

L'oric tells Sha'ik that "Heboric grieves." (707) Having lost his faith, what he must hold onto is the idea that Felisin is worthy of the redemption she has been gifted. His struggle continues because he sees her as losing herself in the grip of the goddess. So there is a transference in Heboric. He wants to be a father figure (a return to his priesthood) – he was an animus projection and now their dynamic has morphed.

Bidithal

Bidithal is a tyrannical father figure. He promotes rules parading as conviction, with the aim of control. "The child must follow the mother's path, Bidithal believes. As the mother was broken inside, so too must the child be broken inside." (344) What is broken and weak needs support, is dependent. He represents the unseen, the ignored—perfect grist for the Crippled God's ideology.

He was a High Priest of Shadow, and with Heboric believing the Whirlwind is a fragment of the shattered warren of Shadow, this little kingdom Bidithal resides in is part of the web of shadows woven through this story.

A blind eye is turned to Bidithal's predilections for young children. While Heboric confronts him, he is in reality powerless, and the others of the camp—Leoman, Toblakai—choose not to act, instead concerned with the power plays in the camp. Bidithal is the apotheosis of all the repressed, forgotten, and ignored aspects—the shadow, indeed.

These paragraphs, as Felisin Younger is drawn into Bidithal's abode, are resonant of the journey into shadow. They also tell us about the Crippled God. If the god had a house, this is what it might look like:

> "She set out across the flagstoned plaza. Hundreds of the camp's destitute had settled here, beneath palm-frond shelters, making no efforts at organization – the expanse reeked of piss and faeces, streams of the foul mess flowing across the stones. Hacking coughs, mumbled entreaties and blessings followed her as she made her way towards the ruin.
>
> The temple's foundation walls were hip high; within, a steep set of stone stairs led down to the subterranean floor. The

sun's angle had dipped sufficiently to render the area below in darkness." (579)

Felisin Younger recalls his words after he had ensnared and mutilated her: "You are to feel nothing, for pleasure does not belong in the mortal realm. Pleasure is the darkest path, for it leads to the loss of control." (594) Bidithal, the twisted father figure, is attempting to normalise the repression of pleasure, putting it into the shadow. This is connected with sexuality, when we consider the genital mutilation. Putting such into the shadow is sadly not unusual in our world. It is an attempt to defy the biological instincts.

Felisin further reflects on those girls that aided him. "They are human, after all, and it is human nature to transform loss into a virtue." (594) The repressed instinct must find an outlet somewhere. Felisin thinks it is a normalisation, a virtue, and that is reaction formation, a defence mechanism that wards off threat by expressing the opposite emotion. Bidithal is making his argument on behalf of the Crippled God. Here is a form of suffering, and the contagion of those negative feelings is plain. The Crippled God, likewise orphaned, made the argument in *Memories of Ice* that others must suffer because of his suffering, though there was no pleasure in it for him. Bidithal, it might be argued, takes some pleasure in others' suffering, though it is rationalised as the hardening of the girls against pleasure.

"I had fashioned, in my own mind, every detail of the cult I would lead." (932) Bidithal also had planned to control the Deragoth, the elemental hounds. His psyche was inflated to the archetypal father – that is, the negative manifestation of the father, the control of power, exerting structure on behalf of divine power. He would damage and deprive the feminine, chain what shouldn't be chained. Such inflation is ill-fated. No surprise, then, that Karsa is the one to emasculate, and then slay this father.

The Bonehunters

The Bonehunters are a shadow cast by the Chain of Dogs. The very existence of the Bonehunters is about turning what was negative—guilt, anger, resentment—into positive energy. In other words, assimilating aspects of the shadow. Collectively, they pour that into an image: the bone held aloft by Grub and the bone fetishes placed about them. It is a potent symbol.

Individually, they must each overcome. And the value of a collective, a community, as discussed in our analysis of *Deadhouse Gates*, becomes relevant here.

Blistig says: "Better we'd died with the rest." (274) They are the words all the guilt-ridden soldiers daren't speak. It is the sentiment of the Squint, trying to drink himself to oblivion. It is survivor's guilt, an inevitable confrontation with the extremity of war and death, and rarely dealt with in fantasy literature.

Gamet acts as a narrator for the army early on. He is suffering from what we might term a superiority complex: "the bluster he often displayed was nothing more than a knee-jerk reaction to his own sense of inadequacy." (278) He is uncomfortable with a rise in status, and therefore aims to bring himself down. This in effect positions him as an outsider from the command of the army, who he views as highly competent and deserving of their position. In turn, this endows him with an assumption of objectivity—similar to Duiker on the Chain of Dogs.

The army sets out, retracing the steps of Coltaine's legacy. Gamet ponders Tavore's journey: "it remains just that. And she now realizes, down in the depths of her soul, that she will stride that man's shadow…all the way to Raraku." (490) History, legacy, is a thing that cannot be escaped, a collective unconscious, as much as our genetic ancestry.

"Show me no seams, lass. I need to hold on to my certainty." (500) Gamet's faith in Tavore is true, in that it hasn't been constructed. He holds the belief that the army relies upon. His fear of that faith being unfounded weighs upon him, but for now he stands as a kind of lens for the soldiers, though they know it not.

Nor are seams visible in Joyful Union. The birdshit scorpion is symbolic of the army. It is an underdog, its danger understated. It consists of cohesive parts, operating together but capable of independent deadly action. Their parting and coming together is also a conjunction, which is a thematic foreshadowing of the end of the series. It also foreshadows the rearrangement of the squads and suggests that they will still function as a whole despite their parting.

Gamet's reluctant to be responsible, but he is also the eyes of the common solider, a "cautious voice" (857) for Tavore. He preserves the structure by taking up his role as Fist again, just as having Fiddler and the vets down among the soldiers is good. Though it takes an insult to wake him up to it: "So cease your selfish sulking, old man, and step back in line." (860) which is perhaps what someone needed to say to Itkovian when he was trapped in his own thinking.

Gamet's redemption is symbolically important for the Bonehunters. He awakes before the impending battle, unable to breathe, his fear and trauma reemerging. He is the lodestone for the shadow under which the army strains. Arising as a spirit himself, he rejoins his soldier self. He is part of the past, and he fights on behalf of the Bonehunters. This is a chance to redeem himself, to achieve the competence and glory he thought he had failed to find. His own instinct had been denied, and what was kept in his shadow—the life unlived—now can be lived out.

He rides with the ghosts of the Wickans and others, giving an answer to the betrayal of the Chain of Dogs. He therefore takes part in the symbolic release of the trauma that still haunts the army. "We've needed our own voice, so that our spirits could march, march ever onward." (954) Freeing their memory, their spirits, the Bonehunters are thus able to move on, no longer burdened by the shadow of the past.

Tavore

What we see of Tavore is a reflection of the reader. Our picture of her is constructed of external impressions and projections. Indeed, everything we know of Tavore up to this book is through Ganoes and Felisin's impressions. "She was not one to spare a moment to sentiment. Cold-eyed, hers was a brutal rationality, pragmatism with a thousand honed edges – to cut open anyone foolish enough to come close." (*MoI* 778)

What is of interest, then, is how she mirrors other characters—both in their impressions of her, and as a comparison with other character arcs. Also, how her story might resonate with mythological motifs.

In a sense, Tavore acts initially as the vessel for shadow projections for the army. And it serves a real purpose, giving them a direction for their doubts, because there is no obvious face for their enemy here in Seven Cities—Pormqual is dead, for example, and his betrayal cannot be answered to their satisfaction.

This gives a curious additional meaning to the fact that Tavore is Felisin's shadow. Felisin projects on Tavore her shadow qualities. Thus there is at some level a truth to the army using Tavore as a shadow vessel in place of the enemy, Felisin, of whom they know nothing.

Gamet reflects, "Tavore had never been free with her thought." (279)

There are powerful layers to this phrasing. We already know that Tavore is closed to others, but additionally, if her thoughts are not free, then they are locked up, chained. We might presume she has never freely accessed her deep unconscious—there is repression at play. Also, the thoughts, if she is not free with them, are perhaps not her own, i.e., what we know of her is not her own thoughts—this mirrors the fact that the reader's impressions are not formed by her point of view.

> "'She knows what's in her.'
>
> 'And it's for us to bring it out into view.'" (512)

Tavore is terse with her command, we see in her meeting with the Fists. She understands others, though, their motivations, deeply. This intuitive nature is similar to Karsa. She is quick to distance herself from the past, the old order, previous command structures. This reflects her personal distancing. She throws Gamet off balance with sharp questions, controlling and redirecting his attention, even manages the same with Pearl who plays similar games himself.

One of the only expressions of open emotion is witnessed by Gamet: "There was a sudden vulnerability in her eyes that triggered a clutching anxiety in his gut – for it was something he had never seen from this daughter of House Paran." (284). She tells him that the Empress is not present here, suggesting that like Adjunct Lorn there is a core of humanity masked by the empire and its roles. She tasks Pearl and Lostara with finding Felisin, which is all the reassurance we'll get that her humanity is preserved for her family. We only see Tavore in brief glimpses, quickly shut down to display on the hardened surface.

Fiddler ponders Tavore's mirroring of Sha'ik, unaware of their relation, and that Tavore also mirrors Coltaine. Both leaders are unproven, taking up a weighty legacy. Sha'ik, too, has to deal with the faith of her army, give purpose to the disparate intentions.

At Vathar Crossing, site of an historical battle, and a symbolic initiation with the crossing of the river, we get the first mention of Tavore as a mother, here to Nil and Nether, the Wickan warlocks in child bodies. "I doubt the Empress intended you to *mother* them, did she?...I am of the opinion that you are proving far too permissive a mother, Adjunct." (649) These words from the trusted Gamet are used to urge a little forcefulness from her—he is drawing out her maternal nature.

Of course, there is the counterpoint to this. Gamet reflects, in his shell-shocked state: "Tavore – she was a child, once. But then the Empress murdered that child." (764) This recalls Lorn's failed quashing of the part of her that was not the Adjunct. But Lorn's humanity came back, her core and her instincts unable to be completely killed. Gamet might think that the child in Tavore was dead, but if there is enough strength at the core of her being, she will be able to maintain her humanity. And if she can integrate those aspects with her duty as Adjunct, then she will survive.

And, though she was indeed a child, as we see in Felisin's reflections on her playing with toy soldiers, recreating battles, there is a maturity, an intention in that play. It warns us that we shouldn't underestimate Tavore. Even in her childhood, real as it was, sought solutions.

"She's made this war personal…*Yes, she would do that. Because it is what she has always done.*" (858) This notion questions her as a commander, as one who should be impersonal but open. Blistig goes on to explain the level of detachment required of a Fist to Gamet. Tavore making things personal is then seen as a weakness, but it also tells us that she takes her goals to heart—they achieve deep meaning for her.

Tavore both takes things personally, and deals with her pain at a deep level of solitude. Discovering that Gamet has died, she once more shows a very brief moment of vulnerability, with Keneb noticing her pallor and a "hand reach down to steady herself" (978) before she dismisses him. T'amber, too, refuses Keneb's suggestion to attend the Adjunct, already aware she would grieve in solitude. Gamet also represented one of the last remaining ties to her old life, her family, and his death leaves her even more alone.

There is therefore a good deal of tragedy in our knowledge that she is killing her own sister when she cuts down Sha'ik. Hearing from Pearl that Felisin is dead also leaves her, to her knowledge, the last of her family alive, indeed Felisin would have been one of the few people with the knowledge that her brother was alive. But now she feels completely alone—but in this state, she is possibly freed to act in ways she may not have otherwise chosen.

The Wickan children's words: "In the dreams that haunted you from the very first night of this march, you saw what we could not see." (991) She has dreamed of chains, of burdens. Though the army is released of its ghosts, one feels Tavore still bears a burden, which is now added to by the knowledge of Felisin's death. Tavore's chains are also the choices she made, with Felisin and no doubt other decisions, and the loss of her own self in service to the role of Adjunct. But the chains are still there to her old life, a possibility foreshadowed by Adjunct Lorn.

The imagery of her dragging ghosts reminds us of Karsa, and it is worth considering whether the ghosts followed, or still follow, Tavore—indeed, whether she drags that burden like the Knight of Chains. And what, then, is her connection to the Crippled God even at this stage of her journey?

The sea rises in Raraku, in answer to Tavore's sword. It is the restoration of balance, life and creation in answer to the death and destruction of the Whirlwind and the history of this desert oasis.

Fiddler / Strings

Fiddler is first seen having undergone a renewal. Not just the change of moniker, but "the rusty hue of his beard in youth had given way now to grey" (270-271). In *Deadhouse Gates* he was acting fatherly, testing the waters of elderhood, but it wasn't conscious, it was instinctive and only happening in glimpses.

The change of name and the outward signs of elderhood suggest a preparedness now. He is reentering the ranks willingly, consciously. He is prepared to assume responsibility. His lieutenant observes: "You're old enough to be the father of most of those marines sitting on the deck behind us." (271-272)

He fathers the army into the world, leads them to their identity, the face they will present to the world. This is the role of the father, archetypally. Where the mother protects the child against the psychic inner forces, the father protects from the social world. He is the model persona. Fiddler's change of name is thus the model of reshaping his persona, played out in the turning of the omen of the bone into a symbol for the army.

His role as father is also played out when in his grief over Whiskeyjack he suggests a course of action to the Wickan youth, Temul. He is confirming the young commander, showing him how to take control of the sniping elders under his command.

"The fire was long dead." (640) Fiddler finds himself riven with doubt, a malaise arising from the knowledge that the army could now do well enough on its own, or so he believes. He questions his own motives in returning to Raraku. "Did I really think I could recapture something in that holy desert? What, exactly? Lost years?" (641)

This refrain is not unlike a parent whose child has flown the nest. He guided Temul's acceptance of the Khundryl, an enacting of the youth's initiation and display to the world. He now feels in a small way that his work is done—in part influenced by the deaths of his friends—but instinct drags him on. Gesler's words cut him: "It's because now you've got a squad, and you're responsible for 'em. *That's* what you don't like, that's what's got you thinking of running." (643) His confirmatory role to date, that he played in *Deadhouse Gates*, for example, and here, has been in passing, a drop of wisdom. Now he has a deeper responsibility, more burdens to shoulder. He must midwife his squad through their birth, and he has to carry that through to completion.

Cotillion

The Patron God of Assassins, a god of Shadow, appears to be having trouble relating to people. Crokus's reflections on Apsalar (the woman Cotillion had possessed) suggest a detachment in the man Cotillion had been. Kalam says: "You need me for something, only you've never learned how to *ask*." (314)

We are circling in on Cotillion in this novel, and understanding for the first time that he is struggling with the revival of his humanity. He offers Cutter his patronage, and when Cutter suggests reciprocity was owed Apsalar, Cotillion says: "Consider this new tact the consequence of difficult lessons." (319) Pressed on regrets, it is apparent that Cotillion is not entirely comfortable with the surrender of humanity that ascendancy had demanded of him, and he intends compensation: "One day, perhaps, you will see for yourself that regrets are as nothing. The value lies in how they are answered." (320) Perhaps it is that he became inflated by unconscious contents when he ascended to godhood.

In the early stages of this story, he is on a recruitment drive: first Kalam, then Cutter, then Lostara Yil, all swept along by his plans.

Cutter's calling of Blind draws Cotillion into the fight on Drift Avalii. After he has got done killing, with Darist and Apsalar lying nearby, "Cotillion's face fell, as if with a sudden, deep sorrow." (533) His apparent sorrow is for both those who have died, and his reminder of his role in Apsalar's life, but also for his being there—his role in the ongoing plans has consequences, and the results weigh on Cotillion's conscience. It has been awakened.

This humanity is apparent when he caresses the dead Hawl after the battle with the Edur. "I made them good at hiding...Good enough to hide even from me, it seems." (659) On its surface, he is talking about his assassins, but he is also talking about his feelings, his humanity. Like the people, like Hawl, however, he is realising that they are not gone. The humanity is coming back.

Jung speaks of the reaction to awareness of unconscious contents, with the extremes being someone who takes that awareness and understanding, and feels able to apply it to everyone else. They have what he terms a 'godlikeness' in their assimilation of contents of the unconscious. This is inflation. A similar example is given by Jung of men (and we should say women) who identify completely with their work, office, or title. It is the adoption of a nature that is actually outside of oneself. This is an over-identification with fantasy, and would result in a weakening of the ego, a crystallisation of the persona.

The counterpoint extreme would be someone who, suddenly exposed to unconscious contents, feels swamped by their power, impotent in the face of powerful forces. This is particularly problematic if one is exposed to the dark nature of the shadow. Such would make one pessimistic, helpless, and despondent, at the whim of nature's darkness.

While these are the extremes of a spectrum, individuation is a balancing function for both. "The aim of individuation is nothing less than to divest the self of the false wrappings of the persona on the one hand and the suggestive power of primordial images on the other."[117]

Personality development is predominantly driven by the need for differentiation and prestige, according to Jung's earlier work. Once a level of prestige is achieved, it becomes valueless as a differentiator from the collective, and one must begin again to develop more personality, lest they become enveloped in the collective. This is another reason titles or status conflated as personhood are unfulfilling, in part because they are infused with too much value, but also in and of themselves don't add significantly to the culture. Also, the collective kills individuality.

Differentiation from the collective is a moral and spiritual issue. When the collective becomes too large, I suspect the desire to differentiate becomes more vital while at the same time more difficult, and this desire can be

---

[117] Jung, C.G., CW7, [269]

leveraged by corporations and ideologues. We think we are escaping conservatism or the parental trap, but it is more an individual instinct for differentiation that is being denied by the size of our collective. When political or corporate actors play on those instincts, and in effect keep you lost by ensuring you all remain the same and there is not real differentiation, then you have a recipe for disaster. Typically the instinct that is frustrated will emerge as shadow projection onto another group.

When morality is gone it is easy to position a group as holding the moral high ground. The collective turns off our individuality and morality, but trains us to repeat the litany of morality. It's hollow, yet insistent. It demands no self-reflection.

Without differentiation, imitation is rewarded. We are under the spell of suggestibility and mental contagion, and this represents a faulty attempt at individuation. We see this in Crokus, in his efforts to imitate Apsalar. He is trying to grow to someone else's tune, to take on their path of individuation. But in doing so, he is avoiding his own shadow.

Cotillion, in his check-in round with his crew, finds Apsalar looking out into the dawn desert. She is reflecting (and we have a rare insight in her point of view, which purposely distances us from Cotillion while giving a new perspective on him) on what the god had left behind in her, and when he appears she tells him she would rather have been left innocent.

"Innocence is only a virtue, lass, when it is temporary. You must pass from it to look back and recognize its unsullied purity." (881) They discuss knowledge, and it becomes a question of what arises first, the growth or the knowledge of it. Innocence is often broken, by a separation or wounding, a soul theft, abandonment. From the outside looking back one can reflect—a theme explored again with Onrack and Trull Sengar. "Changes had come to her." (880) This wording suggests the growth had occurred, and only now is Apsalar able to recognise it, to take from it the knowledge that affirms that growth.

With change, there is often a split, a manifestation of possibility, which allows a path to be chosen. "Knowledge only makes the eyes see what was there all along, Apsalar." (882) Cotillion here speaks of reflection, of synthesising experience with the new stage, the new life, allowing us to understand the past. He is also hinting at his own understanding of what he had lost or left behind with Apsalar.

"We stood in each other's shadow." (882) Some of her is left in him, some humanity, a potential unrealised. He convinces her that Cutter loves her for all of what she is: "Virtues, flaws, limitations, everything." (883) Once again, we can see in this a counter to the Crippled God's focus on flaws—they are part, but not the defining features of a person. Cotillion's argument redeems Crokus for her, and draws her into accepting again the assassin part of herself, which amounts to a sacrifice.

"I like the lad, too" (883) he tells her, which sounds more like a father approving of her choice. "As if he were my own son." (884) There is a tangled skein of projections between these two, and they are not to be unpicked easily, however this conversation feels like Cotillion is finally able to draw close to her, get her to look upon him (at the shadow) and he is consciously attempting to withdraw some of his own projection. In a way, her acceptance of her darker side allows him to reclaim some of his own humanity.

Cotillion, in an unusual way, loves Apsalar, too. He speaks as much for himself as for Cutter. He must love her, because she is part of him now, so to love himself, to show empathy and humanity, to rediscover it, he recognises that love. Love empowers.

Crokus / Cutter

Crokus ponders ascendancy as Apsalar mourns her father: "was it not a mortal's fate, then, to embrace life itself, as one would a lover? Life, with all its fraught, momentary fragility?" (308) He is essentially pondering individuation here. On the contrary, turning away, surrendering to ascendancy, puts everything of life into the shadow.

"He had come, perversely, to know her less and less. Her soul's depths had become unfathomable." (307) On the surface, Crokus is agitated by what he attributes to a darkness between himself and Apsalar. There is trouble connecting and relating, which hearkens back to an anima complex. The dynamic playing out here is of his shadow projection. It is himself that is less and less open and knowable, partly due to his growth and change. What he once was, all his innocence and potential is being bagged up and so he will ascend, in a way, to his new life as Cutter.

It is his own surrender which upsets him, and his response is to harden himself further, make edged his persona.

Cotillion visits Cutter in the night, purportedly seeking Apsalar, but wins Cutter's patronage. This comes with few qualms from Cutter, who appears to be looking for confirmation from a father figure, and an acknowledgment of him as a person he was not going to get from Apsalar. In a curious way, Cotillion could be seen as the masculine aspect of Apsalar, and he needs to build a relationship with that. In a relationship, the anima of a man and the animus of a woman are a substantial part of the dynamic. In that way, the relationship between Apsalar and Cotillion is of crucial importance to Crokus's psychological health.

Cutter is having a crisis of identity (perhaps it is too early in his devotion to Cotillion to have a crisis of faith). He's further distanced from Apsalar—he had hoped Cotillion's attention would bring them closer, bridge their souls. "He'd found himself at subtle war with her, the weapons those of silence and veiled expressions." (434) He doubts his place in the events.

> "This new persona was imposing a certain sense of stricture – he'd thought it would bring him more freedom. But now it was beginning to appear that the truly free one had been Crokus.
>
> Not that freedom ensured happiness. Indeed, to be free was to live in absence. Of responsibilities, of loyalties, of the pressures that expectation imposed." (440)

There is a balance of freedom and responsibility, which we have already explored through Ganoes Paran. They are inextricable: freedom with responsibility, rather than freedom from responsibility. It was a childlike naivete that presumed freedom from burdens in Cutter's former life. The question that arises in Cutter's admission of his persona is whether he is still Crokus at heart, or he has truly left that behind? Is our growth necessarily the adoption of a persona, with its attendant burdens?

Darist, noting Cutter's mourning when he thinks Apsalar has drowned, tells him in truth he mourns for his enjoyment of her company. "Your sorrow is for yourself." (440) This occurs while he considers his previous life, pondering its loss, so in this instance 'yourself' is his old life he mourns. At the same time there is a recognition that he was parting from Apsalar anyway—what he would mourn in her death is what they had before, which was wrapped up in the innocence of his previous life, the looking forward and out with Apsalar. Now he only looks back.

Grief brings into focus the unlived life. Upon his return to Darujhistan in *Toll the Hounds*, this grief for the past will be further explored.

Cutter, in taking up the fight with Darist, believes he is following Rake's example of altruism in fighting for Cutter's own home, Darujhistan, in *Gardens of the Moon*. We can see that the youth is still taking on the attributes of those he admires. We are still waiting to see what he makes of himself, even though to outward appearances he is growing and distinguishing himself.

This is somewhat answered when we see him emerge carrying Apsalar, his path converging on Cotillion. When the god comments on a friend's death, "I thought she was dead," Cutter's shadow bursts through: " 'She is.' Then he snapped his mouth shut. *A damned miserable thing to say*—" (659) He sees the emotional burden on Cotillion, the symbolic and literal ring of corpses, and part of him (the Crokus part, presumably) is still fighting the transition to becoming Cutter, an assassin. Growth never just clicks into place, it is often a chaotic phase, with plenty of back and forth. One must find their way through the uncomfortable parts. "It's not the same! It's not! *We're not*—" (660) Seeing the burden upon Cotillion, Cutter is afraid he won't be able to escape.

Back at sea with Apsalar, he manages to keep his remarks to himself. This could be learning, and it could be a different way of acting towards her than Cotillion. His projections land heavily on Cotillion now, and he has shifted his libido away from her.

"So, Crokus, are you enjoying being the plaything of a god?" (801)

Finally, Apsalar leaves, a withdrawing of the web of projections between them—Crokus, Sorry, Rope, Cutter, Apsalar—and Cotillion charges him with the protection of Felisin Younger. "In your worst moments, think of how Baudin felt." (1010) Erikson is reminding us that Baudin, who we may not have liked, still found in Felisin the possibility of redemption, still found a compassion within him. He fulfilled his duty despite all that he underwent, and whatever lack of appreciation he might have felt.

Once again we see a snide comment from Cutter to his god, and again regret. No surprise that it is in the Temple of Shadow that Cutter must confront this. We often regress after learning, after training ourselves, and after inner work. We might berate ourselves, but it is our nature. Change and growth are messy, they don't lock us into a new state of enlightened perfection. Consciousness must be maintained, else the shadow creeps back into the recesses of the unconscious, from where it can act.

Crokus's story is also one of the young man who continuously falls backwards. His growth entails many backward steps. There is much disillusionment and abandonment, even after he has set himself a goal. Von

Franz said of the shadow: "just like any external person around us, it is a being with whom we must come to terms through—depending on the case—acknowledgment, resistance, or love. It only becomes hostile when it is treated entirely without understanding or is ignored."[118] It can contain elements that are productive, which can be incorporated into conscious life. This is an expansion of the ego, a growth. Not always mere acknowledgment or repression. The Cutter aspect of Crokus is this, the potential to wound, his shadow side, that must also be tempered by maturity and responsibility.

The discernment of what should or shouldn't be incorporated from the shadow is a crucial part of the individuation process. It is the forks on the path where, if one chooses appropriately, he or she can align closer to the ideal self, by choosing that path where meaning in life appears.

The question of Felisin, "What are you to her?" (1010) is the prompting of Cotillion for Cutter to question his place, his responsibility. What burden do you choose to shoulder? By willingly taking a responsibility, a journey undertaken consciously, we allow room for growth, for individuation. Cutter has accepted the burden of his shadow, and now sets forth on the new stage of life.

Lostara Yil

We first see Lostara, recently released from captivity, meeting Pearl. He is an assassin, a man with affectations. She, brusque, cuts through him. She is a killer, too, though her distaste for his profession comes through. When her loyalty is questioned, she stiffens up, there is a tangible change in her, and her loyalty to the empire takes precedence over her loyalty to the Red Blades.

So early here there are unusual signs, suggestive of something unsaid, or merely something unconscious. Her reaction to assassination, and her loyalty to the empire, emerge as though from the unconscious.

As she packs away her Red Blade gear, stripping down her persona, she recalls her history. Abandoned by parents who wanted a son, she spent some years on the streets of Ehrlitan evading temple acolytes who would find such children. Finally she is netted by a priest of Rashan, shadow. Lostara becomes trained as a Shadow Dancer, "a secretive group of men and women for whom

---

[118] Von Franz, 1997, *The Individuation Process*, Insight into the Shadow para. 9.

worship was an elaborate, intricate dance." (387) The shadow of the dancer is what is watched, where the power of the performance lies. Lostara doesn't show great proclivity, it seems. "Her shadow seemed to have a mind of its own and was a recalcitrant, halting partner in the training." (388)

Bidithal was the High Priest of the temple. She remembers the arrival of Delat (Quick Ben) and her performance standing out in his presence. He recognises her desire, its manifestation in her shadow. Repression of desire and sexuality is often attributed to the personal shadow, though it seems Lostara cannot or will not repress it, suggesting she is awakened to her instincts (though she is still a child.) Bidithal, as father, portrays the instinctive and archetypal reaction to repress her performance, to bring her in line.

As she recalls these memories, Dancer/Cotillion visits her. She reaffirms to him her loyalty to the empire, and he recruits her to his as yet unknown plans, putting a deception between her and Pearl.

After their descent in the Imperial Warren and finding the Otataral dragon, Lostara and Pearl emerge in Seven Cities, Pearl carrying the head of a T'lan Imass. She is prodded twice: first by his apparent compassion, after which she is further frustrated by him. Secondly, she notes that her responses to him are cutting more deeply than she first thought: "I asked the question, I should at least let him answer it." (665) This shows Lostara coming to some self-awareness.

Individuation is not something that can be done alone. There needs to be someone or something to reflect you, to project onto, in the same way that we are social beings and cannot discriminate ourselves from the collective completely. Jungian therapists would say this is the value of the therapy, or perhaps a marriage partner. Alone, there is no feedback; development becomes an intellectual exercise. We need to take ourselves out into the world, the real world, to express our instincts, leaving our familiar habits behind. We must ask the questions, and wait for the answers.

Lostara appears to take pleasure in Pearl's suffering, and this may in part be a desire to ground him, to bring him down to something more human in appearance. "She had instead discovered a delicious appeal in flaws." (785) This is somewhat a counterpoint to the Crippled God's notion of flaw as central. In fact, a healthy basis for a relationship of any sort must consider the flaws. Acceptance with flaws, not just in spite of them or imagining them away. A healthy acceptance of imperfection, rather than using it as a rationalisation for suffering. Lostara's attraction is from a strong ego self, rather than low self-esteem.

Lostara's story is one of repressed instinct, perhaps in reaction to that early unconscious expression before Delat. We know her history as a Shadow Dancer, and while she did not step to this role as a calling, it is an expression of a creative aspect of her. That she was not in full control of the wilder aspect of her nature, her shadow responding to her desires, suggests a power and instinctive urge that was not given full expression. It would be fair to say the Shadow Dance was forced upon her, but it revealed something of her—we can only speculate what pleasure she took in it. Her response on escaping the Shadow temple was to join the Red Blades: martial, structured—it is a compensation for her lack of control, a persona compensating for her shadow. Her attraction to Pearl, dusted with pleasure at his pain, threats to kill, and so forth, followed by her almost animal fulfilment of the attraction, also suggests an attempt to repress and rationalise her true feelings, that she was hiding behind formality and structure so as not to lose herself to the wild vagaries of her instinct.

Estés warns that repression of instinct, such as in a creative endeavour (which the Shadow Dance must be), can burst forth with compensatory power:

> "What has erupted from shadow is hard to cap once it has been detonated. Though it would have been far better to have found an integral way to consciously live out one's joy in the creative spirit than to have buried it at all, sometimes a woman is pushed to the wall, and this is the outcome."[119]

The acceptance of Pearl, or her attraction to him, finally reveals itself with a similar release of energy. We could say that Lostara has now attended to her shadow, as she has had Pearl literally walk in it: "But for the moment I'll settle with having you in my shadow." (791). Now she can integrate its contents psychically and symbolically.

Pearl and Lostara's relationship is also a fascinating study of the dynamics of anima and animus clashing: Lostara's firm certainty, Pearl's moods and sentimentality. If we consider the father as the primary animus projection, and recall Lostara was abandoned, then made acolyte in Bidithal's temple, it would be understandable that a negative father complex is affecting her ability to relate, shown by animus possession. There was also a strong projection onto Quick Ben (Delat) that is likely drawing on her libido. Her prickliness wounds Pearl at every turn, draws out of him his wounded anima. She blindsides him symbolically, just as she does literally when she strikes him unconscious.

---

[119] Estés, 1997, p. 254

As the pair confront Tavore following her slaying of Sha'ik, the knowledge that the body in front of Tavore is her sister, Felisin, becomes a weight for Lostara, part of her own shadow that she must carry with her. Just like the chains of blood, a shared burden connects people. She is now a co-conspirator with Pearl, and she draws from him a promise they will reunite.

Despite this final connection, there is an emptiness at the heart of Lostara that has not yet been filled. "Alone?" (989) She can reflect on Tavore's loneliness as the woman walks away. They are alike, for they have both been cut adrift from their family, and both of their stories will entail redemption, a freeing of heart and soul, the creative instinct. They watch the sea rise in Raraku, and Lostara wonders "Why does looking at you break my heart?" (1006) We might answer, because she sees herself reflected in Tavore.

Onrack

Onrack the Broken, a clanless T'lan Imass, is alone, stranded in the Nascent, a fragment of the shattered shadow warren. Here he meets Trull Sengar. His "echoes of curiosity" (322) mark him as unusual among the T'lan Imass: an element of humanity remains. He hasn't surrendered his will and his selfhood to the ritual, to mass consciousness. He doesn't surrender to ennui. "There was always something else to see, after all." (323)

With Trull, under the living statues of the Hounds of Shadow, he ponders the carving out of power:

> "to create an icon of a spirit or a god is to capture its essence within that icon. Even the laying of stones prescribes confinement. Just as a hut can measure out the limits of power for a mortal, so too are spirits and gods sealed into a chosen place of earth or stone or wood…or an object. In this way power is chained, and so becomes manageable.
> …
> Do your Bonecasters also believe that power begins as a thing devoid of shape and thus beyond control? And that to carve out an icon – or to make a circle of stones – actually forces order upon the power?
> …
> Then it must be that we make our own gods and spirits. That belief demands shape, and shaping brings life into being."

(442)

This passage is the crux of the book's eponymous theme. The confinement of the Crippled God's power by limiting it to the Deck's strictures. The construction of the Bonehunters out of shapeless potential. The same for Karsa – wild, barbaric nature tempered by his chains, moulding him into something. He in turn carves out images in the rocks. The Jade statues are also objects invested with power. There is a dialogue not just between freedom and confinement, but of power and belief. The former mirrors the pondering of Crokus. Karsa carves the faces to smash them, driving together these ideas, trapping their essence and unshaping belief.

Erikson here explores the duality of worship and godhood, that the chains work both ways. Elsewhere he delves into the subjugation of groups, of clans and cultures, indeed Trull has just spoken of the captive nature of his own people. But here the notion arises of the subjugation of a god. "The stone has been shaped to encompass them, Trull Sengar. No-one asks the spirit or the god, when the icon is fashioned, if it wishes entrapment." (445)

This precedes Karsa's completion of the carving of his gods, thus bringing them to him in Raraku. In addition, this is what has happened to the Crippled God, as we are aware, being called down to this world for mortal usage. So Erikson is engendering sympathy for non-mortals.

"The renegade kind must be found. They are our...shadows." (554) Onrack's severing of the constrictive chains of culture, through his distinction from the Ritual—that which should and should not be—has allowed him to perceive beyond the norms. That which is repressed is the shadow; those cast out are put in the collective shadow. He has undergone trauma through his wounding, the loss of an arm, "Cheekbone and orbital ridge were both shattered" (550), and now he can see differently. He has opened communication with his unconscious, the shadow. His difference, the initial state of consciousness, made this possible.

Onrack, emerging into his world with Trull, finds his memories awakened to the world as it once was, possibly through the influence of Trull's blood. He recalls his being outcast, how he was fascinated by raw beauty, of a landscape, its inhabitants. This is his curious nature that set him apart. "Art was done in solitude, images fashioned without light, on unseen walls, when the rest of the clan slept in the outer caverns." (670-671) This mirrors the notion of darkness being the preconscious state, before the light of awareness was cast—the birth of consciousness in the collective. It is a metaphor for realisation of the self, the conscious self, as being distinct from the unconscious. Consciousness itself is a two-edged sword; the value of individualism isn't placed above the collective.

"…to separate was to weaken. Where the very breaking of vision into its components – from seeing to observing, from resurrecting memory and reshaping it beyond the eye's reach, onto walls of stone – demanded a fine edged, potentially deadly propensity." (671) The act of perceiving necessitates a perceiver, and thus a differentiation. It is growth of consciousness. At its simplest, fully unconscious, the world simply acts upon us. Each increase in conscious awareness is a growth, further differentiation from the collective.

The state of wonder and awe Onrack's painting elicits in the observer is also symbolic of an enlightenment of consciousness. The painting also reminds us of Onrack's discussion of icons trapping a spirit, but representation also preserves. "I trapped a woman in time." (674) Onos T'oolan, seeing this image of his sister underwent a revelation of consciousness.

According to Neumann, the evolution of culture is mirrored by the evolution of the individual consciousness, and it appears to be that we move from identification with the masses to separation, and thus to spiritual enlightenment: "Myth, art, religion, and language are all symbolic expressions of the creative spirit in man; in them this spirit takes on objective, perceptible form, becoming conscious of itself through man's consciousness of it."[120] Perceiving the self raises consciousness. Just as the child's awareness of itself as a separate entity enlightens consciousness, just as our own 'self-reflection' creates awareness, heightens consciousness.

Representation, in the form of symbol and symbolism, enlightens. When one sees oneself as both symboliser and symbolised, a new level of consciousness is attained. It is a birth, a separation. Erikson is aware that he is both creator and hero. That self-awareness is itself symbolic of growth.

I've deliberately avoided going into depth on authorship and metafiction, a rich set of themes in these books, but this notion of it as a metaphor for raised consciousness is too important to ignore.

> "Whoever speaks in primordial images speaks with a thousand voices; he enthrals and overpowers, while at the same time he lifts the idea he is seeking to express out of the occasional and the transitory into the realm of the ever-enduring. He transmutes our personal destiny into the destiny of mankind,

---

[120] Neumann, 1949, p. 369

> and evokes in us all those beneficent forces that ever and anon have enabled humanity to find a refuge from every peril and to outlive the longest night."[121]

There is safety in the collective, and stepping outside that safety is the separation, the destabilising of culture. There is obviously resistance to that in the Imass. The depiction of Kilava stirs recognition within the unconscious of its own feelings and projections. The art gives the archetype a channel—a symbol—through which it flows, charged, into the consciousness of the culture.

> "He must conquer the ordinary because it represents the power of the old order that constricts him. But conquering normal life—which is the life of the un-heroic—always means sacrificing normal values and so coming into conflict with the collective. If later the hero is honored as a culture-bringer and savior, etc., this is generally only after he has been liquidated by the collective.
> …
> The hero or Great Individual is always and pre-eminently the man with immediate inner experience who, as seer, artist, prophet, or revolutionary, sees, formulates, sets forth, and realizes the new values, the "new images." "[122]

Sacrifice and suffering are inherent in the hero role, Neumann asserts. Indeed, the death of the old, so the new can be reborn, is never without suffering, and it is necessarily a sacrifice. Willing self-sacrifice is essentially heroic.

Neumann further quotes Jung, and the notion that the resonance of great art is in its activation of the archetypes through the creative process.

> "Therein lies the social significance of art: it is constantly at work educating the spirit of the age, conjuring up the forms in which the age is most lacking. The unsatisfied yearning of the artist reaches back to the primordial image in the unconscious which is best fitted to compensate the inadequacy and one-sidedness of the present. The artist seizes on this image, and in raising it from deepest unconsciousness he brings it into relation with conscious values, thereby transforming it until it can be accepted by the minds of his contemporaries according

---

[121] Jung, C.G., CW15 [129]
[122] Neumann, 1949, p. 375

to their powers."[123]

Edinger discusses the 2nd commandment, regarding carved images or likenesses, as proscriptions because such representations are necessarily archetypal:

> "For ancient man the making of an image must have had such a powerful effect on the unconscious that the image immediately became an idol, evoking projection of divine or magical powers. Psychologically, idolatry means the worship of one archetypal aspect or power of the unconscious at the expense of the whole."[124]

The whole, of course, being the greater ideal, as it focuses on the process of individuation. "Evidently the danger of succumbing to the regressive pull of the unconscious is so great at that stage of ego development that fantasy and all the powers of the imagination must be suppressed."[125]

There is also the notion that vested in what is called primitive art is the belief that depiction has an effect on the world. What is visited upon the image will be visited upon the reality. If there is a universality in the depiction, maybe the Imass project the mother onto this image, and if the mother is also the very world you inhabit, it is therefore the highest blasphemy.

This is mere speculation, but how long did civilisation resist image? In a simplified way, we assume that the means and the awareness were the hurdles. It is hard to presume what a culture might have thought by what they didn't do, that which leaves no trace.

Onrack reflects on his similarity to the Unbound: "Like them, I am unburdened. Freed from the Ritual's Vow. This has resulted in a certain…liberation of thought." (780) He was in a way rebirthed in the Tellann fire, his wounds healed as he fused his missing parts with the Unbound, Siballe, destroyed by Karsa. Now, he no longer wants to be freed from existence like the other Imass. There is something fundamental about life, the instinct to carry on. Freed by his initial curiosity, and his ability to think, there is within him an instinct that differentiates him from the

---

[123] Jung, C.G., CW15 [130]
[124] (Edinger, 1986, p. 60)
[125] Ibid., 61

collective. We could read the Ritual as the enactment of cultural bounds, and Onrack's insistent individuality, his wilful refusal to be bound, as in some way heroic.

Onrack calls a halt as they journey with two T'lan Imass in pursuit of the Unbound. This is a simple notion, but it evinces the empathy he has attained for Trull. It shows he is closer to his own humanity. They discuss Trull's story, and Trull says that his understanding was achieved later, after his Shorning. Onrack reflects, "As knowledge flowered before my mind's eye in the wake of the Ritual of Tellann's shattering." (871) This confirms the notion of seeing more clearly as an outsider.

He further explores his perception of Trull as calm and comforting, and realises he has been deceived, that he couldn't see the man's inner wounds. "His heart was incomplete." (872) A telling of a story can reaffirm perceptions, both as glorification and "reaffirmation of our judgement." (872) But when a tale is told such that we might empathise, which is what Trull's telling of *Midnight Tides* aims to achieve in the reader, we are able to have compassion and thus learn. Trull then "prefaces…*everything*" (873) with a discussion of nature's striving for balance. In this way, we are given a frame for understanding all that is to come.

As the Whirlwind Goddess's memories are revealed to us, it comes to light that she was Onrack's mate. Further, that Kilava, with whom Onrack spent a night, was the mother of the humans. This would make Onrack himself at least one of the fathers of the long line of humanity.

Scillara

Scillara rises, cool and numb and forgotten, from Korbolo Dom's cushioned bed. "Advantageous, as well, the rituals her master had inflicted upon her, rituals that eliminated the weakness of pleasure." (727) This is an acolyte of shadow—one of Bidithal's children. Though Scillara is no child. "And life – that time of pain and grief – was but one side of that balance." (728) This woman longs for the end of life's suffering and has been taught that it is a reward for her dutiful work.

Scillara suspects she is pregnant, and feels cold about it. It is a mere practicality. Both the pain she feels, and the hopelessness, along with her dependence on the drug, durhang, leave her adrift. "There had been a time, once, she was fairly certain, when her thoughts had been clear – though, she suspected, most of them had been unpleasant ones. And so there was little reason to miss those days." (830) She has been stripped of meaning, identity almost. She has come to identify and welcome the lack of feeling as an escape from something whose specifics no longer matter.

Estés recalls the folk tale of the Red Shoes, its symbolism for addiction:

> "People who are grabbed and taken away by the red shoes always initially feel that whatever substance it is that they are addicted to is a tremendous savior in one sense or another. Sometimes it gives a sense of fantastic power, or a false sense that they have the energy to stay awake all night, create until dawn, go without eating. Or perhaps it allows them to sleep without fearing demons, or calms their nerves, or helps them not care so deeply about all the things they care so deeply about, or maybe it helps them not want to love and be loved anymore. However, in the end, it only creates, as we see in the tale, a blurred background whirling by so fast that no real life is truly being lived."[126]

Scillara, then, has a similar association to her perceived responsibility to her master, as well as the drug. It is giving her a purpose in exchange for shielding her from a pain she no longer remembers. He life is whirling by, only on a path towards the release of death.

Contemporaneously in the novel, Gamet is undergoing similar desires for flight from his thoughts, seeking death to end his self-judgment. We can also see a reflection here of Sha'ik, whose memories and ability to think are being ever eroded by the influence of the goddess, keeping her from herself. Scillara mirrors Felisin in many ways, and is almost a logical extension of the life of Felisin, had not the Whirlwind Goddess found her.

After killing the guard who would dispose of her, Scillara reflects on her hollow nature.

> "Heavy, and heavier still.
>
> I am a vessel ever filled, yet there's always room for more…Ever filled, yet never filled up. There is no base to this vessel." (833)

With no base, there is no soul. There is nothing underpinning the life left her without pleasure, and so there is no fulfilment. When Heboric rescues her,

---

[126] Estés, 1997, p. 270

and heals her, he says: "it's an odd thing about pleasure. Something Bidithal would have you never know. Its enemy is not pain. No, pain is simply the path taken to indifference. And indifference destroys the soul." (835)

Birkhäuser-Oeri discusses the notion of poison in fairy tales, that it is as much one's reaction to the substance as what is forced upon them. One who has been poisoned has their thoughts and words become hurtful, maternal gestures destructive. "Among women, the ones who have a poisonous influence on other people are particularly those who have failed to achieve some important aim in their lives."[127] This failure to achieve can be by limits imposed on them, not from a failure of character. The poison for Scillara is symbolised by her durhang habit, though in truth is the circumstances she has been raised in, the influence of the father archetype.

She poisons those around her – her animus words – maternal instinct turned to something negative. She spots the faults in others, can barb with insight, but not apply those insights to her own shadow. And tellingly, she doesn't see the redemptive possibility of the child.

Conclusion

Near the end of *House of Chains* we witness L'Oric in a fatherly embrace: "Absurdly – *for a man my age* – he felt at peace. In his father's arms." (983) Balance is achieved, for there is also the nurturing of the father, the comfort of the embrace. We try to escape, but we can also return. "The heart is neither given nor stolen. The heart *surrenders*." (1015)

In addition to the archetypes of father and the shadow, *House of Chains* is about chains and surrender, as counterbalancing notions. Surrender is not necessarily submission; chains are not necessarily confinement.

Karsa Orlong surrenders to his chains, and to the reality of his tribe's history, in order to progress. Cotillion surrendered some of his humanity in the act of ascension. Sacrifice is essential to the birth of the new. Surrender of our hold on the old mentality must occur. On the contrary, when Felisin Younger, helpless before Bidithal, is told she must surrender, there is nothing willing in it—this is a twisted notion of surrender, which merely deadens part of her.

---

[127] Birkhäuser-Oeri, 1988, p. 107

Chains are not mere bindings. We are encumbered with burdens. We can grip that chain and pull. There is a balance inherent in the notion of structure, that some form of binding, of fathering law is necessary to avoid chaos, to avoid society coming apart. Like a ritual, they bind you within a culture, a structure. Breaking those chains is analogous to stepping outside—once outside, we can see with more objectivity. Onrack, shorn from his ritual, sees his fellow T'lan Imass, "what all those who were not T'lan Imass saw." (550) Karsa and Trull, both have perspective on their people, having broken those chains.

Confrontation with the shadow is a type of surrender—a willingness to go down, to surrender our certainty and identification with the persona to the very existence of unconscious depths. That surrender, counterbalanced with strength, allows for safe, wise perception of the unconscious contents.

This book was also a counterbalance to *Deadhouse Gates*. Notions of chains, but a reversal. Not only the re-treading of the Chain of Dogs by Tavore's army, but the drawing together of her and Felisin. *Deadhouse Gates* began with the chained younger sister being sent away; at the end of *House of Chains*, the binding draws them back together in a fierce tug.

Our psychology wants us to individuate, to release and fulfil its potential. There are basic life patterns driven by instinct: attachment to mother, relationship with parents, the social adaptation and differentiation from the parents, finding a partner, reproducing. It is all one story as our body knows and expects it. Even a cliché has some basis in truth. When those instincts are frustrated, then your consciousness is drawn, maybe awakened, and the individuation process has to be attended to. Maybe, while everything is seemingly splendid, there is some sort of deeper potential, something repressed, that you, consciously or not, wish to approach. There's no shortage of shadows, and there's no perfect full totality of meaningful existence. This is to say we don't achieve the end goal by simply allowing the new House in. Growth, individuation, is a constant process. Achieving balance is an eternal struggle when life is riven with many competing tensions.

"It prefaces ... *everything*." (873). Balance, too. This book and those before are the preface to the fulcrum, the midway point of the series.

Civilisation in Transition: Symbols, Innocence, and the Light in the Dark in *Midnight Tides*

Midnight Tides is a book of turning points, the pause before the final descent—or, rather, the brief moments we sit in the discomfort of the unknown or the past, before we begin our ascent towards rebirth. It is a dream, a sojourn into the past, but that idyll always ends, it seems. The outer world cannot help but intrude, material necessity.

This novel is replete with characters lacking agency – those trapped by debt and history, those chained by higher powers and responsibility, those enslaved by their own self-doubt, guilt, indecision. We have already discussed how it is often such fulcrum points, at which there seems to be no correct path, no way out of the funk, in which a light intrudes and individuation begins in earnest.

This book is that held breath.

While the shift in time and setting creates some discomfort in the reader, with the disorientation of a new continent and civilisation, the book also gives us something very familiar in the nature of the Lether economy. It holds up a mirror while offering a rebirth. We return in time to begin again, with just as much chaos, as though to recognise that the first attempt was flawed. More context gives us a stronger foundation.

The tone changes, giving the sense that *Midnight Tides* is a regression into a preconscious state. Symbols are important in both constructing and maintaining culture, and the opening pages are replete with symbolism and superstition.

"Again and again, he shall know death." (34) It is a starting over – we know the shifted setting is told through Trull's story, and he is reevaluating his history as he pieces together the story. The very nature of a psychic rebirth is such that one reevaluates their history, the stories they believed. The Edur are at the mercy of a story that is untrue—when a new story is cruelly mispurposed, it can have ill effects at both an individual and societal scale.

In *Midnight Tides* we are affirming and setting the pattern for the second half, that things repeat, are elliptical, death and rebirth are the eternal cycle.

Udinaas

Udinaas is a fish out of water, a sailor who doesn't like the ocean. He is content, for what it's worth, to be a slave in the Edur village, as compared to being an Indebted, a slave by another name, in Letheras.

He wishes the Edur well in attacking the provocative fleet of ships, but for selfish reasons: the Letherii taking the seals means hunger for him and his fellow slaves. He holds more than a little spite for his own people, or at least for the system under which they labour, slavery by proxy to gold. "Power, status, self-worth and respect – all were commodities that could be purchased by coin. Indeed, debt bound the entire kingdom, defining every relationship, the motivation casting the shadow of every act, every decision." (51) Udinaas understands there is a motive underwritten by greed in the hunting of the seals, and so is able to extrapolate down the line (perhaps by virtue of experience) to who suffers.

We are at the fulcrum point of the series with *Midnight Tides*, so we have the need for balance. Balance can be achieved by a ledger. Gold and debt; slave and master. Udinaas understands that the greed and victory of one necessitates the suffering of another within the Letherii system. As with gold, so with food and hunger.

The Letherii system is founded on the notion that divine favour is deserved, just as failure. This mode of being is fractious, uncompassionate, also unsustainable, because you no longer leverage the wellbeing of the collective, at the detriment to your own ongoing survival and that of your lineage. Or you take that as an end in itself, like a doomsday cult, and that can only be underpinned by hate for humanity, because it deserves its destruction. Inequality is not evidence of injustice, necessarily. As Tehol ponders aloud later, "there resides in all of us the unchallenged belief that the poor and the starving are in some way deserving of their fate." (636) We must be able to disconnect the organising symbol, with its attachment of merit, divinity, morality, and so on. The fallacy that suffering is deserved can only be maintained when underpinned by a cultural myth that we are separate from one another, part of a ledger.

Udinaas wards against the White Crow (which we soon find is itself a tile in the Holds) by drawing a sigil in the sand. This act is seemingly contradictory to the material nature of Letherii, giving a spiritual counterbalance. The Errant is representative of the wild force of nature's whimsy, and the existence or recognition of such a force as foundational to existence remains a presence despite the materiality of Letherii society. It provides an interesting undercurrent of religiosity in the society, but it also perversely provides many in that society with justification for their equating status with gold and divinity.

He is injured when he rescues his love maiden, Feather Witch, from the dragon, "Wyval, spawn of Eleint." (62) Heroically, he had acted on impulse.

Nets on nets, slavery. He thinks there is only freedom in death, sees everything as loss and captivity. But he maintains an identity, a hidden core of self. His holding the Wyval within is a small victory of something hidden, something that the outer slavery cannot see or take away. In fact, his ability to maintain his sense of self is probably the reason the wyval was able to enter him.

Feather Witch, Entropy, and Consciousness

> "the terror of Beginnings, the soul standing before oblivion. A place of such loneliness that despair seemed the only answer. Yet it was also the place where power was thought, and thought flickered through the Abyss bereft of Makers, born from flesh yet to exist – for only the mind could reach back into the past, only its thoughts could dwell there. She was in the time before the worlds, and now must stride forward." (56)

Feather Witch is mentally time-travelling, returning to the pre-embodied state, and here we see the structure of the beginning of the existence of the world. What is proposed is that thought, awareness, existed prior to matter. More appropriately, I think we are dealing with a metaphor for the arising of consciousness from the unconscious. Feather Witch is in the unconscious here, mentally moving back in time, actively playing with it. Before the child exists as an entity separate from parents, with an ego of its own, there is awareness, but it is free-floating. All is one and whole.

Von Franz spoke about the self-regulatory nature of dreams:

> "It is the transcendent function – that is, the symbol-forming spirit – which makes organically possible the transition from a one-sided attitude to a new, more complete one. By symbolically sketching new possibilities of life, it opens up the way for growth. The dream never points exclusively to something known but always to complex data not yet grasped by our ego-consciousness. It points to a meaning we have not yet consciously realized."[128]

Thus, the unconscious presents us with the possibilities for growth, and of making meaning of the world, making sense of it. Perhaps not in that order, but it is there. More concretely, bringing unconscious contents to consciousness opens up possible states, creates options.

The holds and readings represent the unconscious, can be likened to astrology or tarot or dreams or any other psychic spread that might stimulate the symbol-forming nature of the unconscious. Where persistent patterns or stories have arisen, we could presume it is because those symbols and narratives have resonated across time and place.

Time is forward moving, perhaps defined by the increase in entropy – at the least intrinsically connected with it. We evolved in a system bounded by the laws of thermodynamics that determine time as forward moving, so our physiology is likewise bounded by it, our perception of time. But we can mentally (and spiritually?) move across time, backwards and forwards, separating from the conceit of the present.

"Kaschan magic is entropy." (140)

"It's the headlong rush that always troubles me. As if the present is unending." (173)

The body tends towards homeostasis. The less consciousness required to function, the less the brain is required to process, thereby using up less energy. This concords with the concept of entropy. Life and the universe

---

[128] Von Franz, 1998, p. 96

tend towards a resting state, where there are fewer possible states – increasing entropy. But consciousness itself increases possibilities, thus negentropy.

Unconsciousness is preferred for energy conservation. Homeostasis keeps us alive by keeping us physiologically within safe bounds – this happens below our conscious awareness. When something registers outside the thresholds that requires our awareness, heat or cold for example, (discomfort, in short) the conscious mind responds by bringing the state to awareness, with affective valence.[129] So our homeostatic functions are not entropy in themselves, but part of the mechanism of managing it. Consciousness is the threshold. Novelty, challenge, is hard. It is also enlivening.

So at a physiological and affective level, consciousness arises, or is needed, to help the organism maintain homeostasis. In this way, energy is saved, new states can be achieved, new adaptations can occur, thus resisting entropy. This can happen on the scale of moments and on the scale of life stages. Consciousness is therefore adaptive because it helps keep us alive.

But the psyche is not bound by the present as the physiological body is. It can defy time – cast back in time, project into the future – consider possibilities, realise options. This increase in possible states, or state changes arising from psychic activity, along with the decoupling of the psyche from the forward motion of time, could make us consider consciousness, along with the creative faculties of the unconscious presenting us with a constant array of possible thought-states, as in defiance of entropy. It increases life.

The journey of starting at the beginning is one we all take. It mirrors the birth of the world, and it is also a journey that we repeat. Each stage of growth begins a journey anew. Erikson's choice to move back in time to tell this story reveals the cyclical nature of such journeys, and also gifts us the narrative power of travel to times past, to open up the possibilities of interpretation and awareness.

Udinaas (Continued)

Following their injury, Udinaas and Feather Witch commune in the spirit world. While it is new for him, Feather Witch is comfortable here. "We lie side by side, Udinaas, on the blood-soaked earth. Unconscious." (66) She is

---

[129] See Mark Solms, *The Hidden Spring,* (2021)

familiar with the walk in the unconscious. Her power is questioned by the Edur, and she defies them, a confirmation. It also comes to light that the Letherii souls are closed off to Edur magic. What is within them is a life force that is defiant of the nature of repression and stasis.

More, Udinaas is seemingly defying time and place. His unconscious existence is affecting the conscious world.

He dreams of Imass, and Menandore mounts him. Feather Witch arrives in his dream and he insists upon its reality. He encourages himself upon waking to stay the path of his mundane life. "Mend those nets. Weave those strands. *See, I have not lost the meaning of my life.*" (131) He has aroused his consciousness and has been disillusioned to the day-to-day life. He feels an impostor, an outsider because of his contact with the depth of the unconscious world. "Udinaas realized he was among the enemy." (132)

Perhaps drawn by the draconic nature of the wyval within him, a shadow wraith named Wither comes to Udinaas, and tells him that they, the wraiths, are remnants of the betrayed Andii. Memories and truth reside there in the shadow, and this wraith binds itself to Udinaas's real shadow.

"He knew he must hide, only he did not know how." (203) That feeling that he must shelter others from the knowledge of his own explorations, his growth and change, but the unconscious seems to continually intrude, as Udinaas falls into a dream as soon as rest happens. Udinaas has to hide his wounds that carry over, and he told himself he must speak to Feather Witch. But his wounds are revealed at the dinner, and Feather Witch reacts to him with scorn.

Udinaas and Feather Witch represent different ways of holding on to part of themselves while under slavery. She holds on to the culture, which has been transmitted through a score generations, whereas Udinaas holds on to his internal sense of self-worth. He knows he cannot escape the social structure that pervades even the slave population, but his ego is a light he would protect.

"You do not speak as you used to, Udinaas. I no longer know who speaks through you." (269) Udinaas has absorbed the shadow. This book continues the personal journey of integrating parts of the shadow, along with the nature of the archetypal shadow. Udinaas's inner self is now bolstered by the nature of the wyval, as well as the shadow wraith. The strong ego he has maintained is an attractor for other forces.

His saving of Feather Witch has upset their power positions. "Do you think I appreciate owing you my life?" (269) She still lives in the enculturated hierarchical system of the Letherii, and this reversal profoundly affects her.

Udinaas: "You have found yourself…indebted. To me." (269) His heroic sacrifice has embittered and disempowered her. While they speak in their dreams, and Udinaas's fascination with her is plain, he does not leverage this reversal to take advantage of her. He seems content to allow it to play out.

Indeed, he is awaiting recognition:

> "We who are the forgotten, the discounted and the ignored. Why does my heart weep for them? When the path is failure, it is never willingly taken. The fallen. Why does my heart weep for them? Not them but us, for most assuredly I am counted among them. Slaves, serfs, nameless peasants and laborers, the blurred faces in the crowd—just a smear on memory, a scuffling of feet down the side passages of history.
>
> Can one stop, can one turn and force one's eyes to pierce the gloom? And see the fallen? Can one ever see the fallen? And if so, what emotion is born in that moment?" (271)

From recognition, there is empathy, and thus compassion. This is a refrain in the novel. The point was made in *House of Chains*, showing us the broken, telling us the House was sanctified. Now we are seeing a demonstration of why, as we will continue to see throughout the series. If we can assess the self, integrate the shadow, we are able to withdraw projections, to look back, as Udinaas considers it.

The fallen, then, are who an empowered Crippled God can champion—fallen himself, his truth will be revealed once that recognition has been offered to him. In *Midnight Tides*, it is those left behind, the overrun, the forgotten (gods and youngest children), the betrayed, the drowned – these are not so different from the diseased and the disabled, the broken, the burned, and the battered with whom we have already associated the Crippled God. His house has room for these others, and the more we see ourselves in these different guises of loss, pain, and fall, the greater the chance that we might lift ourselves up to a vantage point of compassion.

For Udinaas, it is recognition perhaps not because of his prior station in life, but because of that fiery core of himself that he holds on to, because he demands humanity in spite of being a slave, in spite of being indebted.

When the Sengar brothers arrive back from their quest, Udinaas notes that Rhulad has died and he is indifferent to it. All he knows is that there is work for him. But having sheathed Rhulad's body in coins and wax, we see him instinctively approaching the crying warrior once he has been reborn. We could say that Udinaas became invested in his work, or that partaking of the man's flesh has joined them: "The stench of burnt flesh had painted his lungs, coating the inside of his chest and seeping its insipid poison into his veins." (348) But likely what we see is simply Udinaas's genuine humanity—that gold beneath the wax that he has held onto despite his slavery. He is unable not to comfort Rhulad, pushing through his exhaustion and horror, because the deep vein of compassion within him has recognised a fellow creature sorely used.

> "In the world could be assembled all the manifest symbols to reflect the human spirit, and in subsequent dialogue was found all meaning, every hue and every flavour, rising in legion before the eyes. Leaving to the witness the decision of choosing recognition or choosing denial." (406)

Udinaas here stands on the shoreline (and we pay careful attention to that metaphor) and he is thinking about symbols that arise from the unconscious. Our ability to perceive archetypes as symbols allows us to make sense of them, and to make sense of ourselves in the world. Without a concrete interpretation of the unconscious impulses and feelings, we are compelled without sense or volition. An individuated ego can be in dialogue with the impulses, the symbols acting to transform and release psychic energy, a continued process of raising consciousness. "The creation of such analogies frees instinct and the biological sphere as a whole from the pressure of unconscious contents. Absence of symbolism, however, overloads the sphere of instinct."[130]

The world is replete with images numinous to us, having arisen in connection with our ancestral consciousness. We evolved in those settings, and with cultural influences growing in tandem. The ability to see ourselves reflected in the world—the arising of archetypal symbols—helps create meaning, for it reduces the sway of the unconscious, renders sensible the impulses we feel to be meaningful. It grounds the sense of the outer or divine powers. "Endings and beginnings, the edge of the knowable world." (406) I could be a mere bundle of impulses and reactions, or I can separate the world and myself: past and present, out there and in, conscious and unconscious. A story. Death and life.

But when he realises there will be war, that the world has changed and he couldn't escape into the ocean, Udinaas decides "There was no meaning to be found in lifeless weather, in the pulsing of tides and in the wake of the turning seasons." (437) War has cast all inner meaning aside. The fight is one of survival now. In such a state, the collective unconscious grips us, and we

---

[130] Jung, C.G., CW16 [460]

can no longer differentiate, no longer able to make meaning out of such large, uncontrollable forces. "No meaning to living and dying, either." (437) The insanity, the nature of war, its existence and its results, call all into question.

Just as the Letherii economic ideology stands as a monolith in their society, the power of the coin as a single, reductive symbol carries that weight. With it we may seek to exercise power to achieve numinosity, but it is an empty power. Of course, it is two-sided. "The tyrant was clothed in gold, and the future smelled of blood." (437)

Udinaas witnesses Rhulad's consummation of marriage with Mayen. He stands unseen and unseeing in the shadows. He sees the spark of life reveal itself in Mayen, and it reflects his own holding out of himself despite circumstance. "Had he compassion to feel, he might have understood, and so softened with empathy." (483) He is trying to be disengaged, but he doesn't want to admit that he does have compassion. We have seen it. His very recognition of it in Mayen is the empathy that underpins compassion. Only, he is trying to repress it while he remains detached, feels that is the only way to remain unaffected by the lovers' tragedy.

Udinaas is able to take some control when he sees the doubt and fear in his fellow slaves. "Listen to me. I will tell you a secret. You always like secrets, don't you, Virrick?" (510) Again we can see Udinaas is perceptive, knows how to speak to people. "We slaves have no reason to fear." (510) He takes charge, because the strength is in him, boosted by the wyval blood and Wither's secrets. Now, he has the reflected glory of Rhulad, being the favoured slave. "We need things to return to normal, do you understand? And that task falls to us, the slaves." (510) That sense of control, of confidence, comes from knowing that he holds the spark within himself.

Udinaas oscillates between this strength and doubt. He convinces himself that he is mad, that his whispers aren't real, that he has constructed a fantasy: "Madmen built houses of solid stone. Then circled looking for a way inside." (576) But Feather Witch forces him through the Fire tile into the Refugium. Here he finds his son and the Bentract Imass, confronted with the reality and consequences of his unconscious world.

He had anger, once, he says. Feather Witch begs him to tell: "How? How do you make it go away?" She is filled with despair, hurting. He only looks at her, suggesting that he makes the anger go away through love? Compassion? Perhaps he believes that he has submitted to the despair. "You cannot live like this." (593) Feather Witch senses he has accepted his lot, his helplessness, but in his capacity for compassion there is still hope. He felt guilt at seeing his son, Rud Elalle, and the Imass as they left the refugium, but his grief was for the opportunity he had lost, for fatherhood, for freedom that once was. This mirrors Seren Pedac's guilt once she is made helpless by Buruk's suicide.

The series of passages as the war begins (Chapter 16) is marked by a series of rebirths, a mirror maze of childhood and death. Udinaas and Feather Witch return from the Refugium, where his son resides with the dead Imass. Seren Pedac emerges from the cellar, broken and used, into light and fire, her rapists arriving with the broken corpse of a girl child. She later steps into the sea attempting death, but instead achieves symbolic rebirth. Sandalath's rebirth follows. Rhulad, of course, neck broken, is reborn for the first time since reawakening with the Crippled God's gifts, a child still.

Just prior to Rhulad's death, Udinaas trails the Edur, witnessing the fighting. He can't help offering solace to the dying soldiers left in their wake. This is not guilt driving him, it is something purer. "The apologetic priest, chain-snapped forward step by step, whispering hollow blessings, soft lies, forgiving even as he prayed for someone – something – to forgive him in turn." (609) He gives what he desires—the essence of compassionate attitude. There is no transaction expected, it is given openly.

"Coins had fallen from Rhulad's forehead…" (687) There is the sense that for Udinaas, his indenture is coming to an end as the coins are shed from Rhulad. His investment is becoming detached, and thus he is more free as the symbol falls away from Rhulad.

Udinaas witnesses Hannan Mosag and Mayen in their manipulations of Rhulad, and we connect the scene with his witnessing the sharks and gulls feasting, the Edur hungry for the tainted power they've tasted. Rhulad's attempt to glean truth in Udinaas is waylaid by Wither. "I am unbound, and that has made me useful, for I am proof against compulsion where my kin are not. Can he tell the difference? Evidently he cannot." (692) While these are Wither's words, they apply as much to Udinaas. He is proof against compulsion for the slaves, but also for the Letherii as a whole, and he communicates this nature to Rhulad: "Poor or rich, free or enslaved, we build the same houses in which to live, in which to play out the old dramas." (693)

There is, however, some guilt in Udinaas as he feels his words are manipulating Rhulad, too, the lad's emotions. That he is hiding Wither is a fact, and he understands that Rhulad's emotional connection would result in this being seen as a betrayal. He slows himself as his words reveal truth, insisting that the manipulations come from the poison within him. But in reality it is compassion that halts him—the 'poison' is a projection of his impulse to control, to gain. The same humanity that would protect Feather Witch draws guilt for manipulating Rhulad. That is what Rhulad responds to, what draws him out from the Crippled God's overwhelming power.

"My child." (695) Udinaas then displaces the guilt he felt at leaving Rud Elalle, vowing to stay by the child Rhulad. He is taking the burden of growth, of fatherhood. The burden of a hero is the burden of self-knowledge, knowledge of the Self. This acceptance of burden is a crucial part of the individuation process, and the heroic journey, as a father's responsibility is a continuation of the cosmic cycle.

Udinaas speaks to Hull Beddict about debt and expectation. Hull clears his debt. "I enjoyed speaking with you." (777) He has taught Hull about compassion, in a sense taking the man's burden and allowing him to speak. Then he does the same for Rhulad, absolving him of his grief for drowning a world, assuring him that he expects nothing, and thus winning Rhulad's trust even more.

When the Sengar brothers reunite, it is Udinaas who leads them to Rhulad's tent. He speaks to Trull of what he sees in Rhulad, knowing that Trull too would still hold on to his brother's humanity. "You, all the Edur, you see the sword. Or the gold...I see what it takes from him, what it costs Rhulad...I am his friend. That is all." (788-9)

When the Wyval takes him over on arriving in Letheras, he realises: "A slave. Absolved of all responsibility, nothing more than a tool. / And this, Udinaas knew, was the poison of surrender." (853) Giving over to the possession is both a relaxation, a return to unconsciousness, but an acceptance of slavery. Personal freedom comes at the cost of obligation and the impulse to act. Udinaas has welcomed death on the battlefield, hoping for this release of burdens, but it would not be allowed him. He will awake with bitterness towards Kettle when she has healed him back to life.

Udinaas holds his spark amongst the ashes of his body's existence. Jung, in his autobiography, wrote: "As far as we can discern, the sole purpose of human existence is to kindle a light in the darkness of mere being."[131] Udinaas maintains this spark in the face of his servitude and possession and the expectation that his position has foisted upon him. But he is also the light for Rhulad, and he must balance that expectation with his own growth.

While Udinaas clearly displays the capacity for good, for compassion, and forgiveness, the goal of individuation is the realisation of it first of all, and the integration of it into oneself. That often means forgiving, finding compassion for oneself. Thus, Udinaas's journey is not yet complete.

---

[131] Jung C.G., 1963, p. 358

Seren Pedac

Acquitor Seren Pedac is first met waiting at the top of a hill, looking back down. She is reflective. She is also tired and bent by her work. She is one of a few granted passage into Edur lands – communing with the unconscious, we could say, as the Edur world has a dreamy, ancient quality compared to the wakeful starkness of Lether.

Buruk the merchant has contracted her, "now he owned her. Or, rather, he owned her services as guide and finder – a distinction of which he seemed increasingly unmindful." (70) She shows here her strong ego – she is not inflated to her title or position. Jung used someone who identified as their job as a prime example of that sort of inflation.

> "A very common instance is the humourless way in which many men identify themselves with their business or their titles. The office I hold is certainly my special activity; but it is also a collective factor that has come into existence historically through the cooperation of many people and whose dignity rests solely on collective approval. When, therefore, I identify myself with my office or title, I behave as though I myself were the whole complex of social factors of which that office consists, or as though I were not only the bearer of the office, but also and at the same time the approval of society."[132]

She watches the shadowy figures in obsidian, unaware of the outside world, and heals by touching the stone. But in her soul, there is the grip of meaninglessness, which she initially projects onto those figures:

> "Reflections of ourselves forever trapped in aimless repetition. Forever indistinct, for that is all we can manage when we look upon ourselves, upon our lives. Sensations, memories and experiences, the fetid soil in which thoughts take root. Pale flowers beneath an empty sky." (73)

Hull later reminds her that the path ahead is like the one behind, that we only look ahead. Seren then remonstrates herself for looking back. "I really should stop doing that." (80) So here is a woman who is focused on the past,

---

[132] Jung, C.G., CW7 [227]

longing for the time when she is free of her contract. At this time, she is swimming in a reflection of meaninglessness. But her instinct is striving for freedom—she strains at the head of the wagon train, sees what others do not.

Of her meeting with Hull, an "impending conjoining of broken hearts." (74) She thinks of him as "lost as his flesh and bones." (75) She had "brought him back. At least some of the way." (79) But she corrects herself, thinking it was mere selfishness on her part. This woman is scarred, needs forgiveness.

She is derisive of women's talking, their skein of words. She prefers the company of men. Flight, and silence. She wants to think of herself as pragmatic, to close off the idea of compassion, thinking it weakness and vulnerability. Thinking of the dead Nerek, she wonders at their indifference, and realises that the civilisation cannot afford compassion with its progress. The compassionate would be vulnerable, get left beneath the wheels of the wagon. But in truth, this is rationalisation for the fact that Seren Pedac is stuck.

She wonders if she would save Hull. This is the first indication that she is frozen. In the face of civilisation, an outsourced soul, we forget how to motivate ourselves. It can make us nothing in the sweep of mass-mindedness.

Seren Pedac fought against childhood, wanted to grow up, to prove herself, she tells Hull as she reflects on her childhood. A sort of progress. Watching the Edur children play, unaware of the shadow wraiths about them, she feels a dire resonance. First, there is youth in its beautiful ignorance, unaware of the vagaries of history and the adult world, perhaps reflecting on her own naivete in youth. Then there is the lack of awareness of the true nature of the wraiths.

She speaks to Hull of myths and history, and Seren Pedac believes that "the people live on, and what they carry within them are the seeds of rebirth" (274). She wants to be optimistic of new life, to not be weighed down by history. She wants to distance herself from the mistakes of her people, so that their crimes won't poison her soul. She can't feel she is capable of redemption, for her life has hardened her against her inner self.

Those seeds of rebirth are such as are held by Brys Beddict when he learns the names of the forgotten gods. They are those carried by Tehol by allowing cultures to thrive on the islands. Hull, however, is bitter: "Whatever might be born of that is twisted, weak, a self-mockery." (274) Due to his own influence, he sees no cause for optimism. He speaks of the present, but he longs for the past. Romanticising an unattainable prior state is no more helpful than living purely in the present. His brothers take action, and while Hull is closed to us, it appears he is instead intent on destruction.

Seren is dismissive of the tribes' creation myths. Her notion of rebirth, then, seems predicated on an unseeable future. That she finds herself looking back may well be the pull of that archetypal instinct, the grounding of such myths as she dismisses. It is a hint that what she seeks, which above all is meaning in life, might be found in humble purposes.

She ponders slavery and debt as experienced by the Letherii slaves before speaking to Udinaas. She is unaware that the hierarchies have affixed themselves even within the slave populations. Hers is a mirrored burden to Udinaas's: she is in servitude to Buruk, owned for her services, yet she is free of the daily grind of survival.

Individuation is predicated on a freedom from burdens: a free mind, an evolved consciousness. Free from the burden of parental complexes, the shadow, the engulfing mass consciousness. But also it requires some grounding, in a society, a culture, a history. Debt binds the soul and mind as much as the body. It becomes the way of living. It burdens so that growth is stymied, but such a way of existing also strips the foundation from which a free and healthy mind might advance. A rebirth cannot be considered if one is in freefall; we need ground beneath our feet, even if it is found at the bottom of a descent.

Seren Pedac is at a peak, a turning point, but she must descend before her growth can occur. She must take a similar journey to Brys Beddict, whose descent is meaningful when he ventures into the depths to discover the forgotten gods. If one does not take the descent willingly, it is so often forced upon us by circumstance.

As she awaits the emergence of the Edur after Rhulad's rebirth, Seren Pedac ponders a long term view of existence:

> "She desperately sought out the calm wisdom it promised, the peace that belonged to an extended perspective. With sufficient distance, even a range of mountains could look flat, the valleys between each peak unseen. In the same manner, lives and deaths, mortality's peaks and valleys, could be levelled. Thinking in this way, she felt less inclined to panic." (410)

There is a rationalisation in Seren Pedac, the immobility of one who feels out of control looking for a way to reframe perspective to achieve control. This is done through what she perceives as long term thinking, but is actually just helplessness. Life has ups and downs, just like breathing, like waves upon a shoreline. She wants to mitigate the natural flow and the seeming chaos to achieve balance and stability, but that very impulse for motion is the stuff of life. It appears to be a version of not sweating the small stuff, not being taken in by life's whims, but this is often recognisable as someone not wanting to take responsibility for short term consequences, or stuck unable to act.

It might work, were one able to be the rock in a storm, but if we are merely a blown leaf it is a sign that we are giving over control, it is a surrender of hope. Buruk pins her with his comments, suggesting that what she sees as wisdom is actually despair. "It strikes me you're a sensitive type, Acquitor." (411) Not a rock, then. Though her nature suits her profession. She needs to be perceptive of those small peaks and troughs and shifts in energy.

"Makes you easy to hurt, makes the scars you carry liable to open and weep at the slightest prod." (411) Her assertion of long term thinking is a hope for certainty. Recall, she is standing at a peak but is waiting. She doesn't want to descend. She is therefore at the whim of fate, out of control, and she unconsciously freezes up as a way of asserting some control. We can imagine Buruk understands this all too well, because he too is trapped, not in control, though he escapes with drink rather than hopeful imagining. We often see our flaws in others all too easily.

And Seren Pedac returns in her mind to the notion of words, "Language was war, vaster than any host of swords, spears and sorcery." (412) Here she rationalises her silence, which itself is another form of immobility, and her flight from the company of women. Again, she mirrors Brys Beddict, whose practicality makes him ill-suited to the word games and verbal sparring of the court in Lether.

"There is more in her than she realizes." (428) These prescient thoughts of Udinaas, as he observes the ghosts coming close to her. As she greets Hull returning to the village, they speak of destiny, and Hull further shines insight into Seren Pedac that she refuses or was unaware of. He remarks on "the truth of who you are. You are honourable, in a world that devours honour… I haven't your strength. I could not refashion myself." (489) In Seren Pedac is the potential for a new life, of growth. Her denial of destiny, as "intended to stand in place of ethics, denying all moral context," (489) is her assertion that it is a denial of responsibility. Her own frozenness, her inability to act, is in part fear of this. But her state and the long-term view she tries to take also result in the denial of moral responsibility. She wants others to act, and is relieved when she perceives Hull will no longer be involved.

"It is the best I can do," (489) Hull tells her. He can't be the strong one, to step out on his own. But he believes Seren Pedac can. This is then demonstrated as she speaks against the apprehension of Hull. It seems a small moment relying on Edur law, but for Seren Pedac it is one that required strength.

As they then approach to speak with Rhulad, Hull remarks on her understatement, her "ability to stay level." (492) He perceives a balanced strength in her, in the same way she admires the calm silence of men. "Indecisiveness is generally held to be a flaw, Hull…certainty is the one thing I fear most." (492) Certainty, for Seren Pedac, is too close to destiny. What she wants is decisive action, but not the inevitability of fate. Her need for control has her frozen, in what feels like indecision. Certainty, however, would feel like a lack of control, over her life and fate.

"Destiny." (498) She recalls this notion in her brief exchange with Gerun Eberict, likening the inevitability of the outcomes of the economic system with the lack of control over fate. "Our system appeals to the best and worst within all people" (498). That central symbol, the coin, and the organising notion, debt, homogenises people. It forces us to desire the same things, to want the same unattainable ideal in the myth that we might get ahead. But we only ever stay the same—or, rather, we all lose. But there is destiny, in that there is an inevitability of collapse, to the suffering of those at the bottom. And Seren Pedac doesn't want to be party to the suffering that entails.

Ruin's discussion with Kettle continues the thematic exploration in Seren Pedac, and also tethers her to the child: "proof is achieved by action, and therefore all action – including the act of choosing inaction – is inherently moral. No deed stands outside the moral context." (538) While this is the foundational basis for the Forkrul Assail notion of balance, in itself it speaks to the value of impetus that Seren believes she is lacking. Both she and Trull suffer from inaction, while others like Tehol and Brys choose action in a way that is morally forthright.

Leaving the Edur lands behind, we find Seren Pedac once again waiting atop a peak for Buruk, this time she is hot, weak, though unburdened physically. There is a sense of ending, but she is uncomfortable with going home. We have read a couple of mentions of her estate, a home where she has barely spent any time. The home is the heart and soul, the comforting place. For her to rarely inhabit it is a refusal to look inward. She is searching beyond herself for answers, for action.

She seeks in solitude the freedom from responsibility, not just the unburdening of others' wants. Hearing the spirits in the rock speak of her as a Mistress of a Hold, she thinks of herself as *"Just one more reluctant…lover of solitude…She wanted no new masters over her life. Nor the burden of friendships."* (549) But this is an escape she is not to be allowed, for burdens come in many appearances.

They arrive at the border and she immediately confronts the mages preparing to assault the Edur villages. "There are children—" (553) Hers is a protective instinct, though it is cut short, stymied. Thinking of the deaths of all the Edur, their absence is not an unburdening, rather the unfairness is itself a burden. Similarly, Buruk's suicide, and his revelation of love for her is an unfair burden that she must now carry.

Buruk poisoned her to make her incapable of acting to stop him. This at once recognises her capacity for care, and her ability to stop him, while forcing her to realise she had underestimated her ability to act. He gives her his curse, as she now seeks drunken oblivion. Or she seeks the escape she failed to achieve before. Her helplessness makes her angry because now she truly can't act, and she realises how she could have acted but stopped herself. It is often when our control is taken away from us that we realise what we had, and regret can shift so easily to anger.

"All right." (599) This refrain in the back of her mind as Iron Bars tries to convince her to leave is the voice of her instinct, her conscience, telling her to go with him. But she is still trying to shove it down. Perhaps she feels betrayed by her own instincts, given that they served her poorly before. This can reinforce self-doubt and lead to a spiral of helplessness.

Finally, Seren Pedac steps into the sea to clean herself, an attempted suicide. We recall the notion of the shoreline as "the symbolic transition between the known and the unknown. Between life and death, spirit and mind" (602), and also Udinaas's failed escape into the water, dragged back by the Wyval. This is another rebirth, a painful stinging baptism. It also connects Seren Pedac to Sandalath's rebirth which follows, yet another life given back by the sea.

As they travel further, her wounds weigh on her. She cuts off her hair. She thanks Iron Bars for killing her abusers, but refuses to thank him for saving her. "There was value in pain, if only to remind oneself that one still lived." (700-1) She is immediately accepting that moving beyond pain meant finding pleasure in worse. Iron Bars recognises this desire. "I hurt. But I can make others hurt. Enough so they answer each other leaving…calm." (714) The recognition of the possibility of finding pleasure in others' pain, or not even pleasure but some kind of release, is the same instinct that the Crippled God displays in lashing out.

Seren Pedac regrets her inaction, and her agency has been taken away now causing her lifelong wounds. This leaves her in a place where she no longer knows how to act. She must heal, while also learning again how to exercise her agency. "I know, you're thinking time will bring healing. But you see, Avowed, it's something I keep reliving." (714) The world has forced the fall upon her, her descent into the ocean, but unlike Brys Beddict, it wasn't taken willingly. She must heal as her first step on the ascent.

"Corlo, can you do anything about memories?...Can you take them away?" (753) The mage, Corlo, has been speaking to her about Warrens, and the ability to tap into magic. She wishes for her mind to be convinced that her trauma is forgotten. He argues that she will have an emptiness, a vacuum within. "Besides, the body remembers. You'll react to things you see, smell, taste, and you won't know why. It'll gnaw away at you. Your whole personality will change." (753) Repression of memories to the unconscious can create greater anxiety, with a harder path to access the source of that anxiety. This disconnect is the very definition of neurosis, and it is the psychologist's role to aid one in bridging such gaps and synthesise the discontinuous nature. That is the role Corlo is undertaking here, willingly or not.

"I could make you cry it out," he tells her. Of course, without a physical aspect to the healing, it is merely cognitive therapy, which tends to be woefully inadequate.

> "But you won't fall into the trap of cycling through it over and over again. Release gets addictive, you see. It becomes a fixed behaviour, as destructive as any other. Keep repeating the exercise of grief and it loses meaning, it becomes rote, false, a game of self-delusion, self-indulgence. A way of never getting over anything, ever." (754)

He begins with her, showing her how to reframe—but not just rethinking it, this would be an admission of understanding. A conjunction of the feeling and the thoughts that dance around it. But she must make the journey herself, it has to be earned. If not, there may not be a hole, but it wouldn't strengthen her. Healing creates resilience against future grief and pitfalls.

"You stop the war all in one shot...Regrets, but no self-recrimination, because that's your real enemy." (754) That war, again, is neurosis. If magic is a metaphor—that talent as the ability to make metaphor real—then Seren has the ability to manifest the story, the journey, such that she makes real the concept of her own healing. "Warrens...Forces of nature, proclivities and patterns." (755) They are archetypal, and Seren's instincts are natural talent. The ability to find paths, to see trails, is the notion of arriving at possibilities, of conceiving ways of thinking. She can choose which journey to take, and she chooses to step out of the dark.

Corlo tells her that self-deception was what was keeping her in grief.

"Anything to keep going, right?" (755) That is the very nature she turns to her advantage in healing herself. "She had imposed her own pattern, bereft of nuance, and had viewed her despair as a legitimate response. A conceit of being intelligent, almost preternaturally aware of the multitude of perspectives that was possible in all things. And that had been the trap, all along, the sorcerous incantation called grief…" (756). Not just her post-trauma grief, but that nature made her question and halt in life. Her perceptiveness, her empathy, and sensitivity made seeing others' paths and motives easy, but so much so that she remained passive, aloof from the real world of biology and instinct, her home, so caught up was she in the mind. And for all the wrongs of the world she saw, she internalised the faults. Paralysis results from too much self-criticism.

Her depths conquered, new paths laid in her mind for renewal, Seren Pedac awaits. "The end of one thing brought the birth of another, after all." (920)

Brys Beddict

Where Hull has left civility behind, descending to live in the wilds, and Tehol is up in the clouds (the roof), open to the whimsical air of spirit and inspiration, Brys, the youngest, is a restrained balance of the Beddict brothers. Hull is a "restless ghost" (93) whose presence ever haunts him, and Tehol haunts the whole of Lether.

Like Seren Pedac, he is at the peak looking back. "I believe I stand, here and now, upon the highest reach." (94) Like the book as fulcrum, this is a turning point in the journey, a place of reflection and clear vision. As Quru Kan says, "Clarity ascends…perspective shifts. The world changes." (95) Brys also compares himself to his brothers, who had "ascended their peaks long ago – too early, it turned out – and now slid down their particular paths to dissolution and death." (94) Only, that is one of many journeys. The peak is also the point at which the only way is down—this is symbolic for the Lether economy, and belies the notion of eternal growth. There must be a fall.

Brys Beddict is humble, we see his skill from the words of others, meaning he never reflects or acts with expectation of his own competence. The story then is about what one must do when at a peak. This reflects Seren

Pedac's symbolic peak, from which she is looking back.

Brys is regretful for his brothers, doesn't resent them but is saddened by what he perceives as their demise. However, he is not aware that both of them in their way see clearly by virtue of being outside of the Letherii system. "I wasn't the first to ever make a peak, just the fastest." (105) Tehol shrugs off his victory over the system, aware it is a hollow victory, just a game. Notable, too, is the use of 'peak' to reference a large monetary amount. We can assume that there is no higher goal in that sort of a game—the truer aim would then be to aim for something more spiritually rewarding. Brys is aiming to determine what that might be—service to a higher purpose.

Brys appears forthright, honest with himself and aware of his faults. There is no false modesty in it, for he willingly, if with discomfort, carries the role of King's Champion. He notes and envies Moroch's boldness, for example. This nature and the fact he is "not immune to uncertainty" (96) create the possibility that he will be able to adopt and integrate the nature of his brothers, to create greater wholeness within himself.

As a study of individuation, this is valuable for, as he reflects, Brys is at the peak of his accomplishments in the outer world. There is little more ascent possible when atop a mountain, but such a perspective might reveal the path to a yet higher peak.

Tehol speaks to Brys about their parents, and about how the brothers live out their lives. Each of them has escaped the formality of debt that brought their father to suicide: Hull has escaped to the wild, Brys is beyond need as Champion, and Tehol has played by his own rules. In this way, too, they each live out an aspect of their parents' lives.

Two unseen guards gaze at the back of the King's Champion:

> "They might have wondered at him at that moment, however. The way he stood, as if entirely alone in a large, overwhelming world. Eyes clearly fixed on some inner landscape. Weariness in his shoulders. They might have wondered, but if so it was a brief, ephemeral empathy, quickly replaced by those harder sentiments, envy and admiration." (171)

We briefly step back here from our point of view with Brys Beddict. It is a recognition that he has an inner world, though we are being kept from it, or rather in this case, the writer is allowing him that moment of inner sanctuary, a moment in which to find his self. It is lonely at the top, of mountains and hierarchies, but we leave him to it, as we must, because of that loneliness. We also see here the notion pondered by Seren Pedac, that progress and civilisation leave no room for empathy and compassion.

Tehol is an exploration of the superego—the conscience, if you will, standing above the city and its meddlings, outside the game but playing it. He makes decisions about moral gestures and consequences.[133] Hull is beneath, the id in a Freudian sense, or the instinctual base for Jung, the primal urges, overawed by the games of civilisation. Note, too, the hull of a boat as that which sits partly beneath the surface of the water or the unconscious. Brys, then, is the ego, trying to manage those influences and the parental past, to be something of himself—our stand-in, champion, as we experience the clash of these civilisations.

Tehol could also be seen as persona, aspects of the self constructed through interaction with the world. He is all about appearances—what lies beneath is carefully glamoured by his loquacity and swift logic.

The goal of early development is differentiation of the ego, separation from the influences of the parents and from unconscious control of either the instincts or inflation with the persona. Thus, Brys has a goal to distinguish himself, and we are witness to his efforts to maintain some self while all is in flux about him. His skills are singular, and in that he will find his strength.

For whatever dubious reason, the King's Champion is sent on what seems a mysterious and ill-prepared quest into the depths (of the unconscious) to awaken the Elder god Mael. He finds instead a series of dolmens relating the names and stories of forgotten gods, along with their guardian. After a duel, in which Brys recalls his confidence to allow him to move freely in that world, he aids the guardian with his own blood, and accepts the names of the forgotten gods, assured of his memory and ability to thus keep them alive.

"Stories. So many stories." (248) These gods could be seen as archetypes. To a culture lacking faith, he carries story, heroic and soulful. Memory itself becomes sacred.

He thinks of his application to duelling. "Self-discipline imposed a measure of control over one's fate, which in turn served to diminish the damaging effects of stress…" (375) His focus, his ego control, rules out the intervention of the Errant, or at least minimises it. Consciousness gives some control over the impulses of the unconscious. It is a state of readiness.

His single focus is demonstrated as he is pinballed from Consort to Ceda to Chancellor, at sea in the face of the intrigue, and having just learned of the Ceda's notion of invisible forces in conflict. By choosing to maintain sole focus, he stands outside of the influence of those conflicting forces and impulses.

---

[133] See *A Psychological View of Conscience*, CW10.

Later, as he stands in the Azath grounds, we once again get his practical mind and self-control:

> "A fighter's mind was not in truth emptied during a fight. It was, instead, both coolly detached and mindful. Concentration defined by a structure which was in turn assembled under strict laws of pragmatic necessity. Thus, observational, calculating, and entirely devoid of emotion, even as every sense was awakened." (460)

This is the perceptive detachment of a conscious ego. Brys frames it in the terms of fighting, of that practical necessity, for that is his centring symbol. He is able to perceive what arrives in his mind and not become inflated or emotionally entangled. Though it is misleading to say devoid of emotion, for emotions are at some level the functional prerequisites of conscious interpretation of the world and our sensemaking. Rather, a conscious mind would not be overwhelmed by it, or allow the emotions to rule us unconsciously.

"The past lives on…How do we measure the beginning, the end – for all of us, yesterday was as today and as it will be tomorrow. We are not aware. Or perhaps we are, yet choose – for convenience, for peace of mind – not to see. Not to think." (462) Ruin's speech here stirs up the theme of looping, intertwining time, which reflects both on the scale of the Book of the Fallen, and as a central theme in *Midnight Tides*. We can still be affected by the past. It rises up in us, both in instinct, and at a cultural level. Here, too, is the long time-scale that Seren Pedac wanted to see, recurring at scale. There is no escape from its influences. Ruin's perspective is of such a scale that the days disappear. Seren Pedac thinks she desires escape from that, only she is not long-lived, so in doing so she would forget to live. To choose to be aware, to think, is the raising of consciousness. It is a break from the ease of days finding stability. It is a constant challenge. Yet with it comes something greater, possibility. Brys Beddict maintains the centre, ensures by consciousness he is not fleeing the everyday, and also does not leave himself exposed to the influence of the collective consciousness.

"That which was chained to the earth has twisted the walls of its prison. Beyond recognition. Its poison has spread out and infected the world and all who dwell upon it." (462) In some ways this poison is the acts and words themselves, yet it is also symbolic of our conscious minds having twisted our relationship with the very world that we exist within. We differentiate from identification with the world, see it as a prison, and as a result our relationship with the world has become poisoned. "Your enemy lies in waiting, in your midst. Your enemy hides without need for disguise…it speaks your language, takes your words and uses them against you. It mocks your belief in truths, for it has made itself the arbiter of those truths." (463) The potentiality of our flaws resides within us, and the possibility of it rising to capture our minds – this is the collective unconscious. The Crippled God in some ways represents those words, the twisting of notions of suffering, pain, war, as virtues. This is the game of propaganda (though it is no game in truth, we are suffering under it daily.)

Brys reflects later when considering the impending conflict with the Edur that in defending the King, his greatest fear is to have his agency taken away. "Brys wanted to die honourably, but he was helpless to choose, and that stung." (747) He is able to recognise that while his own centre is strong, to be forced or prevented from acting in accord with that strength leaves one childlike and vulnerable. This mirrors the agency removed from his fellow Letherii, namely Udinaas and Seren Pedac, also Rhulad.

As he awaits the arrival of the Edur, Brys confronts Gerun Eberict and realises the threat to Tehol. Again, he is shackled by his responsibility, obliged to stay and defend the king. "I have no choice in this, Tehol. I'm sorry." (839) However, being honourable and truthful (heroic), clear-sighted, he had set up protection for his brother.

Brys Beddict's tale is one of balance, standing at the peak and having perspective, and maintaining the self in the face of powerful (sometimes conflicting) forces. He mitigates the many buffeting forces by retaining his strong ego.

Rhulad Sengar

Rhulad represents the naïve youth who wants to renew the spirit of his people, the archetypal hero's journey. But his journey is encouraged and co-opted by a poisoned force: the Crippled God in a state of pain and vengeful hatred. The journey then is instructive for what happens when the unconscious is captured by cynical manipulative powers.

"Rhulad seemed unable to keep still, his head turning this way and that, one hand dancing on the pommel of the sword at his hip." (62) He exhibits the energy of desire for battle, he longs to be blooded, a sort of initiation. Trull has already said Rhulad has misjudged him, and against Fear's closed expression he appears here to be seeking outward for examples, guidance, willing to be led.

Jung wrote about the archetype of Wotan in the lead up to the Second World War, and there are some parallels in the Edur. There is a state of readiness in the people, an instinct that is powerful enough to rise despite the civilisation built in defiance of their nature. It is a channel of dried watercourse, into which should enough energy come, the water will once more fill that place:

> "Archetypes are like riverbeds which dry up when the water deserts them, but which it can find again at any time. An archetype is like an old watercourse along which the water of life has flowed for centuries, digging a deep channel for itself. The longer it has flowed in this channel the more likely it is that sooner or later the water will return to its old bed. The life of the individual as a member of society and particularly as part of the State may be regulated like a canal, but the life of nations is a great rushing river which is utterly beyond human control, in the hands of One who has always been stronger than men."[134]

Water that might be enlivened such as by the melting of ice. The Edur soul is raised with the conjoining of the tribes, a symbolic forging of disparate parts, by Hannan Mosag and the power he represents. The Warlock King's shadow wraith is symbolic of the looming shadow of the Edur, the collective unconscious. Personified and solid, the wraith stands behind Hannan Mosag, ready to be the conduit for the unleashing of the Edur's inner savagery.

There is a place of least resistance in the psyche, which the archetype and the man who would fill that place exploits. Jung wrote of the ease of falling into the mindset of not resisting those forces as a type of hysteria:

> "The essence of hysteria is a systematic dissociation, a loosening of the opposites which normally are held firmly together. It may even go to the length of a splitting of the personality, a condition in which quite literally one hand no longer knows what the other is doing. As a rule there is amazing ignorance of the shadow; the hysteric is only aware of his good motives, and when the bad ones can no longer be denied he becomes the unscrupulous Superman and *Herrenmensch* who fancies he is ennobled by the magnitude of his aim.

---

[134] Jung, C.G., *Wotan*, CW10 [395]

> Ignorance of one's other side creates great inner insecurity. One does not really know who one is; one feels inferior somewhere and yet does not wish to know where the inferiority lies, with the result that a new inferiority is added to the original one. This sense of insecurity is the source of the hysteric's prestige psychology, of his need to make an impression, to flaunt his merits and insist on them, of his insatiable thirst for recognition, admiration, adulation, and longing to be loved."[135]

I quote this at length because it speaks so beautifully of Rhulad's character. The immaturity, or lack of consciousness in Rhulad's nature allowed him to be the focus of the archetype (in this case represented by the power of the Crippled God), where it had previously manifested in Hannan Mosag's shadow wraith guardian.

> "In everything, he must win. That is the cliff-edge of his life, the narrow strand he himself fashions, with every slight observed – whether it be real or imagined matters not – every silent moment that, to him, screams scorn upon the vast emptiness of his achievements." (128)

It is a fragile persona, easily slighted. He also has anima projections upon Mayen, we must assume. For all intents and purposes, he is still a child. He is flailing about for independence, yet his society is strict in its rules. Thus he walks in the darkness to achieve what he needs.

Rhulad is wounded by his father's words when Mayen joins the family for dinner. The father complex is here realised. He already strains against the social structure, seeking differentiation. "You have me leashed here in this village and then you mock when I strain." (213) It is a vital comparison to Karsa Orlong in this character. Where Karsa's wilfulness drove him from his village to seek his own glory, the structure maintains a hold of Rhulad. They each are witness to truths of their tribe's history, and each fancies himself the strongest will, without holding the wisdom of his colleagues. Both, of course, come under the eye of the Crippled God. It is interesting to see how their reaction to the world sees their journeys diverge, and eventually converge upon one another.

When travelling to retrieve the sword, Rhulad falls asleep on watch. His reaction to the recriminations of his brothers is heartfelt, and we sense he speaks truthfully, but Trull correctly identifies that Rhulad lacks the sense of

---

[135] Jung, C.G., *After the Catastrophe*, CW10 [424-5]

seriousness in the situation. It is the child in him that speaks in defence, and he feels their disbelief as a betrayal. The stain of this failure would mark him forever forward, before his journey as a man had truly begun. We are reminded of his need to win—this is often a mark of low self-esteem. In Rhulad, it is hidden by bluster, but this failing would shatter that mask, make plain the self-doubting child within.

That child reemerges when Rhulad is reborn the first time from death, crying and grasping for the comfort only the slave, Udinaas, can provide. The one who has not betrayed him. He cradles Rhulad's head in a gesture both too familiar for a slave, and impossible to deny as a gesture of comforting a child.

Just as identification and alienation are the poles of the dynamic between ego and Self, or any other archetype, so the ego interacts with symbols. Edinger discusses this in *Ego and Archetype* and shows the dynamics around symbols are symptomatic of the fundamental lack of meaning in our age. A disconnect has formed with the relation to the unconscious, such that symbols are disconnected from the archetypal foundations from which they arise. Recall that in attempting to define symbols in the Jungian context, we said they arise spontaneously, they are the consciously perceivable manifestations of the archetypes' contact with the conscious ego.

There is a forthright theme in *Midnight Tides*, that of money and the economy, and I want to discuss it at the level of symbol. For this purpose, what we need to know is that the Edur are a kind of pre-modern economy, the Letherii are a sophisticated economy much like our own, with notions of debt and value very formalised. So it is an interesting point that in Rhulad's death he has coins glued to him, before he is reborn and becomes emperor of the Edur. We immediately see when the delegation arrives that the Edur turn the Letherii economic game back on them.

Money, or the coin, is symbolic, and our desire for it is identification with the symbol (rather than the underlying value). Edinger writes:

> "The ego, identified with the symbolic image, becomes its victim, condemned to live out concretely the meaning of the symbol rather than to understand it consciously. To the degree that the ego is identified with the archetypal psyche, the dynamism of the symbol will be seen and experienced only as

an urge to lust or power."[136]

It is necessary to distinguish the collective consciousness and collective unconscious. Jacobi describes how the latter works upon the ego from the depths of the psyche to influence it in specific behavioural directions. The former is rather representative of typical norms, customs and prevailing views in a collective. The unconscious, charged with meaning, magic, and numinosity, manifests the essential nature of humanity, whereas in the collective consciousness symbols are pale copies. But the collective consciousness can seize power, alienating man from his instinctual foundations.

An archetype in the collective consciousness often contains a symbolic nucleus (e.g., a coin). The absolute form of a society in the collective consciousness is individuals deprived of all rights, all meaning. The illusion of freedom, value, and purpose.

> "When the secret contained in it is either made entirely accessible to consciousness and rationalized; or when it has vanished from consciousness...all that remains behind is the husk of the symbol, which then forms part of the collective consciousness. The contents of the collective consciousness are, one could say, empty shells of archetypes, simulacra of those of the collective unconscious, their formal reflection."[137]

Rhulad represents this, the death of the coin. His rebirth cloaked in coinage is the transition of that symbol from collective unconsciousness to collective consciousness, and is the difference in *value* between the two cultures.

> "Only when the collective consciousness and the collective unconscious come into conflict and make a battlefield of our psyche, do we become aware of how hard it is to free our personal individuality, the true core of our personality, from the clutches of these two powers."[138]

Now, obviously these cultures in conflict means Erikson is confronting us with that clash, and the difficulty of individuality in the face of it. It is his hope that at this point our ego has strengthened enough to face this, and its reflection in our own world. Indeed, the same strength was required to confront this destabilisation in the narrative of coming to the Letherii

---

[136] Edinger, 1972
[137] Jacobi, 1925, p. 112
[138] Ibid, p.113

continent.

> "This liberation requires an individual consciousness or ego which is able to differentiate, which has become aware of its limitations and thus knows that it must at all times retain its living bond with the two realms, the collective unconscious and the collective consciousness, if it wishes to maintain the wholeness of the psyche."[139]

"Die, Fear, and claw your way back. Then ask yourself if the journey has not changed you." (417) Fair enough, really. But this statement insinuates strength as well, to achieve something thought impossible, and something spiritually tasking. Finally Rhulad has won, at something. And he then capitalises on his victory, making the Edur kneel, taking Mayen. This too, while shoring up power tactically, is indicative of a fragile personality. When power or victory comes, he is afraid to lose it, afraid it is fleeting, and so makes certain, and takes what he can.

Ruin tells Brys Beddict that Lether is "ruled by greed, a monstrous tyrant lit gold with glory. It cannot be defeated, only annihilated." (464) This is of course foreshadowing Rhulad's rule of the empire, as he physically manifests the symbolic weight and suffering of the gold persona. Rhulad himself is greedy, which arises from his lack of self-confidence or low self-esteem. This nature creates a focus on the persona, which is our ego turned in on itself. That inward gaze shows up as selfishness and greed—lack of ego development means looking for ways to fill the self. And of course, the energy focused on the persona results in complementary energy in the shadow. It is anxiety and self-doubt, Rhulad's inner child looking for ways to compensate for being last, that make him want to win, to dominate, and accumulate.

"I can break the rules that would bind the Edur," he tells Mayen. "The past is dead, Mayen, and it is I who will forge the future." (482) Again we see that glee that the rules might be broken, which is indicative of the negative father complex. Rhulad is the son-hero (bedecked in gold...) escaping from the bindings of the father.

Udinaas reflects on Rhulad's apparent madness and concludes that the man is spiritually damaged by his ordeal, that "The young should not die."

---

[139] Ibid.

(508) The same might be said of symbolic death, the ending of potential. This might be the finality of indebtedness and slavery; indeed, our society presently inducts our young into adulthood under the burden of debt, to great detriment.

Udinaas empathises with Rhulad's loneliness, the control of the god. Rhulad allows Udinaas to speak more honestly than we might expect, and the slave suggests that Rhulad himself is a slave, Indebted. Initially, the emperor agrees, then "We are not the same, slave!" (509) Part of Rhulad refuses the acceptance of debt and weight that come with the god's attention and the Letherii system. (We are reminded of Cutter's denial of Cotillion in *House of Chains*.) But he still wants the comfort of companionship, unable to be vulnerable with anyone else. Udinaas of course recognises Rhulad's plight because he, too, has others within him, shadows whispering in his ear.

"He only whispers advice, helps me choose my words…He but whispers *confidence*." (509) This insistence is obviously hollow, but it confirms that such self-confidence was lacking in Rhulad. The Crippled God is what filled that hole.

Rhulad's story in many ways recreates the biblical fall. He is naïve, as the youngest son, and he seeks knowledge and growth, both in Mayen and in a blooding. "There is deep doctrine in the legend of the Fall; it is the expression of a dim presentiment that the emancipation of ego consciousness was a Luciferian deed. Man's whole history consists from the very beginning in a conflict between his feeling of inferiority and his arrogance."[140] Rhulad's inferiority and arrogance certainly strike us in his pre-death existence. The gift of awareness, of knowledge, then, comes from the Crippled God as Lucifer, though it is, as always, a double-edged sword.

The first half of life is about winning independence. Not just from parents but from what Esther Harding called autoerotic and childish impulses. That succeeding, the individual must be guided by collective mores and attitudes. At midlife, diverse elements may cause conflict. Assimilating conflicts and working through untapped inner potential, spiritual growth, to wholeness, becomes the work.

Freedom from the parents becomes alienation if we are not adapted to the world. A wounded parental image can result in rebellion, allied with

---

[140] Jung, C.G., CW9i [420]

longing for parental love and containment, an idealised image of the parents. Religion, or its symbols, provides a personal and collective container for the archetypes, and aids in the transition without falling into alienation.

Pathological injury can happen from childhood trauma, but it can also be societal, when a myth is disturbed, or religion loses meaning. The energy can be drawn away from, say, a spiritual container into an economic one.

The heroic gains against unconsciousness must be undertaken in each generation, by the individuals in society. A sufficient number of them must experience it and come to their own value, lest the truths instilled by the ancestors degenerate. If custom and myth are treated as just that, and not venerated, they will lose value, and the weight of the unconscious will overrun it – the chaos overtaking the wagon in Dragnipur.

In our world we are taught to have fierce independence, but it often arises out of an inadequate or negative relation to parental archetypes. That is not to say that parents themselves are all inadequate, but more that the social demands of work, along with breakdown of community (drive towards individualism) and the lack of rituals and symbols to act as initiators and containers for projection, create a situation of inadequacy. There is a dissonance between the independence and alienation felt. The search for nurture and containment of parental archetypes, but its wounding and mistrust, alongside the speed of the world's growth and changes challenging the abilities of actual parents to fulfill all that is demanded of them, can only be understood as destabilising for young generations.

At a cultural level, too, we are struggling with the demands of independence, responsibilities, and cause, yet the speed and consequences of our actions, the world-ending capabilities in our hands, has never been more apparent.

We have an instinct for independence, but (economic factors aside) adolescents and young adults are staying within the embrace of the parents longer. What we see is not immaturity, necessarily, but stepping out of that nurturing and protective space with no safety net, just stepping out into the void. The onset of puberty is occurring earlier, which is likely at some level biology being triggered by expectations of earlier responsibility and social demands. Schooling, lack of parental influence, might all trigger an instinctive response. But some combination of the psyche of the adolescent not being ready, and the world not willing to hand over responsibility, while the necessary initiatory rites and processes are no longer there, means the crossing from adolescence to adulthood is coming later.

There is a need to build a container, revive our myths, heal and conjoin our parental archetypes, the masculine and feminine within ourselves and the culture.

Culture, at some level too seems to be prying apart those connections. Culture wars, the relations between men and women, social expectations, belief systems and ideologies, all serving to further the disintegration of individuals and the collective, at the very time when reintegration and deep healing is required. Wounding individuals, disempowering them, leaves them incapable of carrying out their instincts, their responsibilities—and then when a generation is bereft of parental archetypes, their innate need for nurturance, spiritual containment, rules, and maternal sustenance unmet, thrashes about to find something to fulfill its desires. Political, cultural, and social forces are all too willing to embrace these lost children, if only in the name of profit, or perhaps to infuse themselves with some semblance of meaning. We allow ourselves to be embraced, all the while asserting our independence, relaying empty slogans, wondering why we feel so lost.

There are so many symbols and directions available, all vying for our psychic energy, and as a result the collective unconscious is fragmented. Collective power and the containing ability of religious symbols is lost. How can we rebuild or revivify a container without it becoming a cynical, hollow impersonation? When every individual is being schooled that they are the all and the containing self, if only they market themselves right?

Our social and economic systems bear the inherent promise that we don't need any of those containing symbols and myths. What need for safety when you can purchase insurance? A system that sells unconsciousness does not, finally, remove the instincts within us, it merely stamps down or redirects them. Our society promises security, but security comes at the price of loneliness and isolation.

Rhulad is a symbolic and literal manifestation of the Edur abandoning their ideology and going in for something new. He is both broken and sheathed in gold—his outer layers resembling an unholy marriage between the ideologies of the Crippled God and the Letherii materialism. Jung frequently discussed the 'spiritual poverty' of the west that had abandoned Christianity, and at the time was looking to the East for spirituality to fill the hole in the unconscious:

> "Shall we be able to put on, like a new suit of clothes, ready-made symbols grown on foreign soil, saturated with foreign

blood, spoken in a foreign tongue, nourished by a foreign culture, interwoven with foreign history, and so resemble a beggar who wraps himself in kingly raiment, a king who disguises himself as a beggar? No doubt this is possible. Or is there something in ourselves that commands us to go in for no mummeries, but perhaps even to sew our garment ourselves?"[141]

The notion the Crippled God sells Rhulad, that he might shape the new empire in his own reflection, is a lie, or at least a twisted truth as is that god's wont. But the instinct it appeals to is a real one. Rhulad is aware of the descent of the Edur myths, their desacralisation, and so a new operating myth is needed. Symbols rush in to fill that space, it is a powerful vacuum in the collective and individual psyche. Symbols, of course, which have arisen in foreign places from the same instinctive base, the collective unconscious, which accounts for their attraction. But a fulfilling myth is earned, built from the ground up, so to speak, and adopting wholesale another culture's myths will ill fit.

"Choose, woman? I choose nothing." (801) Almost everyone in this book is bound. Slaves, debt, paralysis, agency taken away, all in service to some greater ideal. Indeed, as Udinaas later asks Trull Sengar: "Tell me, when have any of us last had any meaningful choices?" (829)

Udinaas tries to calm Rhulad's urge to lash out following the next battle: "you see clear and true, for that is the terrible gift of pain." (829) His words placate the Crippled God as much as they do Rhulad. For it is true that one's vision may be sharp, but it comes from being hypersensitive to threat. Living with pain makes us expect it. In pain, we need to learn to protect ourselves against outside forces, and those that would take our power. However, Udinaas is not able to take away that pain.

And when Udinaas himself is taken away by the Wyval, there is no defence against madness. "Rhulad's head snapped up, features ravaged with hurt, a dark fire in his eyes." (863) Udinaas kept Rhulad's sanity intact, or rather contained his pain and made him feel less alone. Without it, the pain must lash out.

Finally, Rhulad is alone once again. His adolescence was interrupted by his death, and he failed to break away from the family unit, shackled by a father complex. For all his prowess and promise, his ego is weak, and therefore his inability to break away, to differentiate from the father and the family, will continue to affect him. He is ensnared by the Crippled God, a

---

[141] Jung, C.G., CW9i [27]

kind of cynical societal father figure that takes advantage of him, and he also latches on, childlike, to Udinaas as a caring figure, as much father as friend. And his brothers distance themselves from him. Rhulad had called his agemates his brothers, those who followed, and we recall the scene of Trull's Shorning, who might be those brothers at Rhulad's side, for it was not Fear and unlikely to be Binadas?

The child, unable to be initiated into the social world by a father, will latch on to the peer group, seeking in them the confirmation that the family would not provide. This isn't necessarily because of an abusive or absent father, and in Rhulad we can see that it is the admixture of his personality and his culture which creates a clash. Rhulad seeks victory in his peer group as a compensation for his lack of self-worth. His death means that he never effectively escapes his childhood, and this foreshadows his continual attempts at rebirth, and the theme of *Reaper's Gale*.

Awe and the Coin

The instinct for story can be a healthy outlet for energy. We could see the sun as a hero, but materialism hijacks the sense of wonder. A materialist, rational mindset means we know the sun is not a hero-god riding his fiery chariot across the sky and disappearing into the deep dark of the Great Mother each night before emerging again, thankfully, in the morning. We know the world is spinning.

But there is a way to learn and embody this knowledge in a constructive way. The world isn't *just* spinning. Perhaps our children should be taught that the world is spinning, *and* careering round a huge nuclear ball of fire, which is itself hurtling through space at untold speeds, and we are just part of a vanishingly thin web of fortunate existence that has, at least until now, by chance or design, not been cruelly smote by a passing chunk of rock.

Adapt the tale as you will. But that narrative should leave space for wonder and awe. If the notion of a sun-hero is in fact an anticipation, the archetype within our collective unconscious, for that very numinosity and gratitude, that such wonder and respect in turn conveys some survival value on us as a species through our respect for life and the planet, and one another, then perhaps it is worthy of consideration. If indeed there is such an anticipation in our genome, then to broadly dismiss such a phenomenon as merely the globe's spin effectively frustrates our instinct. Where does that energy then go? Does it turn in on us and reinforce a sense of helplessness and hopelessness, a spiritual sickness?

The solution is not to fall down and worship the sun each morning (though it wouldn't hurt – in fact, some sort of ritual, with gratitude, consciously directed, would likely have enormous individual benefits) but to be conscious of the imbalance. Energy flows, the world moves, but conscious application of energy can mitigate collapse coming about through neglect.

Nor should we hide the rational, factual knowledge, for learning and growth are themselves instinctual and inherently rewarding. But knowledge and understanding could instead bring new directions, bring deeper and entirely new experiences of awe, inviting yet higher levels of spiritual growth and satisfaction, rather than deadening that instinct.

Some or all of that energy, that instinctive drive, will squeeze out from beneath the cruel calloused palm of our enlightened materialism. Jung, in describing the energistic repression of the enlightenment's rejection of the gods:

> "The devaluation and repression of so powerful a function as the religious function naturally have serious consequences for the psychology of the individual. The unconscious is prodigiously strengthened by this reflux of libido, and, through its archaic collective contents, begins to exercise a powerful influence on the conscious mind."[142]

If not channelled or redirected consciously, a vessel then accepting that energy as a replacement will be invested with incredible power.

Into the coin, then, goes the spiritual energy, the libido, that could otherwise be directed into personal or spiritual growth (note here the particularly virulent nature of self-improvement industries that promote financial wellbeing.) At a collective level, economic growth is the container for what could be spiritual growth – the latter, if attended to, possibly mitigating the externalities of our extractive, disruptive 'lifestyles'.

In youth we are still in touch with the sense of wonder. When we enter adulthood (in modern parlance, the workforce) to become responsible members of the community (taxable entities), we take on the burden of responsibility, for ourselves and family, as well as the community. Lacking a ritual initiation, something of that is lost. But more, with the unconscious power of the coin, our economic systems, the assumption of responsibility is

---

[142] Jung, C.G., CW7 [150]

equated with servitude to that system, the assumption of debt. The narrative is also hijacked so that it is hard to question the chains of economic slavery, debt slavery, because instinctively we expected burdens at this time. Obviously, the narrative sneaks into our schooling and our media, to prime its narrative power and expectation.

And so there is a dual effect – there is the natural anticipation of burdens and responsibilities and value for community, and this has some (most?) of its energy leeched away by the economic narrative, so community, family, the collective as a whole suffers. And the burdens, the chains anticipated by the heroic youth turn out to be greater than our psychology or biology anticipated, which has health effects of the individual, the weight sapping our ability to express the totality of our instincts for growth.

Of course, this is before any consideration of the physical effects of the economy on the world, and whatever interactive effect that might have on our physical and psychological health, and that of our communities.

This is not to propose a replacement ideology, merely to illustrate that there is an imbalance. And to describe how such an imbalance might affect the individual through the transfer of psychic energy from instinct into a collective symbol, such as the coin.

Trull Sengar

This is his story, in some manner. He relates his tale to Onrack, and at least the parts where he is present are his telling. Trull is the one who questions the status quo. We already know he ends up Shorn and shackled by his brothers, so every act and word is loaded with dramatic irony, we as readers weigh it closely, but we must also remember that Trull is the storyteller here.

He sees a white owl, and a white crow. He is bothered by Rhulad's behaviour towards Mayen, Fear's betrothed. Fear tells him to teach Rhulad, to guide him. To teach by his actions, rather than expecting the rest of the world to be true and just. Jung recognised the power of the individual, as part of the collective, to be the vehicle for change in the world.

Trull is himself the fulcrum, that which balances the story, which weighs and achieves balance in the telling. "I am pleased you found in my actions a fulcrum by which you could shift the sentiments of the council." (64)

Even in their tribal warfare, the Edur rarely kill. Although the notion of internecine conflict comes loaded with ideas of tribal savagery, there was clearly a structure and polity to such things among the Edur. This way of acting out conflict may have allowed release of the unconscious feelings, without the destructiveness of the soul that death dealing brings.

Now, bound together in their flawed manner under the rule of Hannan Mosag, the Edur are gagging for the chance to unleash those energies, as seen by the quickness with which they would exact vengeance upon the poaching Letherii ships, and the eagerness of the youth such as Rhulad.

Hannan's gesture of using magic to down the ships has a strong effect on the Edur. In part, it is a successful measure to divert the martial energy of the collective, channelling it elsewhere, so the manipulation of energy that is the magic itself is a potent metaphor. The chastising effect also suggests that the Edur are for the first time aware of the true underlying power they represent. It is the shadow surging to consciousness.

Jung, in the shadows of the Second World War, wrote that with advances in technology "no one has stopped to consider that neither morally nor psychologically is he in any way adapted to such changes."[143] The thunderous power of the collective shadow, and the tools at its disposal, far outrun the glacial development of the individual and evolution.

And on a smaller scale, when we expand, colonise, or imperialise other cultures, we do not consider if they want the magical technological progress we bring. This is not to presume an answer, but the question is rarely asked. The question of the effects on the soul of a people is never asked, or if it is, it is wrapped up in rationalisations of development (arguably modern parlance for 'civilising'), and the empowering effects of democracy.

Progress presumes we are at the pinnacle, that it's always forward and up. Building roads and schools and hospitals sounds good, but if it results in dependence on oil, pollution, and the loss of traditional ways of knowing, then how can we presume to understand fully the effects? Again, the answer is not always and not necessarily that we stand back and do nothing because lack of progress is inherently 'pure' and better. But our way of understanding, our egocentric view of progress, precludes the right questions.

Trull, as he stands guard before the dead, sheathed warrior, is immobile. He is weighing his duty up against his suspicions about Rhulad. Indecision can be a failing, but there is no good answer, and were he to follow Rhulad there would be no good outcome—a realisation of his suspicions, or guilt if they turn out to be unfounded. Rhulad later tells him he is "too filled with doubt, brother. It binds you in place—" (135) Such a situation requires us

---

[143] Jung, C.G., CW10, [442]

often to sit with such a tension, it is a time of humbling. For Trull, it is not long before the apparition of the Betrayer, Silchas Ruin, appears. He is thus stripped of his illusions, his fear of the dark disabused. It is not a dream, he tells himself, he is awakened to reality. Now that he is seeing in the dark, his illusions begin to break down. This is further reinforced when he is led down to the place of their dead god's skull, and his notions of mythology are grounded.

It is interesting further to note that the ghost of the Betrayer appears before Trull, just as it had Seren Pedac, when their trust in one close to them is shaken, a suspicion of betrayal.

Trull has a secret, and he is uncomfortable with the revelations. He has learned of the Edur's history, and of the women's knowledge. The women, too, represent a kind of archetypal shadow, with their knowledge, their relation to history carried through time.

Upon their travels, the brothers find a frozen tableau of the past. Trull is traveling through pockets of time, sorcerous perhaps. He finds his doubts about the past further reinforced, cracks in the ground of his convictions. He dreams, coming into his desire, to sexual maturity. We are told the Edur arrive late to their maturity, we presume instead focusing on martial prowess and practicality. Trull's awakening is occurring along with his worldview, a separation, what we might consider adolescent problems.

These travels are a step out of sacred time, into profane time, as Eliade would describe it. Sexual union takes place in profane time, the eternal present of the myth makes profane time possible. Trull is outside of time, delving into his history, going into the ice wastes, bathing in the eternal present of sexual release.

Upon waking, he is angry at Rhulad for falling asleep, and this flows into guilt as he begins to doubt even his recent doubts. This upsets his foundations when he is already questioning his world. He has entered a time of chaos, a time out of time. His goal must be to reestablish a sensible foundation of life, to bring order to the chaos.

His ordeal, running nights through the blizzard, killing wolves and Jheck, is a curious moment. He believed he had died, and perhaps he did. They went through a pocket of time. A hardness thus builds about him, numb to the killing just as his hands were numb to the weapon he wielded.

He reflects later on his ordeal as he awaits the sheathing of Rhulad. His mind protected him from the horror and the death he inflicted, a suppression. This makes a curious comparison to the preservation of memory and story we explore in the novel. That a culture, a god, a myth, might be made of memory, but life and history is as much made of forgetting. Note how Rhulad's future would have been marked by his failing.

Perhaps Trull has forgotten the bad parts—the instinct to repress what we find discomfiting in ourselves—while the others would have the comforting tale of his leading the Jheck away from them bravely. Just as Fear insisted on remembering Rhulad's heroism, thus ending the questions. They travelled, after all, on the ice that had preserved the truth belying the grandiose notions of their cultural history.

Trull aims to live to a truth, a higher value. He is eventually sacrificed for his culture as we know, but his aims are heroic.

In the moments before Rhulad's sheathing, Trull waits alone and considers their situation. He is convinced that they are at the precipice of disaster. "And he could not move." (342) Paralysis is a theme, it appears, but it is not of inaction. It is the fulcrum point, the peak, the moment before momentum takes us over into a descent.

"The world had not crumbled, it had shattered…Like a crazed mosaic, slowly being reassembled by a madman's hand." (433) This image is an ever-present theme in the book. It is also the cracks and flaws in our beliefs and alliances. The pieced together sword, the cracks in the ice, the shattered warren of Shadow, the cracks in the wax sheathing Rhulad as he's rolled over.

The cracks continue to show in the relationship between Fear and Trull, as they all attempt to make sense of Rhulad's rise. Fear recognises Trull's ordeal in the ice wastes, or at least the accepted interpretation of it: "You saved us all when we returned from the ice wastes…" (507) This reaffirms both Trull's place in Edur society, and the confirmation of the narrative as opposed to Trull's knowledge of it. It is notable that at this point, Fear continues to go along with the accepted notion that Rhulad is emperor, despite their prior knowledge. "I seem to recall you shared our mother's doubts—" (506) Trull now calls back to the very traditions that he previously questioned. Almost as if playing devil's advocate. It is not necessarily that he is ever doubtful, or wilfully negative, but he plays an important balancing role by holding accepted notions to account.

His first confrontation with Seren Pedac ends unsatisfactorily. "Is there no room left, Trull Sengar?" (511) While he is considering the heart, she might be speaking of dissent. Trull considers himself a coward, for not opening up to her and her obvious invitation. She saw through him, or at least understood his helplessness.

Trull continues to question his nature as the army marches, and his doubting is called out by Fear and others. "No-one wanted to listen.

Independent thought had been relinquished, with appalling eagerness, it seemed to him, and in its place had risen a stolid resolve to question nothing. Worse, Trull found he could not help himself." (566) This attitude is by no means limited to times of war, but more generally could be attributed to identification with the collective. Certainly, this can be heightened by a figurehead. "...he was becoming as reactionary as they were, driven into extreme opposition...There was nothing of value in such opposed positions of thought." (566) Except perhaps his conscience, his soul. There can be strength in it. We wish him to be more circumspect, too, but his actions are those we would all wish to take and most of us would fail.

These lines of thought are akin to the opposition disguised as balance evinced by the Forkrul Assail. And, for the same reasons, mere counterargument achieves nothing. Synthesis is required, and will not arrive as long as we are entrenched in extremes.

"You will be silent!" (658) Fear's confronting of Trull confirms the notion that Trull is the shadow, or perhaps the conscience of the Edur, which has been relegated to shadow. It is that part which they do not want to confront. He admits his doubts, but at the same time asserting his loyalty—along with blood relations, this makes him impossible to dismiss out of hand. "Like a child, Fear placed his hands over his ears and turned away." (660) This childlike gesture is a clear refusal to hear Trull's arguments. His countering of the notion of the indestructibility of the emperor with "Our brother is doomed to die countless deaths," (660) further shows that his contrariness is grounded in humanity, which increases the cognitive dissonance Fear feels.

Like Udinaas, Trull still has the challenge of applying and assimilating those truths to himself as well.

Trull's sorrow at the battle is answered with his desire to have the demon, Lilac, healed. His rage boils over and he strikes a woman who refuses. Fear's rage, too, tips over and he tries to strike down Trull, incapable of admitting to the doubts and uncertainty that Trull seemingly holds with steady ego. "The Tiste Edur have changed. But I haven't." (771) It is not conservatism that holds Trull Sengar in place, resisting progress. It is him being strong in his self. Thus the split he feels between himself and his family (his people) is a necessary separation of the self-aware ego.

Trull continues to act with what his people consider honour. His refusal to kill Canarth in a duel returns for us some of the honour he lost in striking the woman, and for his naivete. In the throne room, it is Trull's thrown spear that kills the Ceda, saving his people yet again, with a weapon symbolic of barbed precision, like his words.

For all this, he is still taken away and Shorn, betrayed. When truths are uncomfortable, it is seen as a betrayal of the pleasant ignorance a people would choose.

Differentiation and Integration: Balance, Opposition, and Consciousness

> "To achieve peace, destruction is delivered. To give the gift of freedom, one promises eternal imprisonment. Adjudication obviates the need for justice. This is a studied, deliberate embrace of diametric opposition. It is a belief in balance, a belief asserted with the conviction of religion. But in this case, the proof of a god's power lies not in the cause but in the effect...the most morally perfect act is the one taken in opposition to what has occurred before." (537-8)

Ruin describes the nature of the Forkrul Assail to Kettle, as they descend into an underground chamber. There is reversal of perspective. Jungian psychology is intimate with the notions of opposites, and individuation is promoted by some as the integration of our opposites – whether it be the masculine and feminine, or personality types, like extraversion and introversion, or thinking and feeling aspects of our nature.

Opposition is not the only way to find balance. Indeed, the very application of such a notion in the self-certainty of the Forkrul Assail is a demonstration of that oversimplification. The attraction of it, too, is demonstrated in the Crippled God's twisting of words and notions.

In some cases, such as where an extreme exists, application of the opposite might be beneficial, if only to give some impetus for change. But consider that no stable balanced state ever truly exists, rather in life we are constantly affecting the underlying forces that move us along the lever of psychic reality. In other words, we don't merely want balance, we just don't want stasis, whether at an extreme or sitting flush on the fulcrum.

It is difficult to find an analogy, because our psychic state, our personality traits, have no real analogue. They are uniquely hard to grasp, and any abstraction necessarily deprives them of meaning. That said, if we consider ourselves along a continuum, pictured as a lever, then the Forkrul Assail notion of balance is to place a negating counterweight on the opposite end. This is simplistic, and indeed, they found that the most effective result was death or destruction, lifelessness. But we can be moved along that continuum. Change is possible, not just opposition. The difficulty is in finding a metaphor for that functioning at a layer of remove. Instead of feeling more, for example, we must work on those aspects of ourselves that allow us to feel. Instead of adding an opposing amount of introversion to our personality, we might challenge ourselves to seek energy within.

Trull Sengar was described as a fulcrum, because his psychic activity allowed for the possibility of balance. We could consider him not as the balancing force itself, but as the medium through which the action of balancing could be carried out. His questioning is not itself a counterweight, but the opening up of possibility.

So with motion. Instead of stopping, we slow down. Instead of instantly being slower, we must decelerate. To increase velocity, we must accelerate. In mathematics, these relationships are defined by integration and differentiation, terms that are used liberally in psychology, and in this book so far. To stretch a metaphor, then, we must clarify that if we have velocity, we can differentiate the function to determine acceleration, or we can integrate to find displacement and therefore position. Differentiation, then, gives us the rate of change, and integration gives us locatable position, something knowable. It solidifies.

By differentiating ourselves psychically, we are in a sense looking at change because we are separating from the known. By integrating, we are solidifying, and finding ourselves in a new position. It is not necessarily for balance, but for finding where we are, in psychic space.

To feel more, we need to act upon the derivative of our feeling function, in order to then integrate the ability to feel more. This is the process of psychic growth and change. Instead of putting a weight on the opposite end of the scale, we can learn to shift the weight, to shift the scale, even. We train ourselves on how to think, how to exact force upon our psychic state. This increases awareness (consciousness) and the ability to perceive and modify the self, to most effectively find greater balance.

So is awareness, consciousness, the derivative of psychic activity? Consciousness affects time, certainly our perception of it, so is consciousness a fifth dimension? Or should it be conceived as its own evolving state, with greater consciousness moving up a spectrum towards transcendence? And if so, where are its limits?

The Crippled God and Forging

> Pockets of shadow folded in on themselves. Like forged metal. (131)

Seren Pedac speaks of Hull Beddict: "He would drive them to war, if he could. But destruction yielded only strife, and his dream of finding peace within his soul in the blood and ashes of slaughter filled her with pity for the man. She could not, however, let that blind her to the danger he presented." (148) Rightfully, he is hurt, and yet empathy shouldn't be naïve. Lashing out in vengeance only continues past wounds, grows them. We need balance. Compassion, yet the ability to call out when something is wrong. Compassion doesn't mean laying open one's throat.

When Rhulad first appears to the Crippled God, he assails the youth with his disappointment at Hannan Mosag's desire for peace. He insists that it is peace itself that is fundamentally destructive and misled, for all the words and notions are hollow, and it results inevitably in decadence. In *Memories of Ice*, we saw how the Crippled God's values latch on to a thread of truth but misapply the cause. Here again we can question the assertion that peace is the cause of conflict and moral decay, because the Crippled God is misdirecting the level of analysis.

"Peace, my young warrior, is born of relief, endured in exhaustion, and dies with false remembrance." (329) We have elsewhere encountered the notion of nature constantly being at war. Here the god conflates such conflict with the grand exemplary act of large-scale destructive warfare. He asserts that peace, stability, is but a momentary breath before the true state of pain and conflict continues on. Rather, peace should be seen as the goal, much as the nature of the world strives towards balance.

Peace, we might argue, comes with balance. War is necessitated by imbalance. The hollow words and decadence the god decries are the result of imbalance arising during a time of peace, not caused by the peace itself. Rather than war being the true state and peace being the cause of moral decay, war or conflict is a violent response and attempt to reassert a state of balance. This doesn't make it noble, and it doesn't make it inevitable, but rather it could be seen as a split, a neurosis, that occurs when insufficient attention is paid to the state of imbalance—within society, and the self.

By failing to consider the underlying balance, the Crippled God falls prey to misinterpretations, or perhaps these are intentional reworkings of the truth in an aim to leverage human flaws. Perhaps it is human nature to see at too shallow a level of analysis, and thus a god or other ideologue might capitalise on that blindness. Withal seems to appreciate this cynicism when the Crippled God asks him if the words and qualities of warfare affect him: "when I hear them used to raise a people once more to war." (330)

As Ruin and Brys Beddict witness the calling down of the Crippled God, Ruin says, "In its own realm, it was locked in a war. For there were rival gods. Temptations…" (461-2) This memory, the temptation that may have ensnared the god and caused him to be pulled to this realm, may be his anchor to his home realm. Thus, his notions of war as the normal state. Without it he would retain nothing of his home.

"The god is fallen. He crouches now, seeding devastation. Rise and fall, rise and fall, and with each renewal the guiding spirit is less, weaker, more tightly chained to a vision bereft of hope." (464) Again, there is the theme of the series – recursion, round and round. The processes and impulses of life's ups and downs, fall and ascent. Each time around another chance, if you will, to accept the self, to grow and become more whole. To find meaning. We are witnessing in these words the chance for the Crippled God.

That guiding spirit might well be our life's energies fading away as entropy grows on our own scale and on that of the grander cosmic dance. We can hold it back some with consciousness, by sheltering our life spark. With each renewal of ourselves we have less in reserve—for example in adolescence we are replete with growth and expansion energy, but by midlife we might find it fading. We can look within, as Jung exhorts us, for the possibility of individuation. That tightening chain is the past and the conventional paths of life being cleaved to ever more strongly. As life progresses we feel less able to break away, though the impulse to grow never truly abates.

"Yet hope exists. Seek for it…in the one who stands at your side, from the stranger upon the other side of the street. Be brave enough to endeavour to cross that street…Hope persists, and its voice is compassion, and honest doubt." (464) To open ourselves, to experience the other with empathy first and foremost, we will find and guard hope, and compassion. The chance to grow, to take the ascent of rebirth.

"Suffering made manifest, consumed by the desire to spread the misery of its own existence into the world, into all the worlds. Misery and false escape, pain and mindless surrender. *All of a piece.*" (612) Withal continues to provide challenge to the Crippled God's belief system "This god lies." (614) And here in a final assertion, "The more pain you deliver to others, god, the more shall be visited upon you. You sow your own misery, because of that whatever sympathy you might rightly receive is swept away." (623-4)

We can choose to act out with pain. We may be in pain and it can come out as causing pain to others, but Withal is suggesting the conscious choice is met with some cosmic justice.

By now, there's not much to speak well of the Crippled God. There are characters within the Book who are hidden, from whom judgment is withheld, but Erikson is holding this god up as an example. What might be the solution? Not blind balance, for that notion has already been dismissed.

For now the series takes a step back, into the notions of birth and rebirth. We move into another transition, across the water and back into the dark so we may ascend once more.

> "Shorelines were places of worship the world over. ... The verge between sea and land marked the manifestation of the symbolic transition between the known and the unknown. Between life and death, spirit and mind, between an unlimited host of elements and forces contrary yet locked together. Lives were given to the seas, treasures were flung into their depths. And, upon the waters themselves, ships and their crews were dragged into the deep time and again." (602)

Conclusion

> The world has drawn breath ... and now breathes once more. As steady as ever, as unbroken in rhythm as the tides. (919)

Adapted to the world, conscious, in touch with the ability to relate, the shadow confronted, and the parental images consciously appreciated, we are able to go now back to the beginning. To this point, the task of life has been to piece together something out of the aspects of oneself. Now it is about synthesising, making whole.

Without an organising factor, a Self, a central image, we are at the mercy of chaos. The second half of life allows us the opportunity to reassess the preceding stages, build upon them and reintegrate them such that a totality may be achieved.

The impulse for individuation is a gathering of diffuse parts of the inner life to a unity. *Midnight Tides* shows how infusing this gathering with flaws, or attempting to paste over them, dooms them to failure. The nachts know this. Rhulad dies and lives again because there is something fundamental lacking—he has to keep attempting the journey because it is not bringing him to fullness. There is weakness in the foundations – the Tolls, the weak wing of the eternal domicile. Like the Tower of Babel, ascent without conscious integration of the life before invites failure. The Crippled God represents the strain of weakness, the poisoned inner being who capitalises on the flaws where unconsciousness prevails, to hinder growth.

Midnight Tides is just as much about empty vessels: The empty Hold, Kettle, the Fifth wing and the empty palace. There is no firm foundation. Shadow is at work, and it is a collective, archetypal shadow in the Edur. The Crippled God is a symbol of the poison within the shadow. There is a sense of meaninglessness—the hollowness of symbols, the retreading of old paths, the meaninglessness in Seren Pedac, trading one slavery, one emperor, for another.

A home is needed for the soul. This novel is replete with people lost and far from home. Building the nest, Seren's empty estate, the Edur villages burned and left behind or even their original retreat from their realm. Withal's small world needs to be filled with soul: "The nest was empty. The nest needed tearing apart. Rebuilding." (629)

Rise and fall, rise and fall. Each fold in the forging, each death and rebirth, each rebuilding makes the person stronger. And so we go round and round, we do not shy from the journey.

This novel is a confirmation of what came before, as well as preparation for the cycle to follow, the birth anew. I've always struggled with the integration of the journey across ten books, particularly at this inflection point. In some ways it is a reversal of the first half, in others a repetition. From the beginning with a birth in chaos, through differentiation of the individual from the collective, the relating functions of the anima and animus, and relation to the mother and father, to recognition of the shadow, there is a lifetime's work. But now it begins again.

The growth now, however, begins to take place on a higher level. An ascent has already occurred, yet we continually find ourselves born anew—and this very theme is played out over and over in different ways across the second half of the Book. We could perhaps consider the first half of the series to describe the broader conditions of humanity, the collective, from which we must both differentiate and integrate the unconscious components so that the second half, the work of the adult, can begin. For Jung, the second half of life constituted the real work of individuation, for in the first half we are driven almost entirely by patterned behaviour, instinct. We relate to our caregivers, we grow to propagate the species. In that case, we could consider the second movement of the Book, the descent, to reflect the spiritual work of the midlife and beyond. This also represents Jung's place in the pantheon of psychodynamics. Its history began with Janet and Freud and the base instincts, through Adler's relation work, thence to Jung's spiritual opera.

So from the first book, there was explosion. The question of a blank slate or a chain of existence. Mothers and fathers, the ability to relate. Now we are gathering the pieces together in some semblance of narrative, from which stability we can launch forth.

The accumulation phase is completed, the growth of the first half, and now the descent in the second half of life can begin, wherein the strengthening of the soul side occurs.

We are making a nest, so that birth can happen.

We are the Fallen: Birth and Renewal in *The Bonehunters*

We return, then, to birth. But not birth necessarily from a chaotic nothingness, rather birth of a symbol, the Self, an organising centre about which the individuating self can revolve to assimilate the old and new.

This birth is a rebirth, an opportunity to explore such themes with fresh eyes. It is a birth, not from nothing, but out of a conscious descent into darkness. It is, therefore, the beginning of an ascent. A new self, forged in the fire of life experience. No longer a naïve unconscious ego, but a conscious construction of the self as a container, a vessel on the ocean of life.

It may feel like chaos, this rebirth, when the grip we had on the structures that until now gave our life purpose are lost. Undertaken consciously, this rebirth entails sacrifice of the old life, the ego that has been constructed until now.

"There is no linear evolution; there is only circumambulation of the self. Uniform development exists, at most, only at the beginning; later everything points towards the centre."[144] *The Bonehunters* opens with spiderwebs, the first notion of weaving within the book. Along with the symbolism of the protective mother in spiders, it must be noted that the spider typically builds its web from the outside in, beginning with the frame and spiralling ever inward towards the centre. Similarly, the Book of the Fallen has developed a frame of family and home, its collective and the mother and father, an exploration of sisters, of brothers, of building the nest, so that we might undertake this journey inward, beginning with pregnancy and birth.

I see individuation as the full unravelling across the lifespan, and though

---

[144] Jung C.G., 1963, p. 222

there is relatively more similarity in the early stages of life, and many forks in the road have been chosen by life's second half, the full narrative is part of an underpinning instinct across the lifespan. The later builds upon earlier development. And thus the development and processes of early consciousness and separation from the parents for example is not only the unfolding of instinct, but essential for the individuation process, and also analogous to the overall process in miniature. (The same way each stage of life could be conceived as a hero's journey, and therefore the whole of life as a series of journeys. But with a little more nuance.)

Repetition affirms an archetype. By enacting the cosmic play we help to create and recreate it. It creates the world. Thus events that are seen to be repeating, even reversing, are simply part of a rebirth. With the return to rebirth and its themes, we are acting out the beginning much like a ritual of a new year. We mark time, purge the old, and thus allow time to continue its forward march.

Crossing the ocean, the transition from Bridgeburners to Bonehunters, is part of the core of this story. We are shifting to the lower realms now, our journey deepening.

> "The ship goes over the waters of the unconscious. We know that water generally is a symbol of the collective unconscious, therefore the ship has always had the meaning of being something that keeps you afloat and makes it possible for you not to drown in the unconscious. Any philosophy, religious teaching or cultural tradition is such a thing, like a ship that protects us. If we were to go into the unconscious unprepared, we would drown."[145]

The Bonehunters weaves together a series of images revolving around femininity, the maternal, and fertility, in a way that builds upon what we saw earlier with *Memories of Ice*. The moon hovers symbolically over the events of this book, its cycle and its fall and rebirth presaging a renewal. Lunar myths provide coherent theories of death, resurrection, fertility and regeneration, initiation, and so on. Death of the individual, periodic death of humanity is necessary for renewal. The three days of darkness, the seed entombed in the ground, flood, conflagration, all represent the conditions for rebirth.

Eliade places our consciousness of the moon's phases at the centre of much of our self-awareness and our own rhythms, individual and cosmic. Its place at the centre of much of our mythology demonstrates the depth of its

---

[145] Von Franz, 1999, p. 34

symbolism.

> "It was lunar symbolism that enabled man to relate and connect such heterogeneous things as: birth, becoming, death, and resurrection; the waters, plants, woman, fecundity, and immortality; the cosmic darkness, prenatal existence, and life after death, followed by a rebirth of lunar type ("light coming out of darkness"); weaving, the symbol of the "thread of life," fate, temporality, and death; and yet others. In general most of the ideas of cycle, dualism, polarity, opposition, conflict, but also of reconciliation of contraries, of coincidentia oppositeorum, were either discovered or clarified by virtue of lunar symbolism."[146]

The moon is a central symbol in *The Bonehunters*, along with its associations which are as varied and entangled as a spun web. Birth and rebirth are commonly associated to the moon, as it waxes and wanes in the night sky, numinous to us even today. Moon gods and goddesses were associated with fertility, a symbolism cruelly twisted in the plague that swells the bellies of the Seven Cities people.

The prologue of *The Bonehunters* offers us the rebirth of the T'rollbarahl. The rebirth of the moon is from the darkness of the new moon. We also know the myth of Osiris, represented by the moon, who was pieced together from fourteen parts, much like the fourteenth army is reborn in this novel from its disparate survivors of the conflagration in Y'Ghatan.

Scillara

Pregnant, Scillara is a central symbol in this book. She exudes feminine energy through birth and pregnancy, and all the while her own rebirth awaits, or the chance at it at least. She also takes the projections of Cutter, his own lack of purpose fusing with a mother and anima complex.

Greyfrog doesn't speak to her, which suggests her instinct, or her ability to listen internally, is stymied. She is uncertain about the meaning of her pregnancy, reminding us how young she must be. She is still a child in a sense, and thus will inevitably reject the child to save her own possibility of growth.

---

[146] Eliade, 1959, p. 156

Another option, of course, would have been to accept the burden and so grow as a result. There is also part of her that knows she will not love it, she is filled with too much resentment.

Perhaps Scillara's pregnancy could be considered a variation of the virgin birth. Virgin can be read as a quality, or simply translated as unmarried. Heboric uses the healing power of the god upon her, and in doing so quickens her womb, so in that sense there is something holy in it. Greyfrog calls her a "goddess-human." (217) The moon goddesses from various cultures are represented as virgin mothers and bringers of fertility.

She has already surrendered to her fate, just as she surrendered to Korbolo Dom and the men in *House of Chains*, and just as she is willing to surrender to the outlaw men that arrive in the camp, before Greyfrog defends the women's honour. "I can do this. Just like it was before." (110)

Scillara sees a mirror of her trajectory in Felisin, both in the adoption of the drug, and in their physical shape. Felisin is becoming smaller, "I feel more and more like a child. Smaller, ever smaller." (190) She is retreating into herself, while Scillara is becoming bigger. In a way, this could be read as an unconscious adoption of a mothering role, which Felisin is reinforcing by projecting it on to Scillara through her own regression.

"There was something diabolical about this whole pregnancy thing." (212) Where *Memories of Ice* was more focused on the process of motherhood and childhood, in *The Bonehunters* we are turning back to the experience and the process of birth and rebirth, down in the chthonic swamp. "The misery lay in the bearing, in carrying this growing weight, in its secret demands on her reserves." (213) Scillara attempts to give us a cynical viewpoint, but she cannot deny the pleasant sensations, the relaxed mindset she achieves, even while knowing it is her own biology at odds with her rational ego.

Only the body's needs matter, the pregnancy grounding and focusing her, condensing meaning to the singular and the present. As Heboric explains the games of the gods, she can't take interest, knowing they are beyond the everyday reality. "The rules of mortal flesh were all that mattered, the need to breathe, to eat, drink, to find warmth in the cold of night." (267) The cycle of life and death, inescapable, pales into insignificance, or so she thinks – and therefore can dismiss the unborn relationship to her child. Where Karsa Orlong sees a salve in the daily needs and ritual, Scillara sees the shackles of mortal futility.

As their journey with Heboric continues, Scillara continues her litany of complaints about pregnancy. In doing so, she spurns Felisin's worship of her as a mother figure, as elemental feminine. Heboric asserts that her situation is beyond her control: "We each fall into our lives and that's that. Some choices we make, but most are made for us." (548) While this may match her feeling about her pregnancy, it is useful to note that she is exerting control, particularly in her sway over Cutter's attention and the admiration and mimicry of Felisin.

Scillara notices that they are walking old roads, past civilisations, but she sees no rebirth, only death. This mirrors her mentality that she sees only pain and suffering in the pregnancy. If she cannot believe in rebirth, in hope for herself, she can't find that hope for redemption in others. Until now, she hasn't believed it for herself, her situation dominating her life—and that might have been the very gift of Heboric's healing, the chance for finding redemption in herself.

Just before the attack, she ponders the nature of Bidithal's, and thus the Crippled God's, promised paradise. "The numbness within him had made him capable of delivering pain." (575) There is something revealing here—it is not necessarily hurt that causes us to lash out, but becoming used to it, and that makes us, the hurt ones, lose our empathy and compassion. From there, it is but a simple step to not blanche at causing pain. We might even justify it. "This was, she realized, exquisite enslavement: a faith whose central tenet was unprovable. There would be no killing this faith." (575) But perhaps its killing is not the way, the seeking of redress and balance, for that only leads to further loss of sensation. By approaching it with compassion, we might elicit in turn the feeling that makes empathy possible.

They walk into a place of death, "These wetlands died suddenly, in the season of nesting." (576) This of course foreshadows her own impending death during pregnancy. This journey takes place in the same chapter as Mappo awakening from his own web-cocoon, and Paran's journey through the underworld.

She also comments on the deeply rutted road from parent to child. There is a fatalism there, commenting on the inescapability of the path ahead. And then they must go through a basin containing death and ghosts, their path unavoidable, and it leads to their ambushing and death. This is a sudden, fateful descent into the realm of death. There is something of a ritual in the death of this party, the notion of fertility arising out of the burying of the seed and its rebirth from darkness. For Scillara, she needed to undergo a rebirth. And of course, Scillara's baby has now been twice saved.

She immediately disowns the child, at least mentally. Though she fulfils her initial biological role. Along with her and Cutter's healing, we have a sense of birth in Greyfrog, as a smaller version of him is extruded from his corpse (along with Scillara's ability to hear him in her mind now.) And Felisin Younger undergoes a kind of rebirth, as Sha'ik of the apocalypse, this time through the Crippled God's envisioning.

"She had wondered, briefly, if the absence of regret or sorrow…was truly indicative of some essential lack of morality in her soul, some kind of flaw…" (787) Though her abandonment of the child is not really an inversion, because it was expected, it runs against the trope of reluctant mother falling into instant deep love for a child. Indeed, that is the role of biology, and Scillara has reminded us of biological trickery throughout her pregnancy. She is rather taking a stand for her own life—she is already convinced that the negatives of her life would run through her child as well. This way, at least, she grants the possibility of a life for the child and herself. Already, she finds the idea of new adventures in Darujhistan appealing. At a more basic level, the child reminded her of her old life, what was taken from her, and this then is a clean break, a rebirth for herself as much as the child.

As she offers comfort to Cutter, Barathol makes a curious comparison as she exhales smoke: "some demons breathe fire." (910) She no longer represents something numinous as she did in her pregnancy. She is a mother in truth, and is could be said that her attention to Cutter is at times patronising. Though being the 'dragon' side of the mother allows Cutter to fulfil a heroic return to the mother.

Scillara also retains her sense of realism. "Yes, it's a hard thing to take, for anyone. The fact that we're insignificant, irrelevant." (913) Like her detachment from the child, this is not fatalism, but the result of living through the hard knocks. This gives her control over her life—within limited parameters, of course, but that is all that is necessary to undertake the individuation process. "We're the ones who…put things back together… *reassert the normal world.*" (914) Indeed, this is what she aims to do for Cutter.

Chaur's fascination with the sea reminds us here of child and mother. He weeps at contact with the numinous beauty of the water. On the boat, Scillara notes the excitement for Chaur and his laughter. "…blessed music. So unexpected, and in its innocence, so needed …" (915)

Apsalar

Apsalar's journey in this book begins with her sheathed in dust. She washes the dust from her face, the mask, her recent past. She arrives at an inn, and drinks presumably to forget, but the sight of a youngster at the bar recalls Crokus to her mind. She is accosted as she retires upstairs, and her knife speaks for her. "The woman studied the knife in her hand, wondering where it had come from, and whose blood now gleamed from it." (48) She doesn't know who she is, nor does she feel in control of her own actions.

"There was nothing in her – nothing that she could see – worth the overwhelming gift of love." (55) Crokus had believed in the good in her – a compassion, a gift, one that she must learn, and to do that she must see the worthiness in herself. "Cotillion had understood. The god had seen clearly into the depths of this mortal darkness, as clearly as had Apsalar." (55) Only, she misunderstands: Cotillion did see something in her, and he has empathy for her, regret. He doesn't see her as a loss, a tool.

Telorast and Curdle attach themselves to her, dual shadows. They will be the eyes for us as Apsalar attempts to remain hidden.

She is fighting for selfhood, trying to claim defiance where she could. "I was possessed once, but no longer. I still serve, but as it suits me, not them." (77) Despite her insistence that she is just an assassin, "It is simple. It should be simple," (129) her humanity is creeping in: "No more of this weakness ... this ... uncertainty." (130) There is a further moment of humanity when Apsalar is speaking with Cotillion, and recognises it in him. "She reached up with one hand and brushed the line of his jaw, the gesture close to a caress. She caught the sudden intake of his breath, the slight widening of his eyes, but he would not look at her." (131) While what we see is predominantly Cotillion's reaction, we are also seeing a necessary separation for Apsalar. She is searching for her self, her identity, "I'm tired. Of who I am, Cotillion." (131) It is necessary first to differentiate oneself from the identification with the world, ego identification, becoming distinguished as a separate personality. Her reflection of herself in Cotillion and the rejection of what is symbolically self-love, allows that differentiation for her.

An interesting passage occurs beginning with "Four leagues north of Ehrlitan, Apsalar stood facing the sea." (250) That threshold place, between conscious and unconscious, and a place of rebirth. Apsalar is still undergoing the process of differentiating herself from her past lives. She has recently visited Urko who, while having her drugged and immobilised, comments: "The legacy haunts you – you're feeling trapped, caged in." (208) She is here about to venture out despite the promises made to Cotillion, feeling the need "To cast her dagger, to affect, as best she could, a host of destinies." (252)

The passage also begins with Telorast and Curdle noticing Apsalar's menstruation. The etymology of menses is connected with the moon in many cultures. Women are considered taboo during this time, and frequently undergo seclusion, not dissimilar to the disconnection Apsalar undergoes by descending into the shadow realm. Esther Harding notes that similar taboos of setting apart are often observed for birthing women, with the idea of secluding and to "exercise the greatest caution in their contact with the outside world."[147] It is worth raising, if only to affix the image of the moon in our minds, to keep us aligned to the notion of lunar cycles. Rebirth is a connected motif that is commonly ascribed to the cyclical swelling and endarkening of the moon across its month.

There is much in this section of the book about embodiment. Apsalar in general provides an ongoing study in the notion of how our psyche is affected by the memories of our body, in her prior possession by Cotillion. This affects her personality, and her destiny, though she is trying hard to shape that herself.

We saw earlier Mappo's reflection on the stones that buried Jaghut children. He senses the crimes lingering in that place. "Dolomite was said to hold memories…the hauntings in these places was a palpable thing." (98) However, Mappo concludes that the stone itself only holds the brief memory of the heat of the sun, quickly cooled. Scillara, too, reflects on the actions of her body playing out beneath her awareness, despite all her conscious intention.

Apsalar travels the Shadow warren and considers the Edur forest around her:

> "…their presence lingered, but only in the same manner as memories clung to graveyards, tombs and barrows. Old dreams snarled and fading in the grasses, in the twist of wood and the crystal latticework of stone. Lost whispers in the winds that ever wandered across such death-laden places." (255)

Erikson is telling us that we exist in deep time, in buried places. Can we truly be born from nothing if so much is embodied in physical matter, so much instinct unravelling to guide our minds and hearts? All birth, then, is a rebirth.

This, while she has descended beneath the ocean, that ancient womb, walking a shadow forest at the same time. She is in a deep place before birth

---

[147] Harding, 1935, p. 59

here. And she sees a rope, an invitation, and climbs, ascending to greet Ganoes Paran. He mentions Darujhistan, and the memory that arises from her body, the unconscious, startles her: "Whatever confidence she felt she had gained since her time there was crumbling away, assailed by a swarm of disconnected, chaotic memories. Blood, blood on her hands, again and again." (257-8) The image of blood calls back to her menstruation.

She is returning to her pre-Apsalar state, before that part of her was born and matured. We are seeing that despite the nature of rebirth, the prior state still exists at some level within the person. Our past can't be undone, only integrated. The more Apsalar tries to forget (or have her memory taken) or push down the past, the more likely it is to erupt from the unconscious, much like a repressed shadow.

Here we have two characters who have undergone rebirths, both in *Gardens of the Moon* and since. Paran later reflects on their meeting, "he wondered if she would complete her journey, to come out the other end, reborn one more time." (455)

Another interpretation of Apsalar's emergence from the water is of an ascent from the depths, that breaking of the waters signalling a birth. Thus her meeting with Paran elicits the birth, or rebirth, of some part of her, a more human part, similar to what she experienced on her first brush with Crokus in *Gardens of the Moon*. Here, there is a contrast with that novel, where her first encounter with Paran signalled her low point: her assassination of the man came about when her humanity and free will were almost absent.

She rejoins her old squadmates in the aftermath of Y'Ghatan, not dispelling their tension about her. But then she does the shadow dance and holds up the Hounds of Shadow to allow Quick Ben's escape. What is this, if not her asserting her power in the face of the Shadow that once possessed her? Though in the aftermath she explains nothing to Kalam, as though welcoming his wrath. "What she wants … ain't for us to give." (767) There remains a streak of futility and despair in Apsalar, and she is still willing to sacrifice herself to be released of her possession and lack of control over her life.

During the cross-sea voyage, Apsalar finds herself in the company of Squint. An interesting interplay occurs when we realise both that Apsalar knew Squint and hid that knowledge, but likewise he knew her story. We can convince ourselves that our armour is tough, despite the ability to see through others'. Here, in Apsalar's case, that armour is fragile.

She speaks of Crokus: "I loved him too much to see him fall so far into my life, into what I was." (903) Squint tells her off: "You broke yourself and broke him too, I'd think." (903) Descending to the belly of the ship, she finds Cotillion, who speaks of the death of Heboric, and loss of Cutter. She falls into his arms to weep, a mirror of Felisin and Heboric in *House of Chains*.

Her journey in this novel is also mirrored, as she retreats to a room above an inn with a bottle and solitude. Freedom, of a kind.

Cotillion

Cotillion needs Apsalar to find her humanity, to prove to him that it's possible, that having renounced his own he might find it again. It would make meaning of his own actions.

His journey is a balancing act, and he takes it upon himself to basically save the world. In doing so, he must find his humanity, but in the meantime such things seem a distraction, given all the guilt and remorse attached. "The paths ahead were narrow, twisted and treacherous. Requiring utmost caution with every measured step." (85) His aim is to kill the Crippled God to restore the balance in his world.

When Apsalar caresses his face, we see his startled reaction, frozen in the face of the recognition of his glimmer of humanity. However, he is both afraid to take that, and still guilt-ridden over Apsalar.

Later, after his various interventions, including saving Lostara Yil and helping out Kalam, we see Cotillion visit the chamber where Trull and Minala and crew are fighting off the Edur to protect the First Throne. Cotillion is full of guilt here, that he is unable to offer more timely protection, that these people are suffering over again for his cause. He reflects on the state of innocence:

> "There had been times – he was almost certain – when he'd known unmitigated joy, but so faded were they to his recollection that he had begun to suspect the fictional conjuring of nostalgia. As with civilizations and their golden ages, so too with people: each individual ever longing for that golden past moment of true peace and wellness." (841)

With his reawakening humanity, Cotillion is experiencing or re-experiencing memories, and all the attendant emotions.

Monok Ochem asserts that Cotillion is dangerous. He continues: "You think what must not be thought, you speak aloud what must not be said." (848) This assessment of the dangerous path of Cotillion's thoughts is a recognition, in a sense, that he is upsetting the status quo. We can read that as Cotillion deviating from his 'natural' path, but one that facilitates growth. "He now in truth sets out upon an unseen path…" (849)

When Apsalar weeps upon him, the pain of regret leaves Cotillion stricken: "Truths, yes. One after another, one boulder settling down then another. And another. Blotting out the light, darkness closing in, grit and sand sifting down, a solid silence when the last one is in place. Now, dear fool, try drawing a breath. A single breath." (906) This image is what we might imagine to be seen were one to be buried. This is the preparation for a rebirth in Cotillion.

Cutter

Cutter's goal is to find meaning, "a purpose in life." (103) He reflects on Darujhistan, and even amplifies the memory of his chance at being a social climber, though concludes it was a dead end. In the immediate term, his aim is to accompany Heboric, or protect Felisin, "*A path to take, when before there had been none. Even so, it was not the best of motivations. A flight from despair was pathetic, especially since it could not succeed.*" (105)

Presumably he is going to find that it is not the destination, but the journey which will proffer meaning.

Cutter is still seeking his sense of self, and looks for it in the reflection of others. "He sees how cold I've become," (187) he thinks when he sees Heboric's reaction to his assessment of the dead in the monastery. Of Scillara, assuming it is only his control of the conversation, "He rarely made sense when talking to this woman." (189) Though both Heboric and Scillara notice the natural leadership he has displayed, and he offers the role to them both in turn. He is looking for an easy out, a rejection to latch on to so he needn't decide to leave.

Cutter's wound at the attack of the Imass is a mockery of a birthing section. This rather sudden symbolic death and rebirth also appears to sever Cotillion's connection, thus giving him a new life. This demonstrates the joint symbolism of both separation and birth, these images cycle throughout the lifespan and the individuation process.

"It's not good…following anyone's shadow." (785) He was hardened, and now he has lost the purpose of protection which was set him. There is something of a regression taking place, and he is now no longer clearly a leader, especially with the experienced and practical Barathol along with them. Scillara reflects: "Loneliness, then, and a certain loss of purpose…" (786) She aims to keep him distracted from his guilt with flirtation, though this will only keep him from growth, make of him a child. She notes his 'glimmer of enthusiasm' when he speaks of Darujhistan, and this, too, is a kind of childlike wonder.

"What if he falls in love with you?" (909) Barathol asks Scillara. She says he won't, can't. He has a mental block, and it is Apsalar. Or rather, his anima is still projected onto Apsalar as she was when he met her. Returning to Darujhistan will bring him closer to that return.

He begins to undercut himself yet again. It seems that with his own rebirth experience he risks becoming immature and riven with doubts. Scillara insists that he should trust himself. "There's nothing I've done to make that … possible." (913) Scillara is offering him a return to the mother, and Barathol understands intuitively that this risks a regression. These dynamics were discussed with *Memories of Ice*. However, Scillara is smarter than to allow that. She is taking a mother role in a new way.

Karsa Orlong

Karsa projects upon the witch Samar Dev much of his negative anima, fused with a mother complex from having lost his own. He stands in stubborn denial of her and the civility she claims she represents. Their power dynamic is confused from the beginning. They discombobulate one another. His stubbornness undercuts her ingenuity—her mental agility dances about his certainty; and yet, neither will give.

"One who binds risks getting bound in turn…" (68) How does this relate to her life attitude? Does she have difficulty with commitment, or her ability to say what she feels? With her interest in advancement and progression, it calls to mind the progressive mindset, whereby a constant need to shift ideological bounds is masked by a disavowal of conservatism.

When accosted by the town guard in Ugarat, Karsa is typically lacking in subtlety, and his forthrightness undercuts Samar Dev's attempts to soothe

the locals. Here, though, we sense his honesty is from a good place, he does not aim to wound with his words. He wishes, too, to approach the Malazans nearby with peaceful intent. His worldview may not necessarily be coherent, but it is consistent.

Samar Dev does not allow his pronouncements or his bravado, interrupting him. He responds demanding silence. "I am done speaking, witch. Witness." (149) Upon which he uses his actions to speak for him, and battles a K'Chain. When pressed by Samar Dev on what had happened, he tells her, "Nothing important, witch." (160) Unwitnessed, then. It's a dragon slaying, but nothing is saved. Karsa doesn't need external validation for his worldview, and doesn't need to test his beliefs against others' opinions.

"The action of doing things, laborious things, repetitive things, such actions invited ritual, and with ritual came meaning that expanded beyond the accomplishment of the deed itself." (263) Samar Dev reflects on the relative simplicity of the life that Karsa extols in his refutation of devices of convenience. "Among my people…the day is filled, as is the night." (263) In the rituals is a protection against the outpouring of violent instinct. Karsa attributes his own desire for war and slaughter as a disconnect from the life of daily ritual.

We think of necessity and freeing ourselves from its burden, but it has an organising effect on our lives. The notion of ritual, cyclic activity, is not a repressive force against primitive instinct, but a balancing of the psyche. The soothing motion that begets a child's peaceful dream, allowing the mind to find its rhythms, rather than quashing it to a dispassionate blankness with imposed white noise.

In carving gods into rock, and in the shaping of his sword, Karsa had learned patience and the value of long work. Though he still remains restless, he understands better than before that there are necessities that ground us. "I shall do what needs doing in my own time. None can stop me." (265)

Karsa's slaying of the bhederin is more than a side note. Samar Dev wants to believe that Karsa's actions are in aid of proving himself. Baring and Cashford note historical relations of the bull and its horns to the fertility principle, the sun and moon:

> "The sacrifice of the bull was an act of propitiation to the dark phase of moon, sun and year, which guaranteed the return of the light in heaven and fertility on earth.
> The seals and frescoes at Knossos suggest that before the ceremony of the bull slaying, the bull's magical power was

invoked by young men and women vaulting over its back."[148]

So when Karsa vaults the bhederin bull and kills it, it is a sacrifice. The moon is likened to horned animals because of the crescent sweep of the horns. Later, and associated with the sacrifices, the bull began to represent the sun, a masculine energy. The ritual then is a renewal of the kingly power and Karsa, in killing both a bull and a cow, is enacting the conjunction of masculine and feminine energies.

He asserts that the Anibar must grow up, and he is angry with them. He wants to show them his violence. In witnessing, they will be empowered, he says. But this is subtly different to Samar Dev's notion of progress. He doesn't want them to become 'civilised', rather he just wants them to be energised out of their stasis.

"Karsa Orlong was undertaking this journey now as if it had become some kind of quest." (693) As Karsa approaches the Edur invaders at a run, we follow Samar Dev as she first perceives, then runs through, breaking vast spider webs between the trees. These webs can be likened to chains, and to the shatter tattoo upon Karsa's face. He brings slaughter to the Edur, enraged by the imprisoning and torture of the Anibar. This image of breaking chains continues: "Chains cannot hold me, Witch." (810) And now he accepts the invitation of the Edur to duel with their Emperor, Rhulad.

The notable aspect of Karsa's thread is that we are no longer in his point of view, or not often. As he comes into his power and certainty, we are further removed from him. We experienced his growth and realisations, but now that he has matured and wields his certainty, we are less and less invited into his perception of the world.

Mappo Runt

We find Mappo on the shores on the reborn Raraku sea, Icarium splashing about "Like a child unfolding to a new, unexpected pleasure." (97) He sees rebirth, but he also sees about him deeds held in the spirit of a place, in bodies. He wished there was true rebirth in the sea, a cleansing, but he doubts deeds can be separated, doubts his regrets can be washed away. "Said blessing

---

[148] Baring & Cashford, 1991. "Legend of the Minotaur" para 15-16.

would quickly wash off this old hide, my friend. I fear the gift would be wasted…" (98)

And, of course, he reasserts his friendship, "There is no sacrifice involved" (99)

However, later he thinks "I am no friend." Mappo recalls the breaking of his vow, and his sense of duty clashes with his inner feelings. He rationalises this as "Simple, brutal self-interest, the weakness of my selfish needs." (180) This is a common refrain for those who feel guilt, that they are being selfish when motivated by caring for others. But in that state of mind we can forget the greater effect of such caring, that it benefits not just us but others beyond the immediate concern. It is far from selfish to care for another (we wouldn't accuse a mother of a newborn of it), but it is a recognition that all our actions are part of a world system that requires give and take.

Mappo and Icarium stand before the slain dragon Sorrit in the Sky Keep. About them, the melting of ice, the slow drip of Sorrit's blood, the entropy triggered by the otataral spike pinning this dragon – these are as the truth that can't be held back by Mappo. As they discuss the blood, the taint of history embodied in the very life force and passed like a madness to its killers, Mappo and Icarium are speaking in shadows.

Mappo would direct Icarium from the truth, as that truth also lays Mappo vulnerable. His failure, born of love and compassion, weighs too heavily upon him. He can only fail, as he sees it. He is stuck in a bind that has no satisfactory solution – and he would keep his stasis if he could, ever delaying change. But for the melting of ice.

Finally, Mappo undergoes a physical descent to shock him from his stasis. Jung remarks that this outward manifestation is inevitable even if not apprehended consciously:

> "The psychological rule says that when an inner situation is not made conscious, it happens outside, as fate. That is to say, when the individual remains undivided and does not become conscious of his inner opposite, the world must perforce act out the conflict and be torn into opposing halves."[149]

The revelation of Icarium's truths is taken from Mappo's control as the attack of T'rolbarahl separates them. He lies shattered at the bottom of a fissure, near death, when Iskaral Pust extracts him like a broken pup from the vulvic crevice.

Mogora—whom Cotillion soon identifies as being associated with

---

[149] Jung, C.G., CW9ii, [126]

Ardata, the Queen of Spiders—then aids the healing of Mappo with a ritual potent with maternal symbolism: "singing in the Woman's Language… Thousands, tens, hundreds of thousands – the spiders were wrapping about Mappo Runt's entire body…a massive, full moon, hanging so low it seemed within reach." (508) This combination of symbols weaves together some we have already encountered in the novel.

Birkhäuser-Oeri discusses the appearance of the Spinning Woman in folk tales, her connection to fate, and the analogy of the process to the state of dream and fantasy:

> "This character, usually an elderly woman, represents an essential part of the Great Mother. In real life spinning is done almost exclusively by women, but in addition it symbolizes a typically feminine way of behaving. In a man it is the anima which often behaves according to this pattern, while in a woman it illustrates aspects of the Self and the shadow. Spinning symbolizes an activity of mind that takes place in the unconscious—or more accurately the activity of the unconscious.
> Spinning is putting together lots of separate bits to make a continuous whole, in the same way that images are connected in fantasy. The connection grows gradually by a process of association. The deeper and more powerful a fantasy, the more predetermined it is by archetypes and to a certain extent the more inevitable, particularly if it happens unconsciously. So the spinning woman often appears to be the bringer of inevitable destiny."[150]

Wrapped cocoon-like, the invigorating power of the moon enlivening and renewing him, the ritual Mogora undertakes about Mappo could be read as a reinforcement of the symbolic birth his extraction from the fissure represents. However, it could as well be read as a regression—spiders, after all, wrap their prey. Jung noted on the man whose anima, the projection-making function, could not be distinguished from the mother:

> "the enveloping, embracing, and devouring element points unmistakably to the mother…His Eros is passive like a child's; he hopes to be caught, sucked in, enveloped, and devoured. He seeks, as it were, the protecting, nourishing, charmed circle of the mother, the condition of the infant released from every care…"[151]

---

[150] Birkhäuser-Oeri, 1988, p. 116
[151] Jung, C.G., CW9i, [20]

Of course, Mappo is at Mogora's whim, unconscious as he is during the ceremony. However, it might be argued that his stasis, the failure to take the descent consciously, was the precipitating factor in the revelation of his powerlessness in the face of the mother and the feminine. If this is the case, then Mappo's journey must now be one from indecision and stasis to conscious confrontation of the shadow and the feminine. His ability to relate has been stifled by the necessity of his silence and faithful companionship. His rebirth is an opportunity to take such a conscious path.

As he awakens he is being drawn back towards the pain of his life, but the pain is not physical: "this was a searing of the soul, the manifold wounds of betrayal, of failure, of self-recrimination, the very fists that had shattered all that he had been ... *before the fall.*" (555) This way of witnessing the pieces of his life is an opportunity for reflection, a kind of therapy or assessment, the judgment point at his nadir.

When we see the image of threads pulling his life back together, we recall Paran's forced healing in *Gardens of the Moon,* and the notion that there is mental pain, that puzzling together a life and soul is not just as simple as healing the body. What holds our self together is the continuous narrative we perceive. Attempting to join the fragments without that experiential thread will always be fraught. This is reflected in Ardata's musings: "Does it afflict us all, I wonder, the way one's sense of self changes over time? Or, do most people contend, willfully or otherwise, a changeless persistence in their staid lives?" (556)

He learns from Cotillion about the nature of Icarium. "There is, burned into Icarium's soul, something like an infection, or, perhaps, a parasite. Its nature is chaos, and the effect is one of discontinuity. It defies progression, of thought, of spirit, of life itself." (615-6) This reminds me of the telos of the soul. Without a sense of time's passage, of a goal, of something to strive for, that sickness wins, and we are nothing but chaos and impulse. Mappo's role of maintaining a narrative for Icarium is like the teller of myths. He grounds and gives Icarium something to strive for by relating story, weaving Icarium's tale at the expense of his own.

Mappo has been plagued with indecision and the inability to act. When this occurs, the pent up energy often becomes an impulse to anger. The ego necessarily protects itself, and so the frustration and disappointment at oneself is turned outwards, in aggression and hatred. For Mappo, the target is the Nameless Ones: "Sorely used and spiritually abused, Mappo had discovered in them a focus for his hate." (711) Of course, such negativity inevitably infects oneself.

Mappo watches the reunion of Cutter's crew, Barathol holding Chaur, Scillara holding Cutter. "I had ... forgotten." (962) He had forgotten true joy. He was so riven with guilt, his friendship shadowed by duty and deception, that he had let slip the careless passion that truly drives us. He blames himself for Icarium's loss, and is broken by Cutter's condolence. Cutter, meanwhile, has learned to trust himself, and he passes that wisdom on.

Lostara Yil

Lostara parts herself from Pearl's company, frustrated by his inaction. When she is engaged in the fighting in Y'Ghatan we find her assailed, then surrounded by burning oil she blacks out.

Coincident with the ritual which enlivened the moon to heal Mappo Runt, Lostara is also awakened to the amplified light of the moon. We have seen in *House of Chains* that Lostara was afflicted by a suppression of instinct. The moon suggests the natural feminine power is awakening in her, though she is just as comfortable in the shadows it casts.

Cotillion's explanation of his saving her comes with obscure revelations, alongside the confirmation of Cotillion's humanity as one who recalls and appreciates her dance. She reaffirms her ambivalence towards Pearl, though this seems a persona quality, duty above her feelings: "She started, then shrugged. 'A momentary infatuation. Thankfully passed. Besides, he's unpleasant company these days.'" (510) And he alerts her to a 'dire choice' she will face, between the Adjunct and loyalty to the empire.

Finally emerging from the temple where Cotillion left her, she rejoins the burned survivors of the Fourteenth. She notes "They're all wearing rags ... and they're unarmed." (633) Thus, likened to newborn babes, an innocence wreathing them. Her rebirth seems at this stage not as physical as that of the survivors, they having crawled through fire and the underworld. She further considers the physical damage reported of her commander Tene Baralta. This comparison of physical change and battle scars leads to Faradan Sort suggesting "You are still young, Lostara Yil." (633) Even with her rebirth, Lostara feels that she is the endpoint of her history, but Faradan Sort insinuates that certainty and fixedness are signs of inexperience, not yet accepting that which is beyond her control.

Listening, she realises Tene Baralta is corrupted, or at least in danger. Her loyalty will be tested. Following his pronouncement of allegiance to the empress, Lostara retires with him and is seen stripping away his armour in a mirroring of the removal of her own during *House of Chains*. This time rather than finding strength beneath, there is vulnerability, and she kills Tene Baralta. "And once again, the necessary coldness was achieved." (1110) Yet again, as she ends Pearl's suffering with a knife to the heart.

With Lostara Yil, then, the journey will continue towards finding the warmth of compassion. Grub tells her she will take the place of T'amber at Tavore's side in the times to come. She will provide a necessary balance.

Fiddler and the Fourteenth

> "Another hairy moment on this endless march passed by, with only a little blood spilled. The Fourteenth Army was tired. Miserable. It didn't like itself, much…the Fourteenth still waited for a resolution. It wanted blood…" (114)

Fiddler's journey to growth and acceptance of his full self continues. He has established his paternal role with his squad and the army, but he has been worn down by the deaths of Whiskeyjack and the Bridgeburners, he's lonely. Accepting fatherhood is one thing, guiding the birth itself is another. This is exactly what he does by leading his soldiers through the fighting at Y'Ghatan. "Eighteen soldiers – Strings had carried them through." (375) And then as he leads them through the underground and out of the city.

While in the tunnels, as his soldiers are all envisioning their gods and spirits, Fiddler is visited by Hedge. This insinuates that Fiddler's faith lies in his companions, old and new, that he is driven by friendship and love. Hedge tells us that Fiddler's role will be carried through to the finale: "You got to keep going, Fid. You got to take us with you, right to the end" (432).

Fiddler shaves his beard off after emerging from Y'Ghatan, and immediately before reuniting with his old squad members in Kalam, Quick Ben, and Apsalar. Quick Ben remarks, "Reminds me just how young you are – that beard turned you into an old man." Thus, a renewal for Fiddler, once more setting off as a younger man for this next phase of the journey. It also suggests that while Fiddler had acted as a father figure in *House of Chains*, there was premature aging. Retaking the journey will bring him further into his capacity as a father. As they trail the army, Fiddler is seen with babe in arms, even as we have just recalibrated our notions of his true age. "He was carrying one of the children in his arms, a girl, fast asleep with her thumb in her mouth." (635)

As Keneb watches the army boarding the ships for their passage across the sea, he thinks of the loss of the veterans: "The Fourteenth's heart had been cut out at Y'Ghatan…there was a palpable absence in the army, a hole at the core, gnawing its way outward." (773-4) Aside from the vivid imagery of a rat gnawing its way out from a dark place, we can think once again of the notion of finding one's heart. Acting out of compassion is the very purpose of Erikson's message. This army does find its heart, and finally this will be the truth that is faced by the Crippled God. This takes place, notably, as the army prepares for a voyage across the seas, the domain of the Great Mother, the source, back indeed to the heart of the Empire.

"…the Bonehunters may well have been birthed that day in Aren, but it only drew its first breath yesterday." (872) This is not only about the Adjunct's acceptance, but the rejoining of the 'heart' of the army. This results in the birth, indicating why Bottle felt incomplete as they strove to rejoin the army after escaping Y'Ghatan. There is a difference between the physical birth and the infusion of life that is confirmed with a first drawn breath.

Fiddler's game just before the fleet arrives at Malaz affirms his fatherly role. He deals himself both Priest and Soldier of Life, which recognises his dual role, and also in a sense recognises the duality of the Father archetype. The House of Life is relevant because it is ruled by the Queen of Dreams, she of divination, which is what Fiddler is doing in that very game. The cards dealt Keneb, who still represents our eyes for the Fourteenth at a broader level, foreshadows their journey, from Malaz to Lether, and then on to the heart of the Crippled God.

"Killing our own…" (1112) The Fourteenth, this rebirth, occurs in the blood of the citizens of Malaz. It is sacrifice, a brutal rite of renewal, that they may carry on their journey with this season's change. Here, Erikson is offering a summation of the symbols of fertility and renewal seen throughout the book.

Fiddler plays for the fallen. In this way, with this ritual, the spirit lives on in the Fourteenth. The acknowledgement of what is dead creates space for the new. "There was too much compassion within him – he knew that, for he could feel the pain, the helplessness, the invitation to despair…" (1124) There is a recognition here that suffering is pervasive, and Fiddler is confronting the apparent acceptance that one is helpless in the face of that recognition. He is angry because suffering seems inevitable, and there can be no answer to that despair, but still we must seek an answer.

Fiddler's song is one of life, and tells of a spider. "Wild, frantic, amusing. Its final notes recounted the triumphant female eating her lover." (1125) The terrible mother. In the act of conception, the death of the old. The Fourteenth killing their own is also the Empire born anew. There is no answer to the suffering, but with compassion we might live consciously, celebrating birth, not falling to despair.

"Yet perhaps there was a kind of gift in all of this, a measure providing perspective…Children were born to mothers and joyous tears flowed easy down warm, soft cheeks, the eyes brimming with love…" (1174)

Bottle

Bottle's story here is one of connection to the feminine divine, his acceptance of it. This is particularly because of his recent interaction with the Eres'al, a Great Mother figure. His grandmother also provides a maternal presence within him, which he must open up to: "His grandmother would know what to do about this situation" (115). He reflects on his grandmother in a way that speaks clearly to the instinct:

> "Wise in the ways of mortals, seeing through to every weakness, every flaw, reading unconscious gestures and momentary expressions, cutting through the confused surface to lay bare the bones of truth. Nothing was hidden from her." (115)

She may as well be his conscience.

Bottle's challenge is to make himself a vessel for the feminine, but he fears he is overwhelmed by the Eres'al. "I'm not equal to this." (116) He sees a pregnant locust and feeds it to Joyful Union. He's not yet able to allow the pregnancy to be fulfilled by birth, the maternal journey to come to fruition.

Bottle takes the Captain's orders to the squads just prior to the siege at Y'Ghatan. He is becoming our trusted set of eyes, someone we have faith in. Walking out to a midden heap, he considers the path of time, the meeting of the ancient and the new in the once-fertile plain, the differing styles of pottery and art, the forward motion of youth. He and the army's soldiers wear their youth: "eager for a place to stand that didn't feel so isolated and lonely, or filling oneself with bravado to mask the fragile self hiding within." (299) History, its cycles and rebirths, the perspectives lost in eager youth.

"He couldn't be sure of it, but this army felt lost. At its very core was an empty place, waiting to be filled…" (300) Bottle's integration of the ancient and the young, the Eres'al – the old ways and the new – are to fill that space, close the circle. The pregnant Eres'al comes to him as he waits, trying to close that circle of time: "As if all is present, as if every moment co-exists." (301) This is death and rebirth – the conjoining of beginning and end.

In birth, in newness, there is something unsullied. But we have already learned that blood, bone, stone, all contain the past. "Their blood must be drawn into this world's flow of blood…she is the last innocent creature, the last innocent ancestor of our line." (302) The promise of this impending birth is renewal, a cleansing of the bloodlines.

Can a purity then be achieved? Does acceptance of what has come – compassion for self – allow that hope to flare anew? I believe that Erikson wants us to feel that we can grow beyond our past, beyond history, by learning from it. This is an antidote to nihilism.

"Humbled beyond words, filling with shame…Could not encompass this…He could not be her … *her faith.*" (303) Accepting the faith of others is a radical form of compassion, accepting the responsibility to act in such a way as to maximise the wellbeing of life beyond our own. To act as if we are gods, to strive to act as our individuated self. To do less would belie our potential, our responsibility to the earth for bearing us.

Following the conflagration in Y'Ghatan, it is Bottle who leads Strings and the surviving soldiers down into the darkness, into the tunnels, the deeps of history. The darkness beneath the city is a conjoining of the ancient and the new, an escape into the depths of the unconscious, and finally emergence, rebirth into the light. This role is crucial for Bottle's individual journey, but also as a microcosm of the army's rebirth – scouring fire and descent into the dark.

In the tunnels, he is twice entangled: "His forehead caught strands of a spider's web, tough enough to halt him momentarily before audibly snapping." (400) Here he is not to be stranded by the symbolic weave. And again, as he falls down a hole, he fears the worst until: "Sudden tugs, snapping sounds, then more, pulling at him, resisting, slowing his descent./*Gods, webs*—" (407) Gods and webs could well be the beginning of a list. Here the weavings aid him, probably saving his life. Luminous spiders then come, and he feels their rage, but he uses his communicative ability and his wiles to first urge calm and then fear upon the creatures, allowing his safe passage. He is not surrendering to the ensnaring of the goddess here, but nor is he unaffected by it.

Bottle's role here is also instructive in that it shows us how empathy and compassion, in this case for lesser creatures, reaps benefits, and allows safe travel through the darkness. "Compassion existed when and only when one could step outside oneself, to suddenly see the bars from inside the cage." (433) By empathising with others, Bottle is able to raise the life spark of all creatures.

It is the rat's spark that leads them out, that carries them. And of course, the rat is then named Y'Ghatan, symbolic of the life beneath the city. She is pregnant, he soon realises, the seed of life within her resembling the faint life spark of those soldiers Bottle led through the tunnels. "Death, and this long buried seed. *We return. We return to the world…*" (443) Their symbolic death and rebirth is fulfilled.

However, Bottle is concerned about the Adjunct's abandonment of them. He still feels some attachment to the idea of being mothered. "We're dead, you know," (467) he is told, suggesting they are actually in an unborn state, not yet officially rejoining the living.

As the squads begin to return to normalcy as they trail the army, Bottle reflects on the lack of tangible change. "If this was a rebirth, it was a dour one. They'd not emerged innocent, or cleansed. If anything, the burdens seemed heavier." (644) The symbolic change has occurred, recognised by Bottle and the attempt at creating identities and rituals about their experience, but he feels they are too frail and tender for this rebirth to be consecrated. It is as though he has not accepted some truth from it, or synthesised the full meaning of what occurred. "It should have felt … different. Something was missing." (644)

Bottle fixes Quick Ben's dolls, turns Shadowthrone into a hound to help out Paran. Notably, the first thing Bottle spots is the female figure, Quick Ben's sister, who Quick hadn't realised was female. Quick Ben realises the Eres was with Bottle, acting through him. Quick Ben recognises that he has a connection to the old ways, and we are again reminded that Bottle is straddling both worlds. Their comment that he was half asleep takes on greater resonance. Earlier, when the Eres'al confronted him, Bottle thought: "Or maybe I am the conjured, not her." (301) Bottle is the character through which we see the reconciling of these polarities, the numinous feminine, the old and the new.

When approached by the Edur fleets, Bottle again helps Quick Ben with his magical response. He then surrenders to allow the Eres'al through to use him, as a channel. Nil and Nether realise the importance of Bottle, at the least for this channel to the Eres'al: "more important to [Tavore] and her army than Quick Ben, Kalam and Apsalar all put together." (900)

We then get Bottle dealt the Weaver of Life in Fiddler's game. This could directly reference the Eres'al, or could be more broadly symbolic of his connection with the feminine. He is also to go ashore to Malaz Island and retrieve Withal, but first he seeks the assistance of Agayla, the weaver. He still must enlist the ancient feminine to complete his mission.

"Truth is in the touch," (1044) Tavore tells him, somewhat cryptically. They are connected by the aspect of the Eres'al, who resides in T'amber. His warning to the Adjunct to be careful elicits surprise. There is compassion within Bottle, and here he is pivotal in allowing Tavore the recognition of what is within her followers.

In some ways, Tavore's choice to send him ashore could mean that he represents a sort of shadow feminine side to her and the army. His chance here is to unite the feminine.

Corabb Bhilan Thenu'alas

Corabb worships Leoman, a man who has no faith. He wants to believe in Leoman because it is what he rests his own faith upon. Karsa Orlong spoke to the Seven of the roles of the gods – to lift the burden. "To be a god is to know the burden of believers." (682) To offer comfort, solace, compassion. Leoman, faithless, is unable to do so.

Corabb is indestructible. It often seems like divine intervention, the only explanation for his miraculous survivals. This is a counterpoint to the faithlessness of Leoman, as if telling Corabb that he would be right to believe in something greater than the man.

Corabb becomes for us a study case for the Crippled God. He believes those around him are enemies, but he opens up and begins to admire them. His own negative feelings thus turn positive, and he becomes a lesson for how to view others. "Complicated thoughts. It had taken Corabb many hours of frowning regard to reach them, to make that extraordinary leap into the mind of another man, to see through his eyes, if only for a moment, before reeling back in humble confusion." (50)

He is a rare outside view upon the Malazan marines, who the Crippled

God will later look upon in admiration. Corabb gives us insight into the Malazans' ability to regard others with openness, to not give up on someone, no matter that they had fought in the past.

"If not for his commander, Corabb well knew, he would be lost." (51) And so he is. Corabb's perceptions are often at odds with his beliefs, but he chooses to place significance only on what fits his belief. As do we all; this is how faith can be created, and Corabb's faith relies on Leoman. There is so little foundation apart from it that Corabb must double down. "We journey towards something – I know, many here see this as a flight, but I do not. Not all the time, anyway." (65) His ability to reframe his reality based on his perception is demonstrated as he synthesises his hallucinations into his speech: "We are returning to our birthplace. It is the season for that. To build nests on the rooftops." (66) But there is also thematic truth in there, as they are indeed returning to their origin. Corabb is hoping for renewal, a reinvigoration of his faith, but what he will receive is a rebirth in truth.

"Preening with conceit." Here we are speaking of certainty, with Corabb's disbelief that Dassem is not dead, that his worldview is not true, at least that it differs from Leoman. The story of growth is about freeing oneself to knowledge, shedding the cloak of such conceit. In large part it is recognising and accepting that others have a worldview as well. That is the basis of empathy. For many, that comes initially in the mirroring effect of another recognising your worldview.

Corabb's rationalisations continue as he considers the relationship between Leoman and Dunsparrow. "Leoman of the Flails was hiding something from Corabb, and that had never before happened. Her fault. She was to blame." (271) His faith had blinded him to earlier signs of Leoman's intent, or rather he had reinterpreted them. Corabb's is a stubbornness almost a match to that of Karsa Orlong. His insistence on clear demarcations continues when he is challenged by Dunsparrow on the varied nature of those under Malazan conquest: "Malazans were … Malazans, dammit." (275)

And finally, when Corabb is assailed by the truth, he can no longer deny it, he feels himself alone, no longer with the frail ice of his faith to bear him up. "Everything was crumbling inside, and Corabb could feel himself drowning. Sinking ever deeper, reaching up towards a light that grew ever more distant, dimmer." (380) Then in the darkness, alone, he hears the children. Immediately his path is renewed, he has a purpose again, to bring these young lives to safety. Again, it is almost like a divine intervention, a sign from beyond.

This attitude is reinforced when Corabb volunteers to take up the rear with Strings, and then drags the Sergeant through the tunnels. He is unaffected by the scepticism of the soldiers. We know that Corabb can't be killed, so we trust that all will be well, but he also achieves his own awakening. "He had believed them all monsters, cowards and bullies. He had heard that they ate their own dead. But no, they were just people. No different from Corabb himself." (413) This is the awakening of empathy, the scouring clean of the blinders of faith and certainty from the man's eyes. "We must move on." (413) And upon their arrival at the end of the journey, when Corabb assumes they will perish: "So much had changed inside him…Certainty was an illusion, a lie. Fanaticism was poison in the soul, and the first victim in its inexorable, ever-growing list was compassion…*I have cast off my chains.*" (448)

Tavore

> "I've seen people under siege before, but she's raised walls so thick and so high I doubt a dozen irate dragons would get through…" (120-1)

> "She's all edges, but they're for keeping people away, not cutting them." (232)

We finally get a spotlight on Tavore with the visit of Keneb prior to the siege of Y'Ghatan. She is standing firm in her tactics, to the frustration of her commanders: "as I stated earlier, Fist Baralta, I am not interested in assailing the fourth bastion." (304) By giving nothing of her reasons, she risks the doubts of those who would carry out her orders. In a commander who has already earned the faith of her soldiers, this would play differently. "Command does not come from consensus." (305) This solitude and bearing of the risk is her only mode of operation, for good or bad.

Keneb wonders at Tavore's motives when she reminds him that Gamet is dead. Gamet was our eyes in the Fourteenth in *House of Chains*. He was also the conduit of our trust in the Adjunct. She keeps herself close, but she understands that she needs to appear to have the faith of her commanders, the appearance of trust being as important as the reality of it. Keneb's remark on Dujek, that their army will march because they believe the weight of Onearm's host is behind them, is the same sort of faith. Build your own faith until you can act it out in truth.

Blistig's vision: "She was no more than a silhouette, the world behind her nothing but flames, a firestorm growing, ever growing." (389)

There is also the notion that Tavore as mother is making a sacrifice as she sends forth the heroic child, the army, into Y'Ghatan. Only in its differentiation from the mother, in this case the determining of its own identity as an army, independent of the psychological support from the idea of the empire, is she able to release from herself the burden of its dependence and enact her own individuation. Harding discusses the notion of sacrifice of the heroic son from the perspective of the mother: "when her son reaches manhood, he is sacrificed not in spite of her love and protective care but by the edict and consent of his mother." She continues:

> "In these myths the mother is not one, she is dual. She has two aspects: in her light aspect she is compassionate, filled with maternal love and pity, and in her dark aspect she is fierce and terrible and will not tolerate the childish dependence of the son. For his softness and clinging undermine her, just as her oversolicitude undermines him. His childish need appeals too intimately to her own desire to mother him."[152]

In discussing *Memories of Ice* we explored the various natures of mother archetypes. While these can be reapplied here, in short we can note that regardless of the aspect of motherhood being evinced by the Adjunct, it is the act of separation that is relevant here, the sacrifice itself. This paves the way for deeper relationship with the mother as an individual, and for growth in both her and the heroic child. Harding notes: "A woman who has not yet 'sacrificed the son,' that is sacrificed the instinctual maternal within herself, may have no actual children, but will nonetheless carry the maternal attitude into her relationships."[153] And so we might consider that Tavore's conscious sacrifice here is as much a hardening of herself as the army, so that she can face the difficult tasks before her.

"To find what's inside us, you got to take everything else away, you see?" (419) These words from Grub to Keneb suggest the journey of Tavore, our journey in which she is instrumental. The fires scorch the outer self, the armour had to be removed to avoid burning. This journey is inwards from here, following this rebirth.

Tavore tries to get Sinn to talk, but it is a failed endeavour. "Sinn, look at me. Look at me." (422) Faradan Sort is able to communicate to Sinn, at least

---

[152] Harding, 1935 Chapter 14, "Sacrifice of the Son", para. 4-5
[153] Ibid. para 8

to reassure the girl. This happens out of our point of view, perhaps so as not to highlight Tavore's failing and fragility. It shows us there is still work to be done for Tavore's inner self.

Paran, asked by Quick Ben whether Tavore is worthy of trust insists that she will do what is necessary. Quick Ben asks whether for her or her soldiers, and he replies: "For her, friend, there is no distinction." (766) This identification might speak to the protection she would convey upon her soldiers, but it also speaks to the lack of separation.

Something in the inability to give her loyalty doesn't sit right, as though she is too closed. Standing firm and strong falls into character weakness. She is unable to speak of the higher cause. From where she is almost able to give her trust, and accept it from the soldiers, she steps back from that line and it is a long time before we get the opportunity again. I liken it to the inability to make the sacrifice of the child, to let it gain its full independence. It is the sheltering instinct.

She acknowledges Strings is Fiddler, "It is the worst-kept secret in this army, Keneb." (871) This serves to level her with the soldiers, removing the distance of her status, but it is also something to watch given they are the mother and father conjunction at the series conclusion. Acknowledgment opens the door for the blending of the old and the new. In ensuring the newly created Deck gets to Fiddler, she is also showing trust in him.

It is worth noting her reference to T'amber as an apprentice, and the one who sewed the Bonehunters' sigil. The analogy to the ongoing theme of weaving is clear here, and tells us that T'amber represents the feminine aspect of Tavore.

"Humbling, is it not?" Tavore sees the moon come crashing down. "All of our plans ... our conceits ... as if the sheer force of our wills, all of us, can somehow ensure that all else remains unchanged around us, awaiting naught but what we do, what we say." (950) This passage is about as revealing as Tavore can allow herself to be. Fitting that the moon, the divine feminine, is what reveals to her the futility of hiding herself. That is a numinous force that cannot be repressed by the individual. This is a turning point for Tavore, who following this begins her journey toward fullness.

In Fiddler's game she is dealt the Master of the Deck, her brother, Ganoes. She is told, "Even cold iron, Tavore Paran, needs tempering." (1027) This foreshadows the reunion and opposition between her and Ganoes. Fiddler and Tavore are the last two left in the game, which is again a recognition of their duality at the end of the series, as mother and father of this army.

Tavore, following the shattering of the moon, seems to have gained some control. She is offered the loyalty of the Perish, and she is the one who calls Fiddler's game. There is soon after the command to ignore the Empress's orders. She is separating herself from the dependence to the Empress and Empire, finding her own purpose. She senses the loyalty offered her by the troops growing, and she is also aware of the responsibility that entails.

The second half of *The Bonehunters* focuses much on discussions of faith and loyalty, their various facets. Tavore is emblematic of these discussions, the faith offered by her soldiers, and the loyalty reciprocated. How this differs from that offered by worship of gods and other ideals is an interesting contrast.

Grub had intimated, of their return to the beginning, Malaz Island: "But that's when she realises everything." (778) The serene face of the moon has been shattered and, at the time, it seemed so had her plans, whatever they were. We have the hint that all of humanity, civilisation itself, is within her sights. To manage that, her ongoing journey is to restore the archetypal feminine, in herself and to the world.

Laseen speaks to Tavore of truth. "You appear to hold to the childish notion that some truths are intransigent and undeniable. Alas, the adult world is never so simple. All truths are malleable." (1097) In growth, we leave behind our certainties, our perceived duty as the world becomes a more complex place. With faith, the Empress contends, she can turn will and thus revise truth. To challenge would be treason, as a challenge to religious dogma is sacrilege. Tavore's ability to hold tight to a core understanding, a moral belief, is the strength of will that sets her apart.

Tavore has projected the feminine onto T'amber, it seems. It is externalised. And so with T'amber's death she must withdraw that projection and conjoin within herself. In some ways, the two who fight for her through Malaz, T'amber and Kalam, thus represent aspects of her—the cold force of will, and the externalised hidden feminine. It is also interesting to note that as she is about to be finished, it is Fiddler whose face comes into her view to bring her to safety, again foreshadowing their conjunction.

It is in *The Bonehunters* that I feel we see the fullest character of Tavore. Still with her doubts, and still closed off, but not so much that we don't empathise with her plight. It is as though the force of the feminine themes draw those aspects of her out. However, in part due to her traumas and in part to point of view, she becomes more closed off as the army's journey continues in later books. She becomes, as it were, unwitnessed, though so much so that it is to the detriment of her as a character.

Ganoes Paran

It is good to see our erstwhile hero. He has grown into his role in the background of *House of Chains*, but we are allowed his point of view, which, despite his power, is still riven with healthy doubt. This is essential for continued growth. "The Crippled God is finding allies," he tells Apsalar. She asks why. "I don't really know. Compassion?" (259) One wonders if he is truly naïve about the motivations of, say, Tavore and Shadowthrone.

On their parting, Apsalar asks Paran if he is ascended. "You have stumbled onto power, of a personal nature…You begin to see things differently, to think differently." (309) This assessment is accurate of a change in self towards a higher state of growth. "He seemed to have let go of so much…" (312)

> "There were times, Captain Ganoes Paran reflected, when a man could believe in nothing. No path taken could alter the future, and the future remained ever unknown, even by the gods. Sensing those currents, the tumult that lay ahead, achieved little except the loss of restful sleep, and growing suspicion that all his efforts to shape that future were naught but conceit." (452)

This is the attitude of one who has been made a child again. Ganoes Paran has come into his power, grown into a man, but for all that, and his outward role as Master of the Deck, he cannot control the world. The wheel has turned, and he must humble himself before the world. Taking that attitude of humility, knowing that despite all that has gone before the world still can leave us helpless, is the best way to advance, lest we become stuck in our small ponds and petty power games. Tavore comes to a similar realisation as she watches the breaking up of the moon on her journey across to Malaz.

This is also the beginning of the first point of view section with Paran since *Memories of Ice*. Though we have heard of his sanctioning of the *House of Chains*, and learned a little recently of his movements in Darujhistan, and had characters reflect on him in light of his sister Tavore's greater role. We expect, or rather hope, that he has come into his power, wielding it to change the game, yet his musing suggests it is not so clear-cut. Apsalar's meeting with him told us something of his level-headedness, his healthy doubts, and now we can regain his perspective, crucial as it is to the theme of rebirth.

"...this war among the gods would implode into a maelstrom of chaos...This web was growing too fast, too snarled, for any single mind to fathom." (452) He also senses the notion of a web and the interconnectedness with which he must deal, yet he retains doubts about his value in the scheme of the powers at work. Reflecting on Kruppe's visit in the Azath house, we are told, "Eggs have been laid and schemes have hatched! ... You must walk the singular shadow...between life and death." (454) These notions are both foreshadowing and thematically consistent. "He was not the man for this...he was struggling to maintain even the illusion of control." (455) The lesson here is that control is an illusion always. We are seeing in Paran the very nature of his rebirth. Now a reluctant hero, perhaps, where in his former life he was brash and certain. The move to adulthood is a coming into power, a responsibility, and it is often all we can do to hold it all together in some semblance of stumbling control.

Ganath forces Paran to reflect on the idea of followers or worshippers. He is uncomfortable with the idea of his power having consequences in the real world. He had already pushed back against Nightchill and the notion of gods using humans and intervening, now the idea that sacrifices might be made in his name concerns him. This is something that must be accepted, the idea that if you act upon the world there are consequences, that life is not a zero-sum game, and coming to terms with our impact and our choices is necessary for maturity.

> "Burdens were born from the loss of innocence. Naivete. While the innocent yearned to lose their innocence, those who had already done so in turn envied the innocent, and knew grief in what they had lost...He sensed the completion of an internal journey..." (476)

He has achieved the ending of a cycle. The end of naivete has been thrust upon him despite his hope that innocence might remain, in other words he has come fully into his power.

This is quickly demonstrated as he raises the spectres of Raraku's dead to speak to the Bridgeburners' ghosts, "a cacophony of enmeshed lives, each on seeking to separate itself, seeking to claim its own existence, unique, a thing with eyes and voice." (477) We ever strive to differentiate from the masses, as this is a form of birth of the self. This striving echoes after death, because our actions in life are at some level aimed at legacy and immortality. Paran is in touch with the ancient and the new, a conscious rebirth allowing some communion between those worlds, as hinted by Kruppe.

"Certitude is the enemy." (478) For certainty has been shown to preclude compassion, discovered by Corabb, for example. Erikson pits certainty against life, and it ever fails. That understanding allows rebirth, a new stage of consciousness.

The scenes upon the bridge in the underworld are curious, but instructive in asserting Paran's freedom. He speaks of their arrival there as a fulfillment of his visions, but he understands that his next move is within his control. Uncertainty about the future and how to proceed, "I could discard all else and attempt to appease them with precision, never once straying – for fear that it would prove disastrous. Or, I could see all those uncertainties as opportunities, and so allow my imagination fullest rein." (527) Paran is actively exploring his power of free will against the predetermination that his visions offer him. The more opportunities we perceive in life's uncertainties, the greater the control which we can assert. This is also a metatextual moment, as Paran's thoughts might echo those of an author, Erikson as he creates the scene before him, weighing his power and the trade-off between planning and flexibility.

He likens ascendancy to peaks of a mountain range. The pressure of the world means some rise to the top, a combination of the demands of the time and place, coincidence, and consciousness. Biology, psychology, and sociocultural forces interact to shape the individual, and given the right circumstances and impulses of conscious control, we are all capable of individuation, of growth into our capacity. In turn, we shape the society about us, a higher level of collective consciousness becomes the basis from which those who ascend will continue their rise, reaching ever higher towards the Self. This could be seen as a net positive for humanity. Ascendancy and godhood are mentioned as being two-way streets, and this becomes a check on selfish power. Higher states attract worship, which in turn draws power and raises up those beneath.

Tying these ideas together, Paran comments on Hedge's notion that the ghost army are being manipulated. His explanation makes it sound rather like an instinctual, or archetypal, drive for continued progress: "I don't think you and your ghost army are being directly manipulated. I suspect that what calls to you is something far more ephemeral, more primal. A force of nature, as if some long lost law was being reasserted…" (535)

As Paran and the Trygalle wagon flee the guardian of the underworld, we see him turn to face the pursuing beast. This is the archetypal experience of turning to face your demons, and it is the way we might deal with pursuing creatures in a nightmare. He uses his blank card, creativity and intuition, to overcome his fears. On the whole, this section with Paran in the underworld has been focused largely on his internal conflicts. Now he is ready to emerge.

He comes across Onearm's Host, and acts with confidence. "Years ago, Paran would have done … nothing. Succumbed to the rules, the written ones and the unwritten ones." (627) He asserts his own needs, for a bath and sleep, for respect. He knocks out the Captain and the soldier, binding and gagging them. Paran has developed the ability to act with consciousness, and has brought his strength of character into the physical world.

He takes on the role of Captain Kindly, and this notion of playing a role makes him both a player and confirms his own ego strength. His foundations are solid enough that he can step into a role without identifying with it (as he did that of a soldier in *Gardens of the Moon*.) To wear a persona consciously means it is functional, unlikely to fall under sway of identification, and less likely to be seized by the shadow as a result.

There is a curious symbolism in the idea of his taking on the role of Captain Kindly, and indeed there are hidden layers within Paran, including the Hound, and his title as Master of the Deck is also a kind of persona. It perhaps demonstrates that he is confident in taking action now, in standing up to the purported authorities of the world, however he is not yet willing to do so without the layered protection of his personae.

We see in the section where Paran enters the city and confronts Poliel a fulfillment of his ability to act on his convictions, demonstrating his growth as a character. Paran's preference for action over inaction is stated when he comments on the Goddess Soliel: "How has her infamous, unceasing sorrow for the plight of mortals done them any good…It's easy to weep when staying far away, doing nothing." (729) His desire for direct action is then clearly symbolised by his literally walking through the city walls to confront Poliel.

And once his true self is revealed, first to Noto Boil within the city, and then when he emerges to find Dujek has died and the rest of the commanders are aware of his true identity, power is given to him. He is made High Fist and so commands the army. Once his personas are stripped away, the power and attendant burdens are laid upon him.

Paran's taking over of the High Fist role, and the death and celebration of Dujek is a kind of renewal. This might historically occur when kings were sacrificed, symbolically or literally, in the name of renewal and fertility. This would often occur around spring celebrations, tying in to the idea of birth and renewal. And so we come to the idea of the plague as a scouring clean. Paran as the new 'king' fulfils the renewal of that army. Dujek is sacrificed to end the dead time of the plague. The aging king or sovereign in decline is common in fairy tales, as symbolic of a readiness for transition, the old kingdom waning. We might read this transition as specifically Paran's renewal, or the Empire as a whole.

Paran looks upon the High Fist armour he must wear, recalling the donning of armour by his sisters Tavore and Felisin before their confrontation in *House of Chains*. Here, Paran chooses to leave the armour off. This is a recognition, at least unconsciously, that he must maintain his true self, be transparent. This is another role that he doubts his qualification for, but he is not going to hide behind layers of persona. He has been through such a cycle of doubt before, coming into his power. We know now that he needn't doubt, but the inner self continues to grow, and faces challenges over again.

He ponders the expectation his soldiers might have for him to make a speech. He converses with himself about such doubts:

> "I should have said something to them here and now. Warned them not to expect too much. No, that wouldn't do. What does a new commander say? Especially after the death of a great leader, a true hero? Dammit, Ganoes, you're better off saying nothing." (801)

It is in our nature to doubt, for therein lies humility. Unquestioning action does not necessarily speak of growth and maturity. Here, we recall Ganoes in his earlier life, where he likely would have spoken in haste. Wisely, he says nothing, proof again that the role befits him.

For all his doubt and humility, Paran is coming into his individuated self. His various personae are being shed, and he has refused to don the armour of the 'king', the High Fist. He has also achieved recognition from his community: "you rode with one healer into G'danisban and then singlehandedly struck down a goddess...These soldiers are yours, Ganoes Paran." (800)

It may be worth talking about Paran's horse here. It is skittish, and he occasionally tries to wrestle it back under his control. In folklore and fairy tales, a horse can represent the instinctive side of a person, their animal nature. Here we could see Paran's instinct as brimming and bridling. Compare Karsa Orlong's complete mastery of his horse, and thus instinct.

Mathok joins Paran, and there is an interesting twist of fate in that he chooses not to confront Felisin Younger. By doing so he would learn about his sister. "I barely recognize her. She is indeed *fallen*." (986) The way Mathok speaks of Sha'ik reminds us of Felisin Paran in Skullcup.

Heboric

There is regret in Heboric because he couldn't protect either Felisin Younger or Felisin as Sha'ik, even though he was her connection to her past life. He wonders now what value there is in seeing the past if it changes nothing. He feels powerless because he was tasked with this journey by Sha'ik, and by the understanding furnished him by L'oric. Nor did he ask for this dubious gift given by the touch of Jade in the first place.

We have already encountered the notion of time and the ancient lying beneath the new. Heboric's vision has allowed him to see the past, and he has himself undergone a couple of rebirths, or renewals. He shares with us the notion that all the dust and air about, the matter and spirit, are but recycled, they bear the embodied history of past lives and civilisations, just as the ghosts he imagined from the First Empire still lived in the caverns in *Deadhouse Gates*. "Rock was bone. Dust was flesh. Water was blood." (486)

He therefore sees rebirth as only a continuation of prior matter—thus, each of his wanderings, each sleep, is but a preface to another cycle of wakening, not a true rebirth. Of his companions, who cannot see as he does, he thinks: "each night they were as empty things. While Heboric fought on against the knowledge that the world did not breathe, not any more. No, now the world drowned. *And I drown with it.*" (486) He sees both a lack of growth in their emptiness, and death in his own drowning, the weight of knowledge casts his plight into shadow. He is failing to undergo a conscious rebirth, plagued by knowledge of cycles and futility, unable in turn to free the jade prisoners. Yet also unable to die.

"Each time, the return journey was harder, more fraught, and far, far less certain." (486) These drownings, then, are as waves creeping ever higher, smothering him. But something is pulling him back, much as the wyval retrieved Udinaas in *Midnight Tides*. His inability to enact progress is mirrored by the notion of the beast (Treach) within him, a wildness captured in human form, as well as the plight of the jade prisoners. He must free things, yet he feels ever more powerless. "Drowning, I am drowning, and yet … these damned feline gifts, this welter of senses, so sweet, so rich, I can feel them, seeking to seduce me. Back into this momentary world." (487) He cannot drown in history and futility because the animal nature, the alertness to the present, the sensory, is heightened in him. This keeps him straddling the old and the new, always on the cusp of rebirth.

In *House of Chains*, Heboric fought being ensnared, chained, but the inaction he fell into foreshadowed his trapped mentality in this book. "He was the stranger who had come among them; he had done what none other had done: he had reached through the green prison. And they prayed to him, begging for his return." (487) Even his transgression of the jade prison was unwitting, beyond his control. He knows the burden of their regard now, just as Paran has recently learned. He is left powerless, having such outside forces intrude upon him, along with the awareness of history. And yet he cannot go under the water, consciously approach that symbolic death and rebirth, because the animal instinct wants him to live. Though it remains to be seen whether that is indeed the battle waged within him, or whether he risks succumbing to ennui and helplessness but the animal keeps him alive.

"There is a vast dead city awaiting us this day," Heboric announces to his companions. "They buried it intact. Thousands of years have passed, and now the winds and rains have rotted away that solid face. Now, the old truths are revealed once more." (488) This city is a manifestation, or a reversal, of the weight of history Heboric feels drown him—here, the dust is choking. The act of burying is an attempt to forget, and the fact that it has been uncovered—reborn—reinforces for Heboric that such escape is impossible, that history will always return. As Ganath said about the sea to Paran, "It will not last. Nothing lasts." (474) Then, finally, the city mirrors Icarium's dip in that same sea—that awakening of the old had enlivened him. This revelation is twisted now, for Icarium also approaches the city, and he was its destroyer.

"But redemption was not a gift. Redemption had to be earned." (550) Heboric seeks his own redemption by walking back his journey, attempting to right the wrongs. It is notable that he acts with indifference towards the beseeching of the prisoners in jade, which is how he was treated as a priest of Fener. This mirrors the transmission of parent-child attachment.

If redemption must be earned, where does compassion enter the equation? I would argue that compassion must be given to allow for the possibility of redemption, in the self or in another. Heboric is seeing his role as transactional, both with his gods and the prisoners in jade. He has not yet opened freely.

"Deliverance was all he desired now." (577) As they cross the dead field, covered in flies, Heboric reflects on his choices that have brought him here, and he wants to undo. He ponders his role as Destriant: "Harvester of souls…to slay in a god's name. To slay, to heal, to deliver justice." (577)

There is something of shamanic dismemberment in his death here.

Indeed, he is buried, then exhumed, in a classic rebirth symbolism, to be carried to his destination.

"Reach! See my hands! See them! They're reaching – reaching out for you!" (955) With Felisin, Heboric bemoaned the fact that he didn't have the hands to embrace. Now, he realises that he is made Shield Anvil, perhaps always was. In *House of Chains*, he kicked through the Crippled God's lure. Perhaps that wounded god always wanted him, needed someone with the ability to embrace the followers in jade. "The hands … cut loose. Freed. I can't do this … but I think they can." (956) We recall that his hands were gifted a god in *Memories of Ice*. If this was the Crippled God, then the hands have been released to gift Heboric with the power to embrace. It's a curious thing. Perhaps he needed to see the hands himself to believe he had the ability, the gift removing his doubts. But whatever, it is clearly Heboric himself that is able to embrace, or at least the desire to embrace.

If we prevent ourselves from being open, whether through mental block, lack of compassion, or lack of belief in ourselves, we do forget how to care. Compassion can be lost. "I cannot be forgiven. But maybe you can, maybe I can do that, if you feel it's needed…" (958) He could as well be talking to The Crippled God or Fener here.

"One cannot, in any real measure, remember pain." (959) As much as Heboric steels himself for the oncoming souls, the truth is only by living the experience of pain can we truly understand it. In place of that, there can only be compassion. He acknowledges the pain of the gods, and the prisoners, and thus makes it possible for compassion to exist. For forgiveness.

The Moon

"The misshapen moon now cast down a silvery light on the land – it was looking rougher round the edges, Kalam realized, as if the surrounding darkness was gnawing at it – he wondered that he'd not noticed before. Had it always been like that?" (233) Note, this description occurs just before "Good evening, Adjunct." Tavore as the moon, the feminine divine. That which does not cast its own light (point of view character) but only reflects others. The notion of the darkness gnawing at it takes on a sinister meaning.

The notion of the moon waxing and waning suggests death and rebirth. As Baring and Cashford put it, "the gradual 'swallowing' or 'dismemberment' of the moon during its dark phase may have offered an image of the idea that death was necessary to renew the principle of life."[154] Further, then, the idea of the moon being shattered in *The Bonehunters* becomes the end and beginning of a greater cycle. This is a death and rebirth that must be taken internally, it must be experienced at a deeper, mythical level for change to occur to the reader. That is why the images of birth are so strongly reinforced.

The piercing of the moon's light by the projectiles reminds us of the archetypal image in modern life of sperm entering ovum as seen through microscopy. This symbolism confirms that the moon's destruction is not simply an end, but is precipitated by the enlivening of a new state.

That these images appear at this central point in the series is crucial, for it confirms that we are embarking upon heretofore uncharted waters. The old ways are dead and we are forging a new path, a new stage of consciousness being born.

> "The moon is still the primal image of the mystery of birth, growth, decay, death and regeneration. The lunar cycle must have offered a way of comprehending how a seed grows into flower and fruit, which, falling back into the darkness of earth, returns as the regenerated seed."[155]

This description by Baring and Cashford reminds us not only of the thematic lunar elements of *The Bonehunters*, but also is the connective element of the rebirth at Y'Ghatan: the squads buried are the seeds. Some seeds even need fire to open.

Karsa, as he moves through the Anibar's land 'full of omens' notices the strange appearance of the moon and asks Samar Dev about it. "I don't know. It seems to be breaking up. Crumbling. There is no record of anything like that happening before, neither the way it has grown larger, nor the strange corona surrounding it…If it is an omen, it is one all the world can see." (698) Samar Dev's words seem to concur with the idea that this unprecedented occurrence is a changing of a grand cycle.

"The light cast down was muted, dull…that moon's nothing but a blur." (902) Apsalar and Squint's observations of the moon suggest that the feminine is fading, but it also symbolises the armour of Apsalar breaking down.

The final observation of the moon prior to the cataclysm belongs to Scillara. "It was mottled. Strange, like holes had been poked in it." (910)

---

[154] Baring & Cashford, 1991 Chapter 4, Section *The Ritual of Sacrifice*, para.8
[155] Ibid., Chapter 2, para.7

Again, we have a character who had symbolised the numinous feminine noting its separation. We also have a connection to the image of Heboric's hands being jade but mottled black.

Goddesses

We receive many images of matrons and fertility in *The Bonehunters*. The Queen of Dreams has taken residence in the old Y'Ghatan temple of Scalissara, Matron Goddess of Olives. This matron is recalled by her depiction on a statue: "marble arms plump and fleshy, upraised, an uprooted olive tree in one hand, a newborn babe in the other, the umbilical cord wrapped snake-like up her forearm, then across and down, into her womb." (272) This description is redolent of fertility symbolism, the newborn obvious, but the tree as well.

As Leoman leads Corabb and Dunsparrow towards the Queen of Dreams's abode, it is described as an "octagonal edifice…The formal approach was spiral, wending through these smaller domed structures." (275) This conjures a strong image of a spider's web, with the weaver awaiting at its centre.

Cutter, awakening from his wounds, finds himself in the Queen's domain. She is described as "Fair skinned, delicately featured, her long golden-hued hair drawn up and bound in an elaborate mass of braids. One hand was immersed in the pool…" (683) The connection with water suggests maternal or feminine nature, and the unconscious whence dreams arise.

Then we have the Worm of Autumn, D'rek: "the Matron of Decay, the Mistress of Worms…" (923) Fertility goddesses were frequently necessarily also goddesses of death. We see this duality here, with the leaves of Autumn falling to feed the soil, creating fertility, from which a seed grows, born anew. Death and birth are inextricably entwined.

Death and birth also come together in the city of Y'Ghatan. In a chapter epigraph we read, "First and last…Crone and child." (127) It's the beginning and end, the uroboros, a snake biting its own tail. Thus, a place of rebirth. This symbol is important mythologically, and later in the series. "Something is about to be born…" (370) And: "The sun, rising to meet its child." (397)

Trull Sengar

We find Trull in *The Bonehunters* weary and wounded, fighting to stave off his fellow Edur from the First Throne. He has the admiration of Minala and those who fight with him, while at the same time he is carrying guilt and sadness. "And a world in which children were subjected to such things was a world in which compassion was a hollow word" (852)

We see in Trull an example of the counterpoint to compassion being vulnerability. He remarks upon Minala's rage which armours her, and his own lack: "And that is my greatest weakness, that I cannot conjure the same within myself. Instead, I stand here, waiting." (852) We can convince ourselves that vulnerability is akin to inaction, weakness. We are a culture defined by action, the masculine active as opposed to the feminine passive. But here is not found weakness. "Yet, you do not surrender." (852)

By displaying our vulnerability, we might act as armour for others. "Through you, I discover the gift of fighting in defence of honour, the gift of a cause that is worthy." (846)

Trull is healed, to continue fighting. He sees no end to his battles, and no point to the endless fight. "Renewed, once again, to face what will come." (853) In this renewal, he is acting out a small-scale version of his brother's endless rebirths. But where Rhulad is only armour, an empty husk, Trull is bared heart.

Conclusion

> In the seas of reality can be found a multitude of layers, one existence flowing upon another. (34)

We see in *The Bonehunters* the connection between birth and death, understood in the danger of childbirth, here rendered symbolically by Scillara's near death at the time of birth, the idea of spiders who might eat their mate, the image of the plague-ridden children. Death and birth are brought into conjunction by the idea of rebirth. The divine feminine presides over the novel, its power and promise, its need for renewal.

There is a rebirth underway in the world of Malazan, signalled by the impregnation of the moon. This manifests in the destruction at Y'Ghatan (note that this is cyclical too), the images of blood and birth, the culling of the plague that swells bellies like pregnant women. "The old belong to the ways of blood. The new proclaim their own justice." (266)

This rebirth is symbolised by Erikson's weaving aspects of *Gardens of the Moon* into this novel. The return to Malaz with its creaking vane from the first book's prologue, the fulfilment of Paran's career in soldiery, to the death of the moon and its gardens as Apsalar weeps. This is reminder and renewal. It is a return to the beginning, changed.

Birth, of course, also invokes the idea of heritage. This is a tale that reveals layers of history: the buried layers of Y'Ghatan, the manifestations of Shadow walked by Apsalar, including her subsea wandering, the many buried cities encountered across Seven Cities, not to mention the odd skykeep entombed in bedrock.

> Rock was bone. Dust was flesh. Water was blood. Residues settled in multitudes, becoming layers, and upon those layers yet more, and on and on until a world was made, until all that death could hold up one's feet where one stood, and rise to meet every step one took. A solid bed to lie on. So much for the world. *Death holds us up. (486)*

This is history's own web, the skein of civilisation's genetic imprint. "There was no tree of life…no, there was a forest…" (651) This theme closes the loop of the idea of birth, like a snake's first taste of tail, for resurrection and rebirth must come from time's passage, from death. And all that is born must fall to dust. Less the circle of life than the inevitable spiral inwards towards decay.

There is still the notion of the individual journey here, though it is often subsumed by the greater movements in both space and time, and here it is represented in its infancy, it is the individual strands of a web that hold something greater together.

> *"To strive for change, for true goodness in this mortal world, one must acknowledge and accept, within one's own soul, that this mortal reality has purpose in itself, that its greatest value is not for us, but for our children and their children." (672)*

Climbing Into The Light: Initiation and the Death of the Child in *Reaper's Gale*

The shift from childhood to adulthood is marked by the symbolic death of the child. It is a separation, and another instance of rebirth. We continue to journey across the stages of life as stages of the individuation process in *Reaper's Gale*, with Erikson providing us with a study of the varied types of initiation, and myriad aspects of the death of the child.

Initiation, and the rites that often accompany this threshold, is typically a simulated death and rebirth. In *The Bonehunters*, we explored this theme but with a particular focus on its aspects as it relates to infancy, pregnancy, the numinous feminine. In *Reaper's Gale*, we move on through the lifespan journey to adolescence, that cusp of adulthood where the child must die for the journey of the adult to begin. Thus, once again we explore notions of death and rebirth, but with a focus on the death of the child, the various manifestations of that death as a theme. Letting go of the past, its beliefs and behaviours, so that a new self, replete with its responsibilities and burdens, might develop beyond this threshold.

The idea of this initiatory stage presaging death in form and symbol becomes important as this novel is a precursor to *Toll the Hounds*, where such matters attain a more in-depth exploration.

Initiation is the hero's journey in miniature. Journey out, death and rebirth, return changed. It is both a part of the overall individuation process and a short version of it. Its absence in our society has been argued to be the cause of many ills. The fractal nature of this journey can be starkly shown.

> The conclusion of the childhood cycle is the return or recognition of the hero, when, after the long period of obscurity, his true character is revealed. This event may

> precipitate a considerable crisis; for it amounts to an emergence of powers hitherto excluded from human life. Earlier patterns break to fragments or dissolve; disaster greets the eye. Yet after a moment of apparent havoc, the creative value of the new factor comes to view, and the world takes shape again in unsuspected glory. This theme of crucifixion-resurrection can be illustrated either on the body of the hero himself, or in his effects upon his world.[156]

Initiation is constructive for the individual. The passage from childhood often is enacted in the form of a sacrifice. Initiation is a performance of that sacrifice, it also makes acceptable the psychic sacrifice needed for growth. The child contains potential, so there is a desire to stay in that state. The real world can be disappointing, while fantasies are unlimited, and it can be welcoming to retreat to that comfort and potential. Sacrificing that potential and accepting the imperfect nature of life is a crucial aspect of growth.

For groups as well as for individuals, life itself means to separate and to be reunited, to change form and condition, to die and to be reborn. It is to act and to cease, to wait and rest, and then to begin acting again but in a different way. And there are always new thresholds to cross: the thresholds of summer and winter, of a season or a year, of a month or a night; the thresholds of birth, adolescence, maturity and old age; the thresholds of death and that of the afterlife—for those who believe in it. Van Gennep wrote that "to cross the threshold is to unite self with a new world."[157]

The prologue to *Reaper's Gale* shows us a world dying, "Worlds live on, had been the belief – the assumption – regardless of the activities of those who dwelt upon them. Torn flesh heals, the sky clears, and something new crawls from the briny much." (25) Erikson is perhaps presenting us with a lesson about valuing where we live. Perhaps, too, it is a recognition that changing stages of life entail a complete separation, a death in truth. From births, to ends—only, these are sides of a coin, death and rebirth. "Things end. Species die out. Faith in anything else was a conceit, the product of unchained ego, the curse of supreme self-importance." (26)

The realisation of the inadequacy of past knowledge, the death of the ego, is baked in to new stages of individuation. Jacobi attributes that knowledge and independence it offers as the central aspect of the individuation experience:

> "In the individuation process, as understood by Jung, the

---

[156] Campbell, 1949, p. 304
[157] Van Gennep, 1960, p. 20

primary concern is the individual experience of "death and rebirth" through struggle and suffering, through a conscious, lifelong, unremitting endeavour to broaden the scope of one's consciousness and so attain a greater inner freedom."[158]

Children believe they are the centre of the world. The death of the child, psychologically, is in essence the death of their world. In normal growth, that paves the way for rebirth. Even in the death of Kurald Emurlahn, it is the children of Mother Dark that are finding their way to a new world. "For every rebirth is an essential change, a transformation, and the possibility of this is inherent in all living organisms."[159]

Rhulad

"...in every other way he was a child." (107)

Death and rebirth are essential to growth beyond childhood, but Rhulad is unable to make that transition, and so he continually dies and is returned, never fulfilling the growth necessary to take him beyond the childish state.

"What haunted him were the truths of his past." (108) He was immature in *Midnight Tides* before he grasped the sword. Seeking the respect of his brothers, strutting, ever trying to prove himself. He never fulfilled that before the power came to him, and so he did not learn what was necessary, did not achieve internal growth to enable him to transition out of childhood. "To die, only to return, is to never escape." (108) And so, he never escaped his childhood.

Rhulad fails to fulfil a crucial aspect of the heroic journey: sharing his treasure with others. He returns from the dead, from the unknown, over and over, with great power and knowledge of mysteries, yet he clings selfishly to that power. He is ever more fearful and paranoid. His inability to share the wealth of his journey, twisted though it is, symbolised by the coins pressed into his flesh, means he is unable to grow beyond the egocentric nature of the child.

His covetous nature is shown in his response to Trull as he takes the throne. "The one you sneered down upon?" (111) He is still insecure about

---

[158] Jacobi, 1967, p. 62
[159] Ibid, p.61

his inadequacy next to his brothers. He thinks he needs the sword to escape his childhood—the trappings of strength and maturity, rather than coming to it within himself.

Nisall reflects that he pieces himself together each morning, finding some semblance of humanity after his nightly ravings. "She alone was witness to his inner triumph, to that extraordinary war he waged with himself every morning." (113) This gives us hope that there is still a spark of life within Rhulad, and continues to elicit sympathy for him. We are reminded that a child is a symbol of potential.

Receiving our impressions of Rhulad through Nisall gives us a compassionate view. We have rarely seen Rhulad up close, yet our impressions have swung as his deeds and his social position has changed. When the fleet returns, he doesn't want to see his father, fearing Tomad covets his power. The Crippled God can use Rhulad because of this very insecurity, the rift within his family that leaves him in a childlike state. The god has capitalised on his mistrust, and Triban Gnol seeks to do the same thing at a mundane level.

Rhulad is certain that everyone wants his throne—Hannan Mosag, his father, his brothers. It is the childish sense of possession to the exclusion of all else. And his senses are all projection. "Where are my Edur? Why do I never see them?" (265) he beseeches while denying their entry. "They're all frightened of me…" (265) and yet it is Rhulad himself who is riven with fear.

Nisall's arrest shows her continued concern for Rhulad, even in her own darkest hour. She has practiced compassion while seeing the child in Rhulad struggle to coordinate itself in the world. Even as he took the throne she was accepting her fate, but within her there is an inviolable core of compassion. Thus, when she is inevitably hauled off by the patriotists, her surrender is a conscious one, unburdened from vain hope. "I cannot pretend that anything I say will make a difference, will in any way change my fate." (363) It allows her to hold tight to the seeds of compassion within her. Such ego strength reminds us of Karsa Orlong when, chained, he submits to his ordeal. Even in this state, she finally musters empathy for Rhulad's continued plight, against her very captors.

The interaction between Rhulad and his parents provides an interesting study of the dynamic between parents and child, and the attempt at separation. The matter of separation in our modern conception of the myth is linked to our idea of individuality and independence, it renders family as a regression, and to separate necessarily implies independent strength. Tomad and Uruth feel they "must win him back" (630), which rings of the desire for parents to keep the child. There is necessarily a tension between parents and the peer group—the latter being the surrogate family that the child departs to as part of the separation process. "Rhulad repeats his errors…He failed to learn." (630) This is said in relation to his clinging to Nisall, whom they disdained, much as they did Udinaas. They themselves failed to realise that these two were the ones who showed Rhulad compassion.

The discussion of the enslaved kin speaks to Rhulad's desperation to find a peer group to which he belongs. The betrayal he felt from his family in *Midnight Tides*, and the isolation he now feels makes him desperate. His adaptation to a peer group is currently being subverted by Triban Gnol and the Letherii. Rhulad's instinct is being denied, just as we see in his plaintive cry for his brother, Trull.

"Father, we will talk. You and me. Alone. And Mother, yes, you too. The three of us. It has been so long since we did that." (637) This speaks to the sense of betrayal in the adolescent, the confusion of the world and the tension of wanting to separate when most needing solid ground and psychological support.

Adolescence is marked by the withdrawing of projections of the parental archetypes. Rhulad is torn between wanting to reconnect and separate from his parents. He sends them away, to their deaths unknowingly, and so only isolates himself further, and as a result he is still unable to take back his projections and grow in a healthy way.

Watched by the Errant, he of the nudge, the embodiment of precipitating chaos, we witness Rhulad's riven body and mind. This split—neurosis? "Divided soul." (818) Or just a birth, the unfolding of life's paths, the death of those untravelled? "Bifurcation. And he had witnessed when inside crawled outside to a seemingly unseeing world." (818)

Sadly, he is starting to show awareness as the duels begin. He sees through both Hannan Mosag and Triban Gnol who would manipulate him, and he thinks of how he would shape the empire. But it's too late. "Power cares nothing for reason, nothing for justice, nothing for compassion." (634) Harking back to the Errant's thoughts, we see that it is possible that Rhulad is fighting his way through that bind, that he may try and wield his power for good. Does it then become necessary that it is taken from him? Is his gradual awareness instructive for the Crippled God?

In Rhulad's final moments before Karsa ends his plight in the Crippled God's realm, we see Rhulad brighten at the opportunity of asking for Trull's forgiveness. We know by now that Trull would give it and ask for it in return.

Then finally the child dies.

In this moment, the reader is asked to forgive Rhulad, and it is all but impossible not to.

Redmask

Redmask's exile is at an end. He sought to unite the tribes but spoke unwisely. His initiation has occurred, though we have not been shown that reminiscence yet, and he has carried out the heroic journey of going into the unknown. He wishes to share the knowledge he gains with the tribes, he has strange powers in his use of mythical weapons and accompanying K'Chain Che'Malle, but he is stymied.

Redmask reflects on his banishment from the tribes, and how separation is more meaningful than in Letherii society. He is Letherii, we later find, and this has affected the nature of his own separation: "Banishment had not proved a death sentence. Banishment had proved a gift, for with it he discovered freedom." (138) The freedom he considers is that of true separation, which is difficult to attain in a modern society. "He was not as he had once been, no longer the son of his father…" (138) Recall the heroic separation from the archetypal father as explored in *House of Chains*.

Initiation in a traditional setting would take place within strict social structures. The safety net provided by the nature of modern city life, the lack of existential threat in parting from family or clan, perhaps makes it hard to adequately experience separation so as to fulfill the requirements of initiation. Redmask, banished from the tribes, but maintaining the psychological safety of 'civilised' living, experiences instead the freedom, the true separation that he wouldn't get to experience were he raised within a city. And that nature means his banishment is real—not the symbolic separation of a ritual, but the real journey of a hero, into the unknown.

Encountering his old tribe, Redmask speaks to the warriors of the death night, their initiation ceremony, and we begin to see what it entailed: "You must have no shouldermen, for if you did, they would bury you in the earth and force upon you the death night, so that you might emerge, born anew and, hopefully, gifted with new wisdom…" (141) As with many initiation rituals, this transition from childhood to adulthood is a symbolic death, burial, and rebirth—a variation on the broader theme of separation, descent into darkness, return. Eliade, in *The Sacred and the Profane*, describes this transition, and the similarity to Redmask's death night is obvious:

> Initiation includes a ritual death and resurrection. This is why, among numerous primitive peoples, the novice is symbolically "killed," laid in a trench, and covered with leaves. When he rises from the grave he is looked upon as a new man, for he has been brought to birth once more, this time directly by the cosmic Mother.[160]

Initiation, as the death of the child and the emergence into adulthood. It is also the enlightenment, wisdom, as in the emergence from darkness into light.

> In most tribes the initiation rites the young men have to go through are, with small variations, based on the same or a similar archetypal ground-pattern. They represent rebirth ceremonies, that is, the rebirth of the child into manhood, which can take place only if the child is rigorously separated from his previous life and begins a new one.[161]

We can see how this contrasts with Rhulad's lack of true separation from his old life, as it continually arises again. Rhulad is unable to emerge into adulthood, independence.

"Hard lessons, then. But becoming an adult depended on such lessons." (145) That transition is also an accounting of the life that has come before. Individuation and the growth between life's stages necessitates a consciousness of what has come before. That consciousness is the crucial aspect, as it allows us to rise above what is no longer necessary, to put it to rest. "Yet there was value in searing that transition into adulthood, rebirth that began with facing oneself, one's own demonic haunts that came clambering into view in grisly succession, immune to every denial." (165-6)

Redmask demands the proving of those before him: "it will fall to every warrior present to prove his worth." (217) His role is one of upholding tradition, enforcing the rites of separation and initiation: "Your father is gone. You must now let go of his hand and stand alone, Hadralt." (218)

Redmask takes over the army, gets Toc to teach him tactics. He has an elder at his shoulder for a time, but that elder is killed. Following that death, Redmask is less certain, and we see a dawn battle from Toc's perspective. There is uncertainty on both sides about Redmask's intentions. He appears to be afraid to deliver the blow.

---

[160] Eliade, 1959, p. 144
[161] Jacobi, 1967, p. 66

He strangles an elder, the last of his adopted clan, and therefore the remaining link to his past. Afterward, there is uncertainty, haste, and a disastrous battle. In killing the elder, he sought to sever the link to his childhood, but separation is not the death of what's left behind, but the part of oneself that was dependent. "Too many memories of his childhood had slithered into his hands, transforming his fingers into coiling serpents…" (887) The viciousness with which he perpetrates the strangling suggests Redmask's inability to withdraw his own guilt, the truth the elder represented. And now he is haunted by the man's look: "…like a father's regard on a wayward son, as if nothing the child did could be good enough…" (888)

So he is trying to live up to something he is not, making himself more Awl than the Awl. "Am I not more Awl than any other among the Renfayar?" (888)

Ultimately, he is cut down by those whose skin he wears, for failing to achieve victory for those whose trappings and culture he has notionally adopted as his persona. The fact of him literally wearing a mask of K'Chain matron's skin suggests he has identified with his persona. What it hides is the persona of an Awl. In Redmask, it seems we are seeing the result of the superficial aspects of the transition, without the conscious, deep change required to satisfactorily move over the threshold. Each attempt to separate becomes an attempt to adopt a new identity, only resulting in more persona. His attempt to escape Letherii identification is a reaction, and the attempt to adopt K'Chain identity is a literal mask, a caricature.

The two K'Chain Che'Malle might represent an adoptive mother and father, keeping him under the oppressive nature of the parents, or perhaps they are the peer group to whom he escapes, who initiate him into the world. But his failure to rejoin the world and bring back the treasure means he doesn't ever cross the threshold into adulthood. He is never truly himself because he masks himself in yet more personas.

The overly literal or clumsy attempt at separation also shows in his slaying of the elder. He can't truly separate so he has to force it—not by changing himself but by altering his environment in the most drastic way. This is the slaying of the father but, again, too literal, and the result is that he is adrift, rather than independent. The counterweight to persona is shadow, and those which Redmask casts are long indeed.

His is a variation on the theme of the initiate or hero returning, but he doesn't bring the treasure home. I'm not sure if I prefer the interpretation that he doesn't return, or that he doesn't really separate from his origin. It could be either, depending on which persona is considered, but as it turns out he so spurns his origins and cuts the connections that there is no home to which he might return.

Seren Pedac

Without containers or vessels, energies are in chaos. Kettle, and azaths in general, being vessels, represent balance. Rebirth cannot occur if we are stuck. It is a rejection of the call. Without a container for the archetypes, we are exposed to its negatives as well as positives.

Seren Pedac is exhausted from the months of endless flight. "Chained together ... yet ... who holds the means of our release?" (62) One thinks immediately that it is Seren's own individuation that will allow her release.

Kettle's ordeal at the hands of the slavers recalls Seren's own rape. "Seren had her own memories, haunting her every waking moment." (63) She is settled into a role of protector, the only female that Kettle can imprint upon, but she is uncomfortable in that role. She needs to let her past die.

"My task was singular, of course: deliver the fools, then stand well back as the knives are drawn." (77) Here Seren recalls her own role in triggering the war in *Midnight Tides*, and compares her guiding role here to that time. It sets us up to expect that she will respond differently this time. She regrets her inaction, it is her disempowerment, her own shadow. The killing of the old self entails the acceptance of the obligation to act.

"She liked not having to choose; better still, she liked not having to care." (146) Only, we suspect she does care, she just doesn't know how to break through her walls and let compassion in.

As the group come upon a garrison fort, she tries to convince Ruin not to slaughter the people, but she knows she will fail. "She could hurry after him. Attempt one more time to dissuade him. Yet she did not move…*Look at us. Frozen like rabbits*." (152) She has convinced herself again that she is powerless. Detachment is required to separate from the possession of an archetype, to distinguish oneself from the old, yet Seren Pedac, despite her assertions, is still accepting responsibility and guilt for that which she cannot control. "Yet what can I do? Nothing. Besides, it's not my business, is it?" (152) This causes her to shut down even further, just one more regret to hold in her memory.

This inability to act is repeatedly focused on, because passivity and the sense of a lack of control are a response to adversity. Rather than the notion of that helplessness being learned as an adaptation to circumstances, it is now understood that it is in fact a normal reaction, and it is hope that must be learned to defend from and escape adversity. Hope means that we have and can retain control over the world and its unpredictable events—in this way we develop resilience. In turn, this reduces psychological illness and self-destructive behaviours.

Seren Pedac, then, needs a reason to hope. "Grieve for lost potential, the end of possibilities, the eternally silent demise of promise." (403)

Seren Pedac walks between the members of her party, the Tiste at the fore and Udinaas and Fear with Kettle behind. She is the saddle point between these sets of counterbalancing forces. "She thought back, often, on their interminable flight from Letheras, the sheer chaos of that trek, its contradictions of direction and purpose; the times when they were motionless…" (588) Their flight appears random in her mind, but there is attraction, the assertion of order, even if she cannot see it yet, even if she has not acted to instil it.

She still holds to her thought that she is static, helpless. "Easier, isn't it, to just go along, and to keep from thinking too hard." (589) But even then, she sees that their passage creates disintegration around them, impossible to step through the ruins without shifting energy: "their passage was yet further pitching this landscape, and as they walked they gathered to them streams of sliding refuse. *As if our presence alone is enough to shift the balance.*" (589) Seren Pedac is in the process of learning that while she feels isolated, her presence has meaning, in ways she cannot see.

Mockra, the Warren, speaks to Seren Pedac, and we learn more about the creation, and the tension created in dialogue.

> "For the warrens to thrive, coursing in their appointed rivers and streams, there must be a living body, a grander form that exists in itself. Not chaos…a conscious aversion to disorder. Negation to and of all else, when all else is dead. For the true face of Death is dissolution, and in dissolution there is chaos until the last mote of energy ceases its wilful glow, its persistent abnegation." (590)

Van Eenwyk describes how the prevailing scientific view is that dynamic systems dissolve into chaos through entropy, never to renew. However, "The opposite of this idea is contained in models that refer to rebirth, renewal, and rejuvenation. In these models, death gives way to a new state of order, to new configurations and patterns that replace—and sometimes improve upon—

the old ones."[162] This is the rites of passage that lead to new states. The descent into depression (the underworld of heroic myth) can similarly lead to rejuvenation of the self, and of relation with the world and others.

Consciousness allows for a renewal of order, through an intentional psychic dialogue with that chaos. Initiation occurs through an intentional return to birth, to the creation. The symbolic death that occurs in initiation is not merely the creation of a blank slate, but a death of the mindset that occurred before, the innocence and ignorance of a child. The application of conscious will in acting upon chaos is the process of growth. Individuation is a cyclical renewal of order through manifestations of death and rebirth.

For Seren Pedac, magical proclivity is the higher level of existence she is stepping to. For women, initiation is an expansion of powers, capabilities, and experiences—the birth of maternal potential. The warrens are a dialogue, back and forth, a tension not of opposites, as Jung might have it, but merely of distinctions. And from dialogue, a higher understanding might be raised.

This dialogue of the warrens recognises the cyclical nature of dynamic processes, the renewal that occurs within a conscious system. "As K'rul understood, the blood flows out, and then it returns. Weak, then enlivened. Round and round. Who then, ask yourself, who then is the enemy?" (592) The enemy is stasis, despair, and thus entropy and dissolution. It is unconsciousness. The very stasis she fears in herself.

When the ego becomes fixed, the unconscious, through the shadow or dreams, for instance, will interfere and shake the ego from its perspective, create the chaotic dialogue that allows for growth. This impulse to grow and individuate is what is being portrayed by Mockra's appearance in Seren Pedac's thoughts. The balance she seeks in order to avoid thinking about her ordeal, the danger of the bliss of forgetting, is reinforced by Mockra—the projection of pain away from the self. It is through conscious dialogue with the past, her ordeal, Seren Pedac might grow.

Seren Pedac wounds Udinaas twice: first in giving him her knee pain, and then with her careless thoughts that manifest as his being choked by her image of Hull Beddict. This serves two purposes. First, it shows that she is not powerless, perhaps even growing stronger despite her feeling of stasis. Second, it demonstrates the dynamics of the unconscious that Jung proposed. What is not dealt with consciously will boil up with a vengeance from the unconscious. Seren's feelings express themselves as imaginations which hurt Udinaas—that which resided in the unconscious becomes real. Indeed, Seren Pedac solves the throttling by having "conjured into the scene

---

[162] Van Eenwyk, 1997, p. 159

within her mind another figure…" (702) She finds a solution by acting within the bounds of the unconscious. Instinct, here represented by her magic, drives towards growth—if it is repressed, it will explode. That she conjures an image of Trull Sengar to defeat Hull Beddict serves the further purpose of symbolically replacing the old aspects of herself, her former lover, with the promise of the new, the one still on the threshold, awaiting an answer.

Seren Pedac reflects on what she believes to be notions belonging to a child, its naivete, the innocence that the world inevitably takes away: "She had been no different from any other child with her childish dreams of love." (852) She convinces herself that in childhood there is a worldview inherently wrong, and that the harsh reality of the world is what kills the child. "False visions of the world were a child's right, not something to be resented, but neither were they worthy of some adult sense of longing." (852) The death of innocence is the betrayal of the child's potential. The circumscribing of life into social structure necessitates the devaluing of the child's fantasies and visions.

She kills that child within herself, with the notion that she kills what she loves. "I am poison." (866) And so makes herself unable to contact the parts of her inner child that she needs—the notion of innocence, hope.

But her inner child is trying to make its way forward, while she continues to turn the blame upon herself for her misery and loss. "Nostalgia or no, the child still within her was creeping forward, in timid increments." (853) She believes this is an expression of her immaturity and naivete, so of course it must be quashed. And so she kills in herself all notions of a child by necessity, and in doing so disallows herself the wonder and the vulnerability. And without the risk of vulnerability, how could there be compassion?

"The child is me. Still. Always." (871) The death of her inner child is the killing of that which she attributes to her childhood self, the naivete and false visions. It is part of how she convinces herself of her weakness. All the things she will not admit to, good and bad, romance and betrayal. It is her shadow, and she has cast it over her inner child.

Her method of dealing with this is to suffocate and shame that child, while part of her wishes it would return. In order to move on, she feels she must kill the inner child, let it die, so that her adult self can accept the burdens, in turn growing stronger so that she may shoulder them through life. Admissions, that she might release them. "It is what it is to live, child." (871) But in fact it is the acceptance of the burden itself that signifies growth, that raises the child to new status.

She wishes to break Fear's vow, to sting him with a bad impression of her. She can't accept protection, feels it invalidates her sense of internal control. She becomes angry and bitter at the protection he offers.

Even as the confrontation approaches, she is immobile. Fear asks how she will choose. "I don't intend to." (1102) But she has the weapons to make a difference: the spear and her Mockra magic, and aids both Trull and Udinaas once she springs into action. From: "Frozen in shock, Seren Pedac stood rooted to the ground." to: "The will to kill." (1118) Acceptance of the necessity for death spurred her to make a choice. "But alas, Seren Pedac was never good with choices." (1120) And in this moment she acts to defend both.

In the aftermath, Seren Pedac accepts the weight of Trull Sengar. She bears his burden, even as she dreads the damage she will do to him in turn, with her burdens. It appears that she is unaware that the burdens can be shared. Her wanting to take on all her own, the responsibility and blame for herself, is a refusal to share her burdens.

She symbolically allows herself to put all that inner child onto Kettle, and with Kettle's death Seren Pedac releases her own inner child. And then chooses finally acting, accepting Kettle's death, to accept burdens of adulthood, the trade-off of choice. Trull's appearance allows her inner child to surge forward, all the hopes and dreams that she relegated to it are allowed to express once more. And in that renewal of hope she lives again.

In the aftermath, we see Seren Pedac moving stones at the threshold to her house. She struggles with the centre stone—the heart stone—and when Mael arrives, we see her admission that she needs help, and she accepts that help. Finally she is sharing her burden. And thus is gifted with child—the potential, all that was within her, finding in the end healthy expression.

Chaos and Transcendence

While we should not formalise the levels of individuation (the individual's journey is more slippery than that) there are rough milestones, of which the transition from child to adult is a commonly recognised one, and one that in our culture comes with a good deal of psychic upheaval. The notion of spiralling up through levels calls to mind the dynamics of other natural processes. In particular, we can liken the transition through the initiation to adulthood as a period of chaos, and the relative calm on the other side, with the individual at a new phase of power, as a period of relative order. Departure and return, oscillating like chaos and order.

Chaos, or complex dynamics, in nature can often lead to higher levels of order through self-organisation. This gives some weight to the idea of growth being a levelling-up process that arises out of the chaos of psychic conflict. Periods of relative stability, albeit at a higher psychic level, can arise out of conflict and seemingly intractable paradox.

The subjective experience of such growth, on a scale of day to day perception, may well be the fundamental experience of consciousness, which in turn allows empathy and compassion. And these facilitate greater order at the collective scale.

Order is consciousness, chaos is the unconscious. Stability occurs when expectations, symbols, and experiences resonate. Clashes among those set us back into the unconscious as order tries to assert itself—the psyche tries to rationalise the mismatch between expectation and experience, for example, which might remould the complex. This describes well the dynamics of someone being called to individuation.

> We go from stability to instability and hopefully back again. In this case, stability refers to consciousness and the ordering capacities of the ego. Instability refers to the unconscious and its crazy-making jumbling up of conscious categories. Thus, the ego feels stable when reduction, definition, and rationality can accurately describe a situation. When these cannot, as when the ego becomes enmeshed in unconscious dynamics, the ego experiences instability.[163]

These dynamics could as well describe the moment-to-moment basis of consciousness as they do the larger scale of growth or individuation. The processes of the mind may well show self-similarity across these scales, which is why the hero's journey can be both the arc of the day's sun and the lifespan of the self.

So when a significant enough level of chaos is encountered—perhaps driven by the timed expectations of growth inherent in our DNA, a substantial reordering must occur within the psyche. Enough that we are as new people. Our perceptions trigger new results, and so on.

There is something transcendent in the passage to a new stage. The psyche transcending the ego consciousness, by which it can contextualise everything, and thus be renewed. Loss of self can occur in chaos, too.

---

[163] Van Eenwyk, 1997, p. 69

Difficulty, trauma, stress, ill-health can take us out of our context within the world, essentially challenging our very identity.

> The world often feels less real, and we feel more disconnected from others. This form of self-loss, which is deeply impacted by our environment, often results in excessive self-focus, including a fear of loss of control of one's self and a lack of a healthy integration with the rest of one's personality structure.[164]

This state of chaos and insecurity, as discussed in previous chapters, can often be the precipitating state for individuation experiences. Self-actualisation, through transcendent experience, the ego loss inherent in ritual, or the chaos of challenging mental states may all serve similar functions in spurring individuation. They may in fact intersect, as we can see how transcendent experience may arise from ritual, or ritual may be the imposition of balance in chaotic times, and so on. Disorder, too, might precipitate a need for passage or initiation, as in the stereotypical mid-life crisis, or may be part of the very process, for example if a tribe member is torn wailing from his house to be buried in the earth, enacting death.

Kettle

In *Midnight Tides,* Kettle had a kind of divine birth, or was the vessel for the Forkrul Assail heart and the Nameless One, a potential of future power. She came to life, or rather became un-undead. This represents the move from the wholeness of unconscious to the potential of consciousness. Along with that potential there is the vulnerability associated with life. From protection and invincibility (of the ego, say) to vulnerability but life. Her aliveness awakens self-realisation, the awareness of pain, of senses, of need, of loss.

She is also gathering a family, or identifying with characters as family members, so moving away from the abandonment common in the child motif. Abandonment is also necessary at an early stage of individuation, or growth into adulthood, but Kettle has first to gather around her the family upon which she can build a stable base (that construction of home or family

---

[164] Kaufman, 2020, p. 204

being a central theme in *Midnight Tides*.)

Neumann discusses the idea of the kettle as a vessel being archetypally feminine, a vessel of transformation. Dionysus becomes whole after being cooked in a magical kettle of transformation. It is therefore a symbol of fertility, and combined with the motif of a child the idea is resonant with potential and spiritual transformation.

> The kettle of transformation is identical with the sacrificial blood bowl whose content the priestess requires in order to achieve her magical purpose. Here the blood has not yet the later "spiritual" significance of a sacrificial offering, but a magical significance; it "contains" the soul, as the Bible still teaches. The necessity of its use rests on the matriarchal belief that even in the womb no life can be built up without blood. For this reason the kettles of Mexico, the blood bowls, like the caldrons of the underworld, are vessels of transformation on which depend fertility, light, and transformation.[165]

Jung wrote only briefly of the 'Child' archetype, though it deserves mention. He specifically denoted the god-like, or Christ-like nature of the appearance of this archetype, and focused on its appearance in dreams or other unconscious manifestations as part of the individuation process. Rather than appearing nominally as a child figure, "the child motif is extremely variable and assumes all manner of shapes, such as the jewel, the pearl, the flower, the chalice, the golden egg, the quaternity, the golden ball, and so on."[166]

As previously discussed, perhaps the best approach to understanding is to determine what the instinct underlying the appearance of a child archetype might be. In the child, there is purity, potential, as in a seed, the vessel of possibility, of continuity of humanity. Instinct would incline us to protect that innocence. The notion is commonly forwarded of relation to one's inner child, though Jung emphasised the potential of the forgotten aspects of childhood, its nature and conditions creating conflict with the persona we create. Thus the value in, for example, religious retellings, to remind us consciously of that nature. The child is the initial conditions of the process of individuation. The child "paves the way for a future change of personality... it anticipates the figure that comes from the synthesis of conscious and unconscious elements in the personality. It is therefore a

---

[165] Neumann, 1955, p. 288
[166] Jung, C.G., CW9i, [270]

symbol which unites the opposites…"[167]

Kettle's association with the Azath, and thus the acorn of *Gardens of the Moon*, makes her a seed. The seed as a child is a motif in fairy tales. Von Franz[168] discusses one African tale where a son hides away a seed and as it turns into a boy he brings it food and so forth, and another where the child grows and becomes a great medicine man. In the former, the mother is disturbed by the nature of the child and kills it, causing her son to depart and explore the afterlife from which he returns wiser and powerful.

The inner child or child companion is like a connection with the unconscious, similar to a connection with a toy in childhood—an other as a stand-in for the self. Von Franz says that an adult who maintains this connection with the unconscious has a call to creativity. If that call is prohibited from expressing itself, it will come up in a destructive manner.

The relationship between Seren Pedac and Kettle is the one that resonates in *Reaper's Gale*. Kettle is Seren's maintained link to childhood and the creative possibility. By cultivating the compassion for this child, she in turn becomes creative and harbours the possibility of her own life-giving instinct. Thus is her potential for maternity recreated. But the precondition is that Kettle must die, or at least fulfill her telos as a seed.

We also touch on the idea of killing the child in another way. Von Franz suggests that as parents and as a society, when we see unruliness and uncanniness, we tend to quash it in children. Children with unusual talents or precocious abilities are somehow feared, because it is outside the realm of our experience. Our job is to set limits, and yet we are killing the unconscious aspect of the child. We come round here to the idea of the shadow, and what is put in the bag, as Bly put it. The death of the child is in a sense necessary because to live as a child forever is to remain unproductive and unhealthy in society.

Kettle is losing her innocence by seeing how her adopted family treat each other, even as she is returning to life. In the end, it is her death that restores balance, in the form of an Azath, allowing the Refugium to live on.

---

[167] Ibid. [278]
[168] Von Franz, 1997a

Magic as Metaphor for Metaphor

The notion of magic is discussed by Jung as symbol formation and transfer of energy. Illusion is real, in a sense, because it changes your view of the world. "A ceremony is magical so long as it does not result in effective work but preserves the state of expectancy."[169] Like prayer, which may not do what it purports on the surface, but prepares us to act and receive stimuli in a state of readiness, thus changing the outcome had that preparation not taken place. The key, then, is intention.

Good prose is replete with metaphor, but Erikson goes a step further, hinting that magic itself functions the same way as metaphor. In *Deadhouse Gates*, Kulp wonders how to get the ship Silanda through from the liminal space of a warren back to their world:

> He'd hoped he would find inspiration once within the Meanas Warren, some thunderbolt delivering a simple, elegant solution. *With all the grace of poetry. Was it not Fisher Kel'Tath himself who once said poetry and sorcery were the twin edges to the knife in every man's heart? Where then are my magic cants?* (DG, 382)

This use of poetry and sorcery as twin edges of a knife is a metaphor for the dual nature of language. A good metaphor strikes home because it cuts through the distinction between ideas. In magic in Malazan, we have a function that cuts through distinct states of being. A state of chaos or expectancy is created, and in its resolution or ordering, intent creates value.

The concept of metaphor can be understood in terms of the tension it creates between the known and unknown or the conscious and unconscious. Van Eenwyk[170] quotes Jouette Bassler's writing on the Parable of the Loaves, where Jesus (magically) feeds a crowd with a couple of buns: "a metaphor communicates by juxtaposing two not entirely comparable elements, thereby inducing the hearer to extract from the somewhat discordant image a new vision of the primary element." The tension created by the metaphor compels our involvement by shaping our expectations and perceptions in real time.

Basler discusses Wolfgang Iser's theory of narrative gaps or blanks, illustrating the role of tension in the creation of meaning. According to that idea, the interactions between text and reader are generated where there are gaps or blanks in the narrative, as when information is temporarily withheld, there is an interruption in the expected stream of thought or expectations are

---

[169] Jung, CG. CW8 [89]
[170] Van Eenwyk, 1997, p. 74

overturned, links are established between difficult to connect elements, views within or between text and reader are challenged, or inferences must be drawn. These narrative gaps and blanks create tension and compel the reader to complete their understanding of the world and its workings.

We can see how fantasy literature, and in fact the very notion of a functioning magic system is structured on unknowns and the reader's lack of knowledge, defamiliarization. This is very much the same process of sleight of hand in stage magic. Expectations are created, information presented and omitted so as to reinforce expectations or draw attention, misdirecting it, and when the outcome clashes with the perspective created, inference is used to fill the gap made by the impossibility presented.

Consciousness expands to encompass a higher level of understanding. Reality changes, at the least the reality that we create as our conscious mind interacts with the world through the clash of expectations (the world within) and the perception (the world as received).

Erikson's use of metaphor and magic in the Malazan series heightens this tension, setting up expectations and then subverting them. The clash of expectations and perception creates a higher level of understanding as the reader's consciousness expands to encompass a new perspective. Reality changes, at least the reality that we create as our conscious mind interacts with the world. The uncertainty created by the clash of expectations and perception facilitates the potential for growth.

Why does a metaphor strike home, and where is the disparity between the ideas connected? I propose that the same underlying mechanism that explains archetypes is at play. What two ideas might share is some overlap in the subconscious structures at an archetypal level. The surprise of a metaphor resides in bringing them together at a conscious level. What two ideas share is a deeply underlying instinctual expectation, and their fulfilment at a conscious level realises that expectation.

It is not just in the resolution that a metaphor works, but in the state of chaos in between. A metaphor that leads to an interpretation might be considered a well written one, but metaphor that engages the chaos and sets off the search for meaning, for resolution, without guiding to a particular answer, is not necessarily bad. Religious metaphor, for example, and the difficulty of interpretation may well be intended to resist solid conclusions. The chaos arising thus being the very point, encouraging the reader or listener to abide within uncertainty, that condition itself facilitating the potential for growth. Note how the Tanno Spiritwalker's song for the Bridgeburners is "elliptical…like a serpent eating its tail…It's like a spell that remains active,

awaiting resolution." (*HoC*, 481)

This process describes the state of wonder in fantasy. The clash of expectations and perception, a lack of explanation, invites the reader to sit with uncertainty in order to complete their understanding of the world and its workings. This conflict can create greater value and understanding, in both the text and the reader. As Mockra tells Seren Pedac,

> "The construction of language, the agreement in principle of meaning and intent, the rules of grammar – Seren Pedac, what did you think Mockra was? If not a game of grammar? Twisting semantics, turning inference, inviting suggestion, reshaping a mind's internal language to deceive its own senses?" (591)

Metaphor takes understanding and shifts it with the application of a second viewpoint. Dialogue lifts up understanding.

The Hunted

Udinaas

At the end of *Midnight Tides*, when he is taken over by the Wyval, Udinaas thought "His master needed him." (853) This sets up an interesting dynamic, because among the layers of his slavery there is part of Udinaas that considers Silchas Ruin master. Kettle bled on him to keep him alive – the potential and power of the child, returning that life potential to him. So he is conjoined to Kettle in a way, and the anger he shows at the beginning is a protective one. The ex-slave is bitter, and our first sighting of him is taking his revenge on a Letherii slaver. "'Your blood is very thin, Udinaas'... 'Like water'." (65)

Each of the Hunted carry their past and their shadows with them. Ruin's draconian form and his anger hover in his shadow. Kettle's soul, the source of her power. Fear is burdened by Silchas Ruin as myth, and Udinaas as the one he blames for Rhulad's state of mind. Seren Pedac has her own memories, and Kettle as the symbol of the child within herself. Udinaas, of course, has both Wither and the Wyval as the other aspects of himself, reminders of his powerlessness.

"Someone has to be the moral lesson in this epic, right?" (79) However,

I would suggest that Udinaas, too, is capable of change. His role is not merely as counterbalance and commentator to the others.

He provokes Fear, prods at him with his recollections of slave life. It was portrayed as stable, at least, in *Midnight Tides*, but here we begin to get recollections of the true burdens the slaves lived under. Now that he has experienced some freedom, been allowed to speak out, Udinaas is able to share his feelings.

Udinaas mourns the innocence of Kettle. We recall the compassion he had for the child he met in the Refugium, his own child. He is not close, he does not have the experience of love himself to form the attachment, but he understands compassion and innocence. His experience with Rhulad showed him that innocence can still exist in a child, even when outwardly it seems power has twisted the form.

Menandore thinks Udinaas's compassion is fleeting. "He has played with it for a long time…" (474) I think his cynical exterior somehow maintains the compassion, deep within. He has learned to hide it from his many layers of masters. Note that Udinaas dreams he is crippled, thus mirroring the Crippled God. Menandore's assertion that he has no faith or compassion is dismissive, and might be the same dismissal we apply to the Crippled God.

"Each night I receive lessons…in taking control." (476) Order, balance. His initiation is occurring in the unconscious. Dreams within dreams. He reflects on this once his fever breaks, and sees only the many paths closed off. "The strength I felt in those other worlds was a lie. The clarity, a deceit. All those offered ways forward, through what will come, every one a dead end." (586) He has seen the chaos, the many possible states, and in the renewing of a rite of passage, all that possibility collapses down as order is found. A fever broken, he finds clarity, though not the answers he may have wanted.

In the end we see he is connected with Seren Pedac's grief, by way of their shared trauma. We could see this as his empathy, or we could see it as a fellow wounded victim. It could also be that their connection through her Mockra magic has left some thread. It is interesting because she has refused to share her burdens, refused to allow anyone in, and yet Udinaas is able without being asked. We can give compassion and sympathy without needing anything in return.

Udinaas eventually returns to his son in the Refugium, but his son has seen death and lost innocence. While Udinaas wasn't there to initiate his son, he is the one who is vulnerable, able to comfort Kettle. He held Kettle's hand as they approached the gate, he was the one that wanted to stay connected to the child. He believed that her innocence had value. He is the initiating father in his world so that he can repair his relationship with Rud Elalle.

In their final scene, Udinaas allows that he will stay in the Refugium. He is confirming his son's love. He is also coming home himself, to the only family he knows. "Father, you can teach me your greatest skill. How to *survive*." (1256) The child, the ranag calf, crying out, survives, as its kin come for it.

Fear Sengar

The final scenes of *Midnight Tides* are like a prologue for Fear Sengar. "He'd wanted to believe. In all the possible glories. …There had been no great tragedies to mar his youth, and he'd stridden, not stumbled, into adulthood." (*MT* 908) Trull…"gave voice to all my doubts, my terrors, so that I could defy them – so that I could be seen to defy them." (*MT* 909) He thinks he is a failure. He had not seen clearly. He thinks he is the one who betrayed. Finally the weight of all he denied comes down upon him. He would return Father Shadow to his people, bring back the old ways.

These notions give fuel to Udinaas's taunting in *Reaper's Gale*. Udinaas suggests that Fear wants glory still, the return to the old ways, his stalwart insistence on the litany level of life once lived, the stories they were told.

The slave continues to mock his version of Fear's heroic journey. These passages make for interesting reading on their own, and show the self-awareness in Erikson's depiction of his heroes. But they also reveal Fear as being stuck in place, he is unable to exert himself upon the world, pinned between duty and individuality.

What hits home about Udinaas's baiting is not the nature or specifics of the mythical journey he portrays, but the very fact of it deriving from a naïve, childish version of the story. The slave's words unravel the façade of Fear's maturity. He is indeed undertaking a journey of initiation, seeking wisdom in the unknown, and so on. The child he needs to let die is not the one of heroic visions, but the one of his cultural beliefs. He seeks truth, but is reluctant to find it. Udinaas's insinuated narrative is therefore a metaphor for the Edur's operating narrative as a whole.

Balance and opposites

The first encounter on the road to individuation is the ego with the unconscious, or the confrontation with the shadow. The I and the not-I. This is not opposition, though, it is a mere distinction. The opposite of king is neither pauper nor queen—if anything, life and the unconscious are replete with potential complementarities.

The notion that the unconscious manifests the opposite when ego identification occurs therefore takes on more subtlety – we could say that ego identification results in complementary energy manifesting in the unconscious, depending on the complete social, cultural, historical, and psychological context of the individual, and their receptivity, and their stage of the journey of individuation, not merely an opposing, contrary pair.

Greater consciousness, then, is not merely an appreciation of opposition, and supposed 'integration' of it to achieve balance – it is the expansion of consciousness across spectra, such that higher possibilities of awareness, and a greater range of points of view exist. At its widest expanse, there is the potential to synthesise opposing notions or energies on any particular spectrum, though I suspect this is likely only possible with great diligence and experience on a particular matter or sense, and in interaction with widened consciousness across other interrelated spectra of knowledge or skills or perceptions.

This is the very notion of darkness and light. Perception of light doesn't balance darkness—it creates shadow which merely increases the range of possible experience and interactions.

Yan Tovis / Twilight

Her very name suggests transition. The Shore is a place of passage. As life crawled from the great ocean, so the shoreline marks a place of transition.

She encounters Shake witches, and we learn she is the Queen of her people. Yet Yan Tovis has attempted to escape her heritage. Like the inevitable draw of biology, she realises that it was not really escape, and she was working beneath the conscious level to prepare herself.

The shore, and the inexorable rise of the sea is a metaphor for the cosmic oscillation of unconsciousness devouring the conscious. "The Shake knew that in the beginning the world had been nothing but sea, and that in the end it would be the same. The water rising, devouring all..." (514) Entropy inevitably grows as the chaotic fractal of the shoreline is consumed to return to order.

Twilight fled her people and her legacy. Separation was too one-sided, and now she must reintegrate that part of herself, accept the legacy, and reconcile the sides of her character for herself and her people. She stands, as the nature of twilight, at the line where land meets sea, on the precipice between the two states, balancing order and chaos, conscious and unconscious.

The tossing of demonic babies into the sea by the Shake is the same refusal of themselves as Yan Tovis displays. It is a denial of their heritage, and relegation of the shadow to the unconscious. And yet, Twilight's knowledge of the Shore, nagging at her, her drawing of those with Shake blood about her, all speaks to the biological drives within her.

Similarly, Yedan Derryg—both fled, and both are summoned by the shore, for they know not what. Their witnessing of the burning boats is symbolic of their own choices—first the attempt to leave behind their heritage, and now of the stance they must take. In witnessing, Twilight becomes certain she will no longer float upon the depth of the unconscious, but make her stand upon solid ground. "The old ways failed us. Then and now." (597)

Janath

Tanal Yathvanar is Janath's torturer. He is seen as touchy when Karos Invictad reveals awareness of his proclivities. He will take Invictad down with him, and his instinct is to blame others for being found out, rather than accept responsibility for his wrongs. Before we meet Janath, we see Tanal being berated by Karos Invictad, and we are shown that his attitude is somewhat fixed. Janath, too, will make use of that.

Janath tries to bite Tanal with words. She calls him little man. She speaks of the sort of people who fulfil these rules in a tyrannical society: "…small-minded psychotics and perverts. All bullied as children, of course. Or abused by twisted parents…" (85) More than mere understanding of psychology, Janath demonstrates her empathy: "I slip into your head. I see through your eyes. Swim the streams of your thought." (86) We might question whether Tanal's point of view is indeed written through Janath's own perspective. Janath's story shows us that compassion is possible, even when it must be forced at first, surrendered to. To do less is to continue to hide, and so lose one's self.

When Tanal hints at her freedom, she initially shows animation but then quells it within herself. She is determined not to allow herself hope. Notions of inequity pervade the Empire, and the power dynamics between these two are symbolic of that. The importance of holding on to her fundamental values, and the strength required to do so, will be the lessons taught by Janath. But she finds hope, too, which mirrors Seren Pedac's journey.

Tanal Yathvanar defends Invictad, though he has been victimised by the man, "he learned that all emotion had to be scoured from him" (185). This is the transfer of victims lashing out, with Tanal now playing that role upon Janath. Her words and his fear of her twist their balance of power, so that she maintains some control over the situation, even when she is without hope.

Tanal has convinced himself he is in love with Janath, and he expands that to create the possibility in his mind that his love would be reciprocated. He thinks of Karos Invictad, who has wounded him with words: "You and your power, it is all compensation for what you do not understand about the world, for the void in your soul where compassion belongs. Compassion, and the love that one can feel for another person." (273) But compassion is more than just the ability to feel, it is also to empathise. He hasn't shown the ability to understand Janath, but she has him. His view remains egocentric. Van Eenwyk notes that both analysis and life teach us how our self-perception colours our view of others. This is the dynamic of projection.

> Too often—particularly in our most emotionally intense moments—we interact more with our projections (and, thus, with ourselves) than with that which is actually there. When the world fails to confirm our presumptions, we often believe that it is crazy. This further erodes our relationships, leading to a downward spiral whose only remedy is a healthy dose of ego-effacing consciousness.[171]

Tanal's delusions reflect Rhulad's own egocentric creation of his world. His vision clashes with reality, the vision he'd conceived within his imagination, and the clash upsets him, serving to remind him of his lack of control, as much as Invictad's scolding does. "It's all up to me!" (275)

Janath, on the other hand, has trusted reason, her intellect holding firm to her sense of self, batting away at intrusions and firing invective. Now she believes Tanal's physical victory demands her surrender. "And she felt madness reach out to her, an embrace that would sweep away her sense of self, her knowledge of who she had been, once, that proud, smug academic

---

[171] Van Eenwyk, 1997, p. 26

with her pristine intellect ordering and reordering the world." (277) But surrender of direction doesn't necessitate sacrifice of the self. Acknowledgment of her limits—of the binding chains—is necessary, and from there, balance can be sought, temperance achieved. This theme has been explored elsewhere in Malazan, but here with Janath it is a very focused study.

Aniela Jaffe posited that individuation involves the conscious ego surrendering its illusion of freedom, that the ego yield control and authority to the Self, for unrestrained freedom or free will bears no meaning in the absence of direction. Submitting to greater powers does not necessarily encroach upon free will. Consciousness itself is thought to exist as both a blessing and a burden. Self-awareness brings forth the acknowledgment of hidden darkness within. This notion echoes the fall of Adam and Eve, where the price of independence is the relinquishment of security.

There is a compulsion to choose, and that is the expression of consciousness. We can give in to the forces that act on us, complete surrender, or we can choose to act. Janath chooses compassion for her torturer, and in doing so she retains (and eventually regains) her freedom. All the while, her freedom within herself remains undefeated. Acceptance does not necessarily mean resignation. Jung's approach to individuation and finding meaning requires not just surrender but conscious actualisation of the unconscious. In approaching things that way, I believe that we retain our strength, our sense of individuality is not subsumed by the great ocean of existence, and therefore we retain the possibility of meaning. If acceptance is total, and surrender is final, a goal in itself, then we are nothing but meaninglessness. That leads to nihilism, a total surrender to forces that would control our lives and seeing it as a virtue—where, then, is the self?

If we teach ourselves to surrender, then the ego will ever be slave to the unconscious, to the impulses that act upon us. By teaching conscious individuation, it strengthens the individual, even as he or she becomes ever more aware of the depth and strength of those unconscious forces. It is a dance. We meet what comes our way and grow as necessary. But were we to surrender early, or have our growth stymied by society or parents or education that weakens our will and sense of self, the work to regain that self becomes harder.

Consciousness is therefore self-fulfilling. We create ourselves. That is both at the individual and collective level. A conscious self does not surrender its individuality. A conscious civilisation does not oversee its own destruction.

With Bugg and Tehol, seemingly safe, Janath comments that "I do remember what happened, but not even a whisper of emotion reaches me." (424) She is keeping her thoughts close, the emotional responses pinging off the hard shell she's made about her experiences. This appears to confirm the notion that she has not sacrificed her essential self, but rather withdrawn it to such a remote place it cannot be contacted. Like a seed being kept dormant. Erikson is pondering whether even seemingly broken characters might retain their potential, for compassion and fulfilment.

And so, when she is recaptured, and the memory of her trauma returns, that seed is reborn, the conditions right for its germination. With the knowledge of her pain surfacing again, she prepares herself for the ordeal to come.

Just as Janath had her memory buried by Bugg's healing, now that she is captive once more, she must treasure her freedom, keeping it locked within. This she achieves by acting as she understands Tanal Yathvanar wants her to act.

The chains, the tools of her captivity, and Tanal's desire—the psychological tool of her captivity—become her weapons when she finally murders the man as he lies atop her.

A chained one, then, with compassion alive like a spark within the black of a wounded soul.

The Bonehunters

Tavore's army underwent its bloody birth in the previous volume, and now has crossed the ocean as part of its initiation. The first part of initiation is a separation from the old, and this is what has occurred with their voyage, and the unseen speech by Tavore.

Reaper's Gale portrays separation and abandonment in many forms in addition to that of the Bonehunters. The Awl are missing their elders, Rhulad and the Edur are isolated, Clip and the Bluerose Andii are abandoned by Rake. This separation is the death to birth of initiation. Bondage, and flight from it, with Janath, Udinaas, and Feather Witch. We also have Bugg's musings about Icarium: "as lost as any son, a child severed from the thread." (256) This recalls the webs and threads of *The Bonehunters*, and we are also shown that an abandoned child will seek guidance, find a role model in whatever he latches on to (in Icarium's case, it is K'rul.) And of course, Kettle is the abandoned child, and the wounded characters around her show the variations of response.

And so the army's unseen separation serves both to keep Tavore's motives hidden, and to fulfill the function of keeping the ritual taboo. We are not allowed to see because we must ourselves be initiated. This cannot be an intellectual exercise, as Redmask demonstrates to his fellow warriors, it is something that can only be experienced.

"We now cross the world to find the first name that will be truly our own…we sail to give answer." (543) True separation, and unburdened by all past and expectations they must step forward, initiated. The rallying cry that they be unwitnessed takes their deeds beyond ego, beyond the expectation of personal gain. What is done is truly for their own purpose.

The Bonehunters are scattered, uncertain, riven with chaos in other words. There must be a disintegration of the old before rebirth can be attained. Order can be found, a new state of being, when they all come together. So we are learning about the Bonehunters by experiencing their fragmentation, absorbing the chaos. This at once makes them individuals (as units, and as points of view) and part of a whole, which can be likened to the process of initiation, at once a separation and an integration into something greater. And we are getting our own initiation as readers, seeing into the perspectives of these many soldiers, their cases and histories. That is the effect of perspective in all literature, but here Erikson is very consciously presenting the soldiers' perspectives, and some of the enemies', to invite that brief joint perspective, our readerly minds like moths flitting from flame to flame on a dark night's procession.

It is very deliberate that we witness the coming of age of many of these soldiers, in many cases their transition to adulthood or their separation (the death of the child, which is played on with Beak). For example, in Chapter 14 we begin a tour across members of the army with Fiddler's awakening at dusk—a transition period—and for him and Gesler a falling back or reversal, reflection on how they came to be here. This section begins with Fiddler musing on his identity: "He'd wanted to be a soldier named Strings…a new man…he could not convince himself that he had begun anew…" (598) The recognition here is that transition is not always letting go of the past, but integrating it.

Gesler reflects on his path to this point, much of which we have witnessed. "How many battles have we fought, you and me?" (603) Bottle listens to Smiles and Koryk banter of naïve tales told in childhood, that innocence now lost. Corabb is still trying to fit in, likening this army to a pack of animals. Then we meet Trantalo Kendar, an Edur, reflecting on his recent adolescence and apprenticeship, just before he is killed. Hellian ponders the tragedy of a flask half full. Beak plays out a storybook rogue tale and professes love for Faradan Sort, in the way an adolescent might. And then we end with Throatslitter recalling the harsh separation from his father, cast from the family at fourteen. That we end with this symbolism of assassination, separation, mutiny while he observes Tavore and the senior members of the army is itself symbolic. Such passages are frequent through the second half of *Reaper's Gale*, binding the narrative.

It's in the background, but we also see Sinn's progression and her lost childhood. She comes into her power in this novel. "Child of the rebellion. Stolen from the life she should have lived, fashioned by horror into something new." (715) She represents a variation on the theme of the death of the child. It also sets us up for this latter part of the series, where the promise of childhood is frequently contrasted with death and destruction.

With Beak's unveiling of power, it is through Fiddler that we see literally inside the soldiers. He sees their imperfections, their character flaws are shown throughout the novel, but here we are privy to the underlying physical imperfections which, for some, is the very basis of their flaws. About them after is a symbolic purity, while we, and Fiddler as father figure, inherently understand that it is not a literal purity, that beneath there are flaws. We see this through Fiddler because he is the one capable of holding compassion for all those soldiers—he can carry the contradiction.

Beak

"She reminded him of his mother, looks-wise, which should have killed quick any thoughts of the lustful kind…Unlike his mother, anyway, she wasn't the type to browbeat him at every turn, and that was refreshing." (556) It is compelling to consider the mother complex as the fault of son, a failure to grow or of desire to separate. And complex certainly describes Beak's impression of Faradan Sort in this passage. Just as real a phenomenon is the mother that doesn't allow children to grow, wants to keep them as children, they aren't allowed to let it die. This can be as extreme as sleeping with the child. It maintains dependence. Beak, and we presume his brother, had not been allowed to grow. As a result of this stymied development, Beak doesn't know about relating to others.

Without initiation, or with initiation disallowed, there is a kind of inertia from which we are unable to grow. This can speak to the necessity of rites of passage in giving a purpose to the transition from one stage of life to another.

He speaks of his candle in the dark, a light of hope, consciousness. He showed the candle once and everyone died. Tempering such power through initiation and psychic wholeness can be the antidote to such youthful wildness.

The childlike nature is emphasised when we learn that his age when he ran away was nearly thirty. His manner and his story speak to adolescence, but he is merely trapped there. This naïve youthful mentality is exemplified as he ponders his worship of Faradan Sort. He thinks he loves her, though he is simply unused to the attention and respect. "He had never been so happy. This captain was asking him things. Asking for suggestions. Advice. And it wasn't just for show neither. *I'm in love with her.*" (615)

Beak feels some comfort from the notion that the other soldiers are now like him in being unwitnessed. He thinks about anonymous lives, though for him it has meant staying under the radar. This gives us an idea of where we might direct our compassion, even to those we can't see.

"I am learning to tell those moments…When you've convinced yourself how stupid you are." (734) Faradan Sort's assessment shows us that Beak is repressing his own growth. He doesn't know how to come out of his shell, to take command of his knowledge and power, and he quickly retreats when he is noticed. All that turning inwards can result in deleterious effects. "Don't burn me down to the core, Captain. Please." (735)

Beak, at his end, reminisces about his brother suiciding. He had wanted to play, and in his brother's dying moments he was helpless. He is frozen in that moment, the trauma, as much as he is kept a child by his mother and his self-doubt. He joins his brother in the afterlife, which appears to him like a figment of his childhood. He himself remains a child, too.

"Survival, he had found, could only be found through purity." (1057) But is this purity, or innocence? He purifies those within the circle of his magic, returning them to an innocent state, or healing their trauma, even as he dies a child.

This is a variation of the death of a child. Beak does not grow but remains in childhood, a mirror of Rhulad Sengar.

Nimander

As we meet Nimander, we learn he is cursed with inaction. He sees Phaed's nature, but is polite to her, avoidant, almost submissive. He seeks balance in his dealing with her, but sometimes we have to engage the chaos consciously. Sandalath acts as surrogate mother for the Andii, the decisive impulse where Nimander and the others are otherwise in stasis. Nimander thinks of the comfort in following: "Easier to simply follow the commands of others." (568) Without a role model to lead them, he has to find a way to initiate himself to action.

He has the impulse to grow, yet he feels no direction, and no father to guide him. "He was no soldier of darkness, just a young man standing lost in a strange street, a man with nowhere to go – yet driven, driven on at this very moment – to go *somewhere*." (717) He rehearses in his mind what he needs to do, what he knows Anomander Rake would do in stopping Phaed. He is grieving, "She was everything. And she is dead." (719) which gives some rationale for his stasis, and he has introjected the guilt.

"…we are each incomplete…Nimander, who imagines himself leader of this fell family of would-be heroes, who will seek out the ends of the earth in his hunt for … for courage, for conviction, for a reason to do, to feel *anything*." (718) There is a recognition here that the incompleteness in them could be fulfilled by a heroic journey, an initiation. For Nimander, it is to come into his heritage, and to recognise his leadership qualities. Also to accept the respect and admiration of his peers as a leader, in a way that Anomander Rake does not as an ascendant.

Before his confrontation with Phaed, Nimander (in an insomniac haze) is thinking of the living heads upon Silanda, and their bodies beneath the deck. They are ancestors, fathers and mothers that are separated from their bodies, but that the young Andii cannot separate from. Nimander's need to conjoin mind and body is symbolised here, as he is in a state of stasis like those animated ancestors.

"To lead is to carry burdens." (927) To live, alas, is to carry burdens. "Burdens, my love. This is what it is to live, while your loved ones die." (928) It is ambiguous whether this is the ghost of Phaed in his mind, or the beloved he still mourns. It is another burden for him. And so Withal bears his burden of guilt as he sees it, because of his failure to follow through in stopping Phaed. He paralyses himself, seeking only balance, but action, leadership, require the upsetting of that balance.

The Crippled God

Silchas Ruin speaks to a K'risnan, revealing his greater understanding of the Crippled God: "a god in pain is not the same as a god obsessed with evil." (158) This is a recognition that the Crippled God's pain does not necessarily make him evil in intent. Silchas Ruin, while seemingly cold and brutal, is showing compassion for the god. He does not hate, rather he feels pity.

Later, the god himself, speaking through Janall, seems to demand that pity again. "Will you never see? Never understand? I must find the broken ones, just do not expect my reach, my touch. No-one understands, how the gods fear freedom. No-one." (195) We are continuing the shift away from the understanding of this god as the effect he has upon the world, towards the being that resides within, deserving of pity and compassion.

"You have lied to yourself. You all do, and call it faith. I am your god. I am what you have made me." (195) This speaks at once to the reader and Janall, noting that what impressions we have up until now of this god are what are projected from our expectations. It also confirms Ruin's earlier assertion, "perhaps it is the likes of you who have in turn shaped the Crippled God. Perhaps, without his broken, malformed worshippers, he would have healed long ago." (158) The wounded seek the wounded, a twisted convergence, and then their lies give him power.

The god also speaks about power, upending our notion that the god himself is peddling his power to manipulate the world. "You all decry my indifference, but I assure you, you would greater decry my attention…I know what you claim to do in my name…Watch me, mortal, watch me call you on it." (195-6) And of course, the Crippled God knows the consequences of the unleashing of his power: "if I give you what you want, we all die." (196)

At the end, we see the Crippled God attempting to bargain with Karsa. "Let the children witness!" He wants to appeal to Karsa as being dominant over children, but he has grown. No longer desirous of power, of domination. It shows the Crippled God as being focused on that pre-adult mentality.

In addition, it tells us that the Crippled God is at least aware of what is in the heart of people. He may have got it wrong with Karsa, but he is incisive with Rhulad. He offers Rhulad the chance to ask for forgiveness of his brother, Trull. This shows at the least that he is aware, has empathy, even if he twists it for manipulative purposes. But therein lies the potential for compassion.

But for now, we are left with the image of the Crippled God, helpless, bawling, like a child.

Conclusion

Individuation is the overall process of archetypes coming to fruition, expression of the biological process, and has within it the psychological drive towards actualisation. Any deviation or developmental difficulty causes a homeostatic process, which is felt as the sense of getting back on track. As Icarium ponders, the water gets churned and brought along after the canal, the detritus is part of the river, but the water still flows. The natural flow is the shortest path, with all its currents. We can consciously deviate, use that energy for other projects, but at the end of the day, it will still flow.

The Self is a central organising archetype, like the bed of a river, and the unfolding of the process of individuation is the course of the water's flow. We can shift it with consciousness, we can wound it and muddy it and it can contain all manner of resident swimmers. Over time the riverbed is shaped, just as we evolve. But in the end, the water is still flowing the same way.

Perhaps it seems, at times, that we are like Kilmandaros or Rautos Hivanar looking for patterns where none might exist. But it is the sense of pattern that keeps us moving forward.

> "The whole of life may, of course, be viewed as one long process of transition; but it is never a steady progression, and the way is strewn with markers, like milestones which have been eccentrically placed, some fairly close together, others widely apart, and the journey between them is often tedious and uneventful."[172]

Initiation is both a separation and return at once. Separation from childhood and return to the world. "Death and birth. Even in opposition, the two forces are bound, and to define one is to define the other." (253) We go to the child and back, for example Onrack's return to life is an enlivening of

---

[172] Stevens, 2002, p. 182

his childlike nature, from which he and those around him can separate once again.

Reaper's Gale speaks to notions of power, the interplay of those using gods and used by gods. The power of worship, servitude, in chains—those of duty, debt, and literal imprisonment. It turns notions of the worship of immortality on its head, instead we see worship of the mundane: Cuttle's faith in Fiddler, and the army's faith in Tavore. Gods in the mortal realm: the Errant, Fener, Mael. There is the worship of Icarium by Senior Assessor, and of Karsa by the Toblakai. The Emperor is immortal but controlled in a sense by the mortals about him. It is the humanising of devotion, the grounding of worship in the mundane, those just like us. The exhortation not to look for saviours and tricks in godlike authority, but to see the divine, the purity in one another.

In the Refugium we see the death of an innocent place, a time. Onrack's wonder is childlike, and he wishes to defend those kin residing there. It is the belief in childhood, defiance in the face of the assertion that such wonder is merely an illusion—that the stories we tell ourselves are only that. But can stories live? This echoes Seren Pedac and her childish notions of romance, Smiles and Koryk recalling the naïve tales of adventure, and is contrasted by Udinaas's retelling of a heroic tale with the 'realities' of adult life and the outer world reshaping the story. But if there is no sense of wonder, is there only despair?

"In discovering what it is to die, we have been cast out from the world." (1087) The Imass are apart, separate from the natural world—their true parents. This is their descent. Of course, they wish for their innocence back, and their self-portrayal is a reminder, humbling them in the face of the world. Of those within the Refugium, it is said: "Their conceit…has made them real." (1096) Fitting, then, that it is the death of the child returning to life, Kettle, that fixes that innocent place in reality.

Ulshun Pral reflects that the deathless realm of the Refugium "was deathless no longer." (1106) Is it that vulnerability, the very possibility of death that gives innocence its meaning? And so, everyone wants to defend the realm, just as Kilava and Onrack defend their child, including the three T'lan Imass, "And we came here with chaos in our hearts." (1113)

The act of birth, death, rebirth, are symbolic of the cosmology of existence. By taking part in that movement we are replaying and affirming something sacred. It is the ultimate expression of belonging to a cosmic whole, and we enact our gods in the very act of existing.

Could it be said that the symbolic deaths and rebirths which represent growth in our lives are something sacred? Not to lift it to a religiose ideal, but to treat our actions and our heightened consciousness as something profound and numinous might give impetus to the need. It is also an assertion of order at the point of chaos. Lack of initiation means we dwell in chaos for too long, and one can only speculate but that likely leads to physical and mental ill-health.

Without it, we cannot transcend our state of chaos, profanity. So we get stuck in a cycle, where not growing means we cannot initiate the next generation. If we were to characterise the nature of our civilisation, it would be fair to say it is childish in its wants and dependence on structure, hero worship, war, the elevation of political ideologies. At best, adolescent. Individuation, growth at the level of the individual, and the accepting of the burdens and responsibility of such, are the only way to effectively enact change on a large scale, short of catastrophe or paradigm shift.

Even without religion, the instinct persists. The unconscious exists, and it finds expression even when we don't provide the conditions for it. Symbols will arise in our dreams and fantasies. Expressions of our desire for heroism, or initiation, for example, will be latched on to even if they are but pale impressions. But the unconscious, our creativity and our dreams, do offer potential symbols and solutions, if approached with awareness of their symbolic value.

All separations are also unifications. All deaths are rebirths. The second half of life was seen by Jung as separation from the worldly attachments and unification with psychic wholeness. Death, the obvious separation, but we can speculate a soul reunification. At the very least it's a physical reunification with the earth from which we ascended. Death leads to *Toll the Hounds*, and with our awakening compassion we might understand that there is a beauty in it, two sides to grief. It can be approached consciously, and that in itself can render it meaningful, a rebirth.

Seeds in the Ashes: Withdrawal, Reconciliation, and the Middle Passage in *Toll the Hounds*

The themes of separation and return continue, though with variation. This serves to reinforce the cycles of life we've explored, but this time with conscious awareness, so we may apply what we have learned. *Toll the Hounds* focuses on withdrawal and dependence, exploring the process of separation and reconciliation, both in individual lives and across generations. The narrative reflects a conscious reiteration of cycles, imbued with self-awareness and metafictional elements.

The journey towards wholeness involves reconciling the disparate halves of one's life and coming to terms with grief, dependence, and legacy. The motif of return is valuable here, highlighting the importance of reconciliation in finding meaning, and reinforcing the value of separation for growth. This extends beyond the individual, to cultures and even generational transference, fathers to sons.

A vital part of the middle passage or midlife is the perception of the unlived life. The first half with its expansion necessarily cannot be completed, and when we begin to take stock of what has been achieved, it becomes clear that there are aspects of our lives we have ignored or forgotten. Some may regress to try and live out that life in a seeming attempt to attain eternal youth. Some may fall into depression, unable to bear the weight of what's left undone. We mourn for our lost youth and the wasted opportunities, but at the same time undeveloped traits or talents may emerge.

So *Toll the Hounds* deals with both return and the midlife passage, becoming conscious of what was neglected. The second half of life also encompasses the inevitable descent into grief.

> "For the mature person, however, the continued expansion of life is obviously not the right principle, because the descent towards life's afternoon demands simplification, limitation, and intensification—in other words, individual culture. A man in the first half of life with its biological orientation can usually, thanks to the youthfulness of his whole organism, afford to expand his life and make something of value out of it. But the man in the second half of life is oriented towards culture, the diminishing powers of his organism allowing him to subordinate his instincts to cultural goals. Not a few are wrecked during the transition from the biological to the cultural sphere."[173]

Jung here describes the inner shift associated with the middle passage. It is about withdrawing projections, turning inwards to formulate a spiritual self, removing the dependence on the outer world and its material trappings. It is also, perhaps unsurprisingly at this point, a type of return. With the scouring away of the first half, we begin anew, in the spirit of newness and freedom. This internal spiritual journey, and in particular the second half of life, is where Jung focused his studies of individuation.

The midlife passage, though associated with a time in life, is not tied to it. We see that Crokus, still far from midlife, is undergoing his journey into the depths. It is one of reflection, withdrawal of projections. While this descent so often happens around the midpoint in chronological life, the fall may come upon us at other times.

Individuation is a journey towards wholeness. Withdrawing projections is an important part of reconciling the shadow, and in general of accepting and reconciling with the Self – that representation of wholeness that exists archetypally within ourselves. The soul may be no longer satisfied with what has been accomplished, no longer able to bear the burden of its personae.

For many Jungians, and I think for Jung himself, the big work of individuation occurred at midlife. This, for many, is the point at which the individual steps out of the clothes of conventionality and affirms him or herself as the person that will be during the long final descent. It is the familiar pattern, of separation and return, of death and rebirth, though crucially at this point life is no longer in the state of physical expansion, but the beginning of a drawing down. Similarly in childhood the brain expands and new connections are made, while in adolescence a substantial pruning takes place, creating more efficiency. At midlife, then, this takes place at a psychological level: connections and attachments are eroded, but the value

---

[173] Jung, CG. CW8 [113]

of those that remain, the life energy that is invested in them, grows. What holds us together, in best cases, is a psychological and spiritual wholeness, an organisation that defines us.

The shadow emerges as an important aspect at the middle of life. We are able, through analysis or the application of conscious attention, to observe the shadow contents built up over the first half – if we can turn and look. (It is notable the metaphor is commonly one of descent and midlife is the nadir, but also we can use the metaphor of being at the peak before the descent towards death. It is a turning point, and the crucial aspect is the meeting of two halves—inner and outer, upper and lower, past and future.) Cleaning house appears to be an important aspect to enable individuation in the second half of life. Any projections, any archetypal scarring is valuable to deal with, but because the shadow is such an encompassing repository of the forgotten and ignored, it is particularly important at this stage. It is almost as though we are biologically primed to review what has come before.

From *Midnight Tides* we learned that the Letherii don't have a Hold of Death:

> "Our manic accumulation of wealth...Our headlong progress, as if motion was purpose and purpose inherently virtuous. Our lack of compassion, which we called being realistic. The extremity of our judgements, our self-righteousness – all a flight from death...All a vast denial smothered in semantics and euphemisms." (MT 642)

This denial is necessary when the relationship to the world is transacted through material gain. It could be that the material obsession causes a loss of spiritual value; likewise it could be that the hole of a loss of meaning is filled with material gain. Either way, at an individual level this is the sort of self-reflection that might take place at midlife, an honest assessment of our youthful interaction with the world, a slow forced-march down the gallery of our regrets.

In the prologue to *Toll the Hounds* we read: "Speak truth, grow still, until the water is clear between us." (1) This speaks to the nature of the Andii, but also the clearing of the accumulated burdens, the silts churned up by a long life. Characters watch in their dead town as Hood and others appear, they speak of the before-time. And finally, we are witness to the wagon in Dragnipur: its burden ever grows as more fall.

This whole process is one of review and renew, rather than a dramatic shift. With life experience, symbols take on new meaning. Life itself takes on new meaning in new phases. We journey again, and learn more.

> The Self in a human being ... is a dynamic centre of the psyche which seems to be in a state of constant inner flux. That is why no conscious formulation of an experience of the Self can claim to be absolute over a long period of time it has to be re-adapted again and again, so as to keep pace with this changing process.[174]

In the previous chapter we looked at the metaphor of the river for life's flow, the riverbed as the Self. We don't know what might float down the river, nor the shifting of the bed over time. We can only ensure as we journey down the river again that it is clear of blockages, that the water runs clear.

Anomander Rake and Mother Dark

The novel begins with a number of epigraph passages as well as Baruk's reading of Anomander's history, as told in mythology in the tale Anomandaris and other documents. His story in *Toll the Hounds* is like a guiding mythology for the plight of the characters—the carrying of burdens, the sacrifice, and the healing that is possible.

Mother Dark had forsaken Anomander and the Andii for his deed of killing Tiam, which brought down their home world. His actions brought the burdens down on those with him, such as Endest Silann and Spinnock Durav. He has extracted promises, thus making their burdens his.

The mother's curse, her abandonment, takes away their hope and meaning. Healing that old wound is part of the work of midlife.

It should be noted, too, that the symbolism of killing Tiam whose name is an allusion to Tiamat, the Babylonian cosmic mother, distinguishes the archetypal and actual mother in the story. There is the earthly mother with whom we must deal, while at the instinctual and archetypal level there is the necessity to kill or separate from the mother. Killing Tiam was the active heroic quest of slaying the mother; reuniting with Mother Dark is the introverted return, the soul work.

Jung discussed Siegfried as the "ideal masculine type", and in his story the interaction of the hero with the archetypal mother is made plain:

---

[174] Von Franz, 1980, p. 85

"leaving the mother, the source of life, behind him, he is driven by an unconscious desire to find her again, to return to her womb. Every obstacle that rises in his path and hampers his ascent wears the shadowy features of the Terrible Mother, who saps his strength with the poison of secret doubt and retrospective longing; and in every conquest he wins back again the smiling, loving and life-giving mother."[175]

So Anomander's work is an active return to the great mother, but it is also a work of sacrifice. A notable symbolism is played out by the sexual activity of the priestesses of Dark. They engage thus to open a gate to Mother Dark, and so symbolise the return to the mother. "We try as Anomander Rake tries, both of us, seeking to hold on to some meaning, some purpose. He imagines it can be found in the struggles of lesser folk…We fail as he does." (270) Rake is focused on the outer concerns, the priestesses aim to enact the heroic return symbolically. Both are in vain, and meaning is eventually found in sacrifice.

Jung, in *Symbols of Transformation*, wrote of sacrifice in the mythological hero:

> Through sacrifice man ransoms himself from the fear of death and is reconciled to the demands of Hades. In the late cults the hero, who in olden times conquered evil and death through his labours, has become the divine protagonist, the priestly self-sacrificer and renewer of life. Since he is now a divine figure and his sacrifice is a transcendental mystery whose meaning far exceeds the value of an ordinary sacrificial gift, this deepening of the sacrificial symbolism is a reversion to the old idea of human sacrifice, because a stronger and more total expression is needed to portray the idea of self-sacrifice.[176]

The description is redolent of a Christ-type figure, which is certainly an allusion that's in the room as we read of Anomander's plight. The meaning is amplified by his being almost holy and an example the Andii and others think they cannot live up to.

"[Redemption] demands an effort, one with implicit sacrifice and hardship, one demanding all the higher qualities of what we call virtues." (267) Discusssing the Redeemer, Anomander thus distinguishes this from absolution, the one-sided clearing of sin, riven with imbalance. We are shown

---

[175] Jung, C.G., CW5 [611]
[176] Jung, C.G., CW5 [671]

here Anomander's purpose, that his sacrifice will be in aid of redemption, something truly selfless.

"The day we accepted her turning away, Endest, was the day we ran the knives across our own throats." (520) Here Rake speaks of the death of what has come before, the old life. The separation from the parents as the child's life expands trails its consequences out across the lifespan. The echoes of past hurts continue. At midlife, it is as though there is a reckoning, a dalliance with the past and a final withdrawal from the remnants of the parental archetypes.

And so Rake is stepping aside, acknowledging the new generation in a sense. He is consciously learning from his own battle. Endest Silann believes Rake is the only one that was worth following, the only one that can bear the burden, calling back again to Jung's idea of the transcendent sacrifice. With the acknowledgment of the coming generation, we can also relate to the idea that those at midlife are allowing the following generations to accept responsibility, allowing them their own heroic freedom. We must be willing to share burdens, and that which we unwittingly put upon those that come after, as well as our projections.

"Without the blood of dragons...the chaos, Endest – gave us the strength to persist, to cease fearing change, to accept all that was unknown and unknowable." (520) Their longevity takes away an inherent mortal fear, of the numinous approaching of the end of life. But in the Andii this creates the need for consciously approaching oneself, welcoming the chaos. The willingness to perceive and so enable change and growth. (Though here it obviously takes a long time—recognition, perhaps, that we may not see the benefits in a single lifetime.)

And renewal comes from it. In his people, at the least. Jung again, from *Symbols of Transformation*:

> Even on the primitive level, among the Australian blackfellows, we meet with the idea that the life-force wears out, turns "bad" or gets lost, and must therefore be renewed at regular intervals. Whenever such an *abaissement* occurs the rites of renewal must be performed.
>
> ...
>
> In the act of sacrifice the consciousness gives up its power and possessions in the interests of the unconscious. This makes possible a union of opposites resulting in a release of energy. At the same time the act of sacrifice is a fertilization of the mother: the chthonic serpent-demon drinks the blood, i.e., the soul, of the hero. In this way life becomes immortal, for, like

> the sun, the hero regenerates himself by his self-sacrifice and re-entry into the mother. After all this we should have no difficulty in recognizing the son's sacrifice to the mother in the Christian mystery. [177]

Sacrifice and renewal are the movements of the middle passage. The old self is exposed so that the new might flourish. And in making way within ourselves, perhaps we make way for the culture at large. Broadly, this is not much different to the journey of the young and naïve hero, just differently flavoured, an aged wine whose sediment is stirred by the conscious attention to the depths.

The sacrifice of Rake is known to result in oblivion, and we may wonder why is this the ultimate bad ending? Our society, bereft of meaning and the conscious approach to death, almost celebrates atheism and the lack of meaning, like it's a virtue to be a blank slate, but here in metaphor we are exploring the idea that meaning is not just what is left of the ego consciousness, but its legacy, the connections made, and that they ripple through generations. By living and dying well, we improve life for all, not just our promised afterlife. If oblivion was enough, Rake and the Andii would have suicided long ago. They carry on because reconciliation is important, and because they are having some effect.

We are reminded of the notion of chaos as a gift, as a symbol for the spark of consciousness that allows both appreciation for the world and the ability to change it, when Apsalara in Dragnipur realises the audacity of Anomander Rake's plan. "You give us chaos. You give us an end to this." (582) Rake is allowing the chaos to approach the wagon, allowing the necessary intervention that creates meaning by being something, or instigating something that is other than balance and stasis.

If we consider the thematic focus of the series on the idea of compassion, and its counterpoint being indifference, it provides a good analogy for the intervention of chaos against balance. Where there is a tradeoff with compassion, notably in the increase in vulnerability, there is nonetheless an overall tendency toward betterment, at least we hope so. Similarly with chaos—while there are tradeoffs, while there is danger, those are inherent in the act of living. Without that chaos we are in the situation of indifference—there is no movement and thus no chance of progress. In a contented, balanced life, without suffering, without the work and graft of living, we risk pointlessness. And this can then lead to nihilism. We submit to the unknown, we open ourselves to chaos, because therein is the stuff of life beyond the

---

[177] Ibid.

known, the straight and stable, beyond ego and materiality, beyond the present.

In the end it is not just the Andii but all of Rake's shadow legacy, those within Dragnipur, who are redeemed by his return to Mother Dark.

A return home is the ideal in dying. Though we wander, we are also of a place. Homelessness, dislocation, imparts a sense of loss and grief. How can one die meaningfully when one is so lost? Think of the soul of Kedeviss, wandering and in limbo, waiting for Mother Dark to recognise them once more. "The soul was flung away, to wander for ever lost." (735)

Anomander's life shows us that he has made meaning in the act of looking for it, by taking on the plights and fights of others, trying to give purpose to his people. He challenges (implicitly) the Redeemer's followers to find meaning and not to only expect. He demonstrates this in his own quest, and has created meaning in himself and his people, and he hopes that others will take the mantle and the example.

One does not need the eternal faith and support of a god/goddess to create meaning for them. By living in such a way as to seek meaning, it forces Mother Dark to open to him. A saying of the Andii, "Speak truth, grow still, until the water is clear between us" (1) refers to living truly to one's values.

This is the spiritual turning of midlife and the descent towards dying. We realise that which is outside of us is not necessary to provide meaning, but we find it in wrestling with the world. "Whatever Anomander Rake now attempts to do, he does not do it for himself." (900)

The Eye

Ditch thinks about chaos as he is dragged along before being slung atop the wagon: "Life fears chaos...Order battles against dissolution." (472) This brings the race of Dragnipur's wagon from the impending chaos down to the level of our own lives. It is a race, a battle, and yet a necessary tension.

Upon the wagon in Dragnipur, Kadaspala tattoos a godling onto the bodies of the dead. Upon Ditch it takes the form of an eye. "And he was its eye. There to look upon its soul inward and outward." (900)

Consciousness is analogous to the eye. We can only keep small parts in focus, and that focus keeps moving to create a full picture of the world. There is also a blind spot right at its centre, which is the conscious hand of blind

Kadaspala himself. The eye also has a direct connection to the brain, and some consider it to have a special place as part of the central nervous system.

Vision is whole by the joining of the two separate systems. We reconcile two distinct visions of the world. Mother Dark is amorphous, conceptual, has to be perceived and distinguished, so that reunification might occur. This idea of perceiving both inwardly and outwardly before we can make sense of something, to view it from various angles, is very Jungian.

It is also interesting to note that the god that Kadaspala creates only lives for moments, in contrast to the long life of the Andii, the eternity of Dragnipur. It is not just the value of long life but of life well perceived that meaning can arise.

Neumann, in discussing separation and return to the Great Mother, wrote of the fragmentation of archetypes. From numinous wholeness we manage through life to parse and make more sense of the archetypes that once overwhelmed us. "The unbearable white radiance of primordial light is broken up by the prism of consciousness into a multicoloured rainbow of images and symbols."[178]

The work of self analysis is one of discrimination: what are the hangups with the archetypal mother versus my hangups with the real one? This takes on greater resonance at midlife, and makes the role of the hero relevant at that time. The hero, after all, is the one who discriminates. He is the sword that divides. But he is also that which joins it all back again to a meaningful whole. I see here the analogy to the eye, which at once divines detail but also is the window through which consciousness forms an image entire.

Crokus Younghand

His is the work of withdrawing projections, at long last, from Challice. Though he makes rough work of it. First he extracts himself from the crew he's been with, but then he finds he does not really fit with his old life any more. The crossover between the old and the new is inevitable, and it discomfits him.

Challice is our initial witness to the nostalgia of a life now gone: "...the past was a better place to be." (15) She thinks of her unlived life, and knows

---

[178] Neumann, 1949, p. 323

that laid out before her is predictable. She wants to see her jewellery, to capture the feeling of that time, but it is hollow, as we find all accumulated trinkets to be.

"Darujhistan is not the city you left behind years past." (79) Spite argues with Cutter, for he is eager to get back to the city, to see his friends, to act to help the city. He is in a liminal space where he is both keen to act, and nervous about revealing himself. He is also going to find how relatively powerless he is, while his journey so far has been one of coming in to his power. This dual recognition is a humbling necessity.

Cutter's return is not the glorious homecoming he had imagined. He nervously anticipates his entering the Phoenix Inn, the missing friends, and he has a tete a tete with Rallick at the entrance, his new skills and life cutting through the old.

Discomfort inside brings his old self roaring to the surface, feeling like a youngster again. "Even the repetition was in truth nothing but an illusion, a sleight of similitude." (159) He no longer fits the role, but at some level he is unconsciously playing it out. This awkwardness is a conflict within himself. We may find at this stage of life that the old way no longer works, and a new way of operating is required. Jung was keenly aware of such periods of unknowing: "It is usually the moment when a new psychological adjustment, that is, a new adaptation, is demanded."[179] Of course, this requires introspection and the bringing to consciousness of those factors that no longer serve the new life.

When projections clash with our experience of the world, there is the opportunity to learn, to see that the internal model is not accurate. This invitation can allow us to perceive those very projections, and the realisation of a projection is a necessary part of the process of withdrawal. The expectations and assumptions were parts of ourselves. People change, as do we. When something has changed but we wish for it to stay the same, that demonstrates our desire for the projection, not the person in truth.

Challice looks upon her moon ornament as she ponders her old life. It entices her with the bright nostalgia of an unlived life. "The burnished light breathed into her, filled her mind with strange thoughts and hungers growing ever more desperate for appeasement. She was being enticed into a darker world, a place of hedonistic indulgences, a place unmindful of the future and dismissive of the past." (220) And of course, the symbol of the moon marks her as Crokus's desired feminine aspect, which he will soon indulge, regressing. Alongside this, the frequent references to the broken, hazy moon

---

[179] Jung, C.G., CW4, [563]

are notable, as well as how this relates to the archetypal feminine.

Rallick had expected Crokus to come to him and vent: "He would want to explain, wouldn't he? Try to justify his decisions to Rallick, even when there was no possible justification. *He didn't listen to me, did he?*" (230-1) This tells us that Rallick wanted to talk to him, and that the two of them have mutual projections. Both expected something of the old Crokus. Naturally of course, there is actual wisdom in Rallick, and it is with a sense of irony that Crokus continues on his path.

With a sense of inevitability, the descents of Challice and Cutter approach one another. Challice is about to step into her new life, down to rock bottom, willing to be used, so it is not a great step further to welcome Cutter to her. He feels assailed, out of place, and ready to cling on to any lifeline the old life might offer. "I doubt there's a woman low enough for me anywhere in the world." (340) When we submit to regressing in aid of living the unlived life, it is so often found not to live up to our expectations and projections. Just as he is looking at headstones and pondering death, so appears Challice from behind. Both address one another by their former names, to invite the regression.

"I do not stand before a woman, do I? No, I fall into her arms. I change shape to fit each one…" (491) This is Crokus's projection of the anima. It is reciprocal, as she also will try and fit the image she sees to that which he anticipates—the only way to create that match is to change himself. In Challice, he sees what is a formative image of his anima.

"Do second chances even exist?" (491) One must think that second chances cannot exist for the life that wasn't, but sometimes we get a chance to play out what we thought it was we wanted. This will always be weighted by the life lived since. He sees the dark current in Challice's need, recognition that he is not the only one acting out the old life. She remarks: "My life's become a question that I thought no one could answer." (492) And so she sees the attraction of an answer in her past. He recognises that there is something impure, infantile in that reaching back—no, a second chance does not exist here.

But despite his recognition of her misguided notion, he thinks his is just a passive descent. He is losing his agency in the face of the power of his projections. A conscious recognition of that will allow his withdrawal of the projection. But Cutter first needs to live through it, he will find out the hard way there is no substance beneath his anticipations. He sees reflected in Challice the same empty search: "all-consuming, frighteningly desperate, perhaps depthless and insatiable in its need." (560)

But Cutter quickly comes to the realisation, thinking about Scillara, that the past can neither be recalled, nor let go: "some part of him had sought to sever what they had had aboard the ship, as if by closing one chapter every thread was cut and the tale began anew." (561) While the narrative that we construct in life may be a false one, there is a connectedness nonetheless. Choices ring with consequences, and no choice is made in isolation. Sacrifices are necessary.

"Memory did not let go; it remained the net dragged in one's wake" (561). The severing we can achieve is not with our past, nor can we relive it. It must be lived *with*. But this does not discount the damage that can be done with an act, a choice. The severing that can occur is not the shedding of the past, but the future, cessation of possibility. And with that comes the burdens, of regret and more. "…he had gone too far, too far to ever get back what he now realized was precious, was truer than everything he was feeling right now." (561) In trying to recapture the past, he has left himself bereft of another past he now regrets.

This is how life is wrestled with. Whichever paths we choose foreclose on more. And if we remain in the past, then our present suffers. If we try to flee the past, it hounds our heels. And yet, there is still inevitability there, for when they nip our heels we fall, only to rise and learn.

It is only later that Kruppe warns Cutter of this nature of choice, although we know that by this time it is already too late: "Cutter, there are paths that must not be walked. Paths where going back is impossible – no matter how deeply you would wish it, no matter how loud the cry in your soul." (646) By this time Cutter is rushing down paths he has formed. As he considers his adultery, he compares himself to Murillio, a dark echo given that man's corpse has just arrived by wagon in the city. He had previously taken on the roles of Rallick, of Apsalar, and for a brief time the imitation of Icarium. He is still trying to find himself.

Finding out about Murillio's death at the hands of Vidikas, he wants to enact vengeance. He presumes himself to be at the centre of the whole affair, another example of egocentrism, and the same presumptions he showed in *Gardens of the Moon*. He imagines Apsalar speaking to him as he rides: "I gave you a choice, and the choice remains." (732) But he believes his fate is no longer in his hands. "Too late, Apsalar. It was always too late." (732) He gave himself over in his projection, and has not withdrawn it. His conscience is offering him that withdrawal, but he doesn't take it.

After exacting his vengeance upon Vidikas, a witness asks who the boy, Harllo, was, for whom Murillio set out and met his end: "he was a boy nobody loved..." (763) And in his words, we hear Cutter bemoaning his own nature. These are the feelings that set him on to his path, and he is still trying to find that warmth within himself. Indeed, the symmetry of his disposal of Vidikas with the duel at the fete in *Gardens of the Moon* reminds us of Crokus on that night, that it was his first attempt to wrest for himself the love of Challice, his first wound.

Making his way back through the city, Crokus once again ponders his brief history, his lack of agency in how he has dealt with the women in his life. "There was no sacrifice made in being abandoned. There was no courage in doing nothing." (846) Lack of decision is no choice at all. We must determine our convictions and act on them. Studious aloofness is no substitute for an expression of love.

"This is my city...It does not deserve this." (847) We recall that he had feared for his city, before he ensnared himself in his past with Challice. He has failed to defend his home, that which is true within him. The past—Shadow, Apsalar—is rearing up, and that which he thought to reclaim—Challice, the moon—are self-destructing. Indeed, Challice's despair for the innocence of the past drives her to suicide, and we recognise that it is a part of Crokus dying, too. Soon after, though, he introduces himself to Karsa as 'Crokus', as what he once was, so he has shed his persona. That is what has died away.

He has also come full circle, he realises, when he sees Traveller and recognises the role he played in giving him the sword, Vengeance. Crokus in *Gardens of the Moon* was witness to Anomander Rake fighting a demon, saw him as a myth. Now grown, he witnesses the death of that very myth. This is achingly symbolic of his old life and its outlook having died.

Crokus decides to stand in defence of Rake's body, and while he is about to do so out of lack of alternative, he becomes firm in his conviction. He is standing for something greater than himself. This is the moment we witness him growing at long last.

He had thought he was the centre of the story, an expression of egocentrism. The parting with Apsalar made him realise his choice was wrong, and that her story was bigger than him. His realisation on coming home to Darujhistan is that the city didn't need him to save it—again, he was not the centre. People's lives went on without him, and they will continue to do so. These other lives are bigger than him, just as Challice's life is, which is the final realisation for him: that he was not her purpose. Seeing at the end the vastness of power brings it all home, and he settles with the realisation.

What we see here is a mirror of Anomander's journey. Where Rake showed us that the midlife passage is still resonant of the hero's journey in youth, here Crokus fulfills the youthful hero's growth by passing through the relatively mundane affairs of the midlife movement. These two are not so far from one another. The journey is cyclical.

As he sails away from the city, without a grand farewell, his threads not neatly tied, we get a sense of incompleteness. But that is the life: things left undone and regrets that linger. Sometimes we have to return home to remember why we left.

Nimander

Nimander is doing his shadow work. He denies the good in himself. The duality of compassion and vulnerability is clearly visible. The denial of his shadow both disables his finding the inner strength, but also makes him refuse vulnerability, which closes off his compassion. When denied, the shadow clamours for attention, becoming the undeniable focus of the soul.

"I have earned nothing...For all my failures, the community will judge me, and that will be that." (50) He believes himself judged negatively by his peers, his own self-perception a greater burden like many in this novel. He is judged negatively by Clip, but we know that Clip is not a great judge of people. Clip, however, knows that a long life weighs heavily, and we can see Nimander's burdens in the deaths in his past, and the expectations.

Nimander is also burdened by the ghosts that speak to him from the past—the one he loved, and Phaed whom he couldn't kill. This perceived failure, reinforced by her very voice in his head, seems to outweigh the strength within him.

Nimander and his crew come upon the Kelyk plantations and the dead towns attached. Thematically these images amplify what we see in the characters, and also draw parallel meanings. There is grief and addiction, but this is also about dependence. The dead feed the addiction, and so for Nimander, the past feeds his own self-doubt.

"Is this a truth made manifest? Do we all feed on the pain of others?" (178) At the very least, it brings home that we might be blind to it, as dependence can be invisible. There is something resonant in the images about the stasis of life and death. The dying in the fields are still animated, the living are like sleepwalkers.

Kelyk is addictive, and the imagery of the flaccid bodies in the fields dripping black has been likened to our own extractive culture, oil wells dipping and needling in vast rows across fields. It is interesting that the cultural narrative that our society is addicted to oil has coincided with the narrative that addiction is an illness—it has victims. We use that justification to slake our guilt, or to quiet our conscience. This is not to engage in polarised thinking, I am not claiming that addicts are at fault and individual responsibility is the be all. I think the narrative is true to an extent, but it is here twisted. By equating our dependence with addiction, to which we are merely helpless victims, diverts the energy for change, teaches us to be helpless.

The same is true of the narrative of depression as merely, or predominantly, a fault of brain chemistry. It is true, *to an extent*. But both of these narratives conveniently ignore the interactions of our history, individually and collectively, our social context, the interactions with these and our biology and psychology.

Of course, such narratives and their spread are latched on to in service to profit (speaking of dependence…), but at a deeper level it is harmful to society's and individuals' ability to reflect on themselves. In the short term, such lack of reflexive thought diverts away from change. In the long run, I suspect the inability to introspect and understand deep, interconnected causality, makes us weak, dependent, and therefore powerless. Good consumers, yes, and faithful followers.

So what we have here is the idea that we are all too willing to absolve ourselves of responsibility, of blame, for the state of ourselves and the world we are active in shaping. The Redeemer's followers want no expectation placed upon themselves, but this imbalance only weakens their god. It weakens the very culture they are the essential part of.

Phaed, in Nimander's head, reveals that his memory of love was but a delusion, making him question his own grasp of the past. Phaed insists that she can act as the cool rational voice in his leadership. "You need me. I give strength where you are weakest…she cannot help you with the hard choices a leader must make." (180) Phaed here is Nimander's shadow, wishing to be integrated. If he manages that consciously, Nimander will bring the past, and his limitations, to awareness, compensating for his own strengths.

A neurosis is a dissociation within the personality due to the activation of complexes. Phaed's voice is a complex within Nimander. Jung's assertion that the onset of neurosis can trigger individuation means that in becoming conscious of our shadow and our weaknesses, we also become conscious of our strengths and the untapped gold in our nature. Phaed's ghost voice is a split part of Nimander's ego personality because her attitudes and attributes are inconsistent with his view of himself. But all that she represents is in fact within him, if only he can bring it to consciousness.

What is the archetypal basis of this complex in Nimander? Perhaps at this stage we don't know, but the mother is a safe first guess. After all, we are dealing with the manifestation of two women in his life, and we know the Tiste Andii have a little baggage when it comes to Mother Dark. Nimander denies the complex, trying to squash its outpouring, lest it overwhelm him. The question now is whether what Phaed represents is something that needs to be denied (is he just repressing his past?) or whether she is a part of him whose integration will serve him well. Either way, he now appears open to dialogue, the first step to understanding its influence upon him.

Von Franz here describes how these complexes or important unconscious contents will not be denied.

> Every content of the unconscious with which one is not properly related tends to obsess one for it gets at us from behind. If you can talk to it you get into relationship with it. You can either be possessed by a content constellated in the unconscious, or you can have a relationship to it. The more one represses it, the more one is affected by it.[180]

It is in the relinquishing of our ego that we can access the truth, and the unconscious is allowed to express itself in a healthy way. "The less control you have, the greater your talent for leadership seems to become, the qualities demanded of such a person – like those flowers in your hand, petals unfolding." (260) Nimander finds awakening in himself new appreciation for his sisters, Kedeviss and Aranatha, something within his kin is trying to break through to his awareness. "Can you feel me now, Nimander?" (261) It is as though opening himself (whether by volition or not) to the feminine aspects

---

[180] Von Franz, 1980, p. 103

of the unconscious has allowed greater understanding of those parts of his life.

Nimander shows his own willingness to sacrifice, when Gothos sends him into another realm. He is willing to free the builder at his own expense. Does Nimander merely see hopelessness where others see strength and sacrifice? Even Desra is willing to pull him out, as more and more his companions reveal their respect for him.

It is also notable that Nimander is angered by the idea of Gothos collecting people. This recalls Dragnipur, which does the same. And coincidentally with Nimander and his kin bringing new ideals to the Andii, Dragnipur is shattered. Another comparison is made when Nimander must consider carving through the kelyk horde at Bastion. This scene recalls that of Anomander assuming the burden of slaughtering the Tenescowri in *Memories of Ice*. Here, Nimander finds there is another way, and notably he finds it by being open to his kin, almost in complete contrast to the aloofness of Anomander.

After the violence in Bastion, the Tiste Andii group are changed. Skintick wants to know if all the sacrifice is worth it, over a lifespan, watching kin die, and all the losses to the self. "It feels like…dying inside." (518) This could be likened to the old self dying away, the feeling of emptiness and questioning what has come before. Rake is making a symbolic sacrifice in *Toll the Hounds*, on behalf of all. All the lives and losses cannot be undone. Skintick wants to know if it is worth it.

We see through this journey that it is not absence of doubt, but acceptance that defines maturity. Just as we are not courageous in the absence of fear, but in spite of it. Likewise in life, it is not a mistake-free life that rewards one with success, but the ability to carry on in the face of our shortcomings, our regrets, our grief, and imperfections. It is in not giving up, continuing to strive that we actualise.

"Nimander had no choice but to act alone, to trust in the others to follow." (814) In a sense he is here accepting his responsibility, no longer restraining himself in the belief that he is responsible for others, instead acting upon his convictions and trusting the world to respond in kind. Though he still has doubts, of course, he is looking inwardly for the answers. Phaed's ghost responds, and when they are lost in the darkness, it is by looking at his hands, again symbolic of self-awareness, that Aranatha manages to find him.

While Anomander is at the end of his life, Nimander is undergoing the process of midlife, where a final separation from the parents occurs. This can appear as a symbolic abandonment or reconciliation. For Nimander, he is discovering that the literal and psychological support of the parents and the past is going, but he has the necessary strength within himself, and indeed literally has aspects of the parents within himself. He is attempting to get back to his father, to find reconciliation, which echoes Erikson's personal life during the writing of this novel. Generations recur. The history of one will be visited on generations to come. We separate but we are still part of our parents: we are in some ways defined by their traits.

Endest Silann

An old man, once a sorcerer, now a mere castellan is how he introduces himself. He remembers his youth, their arrival into this world, and also is riven by memories of keeping Moon's Spawn hidden beneath the water. His body and mind are fragile like the shattered old palace, and under assault by the memory of the water's pressure.

"We assume the burden as we must. We win through. And life goes on." (39) He sees his own weakness, perhaps he sees only his weakness, living as a symbol of Moon's Spawn beneath the sea. That past action is the great weight of his burdens, threatening to bring him down, to drown him. But as with Nimander, he doesn't yet realise that his own perceived weakness is not what others see.

Endest's mind keeps getting called back to the time before they arrived in this world. He is in this way remembering his youth, and the burden that he took on in promise to Anomander. But he is riven with doubt. "Youth was a time for harsh judgment. Such fires ebbed with age. Certainty itself withered." (109) He ponders that there is a difference in the expectation that the broken might heal, and those who are beyond repair. "A ruined soul should not be stubborn, should not cling to what was clearly a miserable existence." (183) That instinct that we can heal is the expectation of individuation. He withdraws into solitude, to avoid pity he thinks, but perhaps it is fear of connecting. Some part of him is aware that there is the anticipation of a remedy. Just as he is pitying himself, he is called for by Rake. "Endest felt his soul recoil in horror, shrink back into whatever cave it had clawed out for itself…" (184). He needs to find that strength again, to be purposeful, to rediscover meaning.

He ponders rivers, fantasises drowning the one he'd loved beneath the water, seeking enlightenment there. The river speaks of time and its passage, the illusion of stability. "Children will leave. Children will abandon the old ways…" (265) Endest muses on the brevity of youth, the brightness and wonder of his own and what might be lost. This takes on greater poignancy when we discover that he was charged with looking after Nimander and his fellows before they were taken away. He despairs for the loss of youth, but they are returning, and will bring renewal.

And on finding the river, it is not what he'd hoped. This is symbolic of many of the stories in this novel, that search for the actual past being merely a shadow. His discussion with Brood raises an interesting comparison: that he has no truck for forgiveness, but the idea of restitution halts him. In a similar way, we cannot undo what befell us in the first half of life, but we can make amends. It is a question of balance, rather than of cleaning the slate.

Endest ponders trees with his memories of the great blackwood of his home realm, the way wood "crumbles into dissolution" (418). Caladan Brood counters that it is a release of energy. In Endest's memory he had reflected on how the old trees had fuelled the forges creating weapons for war. Here again we see Erikson describing life as exchange of energy. Of course, the dissipation of energy in a life can also be thought of as a buildup in the first half, like an indrawn breath, followed by the slow exhalation in the second.

Accepting his role in Rake's plans (though they are unknown to us), Endest waits, alone. He has run out of belief in what is beyond. He sees the mortal act of living as a betrayal, an evasion of responsibility. And Rake's actions as taking the burden of all their mistakes upon himself. "Is his own burden not enough?" (825) He thinks it is not fair. Though he gives them the opportunity for renewal, a chance, and thus a choice, "He would offer no absolution." (825) Though they can continue to live as though life is indeed a gift. This echoes the time purchased by Hood in Dragnipur, the sacrifice made by the dead for hope.

In his conclusion, he holds back more than he should be able, rises from the river where he found his strength. His strength, inside, was of the memory of the time when he was whole. He acts in the way Rake expected of him, and in that way overcomes his self-doubt long enough.

Dying is Archetypal

Death, or dying, as a process is an archetype, and it has its strongest influence in the second half of life. The expectation or instinct built in to ready us for dying is inherent in our biology. Refusal or inability to conceive or readily appreciate this leads to neurosis.

Not surprising given other life stages, unfolded by biology, follow a similar pattern of death and rebirth. Jung wrote in volume 9i of the notion of rebirth, but I don't think that is archetypal, rather it is a motif. While rebirth is visible everywhere, literal and symbolic, it is not inevitable. However, if dying is archetypal, then rebirth is infused with a sense of wonder, of relief, an invigoration of spirit.

Not the symbol or image of death, say, as represented by a reaper or Hood. Again, the archetype relates to the underlying expectation or instinct, whereas the symbol is produced by the interaction between the archetype and culture and the individual.

We are surrounded by death as cycles, in the falling of flowers, the change of seasons. No surprise then that the image or motif of rebirth or of afterlife exists as a means of consistency with what we see.

> "I am convinced that it is hygienic—if I may use the word—to discover in death a goal towards which one can strive, and that shrinking away from it is something unhealthy and abnormal which robs the second half of life of its purpose. I therefore consider that all religions with a supramundane goal are eminently reasonable from the point of view of psychic hygiene."[181]

Understanding it as a death archetype explains why it feels like an ending, rather than an expectation of rebirth. At a broader scale, this is consistent with the expectations of growth in the first half of life, and descent or dying in the second half.

Rebirth and renewal at each stage is emergent. We are cyclical and patterned. Again, in each case it is something of a surprise, which accounts for the sense of renewal, the feeling of revelation in the rebirth. But the expected trajectory is not forever upwards, that is just a story we have developed to account for the dominion of humanity, and it seems inextricable from the seeming desire to evade or ignore death.

The notion of death as the archetype, the expectation of fall and decay,

---

[181] Jung, C.G., CW8, [792]

contains the greatest explanatory power. Preceded in life, of course, by the rise in the first half. That archetypal rise and descent is as deeply intertwined in our experience of the world as our witness to the sun's passage across the heavens. Jacobi's discussion of individuation touches on Jung's focus on the second half of life, where the goal of individuation is consciously approached. She quotes his statement in the commentary to the *Secret of the Golden Flower*, where he maintains that "Seen in correct psychological perspective, death is not an end, but a goal." She continues: "To confront this goal with the full force of the capacities for growth immanent in the psyche constitutes the real meaning of the second half of life and the highest dignity of man."[182]

We could envisage the trajectory of life as an arc of rise and fall, overlaid by a series of self-similar periods of ascent and decay. The greater scale informs the smaller scale, as if each learning is part of the apprenticeship for our true deaths. How then does this inform how we live in the world? Death is inevitable, of course. But it means we will learn to carry our griefs and burdens, not in the expectation of avoiding death, but by coming to terms with it.

If it is indeed archetypal, it tells us that our biology is urging us to live as though we are dying. It takes that notion out of the realm of platitude, and realises it.

Stevens discusses initiation as an archetype, and posits that: "Belief in reincarnation is also an expression of the initiation archetype."[183] But I believe we should understand the notion of rebirth as the cultural/social reaction, a means of bounding and explaining and guiding the individual through the changes that occur. It is a compelling argument, because it seems the growth stages either side of initiation are themselves archetypal—the archetypal trajectory of life—but do we instinctively expect to come out the other side? It makes more sense to prepare for the psychological and biological expression of ending. This might explain why midlife crises and adolescent loneliness feel like a death of self.

It happens that the changes undergone are particularly meaningful at adolescence, when the physical and psychological forces in the burgeoning adult are at their strongest, the ascent rate of the lifespan arc at its highest, and the threat of such a confluence of forces for the community is at its greatest if unchecked by a containing vessel for myth and ritual. Similarly, at death, without initiation rituals, the process of grief and elderhood, cultural constructs such as reincarnation, there may be a threat to the passage of

---

[182] Jacobi, 1967, p. 26
[183] Stevens, 2002, p. 195

culture and meaning. In other words, such symbolism creates the impetus for growth of culture across time, instigated by the existence of consciousness, without which our trajectory as a species would remain rather flat, just creatures that rise and fall, the greater arc of our species merely at the whim of evolutionary drift.

Just as our society has let slip our responsibility to initiation, we have ignored the archetype of dying, at our peril. There are no shortage of rebirth tales and promises, and yet look at the world we have inherited. If we were to diagnose our culture and its obsession with life and vitality, it would not be laid at the feet of an overabundance of rebirth, rather a lack of attention to dying. Rebirth is supplemental to the fact, but it is an empty promise if we aren't able to attend to the archetypal experience of dying itself.

The belief in reincarnation, then, is supplementary to the deeply ingrained expectation—the archetype—of dying. The sense of renewal and rebirth following initiation or any phase change is likewise supplementary to, or explained by, the greater-scale rise undergone by the individual in the first half of life.

Weight is given to the assertion of the archetypal nature of initiation by the existence of dreams and fantasy that arise spontaneously around transition periods that speak to initiatory imagery. However, these initiatory images themselves frequently have a death or descent as an integral aspect of their representation. The rebirth could be anything, it is greatly variable, but the central, unchanging component is the death—the letting go of the childhood things, the release of the first half, the passing of life itself.

There are contradictory forces at play during periods of initiation. Our biology integrating the continued growth, with cultural assurance, against the psychological, archetypal drive to descend. It is little surprise, then, that adolescence feels chaotic, more perhaps than any other initiatory stage. And at midlife, the underlying ascent has also reached its turning point, so the physiological fall feels greater than before—there is not the symbolic mountain rising beneath our feet. With the lack of initiatory elderhood at this stage, it is no wonder that the individual might feel adrift at this sudden state of descent.

Spinnock, Seerdomin, and the Redeemer

Seerdomin holds back the grief, Spinnock realises, wondering what the difference is between this man and the Andii. The Son of Darkness chafes in his restful position administering benignly over Black Coral. Their discussion of this reveals the same restlessness in each of them. There is more to them, their past and their potential for action much greater than the simple friendship and gaming they undertake. But Seerdomin carries his burden willingly. "There was need, in his mind, to bear his guilt openly, brazenly, to leave himself undefended and indefensible." (104) He prays to the Redeemer, Itkovian, bringing only his company. He seems to want to keep his burden unquestioned, as the Redeemer does. When it is reinterpreted by those around the barrow, it angers him.

Spinnock, meanwhile, with the priestess and his sword, ponders the meaninglessness of rituals. The disappearance of the ritual that Seerdomin once undertook threatens Spinnock's own faith and hope, that there is meaning even if he can't perceive it. He has put his faith in Seerdomin to find that meaning for all of them.

Salind knows that Seerdomin, her Benighted, has turned away, abandoned them. The vulnerability that he fears has closed him down. The compassion with which he approached the Redeemer opened him up, and his task is to accept that duality.

Spinnock remarks on the similarity of his High Priestess and Salind, even noting their hairstyles. Salind, though, wants to speak to her worshiped directly, Seerdomin. Spinnock worships through the High Priestess. So we have the exploration of the different sides of faith and worship playing out through these characters. Salind notices Spinnock's pain. "He answers a need, and so wounded as he now is, *you* begin to bleed." (191)

Salind ponders the weight of expectation placed upon her as High Priestess, and this is contrasted with the expectations placed upon the Redeemer, with no acceptance of the other end of that burdensome chain. Expectation demands denial, knowing our limits, giving freely yet not making ourselves too vulnerable. "Empathy haunted her. Compassion opened wounds…" (271) Salind is ill, poison, she says, for her denial is too strong. Though she denies, the wounds are still there.

"There is no glory in being helpless. Nor is there hope." (272) As Rake discussed with Spinnock, absolution is not enough. The process must be active. We don't cut ties with the old life, but we own it, just as these worshipers must own their responsibility. By conjoining the old with the new, hope may indeed exist. Anomander wants these mortals to be challenged. He wants to find in them hope that people are capable of learning, of denying themselves, their expectations. To make themselves vulnerable, not just weak, for weakness is easy and creates pliable worshipers, but perhaps vulnerable ones are conscious ones, willing to accept the other end of the burden.

Spinnock is rattled by Salind's apparent reaction to direct communication from her god. The Andii would do anything to have such acknowledgment, and to dismiss it as she apparently does, or to make it about her own feelings, startles him. He literally cannot do what she is refusing to do, and he sees only what is lost in the reverence that might be felt. Therein lies the value of a blessing, in the small hope it provides, that it is a lifeline for those that don't have such a direct line to their god.

Seerdomin literalises the choice of new life by weighing up the choice some make between suicide and living on. He makes it about a meaningful existence: "to persist, to live on, demanded courage, and that was only possible when the virtue remained worthy of respect." (422) In this way he is creating a justification for his actions, but also ensuring that it is in service to something other than himself. He doesn't want the Redeemer to cleanse him, he wants no absolution for his choices.

This, of course, takes place after he has hunted and killed the conspirators within Black Coral. That act of balance, for his past crimes as he sees it, gives his actions their deeper meaning. "Irreconcilable. What he had been, what he was now." (423) His actions are not merely a response to the past, this is the choice of a new life, a new direction, though inevitably shaped by the past. He realises that he doesn't need to heal or undo to have something meaningful in his descent: "what he was doing here, with weapon in hand, solved nothing of the conflict within him." (423) Salind realises there is meaning in Seerdomin's refusal to be embraced. By living with his wounds, not smoothing over his past, meaning is shaped by the contours of his history.

The Redeemer, by being compassionate, becomes vulnerable, and this is the route through which he is attacked, by Salind and her possession by the Dying God. This is directly comparable to Spinnock, whose compassion, his vulnerability to love Salind, proved the weakness through which he slips, not realising the gravity of his letting her go. Erikson is reinforcing the duality of worship, of the nature of faith and compassion, that there is an imbalance. Here, we see the inherent vulnerability that comes with compassion. The vulnerability must be reciprocated, else it falls to imbalance.

As Seerdomin leaves for the camp to protect Salind, he mentally notes that "such refusal must be denied." Her desires should be refused. He is acting out the part of balancing the one-sided nature of relationships. Salind's mortal need for answers is then defended by Seerdomin's ability to refuse, to fight back. "If not for your ... uncertainty, your doubts, your *humanity*." (443) The bringing together of the selflessness of Seerdomin with the humanity of the Redeemer creates a balance, a resolution to the question of imbalance between worshiper and worshiped. Neither wants to take.

"We may possess ambition…" (450) Like Seerdomin, the Redeemer as Itkovian has discovered that the notion of seeking ever upwards, while it befits early life, is not enough. These two, sitting together, are finally enjoying one another's company. It is what they both needed, it is their internal reward.

Amongst all of this, the Dying God becomes a study for the Crippled God, how compassion might be offered, and thus defeat the forces that would take advantage of one-sided vulnerability. With compassion, the vulnerability in another is not seen as something to take advantage of, but as something to be met.

"What I gave, I gave freely, a gift, not an exchange." (522) The Redeemer is telling us that compassion means little if there is expectation attached. Seerdomin is being challenged within himself to find that purity of action, to be the one who denies without expectation. He has already lost everything, including his body, and so has nothing to gain. The Redeemer, in being so compassionate is defenceless, vulnerable, and Salind provides the opposite polarity, with her assertion that kelyk, the blood of the Dying God, provides certainty. This is a counterbalance to the childlike trust and openness of the Redeemer. However, it is not a question of which pole to reside, rather it is a constant feat of balance, both in faith and worship, and in the self.

The very attraction he feels for her is like a symbolic harking back to the old life. It is not available to us at midlife, but there is a draw there. It is also a symbolic spin on Cutter's draw towards the life of his adolescent self, and the attractions he felt then. "…she was mesmerizing, this child-woman, this fount of corruption, and the notion that a woman's fall could be so alluring, so perfectly sexual, left him horrified." (672) His conversation with the Redeemer challenges him, it is like a conscience testing itself. He determines that he will fight her, despite the underlying feelings. His notion that he took part in tyranny and hunted down those who didn't comply is symbolic of an unconscious that doesn't let the shadow slide, it shines light on all within oneself and bares it for examination.

Spinnock holds the undeniable force of Kallor at bay, in service to the greater good of Rake, while at the same time Seerdomin holds Salind (the Dying God) at bay for the greater good of the Redeemer. They are mirrored in both acting to serve something beyond themselves.

Redemption, as described later by Monkrat to Spindle: "Maybe it's just doing something, being something, some*one*, and feeling that change inside – it's like you went and redeemed yourself. And nobody else's opinion matters. And you know you still got all them questions…" (894) The work of redemption is internal work, and finally the realisation that finding that inside oneself, imperfect, incomplete, is the closest we get to a satisfying redemption. We can't let go of the past or outrun it, we can't live without regrets. But in aiming to do the work, we find that we can go on.

The Redeemer is shown the truth of redemption in the selfless act of Rake, and presumably in those nearby as the discovery is a kind of contagion. He is certain now that his compassion is not a weakness, but his strength. The Dying God is then allowed to die, no longer kept alive and suffering.

Kallor

Kallor, too, recalls his past in *Toll the Hounds*, when he had ruled and destroyed whole empires and their people. He appears to be in a state of stasis, an unending midlife descent.

"Too much weight was given to history…" (117) He believes himself to be at peace. He doesn't carry burdens of guilt with him, only his simple accoutrements: sword, armour, and a handful of coins. But that peace is the absence of feeling, the absence of meaning. It is the failure to deal with the past.

There is no unlived life to long for in Kallor: "He had lived out his every ambition, after all, lived each one out until all the colour was drained away…there wasn't much in life truly worth the effort to achieve it." (117) And he sees in death no meaning either, which renders him unable to conceive of a life of giving back, which might take him out of his midlife funk.

So the question is, is this all rationalisation for the meaning stolen from him by the curse?

"To the psychotherapist an old man who cannot bid farewell

to life appears as feeble and sickly as a young man who is unable to embrace it. And as a matter of fact, it is in many cases a question of the self-same infantile greediness, the same fear, the same defiance and wilfulness, in the one as in the other."[184]

Kallor ponders the women he had, and the babies he killed. He resists attachment, sees it as a weakness. This spurns the future. There can be no progress without a future.

What he wants now is control of an entire realm. It is the same thing as his previous attempts at rule, just on a different scale. It confirms that he is still repeating the old patterns.

> "The man whose interests are all outside is never satisfied with what is necessary, but is perpetually hankering after something more and better which, true to his bias, he always seeks outside himself. He forgets completely that, for all his outward successes, he himself remains the same inwardly, and he therefore laments his poverty if he possesses only one automobile when the majority have two. Obviously the outward lives of men could do with a lot more bettering and beautifying, but these things lose their meaning when the inner man does not keep pace with them."[185]

If we consider the motion of life as an ascent followed by descent, then we can consider why the perception of the unconscious contents is so prevalent at midlife. In the first half, with the focus on growth and separation from parents, expansion and independence, the biological trajectory is headed upwards. When we are rising, we tend to look upwards, to where we are going. There is no reason we can't look down as we ascend—and indeed, some people may confront the shadow early in life—but it may induce vertigo, we may be overcome by the depths beneath us. But it is typically at the midway mark of life, where the trajectory reaches its turning point, that we take stock. We might look around and think, that's it? And then we look down, able at last to perceive all that has preceded us to this point. And also we can look ahead, to the descent. Then we realise that we still have an entire half of biological life to come, and now that all that sustained us in the first half can no longer do so, how do we live through that? How do we account for the fact that we must find a way to live through that? The answer, so often, is found turning inwards, where the first half of life was sustained by

---

[184] Jung, C.G., CW8 [792]
[185] Jung, C.G., CW11 [962]

achievements and validations external to oneself. Inwardly, we seek for meaning that will sustain us during the descent.

Kallor's refrain is that "Nothing changes." (279) Even Gothos seems to confirm the notion. But I feel that is merely the despair of having no light in the dark. We must make that light, enact change. If we meet the second half of life with bitterness and resentment for those that haven't reached that peak, then what motive is there to change? Perhaps it is to learn to be a guide on that descent, where meaning might be found.

Rites of passage join individuals and groups, recognise the social participation in an individual's life. At midlife, it becomes an internal upheaval, the individual feels excluded from the day to day social, as though they are looking out at a world that is out of touch. This might in some ways contribute to the sense of isolation felt—where before the initiations were focused on strengthening the bonds between individual and society, the midlife descent is at its heart a solitary journey.

"But I will make a place where no fall is possible." (452) If there is no growth, there can be no fall. It is as though the old man were to begrudge the young their success, their growth, or to revel in the descent.

Kallor's brief conversation with an undead dragon shows a side of the man thought long lost. He is awakened to compassion by the idea that the Jaghut had undertaken a war against death. Until now, it has been our experience that Kallor is a pure manifestation of will, having scoured compassion from his soul.

He then sees in his confrontation with Spinnock Durav that Rake has 'sacrificed' him to hold Kallor at bay, and he wonders, emotionally, at the man's ability to draw such reverence. He is not immune to emotion, compassion, it seems. But no doubt he is spiteful and cynical. In fact, even after his meeting with the dragon we are party to his memories of a wife and a horse, and despite what he felt he fancies himself as the avatar of all humanity in its viciousness and hatred, just that he is better at it.

But the Kallor we met in *Memories of Ice*, for example, would have had little qualm in disposing of Tiste Andii. For example, his disdain for Korlat and Orfantal was obvious. So something has occurred to Kallor on this journey that has forced him to reevaluate. It is not his own memories, not a challenge to his perceived superiority, but seeing in others the act of sacrifice, the enactment of their faith.

Kallor is doomed to failure, and so he fits the idea of the Crippled God's worshippers. He embodies that failure to strive. But Kallor is also doomed to persist, and in doing that he still contains the potential for growth. His curse has put him in a bind where he can neither embrace futility, nor perceive the reward for living his life. He is acting out his nature: "Life thrust forth choices, and the measure of a man's or woman's worth could be found in whether they possessed the courage, the brazen decisiveness, to grasp hold and not let go. Kallor never failed at such moments." (811) He sees that despite this nature, ambition leads to inevitable failure. Perhaps what Kallor fails to realise in this is that ambition and action undertaken for solely selfish aims is what leads to their failure.

This lack of recognition is apparent as he rails at Spinnock Durav in the aftermath of their duel. "He does not deserve you!" (867) Spinnock's sympathy for Kallor and his lack of understanding tell us that there is indeed a deserved faith in Rake, that the Andii have agency in their choice to follow him. Kallor is unable to conceive, or perhaps cursed to act as though, there is nothing greater than one's own winning. He is ravaged with grief at the fall of Spinnock, and perhaps some part of him is realising that what they see in Rake is something that he will never win for himself—not the sword or a throne, any of the trappings, but the force of personality.

It must also be remembered that the curse inflicting Kallor in a sense drives him to be what he has become, that symbol of humanity's failure and selfish ambition. The curse means that that is how he is seen, as the persona of his curse, rather than as the man beneath. Spinnock gets a little crack in the mask, but the mask is so thickly welded on at this point we find it hard to believe he will break free.

Traveller: Grief

"Dying was unthinkable…" (97) Traveller has renounced Hood. But death itself? Just as compassion is interwoven with vulnerability, so life is interwoven with grief. It is necessary. So what does he lose in such pronouncements?

> "We have been taught that death is always followed by more death. It is simply not so, death is always in the process of incubating new life, even when one's existence has been cut down to the bones.
>
> Rather than seeing the archetypes of Death and Life as

opposites, they must be held together as the left and right side of a single thought. It is true that within a single love relationship there are many endings. Yet, somehow and somewhere in the delicate layers of the being that is created when two people love one another, there is both a heart and breath. While one side of the heart empties, the other fills. When one breath runs out, another begins."[186]

The question which underlies Traveller's drive, and indeed those long-lived or in their twilight of life—Duiker, Kallor, Endest, even Seerdomin whose challenges may be seen as those of midlife but equally as one who has survived, gifted more time—is what to do with that time. "And what, pray tell, shall we do with it?" (825) What is the meaning of dying and how does that inform the meaning we ascribe to life? When death is ever present, we should value life more. If death is not, then what can life be but a waiting room? And if we, culturally, forsake death or wish it away to unconsciousness, then we are just hoping that life is only an ever-expanding state. Dying is something that must be attended consciously, or we're running against life's rhythms. And what might this do to our descendants, to those who would witness, when they do not see the rhythms unfold?

Stephen Jenkinson speaks about the false dichotomy between meaning in life and meaning at the end of life. "Most everything we know about our life is ending as we die, that is a true thing, but life isn't ending *because* we die." Against the notion that the end of life is the end of meaning in life, he continues: "…when that is your hammer, that is what your dying becomes: the end of the meaning of life."[187] Meaning is not to be made in dying, but in living. It is a journey that takes a life. It is not something to be found at the end, in a sudden rush. Nor does that ending undo or remove responsibility from the life lived. In Rake's sacrifice, we see personified the notion that we can live because we die, not in spite of it. Dying is not life's end, nor its opposite. It is inherent.

Grief, too, is inherent. It is the counterpoint to life, to love. "In love, grief is a promise." (733) The depth of grief is measured by the depth of love, and you cannot have one without the other. The bittersweet nature of love and life is caused by the knowledge of the grief to come, that dying happens and we must face it. To do otherwise can we truly love, live?

> "People will grieve. For the dead, for the living. For the loss of innocence and for the surrender of innocence, which are

---

[186] Estés, 1997, p. 142
[187] Jenkinson, 2015, p. 98

> two entirely different things. We will grieve, for choices made and not made, for the mistakes of the heart which can never be undone, for the severed nerve-endings of old scars and those to come." (551-2)

As Kruppe here extols, grief is not just for the dying, but for that which in life is gone. The old life, youth, our adolescent conceptions of the world. All of it is rendered with the shadow of grief, for all of it will end. This is not cause for sadness in the moment, for disabusing the young of notions of their greatness, but to see it in such terms means we live with it, really with it.

Erikson recognises that in story we can sense that shadow, and feel the grief for the past and gone once more. Thus it is through the trailing of Fisher, the bard, by which Kruppe enlightens us. "Prise loose those old scars. They remind one what it is to grieve. They remind one what it is to live." (552)

Just as the argument is put forward that chaos, or compassion, for all their risks and downsides, further the cause of humanity, so it is with dying. We can choose to die blindly, we can choose no suffering (mentally and emotionally) through sedation and a cultural blindness. But if we live through the concept of dying, approach it consciously, we may learn and leave the world a more caring and less bewildering place after we're gone. To do otherwise is hardly living at all.

"Is not death's gift indifference? Blissful, perfect indifference?" (672) This is not the case, because meaning can be found in it. Meaning can be found in the consideration of a place that embodies death—an afterlife. That is what the Jaghut fought for. That is what could wring a tear even from Kallor's leathern eyes, who had wandered so long he had forgotten meaning.

As Murillio's cart returns with his corpse, we are shown people recoiling from it, from the notion of death itself. "Remonstrance of mortality is a slap in the face, a stinging shock." (700) This is what Jenkinson is explaining in his notion of a death-phobic culture. "Grief is the most solitary of all feelings." (728) And yet it need not be.

"No, nothing wanted to die. When death is oblivion, life will spit in its face. If it can." (831) So we should try to find some meaning, beyond death. Hood says to Draconus, "Let the gods see to their own." (836) The notion that faith can be rewarded by the expectation, or hope, for something other than oblivion beyond dying is played out here. It is not a one-sided expectation, but rather it is created in the very process of faith. We can make meaning.

In midlife we grieve the lost, the life now behind. But grief in and of itself is also a burden. It is one that might teach us that to live with the burdens is the true task of growing, not releasing or running from them.

Stonny and Murillio

Stonny doesn't acknowledge Harllo. He is her burden, the reminder of the past, both of what was lost, in his naming, and the violence enacted upon her. This is a clear mirror of Mother Dark rejecting her children, namely her son Anomander. Lack of trust in her own body, due to her trauma, makes it impossible to be vulnerable. Being vulnerable doesn't necessarily mean regression, it means allowing conjunction between mature masculine and feminine aspects of the self.

Stonny has a role at the duelling school, which is poignant symbolism. The sword cuts to the point, it is an aspect of the logos, where Stonny chooses to dwell. It is also somewhat archaic and ritualistic. A duel is a container for rage, ritual sacrifice as opposed to murder, a more civilised enactment of the outburst of violence. In this way, it is a container for her psychic processes. It is the discipline she needs.

Murillio plays out the puer aeternus—the forever child. He wanted to stay a dandy, forever young. But time and age catch up with him, and this becomes his downfall. However, he saves the child—in that way allowing life to continue, and bringing the child back to Stonny. He is also the reversal of Harllo, who is Stonny's actual child but is forced to grow up too soon.

The journey of the puer or puella is to give something up that is unachievable—it is an ego identity. "Oh, in retrospect, so many regrets this night." (25) We find Murillio at an estate for a dalliance with a widow, and he is charmed instead by the daughter. Older now, but he is still in thrall of that lifestyle, wanting to trade the elder for youth. It is his downfall, as a youth stabs him.

As Kruppe, narrating, later ponders: "in his thoughts he walked the cemetery of his past…while stretching away in his wake was the shadow of his youth…" (91) Midlife contains the process of acknowledging and grieving for the past, dealing with the accumulation of shadow contents from the first half of life. He sees the potential in youth, but he is jaded all the while—he also sees and embodies the futility of it as a lifestyle. His constant reminders of that way of life are in his face as he teaches at the duelling school, and he wishes to force them away, even as he is stuck repeating the pattern. He wants to live his unlived life through them.

Speaking to Cutter in his convalescence, Murillio says, "'I've been granted a second chance and I intend to take it.' 'Meaning?'" (229) The subtle double meaning in Cutter's reply in this the brief exchange is the notion that Murillio will find meaning with his second chance. Tragedy, injury, illness, are often precipitators of the self-reflection required at midlife. They allow or force us to take stock, to realise our limitations, our frailty, our mortality.

Harllo's journey continues to mirror Murillio's, and Stonny continues to attempt to break through. When Harllo goes underground, he is symbolically enacting the heroic journey, reconnecting with the deep past. In this way he is creating, and reuniting the old and the new. Just at this time, Stonny unloads upon Murillio, finally allowing herself to be vulnerable: "like the unlocking of a door once thought sealed for ever more." (401) But with this comes realisation, and her guilt closes her off once more: "Murillio stands apart, desperate to comfort her, to force open all that had now closed between them." (496)

Stonny thought to cut ties with the past, just as other characters have done, but more literally. Even still, the weight of the shadow is there, evidenced by her reaction to Harllo's loss: "to imagine that such a thing could leave her indifferent was not to understand anything at all." (569) While the midlife crisis is stereotypically considered in men, a similar reckoning occurs for mothers when it is time to let their children grow and leave. Symbolically this is the process at play with Stonny, as she is losing her child.

Murillio's second chance, it turns out, is a gift to Stonny: his life for Harllo's. He allows himself to be vulnerable, and acts compassionately, despite her being closed off to him. It is no longer a selfish act, but freely offered. He searches through the dead, keeps trying to find Harllo. This is symbolic of his bearing the weight, the haunting of his past. That is his grief, after all.

His is the refusal that is needed. He doesn't let her push him away.

As we see Bellam Nom follow Murillio to accost Snell, we realise that Murillio's conscious application of his 'second chance' becomes contagious. He affects the youth, who acts in a heroic way. While Murillio falls, tragically, duelling with Vidikas, he has done enough, affected enough people to have it not be in vain. He has taught, and changed some people and this brings about Harllo's return, the ultimate gift to Stonny. This sacrifice reawakens hope within her. This is similar to Rake's actions inspiring the new god within Dragnipur to resist its nature and act selflessly.

It is Bellam's words that break through Stonny's defences. He gives her no choice but to take responsibility, of the two girls. This opening up within Stonny allows her son to come home, finally, when Harllo's own insistence forces the door open for good.

Barathol and Scillara

Scillara, like Cutter and others, also seems older than her years would suggest. She has matured in the intervening time since her escape from Raraku.

> "A single regret could crush a thousand proud deeds, and Barathol Mekhar had more regrets than most mortals could stomach. Nor was he young enough to brazen his way through them, assuming, of course, that youth was indeed a time of bold fearlessness…" (81)

Scillara's perception of Barathol and his burdens also reveals her own uncertainty of what youth might be, for she didn't experience it herself.

Barathol tells Mappo, on their parting, "Some people, I now believe, cannot just … retire. It feels too much like surrender." (82) He is speaking for so many characters in this novel. The burdens of the past, the willingness and the will to go on as before, as though retirement is an acceptance of burdens, but if one keeps working through they might never catch up. But Barathol finds a pleasant satisfaction at least in the work he does. Only, the world is out to stop him.

Barathol reflects on Cutter, and his swift separation from Scillara. "Longing for what could never be found was pointless, a waste of time." (146) He feels youth are quick to cut and run. Though it appears he is lacking some insight. He believes he has let things go, though he is clearly still haunted by his past, it keeps coming back to him unbidden, and the world wants to force him to dance to a different tune.

Letting go is more than just deciding not to think about the past. "Longing will drag you into the stalker's bony arms, and you will have but a single, last look back, on to your life…and you will understand, all at once, all that you have wasted, all that you let escape, all that you might have had." (147-8) He wants it to be easy, a clean break. He thinks to avoid turning to look back gives him that neat separation.

Scillara, ever perceptive: "What to do with the rest of our lives, now there's a worthy question." (149) And it is the question that is rendered clear in midlife, as the actions and the goals of the first half no longer fulfill the soul, but time stretches out in front of us. Barathol wants to start over, "A second chance." (149) This tells us that, after all, he hasn't let go of the past, he is still fleeing it. The goal for him is to integrate the past and the new life. Neither a clean break nor a fresh start, but it might be a rebirth, like what he gave Chaur. That is in his power.

The questions raised by these two remain unanswered, even through the trials they undergo in this book. They survive, at least, and they face the unknown together.

Gruntle

Gruntle, too, is still doing his job, despite his ascendancy. "He was, he considered, too old to be discovering new talents." (71) In a sense, he is denying the shift at midlife, the change of direction, by investing himself further in the old ways. He joins the Trygalle Trade Guild, amplifying his current mode of behaviour in what Stonny sees as a self-destructive attitude.

This line of thinking continues after he goes to see Stonny, "the life he was busy wasting, the pointlessness of all the things he chose to care about…" (223) Again, we are seeing characters no longer doing what they're good at, doing what they've always done. Gruntle, too, needs to find meaning. "They were all cages, and the trick he'd never learned was how to be at peace living in a cage." (225)

Gruntle thinks he will take the earnings and buy some contentment for Harllo and his adopted family. It allows him to give to what he doesn't have in his own life. He feels an attachment to Stonny and her child, as if they are his own family, though his nature does not allow him to settle for that life.

The Bridgeburners

There is not much to say here, but they are retired. These characters are another example of the themes tying this book together. Their past weighs upon them all differently.

Duiker ponders the loss of meaning, in his failed attempts to render the past: "somewhere beneath there must be the thick, solid sludge of motivation, of significance, of meaning…the alternative is … unacceptable." (131) Mallet is likewise riven with regret and searching for some underlying purpose. "I don't like being retired. It's like announcing an end to your worth…" (133) They all, in their search for meaning, are reflecting the same in the other storylines. Do the lives have meaning at all? And what can be created with it after the middle passage?

That question, indeed that quest, was part of Jung's search that unravelled through the process of individuation. It is a question that gains great resonance at midlife, as all that has come before can be perceived, and the future, without the growth and physical ability, stretches out before us like a chasm.

Antsy reflects, in the wake of the attack on the Bridgeburners, on his past. "The mind in the present was ever eager to narrate its own past" (538), and by doing so, Antsy calls into question all that has come before, for himself, for our reading of the narrative. As we age and take stock, we (re)create a narrative, and don't know how much of it is true, "what had been in truth a time as chaotic as the present suddenly seemed like a narration, a story." (538) His reminiscence of childhood defies him, warping, challenging him, proving his disconnection from that past.

He wants to forget the past, in a way, but he also needs it, to recapture the feelings and attitudes that kept him going. Casting off the past, or drowning it—"Gallons of ale wasn't helping." (539)—doesn't work. But nor is it necessarily truthful when it does arise. So memory and the past is an act of faith. We accept it, and move forward despite it.

At the end it is Spindle's finding Monkrat to remind him of the soldier's way in this empire, that speaks to rightful action. "We had the chance – the privilege – of doing the right thing." (820) The power that comes with being a soldier, wielding its weaponry, must be counterbalanced by the freedom to act in the service of humanity. Therein lies their capacity to maintain a sense of self, a sense of meaning. "…when I see these uniforms I see compassion and truth. The moment those virtues fail, then the gods help you, for no armour is strong enough to save you." (820-1)

Conclusion

In many ways, the outcomes in this novel are of characters accepting their nature. In the growth phase of life we create a persona, whereas at midlife we expose it to scrutiny, laying bare and understanding our true selves, if we've the courage. The acceptance of the self, first, and living a life consistent with that inner self and true purpose is essential for creating meaning in that descending phase. But knowing, too, that we can consciously intervene, we can act against our seeming true nature, add a little chaos, to guide the flow of life, to grow, and to maybe make the world a better place.

Hood is discontented with how his outer person has come to be represented by the nature of death. Kallor is represented by his curse. The nature of Nimander, the son, becoming like his father, Anomander. There are brief musings on DNA. Of course, the various associations with the Redeemer and how a god or faith may or may not be the outer nature that is represented. The many characters who want to find a new life, or a new career, but are drawn to be what they are. All of these are aspects of people being their outer manifestations (personae) or pushing against those. But is there an inevitability, as there seems to be with Crokus, that life or fate will force us to play out those threads we have set in motion? How much room is there for the hands at the pottery wheel?

So then, what about the Crippled God? For the Crippled God, "the flaw is the virtue. Salvation arrives with death and it is purchased through mortal suffering. There is no perfection of the spirit to strive towards, no true blessing to be gained as a reward for faith." (745) This is, in a way, anathema to the idea of individuation. In spite of flaws, Jung would have it that the striving is the thing. Could it be that such ideology can thrive in a time and place when there is no sense of something greater? Nothing given in return for faith, no reward in the world in return for our living and striving. If we are lost and lonely, then any promise of salvation will do. The work of life is to remind ourselves that we are not lost.

> "That in living, one recounts the lives of all those long gone, long dead, even forgotten. Recounts all the demands of necessity…and the urges of blessed wonder – a finger tracking

> the serpent's path, a breath against stone. Weight and presence and the lure of meaning and pattern." (748)

This is not a nihilistic notion. We mark stone, we narrate our stories, because in that way we remind ourselves and those who might come after, that we are. "I, Samar Dev, once was. And am no more." (748)

Is that the only faith we need, that we exist and that is enough? We mark ourselves, and we mark for each other, that a finger might trace us, and so become aware. And it is that awareness itself that makes it worthwhile, even as it makes us feel small and lonely and insignificant.

So too within a life, that we might see our past and patterns, and take a step beyond them. And so, too, in grief we might recognise our own mortality, and learn what it is to live.

Kruppe's narration throughout the novel is an example of the sort of compassion we are being asked to consider by Erikson. How he slides into the minds of the characters, finds empathy for those we might not even glance at—Chaur, the ox, etc.—and his very dance itself is the enactment of conscious empathy. Deeper, we get to witness Hood's walk into the city, and here we see what I believe to be Erikson's will inserting itself into the story. Hood changes the outcome for the guard who is close to death—this one time, the Lord of Death chooses to enact what he sees as justice for the compassionate guard, whose "soul shines." (796) Again, an example is set. The author, through Kruppe's narration, is begging that we find such compassion within ourselves, asserting that even the god of death can defy his very nature to save one soul.

> "The alchemist knows: the wrong catalyst, the wrong admixture, ill-conceived proportions, and all pretence of control vanishes – the transformation runs away, unchained, burgeons to cataclysm. Confusion and fear, suspicion and then war, and war shall breed chaos. And so it shall and so it does and so it ever will." (578)

And so, we must remain ever conscious, ever diligent.

What Is, Was: Alchemy, Fire, and Renewal in *Dust of Dreams*

Alchemy, for Jung, was a model for the soul's journey of transformation. The opus of alchemical investigation is the very process of inner work projected on to the physical world. This is a fine metaphor for the process undergone by the writer and the reader, in approaching the transformative process of living through the Book of the Fallen. In consciously undertaking the process, we are seeking fullness within ourselves.

Jung's writings and lectures on alchemy, which were the focus of the latter part of his life and constitute a good chunk of his collected works, are often approached with frustration. They do not seem to be contiguous with his prior work (though hints are scattered throughout his earlier work), rather a contraction of his mind into ever more esoteric pursuits. But there is something in it. Jung believed this philosophy was the perfect metaphor for the process of self-growth, individuation.

The latter half of his life was, if not consumed by, supported by alchemy. It appears that what Jung was searching for, what he sensed was missing in his vast earlier theories, was something central. Whether he found this in alchemy, or whether he merely sensed a similar search, the work of kindred spirits, is unclear. But it is also around this time that the term Self begins appearing in his works. It is almost as though alchemy was the work of Jung's own individuation, the metaphor for, and process of, his own spiritual attainment during the second half of his life.

Though it appears mystical and arcane to us now, Jung was not alone in considering alchemy an important line of research. *Psychology and Alchemy*, published now as Volume 12 of Jung's Collected Works, was the first volume translated into English, on the premise that it was the topic that at that time was apt to capture the public consciousness. The writings seem to come with their own language, an array of symbols and concepts that one must wrestle with to follow the narrative. Indeed, it goes deep, but I don't think one must understand the specifics to appreciate the symbolism. The defamiliarization that is at play is no different to entering a fantasy world.

Alchemists often had slippery definitions of their symbols, partly because there were many different ideas over a long period (it is worth keeping in mind that this was not a brief diversion limited to a handful of medieval quacks, but many centuries' worth of scientific pursuit), but also because the writings were often secretive and coded. Fundamentally, as a philosophy, alchemists believed that all is alive, all matter. They desired to transform material by finding its essence, the elusive Lapis Philosophorum or Philosopher's Stone. With this, it was supposed that one could transmute base metals into gold, heal and bestow eternal life, and of course, enlightenment.

The Magnum Opus was the ongoing work of the search. The work contained various methods and stages of separation and recombination, death and rebirth, to refine and achieve a state of pure being. Masculine and feminine aspects (and other dualities) are united in a hieros gamos (divine marriage), to transcend or bear a child that defeats death. This union of opposites is the ultimate stage of the alchemical work.

While the practical, physical goals of alchemy were doubtless important to practitioners and the spread of alchemy (or at the least that oversimplification permits its persistence in modern consciousness), it is clear that the aspect of spiritual transformation in the work was of high importance, even to the earliest known works, back to references contained in Egyptian myth, such as the notion of Osiris being the *prima materia*, sealed, bathed, dismembered and reconstituted and so forth. Von Franz notes it wasn't a literal immortality that was sought (though it's likely that was a motive for some), but an understanding of something fundamental to humanity: "The search for immortality was actually the search for an incorruptible essence in man which would survive death, an essential part of the human being which could be preserved."[188]

The goal of the process of individuation is to merge all the parts of the psyche into some sort of unity, to achieve spiritual wholeness: from the original unity pre-birth to the differentiation of birth and development, the self-similar connections and separations through the lifespan, to the final manifestations of Self. Jung identified that a parallel goal exists in the alchemical work, the goal sometimes called the philosopher's stone. Jung

---

[188] Von Franz, 1980a, p. 93

believed this aim was akin to undergoing the individuation task, though in a material way.

During the Book of the Fallen, to this point we have entered with naïve expectations, experienced chaotic birth into the world, undergone variously the separations and unity of the collective, worked through archetypes of the parents, the animus and anima, the shadow, and then traversed the symbolic lifespan over again, from birth, through initiation, and the middle passage. Now, in its final movements, we will coalesce once again towards wholeness and unity.

As a reader it seems that from this point forward is where the dialogue between the conscious and unconscious, if you will, seems to be openly engaged in the pages. The 'work', as we may put it in an analytical sense, has been done, the groundwork laid, the patterns formed and the questions raised. It might also be noted that what Erikson has shown up until now is from true experience, but hereon it is exploratory. The real completion of the process of individuation happens not in instructive form, but in iteration and to some degree apart. We are on our own now. But we have all that we need.

These final two novels are at once dreamlike, and completely logical given what has come before. It is not in the author's purview to give us answers, but to allow us to find them for ourselves, maybe in ways that we cannot quite articulate.

Alchemy is about transformation and realisation of potential. The alchemical opus, then, is the inner work projected out onto matter. The process of seeking the philosopher's stone, the transformation of matter into the pure substance of life, is a work of seeking perfection and underlying meaning, the spiritual essence. As Jung puts it, "The goal is important only as an idea: the essential thing is the *opus* [the work on oneself] which leads to the goal: *that* is the goal of a lifetime."[189] Individuation is likewise such a conscious relation to the self.

The process, like the alchemical opus, is the work of individuation. In striving, we are approaching wholeness. If we aren't conscious of it, we cannot strive. But it is an ideal not meant to be achieved. In the search for meaning in human life, an underlying archetypal pattern is revealed. The sustained efforts of the alchemists to formulate an understanding made it so. Not only striving for meaning, but striving to form a metaphor for the self. To know itself, to know the gold within.

It should also be noted that alchemy operated under an entire philosophy, related to religion, the stars, as well as the inner world. There was intercom-

---

[189] Jung, C.G., CW16 [400]

nectedness, and vital life spark in all things—what we might nowadays consider panpsychism. So working on what we might consider inert matter was not just a vain pursuit, nor merely allegory. The divine essence is the underlying search. It is associated with turning base metals into gold, or to gift eternal life. At the base of these is the belief that in all matter there is spirit, and by seeking the fundamental essence, all manner of transformation is possible.

Dust of Dreams is a book of lasts, people who represent the culmination of their people or the final argument of their beliefs. This finality is people laid bare, burned down to their alchemical essence.

The book opens with unfamiliar scenes, tragedy visited upon peoples and spirits broken. We will journey to recapture and consolidate the essence of humanity, completing our cycle on this journey of individuation.

Kalyth, gifted awareness beyond her senses, sees herself as the embodiment of an omen: "Death arrived winging across the face of the setting sun…driven to earth as all things were, eventually." (41) And so the spirit of the sky is conjoined to the matter of the earth beneath. This is a divine marriage, the conjunction, two become one. We see the vision of the assassin, formed of two sets of eyes, one above and one below, conjoined to create a greater vision of the world: "after a time Gu'Rull was able to enforce the necessary separation, so that the vistas found their proper relationship to one another, creating a vast panorama of the world beyond." (43)

As above, so below.

Kalyth

Kalyth is the last of her kind, mirror to the Matron of the K'Chain Che'Malle, who has adopted her as Destriant. This is an attempt to humanise and to capture the power of human worship. It also reflects her as the spiritual aspect to the Matron's matter (mater, mother).

She is set what she believes to be an impossible task, and has no talent to undertake her role. "I am blind to whatever it is a Destriant needs." (39) The opening of the book is replete with visions, of eyes not functioning and those taking in new vistas. It is symbolic of the coming of vision, of consciousness being born. For Kalyth, the impossible task is the spiritual work, and to undertake it in spite of the futility is where the value can be found. "And this, she now understood, was the penance set upon her soul." (39)

She feels that she has committed a betrayal when she fled in the face of her tribe's slaughter. In part, this would be a kind of survivor's guilt. In part, it is that she is at a loss as to how to proceed.

She ponders the rituals of the Spotted Horse, her tribe's way of mixing herbs to go on a spirit journey. The specific preparation and mixing of the contents, the notion that alone they would kill, and in incorrect proportions, sounds alchemical in nature: "Seven herbs, softened with beeswax and rolled into a ball and then flattened into an oblong disc that was taken into the mouth and held between lip and gum." (194) And its effects appear to be a kind of spiritual rebirth: "To journey into this realm was to be cleansed, made whole, purged of all regrets and dark desires." (195)

And then, of course, though uninitiated she takes the journey. She is not sure what she seeks, some sort of connection to her people, some answers to her lost state, perhaps.

In her vision she sees the falling to dust of the past, the sweep of history, its vastness. "Such knowledge could crush a soul with its immensity, or drown it beneath a deluge of unbearable futility." (200) Erikson in this series is showing us the nature of separation against the backdrop of the rise and fall of history and civilisations. But at another level it is something we all experience, the infant realising its separation from the mother, for example. It is the awakening of self, the burgeoning of consciousness. Kalyth understands this separation of self from the world in terms of the seeming insignificance of the individual in the face of history's disinterest: "the self became an orphan, bereft of all security, and face to face with a world now become at best a stranger, at worst an implacable, heartless foe." (200-1) This separation explains the feeling of loneliness, but the question becomes how to combine again the sense of connection. "But how could one step back into the world?" (201) It is the separation itself that wounds, and spiritual health is to be found in healing those splits. Curiously, in our world typically a psychedelic experience would enlighten the connection, rather than separation, though perhaps the understanding of separation must come first.

She finds Heboric digging, it seems, or rather thrusting his hands beneath sand. He speaks as though there is arcane knowledge to which he is not party. "There must be some other secrets involved. Quenching in water or manure piles…" (202) Coming out of the vision, she questions its veracity, thinks it meaningless because she hadn't had a specific purpose. "…willpower alone was not enough, particularly when she had no real destination in mind" (209). But perhaps the intention is enough. She has brief visions of a war gone or to come, ruined K'Chain mechanisms, and twin suns blazing.

As the K'Chain bring her to the site of a dead dragon, she is wondering what she has to offer them as Destriant, only knowing of the excoriation of her past, the awareness of endings and dust. But the K'Chain Che'Malle are willing to renew their ways with new blood, with the nature of humanity. They see this as a renewal, if we are not to believe it is mere madness.

She finds a fang of an Otataral dragon, and this begins a discussion of opposition. "The Nah'ruk…spoke of forces in opposition, of the necessity of tension." (376) Jungians, then. But it reveals that the K'Chain are aware and open to the possibility of a multitude of forces all influencing each other. It is no wonder then that the battle to come is against the Nah'ruk.

"If all remains within…then there is no reason for anything to exist, no reason for creation itself. If all is ordered, untouched by chaos, then the universe that was, is and ever will be, is without meaning. Without value." (376) This touches on notions of the alchemical process and individuation. Remaining within means to not change, and not be open to the outer world. We must rejoin the world when the individual work has been done, be open to its influences. The passage also means we cannot remain in the conscious world, unexposed to the unconscious, if we expect to grow. There are places we must look. The K'Chain are aware that a little chaos is a catalyst, creates progress. This might give an insight into the nature of the Shake and their drop of demon blood.

And we have here the refutation of simple polarity and forced balance. "In that tension, meaning will be found. In that struggle value is born." (376) It is in the constant monitoring of forces to find balance, that the work is done, not in the end state of maintained stasis or, worse, the state of stasis untouched in the first place.

The lesson is that recognition of what is outside of us—whether that is in the form of our gods, culture, ideology, whatever—must necessarily create empathy: "And if your god has a face, then so too does that other. In such comprehension, Destriant, will you come to grasp the freedom that lies at the heart of all life; that choice is the singular moral act and all one chooses can only be considered in a moral context if that choice is free." (376) And so, to the Crippled God. Just as the K'Chain are compassionate to the lives they take, it is a consciousness, profound.

Kalyth travels to observe the Otataral dragon. She understands that in freeing it, its opposite will also be freed. Balance will thus be enacted. And so the act of trying to create balance by acting upon the world with a force of great extremity is misguided. A conjunction is in the offing—the goal of the alchemical process, the uniting of the opposites, just like in individuation. She sees that opposition, the nature of it, makes of our actions something futile— we create enemies, "we each fashion our 'others' and chart the course of our lives as that eternal campaign, seasons of gain, seasons of loss." (380)

And so Kalyth offers the K'Chain a different way. "Find your faith in each other. Look no further." (381) In a sense this is the rallying cry of the Book of the Fallen, and certainly echoes Tavore in *Dust of Dreams*, who no longer wants to be used by the gods, who wants to champion mortals' compassion. In one another, in ourselves, we will find something sacred, and perhaps rise beyond the 'natural' state of endless conflict. But it is work, and it goes on. "Somewhere, out there, you will find the purest essence of that philosophy." (381) Perhaps she speaks of the philosopher's stone. There in the Bonehunters where reside Gesler and Stormy. But it is not just them, it is the act itself: "Worship the sacrifice they will make, for they make it in the name of compassion – the only cause worth fighting and dying for." (381)

Kalyth recalls a rite of her tribe, that of a clay 'vessel' being created when a child is born. In alchemy, the vessel is symbolically as important as the material itself in some writings. It is often depicted as containing Hermes/Mercurius, meaning the spirit is contained within the matter. The work is carried out within the vessel, meaning it is a symbol for the self, within which transformation is taking place.

Kalyth recalls the elemental dispositions, and we are shown that upon death the vessel is placed within the flames of the hearth: "Fire was the Brother and Husband Life-Giver of the Elan…the clay figurine – born of Water, Sister and Wife Life-Giver – finally shattered in the heat, thus conjoining the spirit-gods…" (471) This elemental duality and the conjunction at the end of the opus is redolent of alchemical symbolism. The opus has as its end point the conjunction of the oppositional natures, typically spirit and matter, like air and earth, also the divine marriage, sometimes depicted as divine Brother and Sister.

"Kalyth had lost her figurine…" (472) This loss reflects her sense of being adrift, of being in a kind of purgatory with her tribe gone and her soul nowhere to go. She is disconnected from the world, her reality, ego and Self seeking conjunction. Without that protective 'vessel' of culture, her conception of life and mortality is shaken. In recalling the bhederin's long dying, its "stubborn defiance" (472), she is concluding that there is no neat throughline in life and death. The vessel, then, also represents the containing myth of her people.

The clash of elemental forces is brought home as she and the K'Chain

Che'Malle are fleeing the storm. The black clouds are symbolic of the confusion of the early stage of the alchemical process. The lightning is representative of an awakening from the confusion—enlightenment of the chaos, a bolt from the blue. Though we know that these clouds hide a particular embodiment of chaos in the form of the skykeeps. The storm brings together the air, the fire, and the rumbling of the earth. This is a place bereft of water, though they pass through "a pan of parched clay crusted with ridged knuckles of salt." (475)

Kalyth begins to take strength in her role. Though she still doubts, she is able to instruct the K'Chain Che'Malle, to give them faith through her words. She even stands up to the assassin, Gu'Rull. In her death realm she encounters the Bridgeburners, and takes heart in their being the guardians of that place. So long without human contact, it is a comfort to her, and she no longer fears. She had thought of herself "A vessel empty, longing to be filled by a hero's bold fortitude" (634), but that strength is instead filling her from the inside.

"The world narrows – but how is it I even know this? What part within me is aware of its own measure?" (640) Self-awareness, the accepting of her limitations, and the embracing of her strengths, these are the outcomes of her journey so far, with work still to be done. The balancing of forces, both within her and without, is the work of individuation. "Against the cold that slays, you must answer with fire." (638) While this evokes particular associations within the story, it could also be the cold of judgment being balanced with the fire of compassion. Taking the lead once again, Kalyth commands Gunth Mach to allow her to ride—the taming of the beast, often depicted as a lion or unicorn in alchemical symbolism, representing the connection of one's animal nature, its mastery. The strength shown is not physical, but that of discipline. And for Kalyth, it is an awakening of life: "she could feel her frailty falling away from her soul like a cracked seed husk." (640) The seed being the most archetypal vessel.

As a result of her realisations, Kalyth begins to feel empathy for the creatures she accompanies—or perhaps it is the empathy that comes first. She mourns a dead one, and they are surprised at her emotion. Both species are beginning to find that empathy for one another, and both are disappointed in themselves, feeling unworthy. "We will show you the horrors of the modern world you so want to be a part of," (721) Kalyth thinks. Gunth Mach reflects that she is the last Matron, and in Kalyth lies their hope of renewal.

Kalyth is witness to the raising up of the K'Chain Che'Malle nest.

Uprooted, what was fixed has become volatile. Within the stone dragon is a spark of life which lifts it to the sky.

"She also broke ten thousand years of changing nothing…" (1252) The Matron, in planning for the future and enjoining with the humans and their mentality, has broken the grounding shackles of static tradition. The sacrifice then gives the Che'Malle hope.

As the battle approaches, Kalyth finds herself disappointed in Stormy and Gesler, at their martial nature, their apparent cold conviction. She is struck by what appears to be the inhumanity of them, machine-like, just as she was alienated by the Che'Malle at the start. But after the battle, when they have survived, she understands the Matron's faith in the humans, and she finds it in herself, a faith in humanity.

Fire and Dragons

"Take a scintillating, flaring arm of the sun's fire, give it form, and upon the faint cooling of the apparition, a man such as Rud Elalle might emerge…" (126)

These seeming alchemical tempering instructions introduce yet another aspect of fire and burning. We have the Wastelands and Elan, and the scouring away of the peoples. Sinn and her precocity with fire and magic. Run'Thurvian melting down and excreting strangely yellow fluids, just as the gods Ursto and Pinosel do in Seren Pedac's house: "burned and burned, and beneath the flames they were *melting like wax*."(168). The sun awakening as the Watch is banished. Images of fire and burning and confusion following the prima materia of the prologue.

Paracelsus, a giant of alchemy, wrote: "By the element of fire all that is unpurified is destroyed and taken away." It is at once a force of life and an ordeal. Gesler and Stormy went through fire and were cleansed, so Kalyth searches for her 'hands of fire.' Both symbolic and literal fire in this novel are used to purify and uncover the essence of the humanity beneath. In a psychological sense, the process of fire is to remove egoic desires, leaving the aspects of the Self, a purer outcome, one not at the whims of the unconscious.

And we have dragons. The serpents that open the book, then dragons to the fore, with the vision of one pinned (Korabas) in Heboric's recollection,

Rud Elalle and Silchas, Telorast and Curdle. The K'Chain assassin, Gu'Rull becomes a kind of winged serpent, as he grows new feathered scales to allow flight. And then we see Ublala Pung disinter some dragon bits and dress up as a dragon slayer. (534)

"To the Blood of the Eleint, Udinaas, any notion of community is anathema. ...Once the draconic blood took hold of us, we were driven apart." (106) So what are the dragons representing, thematically? Jung wrote of dragons in alchemy thus: "The dragon in itself is a *monstrum*—a symbol combining the chthonic principle of the serpent and the aerial principle of the bird."[190] He then likens it to Mercurius, or Hermes, the winged symbol and messenger, both the prima materia and the symbol of the union of opposites at the pinnacle of the alchemical work. "When the alchemist speaks of Mercurius, on the face of it he means quicksilver, but inwardly he means the world-creating spirit concealed or imprisoned in matter."[191] In this book and the last, it's going to be a bringing together of contrary forces, the work of solitary figures becoming a conjunction.

The dragon or serpent itself has an association with fire, or sulphur. It also is worth discussing the image of the crucified serpent, which frequently appeared in alchemical texts based on the notes of Nicholas Flamel. In the Book we have had images of dragons impaled, notably the otataral dragon, Korabas. The crucified serpent can be taken to mean a fixing of the volatile substance, the sacrifice of Mercury during the opus.

Setoc

Setoc is not the last of her kind, necessarily, but the last of her family, and she becomes transformed into something else. "The holder of a thousand hearts." (225) She was raised by wolves. "Wolf gifts. Milk she had suckled, milk of blood, milk of a thousand slain brothers and sisters." (225)

She is a symbol of the wild, and she insists that it is the wildness itself that must be worshiped. That is the purity, or at least the unbroken state. "The enemy, Great Warlock, is peace." (232) This notion of peace and war likened to the wild and the civilised calls back to discussions of balance and

---

[190] Jung, C.G., CW12 [404]
[191] Ibid.

chaos.

She accompanies Torrent and Cafal as they escape the Gadra clan. The newness, youth and novelty, of her and Torrent are in this case notable by the envy and lust they elicit. It is not a pleasant assimilation, nor a healthy conjoining for these two. They experience a burning: "White fire erupted around them…Searing heat, stunning cold." (387) They find themselves buried in a barrow.

Setoc is now separated from her gods in this place. But in calling out to the dead wolves of this world they find themselves in, Setoc becomes overwhelmed. First, the last wolf to have been hunted comes, and we see that she has the compassion for this creature that the K'Chain Che'Malle spoke to Kalyth about. "She felt, as well, as the beast's lifeblood spilled into the churned-up soil, its surrender, its understanding – in that final moment – that its terrible loneliness was at last coming to an end." (395) She sees in the fact of their death the consequence of the attitude of polarity, of opposition, that a mind and attitude in conflict, embattled, isolated, creates: "she saw, with mounting horror, a legacy of such hateful, spiteful slaughter that she cried out, a shriek tearing at her own throat." (395) This comes after her innocent question to Cafal about who would hunt wolves to extinction. Having grown amongst wolves, and away from civilisation, it does not make sense in her world that such callous disregard would exist.

"She wept like the last child on earth, the last living thing, sole witness to the legacy of all that her kind had achieved. This desolation. This suicidal victory over nature itself." (396) She is the last child in the sense that she is the last innocent, the only one not corrupted by civilisation. And so she stands as the witness to civilisation, the only one worthy of judging its failings. What we see in Setoc, along with Kalyth, and Badalle to some extent, is a reader for Tavore. She is unique, standing outside, and so we can observe through her eyes the attitude we are being encouraged to take.

Setoc dreams of apocalypse, she is the Destriant of the wolves. And she cares for Tool and Hetan's kids. The images of destruction she perceives are representative of an inner separation. She embodies a god of war, but is also a protector. She ponders whether the selves we portray are within our control, as she remembers a man with a lost mind who wore the skin of a wolf: "The self could become lost in more subtle ways, could it not? *Today I am this person. Tomorrow I am another. See the truths of me? Not one is tethered. I am bound to no single self, but unleashed into a multitude of selves. Does this make me ill? Broken?*" (1019) She has undergone separation both from her past worlds, and within herself. She is trying to pin down an identity, and at a spiritual level she is aiming to reconcile the ghosts of the wolves she brought with her to this world, and the world as it is. "The twins walked five paces in front of her. They were one split in two. Sharp-eyed round faces peering into the mirror, where nothing could hide." (1020) She recognises that in the conjunction of opposites, the revelation of the self can be found.

Badalle and The Snake

Jung claimed that alchemy is a path, "not straight but snakelike, a path that unites the opposites, reminding us of the guiding caduceus, a path whose labyrinthine twists and turns are not lacking in terrors."[192] The serpent, often interchangeably with a dragon, is a common motif in alchemical imagery. Most familiar is the snake eating its own tail, the Ouroborus. This symbol contains unity: beginning and end, conscious and unconscious, holding and held, as well as the union of all into one. It shows that the alchemical process is circular and self-contained. It is both the prima materia, the original state, and its end point, the philosopher's stone. "Days and nights were a tumbling cavort, round and round with no beginning and no end. Jaws to tail." (417)

In addition to the ouroborus, alchemy is associated with another familiar serpentine symbol, the caduceus, two snakes entwined on a staff. While both are symbolic of conjunction, the caduceus is the conjunction of opposites, or duality, particularly the above and the below, spirit and matter. It is also renewal and healing, as we can see in its use as a medical symbol.

The ouroborus is not unique to alchemy, rather it has associations with many creation myths. In the ouroborus, we are witness to the cycle of birth and death, both cosmically, and of the individual or hero. "Just as the uroborus fertilises itself in the mouth by eating its own tail, so 'its own waste provides its own food,' an ever-recurrent symbol of autonomy and self-sufficiency."[193] In *Dust of Dreams* and on into *The Crippled God*, we are witness to many inversions and returns to childhood, the playing out of the cosmic cycle. Badalle is witness to children carrying babies, at once young and old. Badalle acknowledges that Rutt is the head of the snake, and he holds the child Held. Held is the seed in the dark womb of the earth. Thus Rutt

---

[192] Jung, C.G., CW12 [6]
[193] Neumann, 1949, p. 33

represents the beginning and the end, that childhood is at once the future and past. These children are old beyond their years.

"This snake had forgotten how to eat." (29) And so indeed, how to begin again.

> "the uroboros, the circular snake biting its tail, is the symbol of the psychic state of the beginning, of the original situation, in which man's consciousness and ego were still small and undeveloped. As symbol of the opposites contained in it, the uroborus is the "Great Round," in which positive and negative, male and female, elements of consciousness, elements hostile to consciousness, and unconsciousness elements are intermingled… a symbol of a state in which chaos, the unconscious, and the psyche as a whole were undifferentiated—and which is experienced by the ego as a borderline state."[194]

A river, too, winds like a snake; generative ground water is the life force of rebirth. Badalle is a poet. The transformative character of the feminine leads to birth of the eloquent spirit. "What we later designate as poetry originates in magical incantation and song, rising spontaneously from the unconscious and bringing its own form, its own rhythm, and its own sensuous images up with it from the depths."[195] Such incantations are related to spirit possession, rising up from the transpersonal unconscious, overpowering and making the speaker its instrument.

Badalle thinks of herself and Rutt and Held as a kind of symbolic triad that heads the Snake, and doesn't like the insinuation of the girl Brayderal into their 'family': "as if she wanted to be part of something. Something made up of Rutt and Held and Badalle. But whatever that something was it had no room for Brayderal." (234) Saddic moves in her shadow. "Saddic worshipped her, but he would not draw closer to her, not yet, because there would be no point." (236) He is also the commentary for Badalle as a meta-narrator. "Badalle had knowing told an untruth about Visto…Why had she done that?…*Her words weren't for him because he was gone. They were for us. She was telling us to give up remembering.*" (237) He notes that she names things, giving life and language.

Saddic is writing a book of their journey, recording her poems. This is a book of the fallen in miniature, a microcosm of our journey. "We got to lighten the load / Cut down on what we carry" (419) The book would have

---

[194] Neumann, 1955, p. 18
[195] Ibid. p. 297

empty pages, Badalle thinks, for their silences. The words they have cannot communicate the horror that the children are living, the despair that Erikson is trying to communicate. Words will never be enough. And so, in his way, he gives us a mirror of the greater journey, complete with narrators and witnesses without the words, the experience, to communicate it. Or, perhaps, their way of speaking of it is the most pure.

In doing this, Erikson shows us that we are at once incapable, and all too able, to live this experience. It resonates and alienates at the same time. We try to find compassion for these children and their plight, even as their difference, their distance, is being highlighted. Even when it is hopeless. Even when all is seared away to silence. The child, Held, is that spark of hope and possibility, the life essence, that we must grasp and carry. Held is the prima materia.

"Her mind was free. Free to make beauty with a host of beautiful, terrible words." (630) In a metafictional passage, we are witness to Badalle's mind floating free of her body, escaping the pain, and being able to witness and experience beyond her mortal body. It is clear in the juxtaposition of beautiful and terrible that language can invoke both, aiming to express what is beyond the words. "There was no pain in this place." (631) It is both her escape and her particular talent.

"She could be an adult here…" (631) With that escape, she imagines the carefree life that adulthood might be. These children are adrift from the caring containment of family, they are orphaned. All they know is the pain, flight and fear. "The adults don't care." (631) This plays with the notion that with civility, maturity, comes the expectation of a firm grasp of reality, what is important. No longer willing, if even able, to let loose our minds to fly like Badalle. And at the same time, it is a finger pointed at the reader, as Erikson holds up to us the horror of the Snake, and begs us to let our minds conjoin with one in pain. "Even words, especially words, could not penetrate those walls…" (631) With adulthood come the defences, seeking to protect our vulnerability, but in building up those walls we close off compassion. The walls define the limits of our empathy.

The free mind of the poet-child is the freedom to experience and express. The crystallised enclosure that is a defined self, the hardened barrier to the freedom Badalle imagines, and all it contains, only falls to dust, like all material things. "She wondered what adults owned, these days. Apart from this murderous legacy, of course." (632) Her freedom, though, is eternal.

"So many fallen…I could list them. I could make them into a book ten thousand pages long. And people will read it, but only so far as their own private borders, and that's not far. Only a few steps. Only a few steps." (632) Her attempt to render the memory of the fallen, a thing different from the unconstrained nature of her soaring perspective, the one remembered by Saddic, is analogous to the helpless feeling of uncertainty Erikson must have felt in rendering this Book of the Fallen. It cannot be experienced, not in the way of Badalle's own floating mind. Committing it to paper necessarily draws away some of the reality. And as the Snake takes this interminable journey, Erikson needs us to keep walking alongside it, to resist putting up our defences, to take more than only a few steps. By staying with it, we will allow ourselves to open to compassion. "One long scream of horror, Badalle. Ten thousand pages long. No one will hear it." (632) The attempt to portray it in its fullness, even as the author knows it is in vain. "I am Badalle, and all I have is words." (633)

The image of Badalle both flying above and walking below calls up the alchemical depiction of a double ouroborus, a winged serpent and one without wings biting one another's tails in a circle. This is a depiction of circulation, changing the fixed to the volatile and back again, a state spiralling closer to the work's completion. The perspective must be allowed to fly free, and then be brought back to reality again, so we might as readers engage in reflection. It is the principle of change, and in a sense reflects the alchemist's attempt to overcome mortality. The static rendering of experience on paper circulates back and forth with the direct experience of the free mind. At the same time, Kalyth is returning from her own dream, where she finds faith in adult humans, and courage and strength in the physical world. This is what Badalle must still find.

This flying is also associated with the alchemical stage of sublimation—a freeing of spirit to air, accompanied by images of ascent and flying, often by a white dove. From a psychological perspective, this can give perspective over a problem, however being stuck in the air (too much in the mind), can prevent us from dealing with the real problem 'on the ground'. The sublimation will usually be followed by a fall, which we see in Badalle, with her wings burning away.

Badalle witnesses the power of the sun's fire upon the body of a creature, and again this reads almost like an esoteric instruction to an alchemist trying to uncover gold: "No wind had come to scatter the scale, and the relentless sun had eaten away the toxic meat from around the bones, and had then bleached and polished those bones to a fine golden lustre." (818) There is a hard reality beneath the brief flit of life that dances over the mineral frame beneath. Paracelsus: "Fire separates that which is constant or fixed from that which is fugitive or volatile." Similarly, the flight of Badalle's imagination is under threat of being crushed by reality: "Her wings were shrivelled, burnt down to stumps. Flying was but a memory, finely dusted with ash, and she found nothing inside to justify brushing it clean." (819)

She ponders the gods above, the power of inaction, its omnipotence. Again, we feel this is a cry for our attention and action. Badalle gazing up to the sky, beseeching, gazes right into the reader's soul. And we are again party to the likeness of parents and children: "*The Fathers drove us out. They were done with children.* Now she believed the fathers and mothers of the gods had driven them out as well..." (821) There is the sense of abandonment, as though only that could explain the inaction that underlies a lack of compassion. A return to the welcome of open arms, the conjunction of mother and father, will provide real hope for Badalle.

As she holds Rutt, she thinks: "I have flown to where the sun sets, and I tell you, Rutt, we are marching into fire. Beautiful, perfect fire." (823) This brings back the power of the sun, but with a hopeful, cleansing sense. Note the duality of the destructive, wild force of fire and sun, compared to the warming, lifegiving effects. She and Rutt support one another, both failing and yet giving the other what is needed to stay upright. While unseen here, the child, Held, hovers thematically between them. They play the mother and father, until such time as their own can be returned to them.

Badalle's role as a containing vessel is reinforced when we see Hetan's death, and then Badalle's imagination floats across the scene, tells us that she held Hetan's soul at her end. She holds the souls of the suffering while the gods remain indifferent.

"Held. Held is the secret. One day, everyone will understand. Do you think it matters, Saddic? Things will be born, life will catch fire." (943) In Badalle and the Snake, we have a hope in the face of what appears to be utter despair. This becomes a counterpoint, finally, to the Crippled God's purported ideals, and also gives us a study in which to understand him, as he is also in a state of apparent hopelessness. The god is called to mind as Badalle recalls the nature of cities and temples. "Those temples, they were like giant fists built to batter us down, to take our spirits and chain them to worldly fears. We were supposed to shred the skin from our souls and accept the pain and punishment as just." (944) Power maintains weakness, and so feeds upon it, for material wealth or, in the Crippled God's case, for the power he represents. Chained, their power and agency are leeched away. "The temples told us we were flawed and then promised to heal us." (944) Recall, the presumption of the Crippled God's outlook, that because we all suffer, suffering is what defines life, and therefore it must be worshiped. For the Crippled God and his followers, the salvation occurs in death, though the same fundamental process is at work in Badalle's temples. And yet, despite their situation, Badalle insists on something more: "It is what we can bear…But there is more to life than suffering." (951)

"The sun made the world white, bitter with purity. This was the perfection so cherished by the Quitters." (948) Again, we see its duality, in that it reveals while providing life. Erikson keeps shining that bright and burning light. It also reflects the need for balance—feminine moon against the masculine sun. Her magic, when attacked by the Quitters, manifests as waves of light, of fire: "She felt fire in her limbs, saw blinding incandescence erupt from her hands. Truth was such a rare weapon, and all the more deadly for it." (949)

When the children are inside the crystal city, Icarias, Badalle reinforces the notion of her reversal from child, and the aspect of children in others. "Badalle was still a child, should one imagine her of a certain age, but she walked like a crone, tottering, hobbling." (1112) It remains for her to reconcile these, to undergo another reversal and find the child again.

For Badalle, transcendence is growth, which is why her mind flees her body. Beyond the confines of the mortal world that has so wounded them. She wonders at the expressionless stare of the dying boy: "oh, the horror of that…to wonder who was trapped inside, and why they'd given up getting out." (1113) For now, childhood is to be escaped.

And she becomes a witness again for us and she flies and dreams. "I grow wings. I fly across the world, across many worlds." (1114) This serves both as the metaphor for her escape, and to give us witness to what is happening in the story. "She'd dreamed of children. Looking down from a great height. Watching them march in their tens of thousands…Children, but not *her* children." (1114) Again, the reversal of her as mother, or its potential—of those she observes as being children. In this case it is the Bonehunters she witnesses. There is some resonance with the intention of Kalyth, even though what she is seeing is likely the perspective of the Che'Malle assassin, Gu'Rull.

> "She dreamed her eyes – and she had more of those than she should, no matter – fixed upon the two burning spots she sought. Bright golden hearth-flames – she had been tracking them for a long time now, in service to the commands she had been given…To steal *fire*." (1115)

The fires here are Stormy and Gesler, though it is likely that the words have a double meaning. The many eyes can be read as many perspectives of Badalle as an author.

Such multiple meanings recur when Badalle hunts Brayderal, with a shard of the crystal palace as a sword in her hand, which she then names Fire. "Where is my child of justice / I have a knife that will speak true / To the very heart" (1116) On the surface, this is the hunting of the other girl, whose Assail blood represents justice. But it could also be read as the child of justice being Tavore. She has just witnessed the Bonehunters as children, and we have read of Tavore's intentions as just. The knife to the heart is resonant with the final act of redeeming the Crippled God's heart.

Blood and Wounding

> "Someone drew a knife and carved a new pattern here." (278)

Alongside the discussions about the new imposition of warrens in the Letherii capital, there are images of wounding and blood aplenty. Lostara's knife, Brys as a weapon.

Magic, too, is inherently attuned to blood. Bottle and Ebron and Deadsmell chat about the idea of magic coming from K'rul's blood, and the fresh blood revealed by Fiddler's reading tapping the new warrens of Icarium. "when we use sorcery, we're feeding on K'rul's blood." (265)

> "'What is the threat to Letheras, should it continue to … bleed?'
>
> The old man [Bugg/Mael] made a face that suggested he'd just tasted something unpleasant." (278)

This is a revival of the notions of poisoned blood from earlier in the series, now coming to a conclusion. Of course, it is inherently ties to the Crippled God's heart, which is captured by the Forkrul Assail and to which the army will soon march. Blood is the life essence, the symbolic life force.

> "The reading gave that wound a sharp poke. Blood flowed out, and in this instance, *blood is power*." (279)

In relation to alchemy, we might recall the idea of the holy grail, which is symbolically likened to, and sometimes referred to as the philosopher's stone.

The grail contains the blood of Christ, at least in some versions of the tale. So in the grail story one aspect is the eventual death of the Fisher King, which enlivens the land around, a wasteland. This symbolism of sacrifice of the old to renew is frequently likened to ushering in a new paradigm, renewal, which is a theme played with in *Dust of Dreams*, and also harks ahead to the final chapters of *The Crippled God*.

Tavore

> Guidance is necessary and, indeed, pressing. (86)

Brys Beddict observes Tavore and the Malazans at the reading: "They were adrift, and it was all Tavore could do to hold the army together…" (164) Indeed, Fiddler covertly reveals Tavore's card as Chain, that which binds both ways. She is bound to her soldiers and they to her. Of course, we don't understand the consequences of that, and Tavore's audacious plan, but it weighs upon her, "it's the price of living." (192) As the reading gets underway, Tavore attempts to recast the uncertainty as part of her plan. "Sometimes, Sergeant, mistakes are necessary." (165)

"If only your chains didn't reach right into the heart of the Bonehunters…" (192) The symbolism of the heart is a direct connection to the Crippled God's captured heart. It is also reminiscent of references to knives and blood and wounding.

Bugg talks to Seren Pedac about power, and this is relevant to Tavore. "Presence, Acquitor, is power's truest expression." (176-7) What Tavore is doing is invoking her presence, to embrace the Crippled God on our behalf. She is the rock in the river. "Everything now was about control – and this, Bugg understood, came from that ineffable strength within a woman who was or would be a mother." (177) Tavore is to be the mother: for the army and, by extension, for the world. This will be the redemption of the feminine, the maternal.

But she also plays out the family role as sister. Discussion of her brother as Master of the Deck leads her to reveal their split nature to Brys. He comments: "regret must serve as the place to begin. Reconciliation does not demand that one side surrender to the other." (187) This gives her the notion that redemption is possible for her and Ganoes. It is also the process of the conjunction that two become one, not that one subsumes the other.

"Something was driving the Adjunct, her very own fierce, cruel obsession." (246) Lostara, and Quick Ben and others, are witness to the Adjunct coming out of her vessel of containment as she reveals the plan to cross the Wastelands. She speaks to Quick Ben about the gods, the Crippled God, the nature of the Forkrul Assail. She is enlivened by the goal, and adamant in her defence of mortals. "The gods can have their war. We will not be used, not by them, not by anyone." (247)

Fundamental to the alchemical quest is the need to be like god, to transcend body and time, to unite the opposites. This was not a blasphemous pursuit, rather one of adoration. I think this is what Tavore is achieving with her obsessive work. She aims to be beyond herself, beyond mortal capacity and to extend godlike compassion, and in doing so, the chain of complementarity influences the Bonehunters and, in turn, the Crippled God. It influences the reader and the writer to be beyond themselves, to take all upon themselves and so grow. She transcends humanity.

Lostara Yil's observations call to mind fire imagery: "Something blistered in this chamber now, touching like fire everyone present…" (254) Tavore has made herself the focus, made herself more than her corporeal body, and thus invites godlike devotion, wisdom, and soul. This becomes contagious, lifting those around her: "If a god showed its face in this chamber at this moment, six fists would vie to greet it." (254) Lifting herself and those around her is a lifting up of the mortal through the alchemical process, through individuation.

Fiddler, with the sergeants, hints at the nature of the Adjunct's mission: "Surviving isn't what all this is about!" (543) With the interesting side note: "The Adjunct's not our Hood-damned mother." (543) When next we see Tavore, Lostara Yil notes that she has physically devolved. "She'd lost weight, further reducing the few feminine traits she possessed." (563) There is a sense of her being distilled down to her essence, an alchemical dissolution.

"Legacies are never what one would hope for…" (564) Here she is confirming our growing suspicion that Tavore is making a hard decision in the name of humanity, not for any personal gain, and perhaps at great cost. It puts a spin on how we live our lives to grow a legacy, but she is demonstrating that doing just the opposite is the outcome of meaningful striving. She decides to live for what's right—to live for the living. Like her own physical form in this moment, she reflects that the accumulation of deeds is not a record of a life: "The wax is smooth, the past melted away – if it ever existed at all." (564)

The notion of Tavore as acting upon, or being the vessel for alchemical transformation of, the Bonehunters is reinforced when Lostara Yil speaks to her of the seeming struggle to achieve order prior to the march. "I give them this touch of chaos, of near anarchy." (565) We have discussed previously about the value of chaos in being a precipitating factor to change. For Tavore this is what she mentions in relation to Keneb and Blistig, the chaos inciting them to rise above. But additionally, the initial state of alchemical opus is chaos, confusion. Separating out the elements to find order is part of the initial phase. She is allowing that chaos to exist, trusting that she has the tools to bring order upon it. Bugg/Mael gifting her a dagger which appears to be related both to water and blood continues this idea of her having tools at her disposal. We have already seen her likened to fire, and now we can add water to her kit, along with the transformations in her physical self.

Our sense of Tavore's isolation, or separation, is confirmed by Sinter as she speaks with Kisswhere and Masan Gilani. Masan tells them: "We don't think we're off to kill the Chained One. In fact, it's those chains we're after. Well, the Adjunct, I mean. What she's after." (994) It is the chains themselves, what they represent, that she seeks to undo. In so doing, she has taken that burden upon herself.

> "She's locked in a room, a prison of her own making. In there, she hears nothing, sees nothing. In there, she is absolutely alone. And holding on with white knuckles. It's her burden and she won't dump it on anyone else...She's put herself between us and the truth – but it's killing her." (996)

This revelation comes at the same chapter that Badalle is fighting off the Forkrul Assail: "Truth was such a rare weapon, and all the more deadly for it." (949)

The notion of separation creates an awareness of the opposites, in a Jungian sense. Awareness of the ego necessarily separates it from the world. This is a coming of consciousness. It then creates the conditions for a conjunction to occur, to reintegrate.

The Imass following Onos T'oolan have their inner turmoil as they wander in search of unknown purpose. Kalt Urmanal reflects that such turmoil weakens their army and Onos's leadership. This is a clear parallel to the Bonehunters. "Kalt knew that wars raged within each and every one of them. He could feel as much, swirls of conflicting desires, awakened hungers and needs. An army must kneel before a single master." (1090) Seemingly without purpose, their leader shrouded in mystery: "From the First Sword himself, however, there was nothing. Not a single wisp of thought escaped him, not a hint of emotion. Was he simply lifeless, there in his soul?" (1092) Such questions have arisen of Tavore, though here the Imass give us an answer. "Faith is a strange thing…Perhaps, Nom Kala, the First Sword seeks to awaken it in us once more." (1093) The nature that Tavore hides is thus revealed. "Instead, he shows us the freedom of mortality, which we'd all thought long lost." (1094) With these passages Erikson is humanising the Bonehunters as well as the Imass for the reader. It makes their singular decisions and their outcomes more profound, more impactful, not just an army crossing the wastes, not just the fodder behind a hero; heroes, all.

The Bonehunters

The army is searching for its place once again, confident in itself, but in a new and strange location. They cling on to their identity as Malazans, using it as something that distinguishes them, for example in their notion of 'Braven Sergeants' when training the Letherii.

Bottle ponders the fragility of the life of a soldier. "A soldier knew what was real and what was ephemeral. A soldier understood how thin, how fragile, was the fabric of life." (263) He is estranged and bemused by the seeming ignorance of people going about their daily lives. He wonders whether in their nature there is greater strength than that of the soldiers, because they have not been broken by the very fragility of the soldier's outlook: "because once you become aware of that fragility, there is no going back." (263) It is like life stripped away to its essence, none of the civilised personae remain. Once awakened to this consciousness, or rather once the unconscious has been touched, there is no putting it away again.

The Bonehunters are the example of an old pattern reforming into something new, with a fundamental shift at its core. This symbolises the evolution of the magic of the Letherii continent, as the newer, more 'civilised' magic of warrens begins to take over. However, even this is infused with something new, tainted as it is with Icarium's effects. As Brys Beddict mentions, "it seems there is a quiet revolution under way, and I suspect that when the dust has settled, the entire discipline of sorcery will be transformed."(242) This quiet revolution is further explored within the Bonehunters' mages, and is symbolic of the revolution in outlook that the reader undergoes through these final two books: at once strange and familiar, changed but affirmed. Our understanding both shifts and coalesces upon what has already been read. For now, there is some uncertainty. We are back in the chaotic birth phase, trying to ground ourselves once again: "And now, it's all ... jumpy, twisty." (264) Bottle says: "I think what we're dealing with here is the imposition of a new pattern on to the old, familiar one." (265) When Quick Ben speaks of Icarium's actions, he says: "someone...attempted to impose a new structure upon the already existing warrens of sorcery." (277) We could also liken it to the imposition of order on chaos, or rather the restraining of a wild-natured power: "The local mages. They used raw sorcery, pretty much Chaotic and nothing else. No warrens. But now there's warrens here." (267) And: "The power, so raw here, is elsewhere refined, aspected, organized into something like themes." (277)

Quick Ben and Bottle examine the Cedance in the old palace, finding it alive, and are surprised that it hasn't died. "The magic here should be waning. We've unleashed the warrens, after all...We've slammed the door on Chaos." (343) The belief that closing out the chaos with a new order creates a finality is challenged here. The old still finds a way to absorb the new, making of it something new again. Order isn't immune to chaos. This can be likened to the Bonehunters themselves, separated from the old ways, the empire itself, trying to forge something new, but still being influenced by their history and training. The way they are blending the Malazan training styles with the Letherii armies, also creates an admixture of styles, both learning, just as cultural assimilation is never as simple as replacement—this is argued in the story of Torrent of the Awl, and also the Barghast. It is also mentioned in passing that the lesson of Kallor's destruction would not be lost on Shadowthrone—so we might presume that Shadowthrone's plan in taking down the old order might not be so simple as destroying the old pantheon.

And then Grub and Sinn further explore the notion, but as children they represent the symbolic aspect of a generational shift, along with the paradigm shift: "you and me, Grub, we're going to leave all the old people behind." (268). The question that is left is, does the old get left behind completely, or refined? So we're looking at a reshaping of the old, progress, its price and upheavals, which is contrasted against, e.g., the Forkrul Assail, who represent stagnation. They wander together as ghosts in a burned, ruined world, a warren as she says. They see a parade of the past, wagons and a warrior king, and a priest who comes forward to touch them and thus see into the future. This is an emotional revelation for the priest who, Sinn tells us, believes that his ways and his civilisation are immortal. "He believed in the sun god! He believed in immortality...*They do, we do, everyone does!*" (369) These children and their power represent the revelation of life's eternal march, the decay of the past and the new order to come.

Note, too, Stormy's dream. "Clouds on the horizon. Black, advancing in broken lines." (334) Marie von Franz gives us this in relation to the same image occurring in the Aurora Consurgens, an alchemical text:

> "The black cloud is a well-known alchemical symbol for the state called the nigredo, the blackness which very often occurs first in the opus; if you distill the material it evaporates and for a while you see nothing but a kind of confusion or cloud, which the alchemist compared to the earth being covered up by a black cloud.
>
> In the language of antiquity the cloud also had a double meaning, being sometimes compared to confusion or unconsciousness."[196]

The first task for the army upon readying to leave Lether is to draw back together. They are scattered and fragmented. Premonition is rife, with Deadsmell reflecting on death and the emptiness in the eyes with Bottle, Hellian's flashback to a dead fish, and Fiddler's reminiscence again on the Bridgeburners as well as the unintended death of people, while soldiers lie in fever nearby.

Dissolution into elemental components (Earth, Fire, Wind and Water) in the alchemical process can be likened to Jung's psychological types (Sensing, Feeling, Thinking, Intuition). The therapeutic/individuation process entails an awareness of these aspects, and thereupon a balancing of them. Fiddler, in bringing together the sergeants, allows them to determine their strengths, those soldiers who display certain attributes. This awareness raising process gives a fuller picture, whereby they might address the weaknesses and find more balance.

This happens too at the individual level. We have a dominant and an inferior function, which can be portrayed along an axis (and gives Jungians another reason to invoke opposition). If I were a thinking type, my feeling function would be inferior, for example. Jung explored the dynamics in depth[197] and later Jungians took these ideas and ran with them, but the specifics are not necessary to understand for our purposes. Initial stages of analysis or individuation bring the less developed functions to consciousness, that they might be activated, and so balance brought to the individual.

---

[196] Von Franz, 1980a, p. 208
[197] See CW6, *Psychological Types*

As the journey of the army begins, we see Cuttle and Gesler reinforce the notion of history and its telling, this time on an individual level. The story of the army allows Erikson to lay out the theme at a broader scale of the arc of the Bonehunters, as well as how this plays out at the scale of each soldier.

> "Histories, they're just what survived. But they're not the whole story, because the whole story can never be known. Think of all the histories we've gone and lost. Not just kingdoms and empires, but the histories inside every one of us, every person who ever lived." (779)

And so, within an individual, there are threads and tales, ideas and unconscious aspects who don't survive the enduring narrative of ourselves. But this story of the self also relates to how we see our place in the grander narrative of history. The lure of history and grand stories is that they give us something to live up to. Comes a certain point, we realise that we aren't those heroes, we aren't the shapers of history. But maybe it doesn't take away from a life well lived. Maybe we can make an opus that doesn't uncover gold, but enriches our lives no less.

This notion is also played out as Olar Ethil challenges the understanding of the other Elder Gods. She points out that even the Crippled God is as nothing to the forces playing out in the world, the return of the beasts, the time of the Imass, Andii on the Road to Gallan, Jaghut cruising again together. "None of you understand anything. Too long hiding from the world. Things are coming back. Rising. The stupid humans have not even noticed." (772) Until now, the battle appeared to be the old gods and the new gods, but she is showing that even that is oversimplified. We invent the notion of opposition to simplify, perhaps even to enforce an understanding that gives us some agency in the face of history's sweep. If even the history itself is a constructed narrative, and that of our individual selves is moulded and shaped like wet clay, and the notion of the tension between the past and future is but a side note, no wonder it would make a soldier feel helpless. The inner battle for these soldiers is finding and maintaining humanity in the face of such forces beyond our comprehension, let alone our control. "No matter the scale, no matter the pretensions of the things within that circle, no matter even their beliefs, they travelled in profound ignorance of the vastness of the universe beyond." (785-6)

Their mages reeling from Draconus's arrival, a manifestation of dark, the Bonehunters march across the Wastelands, scattered, isolated. Koryk wanders out alone, Corabb is lost, Fiddler makes noises about family and keeping everyone together. The mood is one of dread anticipation, and the reader feels a fall must occur. This is presaged by Gesler and Stormy, with the latter relating strange dreams, "Stuff falling out of the sky." (976) Dreams of falling objects—planes, stars—are related to the alchemical coagulation. It is a grounding, or fixedness, ego formation. These two are becoming the roles they will inhabit, no longer the volatility of fire, nor able to mould themselves to the nature of the army. They are apart.

There is also the aspect of separation occurring. Each of the soldiers, and the army as a whole, feel isolated. Sinter and Kisswhere with Masan Gilani decide to send the latter two away from the army, to make contact with others. This comes with their understanding of the nature of Tavore's gambit, and the realisation that they are journeying to free the Crippled God. Sinter decides that justice is worthy of their loyalty. From their state of chaotic separation, they aim to draw Tavore closer, and thus keep the army connected.

The gloss of war and armies has worn off, the Bonehunters are as frayed as ever. Keneb muses on his failure, on Blistig's attempts at reflected glory. Koryk is still lost and alone, and is thus a symbol for the marines. "Whatever happened to glory?" (1154) Corabb thinks of how the leadership of personality made Leoman dangerous, and that he'd follow Tavore because she cared. Though there are still many that need to reconfigure their notions of worth and glory.

But in their final movement, it is a disintegration that occurs. The arrival of the Nah'ruk, darkness, lightning, mages and heroes acting alone. The literal disintegration of the bodies of soldiers. "But he felt himself being torn apart. He felt his mind shredding. He could not do much more of this. Yet Bottle did not relent." (1225)

Fiddler

The squads have to hunt Fiddler down to get him to do a reading. He is reluctant to be involved. He doesn't want anything to do with Hedge. That is the past, what has been separated from his conscious self. To invite it back in would, to him, be a kind of regression. He must look towards the future.

As he begins the reading, reiterating his reluctance, Tavore tells him "you know my desire in this – more than anyone else here, you also know my reasons." (166) This speaks to a knowledge we didn't know Fiddler possessed, or perhaps Tavore understands that Fiddler has a way of accessing the knowledge. Von Franz spoke of a motif in alchemical literature of a secret that cannot be written or spoken, "not because one *wants* to make a secret of it, but because it is inexplicable and irrational and very complex."[198] In part it is similar to trade secrets, one not wanting to reveal the inner workings, but the other aspect of it is the idea that something is being shared that is ineffable, something that connects them, a sympathy not unlike the analytic relationship. Tavore and Fiddler share some understanding that arises because of the scale and nature of what is to come.

"No one here was found. No one was claimed. Adjunct, they were *marked.*" (173) The characters attending the reading are shown what will be demanded of them as we approach this story's conclusion. "I think I can see the end." (173)

Fiddler's confrontation with Hedge furthers the idea of progress and refinement. Fiddler represents the army, in a sense, and has fathered the reader through the shift from the Bridgeburners to the Bonehunters. To him, Hedge is the chains of the old ways, his past life. "And then you died. So I went and got over you. And now you show up all over again." (270) In a way, we are seeing Fiddler's insistence on continuing forwards, the strength in maintaining that and not a falling back to the lure of the old and comfortable.

As he speaks on this later to Cuttle, the army is in a liminal space, about to leave Lether. The soldiers are reflecting on the nearness of death. For Fiddler, Hedge is not quite there, in a similar way. "Back and yet, not back." (452) It is Fiddler's contention that the tension between two polarities must be held. We must bear witness, lest we become overly optimistic and so blindly careless, or pessimistic and riven with despair: "a place where you can settle into doing what you can, hold fast in your fight against that suffering. And that's an honest place, Cuttle." (469) While he diverts Brys's contention that this is heroism, and he spurns Cuttle's worship, we can see that he is carrying the flag for the army's compassion.

That compassion again shows through when he brings the sergeants together for a drink, a revival of an old tradition from the Bridgeburners. While this again shows the blending or the evolution from old to new, it is even more important in humanising Fiddler. His outburst in defence of the Adjunct suggests both that he knows more than he is letting on, and what is at stake. He is still coming to terms with that in himself, while feeling the pressure of holding it together for the squad, if not the army as a whole. As Bottle later thinks of him: "He was the iron stake driven deep into the

---

[198] Von Franz, 1980a, p. 68

ground, and no matter how fierce the raging winds, he held fast – and everyone in turn clung to him, the whole damned army, it seemed." (785)

Ash and Coagulation

Coagulation, separated from previous elemental associations of fire and water in the alchemical process, is a cooling and hardening. Solidifying into something concrete.

> "It doesn't disappear into the air by volatilizing nor pliantly adapt itself to the shape of any container as does water. Its form and location are fixed. Thus, for a psychic content to become earth means that it has been concretized in a particular localized form; that is, it has become attached to an ego."[199]

This can be likened to the hardening and manifestations that take place contemporaneously in the novel, of Icarium and Draconus. "The sky above was devoid of all light, but the ashes drifting down were visible, as if each flake was lit from within." (925) Following the nigredo stage in alchemy is the albedo, whiteness. The transition can be marked by divine intervention, the image of lightning striking a vessel, thus the awakening of these forces and the electricity within the darkness and within Kalse Rooted.

As darkness is descending across the Wastelands, there is a cooling taking place. Saddic beseeches Badalle: "I am cold, tell me again about the fires." To which her thoughts give us: "But these fires were burned down to cinders and ash." (872)

This cooling is associated with the descent and manifestation of Draconus, the pure darkness he embodies. The battlefield upon which the Barghast confront the Akrynnai is studded with ice, an image that mirrors various appearances of white or ash beneath feet in the novel at this time. For example: "He pictured a Letherii soldier standing atop a heap of bones – a mountain of white that was all that remained of Torrent's people." (890) And, of course, at the Shore, the strand is ground bone parts.

---

[199] Edinger, 1985, p. 85

Icarium

> He was many, but he was one. (46)
>
> He is trapped in the vessel of the minds. (309-10)

Two of the personalities argue about the value of knowledge. "What difference does knowing make...It eases the fire in my soul...The fire is the reason for living." (311) He considers the notion of self-delusion: "When the self was a monster – who wouldn't hide from such a thing?" (319). That's what all this is for Icarium, a way to avoid thinking, analysing himself. We instead identify with aspects of ourselves, or with other people. He is, like the writer perhaps, working through his understanding by dipping in and out of the minds of various characters, taking on personae.

The world is unknowable, and Icarium wants to force structure on to it. To feel that control. He is indignant at the gods. It is the bounding structure of the old ways he seeks to escape, and so create his own.

They ascend the dragon, Kalse Rooted. Such ascension itself is obviously symbolic. We recall Kalyth's initial ascent, and it can be likened to the Hermetic ascent of the heavens, which itself is likened to the chakra system, here seen as Root, Feed, Womb, Heart, Eyes, Brow.

During the journey they each are reviewing their lives, or their deaths, and their nature. Taxilian reflects on his search for the ideal moral machine: "such a machine, he now knew, would quickly conclude that the only truly just act was the thorough annihilation of every form of intelligent life in every realm known to it." (408) This is another example of the argument of cleansing balance against the slow corrective act of nature's drive for balance. Icarium, it turns out, is horrified by this argument, giving a nuanced argument for leaving certain things to nature: "Leave such things to nature, to the forces not even the gods can control...Nature may be slow to act, but it will find a balance – and that is a process not one of us can stop, for it belongs to time itself." (409)

These seven aspects of Icarium may also represent the seven planets, and the seven stages of alchemical transformation. "The seven are an obvious allusion to the seven planets and hence to the metals which in the alchemical view spring from the hermaphrodite Mercurius."[200] Icarium is in a sense working through them, and they are whittled away until only his essence remains, something new and pure. The task of alchemy is to redeem the spirit, the anima mundi, trapped within the elements, matter. It is redeeming man himself, then redeeming nature through him. Redeemed, one can undertake redemption on behalf of mankind. It could be said that Icarium redeems the matron, the maternal, in helping to enliven the Rooted.

His ghost observes the K'Chain drone, Sulkit, being born. A prima materia, it is all potential, affected by the chemical signals as it takes shape. "Two newborn eyes opened, seven distinct lids peeling back in each one…constructing an ever more complete comprehension – heat, current, charge, composition – and many more…" (492) This is a birth of consciousness.

"In some ineffable, fundamental way, they were pulling apart." (656) And in Icarium they would draw back together again? The process of self-knowledge, beginning with disintegration and ending with integration.

Sulkit sees the ghost. "The realization stunned him. And all at once he could feel something – *my own body* – and with it jarring pain in his hands, the ache of abuse." (659) Turning the light of awareness onto the self, the unconscious becomes conscious, if even just for an instant, and that awareness can be a revelation. Icarium then ponders the nature of a blink. "You can't even be sure how long that blink lasted. A moment, a thousand years." (661) Time is lost forever in unconsciousness. Its antidote is the maintenance of consciousness.

The ghost of Veed arrives, ostensibly to slay all the other aspects of Icarium. What takes place is Icarium questioning all the memories within himself, assimilating them into himself, and refining it all down into his self. He is making the unconscious conscious. The solidifying of Icarium from ghost to solid body represents this shift, a coagulation into ego. The broken mechanism upon which Rautos gazed was the metaphor for this broken soul, and each of them represents in some ways a guilt he carries: "we're just back inside you, old friend. We're the stains on your soul." (915) Each of these autonomous personalities amount to the complexes. While Icarium has now recognised them as part of himself, there is still some way to go to assimilate them into his Self, completing the journey of individuation.

Finally, we are witness to the city that Icarium created, Icarias. It traps time with the play of light in crystal, and it appears to be the most successful attempt of Icarium to preserve time. It draws Jaghut together, and Che'Malle,

---

[200] Jung, C.G., CW12 [410]

which connects him to them and likely an interaction between the two races and their technologies. But all is not perfect in that city. "Broken. His heart is broken." (1119)

Icarium is, in a sense, a catalyst. "My flesh is stone. My blood rages hot as molten iron. I have a thousand eyes. A thousand swords. And one mind." (1261) He has made a lesser conjunction within himself, accepting the aspects of the ghosts within, though it is still a battle. "He felt himself tearing loose, moments from being ripped from his flesh of cracked stone, his bones of tortured iron." (1264) He has identified with the mechanism he controls.

His final act, after reconciling the aspects of himself, is to heal the wound in the sky, the gate from the warren, with his new magic. This faith is found in the awareness that there is something new to be born, children aspected to his new magic. "This is the day of fire, Icarium. The children wait. The children hear." (1265) This notion of potential is furthered by his use of the Errant's eye as a seed for an azath. Sealing the gate with his mechanism and his soul, the sky and earth are joined, and he becomes stone.

Tanakalian

"Too young, woefully inexperienced, and dismayingly inclined to rash judgement..." (114) He is raging against this impression of him. "You ... you are ... *insufficient*." (117) But he rather thinks of himself as conscious, as careful in his judgments. "It is my essence that I am able to weigh my judgement." (118) He represents progress in the face of tradition, the certainty he perceives in Mortal Sword Krughava. It is rather the work to marry the two, to find balance. "The world has changed – we must change with it." (118)

He is disaffected by Krughava, the clash with the youthful vision of heroism he perceived upon seeing her, and the understanding that virtues are not one-sided. In his mind he is exploring the messy complexity of nature. Perhaps seeking the essence. Their natures need to be in balance.

Krughava, in response to Tanakalian's thoughts about choosing a new Destriant, says: "None of our elders happen to be very old." (288). Again we are looking at the notion of old versus new being played out, and weighed against one another. Tanakalian perhaps represents the overly ambitious drive to progress, the dangers of discarding the old ways, which he sees as representing a stifling impediment to human will and progress. He sees Krughava in turn as representative of the old ways, though it is likely his perception of her is coloured by his desire to cast everything in the terms of that battle of tradition and progress.

"In Krughava's mind, Tanakalian well knew, a holy war awaited them…" (290) Here Tanakalian casts Krughava's mind as seeking the glory of confirmation of the traditional ways of the Grey Helms. He too shares her "sense of purpose, fate's bold promise," (290) but he considers it in service to bringing change, to reshaping the world.

The disavowal of tradition rings hollow, because progressivism is energised only by that rejection, not by forward thinking. True progression would build upon, not merely reject tradition. Or if building something new, do it to show a better way. The energy here is only focused in tearing down.

As he watches the Mortal Sword move amongst the soldiers, their respect obvious, Tanakalian can only understand it as a constructed narrative. The story he observes being played out is only that, a deliberately framed story that the actors play out for the sake of history. Disconnected from the feeling, he cannot understand the true emotions that might underlie people's actions. "You are witness to the manufacture of delusion, the shaping of a time of heroes." (682) This unseats us as readers, for we are indeed being fed a selective telling of events. Yet in Tanakalian, it is the suspicion of all that is traditional, the certainty that his truth is more pure, that blinds him to the possibility of the underlying truth to a tale.

"My indecision stings you into impatience." (1041) He is frustrated by a lack of progress. "What we do is not in service to ourselves, but to all of you." (1044) It seems as though Tanakalian understands what Tavore aims to achieve, but his feeling is that Krughava doesn't. By assuming that she wishes to achieve a legacy, he disdains her actions. His own understanding of the glory is riven by futility. When Krughava challenges his notion of Tavore's selfishness, the realisation comes that he sees the glory will in fact be found because they will lose. And so, if they will lose, he has already given up hope. Glory without hope is a different thing altogether. That one eye on the future is in fact turned towards death—the afterlife.

With the arrival of Kisswhere and the decision to ride to the Malazans' aid, Tanakalian reveals himself: "this is not the place…That time is yet to arrive…" (1180) Either his notions of glory will not be fulfilled in this manner, or he wants to keep the armies apart. "Brother Tanakalian, you are not the arbiter of destiny, no matter the vast breadth of your ambition." (1181)

Tanakalian's story seems to teach us about the presumption of others' narratives. In focusing on the metanarrative we live too much in our heads, and disconnect from feeling. Tanakalian's expectations and presumptions clash with reality, and he is thus isolated despite his own story which renders him as a hero in waiting.

Yedan Derryg and Yan Tovis

Yedan Derryg is faced with unknowns. Uncertainty is the order of the day at the beginning of this book, everything in flux. The tides, the blurring of the moon, blood in water, all seeking clarity. "The night sky, so familiar...was now revealed to him as strange, jarred free of the predictable, the known..." (119)

Twilight must lead her people. The arc of their story is of brother and sister conjoining, to mirror the Parans. "The loss of a brother – again – *again*." (146) It is also symbolic in being the conjunction of the sea and shore, and with twilight being the liminal time between night and day. "Sometimes the verge between the two grew very narrow indeed." (124)

Yan Tovis walks through a desolate, grey world, the remnants of logging work about her. This journey into the dark and the past is filled with imagery of decay and rubbish. She ponders the King's suspension of these operations—a new system to replace the old—one that offers rebirth and not just extraction.

Yedan insists she take him with her, brother and sister together. "Then find a worthy mate – a king..." (305) There is the notion that she needs to be conjoined with her opposing aspect in some way to achieve leadership for her people.

Yan Tovis speaks to the witches of their home and the road there, wonders: "What so fouled the water that we could no longer live there?" (413) We hark back to the notion of water running clear in *Toll the Hounds*, this time with the added symbolism of the alchemical notion of purification. For the Shake, this might reflect the notion of too much chaos in the water. They managed with a little reptile in the water, but too much breaks them.

Returning home is more than just a physical act. As Yan Tovis walks along Gallan Road, she symbolises progress: "the best course is simply to place one foot in front of the other, and think not at all of fate or the cruel currents of destiny." (497) While that forward momentum is blind, theirs is also a return. It is a recombination of the old and the new, not a 'progressive' discarding of the old. The very notion "they need only follow their Queen" (497) is one of faith and trust, an old way and an old title. That the witches are taking power and youth from her blood is a potent metaphor for the old being cast aside in favour of the new, "the sloughing away of wrinkles, dread aches, frail bones" (498). Their path is a river of her blood, a path and a gate. She is holding them on the path, for to step off it is to find the cursed knowledge, the horror that awaits in the dark. "No, best they know nothing." (498)

Yedan Derryg observes the three suns, and that his people, the Shake, have withered beneath the onslaught of the world. "Generation upon generation, they had made themselves *small*, as if meekness was the only survival strategy they understood." (500) Agency needs to return to these people. He muses on the Letherii adaptability of the islanders, and there may be within that a metaphor of the island and the shore, and how they combine to be reshaped and adapt.

He rides off the path to confront the Liosan he knows dwell in that place. It is a realm of "cold judgment" that contains "sworn enemies of the uncertain Shore" (506). He is surprised to find a Forkrul Assail there, though the notions of judgment make sense to the reader. He and his people are able to hold contradictions in mind—the value of consciousness and the pause of uncertainty: "a thing could be both one and the other, or indeed neither." (506)

"In this place, however, the blended flavours of compassion were anathema to the powers that ruled." (507) It appears that what is anathema to compassion is the certainty, the dispassion, of the Forkrul Assail and their ilk. It is the difference between judging and withholding judgment. The watch is the time of night that seems beyond time, a held breath in the dark. This is a lovely metaphor for the withholding of judgment, waiting, that is tied to compassion. "We have time, Queen." (512)

Alchemical texts speak of the laborious nature of the opus, the courage required to undertake the seeking, and of course insist that what is sought is both within and without. Yan Tovis, along the Gallan Road, trying to find a way off for her people, blind and attempting to solve a riddle, is like the blindfolded alchemist, lost in the darkness and confusion of the early stages of the alchemical process.

> "Will the light never return? Is the joke this: that salvation is all around us, even as we remain for ever blind to it?

> Because we believe … there must be a road. A journey, an ordeal, a place to find.
>
> We believe in the road. And in believing we build it, stone by stone, drop by drop…" (608)

The individuation process is the very walk upon that road, building it ourselves, with our own blood. We create the shape of a journey by our belief in the notion of it, in the illusion of progress. "…the darkness comes from *within*." (608) And so, like all revelation, we come to understand that meaning comes from within—that the destination is not one, rather it is the road itself we bleed out before us that gives us something upon which to walk. Awareness of the self and its potential are the goal of individuation, much as in alchemy. Redemption of humanity through redemption of the self.

The return to Kharkanas is at once a set of images of clashing opposites, and the containment of an alchemical *solutio*. The latter is like a return to the womb, a containing vessel. The return home for the Shake is such. Within the embrace of that place, rebirth is offered. It is the vessel within which the conjunction will take place.

"They stood facing one another in extremity, across a gulf that could not be bridged." (875) Their complementarity is highlighted as they encounter the Shore. He is the archetypal masculine, active, to her passive indecision: "doomed to react and never initiate, a mind that simply held itself in place, passive, resigned to whatever the fates delivered." (875) Of course, both will find a balance within themselves as well as complement one another.

The return of Mother Dark to Kharkanas is a complementary image to the darkness sweeping across the Wastelands elsewhere in the story. But it is also here presented as the darkness from which light awakens. "We gift the living with light and darkness and shadow. The truth of our natures cannot be found in the absence of that which we are not." (877) Here is a recurrence of the image of light and conscious awareness, but also the notion reflects Yedan's and Yan Tovis's complementarity, an acknowledgement that they cannot exist in the absence of their inferior functions. They need one another and the aspects they represent. Their understanding of the history of their people is complementary, and we see them trading their understanding, to conjoin into a more complete picture.

The Maternal and Conjunction

Throughout the text, there have been hints at the idea of the feminine being returned, the importance of bringing that element back to prominence. While the concept of conjunction is brought to fruition in the final volume, here in the penultimate stage the groundwork is laid.

We have Olar Ethil's return as the archetypal mother, the awakened one. She represents in some ways the aspects of the feminine, but as she has been asleep, those elements are not in balance. Thus she comes across as the negative aspects of that archetype. She tells Torrent as they wander the Wastelands: "Once, long ago, spirits of earth and wind thrived in this place…" (1012) We understand that there are elements that have been in paucity. Just like Jung's idea of inferior aspects of psychological typology, these elements need to be returned to consciousness and thus bring fullness and consciousness, or bring life to the Wastelands.

Mother Dark's return mirrors this is many ways. She has awakened, and we see darkness clashing with light on the battlefields of the Wastelands. Her return is not complete, though. With it, the light upon the Shore is also returned, and it is up to the Shake to keep them at bay (or in balance). As Sandalath returns to Kharkanas, she acknowledges that while Mother Dark has returned, she is still not completely conscious: "She is no longer turned away, but in mourning. Her eyes are averted, downcast. She is here, yet behind a veil. Mother, you make this a most bitter gift." (1062)

The symbolism of the moon and its shattering has already taken place in *Toll the Hounds*, but in this volume the timeline catches up, and we get a different set of observations of the event. With the Khundryl, Hanavat, pregnant, steps out into the night. She feels burdened, and having had many children already is disabused of the supposed bliss of childbearing. She likens herself to the moon in myth: "She was the wandering moon of her people's legends…" (1055) But we know the steady, predictable nature of the moon has been broken, representing the lack of feminine: "No, the moon had been struck a mortal blow. She was dying." (1055)

But there is a hint that it is not completely absent. Hanavat sits with two other women: "Hanavat sat down, forming the third point to this triangle surrounding the fire." (1056) This is imagery of balance and containing the fire—a vessel containing a life spark or consciousness. "Was a scent released upon the air? Did it drift through the entire camp of the Khundryl Burned Tears?" (1059) Here we see that while the feminine or the maternal is reawakening, there is still an absence of sorts.

Spax watches Krughava (herself unbalanced, the triad of leadership of the Grey Helms currently broken) remain unaware of the masculine attentions of Gall. Here we see that the feminine or maternal has not yet awakened.

In Tavore these images and symbols coalesce and find greater resonance in the final volume.

Lostara Yil

We come upon Lostara Yil cleaning her blade, scrubbing and scouring. Something of the work affects her, too. "The bones of her hands ached. They felt heavier these days, as if the sand had imparted something to her skin, flesh and bones, beginning the process of turning them into stone." (82) This should call to mind Kalyth's vision of Heboric's hands plunging into the sand and being revealed as otataral (rust coloured stone).

She feels an urge to continually clean her blade, it being the weapon she used to end Pearl's life: "driving a knife through the heart of the man she loved was bound to leave an indelible stain on her soul. The knife had become a symbol – she'd be a fool not to see that." (244) Along with other symbols, this is a mirror to Tavore's blade gifted by Mael, which Lostara is later revealed to be responsible for carrying, making her Tavore's shadow in a way.

She listens to Quick Ben and Tavore, and the planning, filling in what she knows about Shadowthrone and his plans in her mind. She gets a picture of the scale of what they are about to undertake, and she is our witness to the burgeoning fire in Tavore. It is curious to note that they speak of Shadowthrone's adoption of Kallor's burnt realm as his warren, an image of life rising from the ashes.

"With that knife, Lostara could cut herself loose whenever she liked." (799) She feels bound, even as the army is on the move, perhaps by the greater movement of the world, perhaps simply to Tavore. The image of them distinct but connected as they supper together in silent bubbles is revealing. Lostara feels a lack of agency, holding on to her salvation with the knife she works—it represents the power of her mind to discriminate. She continues to work the knife, polishing it as though to reveal the gold beneath.

"It was him. But you let him go." (1001) The death of someone close challenges the ego to individuate. Projections must be realised and the person can either fall into unconsciousness, thus despair and regression, or consciousness can be raised, allowing the ego to separate from identification with the relationship. The same occurs at different scales at the separation or death of parents, and other close relationships. Alchemically, a separation must occur to pave the way for a conjunction.

Conclusion

"I am readying myself … to wield a most formidable weapon. They thought to hide it from me. They failed. Weapons must be tempered and tempered well…The key to everything, you see, is to cut clean, down the middle." (203) This is the notion of discrimination, to see clearly a separation so as to enable the conjunction of opposites. We might be tempted to think of the weapon here as Heboric's hands, but perhaps the heart is the weapon, that which yields compassion.

Cutting down the middle calls to mind Tavore and the Crippled God, and the journey to bring them together. To create a separation can be to remove the possibility of compassion, to stop us from acting beyond ourselves and our capacity. But when the separation is perceived, a conjunction becomes possible. "It is a flaw…to view mortals and gods as if they were on opposite sides…when the blade comes down, why, they are for ever lost to each other." (204)

So a major theme overall in *Dust of Dreams* is that of burning away the old to make something new. The distinction between old and new is a false one, just as there is no true separation of past and future, but through our perception of an infinitesimal present. A tension exists, a balance is sought, in making progress as both an individual and society, while not completely and rashly discarding the old. This very act of seeking the balance is the act of progress.

We have all the varied extremes of this duality: the magic system changing, Fiddler and his old life, youth and new generations, Tanakalian and his disdain for tradition, the Forkrul Assail and their stagnant insistence on balance, the Snake and its integration of eternal youth, and the hope therein, the Letherii reinventing their army to become more like the Malazans. Certainly, the hobbling of Hetan is a defeat of forward thinking by an inhumane view of tradition.

So in *Dust of Dreams*, though we are purifying and burning the old, it is not its removal, just as in an individual's life their history and their heredity cannot be entirely escaped. Growth is the blending of the old and new: endings, progress, assimilation. It is the story of people who are the last of their kind: Kalyth, the Matron, Setoc, Badalle. Torrent and his horse: "like one last drop of blood refusing to soak into the red mud" (217). These remnants of the past exist as the fulcrum point for a future that is at once the old and new, a vessel for the alchemical work to find fruition.

And there is the hint of conjoining to come: Kalyth and the K'Chain, the brother and sister pairs of Twilight and the Watch and, of course, the Paran siblings. New blood, if we are to take Icarium's actions literally. But it all leads back to the idea of reconciling the old and the new, itself a conjunction.

This is a study of the stories and histories we weave, how they will be remembered, and how they evolve. Who records it, and therefore who gives the material shape? Thus, we have Badalle and her imagined book of the fallen, Tanakalian's skepticism, Tavore's unwitnessed, the memory of Icarium, and so many stories forgotten as their last twig of memory is snapped, like Gunth Mach reflecting on the end of the Matron's line.

In many ways it is also about the breaking of the feminine—Olar Ethil, Hetan, the Matrons, and the shattered moon. It is in need of repair. And it is in the women of this novel that we find the seeds of redemption: Tavore, Badalle, Kalyth, Gunth Mach, Setoc, Sinn, and others.

Because our nature is expansionist, progressive if you will, we seek to grow and conquer, as does all life. It behoves us to be conscious of balance, of the past, of weighing tradition and progress. In conscious growth, perhaps we achieve compassion, a betterment for all, a humanity.

Can the humanity of a Fiddler balance the expansionist wars of empire? Can the compassion of Tavore justify the blood spilled along the way? I think these are the wrong questions. If we act with compassionate intention, learn as we go, then the opus we undertake, our personal journey, is one of growth. It will not be pure and shiny, for that is the misguided notion of the Forkrul Assail. It is the tales of our childhood. Humanity needing to learn the same lessons over and again, civilisations rising and falling, should not be cause for nihilism and the presumption of insignificance, nor justification for the darker aspects of our nature, either individually and culturally. But nor should such understandings be swept under the rug of our consciousness.

In the end, the K'Chain Che'Malle find faith in humanity. Their embrace of new ways enlivens them, but not at the expense of their identity, of the old ways.

That faith in humanity is what we will seek in the final volume.

Unchained Hearts: Redemption, Conjunction, and Return to Childhood in *The Crippled God*

> "the widening of consciousness is at first upheaval and darkness, then a broadening out of man to the whole man."
> Mysterium Coniunctionis [209]

Conjunction is the joining of the opposites to achieve the final stage in creating the philosopher's stone. It results in the rubedo, the final red stage of alchemical transformation. Another image of the stone is that of the anima mundi, the soul of the world. This way, the stone is depicted in alchemical texts by a heart within a mandala made up of the four physical elements. The heart is the centre of a quincunx, thus the quintessence, the fifth element. A similar image is derived for the World card in the tarot. The conjunction is often symbolised by marriage or sexual union, a hieros gamos, between Sol and Luna (sun and moon), King and Queen, divine brother and sister, and other such depictions of the opposites. It is the conjunction of ego and Self, the culmination of the individuation process.

Jung's volume *Mysterium Coniuntionis*[201] is a culmination of his alchemical studies, and to his mind the ultimate conception of the goal of psychic wholeness. Its opening line states: "The factors which come together in the coniunctio are conceived as opposites, either confronting one another in

---

[201] Jung, C.G., CW14

enmity or attracting one another in love."[202] As can be seen, it takes as its central premise the union of opposites, and opposition is a notion which I have strained against in this study. Conceived as complementarities instead of opposites, we will see how conjunction of complementary forces, the union of the past and present, conscious and unconscious, can aid us to become whole. It is not in paradoxical opposition or negation that wholeness is achieved, though it may feel that way when one is pulled in multiple directions or must make choices with consequences, but in conscious choice. In bringing together complementary aspects we can achieve wholeness and redemption.

Conjunction is a return to wholeness, but a return changed, having experienced all that we have. The return is fulfilling because we have grown, become more conscious along the way. It's the journey, after all.

> I had learned meanwhile that the greatest and most important problems of life are all in a certain sense insoluble. They must be so because they express the necessary polarity inherent in every self-regulating system. They can never be solved, but only outgrown. ... This "outgrowing" ... on further experience was seen to consist in a new level of consciousness. Some higher or wider interest arose on the person's horizon, and through this widening of his view the insoluble problem lost its urgency. ... What, on a lower level, had led to the wildest conflicts and to panicky outbursts of emotion, viewed from the higher level of the personality, now seemed like a storm in the valley seen from a high mountain-top. This does not mean that the thunderstorm is robbed of its reality, but instead of being in it one is now above it.[203]

The final act, the last two novels of the Malazan Book of the Fallen, is two as one. Conjoined, these two novels represent the final stage of our journey. Further, there is a disintegration in structure: where all prior books contained four main sections, 'books', *The Crippled God* contains seven, its own ascent through the stages.

We will find the stone, the stone that is our heart, and we will unchain it to bleed compassion. Alongside these notions of compassion and redemption, we explore again the idea of balance through the Forkrul Assail and others. And, finally, there are children throughout the novel. Children are hope and the future, but also we need to reclaim that childlike wonder, we need to become as children again—innocent, vulnerable, our hearts not

---

[202] Ibid. [1]
[203] Jung, in *The Secret of the Golden Flower*

hardened to the world—so we can let the compassion in. Finally, as a child again, we are reborn, and so the series comes full circle.

> Years later I discovered the butterfly is a symbol of the human soul. I also discovered that in its first moments out of the chrysalis the butterfly voids a drop of excreta that has been accumulating during pupation. This drop is frequently red and sometimes voided during first flight. Consequently, a shower of butterflies may produce a shower of blood, a phenomenon that released terror and suspicion in earlier cultures, sometimes resulting in massacres. Symbolically, if we are to release our own butterfly, we too will sacrifice a drop of blood, let the past go and turn to the future.[204]

Tavore

Mael and K'rul speak of Tavore in the opening chapter, and even they are in awe of her. "There is such pain in her … no, I dare not get close." (34) We are seeing her as author and reader, Erikson's explainer for what he has done and what is to come. "Is this to be a voyeur's game, K'rul? Into a woman's broken heart?" (34-5) Were we allowed in to her perspective we would understand, but the gods are questioning whether that understanding is worth the pain. She is closed for a reason, and to have faith means to trust in her reasons. "Her heart must remain her own, immune to all assault." (35) If a hero entails sacrifice, then Tavore has sacrificed everything, including her humanity, which is signalled to us by the lack of her point of view in earlier books. When Deadsmell heals her of her headaches, letting him in just briefly, he is bereft when done by the damage, the overwhelm.

Tavore encapsulates the idea of reconciling opposition. Jung writes of the *coniunctio oppositorum*: "The brother-sister pair stands allegorically for the whole conception of opposites. These have a wide range of variation: dry-moist, hot-cold, male-female, sun-moon, gold-silver, mercury-sulphur, round-square, water-fire, volatile-solid, physical-spiritual and so on."[205] Think of all the aspects of such complementarity that Tavore fulfills: the bringing of water to the desert, hot iron and cold iron. Jung thought of

---

[204] Woodman, 1985, p. 14
[205] Jung, C.G., CW12 [436]

androgyny as symbolising the search for wholeness, its potential. It is the state of trying to reconcile opposition. We have been given descriptions of Tavore as sexless, with no effort made to highlight her femininity. Now, this could be a depiction of one who is lacking the feminine, or as one who is more androgynous as Jung described, one on the quest for reconciling those opposites in creative fashion.

And we do see both at work, she plays a reconciling role, the chain that binds things together, the conjunction of spirit and matter, of binding the army. But she also fulfills the feminine role, coming into her materiality (her motherhood) as Badalle describes her as mother, and she is actively the feminine aspect of the divine conjunction of brother and sister.

"You made us into something..." (276) Stormy's observation affirms the notion that she is a catalyst, or a vessel for the army. She is able to contain their compassion and so carry them to the end of their goal. "And she held something in her hand..." (381) Krughava believes Tavore holds compasssion, contains it, but they also believe that she has lost her faith, that in taking the Bonehunters across the desert she is allowing that compassion is not enough, and so the world is not worth saving. This is countered when the Fists approach Tavore in her command tent. They challenge her with the rumours amongst the soldiers, and Ruthan Gudd draws out her surprise that she might be followed for herself. We can only assume that such surprise is genuine, as it is close to the first time that her stolid mask has been broken. She is challenged to give them meaning, to give the soldiers and commanders a meaningful cause. "We don't dare look across into the eyes of a suffering god. But, Kindly, she dares...She'll feel all the compassion none of you can afford to feel." (404-5)

Tavore offers a counterpoint to the faith and worship that they expect to pull an army along. She reflects, instead, the Crippled God's suffering. She takes on compassion for him, so that worship is not required. "So look across, then, across that vast divide...*Look into his eyes, Kindly, before you choose to turn away.*" (400) She offers them a human face, to see the brokenness, the suffering in her, and then apply that to the Crippled God.

Jung's work on the *Psychology of the Transference* (CW16) is an analysis of alchemical pictures and process as it relates symbolically to recovering wholeness within the therapeutic process. This analogy for the wholeness of the self through individuation is clear. Tavore takes on the Crippled God in some ways, in the form of a transference. She becomes chained, at the very least to the army, to duty. "the doctor is bound to influence the patient, but this influence can only take place if the patient has a reciprocal influence on the doctor. You can exert no influence if you are not susceptible to influence."[206] Compassion is a two-way street, it's not mere altruism. It is not just a superficial decision to feel compassionate. She takes his burdens in so many ways. Her anger at the gods is likely influenced by the hurt transferred to her by understanding the Crippled God's chaining and pain.

This process of transference and countertransference speaks to a deeper nature of relationship and openness to change. We must be open to change to be able to exert change. Susceptibility to influence is like the vulnerability that accompanies compassion. The Crippled God cannot have his heart freed without opening it to the understanding of the compassion of the soldiers, thus becoming able to reciprocate. We cannot know the self without opening to the unconscious.

Abrastal and Spax discuss that they are haunted by Tavore, by her face. "Bleak, then," Spax calls it. "Nothing regal in her clothes. Not a single item of jewellery. No paint on her face, or her lips, and her hair – so short…" (496) She is comfortable in her nature, and thus is not at war with nature. She represents humanity at peace with itself, seeking harmony. She seeks no glory, offers no rousing speeches, hides behind no god or cult. She lets others come to their understanding. Could she avoid some problems, in theory, with better communication? Perhaps, but this is a symbolic character. She is archetypal, of all that we hold inside. She is opaque, but there is no mask.

Tavore represents an individuated person in and of herself, because she is, for all her flaws and suffering, an individual in the truest sense. She does not look to outward affirmation, does not conform to the collective. Jacobi writes of the individual: "To those who are not recognized by the collective, who are rejected and even despised, it can restore their faith in themselves, give them back their human dignity, and assure them of their place in the world."[207] Tavore is comfortable in her self, and while her journey is not quite completed, we feel that she has done the work of self-realisation.

As will be seen later, Krughava's faith being challenged is an example of the clash between the social and the individual desires, which can magnify the axis of one's conscience. Tavore contains the paradox, and in a sense shows an extreme example of the pure application of conscience, seeming not to bend at all to the social pressures. She acts because there is an internally realised justice to her path. A loss of faith is sometimes essential—without questioning there would be no evidence of the guiding hand of conscience.

She contains the god-image, the Self, by reflecting the Crippled God's

---

[206] Jung, C.G., CW16 [163]
[207] Jacobi, 1967, p. 83

brokenness. Part of Tavore's closed nature may in fact be that she is driven by the underlying archetype of the Self—the god-image or conscience within. To presume that she knows and has judged all the possible outcomes through ego consciousness would be an inflation, that she has a conscious grasp of all that is happening. She is rather guided by a deep knowledge, an archetypal instinct—the gods, the unconscious, the nature of the feminine, are all her guides. Her faith is not in a god but in humanity as a collective, something beyond the individual. And her goal in aligning with that purpose is the path to individuation.

> Only consciousness of our narrow confinement in the self forms the link to the limitlessness of the unconscious. In this consciousness we experience ourselves concurrently as limited and eternal, as both the one and the other. In knowing ourselves to be unique in our personal combination—that is, ultimately limited—we possess also the capacity for becoming conscious of the infinite.[208]

"The only ones who will not turn away from us. You are our mother." (633) These words from Badalle cause a physical reaction from Tavore, as though she understands the symbolism in them. She is still torn by the death of the child under her care, her sister Felisin. The impact upon her perhaps shows her reluctance to adopt the mother role once more, that she had hoped to keep herself apart. That is partly why she does not open to the army. But a family needs the mother to be emotionally available.

That mother-nature also calls back to the philosopher's stone, which is said to bear children in that all base metals it touches also turn into the philosopher's stone. This is the contagious nature of the individuating person. Tavore's journey becomes something those behind her take on, not by compulsion or persuasion, but by experiencing the rightful attitudes being displayed by her, just as we would experience the journey of a hero in myth.

Chapter 20 of *The Crippled God* begins with the birth of Hanavat's child, and runs through images and memories of childhood and mothers, notably members of Fiddler's old squad. "It's innocence that is sacred." (768) At the beginning of the chapter, witnessing the birth alongside Badalle, Tavore is uncomfortable, draws her hand away from Badalle. "Mother, when will you let yourself feel?" (766) And the chapter ends with her returning water to the Wastelands, her own form of alchemical creation, of mothering.

Drama aside, this turnaround in Tavore strongly suggests that in addition to being an implacable force, she is also in fact working through her own

---

[208] Jung C.G., 1963, pp. 357-8

growth. Much of her reluctance comes not from supreme confidence and unknowability, but from a refusal to be open to her maternal nature, to be vulnerable. We already know that vulnerability is the necessary complement to compassion. And it is in her vulnerability that she finally seals the loyalty of the army behind her.

The image of water being restored to the wasteland is of life, fertility. The conjunction of conscious and unconscious through magic and strength. The beginning of something new, and a redemption for the world. It shows Tavore's capacity for renewal and fecundity. It is rebirth, the alchemical solution, it is the reemergence of the feminine principle to this barren place of old death. Soul and body, in contact once more. She is symbolically allowing herself to feel, as Badalle had beseeched.

Kalam's recall of her manner of extracting loyalty gives us further insight into Tavore's nature. "All at once, it's as if she's somehow laid bare your soul and there it is, exposed, trembling, vulnerable beyond all belief…" (870) The vulnerability she draws out is her own, mirrored. It allows her to communicate compassion without weakness. It is openness, and she is genuine. It is perhaps not what is expected, and if the other is closed to compassion, or not willing to be vulnerable, then her approach will fall flat. That is why her persistence pays, as we see with Blistig. It is what Erikson is asking of the reader, to be open as he is promising to be vulnerable to us.

Tavore directly addresses the notion of children, and even as she says she is no mother, she shows us that she is symbolically referring to the future:

> "It is not enough to wish for a better world for the children. It is not enough to shield them with ease and comfort. Lostara Yil, if we do not sacrifice our own ease, our own comfort, to make the future's world a better one, then we curse our own children." (1030)

This is the faith that the world is worth fighting for. We don't need to search for a reason to fight, because when we embody the idea of progress through a better world the reasons are self-fulfilling. Individuating, she sees beyond the ego. Even if we don't know what the future holds, acting as though it exists necessitates a compassionate approach, even to those unborn. Self-sacrifice is inherent, and when Fiddler likens her to "a starved child under that armour (1037) we are called back to the hunger and sacrifice of mothers in *Memories of Ice*, and the armoured child, Felisin, she killed in *House of Chains*.

"The three horses were waiting, two saddles as yet unfilled. Slouched in the third one … Banaschar looked up, nodded in greeting. 'Captain.'" (1033) The triad of Tavore, Fiddler and Banaschar set of together. Mother, Father, and Priest. Off to an alchemical marriage.

Banaschar tells Ruthan Gudd that Tavore won over D'rek, "she simply refused to waver from her path, and by that alone she has humbled the gods." (1063) She hasn't inflated her ego to the level of the gods, but in her determination and focus has brought them to her level, a key aspect of conjoining ego and Self. She reflects on this later with Banaschar, whom she was surprised stayed by her. He is a symbol of faith, that it is not blind, nor is it owned by such as a god. The power to choose is just as important.

As she then stands before the regulars, she tells them their stories, surprising them and the reader. She knows them because she has held them inside her. By doing that she evinces the compassion she expects in turn. By carrying her soldiers through their stories, she lifts them up as well as her. This is the very gift that the Crippled God gives the marines, by listening to their words. "Except for the soldier either side of you. *They* shall witness." (1112) She thus invites them to carry one another's stories, and so exalts them again, shows them they may have the compassion within them.

We finally believe she is done, when Ganoes arrives to support them in battle with the Host. She releases her almighty scream, finally letting out all that she held within her, vulnerable, all else stripped away. The vulnerability that she has held back on in answer to the compassion she has shown. And her brother comes. "I lost her! Oh, Ganoes, *I lost her!*" (1139) She reveals the pain of the loss of the child, Felisin, as it returns in her: "As she collapsed into his arms, frail as a child, Ganoes held her tight." (1139) Conjunction of divine brother and sister, this is the final stage of the alchemical process.

Tavore and Fiddler become the mother and father. We saw Fiddler's growth into the father role, and now we see Tavore evincing a connection to her feminine side, her creativity (the water of life), protection and so on. Now, as mother-hero, she can redeem the world.

In *The Undiscovered Self,* Jung discusses that redemption or change in the world is down to the individual. It is where we have control, it is where change is possible within the means of us as people. One affects many, and many together can change the world:

> What does lie within our reach, however, is the change in individuals who have, or create for themselves, an opportunity to influence others of like mind…anyone who has insight into his own actions, and has thus found access to the unconscious, involuntarily exercises an influence on his environment.[209]

---

[209] Jung, C.G., CW10 [583]

Badalle

Saddic is collecting things, sticks and rocks. He is trying to figure out how to play again. Badalle doesn't like them, but that is because they would bring memories of the past. She shies away from that, unconsciously having hardened herself against it. Meanwhile, in Icarias, the children are all trying to play roles and find their true inner child:

> "Older boys became pretend-fathers, older girls became pretend-mothers, the young ones scampered but never for long – they'd run, as if struck with excitement, only to falter a few steps, faces darkening with confusion and fear as they ran back to find shelter in their parents' arms." (114)

"What does the child want, that you did not have first? What do you own that the child does not want?" (194) These words in Badalle's mind reflect at first the notion of legacy in humanity, that the material gains and extractive desires we obtain will be coveted again by future generations. The child wants what the parents had. But the child also wants what its older siblings have. This is the nature of desire. We know that Badalle is sympathetic to the various women of the Wastelands, that her thoughts reach them at times. It might be considered that these are Tavore's thoughts reaching Badalle, her pondering of the child that was Felisin, a reflection upon the nature of that child and what was lost, for Felisin's loss was instrumental in Tavore's journey—she lost the child, and that must be redeemed.

"Children are dying. Still dying. For ever dying." (282) And the Shards feed upon them, and they feed upon the Shards. It is nature. "We go round and round and this is the story of the world." (283) The notion of whether the world is worth saving is rendered in stark detail as we witness the Snake once again journeying through the Glass Desert. Mappo's conclusion that the world is only worth saving if compassion exists, and that he failed in not saving the children, is brought home by Badalle, for if the children cannot be children, what innocence is there? Saddic's attempt to recall the instinct of childhood through playing with toys is initially met with disgust from Badalle, but he is merely holding on to the idea of childhood, just as Rutt holds Held. Letting go of the child's innocence within and in the outer world, is to leave nothing to save.

"We must live to see the day when a new colour finds Held's eyes, when Held goes back to being Born." (283) She wants to reclaim all that innocence and potential for these children again. They are going by instinct, trying to survive. "Our own mothers and fathers, lying together, trying to make babies. We can only go back to what we knew…" (284) Not being able to hold on to their childhood, they are acting out a more developed state, but maybe they aren't physically or psychologically ready for it. And in finding the embrace of family again, they will be allowed to relax into their true childhood state. "There is a great family, and they are rich in all things. In food. In water…to show us that the future still lives…And there is a mother who leads them, and all her children she holds in her arms, though she has never made a Born." (284) It is Tavore, as matron, who will be able to contain and redeem these children.

Badalle discovers the nature of the flies and butterflies and Shards and so forth to be that of D'ivers, an old god. This is another example of dissolution, but in this case, there will be no rejoining of the component parts—only lifelessness remains. Of the flies and butterflies: "One white, the other black. Only the extremes remained: from the unyielding ground below to the hollow sky above; from the push of life to the pull of death…" (510) These revelations come after Krughava has been considering the contradictions within people, whether those contradictions can be held. And Badalle asks us, the readers, to hold difficult questions, to hold these children in that liminal state between life and death, between childhood and adulthood, as she relates the evidence of their plight.

After they have encountered the Bonehunters, Badalle sits on a wagon. She looks behind, and then she looks forwards. Erikson then applies a structural technique using this as a flashback. "She thought back." (629) This chronological technique is used a handful of times to open chapters in this novel, and is notable for its break with the conventions of the series so far. Time is not so much coming unstuck as the past is catching up with the present. We were never going to outrun it, slouching along like those bearing Dragnipur's chains. Here it represents the fact that Badalle now has a past— no longer just one foot in front of the other through the desert, the eternal suffering, there is a winding back to the time before.

"And now Badalle saw a new Snake, coming out of the sunset, and this one was of iron and chains, and she knew that she had seen it before, in her dreams." (632) Now enmeshed within the Bonehunters, we have two snakes conjoined, forming the symbolism of the caduceus, renewal and healing. Intertwined, they represent the unity of a duality.

The Snake again bites its tail as Rutt awakens to the cries of Hanavat's baby, and steps forward to take it in his arms. "And what Rutt carried in his arms was us, all that way. He carried us." (794) Now he carries a reborn Held, a Born, and this is a gesture of hope, the return of the life of the child. And so all the innocence and hope of the children in those entwined Snakes.

Ganoes Paran

We find Ganoes looking out over a wall, a city in flames, a reflection of the past: a child trying to comprehend forces beyond his control, and no doubt Ganoes sees himself there. While Noto Boil is put off by the children they've freed, Paran is happy to let them be. "Haven't you noticed, today's the first day they're finally behaving like normal children. What does that tell you?" (45)

The many children in the novel represent the reintegration of childlike aspects of play and wonder. The children need to be united with the worn-out soldiers. In this way we can reconnect to the purpose of life, give answer to the notion that 'children are dying' that has rung through the books since *Deadhouse Gates*. Ganoes is like a father to the army, to these children, and more specifically to the future they represent. Like Fiddler, he has adopted the abandoned children, and is acting out a fatherly role to mirror his role in the army.

The soldiers are attached to him, and it is Quick Ben and Kalam who comment on his easy way of command. "Our old captain here is now leading the whole army. You say Tavore *asks* because for her that's what's needed. But her brother, he just *expects*." (871) He has come into his power, and has come into the mundane role in the army, a fullness of self, though he still has his doubts. Those doubts don't seem to slow him much, and rather suggest a man who is conscious of himself and his flaws, though doesn't let them rule him. He has become the complement to Tavore, as noted by his old squad mates, and is thus ready to complete the family conjunction.

The Crippled God

The Crippled God, Kaminsod, is our god, or rather our potential Self. We have damaged it, the spiritual existence of our world, or the god archetype, and the Crippled God is therefore the metaphor of our god archetype. So in a sense Erikson is making a speculative point—if we kill our god, where does it go?

The conversations within the jade can be seen as Erikson's internal dialogue on what that understanding of god and society means to him, at least at the time that this was being written. Now, the conversation with Shadowthrone is Erikson speaking to the reader, making his case. Or perhaps it is the writer and his shadow, conscious and unconscious, meeting at last to work things through. This final volume does not explain all, but gives the opportunity for the writer to finally reveal intent. It is still up to the reader to take up his or her end of the chain and put it into practice.

The god's heart literally needs to be freed, and that is Tavore's ostensible journey. We could say her brother enables, and she completes, the task, showing the value of two aspects conjoining in their purpose to create something. The necessity of not just the youthful fight but the hard edges combining to enable purpose. I like to think also that without Felisin's sacrifice, Tavore wouldn't have been able to complete this task; the dying of the child within Tavore a necessity, rather than Felisin's death simply being circumstantial.

From the beginning of *The Crippled God*, it is clear that Kaminsod's perspective has changed, and it is through contact with the world. "I once looked upon them with contempt." (29) No longer isolated, being able to reach out has made him vulnerable in turn—the reflective nature of faith that has been so deeply explored within the series. "They wanted my pity. They have it. I am the god that answers prayers…My pain, which I held on to so selfishly, now reaches out like a broken hand." (29) In answering prayers, he touches mortal lives. By doing so, if only to share his pain, he creates a connection. The value of that connection changes both him and the mortal he touches.

Ruthan Gudd thinks of him, as the last two Tlan Imass arrive to complete the House of Chains, that "He is as unwitnessed as we are." (540) His journey was being undertaken beyond our knowledge, all through the series. That journey, of growth and individuation, is something we don't see in others, and we can easily discount the possibility of their humanity and suffering at our peril.

In some ways, I like to think of the Deck of Dragons, especially with its associations with gods and ascendants, living myths if you will, as representative of the collective unconscious. The impact it has on mortal lives is made literal in fantasy and myth, and Erikson applies that metaphor freely. It also means that while Tavore is focused on the mundane, Ganoes is more in touch with the archetypes, the unconscious. Bringing those two together, in conjunction, frees the wounded heart and reinforces compassion as the goal, even though it entails sacrifice. No victory prevents pain and sacrifice, just like no transformation or rebirth is possible without the death of the old self.

By chaining one's heart, pain and suffering embroil you. It becomes your focus, your sole way of relating. Only through deep abiding compassion (Tavore running point, but many others coming to the same conclusions) can we allow it to be freed. In fact, one might understand it as Tavore needing not only to take it upon herself, but needing there to be many others coming to the same realisation to effect change. Both the trust of her soldiers, the Bonehunters, as well as other characters finding their compassion, and altogether there is enough psychic change in the collective that the world can be saved. Sounds grandiose, and plotwise is probably a little speculative, but I don't think she could have done it on her own.

The Forkrul Assail have possession over his heart: "that blackened, rotted abomination, the boulder that was – or, perhaps, encased – the heart of an alien god." (185) Here we see clearly the connection between heart and stone as is thematically arrayed through the book and the series. Heart and stone, the anima mundi.

Alchemical representations of the philosopher's stone can be seen as a mandala, with the heart (soul) at the centre of a quincunx, and the four base elements (air, fire, water, earth) at the corners. Finding the heart is one symbolic outcome of the alchemical opus. What does it mean that the Forkrul Assail have possession of it? Stasis and balance, the holding back of consciousness and progress, which stops us from seeking the soul. It prevents compassion.

Alchemy is in essence the search for the philosopher's stone, a substance that is so essential that it is able to turn base metals into gold, and offer eternal life, and so forth. That essence can be sought in all matter, symbolised here by the blood within the stone. Because in death, something is missing, that something being the basic essence of life. To try and distil that out of material (for it was believed all matter contained that essence), is to find something essential to life.

Reborn, the Crippled God tells Fiddler: "I wish I could understand." (1089) He seeks to know what drives the selfless actions of those marines, of the Malazans descended from Kellanved. This echoes our own search and the wish to understand what it is that drives the best in us. Our instinctive desire to comprehend and emulate the heroes and heroines of our stories. It will be by riding their perspectives, by listening to their words that he will learn, by exercising empathy first and foremost.

He wonders of the souls of his followers, lost without him for so long: "Did they struggle to hold on to their faith, with their god vanished for so long?...Did they now wander without purpose, in the horror of a meaningless existence?" (1106) If we are abandoned by a god, or if we abandon the faith that we understand god to be, we lose our faith in something bigger. We need something to fill its place, and if there is nothing does nihilism result? If it reflects our worst attributes, then the world is at our mercy. This reflects back to Hedge's notion "we might see that god we made out of the best in us." (1090) Keeping faith is holding to the good, knowing it is still alive and there, and maybe it just needs freeing and a little love.

He hears the marines laughing as they defend him on the barrow. He admires them for their skill, their tenacity, and more, but it is their nature in this moment that awakens him: "the Crippled God, who had been listening, now heard." (1147) They awaken his emotions. Something that isn't pain, even in the face of their seemingly hopeless situation. And so their stories will be made immortal, just as the soldiers' faces and memories are carried in Fiddler's mind—he will construct a book of the fallen.

He is uncertain of his ability to chain Korabas, at first not wanting to, because he knows what it is like to be chained. But when he realises she accedes, he does not know how to enact his power. It is love that is universal, those emotions awakened by the marines, and so he can latch on to that.

If we consider Kaminsod as the author of the Book of the Fallen, our author, we can see he shows us how the various journeys portrayed across the books have combined to create a grander narrative journey, a body of mythology if you will. It frames our understanding of the journey taken by us and the author, and gives us cause to reflect on what has led to this point. What has changed, why those stories were meaningful, how we have grown.

We strive to achieve self, but we never truly live up to the ideal. It is in that futility, in the striving, the journey, that meaning is to be found. "For this, my Book of the Fallen, the only god worthy of its telling is the crippled one. The broken one. And has it not always been thus?" (1147) Not only must we fall to rise, we have to be able to step in to the minds of others.

"And only the fallen can rise again." (1147) He honours the fallen in turn, his journey as author of this book a redemption of his heart, a freeing of his compassion, in return for that shown by his redeemers in literally redeeming his heart. To do so, he must draw that compassion out of us, redeem us, guide us to individuation, because it is the only way to truly show the sacrifices made, the humanity shown in the mission to free him: to make us feel it.

Beyond the clear metafictional aspect, we can think of the very idea of this wounded, suffering creature. Isolated, broken, he has to piece himself together to make sense of the world he has found himself within. He must attain what agency he can, and finally the heart is what is redeemed—there is a knife because there is no happily ever after, it is ever another wounding. He is a metaphor for the author. He reaches out to try and shape events, to hopefully influence the world beyond his small, chained realm.

Kaminsod's notions of suffering have been tempered. He lashed out, became helpless after his misadventure with Rhulad. Erikson was playing on the trope of the hero who takes the sword for the god and becomes the great champion. Now, as Kaminsod witnesses the acts of the Bonehunters, he understands or finds again compassion, finds his heart. He sees true heroism.

This storyline also has clear associations with hero myths, such as freeing a captive. The captive is the Crippled God's heart which, if we analyse the Crippled God as a god of our universe, means the captive is the reader's humanity, the treasure our compassion. The captive is also Tavore's own feeling side, which is redeemed along with the Crippled God. We might also recall Osiris, a dismembered culture-hero, whose resurrection and recombination is symbolic of the conjunction of soul and body.

This final volume is much about the redemption of the feminine, with all the women who help. At the end, Tavore, Lostara, Badalle and others converge to fulfil the heroic freeing of the captive. Tavore is mother because she contains the multitude, she holds all within her until it is able to be released. By redeeming the feminine aspect, our feeling side, releasing the captive allows escape from the dominance of the Great Mother archetype. By freeing that feminine aspect, Tavore takes on the mother archetype, her own creative aspect. Thus can Badalle recognise her as Mother.

While he dies, and is clearly surprised by it, we have come by this point to understand that freedom, rebirth, is a gift in itself, if only for a short time.

Forkrul Assail

The Forkrul Assail are an exploration of opposition and extremity. They invite consideration of homeostasis and balance, stagnation, versus chaos in the form of life and progress. Their notion of justice and balance is compromised by growth. Their judgment ends with destruction.

The Forkrul Assail display a moral certainty, which Erikson has held up as dangerous and deluded through the series. The ability to introspect and consider the nature of life is apparently absent, and so fearing stagnation, unable to compromise, they embrace destruction. The logic itself is hard to argue, but because its fundamental pillars are inhuman and mechanistic, they are horrifying. A similar notion is attributed to Burn's gambit, and also Rake's actions, with the idea that no one can decide on the end of all life based on a simple decision, much as that might end the uncertainty. Brood thus gives us his reason for denying Burn, and balance is achieved in the unknowing, the appearance of stasis.

As Jung had it, psychic energy is constantly in a dynamic state, ever sliding along a spectrum between chaos and order, tension and stagnation. Knuckles ponders his past, "The laws are not what they seem. Order is an illusion. It hides its lies in your very eyes, deceiving all they see. Because to see is to change what is seen." (191) This understanding, confirmed by the science of perception, puts a lie to the notion that we can swing to one end of a polar opposition. If we are alive, then we are changing, changed.

The Forkrul Assail want only balance, a return to some imagined original wholeness, thus stagnation. For all our flaws as individuals and as civilisations, the possibility of growth, of advancement, of meaning and wholeness, only exist with a touch of chaos—we have to take the good with the bad. That is the dance of life. Otherwise, we stagnate into self-hatred and nihilism, inhumanity.

Let's briefly summarise what we have learned about the Forkrul Assail, and see how their notion of purity and balance is unsustainable.

In *House of Chains*, Cynnigig explains:

> "such adjudication is invariably bloody. Rarely indeed is anyone satisfied. Rarer still that anyone is left alive. Is there justice in such a thing, I ask you? Oh yes, perhaps the purest justice of all. On any given day, the aggrieved and the aggriever could stand in each other's clothes. Never a question of right and wrong, in truth, simply one of deciding who is least wrong." (*HOC* 692)

In *Midnight Tides*, Silchas Ruin speaks ominously of the Assail to Kettle, how he refutes their fundamental notion of balance:

> "It is not that I am blind to the way in which force is ever countered, the way in which the natural world strains towards balance. But in that striving I see no proof of a god's power; I see no guiding hand behind such forces. …Chaos needs no allies, for it dwells like a poison in every one of us. The only relevant struggle for balance I acknowledge is that within ourselves. Externalizing it presumes inner perfection, that the internal struggle is over, victory achieved." (*MT* 539)

For Ruin, it is implicit in the striving for balance that it is never achieved. He certainly doesn't see it in himself. He asserts that the Forkrul Assail aim to act on behalf of the imagined existence of an active striving for balance. However the grand gesture of resetting the balance is unthinkable. The balance for city life is…nature. Not the razing of all cities and killing the inhabitants. The notion of active balancing, presuming to do nature's work, is different to the slow, homeostatic balancing that naturally occurs, as life finds equilibrium. It could be considered that such natural balancing is in fact progressive, because it presumes growth, whereas the Assail are trying to stifle forward movement, in the name of balance.

In *The Bonehunters*, Paran learns about the Errant: "The Errant's enemy was ennui, stagnation. This is why the Forkrul Assail sought to annihilate him. And all his mortal followers." (*BH* 475) And in Toll the Hounds, Caladan Brood speaks of their ongoing war with the Jaghut, calling them "the purest manifestation of arrogance and separation." (*TTH* 419)

By now we have a flavour for this people, and we are familiar with some of the ideas Erikson has wrestled with through the series. "Nature insists on a balance—" (*DOD* 252). Here we finally get a discussion about the Assail, Quick Ben and Tavore philosophising about the nature of justice. "The whole notion is founded on a deceit: that truths are reducible—" (*DOD* 252) The justice they speak of here is a justice wielded with the intent to end the vagaries of life, one that enslaves the heart. "Justice of a most terrible kind." (*DOD* 253) Their plans are world-ending. It is the extremism of their belief that all life is imbalance and thus harmful to balance. It is a similar extremism as evinced by the Crippled God in *Memories of Ice*. Is he influenced by them because they have captured his heart? Or does this show that the pain and psychological torture of captivity, freedom denied, tends to lead us to extreme viewpoints?

Perhaps there is consequence to all life, we leave marks, we cost the world. But it is life, after all, part of the same cosmic dance. A return to imagined static bliss, or a scouring clean, is not necessarily an effective answer to this problem.

In their battle with Badalle, we get an indication of what is anathema to the Forkrul Assail outlook. Approaching the city where the Snake will find refuge, Sever tells the others that they cannot storm the city. Adroit responds: "Its own beauty, yes. To challenge would be suicide." Sever concedes: "We cannot. It is absolute. It shines." (*DOD* 946) The nature of beauty, of a liveliness in a lack of static order, of the very existence of the hope of childhood represented by the Snake, is what they are threatened by. But it is not the beauty itself that threatens them, it is the way that undermines their certainty. If beauty can exist for its own inherent value, then their outlook is challenged. Badalle is free to make beauty with her poetry, her soul flying free is a wonder that cannot be abided in the Forkrul Assail worldview. Thus she is able to challenge them with the fire of her words and truth.

Now in *The Crippled God* we finally get their nature from their own perspective. First, from the angry and bitter Calm: "in their place, beneath stones, bound in roots and dark earth, they were witness to the corruption of justice, to its loss of meaning, to its betrayal." (25) The Forkrul Assail notion of justice, as we have seen, is itself very specific. They see themselves as arbiters of balance, and any life beyond their order is a danger to that. "Gods and mortals, twisting truths, had in a host of deeds stained what once had been pure." (25) Purity is always lost—and so their battle is a never-ending one. Their notion that such words are twisted mirrors how we as readers see them. They rail against civilisation and its liveliness and its spark that breaks the pure dark, and so the only final solution they see is the scouring clean of all that life. As she observes the desolate wastelands: "not even a single herd remained, domestic or wild. There was, she observed, admirable perfection in this new state of things." (42)

Ascending to the presence of the Crippled God's heart, Sister Reverence confirms for us that it is humanity that the Forkrul Assail wish to cleanse from the world, returning it to an ideal state. "Judgement upon humanity. Judgement upon this broken, wounded world. We shall cleanse. It is not what we chose for ourselves. This burden in truth does not belong to us, but who will stand to defend this world?" (184)

It is interesting to speculate on the history of the Forkrul Assail, because we might think that time and our perception of it has some bearing on the instinct of forward motion-growth, evolution, the instinct to reproduce, and to produce anything, which presumes a future. Their notion of balance must have come late in their evolution, because such extremes cannot maintain a civilisation. Perhaps they came to their current evolution and feared losing it.

"Our answer is annihilation. Our cull shall be absolute. Our cull shall be the excision of an entire species." (337) This is another encapsulation of the Forkrul Assail war against humanity. However, these musings by Sister Calm remind us that the notion has been twisted. She had thought there could be balance, a smaller cull from which nature would recover. But the Pures were poisoned by the Crippled God's heart, or the power it represented, the ambition. "We could be made children once again." (337) But that rarely goes the way you think. A return to childhood is a spiritual move, and coloured by what has come before.

Paran challenges the Forkrul Assail. He is up against the notion of detachment, which was mentioned by Mhybe. He has learned. "Those pathetic needs I talked about? They all come down to power." (674) He challenges their notion of dominance, their right to kill. That is life all the way up, and we are being shown that just as we cannot remark at the injustice of one predator killing another, they cannot because they are doing it to humans. There must be self-awareness before we accuse. It is through the metaphor of humans not being the top of the food chain in this world, by showing us as the victims, that we may garner some understanding of that.

"They judged their own god and found him wanting. And for his imperfections, they finally killed him." (706) Certainty is self-destructive, isolating. Not only is all beneath the Forkrul Assail judged, but all that might be beyond them. If we are certain of our own rightfulness and purity, then what need for gods? Who can ever live up to our lofty standards? If we are pure, we don't want flawed heroes and deities. The purpose of those is to stand beyond and above us, but if we are already perfect, then what do we have to strive for? That is ego inflation, and if we decide we do not need the Self archetype, then there is no growth, only stagnation.

"And for all that we Forkrul Assail can but aspire to true perfection, justice stands outside and its state of perfection cannot be questioned." (829) Again displaying certainty, the Assail are holding up what Jung called the Self image, that which we are striving to attain in the individuation process. It is beyond us, gives us a target, and indeed it is archetypal perfection. But the recognition that we cannot achieve it does not mean that growth and change are impossible. Conscious appreciation of the difference between ego and Self gives the impetus for growth, and the hope that over time we can all grow and find more balance in the world. They put themselves in contrast to the Crippled God's ideology of celebrating imperfection—and indeed they are polar extremes on the surface of it. But they are more similar than that: because suffering and imperfection exist does not make a life of pain and meaninglessness the only true way.

When Badalle steps up and summons their god as Shards in the final battle, she is providing a balance to the claims of the Assail. She recalls the Inquisitor coming to her people:

> "He told them they had to die. To answer ancient crimes.
> Perhaps he was right.
> But that did not mean he had the right." (1121)

The presumption of the Forkrul Assail is that they are the hand of justice, when the world gives its own. Far from balance, this is a sword's point leaning on the scales. Her summoning provides a true balance, because it is the god that they destroyed in the first place. It enacts its own revenge.

In many ways, the Forkrul Assail are the apotheosis of stagnation and the soul that won't grow. In that sense, they stand against the very purpose and message of the series, and we can see that they ultimately fail, whereas the Crippled God himself undergoes growth and change.

Fiddler and the Bonehunters

From the disintegration and chaos of separation, the Bonehunters must be pieced back together. Polished away to a bright pure core, all the excess is gone. Now their essence must undergo rebirth so as to fulfill their purpose.

We see that rebirth first through the mind of Bottle, who had split his mind to become many. His awakening is a tour of the elements and of the senses:

> "The smell of burning grass. Wetness against one cheek, cold air upon the other, the close sound of a click beetle. Sunlight, filtered through shut lids. Dusty air, seeping into his lungs and then back out again. There were parts of him lying about. In pieces." (88)

This is also the awakening of consciousness, at multiple levels. Each awakening is a piecing back together of the mind and soul, each rebirth builds upon what has come before, memories and history. This awakening becomes the rebirth for the Bonehunters after the ordeal of their disintegration and their burning away. What is left is hardened, pure of intent.

All the pieces, all the elements are in place for the journey to individuation. The awakening and reconciling of body and soul is itself a form of conjunction, and here it paves the way for the larger scale conjoining of all spirit and matter, inner and outer: heart and stone.

Dissociation and reintegration are shown by the soldiers, all bewildered in the wake of the battle with the Nah'ruk, but this is the natural process of growth and expansion. Wholeness without dissolution is no growth at all; remaining in a state of disintegration invites chaos. For all these soldiers, and for the army as a whole, it is vital that they experience coming back together. To rejuvenate literally means to restore a state of youth.

Their memories are what anchor them. Kisswhere ponders her training in the army. Stormy and Gesler (although not physically connected to the Bonehunters) wonder at their mistakes and regrets. The camped army recalls the faces of the dead, trying to make space for their gear and flags. Reintegration occurs, squads get swallow one another up, recombined.

Fiddler "answers only to the Adjunct." (158) He has been made a captain. "To fit into a new thing you had to leave the old thing behind, and that wasn't as easy as it sounded, since it meant accepting that the old thing was dead" (254) The marines under Fiddler are now separating from Tavore and the rest of the army. The separation of old and new is both in Fiddler's old life, and the Bonehunters as they once were, now that so many have been killed.

The Glass Desert can be seen as a kind of Hermetic vessel, impenetrable and blind to the outside, it is where the final transformation takes place. "…no one can find us out here. Right?" (413) Various stages of dissolution and coagulation eventually result in the transformation of the prima materia into the philosopher's stone, this is the alchemical process, and symbolically the individuation process in a nutshell. "We're an army not thinking about loot." (416) Their discussion shows that change has occurred, but crucially that they are no longer interested in the physical aspect of gold—what they seek is the spiritual gold at the end of the journey.

Fiddler watches the Khundryl youth who track close to his soldiers, more children who have lost too much. "Children always made him feel awkward." (445) Though this isn't fooling us. They are comfortable near him for the same reason the squads gravitate towards him. They feel they can trust him as a protector, as a father.

He speaks as though to the Crippled God, and we might consider it a prayer. He knows the suffering, and they will do what they can: "whatever we manage to do, it will have to be enough." (445) He wonders about the writing of a Book of the Fallen, a history of this journey, how the individuals wouldn't be seen, how their motives would be misconstrued. And perhaps the god hears that prayer, and in his own portrayal he will render the individuals, the fact that there is suffering and vulnerability in all of us, that their motivations matter.

"And so there was no letting go, not from any of this." (556) Fiddler provides both a balance and contrast to Tavore as the Bonehunters approach their destiny. He draws the soldiers and the children to him, he is open, and we are party to what haunts him in his thoughts, as opposed to the very closed nature of Tavore, though she is also a magnetic draw to those around her. She has the faith he lacks, perhaps, and so they will each take something of the other in their manner of conjunction. Conscience, or merely the memories of his wrong choices resurfacing, make Fiddler aware that he can't take the easy road by letting go or escaping, if he wants to be true to what he is.

"Adjunct, you were right to seek this war." (636) Fiddler shows us that they had to take this journey to discover the suffering, of the children in this case but also how it can be reflected in themselves, and by taking the journey they have discovered what is right, even if the cost is their own lives. But he still doubts they can be what Tavore expects of them, only mortal as they are.

Badalle says of Fiddler, "This father, Rutt, is a good father." (631) He looks into Rutt's eyes, like Tavore challenged Kindly to look into the Crippled God's. "She saw him recoil, saw him look up and stare hard into Rutt's slitted eyes." (631) He fights against the instinct to withdraw, and by taking that moment to gaze into Rutt's eyes, he sees the suffering, really sees it. And despite the unlikelihood of their survival he chooses to give them water anyway. It is right. And the children of the Khundryl follow his lead.

"Fathers and mothers, but children all. And there – I see her – that is their one mother – I see her. She comes." (632) The army of the Bonehunters are adults, here in Badalle's world, but they are also contained by Tavore. They are being carried, and made anew. They are seeing the world anew.

"The tremulous arrival of a child into every knot of soldiers seemed to have a strange effect upon them. Arguments fell away, glaring eyes faded, resentments sank down." (646) There is a juxtaposition in the notion of warring soldiers and the comforting arms of a parental embrace. The gift goes both ways. The soldiers see something outside themselves, something greater, which takes away the ego-level concerns. They understand so that they can embody what Tavore needs them to be. The children, many dying in the soldiers' arms, have finally come home to their mothers and fathers, and can rest. The soldiers in some way take on the child's aspect, a conjunction, an embrace like that of a Shield Anvil. "We can die in the arms of men and women, men and women who for that moment become our fathers, our mothers." (765)

Fiddler feels the cut in Tavore's hand, when she uses her otataral knife. It is an indication that they share something. There is already a connection, but it will be symbolically consummated when they ride with Banaschar to plant the Otataral sword.

Fiddler undergoes another conjunction, this time the old and new, as he embraces Hedge when the marines and heavies leave the army behind. In their initial confrontation, Fiddler pushes Hedge away literally and metaphorically, but we see Fiddler's grief because he wanted to protect Hedge and indeed those parts of himself. He shows vulnerability to the reader when he breaks down, and it is in the salute to the regulars, and the embrace of Hedge, that he opens up and becomes vulnerable to those around him.

As the marines and heavies march out on their final mission, they are witnessed by the regulars, and witnessed by the reader as we ride with their thoughts almost for the last time. Memories and regrets, possible futures. It doesn't matter that we witness them, because they have embodied the intention to be unwitnessed. That intention alone has set them on their path, ensured the growth in themselves.

As they prepare to defend the Crippled God's hill, Fiddler wonders how to find meaning in his soldiers' deaths. "If only they knew, the fools. I'm as lost as they are." (1084) But the marines don't seem lost—they have their jobs, their banter. They know their roles and they are content. And they have Fiddler.

Cotillion and Lostara Yil

Cotillion is now living with his past, what was awakened through his possession of Sorry. An initial attempt at retaining some humanity, or maybe he is shown some humanity in that fight, and that sets him on the path. Either way, it seems on reflection that his choice was odd, in possessing Sorry, but if we see it as a necessary trigger for his individuation journey, it makes sense.

He still wants victory, he has a goal, but he is worn and weary. When

Edgewalker tells him he cannot win, "That doesn't mean I have to lose, does it?" (23) This is a refrain taken up later by Shadowthrone. From Cotillion, it is more human in the idea that victory is not a selfish one, but a net benefit for the world. He feels his physical body: "His throat felt tight...The muscles of his shoulder ached and dull thunder pounded behind his eyes...feeling ... *mortal*." (30) This is a further clarification that his humanity is returning.

In Lostara Yil's defence of the Adjunct, the Shadow Dance, Cotillion took over. She felt out of her body, not in control. It is a level of unconscious. "I have never felt such rage. It burned right through me. It scoured me clean." (155) Indeed, she feels healed in her heart, of her loss. The realisation that she had to let go of control to heal that sense of abandonment.

She was protecting an image she created, a projection, now she can no longer hide from her reality. Her grief is for what she used to be. Now she feels freer. But she has also been distilled to her essence, and come out the other side with a pure core. "But no mortal could stand in that blaze and not come through either burned to ashes, or reborn." (155)

But has Cotillion taken something? Does she need to have a conscious conjunction now? Is she whole? Cotillion comes to her, and we learn that what she took from him was his anger. Now, stripped of it, he is weary, lonely, and struggling to maintain the purpose. In return, he felt the love in her, was reminded of it, and is now trying to deal with the guilt of his possession of Sorry, knowing that loss of love runs deep. "All of it, so terribly *wrong*. Love ... I'd forgotten." (266) His use of Sorry was exploitive, just as we have been exploring the notions of humanity's exploitation of the world, of extracting the power from the Crippled God. Now, Cotillion brings it back to a human level for us.

"I'm trying to give you some of your humanity back." (265) He denies the chance to feel it again, but without it he is bereft. Can he find it without the need for possession? Is that the true regaining of his humanity? He sees, admires, but needs to feel compassion and love for its own sake. He wants to feel it, but all he can give in exchange is the sorrow and emptiness, the guilt and the hopelessness. And so he must bear that for himself.

He has a tradeoff, he has given these people more time, but is concerned that he has only extended the suffering to its inevitable conclusion. But Lostara Yil maintains there is more than just that, there are gifts in his actions. "There must be, Cotillion. They exist. They always do." (266)

And so Cotillion returns to the place that we met him, the road where he met Sorry, that place of regret. Cotillion's regrets have piled up, and they are finally coming home, with us being shown the implications of his actions since *Gardens of the Moon*. His possession and inhumanity, his choice to let children die, and the consequences of his choices as ascendant. He is still trying to make amends. His life journey is showing him those consequences, that we can't undo them, but might choose to live consciously, and in that way children might be redeemed, and the future contain hope again. This very consciousness, and his awareness of it, is what allows him to maintain a grip on his own humanity. Without that awareness, should he choose to, he could avoid the regret—but lose all humanity in the process.

He kills the Crippled God, as a final act of mercy. Where the gods wanted to kill him for hate, the Forkrul Assail for power, Cotillion kills to ease suffering. It is mercy, and compassion.

Apsalar and Crokus reunite in the end, and this too is Cotillion's parts healing.

Twilight – The Watch

"We are children here." (175) The Shake siblings are apart but need to come together in conjunction to rescue their people, to renew their world.

These two and the people that follow them stand between Lightfall and Sandalath, Queen of Darkness. They are the intermediate state. Without them to hold back the light, the Liosan will destroy civilization. Therefore they are what provides the balance between the two extremes.

She is supposed to kneel, to surrender. Yedan is like a wall himself. Both refuse to yield part of themselves, though they know it is the right thing to do. "We see each other, yes, and neither of us does a thing to reach across." (457)

Yedan repels the first breach, and Yan Tovis thinks about how he hardens groups of soldiers in turn. "And, as they begin to fall, why, he'll have a new crop of veterans to draw from." (456) He is able to forge something, to be a central point just like Tavore or Fiddler, and give those others a reason to fight that is just. He does it by being his true self.

In Sanadalath's memories, she recalls Rake saying of the Liosan coming through Lightfall, "There are children who will have their way." (468) This shows how the storyline connects to that of the new gods coming into the world, the presumption of humanity taking over the peace of the world. The new forces its way in, and the Shake represent the balance.

"This is their fight." (470) It gives the Shake and those with them meaning. They don't fight for the riches and the glory, nor the need to be witnessed. They reflect the Bonehunters in this way. "You can win even when you lose. Because, even in losing, you might still succeed in making your point. In saying that you refuse the way they want it." (471) Here Yedan Derryg echoes Cotillion from the novel's opening. Cotillion, of course, showed by his actions how he wanted to be, losing notionally but retaining his humanity in a just action.

When the Imass arrive in the Bonehunters' camp, Nom Kala is forced to question why they should keep bearing suffering, and she has no answer. Similar questions arise for those at the breach of Lightfall. Why continue to suffer if it is inevitable, if the outcome is doomed? Justice, the end of suffering, saving the world: these are all good reasons, but we are seeing people explore their motives and finding they are not enough. There is a faith in something greater beyond them, and in living as though there is, meaning can be made. The reasons on their own are not enough, but continuing to question is part of that very journey. We also see Erikson bringing the question back down to the individual level—when high-minded morals and faith are taken to their endpoint, it is still at the individual level that action must be taken, choices must be made. We are not subsumed by greater purpose.

Yan Tovis and Sandalath are both isolated queens. They mirror one another in being apart from their people, held there by a history they feel disconnected from. "Neither of us can withstand the weight of this crown." (589) They both feel the burden of leadership, but it's what's needed somehow.

Pully and Skwish are as children. "They're little girls now." (588) Using the power of Yan Tovis's blood they get even younger, another example of the return of the child.

"What right do we have to choose destiny? Only the defeated kneel." (725) In the end, Yan Tovis kneels to the people who are fighting. This symbolic act confirms that we are not bound, fated, but can choose. It is the choice of those who fight for this cause that she respects, and she is paying tribute to that power.

The arrival of the Andii wrap the themes of this plot up nicely. Spinnock, leading the Andii to battle thinks about the times they taken on causes on behalf of others, that it had no meaning. But there was a purpose to that, after all. By fighting for causes that were just and selfless, they created a situation where they were able to find meaning, and were not hopeless at this end, but able to come home, to fight for themselves, to accept the sacrifice on their behalf. We can't always see the benefit ahead of time, we can't always act with expectation of benefit in our lifetime.

Yan Tovis struggles again to get to Yedan Derryg as he is dying, she cannot seem to reach him, still separated. "As far away as hope. And that is a shore I will never reach." (745) As the witches die, turned by her power back to children, she feels that power to move return, and finally she reaches her brother. There are conjunctions of opposites everywhere here. Forces of darkness arrive, black and white dragons do battle in the sky, brother and sister are united, and Yedan says he is home, his doubts gone, the breach between them closed.

The dead children return power to Yan Tovis. Sandalath awaits the return of her child, who is dead, while Korlat, her other child, is as dead to her. And the Son of Darkness's death has allowed the return home of the Andii to their mother. Here in the culmination of the battle of Lightfall, the theme of return of childhood is battered askew, explored from these different angles. And the Letherii, the guilty, stand ready to defend the children, where others in the novel had failed. These inversions of what we have seen thematically through the book provide an interesting contrast to those other threads.

Tanakalian

The Grey Helms are hounded by talk of betrayal. Meanwhile, Tanakalian is still projecting a lust for glory upon Mortal Sword Krughava, and thus he is blind to the betrayal. "You seem bent on forcing my hand. Is there room for only one on that pedestal of yours?" (122) She, in turn, doesn't trust him. "Already a legend is taking birth, and yet we saw none of its making. We played no role." (123) He is covetous of that grand legacy, and believes the Grey Helms deserve a part in it.

Tanakalian again has as his major fault a certainty, about the world and about others. Such certainty precludes empathy, and so he is unable to step inside the minds of others. Casting himself as the main character in his narrative, he is doomed to misjudge those around him.

He decides to challenge Krughava. He thinks the betrayal is of their deities, the Wolves, by Krughava swearing to Tavore. He rationalises everything by telling himself that he has been forced into the position. This is not a strong ego position.

"Oh, how he had longed for this moment, how he had conjured this scene…*This precise scene.* And in his mind he had spoken all he would now say…" (370) The very manufactured glory that he resents Krughava for, the story being invented in *Dust of Dreams*, is now revealed as the nature of Tanakalian. He operates entirely within that practiced story. He has prepared so much for the moment that he has lived it in fantasy over and over. So stuck within it, it has become a complex, and any deviation from how it has been anticipated in his mind would shatter the persona thus constructed. What rises up in its wake would be the unconscious, neglected: the shadow.

"…are we to be human, or are we to be humanity's slayers?" (374) He lays out the contradictions of their faith—that no side in this war suits their leanings with a logical outcome. "It is not glory we seek…" (375) His words shake Krughava, but not because he saw her true, but perhaps because she was as blinded by her faith as he, in her way. Hers was for Tavore.

"Gods, the supreme egoism of this creature!" (377) His view of Krughava is classic projection. Only able to see his world through the lens of manufactured story, he presumes she does the same, and could not see true heroism, compassion, when it exists. Just as he couldn't believe the respect she had earned from her soldiers.

It might be argued that Tanakalian is experiencing an encounter with the Self, leading to an inflation of his ego to godlike status of the suprapersonal. He believes that what he is doing transcends him, whereas Krughava, in contrast, comes to realise that her inflated sense of connection to Tavore was misguided, and so is brought back down to the human level.

The Liosan, in their efforts to breach Lightfall, provide another good study for Tanakalian's mentality. Aparal Forge wonders at the humans defending the breach, and he presumes that their motives are short sighted: "the legacy they sought was more often than not a selfish one, the private glory of immortal notoriety or fame." (462) These creatures in their certainty fail in presuming there is no purpose to people, that their acts cannot be selfless, and that is to miss the very humanity beneath. It is the same as presuming the Crippled God is a villain. We are being reminded constantly, shown that such thought is flawed.

Krughava ponders her usurpation, the fact that Tanakalian revealed contradictions in her faith, a flaw in logic. "…where was the crime in that most human of capacities: to carry in one's heart a contradiction, to leave it unchallenged, immune to reconciliation; indeed, to be two people at once…" (498) From being 'two people at once' it is conjunction that creates wholeness. Of course, it is no crime, and Jung was explicit on the idea of holding the tension of the opposites, as he called it. From holding the tension of an unanswerable question, a psychic conundrum, something new would often arise, as a child from an alchemical marriage. This paradoxical situation is very often the trigger to undertaking the individuation work in earnest, as the very nature of the contradiction can raise consciousness in an individual.

Tanakalian cannot hold that contradiction, sit in the discomfort. Like the Forkrul Assail or the Liosan, he demands certainty.

> Conscience may indeed demand that the individual follow his inner voice even at the risk of going astray. If he refuses to obey it, and, for fear of taking the wrong road, adapts to the generally accepted, traditional morality, he will nevertheless feel uneasy because he has been untrue to his real nature.[210]

The clash between the morality of the masses, the accepted social way, and the inner desires, the ethical choices of the individual, is a frequent conflict in those undertaking the journey of individuation. Krughava's realisation of the paradox of their faith is a good example of this. Choices that cause us to deviate from our individuating path tug at the conscience. The breaking of the quandary often results in a third path, what Jung referred to as a creative solution, but again, this usually requires sitting in the discomfort for some time.

> "There is no light without shadow and no psychic wholeness without imperfection. To round itself out, life calls not for perfection but for completeness; and for this the 'thorn in the flesh' is needed, the suffering of defects without which there is no progress and no ascent."[211]

Now, with his ideology stripped down, his army taken from him by Setoc, and his actions tyrannical, his gods not answering, he realises the nature of all their beliefs.

> "In the end, we are no different from every other cult, every other religion. Convincing ourselves of the righteousness of our path. Convincing ourselves that we alone hold to an immutable truth. Secure in the belief that everyone else is damned." (850)

He is no different in that, but he also realises that is how he chose to act. He

---

[210] Jacobi, 1967, p. 114
[211] Jung, C.G., CW12 [208]

is lost.

"[W]e are not wolves…when we act, we are privileged, or cursed, to know the consequences." (949) Krughava appeals to humanity, our ability to perceive and be self-conscious despite our nature. But for Tanakalian it is not enough. "I am the hero! I am!" (951) Consequences be damned, he kills both women, his god too, egocentrism and venality winning out.

Brys and Aranict

Brys's journey is also one of finding his humanity again. In *Dust of Dreams* he was awakened to his nature by Aranict, and their love. Now, he must consolidate that, and maintain it in the face of what is perceived as a higher duty, a responsibility that comes along with his rebirth.

Brys and Aranict ponder their connection. They don't reflect one another – they do not have the polarity of opposites. Their love accounts for their difference. "You are not my mirror, Aranict. You are something *other*. I am not reflected in you, just as you are not reflected in me." (125) This recognition of the other, and its assimilation, is the basis for self and external growth. But it is growth that is available for one who is already whole in themselves, the person who then flourishes when they can open their individuated self to the world.

Fundamental to the idea of alchemy is the union of opposites. I have discussed earlier that the concept of opposition is perhaps too polarised in its thinking, that complementarity is a better phrase. Here Jung clarifies it:

> "the problem of opposites called up by the shadow plays a great – indeed, the decisive – role in alchemy, since it leads in the ultimate phase of the work to the union of opposites in the archetypal form of the hieros gamos, or "chymical marriage." Here the supreme opposites, male and female (as in the Chinese Yang and Yin), are melted into a unity purified of all opposition and therefore incorruptible."[212]

Again, think of the discussions of balance and chaos in these books. Balance is not the opposite to any particular state, not a static goal in itself as the

---

[212] Jung, C.G., CW12 [43]

Forkrul Assail would have it, but it is an active process in reconciling complementary forces.

After seeing off the Bonehunters into the Glass Desert, Brys has taken on some of Tavore's silence, and Aranict calls his attention to it. It is the nature of being closed, and keeping both the suffering and compassion within. Brys is already brimming with the names of gods, and he either doesn't have the room, or is not a strong vessel like Tavore, to contain all that for his army. Likely, what is missing is the feminine counterpart, which is why Aranict is able to draw him from that silence. As his counterpart, rather than his mirror, she is able to be the counterweight to his resurrected self, allowing him an anchor to his humanity.

He feels the loneliness of the stranger beneath the ocean. "Relief. From the terrible pressures, the burdens, the *darkness*." (367) From the darkness, loneliness. "Am I here to feel once more what it is to be human, to be alive? No. There is more, my love. There is more." (368) Connection, not just moving through from birth to death. For in his dreams he sees this figure reaching out a hand in need. And he thinks about the loneliness at the end of life: "immense, devastating loneliness…It was all he needed. It was all anyone needed. *A hand to take ours…to assure us that our loneliness…has at last come to an end.*" (837) For Brys, Aranict provides that hand. "She held tight on to his hand. As if that could help, when she knew that it could not." (849)

Lonely, forgotten, abandoned gods are recalled by Brys as he confronts the Pure. And Aranict catches him, she held tight to his humanity and that enabled her to save him. By connecting with her, he has stayed his own loneliness – his humanity a tether which keeps him in this world.

Setoc and Humanity

"But the ghost wolves – and all the other fallen beasts – they look to me." (221) Setoc is at a decision point, where she must choose between the unknown, her destiny, on the path of wolves, or the comfort and destructiveness of civilisation.

"You empty the land. You break the earth and use it until it dies, and then your children starve." (221) She laments the humans' use of the land, that they drain its power just as the Forkrul Assail considered using the Crippled God: the power is chained, that it is the natural thing to do. This makes Setoc sympathetic to their idea of cleansing the land of humans, but she decides that is not her destiny. The beasts within her want that, but she maintains some humanity. Perhaps then freedom is release from the need to choose in which way the destruction flows. True freedom, to live like the beasts, to Setoc means to remove the necessity for destruction and violence that is inherent in civilisation.

This is taking place while Rud Elalle considers the notion of surrendering to the Eleint tendencies, and maintaining that draconic form. We also see Gruntle surrendering to fighting humanity on behalf of the beasts. His internal discussion with Kilava gives us a perspective on the extreme argument of the Forkrul Assail. "Tell me, Gruntle, how does one measure these things? How does one decide which life is the more precious?" (233) Life entails death, extraction and exploitation. Can we let life be, simply because it is life? Does thoughtless action beget the need for vengeance? And then at what point do our actions as a civilisation get considered thoughtless, and require the cleansing discussed in this novel?

Is it enough to ensure we do not cause undue suffering, as of the exploitation of one chained?

"...to be blameless." (234) Or rather, thoughtless. Gruntle wonders if being in the beast mind absolves him of the guilt, the trail of blame. It is the question Setoc doesn't ask, whether the freedom she considers is truly free of blame. We can turn away from the destruction we cause, the suffering. We can acknowledge it, and carry the guilt. Somewhere in between is conscious living, without the soul-crushing burden.

It is clear that the innocence and potential of a child is held up against the notion of its inherited guilt, and the inevitable suffering it will cause. Whether that deserves cleansing is the central question. Mappo is the one who lives the trade-off at the larger scale. "He stood between the world and Icarium. Why? *Because the world was worth saving. Because there was love, and moments of peace. Because compassion existed, like a blossom in a crack of stone, a fulsome truth, a breathtaking miracle.*" (235) In choosing to walk away from the children, giving them up, he has walked away from the very things that make the world worth saving. "If I harden myself to compassion, then what am I trying to save?" (235) We don't all get the chance to save the world, but Mappo's struggle is showing that right living should be the precursor.

Consciousness, humanity, self-awareness, such incredible adaptations, lifting us out of the thoughtlessness of bestial actions. But with that awareness comes the awareness of consequences—the double edge of consciousness. If we choose to remain ignorant, then we are choosing inhumanity.

"We must be free to speak – all of us. We must be free to object, to argue…" (832) Setoc, feeling the beast gods in her, maintains the sense of humanity. Her argument is a variation on the idea of the power of words in this novel. Where the Forkrul Assail have their magical voice, and Badalle uses the magic of words, here Setoc claims that the mundane nature of human communication gives us a means by which to lift ourselves above savagery and callous destruction. Even quiet words have power. Setoc is positioning herself against certainty, as fanaticism and certainty don't allow for clarity and self-awareness, don't allow for humanity.

Ending

The end of the novel is a blood-stained baptism for many. There is the reanimation of the Imass, but the work is not finished: they still have to find their soul, their humanity. In alchemical imagery, the blood is what animates to shift to the final stage of the opus. Jung spoke of the final shift towards wholeness in the process:

> But in this state of "whiteness" one does not live in the true sense of the word, it is a sort of abstract, ideal state. In order to make it come alive it must have "blood," it must have what the alchemists call the rubedo, the "redness" of life. Only the total experience of being can transform this ideal state of the albedo into a fully human mode of existence. Blood alone can reanimate a glorious state of consciousness in which the last trace of blackness is dissolved, in which the devil no longer has an autonomous existence but rejoins the profound unity of the psyche. Then the opus magnum is finished: the human soul is completely integrated.[213]

This sense of integration is the rebirth into a new state, a new innocence and vulnerability, but with the life solid behind us. Here in the novel, the death of the war god brings the life, a neat inversion, revealing the vulnerability beneath the façade of war.

All the elder races return, all the elements—fire, ice, blood, stone—clash,

---

[213] McGuire & Hull (Eds.), 1977, p. 229

in these frail moments. Gesler and Stormy go through fire again. It is a series of returns, to life, to the past. Symmetry running through the late chapters, calling back to the journey we have undertaken. Finally, the children return to Onos Toolan.

As with each book, we close at dawn, for there is always a new day to begin again. *The Crippled God* brings us full circle in many ways. It is at once a return to the beginning, and a redemption of what has been lost, a return to an innocent state. But that innocence is not purity, for it contains the seeds of all of life's unfolding, with its complexities and complementarities, and propensity for hurt and destruction that is inseparable from being human.

We take this ride again and again, round and round, each time with greater consciousness. Both for the individual in his or her lifetime, and as each generation unfolds, we hope to do better.

Conclusion

> The leitmotif or kernel of a story represents an archetypal juncture in the psyche. That is the nature of archetypes...they deposit some nuance of themselves at the point of contact with the psyche. As symbolic representations, they sometimes leave behind an evidence – wending their ways into the life stories, dreams, and ideas of every mortal. Dwelling who knows where, the archetypes constitute, one might say, a set of psyche instructions that traverse time and space and enwisen each new generation.[214]

Such is the archetypal effect of the Book of the Fallen. Readers are being shifted, lives changed, by this archetypal pattern of growth – individuation – acting as a guide through significant life periods.

Not only does Erikson employ the power of story to its fullest capacity in teaching, showing, and guiding, it is a timely addition to our mythology of humanity. It is a shining light in a time of disconnection and discontent, and it makes this reader, for one, feel less alone, feel there is meaning to be had, even in the face of hopelessness and helplessness.

"Despair or wonder. Between the two, which would you choose?" (TCG, 838) Erikson doesn't shy away from showing us the worst in humanity, its loss beneath dust. He even makes strong arguments against its nature. But in the end it is hope that prevails, that humanity can be better, worth saving, that the heart can be redeemed. It is our consciousness and compassion that enable us.

In the writing of the books, Erikson is looking for the answers to these questions, trying to free his burdened heart, that we as readers might do the same. It is in the questioning, after all, that the journey takes place. And it

---

[214] Estés, 1997, p. 355

shouldn't be easy—no transformation, no death and rebirth is. We should assume that this journey was especially profound for Erikson in the writing, but for those of us who read over the course of ten years or more, and those of us reading or rereading now, it is still a long journey. There is still unpleasantness to be had. Aniela Jaffé referred to the unconscious journey as a religious one:

> "Courage and inner strength are needed to pay serious attention to the voices and images that crowd into consciousness, to endure the encounter with the numinous figures, to understand them and take their meaning to heart. [Jung:] 'The spiritual adventure of our time is the exposure of human consciousness to the undefined and indefinable.' But the adventure is successful only when the descent into the unconscious changes from passive exposure into active participation. By taking up an attitude towards it, consciousness delimits itself from the unconscious, broadens its scope so that the personality can unfold."[215]

We know that we share this experience with other readers, and of course with the writer, who reminds us meta-textually in case we were to forget. And there is the value in building the collective experience via the shared traumas as in the Chain of Dogs. But our journey is at the same time deeply personal. It is contextually dependent on our time and place. The me that read this as a young adult is far different from the man reading it at life's midpoint. Its value as a story has grown, and this very work is hopefully a testament to that.

Growth of consciousness in the individual can protect us from unconscious integration into masses. But that must occur consciously. Therein lies the value of the individual journey. As Jung acknowledged, the sole sense of human existence is "to kindle a light in the darkness of mere being,"[216] that is, to create consciousness.

The individuated person is freed from the compulsions and complexes associated with archetypes. Working through each of them by repeated circumambulatory exposure gives the reader a way to check in, to reflect, to be more conscious of their status and their change. When unconscious of archetypal forces, they have power over us. Rereading is a way to ring the bell again, test if that still has power over us, reflect on how we used to feel.

This work is, for me, a reread, a finding again of my own compassion

---

[215] Jaffé, 1970, p. 55
[216] Jung, C.G., 1963, p. 358

that I had lost during trying times, and finally the synthesis of Jung's ideas in my own mind—removing their mystery, coming to understand them, empty myself of them and, finally, to move past their abstractions. It is disenchantment, a clearing of the slate for me. As we age, we need to retain the sense of wonder, but also to simplify. It's the downward slope now, after all.

If we are to approach the experience of the unconscious or the journey of individuation honestly, then we find that reaching the goal of our quest does not bestow wisdom, nor lift us to lofty heights from which we might judge others. Compassion is not the ignoring of the bad, or the forgetting of our failings. It is self-love in spite of those. It is not something we can claim so as to set ourselves above others, nor is it a fetish we wear to scorn those who don't appear to be compassionate, or who haven't completed their journey. Doing so proves the opposite. If one is compassionate they could empathise with even those people, and understand they still have a way to go. Be the one who offers succour to the broken.

> "So long as one continues to develop, inner peace, even for those whose life has been enriched by an encounter with the unconscious, is only a breathing space between the conflict solved and the conflict to come, between answers and questions that throw us into turmoil and suffering, until new insights or new transformations bring a fresh solution and the inner and outer opposites are once again reconciled. The experience of meaning – which is what, ultimately, life is about – is by no means equivalent to nonsuffering; yet the resilience of the self-aware and self-transforming consciousness can fortify us against the perils of the irrational and the rational, against the world within and the world without."[217]

Do we need hero stories in our time? We need stories in our time, that is an eternal truth. Stories that bind us and teach us. Joseph Campbell asserted that myths,

> And their understood function is to serve as a powerful picture language for the communication of traditional wisdom. This is true already of the so-called primitive folk mythologies. The trance-susceptible shaman and the initiated antelope-priest are not unsophisticated in the wisdom of the world, nor unskilled in the principles of communication by analogy. The metaphors by which they live, and through which they operate, have been brooded upon, searched, and discussed for centuries—even millenniums; they have served

---

[217] Jaffé, 1970, p. 56

whole societies, furthermore, as the mainstays of thought and life. The culture patterns have been shaped to them. The youth have been educated, and the aged rendered wise, through the study, experience, and understanding of their effective initiatory forms. For they actually touch and bring into play the vital energies of the whole human psyche.[218]

We have plenty of hero tales – some even announcing themselves as such – but do they teach? Do they take the journey before the telling? I think our culture's tales are quick hits, a sugar rush of sweet lipservice to the journey. A feelgood momentary reflection that we can live with a click and then go back safely to our village, the real dragons remaining unfaced. We want the water to lap our toes and to dream of the treasure, but we don't want to drown.

We should see history, see wildness in our world, see our shared unconscious, and our difference, and revel in it all. We need to see heroes around us, support one another. I think individuality isn't what we need, but maybe individuation can save us all. The hero should return with treasure, bring a new culture. We change, and we create change, too. Whether in the collective or in a relationship, individuation can rarely occur as a solitary journey. Rare is the hero that succeeds without magical assistance. We need relationships on which to explore our projections, and the village to return to.

Don't wait for the world to change, don't wait until you know the journey's end. All our journeys end the same way, it looks like, but we can determine to some extent how we get there, what meaning we extract along the way. Take the journey so you can speak with authenticity. Be an elder, so you too can guide by story and by action. Find your voice. Live through many stories, and find all those parts of yourself within. Swim in the myths of our forebears, that we might wade across our time's rushing river. Let the images in, that they might feed our souls.

Individuation surely has an adaptive function, if indeed it represents a genetically imprinted psychological instinct. It arises from the deep unconscious, as Jung taught us. Learning through story is clearly a selective mechanism. The hero, any individuating character we witness, is a guide, is adaptive for the collective.

We might say the theme of the Book of the Fallen is compassion. But how do we learn it, in the end? We read the books, right? But why does it work? That growth is deep, it's beneath conscious awareness. The creation

---

[218] Campbell, 1949, p. 238

of fullness, wholeness, meaning: individuation. It works on us like a mythology – we are reading the many stories, living their threads, and we are becoming sensitive to them. Knowing that doesn't take away the magic, at least not for me. In fact, it enriches the meaning, being able to consciously understand character and transformation in this way.

Is there room for this new mythology? Culture needs refreshing, and so do its myths. In reading Erikson, we are witness to an elder delivering a message and acting as spiritual guide. The value of this is immense, and our civilisational moment is howling for it. And the Jungian lens tells us how we can work in it consciously, to understand the shared experience we've had.

We can be riven by a sense of futility. No matter how much you do, the system is still bound for collapse and catastrophe. But an individuated, conscious self is more ready to step into a new world—whether that comes about by collapse, scientific revolution, or mass shift in consciousness. Primed for the trials, responsibilities, and opportunities of a new world.

> "One of the least discussed issues of individuation is that as one shines light into the dark of the psyche as strongly as one can, the shadows, where the light is not, grow even darker. So when we illuminate some part of the psyche, there is a resultant deeper dark to contend with. This dark cannot be let alone."[219]

Bewilderment is better than destructive certainty. That is not to say that we should never be confident in our knowing, but to have willingness to let go of some certainty, to surrender, so that answers might arise. Silence, so the unconscious might speak through us.

To be individuals we have to find our own telling of the myth, a throughline in the mire of stories. Where are you similar or apart from your ideals? Where are your complexes exerting too much control on behaviour or relating? Where are your instincts repressed or too free? Don't fall into collective myths, or collective idealisations including stereotypes. Don't latch on to one idealised hero as a projection of your own desire for growth. Don't let superficial culture build you. Get in touch with instinct. We are often drawn to personalities because we lack relation, and we are relating to their ideas, but so often we elevate the individual communicating those ideas. It all becomes out there, rather than internal. And internally is where we need to direct our relating energies if we desire conscious growth.

Chaos and balance; order and disorder. Malazan teaches us that our

---

[219] Estés, 1997, p. 58

actions invite repercussions, convergence. A dynamic system is in constant flux, always in tension and conflict. Our actions can have unpredictable and amplified impacts, not only now, but throughout the course of history. In consciously engaging with the chaos and order within ourselves, we are playing a hero's role in the greater conflict.

The ego and Self play out the same dynamics of separation and return as the hero's journey, as do we in our lives. Depart from home, return changed, and hopefully in time we will reconcile the differences. Consciousness must maintain itself against the force of the unconscious. A strong, stable ego permits return and reintegration. To me, it would be a goal to be able to accept and reconcile those that return, to be the elder who welcomes back the hero, reintegrates him or her into the community. It is part of the nature of being an elder. But remember that reaching the goal of our quest does not bestow wisdom, nor lift us to lofty heights from which we might judge those still on that road. We all become children again, after all.

Prayer and magic may not be able to change the objective world, but it is only a rational worldview that dismisses them for that reason. It can change the inner world, the consciousness. In the same way, don't doubt that change in the self, the hard work that is unseen or unnoticed, the quiet heroism, has real effects on the world, on your community and family. It can be unwitnessed. Change in the inner world — growth in consciousness, a transformation — is real change, and in turn has real effects on the outer, 'objective' world. The treasure we attain is the soul itself.

Cultures ritualise the rebirth of seasons because they believe it enacts the world's rebirth. If they don't greet the sun, it won't rise. We can embrace that wild awe, enact transformation of the self, believe that it will grow the consciousness of the world around us. Do it like the fate of the world depends on it.

Jung's work speaks to the fact that our civilisation, having shifted from collective to individualised, brings with it a concomitant responsibility: that meaning, choices, values of life are no longer found within the collective, but within your own soul. No longer do we take our values from mediating authorities, like religion, nor should we through political organisations or mass media. Failure to take that responsibility, at an individual or even generational level, leaves us open to the influences of the collective unconscious.

The continual erosion of the outer certainties in life appears to have come about because we lack a containing myth. The realisation of our own constructive power for our myths and narrative, our society, our selves, triggers the instinct to individuation. We could see it as a uniquely modern, western pursuit of self-improvement, but I think it is more appropriately seen as an opportunity given our success, and an instinct that can now be tamed and fulfilled. We needed the cultural and biological conditions to be right, just as the individual needs all that, the social framework, the time to understand his history and background. It is a privilege, in other words. And it retains for us the mythology of the collective unconscious, provides a framework when the reality of the world around us seems no longer stable.

> "One of the most fatal of the sociological and psychological errors in which our time is so fruitful is the supposition that something can become entirely different all in a moment; for instance, that man can radically change his nature, or that some formula or truth might be found which would represent an entirely new beginning. Any essential change, or even a slight improvement, has always been a miracle. Deviation from the truths of the blood begets neurotic restlessness, and we have had about enough of that these days. Restlessness begets meaninglessness, and the lack of meaning in life is a soul-sickness whose full extent and full import our age has not as yet begun to comprehend."[220]

Lacking awareness of our unconscious impulses does not lessen their effect on our lives; arguably their effect is even greater. Perhaps we introject the feelings to our ego, causing us to rationalise a belief that our actions and unconscious impulses are part of our central self—thus giving them power. Similarly with individuation itself. Growth happens without our conscious awareness, but the notion of individuation also contains the idea of approaching fullness and realising potential. Jung emphasised that this could not be done through only the unconscious, but with the cooperation of a strong, conscious ego. A conscious approach to growth helps us realise that potential. We will become what we will become, but with consciousness, we can become more of what we could have been.

Unconscious, our baggage grows, the weight of chained things. What we carry from phases of our life bears down upon us, thus infantile impulses might rear their heads later, adolescent impulsiveness recurs at midlife, and so on. These deleterious impulses might not emerge as full-blown neuroses—they may escape notice altogether—but we can only speculate at the unrealised potential of human energy and capacity. The obvious analogy being the unrealised human potential of an oppressed or hungry population

---

[220] Jung, C.G., CW8 [815]

who are too focused on survival to reach for spiritual heights.

Jung stressed, particularly in the age of burgeoning nuclear power, after the horrors of the Second World War, that consciously approaching individuation really is a matter of life and death for civilisation. Our potential for destruction is great. Unconscious progress necessarily doesn't consider its consequences. A distracted, hopeless population is exposed to the influence of mass movements and cynical manipulations that defy our instincts.

This rings similar to what Draconus tells Paran of the imbalance between chaos and order:

> "Devastating, civilization-destroying wars, civil wars, pogroms, wounded and dying gods – you and your kind progress at a perilous pace on the path forged by Chaos. Blinded by rage, lusting for vengeance, those darkest of desires…Where history means nothing. Lessons are forgotten. Memories – of humanity, of all that is humane – are lost." (*MoI* 972)

A narrative keeps the archetypal forces under control. We create a story, and the ego strives for wholeness. In living out the journey of individuation, we fulfil both a creation myth, and the journey and history of humanity in achieving the fullness of meaning and consciousness we have attained. When our individual state has achieved some sort of stability and wholeness, we turn and seek to lift up the collective. Our individual journey in the physical plane isn't going to change: we're all heading to the same place. So the only way to achieve greater consciousness, as we instinctively want to, is to lift the story itself up to a higher plane of being. In the second half of life, we synthesise and integrate what has happened, and if successful we can turn our attention to lifting up the collective.

If we atrophy from the unconscious, we lose the drive for wholeness. This can happen at any stage, alienation, and it can happen culturally. Our cultural apparatus in this age enables immense connection, though connection is not always conscious—the collective consciousness is in play, and the cynical drive for power and control in our political, economic, and technocratic spheres appeal to the collective, and with the immense reach and power of our symbols and technology, the fight to maintain individual, individuating consciousness is harder.

But at the same time our potential for knowledge is increased. The risk and reward of the journey and its treasure is ever greater.

We can train our consciousness, the mechanism that will defend against that mass hypnosis, but also exercise our ability to see and relate to symbols, myths, art, and dreams. I reiterate, this is the power of literature and art, the value of an elder like Jung or Erikson, to guide us in that process, to rekindle the fire of the soul.

Our actions and our very words are short-circuited by the values and language that the unconscious would impose. Routing those symbols through consciousness allows us space and time to apprehend our own thoughts and feelings, to reflect on their source, and so on. Consciousness, in many ways, is that action, that space. Here, again, is the value of story, and in particular this story. For those who read the Book of the Fallen over the course of many months, or many years, it exercises our consciousness and humanity. Its themes circumambulate humanity, individuation. It gives space for self-reflection, for compassion. It is a heroic journey, a modern myth.

Neumann, in the wake of the second world war, wrote of the disintegration of value systems, and how the individual is left adrift, prone to fall prey to powerful archetypal contents. The words resonate today:

> "The grotesque fact that murderers, brigands, gangsters, thieves, forgers, tyrants, and swindlers, in a guise that deceives nobody, have seized control of collective life is characteristic of our time. Their unscrupulousness and double-dealing are recognized—and admired. Their ruthless energy they obtain at best from some stray archetypal content that has got them in its power. The dynamism of a possessed personality is accordingly very great, because, in its one-track primitivity, it suffers from none of the differentiations that make men human."[221]

The powers play upon our unconsciousness by inviting your projection onto hollow signs, mere effigies of the powerful symbols, that appeal to our inherited instincts. Our politics, our desire for social life, our value of the symbolic, our need for heroes, all being played by people and forces who are, at best, unconscious of their actions and the consequences; at worst, desirous of power and the schism of conscious and unconscious in the people. And as in all cases, we must begin inside.

This doesn't mean cast out all, cancel all the culture, rewrite history, burn the texts. History and heredity is inescapable, and must be integrated as with any aspect of the unconscious mind. One can only hope that the times we live in, for all their suffering, are merely the necessary wounding preceding the ascent, that we will rise up in meaningful consciousness, that we will find balance and reconnect with our nature and with all that exists around us.

---

[221] Neumann, 1949, p. 391

Jung's take on psychology and humanity will be relevant as long as we are human. It is a study of the soul. In the same way, art and literature will always be meaningful for humanity as long as it deals with that very struggle, how to exist as a human in the world. These two things synthesise together to give us, not a roadmap, but a whisper, that there is a journey in the offing, should we wish to accept the call.

So will we be reborn.

> Everything young grows old, all beauty fades, all heat cools, all brightness dims, and every truth becomes stale and trite. For all these things have taken on shape, and all shapes are worn thin by the working of time; they age, sicken, crumble to dust—unless they change. But change they can, for the invisible spark that generated them is potent enough for infinite generation. No one should deny the danger of the descent, but it *can be* risked. No one *need* risk it, but it is certain that some one will. And let those who go down the sunset way do so with open eyes, for it is a sacrifice which daunts even the gods. Yet every descent is followed by an ascent; the vanishing shapes are shaped anew, and a truth is valid in the end only if it suffers change and bears new witness in new images, in new tongues, like a new wine that is put into new bottles.[222]

---

[222] Jung, C.G., CW5 [553]

Primary References

The primary reference material for this text is The Malazan Book of the Fallen, by author Steven Erikson. These are the editions used.

Gardens of the Moon. (1999) Tor, New York. 2005
Deadhouse Gates. (2000) Tor, New York. 2006
Memories of Ice. (2001) Bantam, London. 2002
House of Chains. (2002) Bantam, London. 2003
Midnight Tides. (2004) Bantam, London. 2005
The Bonehunters. (2006) Bantam, London. 2007
Reaper's Gale. (2007) Bantam Press, London.
Toll the Hounds. (2008) Bantam Press, London.
Dust of Dreams. (2009) Bantam, London. 2010
The Crippled God. (2011) Bantam, London. 2012

The Collected Works of C.G. Jung is typically referenced by volume and paragraph number. An electronic version was primarily used in preparation of this manuscript, based on the R.F.C Hull translation.

Jung, C.G., (1967) *The Collected Works of C. G. Jung* (2nd ed.). (H. Read, et al., Eds.). (R. F. C. Hull, Trans.). Princeton University Press.

Bibliography

Baring, A., & Cashford, J. (1991). *The Myth of the Goddess: Evolution of an Image*. London: Arkana.

Birkhäuser-Oeri, S. (1988). *The Mother: Archetypal Image in Fairy Tales*. Toronto: Inner City Books.

Bly, R., & Woodman, M. (1998). *The Maiden King: The Reunion of Masculine and Feminine*. New York: Henry Holt and Co.

Campbell, J. (1949). *The Hero With a Thousand Faces*. New Jersey: Princeton University Press. 2004.

Edinger, E. (1972). *Ego and Archetype*. Boulder, CO: Shambhala.

Edinger, E. (1985). *Anatomy of the Psyche: Alchemical Symbolism in Psychotherapy*. La Salle, Illinois: Open Court.

Edinger, E. (1986). *The Bible and the Psyche: Individuation Symbolism in the Old Testament*. Toronto: Inner City Books.

Eliade, M. (1949). *Cosmos and History: The Myth of the Eternal Return*. New York: Harper and Brothers.

Eliade, M. (1959). *The Sacred and the Profane: The Nature of Religion*. New York: Harcourt, Brace & World.

Estés, C. P. (1997). *Women Who Run With the Wolves*. New York: Ballantine Books.

Hannah, B. (2000). *The Inner Journey: Lectures and Essays On Jungian Psychology*. Toronto: Inner City Books.

Harding, M. E. (1935). *Woman's Mysteries: Ancient and Modern*. Boston: Shambhala. 2001.

Harding, M. E. (1965). *The Parental Image: Its Injury and Reconstruction*. Toronto: Inner City Books. 2003.

Jacobi, J. (1925). *Complex/Archetype/Symbol in the Psychology of C G Jung*. New York: Routledge. 2013.

Jacobi, J. (1967). *The Way of Individuation*. New York: Meridian. 1983.

Jaffé, A. (1970). *The Myth of Meaning in the Work of C.G. Jung*. London: Hodder and Stoughton. 2012.

Jenkinson, S. (2015). *Die Wise: A Manifesto For Sanity And Soul*. Berkeley: North Atlantic Books.

Jung, C. (1964). *Man and His Symbols*. Aldus Books: London.

Jung, C. G. (1963). *Memories, Dreams, Reflections*. London: Fontana Press. 1995

Jung, E. (1955). *Animus and Anima*. Putnam, CT: Spring Publications Inc. 2004.

Kaufman, S. B. (2020). *Transcend: The New Science of Self-Actualization*. New York: Tarcher Perigee.

Le Guin, U. K. (1979). *The Language of the Night: Essays on Fantasy and Science Fiction*. New York: Putnam.

McGuire, W. & Hull, R.F.C (Eds.). (1977). *C.G. Jung Speaking*. Princeton: Princeton University Press.

Neumann, E. (1949). *The Origins and History of Consciousness*. New Jersey: Princeton University Press. 2015.

Neumann, E. (1955). *The Great Mother: An Analysis of the Archetype*. New Jersey: Princeton University Press. 1974.

Shaw, M. (2014). *Snowy Tower: Parzival and the Wet, Black Branch of Language*. Ashland, Oregon: White Cloud Press.

Stevens, A. (2002). *Archetype Revisited: An Updated Natural History of the Self*. London: Brunner-Routledge.

Van Eenwyk, J. R. (1997). *Archetypes & Strange Attractors : The Chaotic World of Symbols*. Toronto: Inner City Books.

Van Gennep, A. (1960). *The Rites of Passage*. Illinois: University of Chicago Press.

Von Franz, M.-L. (1980). *The Psychological Meaning of Redemption Motifs in Fairytales*. Toronto: Inner City Books.

Von Franz, M.-L. (1980a). *Alchemy : An Introduction to the Symbolism and the Psychology*. Toronto: Inner City Books.

Von Franz, M.-L. (1997). *Archetypal Dimensions of the Psyche*. Boston, Mass.: Shambhala.

Von Franz, M.-L. (1997a). *Archetypal Patterns in Fairy Tales*. Toronto: Inner City Books.

Von Franz, M.-L. (1998). *C.G. Jung : His Myth in Our Time*. Toronto: Inner City Books.

Von Franz, M.-L. (1999). *The Cat : A Tale of Feminine Redemption*. Toronto: Inner City Books.

Woodman, M. (1985). *The Pregnant Virgin*. Toronto: Inner City Books.

Woodman, M. (1990). *The Ravaged Bridegroom: Masculinity in Women*. Toronto: Inner City Books.

About the Author

Michael Woods lives with his family in Perth, Western Australia.

www.ingramcontent.com/pod-product-compliance
Lightning Source LLC
Chambersburg PA
CBHW060048190426
43201CB00034B/435